HFT 4286: Hospitality Communication

Professor Vicki Lavendol, SPHR

Rosen College of Hospitality Management

University of Central Florida

| PEARSON COLLECTIONS |

Cover Art: Courtesy of EyeWire/Getty Images

Attention bookstores: For permission to return any unsold stock, contact us at pe-uscustomreturns@pearson.com

Pearson Learning Solutions, 501 Boylston Street, Suite 900, Boston, MA 02116

A Pearson Education Company
www.pearsoned.com

ISBN 10: 1323515674
ISBN 13: 9781323515679

Printed in the USA

Table of Contents

Hospitality Communications

HFT 4286

Rosen College of Hospitality Management

University of Central Florida

Rosen College of Hospitality Management at the University of Central Florida is the leader of select colleges offering undergraduate and graduate degrees in Hospitality Management, Event Management, and Restaurant Management. Hospitality Communications is a senior level course with multiple prerequisites providing sound foundations for success.

This custom Hospitality Communications text is a blend of the most current and relevant concepts in business communications. All classroom learning activities are direct applications of these professional communication principles in the hospitality industry. The publisher of this text provides homework assignments and quizzes along with a full e-text. There are also multiple additional resources.

Every business communication assignment is focused solely on application in the hospitality industry. Students also create and deliver professional presentations as members of a team. Individual writing assignments and quizzes round out the assignments for this course. Attention to detail is critically important, along with following accepted business communication practices.

During the semester students learn to present themselves as hospitality professionals. Students create a personal professional portfolio including a resume, cover letter, self-introduction, business card, marketing plan, and networking plan. There are multiple opportunities for presentations to the class, as well as multiple written assignments; all following professional hospitality communications standards.

Students profess that no other course focuses on professional success like Hospitality Communications. Different learning styles are targeted. Each semester listening, reading, writing, speaking, and presenting are practiced. Students build relationships; a strong network in the industry is a wonderful foundation for a hospitality career. Just another benefit by Rosen College of Hospitality Management.

Professor Vicki Lavendol, SPHR

Rosen College of Hospitality Management

Developing and Delivering Business Presentations

LEARNING OBJECTIVES

After studying this chapter, you will be able to

1 Highlight the importance of presentations in your business career, and explain how to adapt the planning step of the three-step process to presentations.

2 Describe the tasks involved in developing a presentation.

3 Describe the six major design and writing tasks required to enhance your presentation with effective visuals.

4 Outline four major tasks involved in completing a presentation.

5 Describe four important aspects of delivering a presentation in today's social media environment.

ON THE JOB: COMMUNICATING AT
PRINCIPATO-YOUNG ENTERTAINMENT

The Serious Side of the Comedy Business

The business of being funny can be profoundly unfunny these days, particularly for comedians who want to break into movies and television shows. Fewer movies are being made, and the audience for television and online shows is so fragmented that trying to build a fan base is an uphill struggle. Making the situation even worse for comedians, many of whom are writers at heart, is the seemingly unstoppable growth of reality shows, which require neither writers nor actors in any conventional sense.

John Shearer/Getty Images

Talent agent Peter Principato (*right*, with actor Will Arnett) coaches his comedian clients to hone their presentations before pitching movie and TV show ideas to studio executives.

From Chapter 14 of *Excellence in Business Communication*, Twelfth Edition. John V. Thill, Courtland L. Bovée. Copyright © 2017 by Pearson Education, Inc. All rights reserved.

Talent agent Peter Principato knows this landscape as well as anyone, and as he puts it, "There's less and less real estate every year." Studios are increasingly reluctant to "green-light" projects, particularly with the young and not-quite-top-of-the-marquee talent that is the specialty of Principato-Young Entertainment, the Beverly Hills company he cofounded with producer Paul Young. But comedy is in Principato's blood, so he works overtime to make his clients successful, even in this challenging environment.

In the entertainment industry, the road to success often starts with "the pitch," a brief presentation to one or more studio executives by an individual writer, actor, director, or producer or by a team of these people. If the executive is intrigued by the concept, it might be discussed further within the studio, and eventually a decision will be made about funding production.

With so much riding on this brief presentation, you can imagine that it's a high-anxiety event for the presenters, requiring vital communication skills. In fact, the ability to pitch effectively is so important that it has its own slang term: being "good in a room."

Pitches can fall flat for a number of reasons, whether the concept is not a good fit for a particular studio, the idea is so unusual that executives are unwilling to risk investing in it, or the pitch is poorly presented. A presenter may fail by being unable to summarize what a new show or movie idea is all about, by smothering executives in too many details, or by trying too hard to sell the concept.

The pointers Principato gives his clients constitute good advice for presentations in any industry, but they're vital in the entertainment industry. First, come up with a single compelling sentence that describes the show or movie. If presenters can't do this, chances are they haven't thought the idea out well enough, or the idea is so complicated that it would be too risky or too expensive to attempt. This one-line summary is essential for another reason, in that the first studio executive to hear the pitch will usually need to share it with other executives or potential financiers before a decision can be made. A catchy, succinct idea is a lot easier to repeat than a rambling, confused concept.

Second, expand on that one sentence with a single paragraph that builds interest by substantiating the concept and helping the listener envision what the show or movie would be like. Third, for a proposed series, explain how the concept would play out, week by week, by describing several episodes. Fourth, fill in the "big picture," such as by describing how the show would look on screen or by rounding out the main characters.

You've probably noticed how this advice follows the classic AIDA model of getting attention, building interest, increasing desire, and asking for a decision, which is what makes Principato's advice valuable for just about any profession.

The funny business is tough and getting tougher, but Principato is clearly doing something right. Principato-Young continues to expand and attract more of the young comedians who might be box office stars for the next several decades. And his love of comedy and comedians continues to motivate Principato himself. As he describes it, having his job "is like getting to hang out with your favorite band."[1]

WWW.PRINCIPATOYOUNG.COM

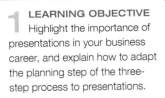

1 **LEARNING OBJECTIVE**
Highlight the importance of presentations in your business career, and explain how to adapt the planning step of the three-step process to presentations.

Presentations involve all of your communication skills, from research through nonverbal communication.

Creating a high-quality presentation for an important event can take many days, so be sure to allow enough time.

Planning a Presentation

You might not pitch the next Oscar winner to a studio executive as Peter Principato (profiled in the On the Job chapter opener) hopes to do, but wherever your career takes you, speeches and presentations will offer important opportunities to put all your communication skills on display, including research, planning, writing, visual design, and interpersonal and nonverbal communication. Presentations also let you demonstrate your ability to think on your feet, grasp complex business issues, and handle challenging situations—all attributes that executives look for when searching for talented employees to promote.

Planning presentations is much like planning other business messages: You analyze the situation, gather information, select the best media and channels, and organize the information (see Figure 1). Gathering information for presentations is essentially the same as it is for written communication projects. The other three planning tasks have some special applications when it comes to oral presentations; they are covered in the following sections.

On the subject of planning, be aware that preparing a professional-quality business presentation can take a considerable amount of time. Nancy Duarte, whose design firm has years of experience creating presentations for corporations, offers this rule of thumb: For a 1-hour presentation, allow 36 to 90 hours to research, conceive, create, and practice.[2] Not every 1-hour presentation justifies a week or two of preparation, of course, but the important presentations that can make your career or your company certainly can.

ANALYZING THE SITUATION

As with written communications, analyzing the situation involves defining your purpose and developing an audience profile (see Table 1). The purpose of most of your presentations will be to inform or to persuade, although you may occasionally need to make a

Developing and Delivering Business Presentations

1 Plan →	**2** Write →	**3** Complete
Analyze the Situation Define your purpose and develop a profile of your audience, including their likely emotional states and language preferences. **Gather Information** Determine audience needs and obtain the information necessary to satisfy those needs. **Choose Medium and Channel** Identify the best combination for the situation, message, and audience, including handouts and other support materials. **Organize the Information** Define your main idea, limit your scope and verify timing, select the direct or indirect approach, and outline your content.	**Adapt to Your Audience** Adapt your content, presentation style, and room setup to the audience and the specific situation. Be sensitive to audience needs and expectations with a "you" attitude, politeness, positive emphasis, and bias-free language. Plan to establish your credibility as required. **Compose Your Presentation** Outline an attention-getting introduction, body, and close. Prepare supporting visuals and speaking notes.	**Revise the Message** Evaluate your content and speaking notes. **Master Your Delivery** Choose your delivery mode and practice your presentation. **Prepare to Speak** Verify facilities and equipment, including online connections and software setups. Hire an interpreter if necessary. **Overcome Anxiety** Take steps to feel more confident and appear more confident on stage.

Figure 1   The Three-Step Process for Developing Business Presentations
Although you rarely "write" a presentation or speech in the sense of composing every word ahead of time, the tasks in the three-step writing process adapt quite well to the challenge of planning, creating, and delivering oral and online presentations.

TABLE 1   Analyzing Audiences for Business Presentations

Task	Actions
To determine audience size and composition	• Estimate how many people will attend (in person and online). • Identify what they have in common and how they differ. • Analyze the mix of organizational position, professions, language fluencies, and other demographic factors that could influence your content and delivery choices.
To predict the audience's probable reaction	• Analyze why audience members are attending the presentation. • Determine the audience's general attitude toward the topic: interested, moderately interested, unconcerned, open-minded, or hostile. • Analyze your audience's likely mood when you speak to them. • Find out what kind of supporting information will help the audience accept and respond to your message: technical data, historical information, financial data, demonstrations, samples, and so on. • Consider whether the audience has any biases that might work against you. • Anticipate possible objections or questions.
To gauge the audience's experience	• Analyze whether everybody has the same background and level of understanding. • Determine what the audience already knows about the subject. • Consider whether the audience is familiar with the vocabulary you intend to use. • Analyze what the audience expects from you. • Think about the mix of general concepts and specific details you will need to present.

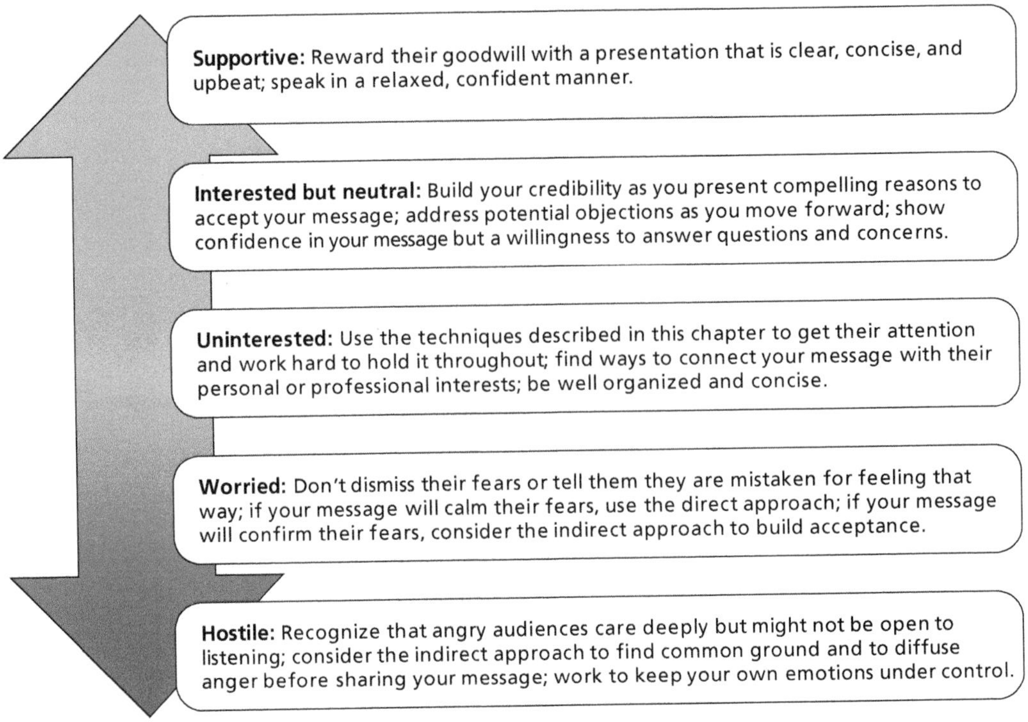

Supportive: Reward their goodwill with a presentation that is clear, concise, and upbeat; speak in a relaxed, confident manner.

Interested but neutral: Build your credibility as you present compelling reasons to accept your message; address potential objections as you move forward; show confidence in your message but a willingness to answer questions and concerns.

Uninterested: Use the techniques described in this chapter to get their attention and work hard to hold it throughout; find ways to connect your message with their personal or professional interests; be well organized and concise.

Worried: Don't dismiss their fears or tell them they are mistaken for feeling that way; if your message will calm their fears, use the direct approach; if your message will confirm their fears, consider the indirect approach to build acceptance.

Hostile: Recognize that angry audiences care deeply but might not be open to listening; consider the indirect approach to find common ground and to diffuse anger before sharing your message; work to keep your own emotions under control.

Figure 2   Planning for Various Audience Mindsets
Try to assess the emotional state of your audience ahead of time so you can plan your presentation approach accordingly.

Try to learn as much as you can about the setting and circumstances of your presentation, from the size of the audience to seating arrangements.

collaborative presentation, such as when you're leading a problem-solving or brainstorming session.

Try to anticipate the likely emotional state of your audience members. Figure 2 offers tips for dealing with a variety of audience mindsets.

As you analyze the situation, also consider the circumstances. If some or all of the audience members will be in the same room with you, how will they be seated? Can you control the environment to minimize distractions? What equipment will you need? If some or all of your audience members will be online, how will the meeting system you're using affect their ability to hear and see you and your presentation materials? Such variables can influence not only the style of your presentation but the content itself.

REAL-TIME UPDATES
LEARN MORE BY WATCHING THIS VIDEO

Dealing with the difficult four

Get advice on dealing with four difficult audience members: the Resister, the Expert, the Dominator, and the Rambler. Go to http://real-timeupdates.com/ebc12 and click on "Learn More in the Students section."

SELECTING THE BEST MEDIA AND CHANNELS

For some presentations, you'll be expected to use whatever media and channels your audience, your boss, or the circumstances require. For example, you might be required to use specific presentation software and a conference room's built-in display system or your company's online meeting software.

For other presentations, though, you might be able to choose from an array of presentation modes, from live, in-person presentations to *webcasts* (online presentations that people either view live or download later from the web), screencasts (recordings of activity on computer displays with audio voiceover), or *twebinars* (the use of Twitter as a *backchannel* for real-time conversation during a web-based seminar[3]).

ORGANIZING A PRESENTATION

Linear presentations generally follow a fixed path or from start to finish.

The possibilities for organizing a business presentation fall into two basic categories, *linear* or *nonlinear*. Linear presentations are like printed documents in the sense that they are outlined like conventional messages and follow a predefined flow from start to finish. The linear model is appropriate for speeches, technical and financial presentations, and other presentations in which you want to convey your message point by point or build up to a conclusion following logical steps.

In contrast, a nonlinear presentation doesn't flow in any particularly direction but rather gives the presenter the option to move back and forth between topics and up and down in terms of level of detail. Nonlinear presentations can be useful when you want to be able to show complicated relationships between multiple ideas or elements, to zoom in and out between the "big picture" and specific details, to explore complex visuals, or to have the flexibility to move from topic to topic in any order.

Nonlinear presentation can move back and forth between topics and up and down in levels of detail.

The difference between the two styles can be seen in the type of software typically used to create and deliver a presentation. Microsoft PowerPoint, Apple Keynote, and similar packages use sequences of individual slides, often referred to as a *slide deck*. They don't necessarily need to be presented in a strict linear fashion, because the presenter does have the option of jumping out of the predefined order, but in most presentations using slides the speaker moves from start to finish in that order.

Prezi is the best-known nonlinear presentation software and doesn't use the concept of individual slides. Instead, you start from a main screen, or canvas, which often presents the big-picture overview of your topic (see Figure 3). From there, you add individual objects (including blocks of text, photos, or videos) that convey specific information points. When you present, you can zoom in and out, discussing the individual objects and their relationship to the big picture and to each other. You can also establish a narrative flow by defining a path from one object to the next, which also lets people view the presentation on their own[4] (and effectively turns a Prezi presentation into a linear presentation).

Prezi is sometimes viewed as a more dynamic and engaging way to present, and it certainly has that potential. However, keep several points in mind if you have a choice of which approach to take and which software to use. First, match the tool to the task, not the other way around. A detailed technical discussion might need a linear presentation, whereas a free-form brainstorming session might benefit from a nonlinear approach. Second, if they are used well, software features can help you tell your story, but your story

Remember that presentations—using any software or system—are not about flash and dazzle; they are about sharing ideas, information, and emotions with your audience.

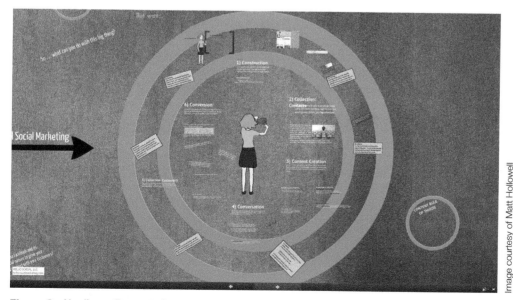

Image courtesy of Matt Hollowell

Figure 3 Nonlinear Presentations
Nonlinear presentations, particularly those using the cloud-based Prezi system, give the presenter more freedom in zooming in and out from the big picture to the details and covering topics in any order.

is what matters—not the software. If they are used poorly, software features only get in the way. (Overuse of zooming in Prezi is a good example.[5]) Third, despite their reputation, PowerPoint and other slide programs aren't limited to creating boring, linear flows of bullet points (see "Choosing Structured or Free-Form Slides").

Defining Your Main Idea

Regardless of which overall approach you take, a successful presentation starts with a clear statement of the main idea you want to share with your audience. Start by composing a one-sentence summary that links your subject and purpose to your audience's frame of reference. Here are some examples:

> Convince management that reorganizing the technical support department will improve customer service and reduce employee turnover.
>
> Convince the board of directors that we should build a new plant in Texas to eliminate manufacturing bottlenecks and improve production quality.
>
> Address employee concerns regarding a new health-care plan by showing how the plan will reduce costs and improve the quality of their care.

Each of these statements puts a particular slant on the subject, one that directly relates to the audience's interests. By focusing on your audience's needs and using the "you" attitude, you help keep their attention and convince them your points are relevant.

Limiting Your Scope

Limiting your scope is important with any message, but it's particularly vital with presentations, for two reasons. First, for most presentations, you must work within strict time limits. Second, the longer you speak, the more difficult it is to hold the audience's attention levels, and the more difficult it is for your listeners to retain your key points.[6]

The only sure way to know how much material you can cover in a given time is to practice your presentation after you complete it. If possible, complete a dry run in front of a live audience in order to simulate real-life speaking conditions. As an alternative, if you're using conventional structured slides, you can figure on 3 or 4 minutes per slide as a rough guide.[7] Of course, be sure to factor in time for introductions, coffee breaks, demonstrations, question-and-answer sessions, and anything else that takes away from your speaking time.

Approaching time constraints as a creative challenge can actually help you develop more effective presentations. Limitations can force you to focus on the most essential message points that are important to your audience.[8]

Choosing Your Approach

With a well-defined main idea to guide you and a clear notion of the scope of your presentation, you can begin to arrange your message. If you have 10 minutes or less, consider organizing your presentation much as you would a letter or other brief message: Use the direct approach if the subject involves routine information or good news, and use the indirect approach if the subject involves bad news or persuasion. Plan your introduction to arouse interest and to give a preview of what's to come. For the body of the presentation, be prepared to explain the who, what, when, where, why, and how of your subject. In the final section, review the points you've made and close with a statement that will help your audience remember the subject of your speech (see Figure 4).

Longer presentations are often organized more like reports. If the purpose is to motivate or inform, you'll typically use the direct approach and a structure imposed naturally

If you can't express your main idea in a single sentence, you probably haven't defined it clearly enough.

Limiting you scope ensures that your presentation fits the allotted time and your content meets audience needs and expectations.

The only sure way to measure the length of your presentation is to complete a practice run.

Organize short presentations the same way you would a letter or brief memo; organize long presentations as you would a report or proposal.

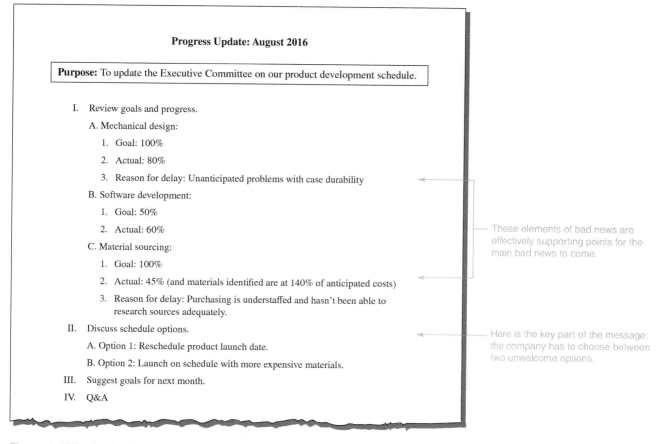

Progress Update: August 2016

Purpose: To update the Executive Committee on our product development schedule.

I. Review goals and progress.

    A. Mechanical design:

        1. Goal: 100%

        2. Actual: 80%

        3. Reason for delay: Unanticipated problems with case durability

    B. Software development:

        1. Goal: 50%

        2. Actual: 60%

    C. Material sourcing:

        1. Goal: 100%

        2. Actual: 45% (and materials identified are at 140% of anticipated costs)

        3. Reason for delay: Purchasing is understaffed and hasn't been able to research sources adequately.

II. Discuss schedule options.

    A. Option 1: Reschedule product launch date.

    B. Option 2: Launch on schedule with more expensive materials.

III. Suggest goals for next month.

IV. Q&A

These elements of bad news are effectively supporting points for the main bad news to come.

Here is the key part of the message: the company has to choose between two unwelcome options.

Figure 4 Effective Outline for a 10-Minute Presentation
Here is an outline of a short presentation that updates management on the status of a key project; the presenter has some bad news to deliver, so she opted for an indirect approach to lay out the reasons for the delay before sharing the news of the schedule slip.

by the subject: comparison, importance, sequence, chronology, geography, or category. If your purpose is to analyze, persuade, or collaborate, organize your material around conclusions and recommendations or around a logical argument. Use the direct approach if the audience is receptive and the indirect approach if you expect resistance.

No matter what the length, look for opportunities to integrate storytelling into the structure of your presentation. The dramatic tension (not knowing what will happen to the "hero") at the heart of effective storytelling is a great way to capture and keep the audience's attention.

Using a storytelling model can be a great way to catch and hold the audience's attention.

Preparing Your Outline

An outline helps you organize your message, and it serves as the foundation for delivering your speech. Prepare your outline in several stages:[9]

- State your purpose and main idea, and then use these elements to guide the rest of your planning.
- Organize your major points and subpoints in logical order, expressing each major point as a single, complete sentence.
- Identify major points in the body first, then outline the introduction and close.
- Identify transitions between major points or sections, then write these transitions in full-sentence form.

In addition to planning your speech, a presentation outline helps you plan your speaking notes.

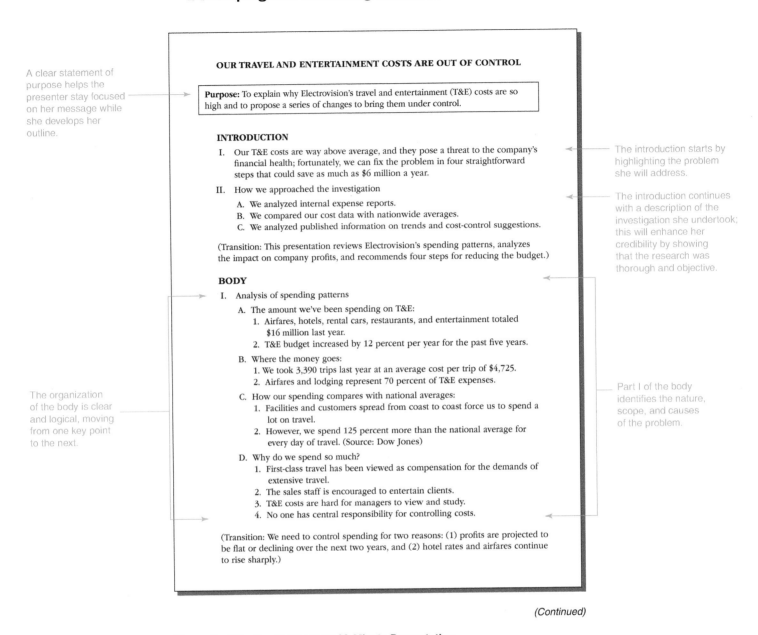

A clear statement of purpose helps the presenter stay focused on her message while she develops her outline.

The organization of the body is clear and logical, moving from one key point to the next.

OUR TRAVEL AND ENTERTAINMENT COSTS ARE OUT OF CONTROL

Purpose: To explain why Electrovision's travel and entertainment (T&E) costs are so high and to propose a series of changes to bring them under control.

INTRODUCTION

I. Our T&E costs are way above average, and they pose a threat to the company's financial health; fortunately, we can fix the problem in four straightforward steps that could save as much as $6 million a year.

II. How we approached the investigation
   A. We analyzed internal expense reports.
   B. We compared our cost data with nationwide averages.
   C. We analyzed published information on trends and cost-control suggestions.

(Transition: This presentation reviews Electrovision's spending patterns, analyzes the impact on company profits, and recommends four steps for reducing the budget.)

BODY

I. Analysis of spending patterns
   A. The amount we've been spending on T&E:
      1. Airfares, hotels, rental cars, restaurants, and entertainment totaled $16 million last year.
      2. T&E budget increased by 12 percent per year for the past five years.
   B. Where the money goes:
      1. We took 3,390 trips last year at an average cost per trip of $4,725.
      2. Airfares and lodging represent 70 percent of T&E expenses.
   C. How our spending compares with national averages:
      1. Facilities and customers spread from coast to coast force us to spend a lot on travel.
      2. However, we spend 125 percent more than the national average for every day of travel. (Source: Dow Jones)
   D. Why do we spend so much?
      1. First-class travel has been viewed as compensation for the demands of extensive travel.
      2. The sales staff is encouraged to entertain clients.
      3. T&E costs are hard for managers to view and study.
      4. No one has central responsibility for controlling costs.

(Transition: We need to control spending for two reasons: (1) profits are projected to be flat or declining over the next two years, and (2) hotel rates and airfares continue to rise sharply.)

The introduction starts by highlighting the problem she will address.

The introduction continues with a description of the investigation she undertook; this will enhance her credibility by showing that the research was thorough and objective.

Part I of the body identifies the nature, scope, and causes of the problem.

(Continued)

Figure 5 Effective Outline for a 30-Minute Presentation
This outline clearly identifies the purpose and the distinct points to be made in the introduction, body, and close. Notice also how the speaker has written her major transitions in full-sentence form to be sure she can clearly phrase these critical passages when it's time to speak.

- Prepare your bibliography or source notes; highlight those sources you want to identify by name during your talk.
- Choose a compelling title. Make it brief, action oriented, and focused on what you can do for the audience.[10]

You may find it helpful to create a simpler speaking outline from your planning outline.

Many speakers like to prepare both a detailed *planning outline* (see Figure 5) and a simpler *speaking outline* that provides all the cues and reminders they need in order to present their material. To prepare an effective speaking outline, follow these steps:[11]

- Start with the planning outline and then strip away anything you don't plan to say directly to your audience.
- Condense points and transitions to key words or phrases.
- Add delivery cues, such as places where you plan to pause for emphasis or use visuals.
- Arrange your notes on numbered cards or use the notes capability in your presentation software.

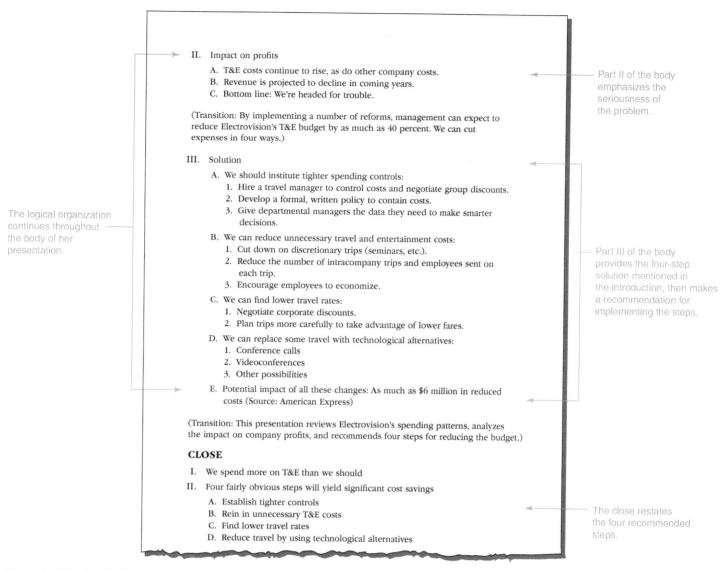

II. Impact on profits
  A. T&E costs continue to rise, as do other company costs.
  B. Revenue is projected to decline in coming years.
  C. Bottom line: We're headed for trouble.

(Transition: By implementing a number of reforms, management can expect to reduce Electrovision's T&E budget by as much as 40 percent. We can cut expenses in four ways.)

III. Solution
  A. We should institute tighter spending controls:
    1. Hire a travel manager to control costs and negotiate group discounts.
    2. Develop a formal, written policy to contain costs.
    3. Give departmental managers the data they need to make smarter decisions.
  B. We can reduce unnecessary travel and entertainment costs:
    1. Cut down on discretionary trips (seminars, etc.).
    2. Reduce the number of intracompany trips and employees sent on each trip.
    3. Encourage employees to economize.
  C. We can find lower travel rates:
    1. Negotiate corporate discounts.
    2. Plan trips more carefully to take advantage of lower fares.
  D. We can replace some travel with technological alternatives:
    1. Conference calls
    2. Videoconferences
    3. Other possibilities
  E. Potential impact of all these changes: As much as $6 million in reduced costs (Source: American Express)

(Transition: This presentation reviews Electrovision's spending patterns, analyzes the impact on company profits, and recommends four steps for reducing the budget.)

CLOSE

I. We spend more on T&E than we should
II. Four fairly obvious steps will yield significant cost savings
  A. Establish tighter controls
  B. Rein in unnecessary T&E costs
  C. Find lower travel rates
  D. Reduce travel by using technological alternatives

The logical organization continues throughout the body of her presentation.

Part II of the body emphasizes the seriousness of the problem.

Part III of the body provides the four-step solution mentioned in the introduction, then makes a recommendation for implementing the steps.

The close restates the four recommended steps.

Figure 5 **Effective Outline for a 30-Minute Presentation** *(continued)*

Developing a Presentation

Although you usually don't write out a presentation word for word, you still engage in the writing process—developing your ideas, structuring support points, phrasing your transitions, and so on. Depending on the situation and your personal style, the eventual presentation might follow your initial words closely, or you might express your thoughts in fresh, spontaneous language.

2 LEARNING OBJECTIVE
Describe the tasks involved in developing a presentation.

ADAPTING TO YOUR AUDIENCE

The size of your audience, the venue (in person or online), your subject, your purpose, your budget, and the time available for preparation all influence the style of your presentation. If you're speaking to a small group, particularly people you already know, you can use a casual style that encourages audience participation. A small conference room, with your audience seated around a table, may be appropriate. Use simple visuals and invite

Adapting to your audience involves a number of issues, from speaking style to technology choices.

your audience to interject comments. Deliver your remarks in a conversational tone, using notes to jog your memory if necessary.

If you're addressing a large audience or if the event is important, establish a more formal atmosphere. During formal presentations, speakers are often on a stage or platform, standing behind a lectern and using a microphone so that their remarks can be heard throughout the room or captured for broadcasting or webcasting.

CRAFTING PRESENTATION CONTENT

Like written documents, oral presentations are composed of distinct elements: the introduction, the body, and the close.

Presentation Introduction

An effective introduction arouses interest in your topic, establishes your credibility, and prepares the audience for the body of your presentation.

A good introduction fires up the audience's interest in your topic, establishes your credibility, and prepares your listeners for the information and insights you have to share. That's a lot to accomplish in the first few minutes, so give yourself plenty of time to develop the words and visuals you'll use to get your presentation off to a great start.

Getting Your Audience's Attention   Some subjects are naturally more interesting to some audiences than others. If your presentation involves the health, wealth, or happiness of your listeners, most people will be interested, regardless of how you begin. With other subjects, though, you need to use some imagination to pull people in. Here are seven ways to arouse audience interest:[12]

Spend some time thinking about the best technique to capture the audience's attention and interest with your opening remarks.

- If it's appropriate for the presentation, encourage your listeners to unite around a meaningful business objective. For example, if the company is struggling and your presentation offers a turnaround solution, you could start by urging your listeners to join together for the common good.
- Open with a brief story that makes a point relevant to your presentation. Be sure to keep it brief and directly on topic so listener attention doesn't start to wander.
- Consider using a prop or some other kind of visual that relates to your main idea. This gives you an opportunity to be clever and creative, as long as it's appropriate for the setting. If your presentation is about how the company's outdated policies keep customer service agents from offering top-quality service, you might walk on stage with yours hands tied together to illustrate employee frustration about having their "hands tied" by rigid policies. To point your listeners in the direction of your main idea, ask a question that your presentation will end up answering. If you're sharing the results of a consumer research project, for instance, you might open with "Why do some consumers reject our products and buy from one of our competitors?"
- Surprise or shock your listeners with an important and relevant statistic or detail, such as "If we could cut product returns in half, we would save enough to give every person in this room a 10-percent raise."
- In the right circumstances, you can open with some appropriate humor that helps endear you to the audience, shows empathy with your listeners, or sheds some light on your subject matter. Humor needs to be approached with great care, however. If you open with a joke that is irrelevant, offensive, or simply not funny, you'll dig yourself into a hole before you even start your presentation.
- Open with a bold and specific promise about how the presentation will help your audience by providing valuable insights, information, or inspiration.

Regardless of which technique you choose, make sure you can give audience members a reason to care and to believe that the time they're about to spend listening to you will be worth their while.[13] The more you can make your opening about your listeners and their concerns, the more likely they will be to lock in your message and stay tuned.

Building Your Credibility   Audiences tend to decide within a few minutes whether you're worth listening to, so establishing your credibility quickly is vital.[14] If you're not a well-known expert or haven't already earned your audience's trust in other situations, you'll need to build credibility in your introduction. If someone else will introduce you, he or she can present your credentials. If you will be introducing yourself, keep your comments brief, but don't be afraid to mention your accomplishments. Your listeners will be curious about your qualifications, so tell them briefly who you are, why you're there, and how they'll benefit from listening to you. You might say something like this:

> I'm Karen Whitney, a market research analyst with Information Resources Corporation. For the past five years, I've specialized in studying high-technology markets. Your director of engineering, John LaBarre, asked me to talk about recent trends in computer-aided design so that you'll have a better idea of how to direct your development efforts.

If someone else will be introducing you, ask this person to present your credentials.

This speaker establishes credibility by tying her credentials to the purpose of her presentation. By mentioning her company's name, her specialization and position, and the name of the audience's boss, she lets her listeners know immediately that she is qualified to tell them something they need to know.

Previewing Your Message   In addition to getting the audience's attention and establishing your credibility, a good introduction gives your audience a preview of what's ahead. Your preview should summarize the main idea of your presentation, identify major supporting points, and indicate the order in which you'll develop those points. By giving listeners the framework of your message, you help them process the information you'll be sharing, Of course, if you're using the indirect approach, you'll have to decide how much of your main idea to give away in the introduction.

Offer a preview to help your audience understand the importance, the structure, and the content of your message.

Presentation Body

The bulk of your presentation is devoted to a discussion of the main points in your outline. No matter what organizational pattern you're using, your goals are to make sure that the organization is clear and that you hold the audience's attention.

Connecting Your Ideas   In written documents, you can show how ideas are related with a variety of design clues: headings, paragraph indentions, white space, and lists. However, with oral communication—particularly when you aren't using visuals for support—you have to rely primarily on spoken words to link various parts and ideas.

For the links between sentences and paragraphs, use one or two transitional words: *therefore, because, in addition, in contrast, moreover, for example, consequently, nevertheless,* or *finally.* To link major sections of a presentation, use complete sentences or paragraphs, such as "Now that we've reviewed the problem, let's take a look at some solutions." Every time you shift topics, be sure to stress the connection between ideas by summarizing what's been said and previewing what's to come. The longer your presentation, the more important your transitions. Your listeners need clear transitions to guide them to the most important points. Furthermore, they'll appreciate brief interim summaries to pick up any ideas they may have missed.

Use transitions to repeat key ideas, particularly in longer presentations.

Holding Your Audience's Attention   A successful introduction will have grabbed your audience's attention; now the body of your presentation needs to hold that attention. Here are a few helpful tips for keeping the audience tuned into your message:

- Keep relating your subject to your audience's needs.
- Anticipate—and answer—likely questions as you move along so people don't get confused or distracted.

REAL-TIME UPDATES
LEARN MORE BY VISITING THIS WEBSITE
The latest tools and trends in presentations
From design trends to new software tools, this blog covers the newest ideas in presentations. Go to http://real-timeupdates.com/ebc12 and click on Learn More in the Students section.

The most important way to hold an audience's attention is to show how your message relates to their individual needs and concerns.

- Use clear, vivid language and throw in some variety; repeating the same words and phrases over and over puts people to sleep.
- Show how your subject is related to ideas that audience members already understand, and give people a way to categorize and remember your points.[15]
- If appropriate, encourage participation by asking for comments or questions.
- Illustrate your ideas with visuals, which enliven your message, help you connect with audience members, and help them remember your message more effectively (see "Enhancing Your Presentation with Effective Visuals").

Presentation Close

The close of a speech or presentation has two critical tasks to accomplish: making sure your listeners leave with the key points from your talk clear in their minds and putting your audience in the appropriate emotional state. For example, if the purpose of your presentation is to warn managers that their out-of-control spending threatens the company's survival, you want them to leave with that message ringing in their ears—and with enough concern for the problem to stimulate changes in their behavior.

Plan your close carefully so that your audience leaves with a clear summary of your main idea.

Restating Your Main Points   Use the close to succinctly restate your main points, emphasizing what you want your listeners to do or to think. For example, to close a presentation on your company's executive compensation program, you could repeat your specific recommendations and then conclude with a memorable statement to motivate your audience to take action:

When you repeat your main idea in the close, emphasize what you want your audience to do or to think.

> We can all be proud of the way our company has grown. However, if we want to continue that growth, we need to take four steps to ensure that our best people don't start looking for opportunities elsewhere:
>
> - First, increase the overall level of compensation
> - Second, establish a cash bonus program
> - Third, offer a variety of stock-based incentives
> - Fourth, improve our health insurance and pension benefits
>
> By taking these steps, we can ensure that our company retains the management talent it needs to face our industry's largest competitors.

Repetition of key ideas, as long as you don't overdo it, greatly improves the chance that your audience will hear your message in the way you intended.

Plan your final statement carefully so you can end on a strong, positive note.

Ending with Clarity and Confidence   If you've been successful with the introduction and body of your presentation, your listeners now have the information they need, and they're in the right frame of mind to put that information to good use. Now you're ready to end on a strong note that confirms expectations about any actions or decisions that will follow the presentation—and to bolster the audience's confidence in you and your message one final time.

Some presentations require the audience to reach a decision or agree to take specific action, in which case the close should provide a clear wrap-up. If the audience reached agreement on an issue covered in the presentation, briefly review the consensus. If they didn't agree, make the lack of consensus clear by saying something like "We seem to have some fundamental disagreement on this question." Then be ready to suggest a method of resolving the differences.

If you expect any action to occur as a result of your speech, be sure to identify who is responsible for doing what. List the action items and, if possible within the time you have available, establish due dates and assign responsibility for each task.

Being a Team Player

Professionals know that they are contributors to a larger cause, that it's not all about them. Just as in athletics and other team efforts, being a team player in business is something of a balancing act. On the one hand, you need to pay enough attention to your own efforts and skills to make sure you're pulling your own weight. On the other hand, you need to pay attention to the overall team effort to make sure the team succeeds. Remember that if the team fails, you fail, too.

Great team players know how to make those around them more effective, whether it's by lending a hand during crunch time, sharing resources, removing obstacles, making introductions, or offering expertise. In fact, the ability to help others improve their performance is one of the key attributes executives look for when they want to promote people into management.

Being a team player also means showing loyalty to your organization and protecting your employer's reputation—one of the most important assets any company has. Pros don't trash their employers in front of customers or in their personal blogs. When they have a problem, they solve it; they don't share it.

CAREER APPLICATIONS

1. If you prefer to work by yourself, should you take a job in a company that uses a team-based organization structure? Why or why not?
2. You can see plenty of examples of unprofessional business behavior in the news media and in your own consumer and employee experiences. Why should you bother being professional yourself?

Make sure your final remarks are memorable and expressed in a tone that is appropriate to the situation. For example, if your presentation is a persuasive request for project funding, you might emphasize the importance of this project and your team's ability to complete it on schedule and within budget. Expressing confident optimism will send the message that you believe in your ability to perform. Conversely, if your purpose is to alert the audience to a problem or risk, false optimism will undermine your message.

Whatever final message is appropriate, think through your closing remarks carefully before stepping in front of the audience. You don't want to wind up on stage with nothing to say but "Well, I guess that's it."

> Make sure your final remarks are memorable and have the right emotional tone.

Enhancing Your Presentation with Effective Visuals

Slides and other visuals can improve the quality and impact of your presentation by creating interest, illustrating points that are difficult to explain in words alone, adding variety, and increasing the audience's ability to absorb and remember information.

You can select from a variety of visuals to enhance presentations. Don't overlook "old-school" technologies such as overhead transparencies, chalkboards, whiteboards, and flipcharts; they can all have value in the right circumstances. However, most business presentation visuals are created using Microsoft PowerPoint, Apple Keynote, or Google Documents for linear presentations and Prezi for nonlinear presentations. Presentations slides and "Prezis" are easy to edit and update; you can add sound, photos, video, and animation; they can be incorporated into online meetings, webcasts, and *webinars* (a common term for web-based seminars); and you can record self-running presentations for trade shows, websites, and other uses.

Presentation slides are practically universal in business today, but their widespread use is not always welcome. You may have already heard the expression "death by PowerPoint," which refers to the agonizing experience of sitting through too many poorly conceived and poorly delivered slide shows. In the words of presentation expert and author Garr Reynolds, "most presentations remain mind-numbingly dull, something to be endured by presenter and audience alike."[16]

That's the bad news. The good news is that both linear and nonlinear presentations can provide an experience that is satisfying, and sometimes even enjoyable, for presenter and audience alike. Start with the mindset of *simplicity* (clear ideas presented clearly) and *authenticity* (talking *with* your audience about things they care about, rather than talking *at*

> **3 LEARNING OBJECTIVE**
> Describe the six major design and writing tasks required to enhance your presentation with effective visuals.

Thoughtfully designed visuals create interest, illustrate complex points in your message, add variety, and help the audience absorb and remember information.

MOBILE APP
With Apple Keynote, you can create and deliver presentations on your iOS mobile devices.

Focusing on making your presentations simple and authentic will help you avoid the "death by PowerPoint" stigma that presentations have in the mind of many professionals.

them or trying to be a "performer"), and you'll be well on your way to becoming an effective presenter.

CHOOSING STRUCTURED OR FREE-FORM SLIDES

Structured slides are usually based on templates that give all the slides in a presentation the same general look (which usually involves a lot of bullet points); free-form slides are much less rigid and emphasize visual appeal.

Free-form slides often have far less content per slide than structured designs, which requires many more slides to cover a presentation of equal length.

For linear presentations, the most important design choice you face when creating slides is whether to use conventional, bullet point-intensive **structured slides** or the looser, visually oriented **free-form slides** that many presentation specialists now advocate. Compare the two rows of slides in Figure 6. The structured slides in the top row follow the same basic format throughout the presentation. In fact, they're based directly on the templates built into PowerPoint, which tend to feature lots and lots of bullet points.

The free-form slides in the bottom row don't follow a rigid structure. However, free-form designs should not change randomly from one slide to the next. Effectively designed slides should still be unified by design elements such as color and font selections, as can be seen in Figures 6 (c) and 6 (d). Also, note how Figure 6d combines visual and textual messages to convey the point about listening without criticizing. This complementary approach of pictures and words is a highlight of free-form design.

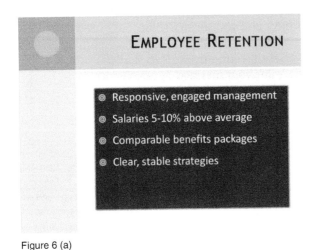

Figure 6 (a)

Figure 6 (b)

Figure 16 (c)

Figure 6 (d)

Figure 6 Structured Versus Free-Form Slide Design
Compare the rigid, predictable design of the two slides in the top row with the more dynamic free-form designs in the bottom row. Although the two free-form slides don't follow the same design structure, they are visually linked by color and font choices. Note that Figure 6 (d) is a humorous way of conveying the first bullet point in Figure 6 (b).

Advantages and Disadvantages of Structured Slides

Structured slides have the advantage of being easy to create; you simply choose an overall design scheme for the presentation, select a template for a new slide, and start typing. If you're in a schedule crunch, going the structured route might save the day because at least you'll have *something* ready to show. Given the speed and ease of creating them, structured slides can be a more practical choice for routine presentations such as project status updates.

Also, because more information can usually be packed on each slide, carefully designed structured slides can be more effective at conveying complex ideas or sets of interrelated data to the right audiences. For example, if you are talking to a group of executives who must decide where to make budget cuts across the company's eight divisions, at some point in the presentation they will probably want to see summary data for all eight divisions on a single slide for easy comparison. Such a slide would be overcrowded by the usual definition, but this might be the only practical way to get a "big-picture" view of the situation. (The best solution is probably some high-level, summary slides supported by a detailed handout, as "Creating Effective Handouts" explains.)

The primary disadvantage of structured design is that mind-numbing effect Garr Reynolds describes caused by text-heavy slides that all look alike. Slide after slide of dense, highly structured bullet points with no visual relief can put an audience to sleep.

Structured slides are often the best choice for project updates and other routine information presentations, particularly if the slides are intended to be used only once.

Advantages and Disadvantages of Free-Form Slides

Free-form slides can overcome the drawbacks of text-heavy structured design. Such slides can fulfill three criteria researchers have identified as important for successful presentations: (1) providing complementary information through both textual and visual means, (2) limiting the amount of information delivered at any one time to prevent cognitive overload, and (3) helping viewers process information by identifying priorities and connections, such as by highlighting the most important data points in a graph.[17] (Of course, well-designed structured slides can also meet these criteria, but the constraints of prebuilt templates make doing so more of a challenge.)

With appropriate imagery, free-form designs can also create a more dynamic and engaging experience for the audience. Given their ability to excite and engage, free-form designs are particularly good for motivational, educational, and persuasive presentations—particularly when the slides will be used multiple times and therefore compensate for the extra time and effort required to create them.

Free-form slides have several potential disadvantages, however. First, effectively designing slides with both visual and textual elements is more creatively demanding and more time-consuming than simply typing text into preformatted templates. The emphasis on visual content also requires more images, which take time to find.

Second, because far less textual information tends to be displayed on screen, the speaker is responsible for conveying more of the content. Ideally, of course, this is how a presentation *should* work, but presenters sometimes find themselves in less-than-ideal circumstances, such as being asked to fill in for a colleague on short notice.

Third, if not handled carefully, the division of information into smaller chunks can make it difficult to present complex subjects in a cohesive, integrated manner. For instance, if you're discussing a business problem that has five interrelated causes, it might be helpful to insert a conventional bullet-point slide as a summary and reminder after discussing each problem on its own.

Well-designed free-form slides help viewers understand, process, and remember the speaker's message.

Free-form slides can require more skill and time to create, and they put more demands on the speaker during the presentation.

DESIGNING EFFECTIVE SLIDES

Despite complaints about "death by PowerPoint," the problem is not with that software itself (or with Apple Keynote or any other presentation program). It is just a tool and, like other tools, can be used well or poorly. Unfortunately, lack of design awareness, inadequate training, schedule pressures, and the instinctive response of doing things the way they've always been done can lead to ineffective slides and lost opportunities to really connect with audiences. And although Prezi is sometimes promoted as the antidote to

Use presentation software wisely to avoid the "death by PowerPoint" stigma that presentations have in the mind of many professionals.

PowerPoint, using Prezi does not guarantee you'll end up with an effective presentation; it, too, can be misused and wind up creating a barrier between the speaker and the audience.

Another reason for ineffective slides is the practice of treating slide sets as standalone documents that can be read on their own, without a presenter. (The emergence of websites such as SlideShare might be contributing to this problem, too, by making it so easy to share slide sets.) These "slideument" hybrids that try to function as both presentation visuals and printed documents don't work well as either: They often have too much information to be effective visuals and too little to be effective reports (in addition to being clumsy to read).

As the section "Creating Effective Handouts" explains, the ideal solution is to create an effective slide set and a separate handout document that provides additional details and supporting information. This way, you can optimize each piece to do the job it is really meant to do. An alternative is to use the notes field in your presentation software to include your speaking notes for each slide. Anyone who gets a copy of your slides can at least follow along by reading your notes, although you will probably need to edit and embellish them to make them understandable by others.

However, if creating slideuments is your only option for some reason, be sure to emphasize clarity and simplicity. If you have to add more slides to avoid packing individual slides with too much text, by all means do so. Having a larger number of simpler slides is a better compromise all around than a smaller number of jam-packed slides. Remember that the primary purpose of the slides is supporting your presentation, so make sure your slides work well for that purpose.

> "Slideuments" are hybrids that try to function as both presentations slides and readable documents—and usually fail at both tasks.

> Rather than packing your slides with enough information to make them readable as standalone documents, complement well-designed slides with printed handouts.

REAL-TIME UPDATES

LEARN MORE BY VISITING THIS WEBSITE

Advice and free templates for more-effective slideuments

The free ebook and a pair of PowerPoint templates will help you make more-effective slide-document hybrids. Go to http://real-timeupdates.com/ebc12 and click on Learn More in the Students section.

Designing Slides Around a Key Visual

> Organizing a slide around a key visual can help the audience quickly grasp how ideas are related.

With any type of presentation, it is often helpful to structure specific slides around a key visual that helps organize and explain the points you are trying to make. For example, a pyramid suggests a hierarchical relationship, and a circular flow diagram emphasizes that the final stage in a process loops back to the beginning of the process. Figure 7 shows six of the many types of visual designs you can use to organize information on a slide.

Writing Readable Content

> Use slide text sparingly and only to emphasize key points, not to convey your entire message.

One of the most common mistakes beginners make—and one of the chief criticisms leveled at structured slide designs in general—is stuffing slides with too much text. Doing so overloads the audience with too much information too fast, takes attention away from the speaker by forcing people to read more, and requires the presenter to use smaller type.

Effective text slides supplement your words and help the audience follow the flow of ideas (see Figure 8). Use text to highlight key points, summarize and preview your message, signal major shifts in thought, illustrate concepts, or help create interest in your spoken message.

Creating Charts and Tables for Slides

> Charts and tables for presentations need to be simpler than visuals for printed documents.

Charts and tables for presentations need to be simpler than visuals for printed documents. Detailed images that look fine on the printed page can be too dense and too complicated for presentations. Remember that your audience will view your slides from across the room—not from a foot or two away, as you do while you create them. Keep the level of detail to a minimum, eliminating anything that is not absolutely essential. If necessary, break information into more than one chart or table. It may also be useful to provide detailed versions of charts and tables in a handout.

MOBILE APP

authorSTREAM lets you replay webcasts and other recorded presentations on your mobile device.

Selecting Design Elements

As you create slides, pay close attention to the interaction of color, background and foreground designs, artwork, typefaces, and type styles:

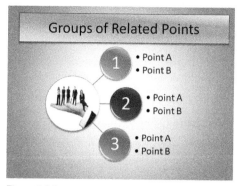

Figure 7 (a)

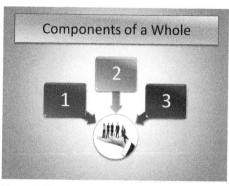

Figure 7 (b)

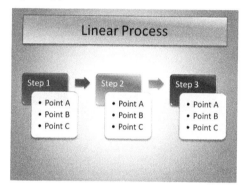

Figure 7 (c)

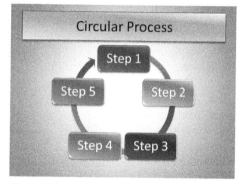

Figure 7 (d)

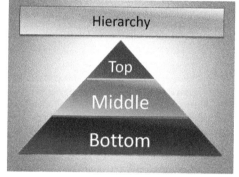

Figure 7 (e)

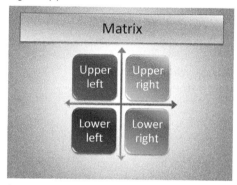

Figure 7 (f)

Figure 7 Using a Key Visual to Organize Points on a Slide
Simple graphical elements such as these "SmartArt" images in Microsoft PowerPoint make it easy to organize slide content using a key visual. Whether you're trying to convey the relationship of ideas in a hierarchy, a linear process, a circular process, or just about any other configuration, a key visual can work in tandem with your written and spoken messages to help audiences get your message.

- **Color.** Color is a critical design element that can grab attention, emphasize important ideas, create contrast, influence acceptance of your ideas, improve retention, and stimulate a variety of emotions (see Table 2 on the next page).[18] Color is powerful, so use it carefully.
- **Background designs and artwork.** All visuals have two layers of design: the *background* and the *foreground*. The background is the equivalent of paper in a printed document, and the elements in the foreground are the essential content of your slides. Make sure the background stays in the background and doesn't distract viewers or compete with the foreground. (Note that many of the template designs in presentation software have backgrounds that are too distracting for serious business use.)
- **Foreground designs and artwork.** The foreground contains the unique text and graphic elements that make up each individual slide. Foreground elements can be

Color is more than just decoration; colors have meanings themselves, based on both cultural experience and the relationships that you established between the colors in your designs.

Make sure the background of your slides stays in the background; it should never get in the way of the informational elements in the foreground.

19

Writing Readable Content

To choose effective words and phrases, think of the text on your slides as guides to the content, not the content itself. In a sense, slide text serves as the headings and subheadings for your presentation. Accordingly, choose words and short phrases that help your audience follow the flow of ideas, without forcing people to read in depth. You primarily want your audience to *listen*, not to *read*. Highlight key points, summarize and preview your message, signal major shifts in thought, illustrate concepts, or help create interest in your spoken message.

Figure 8 (a)

Writing Readable Content

- Text should be a guide to your content
- Use bullets like headings and subheadings
- Help audience follow the flow of ideas
- Encourage audience to *listen*, not *read*
- Highlight, summarize, preview, illustrate

Figure 8 (b)

Use enough text to help your audience follow the flow of ideas— and not a single word more.

Figure 8 (c)

Just enough

Figure 8 (d)

Figure 8 Writing Text for Slides
Effective text slides are clear, simple guides that help the audience understand and remember the speaker's message. Notice the progression toward simplicity in these slides: Figure 8 (a) is a paragraph that would distract the audience for an extended period of time. Figure 8 (b) offers concise, readable bullets, although too many slides in a row in this structured design would become tedious. Figure 8 (c) distills the message down to a single thought that is complete on its own but doesn't convey all the information from the original and would need embellishment from the speaker. Figure 8 (d) pushes this to the extreme, with only the core piece of the message to serve as an "exclamation point" for the spoken message. Figure 8 (c), and especially Figure 8 (d), could be even more powerful with a well-chosen visual that illustrates the idea of following the flow.

TABLE 2   Color and Emotion

Color	Emotional Associations (for U.S. audiences)	Best Uses
Blue	Peaceful, soothing, tranquil, cool, trusting	Background for electronic business presentations (usually dark blue); safe and conservative
White	Neutral, innocent, pure, wise	Font color of choice for most electronic business presentations with a dark background
Yellow	Warm, bright, cheerful, enthusiastic	Text bullets and subheadings with a dark background
Red	Passionate, dangerous, active, painful	For promoting action or stimulating the audience; seldom used as a background ("in the red" specifically refers to financial losses)
Green	Assertive, prosperous, envious, relaxed	Highlight and accent color (green symbolizes money in the United States but not in other countries).

Source: Claudyne Wilder and David Fine, *Point, Click & Wow* (San Francisco: Jossey-Bass Pfeiffer, 1996), 63, 527.

either functional or decorative. *Functional artwork* includes photos, technical drawings, charts, and other visual elements containing information that's part of your message. In contrast, *decorative artwork* simply enhances the look of your slides and should be using sparingly, if at all.

- **Typefaces and type styles.** Type is harder to read on screen than on the printed page, so you need to choose fonts and type styles with care. Sans serif fonts are usually easier to read than serif fonts. Use both uppercase and lowercase letters, with generous space between lines of text, and limit the number of fonts to one or two per slide. Choose font sizes that are easy to read from anywhere in the room, usually between 28 and 36 points, and test them in the room if possible. A clever way to test readability at your computer is to stand back as many feet from the screen as your screen size in inches (17 feet for a 17-inch screen, for example). If the slides are readable at this distance, you're probably in good shape.[19]

Many of the typefaces available on your computer are difficult to read on screen, so they aren't good choices for presentation slides.

REAL-TIME UPDATES
LEARN MORE BY READING THIS ARTICLE
Inspire your presentations with advice from these bloggers
These visual design specialists offer advice and inspiration that can benefit all business presenters. Go to http://real-timeupdates.com/ebc12 and click on Learn More in the Students section.

Maintaining design consistency is critical because audiences start to assign meaning to visual elements beginning with the first slide. For instance, if yellow is used to call attention to the first major point in your presentation, viewers will expect the next occurrence of yellow to also signal an important point. The *slide master* feature makes consistency easy to achieve because it applies consistent design choices to every slide in a presentation.

Design inconsistencies confuse and annoy audiences; don't change colors and other design elements randomly throughout your presentation.

Adding Animation and Multimedia

Today's presentation software offers many options for livening up your slides, including sound, animation, video clips, transition effects, hyperlinks, and zooming. Think about the impact that all these effects will have on your audience, and use only those special effects that support your message.[20]

Functional animation involves motion that is directly related to your message, such as a highlight arrow that moves around the screen to emphasize specific points in a technical diagram. Such animation is also a great way to demonstrate sequences and procedures. In contrast, *decorative animation*, such as having a block of text cartwheel in from off screen or using the zooming and panning capabilities in Prezi in ways that don't enhance audience understanding, needs to be incorporated with great care. These effects don't add any functional value, and they easily distract audiences.

You can animate just about everything in an electronic presentation, but resist the temptation to do so; make sure an animation has a purpose.

Slide transitions control how one slide replaces another, such as having the current slide gently fade out before the next slide fades in. Subtle transitions like this can ease your viewers' gaze from one slide to the next, but many of the transition effects now available are little more than distractions and are best avoided. **Slide builds** control the release of text, graphics, and other elements on individual slides. With builds, you can make key points appear one at a time rather than having all of them appear on a slide at once, thereby making it easier for you and the audience to focus on each new message point.

If you use transitions between slides, make sure they are subtle; they should do nothing more than ease the eye from one slide to the next.

A *hyperlink* instructs your computer to jump to another slide in your presentation, to a website, or to another program entirely. Using hyperlinks is also a great way to build in flexibility so that you can instantly change the flow of your presentation in response to audience feedback.

Hyperlinks let you build flexibility into your presentations.

Multimedia elements offer the ultimate in active presentations. Using audio and video clips can be a great way to complement your textual message. Just be sure to keep these elements brief and relevant, as supporting points for your presentation, not as replacements for it.

INTEGRATING MOBILE DEVICES IN PRESENTATIONS

Smartphones and tablets offer a variety of ways to enhance presentations for presenters as well as audience members (see Figure 9 on the next page). For example, you can get around the problem of everyone in the audience having a clear view of the screen with systems that broadcast your slides to tablets and smartphones. In fact, these systems can

MOBILE APP
SlideShark lets you present and share PowerPoint slides with mobile and PC users.

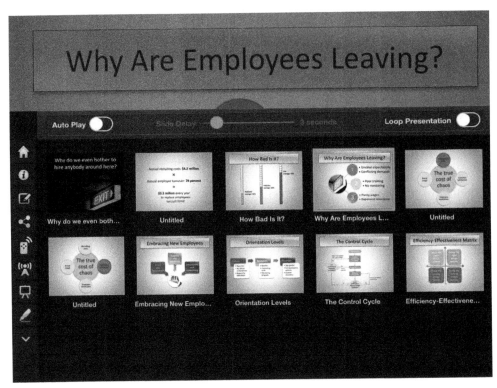

Figure 9 Using Mobile Devices in Presentations
A variety of mobile apps and cloud-based systems can free presenters and audiences from the constraints of a conventional conference room.

eliminate a conventional projection system entirely; everyone in the audience can view your slides on their mobile devices. You can also broadcast a live presentation to mobile users anywhere in the world. Each time you advance to a new slide, it is sent to the phone or tablet of everyone who is subscribed to your presentation.[21]

Completing a Presentation

4 LEARNING OBJECTIVE
Outline four major tasks involved in completing a presentation.

The completion step for presentations involves a wider range of tasks than most printed documents require. Make sure you allow enough to time to test your presentation slides, verify equipment operation, practice your speech, and create handout materials. With a first draft of your presentation in hand, revise your slides to make sure they are readable, concise, consistent, and fully operational (including transitions, builds, animation, and multimedia). Complete your production efforts by finalizing your slides, creating handouts, choosing your presentation method, and practicing your delivery.

FINALIZING YOUR SLIDES

Electronic presentation software can help you throughout the editing and revision process. For example, the *slide sorter* view (different programs have different names for this feature) lets you see some or all of the slides in your presentation on a single screen. Use this view to add and delete slides, reposition slides, check slides for design consistency, and verify the operation of any effects. Moreover, the slide sorter is a great way to review the flow of your story.[22]

In addition to using content slides, you can help your audience follow the flow of your presentation by creating slides for your title, agenda and program details, and navigation:

- **Title slide(s).** You can make a good first impression with one or two title slides, the equivalent of a report's cover and title page.

- **Agenda and program details.** These slides communicate the agenda for your presentation and any additional information the audience might need, such as hashtags and WiFi log-in information.

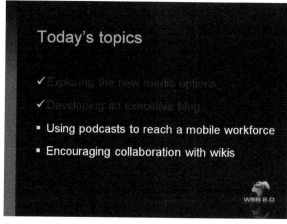

Figure 10 (a)

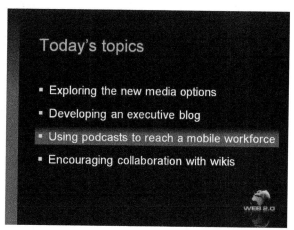

Figure 10 (b)

Figure 10   Blueprint Slides
Here are two ways you can use a *blueprint slide* as a navigational aid to help your audience stay on track with the presentation. Figure 10 (a) visually "mutes" and checks off the sections of the presentation that have already been covered. In contrast, Figure 10 (b) uses a sliding highlight box to indicate the next section to be covered.

- **Navigation slides.** To tell your audience where you're going and where you've been, you can use a series of **navigation slides**. A simple way to do this is to repeat your agenda slide at the beginning of each major section in your presentation, with the upcoming section highlighted in some way (see Figure 10).

  Navigation slides help your audience keep track of what you've covered already and what you plan to cover next.

  Figure 11 on the next page illustrates some of the many options you have for presenting various types of information. Note that although these slides don't follow a rigid structure of text-heavy bullet points, they are unified by the color scheme (silver background and bold color accents) and typeface selections.

CREATING EFFECTIVE HANDOUTS

Handouts—any printed materials you give the audience to supplement your talk—should be considered an integral part of your presentation strategy. Handouts can include detailed charts and tables, case studies, research results, magazine articles, and anything else that supports the main idea of your presentation.

Use handout materials to support the points made in your presentation and to offer the audience additional information on your topic.

Plan your handouts as you develop your presentation so that you use each medium as effectively as possible. Your presentation should paint the big picture, convey and connect major ideas, set the emotional tone, and rouse the audience to action (if that is relevant to your talk). Your handouts can then carry the rest of the information load, providing the supporting details that audience members can consume at their own speed, on their own time. You won't need to worry about stuffing every detail into your slides, because you have the more appropriate medium of printed documents to do that. As Garr Reynolds puts it, "Handouts can set you free."[23]

For a quick review of the key steps in creating effective visuals, see "Checklist: Enhancing Presentations with Visuals."

CHOOSING YOUR PRESENTATION METHOD

With all your materials ready, your next step is to decide which method of speaking you want to use. Speaking from notes (rather than from a fully written script) is nearly always the most effective and easiest delivery mode. This approach gives you something to refer to as you progress while still allowing for plenty of eye contact, a natural speaking flow, interaction with the audience, and improvisation in response to audience feedback.

In nearly all instances, speaking from notes (rather than a full script) is the most effective delivery mode.

Left: This introductory slide is a blunt attention-getter, something that would have to be used with caution and only in special circumstances.

Right: This simple math equation gets the point across about how expensive high employee turnover is.

Left: This stylized bar graph sends a stark visual message about how bad the company's turnover really is.

Right: This slide is essentially a bullet list, with three groups of two bullets each. Repeating the photo element from the introductory slide emphasizes the message about employee turnover.

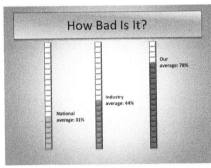

These two *navigation slides* show one way to introduce each of the four subtopics in this particular section. As the highlight moves around the central circle, the audience is reminded of which subtopics have been covered and which subtopic is going to be covered next. And each time it is shown, the message is repeated that all these problems are the "true cost of chaos" in the company's employment practices.

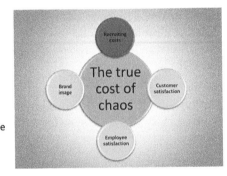

Left: This slide introduces three key points the speaker wants to emphasize in this particular section.

Right: This slide shows a linear flow of ideas, each with bulleted subpoints. This slide could be revealed one section at a time to help the speaker keep the audience's attention focused on a single topic.

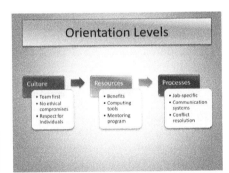

Left: This flowchart packs a lot of information onto one slide, but seeing the sequence of events in one place is essential.

Right: This simple visual highlights the presenter's spoken message about being careful to choose the right tasks to focus on and then completing them quickly.

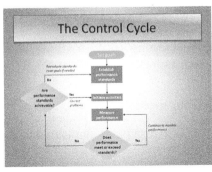
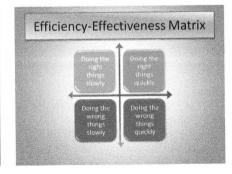

Figure 11   Designing Effective Visuals: Selected Slides
These slides, from a presentation that addresses a company's high employee turnover rate, illustrate the wide variety of design options for creating effective, appealing slides. (All the slides were created using features in PowerPoint.)

CHECKLIST: ✔ Enhancing Presentations With Visuals

A. Plan your presentation visuals.
- Make sure you and your message, not your visuals, remain the focus of your presentation.
- Follow effective design principles, with an emphasis on simplicity and authenticity.

B. Choose structured or free-form slides.
- Structured slides using bullet-point templates are easy to create, require little design time or skill, and can be completed in a hurry. Best uses: routine, internal presentations
- Free-form slides make it easier to combine textual and visual information, to create a more dynamic and engaging experience, and to maintain a conversational connection with the audience. Best uses: motivational, educational, and persuasive presentations

C. Design effective slides.
- Avoid the temptation to create "slideuments," slides that are so packed with information that they can be read as stand-alone documents.
- Use a key visual to organize related ideas in a clear and meaningful way.
- Write text content that will be readable from everywhere in the room.
- Write short, active, parallel phrases that support, not replace, your spoken message.
- Limit the amount of text so that your audience can focus on listening, not reading.
- Use color to emphasize important ideas, create contrast, isolate visual elements, and convey intended nonverbal signals.
- Limit color to a few compatible choices and use them consistently.

- Make sure your slide background doesn't compete with the foreground.
- Use decorative artwork sparingly and only to support your message.
- Emphasize functional artwork—photos, technical drawings, charts, and other visual elements containing information that is part of your message.
- Choose typefaces that are easy to read on screen; limit the number of typefaces and use them consistently.
- Use slide masters to maintain consistency throughout your presentation.
- Use functional animation when it can support your message.
- Make sure slide transitions are subtle, if used at all.
- Use builds carefully to control the release of information.
- Use hyperlinks and action buttons to add flexibility to your presentation.
- Incorporate multimedia elements that can help engage your audience and deliver your message.

D. Complete slides and support materials.
- Review every slide carefully to ensure accuracy, consistency, and clarity.
- Make sure that all slides are fully operational.
- Use the slide sorter to verify and adjust the sequence of slides, if needed.
- Have a backup plan in case your electronic presentation plan fails.
- Create navigation and support slides.
- Create handouts to complement and support your presentation message.

In contrast, reciting your speech from memory is nearly always a bad idea. Even if you can memorize the entire presentation, you will sound stiff and overly formal because you are "delivering lines," rather than talking to your audience. However, memorizing a quotation, an opening statement, or a few concluding remarks can bolster your confidence and strengthen your delivery.

Reading a speech is necessary in rare instances, such as when delivering legal information, policy statements, or other messages that must be conveyed in an exact manner. However, for all other business presentations, reading is a poor choice because it limits your interaction with the audience and lacks the fresh, dynamic feel of natural talking.

Another important decision at this point is preparing the venue where you will speak. In many instances, you won't have much of a choice, and in some situations, you won't even be able to visit the venue ahead of time. However, if you do have some control over the environment, think carefully about the seating for the audience, your position in the room, and the lighting. For instance, dimming the lights is common practice for many presenters, but dimming them too far can hamper the nonverbal communication between you and your audience and therefore limit opportunities for interaction.[24]

PRACTICING YOUR DELIVERY

Practicing your presentation is essential. Practice boosts your confidence, gives you a more professional demeanor, and lets you verify the operation of your visuals and

The more you practice, the more confidence you'll have in yourself and your material.

equipment. A test audience can tell you if your slides are understandable and whether your delivery is effective. A day or two before you're ready to step on stage for an important talk, make sure you and your presentation are ready:

Make sure you're comfortable with the equipment you'll be expected to use; you don't want to be fumbling with controls while the audience is watching and waiting.

- Can you present your material naturally, without reading your slides?
- Could you still make a compelling and complete presentation if you experience an equipment failure and have to proceed without using your slides at all?
- Is the equipment working, and do you know how to work it?
- Is your timing on track?
- Can you easily pronounce all the words you plan to use?
- Have you anticipated likely questions and objections?

If you're addressing an audience that doesn't speak your language, consider using an interpreter. Send your interpreter a copy of your speech and visuals as far in advance of your presentation as possible. If your audience is likely to include persons with hearing impairments, be sure to team up with a sign-language interpreter as well.

When you deliver a presentation to people from other cultures, you may need to adapt the content of your presentation. It is also important to take into account any cultural differences in appearance, mannerisms, and other customs. Your interpreter or host will be able to suggest appropriate changes for a specific audience or occasion.

Delivering a Presentation

5 LEARNING OBJECTIVE
Describe four important aspects of delivering a presentation in today's social media environment.

It's show time. This section offers practical advice on four important aspects of delivery: overcoming anxiety, handling questions responsively, embracing the backchannel, and giving presentations online.

OVERCOMING ANXIETY

Preparation is the best antidote for anxiety; it gives you confidence that you know your material and that you can recover from any glitches you might encounter.

Even seasoned pros get a little nervous before a big presentation, and that is a good thing. Nervousness is an indication that you care about your audience, your topic, and the occasion. These techniques will help you convert anxiety into positive energy:[25]

- **Stop worrying about being perfect.** Successful speakers focus on making an authentic connection with their listeners, rather than on trying to deliver a note-perfect presentation.
- **Know your subject.** The more familiar you are with your material, the less panic you'll feel.
- **Practice, practice, practice.** The more you rehearse, the more confident you will feel.
- **Visualize success.** Visualize mental images of yourself in front of the audience, feeling confident, prepared, and able to handle any situation that might arise.[26] Remember that your audience wants you to succeed, too.
- **Remember to breathe.** Tension can lead people to breathe in a rapid and shallow fashion, which can create a lightheaded feeling. Breathe slowly and deeply to maintain a sense of calm and confidence.
- **Be ready with your opening line.** Have your first sentence memorized so you don't have to improvise your opening.
- **Be comfortable.** Dress appropriately but as comfortably as possible. Drink plenty of water ahead of time to hydrate your voice (bring a bottle of water with you, too).
- **Take a three-second break if you need to.** If you sense that you're starting to race, pause and arrange your notes or perform some other small task while taking several deep breaths. Then start again at your normal pace.
- **Concentrate on your message and your audience, not on yourself.** When you're busy thinking about your subject and observing your audience's response, you tend to forget your fears.

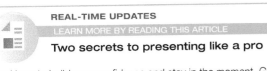

REAL-TIME UPDATES
LEARN MORE BY READING THIS ARTICLE
Two secrets to presenting like a pro
Read how to build your confidence and stay in the moment. Go to http://real-timeupdates.com/ebc12 and click on Learn More in the Students section.

- **Maintain eye contact with friendly audience members.** Eye contact not only makes you appear sincere, confident, and trustworthy but can give you positive feedback as well.
- **Keep going.** Things usually get better as you move along, with each successful minute giving you more and more confidence.

HANDLING QUESTIONS RESPONSIVELY

Whether you take them during a formal question-and-answer (Q&A) period or as they come up during your presentation, questions are often one of the most important parts of a presentation. They give you a chance to obtain important information, to emphasize your main idea and supporting points, and to build enthusiasm for your point of view. When you're speaking to high-ranking executives in your company, the Q&A period will often consume most of the time allotted for your presentation.[27]

Whether or not you can establish ground rules for questions depends on the audience and the situation. If you're presenting to a small group of upper managers or potential investors, for example, you will probably have no say in the matter: Audience members will likely ask as many questions as they want, whenever they want, to get the information they need. On the other hand, if you are presenting to your peers or a large public audience, establish some guidelines, such as the number of questions allowed per person and the overall time limit for questions.

Don't assume you can handle whatever comes up without some preparation.[28] Learn enough about your audience members to get an idea of their concerns, and think through answers to potential questions.

When people ask questions, pay attention to nonverbal signals to help determine what each person really means. Repeat the question to confirm your understanding and to ensure that the entire audience has heard it. If the question is vague or confusing, ask for clarification; then give a simple, direct answer.

If you are asked a difficult or complex question, avoid the temptation to sidestep it. Offer to meet with the questioner afterward if the issue isn't relevant to the rest of the audience or if giving an adequate answer would take too long. If you don't know the answer, don't pretend you do. Instead, offer to get a complete answer as soon as possible.

Be on guard for audience members who use questions to make impromptu speeches or to take control of your presentation. Without offending anyone, find a way to stay in control. You might admit that you and the questioner have differing opinions and offer to get back to the questioner after you've done more research.[29]

If a question ever puts you on the hot seat, respond honestly but keep your cool. Look the person in the eye, answer the question as well as you can, and keep your emotions under control. Defuse hostility by paraphrasing the question and asking the questioner to confirm that you've understood it correctly. Maintain a businesslike tone of voice and a pleasant expression.[30]

EMBRACING THE BACKCHANNEL

Many business presentations these days involve more than just the conversation between the speaker and his or her audience. Using Twitter and other electronic media, audience members often carry on their own parallel communication during a presentation via the **backchannel**, which presentation expert Cliff Atkinson defines as "a line of communication created by people in an audience to connect with others inside or outside the room, with or without the knowledge of the speaker."[31] Chances are you've participated in a backchannel already, such as when texting with your classmates or live-blogging during a lecture.

The backchannel presents both risks and rewards for business presenters. On the negative side, for example, listeners can research your claims the instant you make them and spread the word quickly if they think your information is shaky. The backchannel also gives contrary audience members more leverage, which can lead to presentations spinning out of control. On the plus side, listeners who are excited about your message can

Don't leave the question-and-answer period to chance: Anticipate potential questions and think through your answers.

If you don't have the complete answer to an important question, offer to provide it after the presentation.

If you ever face hostile questions, respond honestly and directly while keeping your cool.

Twitter and other social media are changing business presentations by making it easy for all audience members to participate in the backchannel.

27

build support for it, expand on it, and spread it to a much larger audience in a matter of seconds. You can also get valuable feedback during and after presentations.[32]

Resist the urge to ignore or fight the backchannel; instead, learn how to use it to your advantage.

By embracing the backchannel, rather than trying to fight it or ignore it, presenters can use this powerful force to their advantage. Follow these tips to make the backchannel work for you:[33]

- **Integrate social media into the presentation process.** For example, you can create a website for the presentation so that people can access relevant resources during or after the presentation, create a Twitter hashtag that everyone can use when sending tweets, or display the Twitterstream during Q&A so that everyone can see the questions and comments on the backchannel.
- **Monitor and ask for feedback.** Using a free service such as TweetDeck, which organizes tweets by hashtag and other variables, you can monitor comments from people in the audience. To avoid trying to monitor the backchannel while speaking, you can schedule "Twitter breaks," during which you review comments and respond as needed.
- **Review comments point by point to improve your presentation.** After a presentation is over, review comments on audience members' Twitter accounts and blogs to see which parts confused them, which parts excited them, and which parts seemed to have little effect (based on few or no comments).
- **Automatically tweet key points from your presentation while you speak.** Add-ons for presentation software can send out prewritten tweets as you show specific slides during a presentation. By making your key points readily available, you make it easy for listeners to retweet and comment on your presentation.
- **Establish expectations with the audience.** Explain that you welcome audience participation, but to ensure a positive experience for everyone, comments should be civil, relevant, and productive.

GIVING PRESENTATIONS ONLINE

Online presentations give you a way to reach more people in less time, but they require special preparation and skills.

Online presentations offer many benefits, including the opportunity to communicate with a geographically dispersed audience at a fraction of the cost of travel and the ability for a project team or an entire organization to meet at a moment's notice. However, this format also presents some challenges for the presenter, thanks to that layer of technology between you and your audience. Many of those "human moments" that guide and encourage you through an in-person presentation won't travel across the digital divide. For instance, it's often difficult to tell whether audience members are bored or confused, because your view of them is usually confined to small video images (and sometimes not even that).

To ensure successful online presentations, keep the following advice in mind:

- **Consider sending preview study materials ahead of time.** Doing so allows audience members to familiarize themselves with any important background information. Also, by using a free service such as SlideShare, you can distribute your presentation slides to either public or private audiences, and you can record audio narrative to make your presentations function on their own.[34] Some presenters advise against giving out your slides ahead of time, however, because doing so gives away the ending of your presentation, so to speak.
- **Keep your presentation as simple as possible.** Break complicated slides down into multiple slides if necessary, and keep the direction of your discussion clear so that no one gets lost.
- **Ask for feedback frequently.** You won't have as much of the visual feedback that alerts you when audience members are confused, and many online viewers will be reluctant to call attention to themselves by interrupting you to ask for clarification. Setting up a backchannel via Twitter or as part of your online meeting system will help in this regard.
- **Consider the viewing experience from the audience members' point of view.** Will they be able to see what you think they can see? For instance, webcast video

is typically displayed in a small window on-screen, so viewers may miss important details.

- **Allow plenty of time for everyone to get connected and familiar with the screen they're viewing.** Build extra time into your schedule to ensure that everyone is connected and ready to start.

Last but not least, don't get lost in the technology. Use these tools whenever they'll help, but remember that the most important aspect of any presentation is getting the audience to receive, understand, and embrace your message.

ON THE JOB: SOLVING COMMUNICATION DILEMMAS AT
PRINCIPATO-YOUNG ENTERTAINMENT

You share Peter Principato's love of comedy, and now you get to learn from his decades of experience in the business. You've joined Principato-Young as an apprentice talent manager, working side by side with Principato to coach comedians through their careers and to pitch TV and movie ideas to studio executives.

Principato was struck by the rapport you established with Lysette Laria, a new client, and he has asked you to team up with Laria to pitch a new weekly situation comedy she created, tentatively called *You Just Missed Me*. In it she will play a character on the run from the mob who hides in plain sight in various professions—impersonating a new character every week and generally making a mess of every job she steps into.

1. You and Laria know how important an attention-getting opening is when it comes to pitching a new show. You have a meeting with a studio executive next week, and you've brainstormed five possibilities. Which of these should you use?
   a. You don't want to miss *You Just Missed Me*!
   b. *You Just Missed Me* gives comic treatment to a fear that many of us have or can imagine having: being uncovered as a fraud.
   c. Just imagine what it would be like to go to work in disguise every day with the fear that your real identity might be uncovered.
   d. *M.A.S.H., Cheers, Seinfeld, Friends, The Office*—which sitcom is next to join these classics in the pantheon of money-making shows?
   e. Imagine all the trouble you could get into by clumsily faking your way through a new profession every day of your life, all while running from a bunch of bad guys who are as clueless as they are heartless.

2. When Laria first described her show's concept to Principato, he chuckled at the comic possibilities but then went glum when he stopped to consider the cost and complexity of producing a show set in a different location every episode. He knows any studio executive will have the same reservations. How should you and Laria handle this objection in your pitch?

   a. Emphasize that if the show turns out to be as popular as you honestly believe it will be, it will generate high ratings, which will lead to higher advertising rates, which will then pay for the higher production costs.
   b. See if you can identify any other successful shows that have had to use a variety of sets and use them as justification for whatever *You Just Missed Me* is likely to cost.
   c. Explain to the studio executive that you will adapt the episode storylines to fit the studio's existing sets, whatever those are.
   d. Do some research to find out which shows and movies this studio has produced in the past and which of those sets are still available. Then sketch out two or three episodes that could adapt these specific resources to help keep costs down.

3. You've seen Laria perform in comedy clubs a dozen times, and on stage she is witty, chatty, and relaxed. Unfortunately, off stage she is withdrawn and fidgety, giving the impression that she is either terrified to be in someone's presence or so bored she can't wait to leave. Neither impression will help in a pitch meeting where you're trying to sell her as the capable star of a show that will cost millions of dollars to produce. How should you handle the situation?
   a. As awkward as Laria is in one-on-one settings, she will be the star of the show, so she simply has to step up and perform in the pitch meeting. Let her give the presentation and just hope her on-stage persona somehow comes through. Or hope that the studio executive finds her quirky personality appealing somehow.
   b. Send her for some emergency training sessions so that she can become "good in a room." Then let her give the presentation.
   c. You are comfortable giving presentations and actually enjoy meeting with executives, so you should give the presentation yourself. Laria will come along, but only as a prop and proof that she exists, without saying anything beyond simple introductions.

d. You should give the bulk of the presentation but plan it so that Laria can weave in a few of her comedy routines along the way, as though she were on stage. This will show off her talents without draining the life out of the presentation.

4. Principato warned you that some studio executives can be blunt, but that didn't prepare you for the shock you received after you and Laria gave your pitch. The executive sat silently for a long moment and then without even looking at you, asked in a derisive tone, "Seriously? Is that the best you can do?" How should you respond to this hostile question?

a. Respond with confidence, saying, "Yes, it absolutely is the best."

b. Respond with a question, asking the executive if he has specific concerns about the show.

c. Respond with an air of submissive respect, saying, "Well, if you don't like it, I suppose we could tweak the format or come up with something else."

d. Respond with confidence, saying, "Yes, it absolutely is the best, and we're happy to walk out of here and pitch it to another studio."

Learning Objectives Checkup

Assess your understanding of the principles in this chapter by reading each learning objective and studying the accompanying exercises. You can check your responses against the answer key.

Objective 1: Highlight the importance of presentations in your business career, and explain how to adapt the planning step of the three-step process to presentations.

1. ____ presentations are outlined like conventional messages and follow a predefined flow from start to finish; ____ presentations don't flow in any particularly direction but rather give the presenter the option to move back and forth between topics and up and down in terms of level of detail

2. Which of the following is the best way to know how much material you can cover in a given amount of time?
   a. Divide the amount of time you have for your presentation by 20 to figure out how many slides you can show.
   b. Figure on one or two slides per main heading in your planning outline.
   c. For the equivalent of 100 words of written speech, plan to create one slide.
   d. Complete a dry run in front of a live audience after you've developed your speaking notes, slides, and other materials.

3. If you are facing an audience that is apprehensive about what you might have to say in a presentation, which of the following approaches is best?
   a. Even if your presentation will confirm their worst fears, use the direct approach to confront the negative emotions head-on.
   b. If your message will calm their fears, use the direct approach; if your message will confirm their fears, consider the indirect approach to build acceptance.
   c. Ignore the emotional undercurrents and focus on the practical content of your message.
   d. Diffuse the situation with a humorous story that dismisses the audience members' fears.

Objective 2: Describe the tasks involved in developing a presentation.

4. Which of the following is the best way to arouse interest in a presentation to a group of fellow employees on the importance of taking ownership of the problem whenever a customer calls in with a complaint?
   a. "If customers leave, so do our jobs."
   b. "Everything we want as employees of this company—from stable jobs to pay raises to promotional opportunities—depends on one thing: satisfied customers."
   c. "How are customers supposed to get their problems solved if we keep passing the buck from one person to the next without ever doing anything?"
   d. "The company's profit margins depend on satisfied customers, and it's up to us to make sure those customers are satisfied."

5. If you suspect that your audience doesn't really care about the topic you plan to discuss, how can you generate interest in your presentation?
   a. Look for ways to help them relate to the information on a personal level, such as helping the company ensure better job security.
   b. Speak louder and, if possible, use lots of sound effects and visual special effects in your presentation.
   c. Show your passion for the material by speaking faster than normal and pacing the room in an excited fashion.
   d. Show that you care about their feelings by saying up front that you don't really care about the topic either, but you've been assigned to talk about it.

6. If you're giving a presentation in a subject area you've researched thoroughly but in which you don't have any hands-on experience (suppose your topic is coordinating a major facility relocation or hiring a tax attorney, for instance), which of these steps should you take to build credibility?
   a. During your introduction, explain that your presentation is the result of research that you've done and briefly explain the extent of the research.
   b. Explain that you don't have any experience in the subject area, but you've done some research.
   c. Emphasize that you know a great deal about the subject matter.
   d. Sidestep the issue of credibility entirely in the introduction and let your knowledge shine through during the body of your presentation.

7. Which of the following would do the best job of holding an audience's attention during a presentation on the growing importance of social networking in corporate communication? In this particular case, the audience members are all managers of the same company, but they represent a half-dozen countries and speak four different native languages (although they all have basic English skills).

   a. "Social networks are now an important feature in the corporate communication landscape."

   b. "Successful managers around the world now view social networks as an essential tool in their communication efforts."

   c. "Millions of customers and employees are now hip to the latest wave to blow through corporate communication, the clumsily named but nevertheless vital social network."

   d. "I personally get dozens of interesting social networking updates every day, which is solid evidence of how important social networks have become."

8. Your company recently relocated from another state, and the owners are eager to begin building a positive relationship with the local community. You've been asked to speak to employees about volunteering in various community organizations. Which of the following statements does the best job of communicating the owners' wishes while appealing to employees' personal interests?

   a. "Becoming involved in community organizations is a great way for you and your families to meet new people and feel more at home in your new city."

   b. "Becoming involved in community organizations shows our new neighbors that we're an organization of positive, caring people—and it's a great way for you and your families to meet new people and feel more at home in your new city."

   c. "We really owe it to our new community to give back by volunteering."

   d. "The owners feel it is vital for us to become more involved in the community."

9. Which of these techniques is mentioned in the chapter as a way to hold an audience's attention during a presentation?

   a. Speak louder than average.

   b. Tell people that management expects them to pay attention.

   c. Use clear and vivid language.

   d. None of the above.

Objective 3: Describe the six major design and writing tasks required to enhance your presentation with effective visuals.

10. Which of the following is an advantage of structured slide designs over free-form designs?

   a. Structured designs are more colorful and therefore keep audience attention better.

   b. People are accustomed to structured designs, so they are more comfortable with them.

   c. Structured slides are generally easier to create than free-form slides.

   d. Structured slides are cheaper.

11. Which of the following is a benefit of organizing a slide around a key visual such as a pyramid or a circular flow diagram?

   a. Slides without key visuals are always boring and repetitive.

   b. The key visual shows how the various ideas are related, making it easier for viewers to grasp your message.

   c. With a key visual to rely on, the speaker doesn't have to know the subject matter quite as thoroughly.

   d. You can use the key visual for every slide, making your presentation more consistent.

12. Which of the following is a problem that results from cramming too much text on a slide?

   a. It forces the audience members to spend more time reading than listening to speaker.

   b. It forces the presenter to use smaller type on the slide.

   c. It overloads the audience with too much information too fast.

   d. All of the above are problems that result from cramming too much text on a slide.

13. Charts and tables used for presentations should be

   a. Simpler than charts and tables used for printed documents.

   b. More complex than charts and tables used for printed documents.

   c. Exactly the same as charts and tables used for printed documents.

14. Slide _____ control how one slide replaces another, whereas slide _____ control how text and graphical elements are revealed on an individual slide.

15. Why is consistent use of colors, typefaces and type treatments, size, and other design elements important in presentations?

   a. Consistency is not important; in fact, it's a sign of a dull presentation.

   b. Consistency shows that you're a smart businessperson who doesn't waste time on trivial details.

   c. Consistency simplifies the viewing and listening process for your audience and enables them to pay closer attention to your message rather than spending time trying to figure out your visuals.

   d. Consistency shows that you're a team player who can follow instructions.

Objective 4: Outline four major tasks involved in completing a presentation.

16. How does the completion stage of the three-step writing process differ between reports and presentations?

   a. Completion is exactly the same for reports and presentations.

   b. Presentations are never proofread or tested ahead of time; doing so would destroy the spontaneity of your delivery.

   c. You never revise presentation slides because they're locked in place once you create them.

   d. The completion state for presentations involves a wider range of tasks, including testing your presentation slides, verifying equipment operation, practicing your speech, and creating handout materials.

17. What advice would you give to a novice presenter regarding practicing before a big presentation?

   a. Don't practice; it destroys the spontaneity you need to give an upbeat presentation.

   b. Make multiple practice runs, a half dozen if needed, to make sure you can deliver the material smoothly and confidently.

c. Write out a script and memorize it word for word; you can't risk forgetting any key points.

d. One practice session is adequate; use the extra time to polish your presentation slides instead.

18. What is the best approach to developing handout materials?

a. Create them after you've planned, developed, and tested your presentation so that you can see which points are confusing and could benefit from additional support.

b. Wait until you give the presentation and then ask your viewers what they would like to see in terms of additional information.

c. Always follow the lead of whatever the more experienced presenters in your department do; they've already set audience expectations.

d. Plan your handouts as you plan and create your slides so that you maintain an effective balance between information that you'll cover during the presentation and information that is better suited to a printed handout.

Objective 5: Describe four important aspects of delivering a presentation in today's social media environment.

19. Which of the following is an effective way to respond if you feel nervous right before giving a presentation?

a. Think up a short joke to begin your presentation; the audience's laughter will help you relax.

b. Begin your presentation by telling people that you're nervous and asking them to be sympathetic if you make any mistakes.

c. Begin your presentation by telling the audience how much you dislike speaking in public; most of them dislike public speaking, too, so they'll be more sympathetic toward you.

d. Remind yourself that everybody gets nervous and that being nervous simply means you care about doing well; use the nervousness to be more energetic when you begin speaking.

20. Which of these actions should you take when an audience member asks you a question?

a. Observe the questioner's body language and facial expression to help determine what the person really means.

b. Nod your head or show some other sign that you acknowledge the question.

c. Repeat the question to confirm your understanding and to ensure that the entire audience has heard it.

d. Do all of the above.

21. If you receive a question that is important and relevant to the topic you're presenting but you lack the information needed to answer it, which of the following would be the best response?

a. "I'm sorry; I don't know the answer."

b. "You've asked an important question, but I don't have the information needed to answer it properly. I'll research the issue after we're finished here today and then send everyone an email message with the answer."

c. "Let me get back to you on that."

d. "I'd really like to stay focused on the material that I prepared for this presentation."

22. What is the best strategy for using the Twitter-enabled backchannel in a presentation?

a. Build automated Twitter feeds into your presentation slides that send out capsule points as you move through the presentation, but ignore whatever audience members might be doing on Twitter and stay focused on your presentation.

b. Announce up front that the use of Twitter and other messaging tools is forbidden during the presentation; the audience's job is to pay attention to you, the speaker.

c. Embrace the backchannel fully, including building in automated feeds from your presentation, providing a hashtag for everyone to use making it easy to follow tweets related to the presentation, and take occasional Twitter breaks to check for feedback and questions from the audience.

d. Ignore it; you can't stop people from tweeting during a presentation, so you might as well just accept that they are going to do so.

23. Which of the following is a disadvantage of conducting presentations online?

a. The lack of audio communication

b. The inability of most people to participate, since businesses have different Internet connection speeds

c. The inability to use PowerPoint slides online

d. The shortage (or sometimes complete lack) of nonverbal signals such as posture, which can provide vital feedback during a presentation

24. Which of the following is an advantage of online presentations?

a. Lower costs as a result of less travel

b. More opportunities for employees to meet customers in person

c. The ability to multitask during meetings

d. All of the above

Quick Learning Guide

LEARNING OBJECTIVES

1 Highlight the importance of presentations in your business career, and explain how to adapt the planning step of the three-step process to presentations.

2 Describe the tasks involved in developing a presentation.

3 Describe the six major design and writing tasks required to enhance your presentation with effective visuals.

4 Outline three special tasks involved in completing a presentation.

5 Describe four important aspects of delivering a presentation in today's social media environment.

KEY TERMS

backchannel A social media conversation that takes place during a presentation, in parallel with the speaker's presentation

free-form slides Presentation slides that are not based on a template, often with each slide having a unique look but unified by typeface, color, and other design choices; tend to be much more visually oriented than structured slides

navigation slides Noncontent slides that tell your audience where you're going and where you've been

slide builds Similar to slide transitions, these effects control the release of text, graphics, and other elements on individual slides

slide transitions Software effects that control how one slide replaces another on-screen

structured slides Presentation slides that follow the same design templates throughout and give all the slides in a presentation the same general look; they emphasize textual information in bullet-point form

CHECKLIST:

Enhancing Presentations With Visuals

A. Plan your presentation visuals.
- Make sure you and your message, not your visuals, remain the focus of your presentation.
- Follow effective design principles, with an emphasis on simplicity and authenticity.

B. Choose structured or free-form slides.
- Structured slides using bullet-point templates are easy to create, require little design time or skill, and can be completed in a hurry. Best uses: routine, internal presentations
- Free-form slides make it easier to combine textual and visual information, to create a more dynamic and engaging experience, and to maintain a conversational connection with the audience. Best uses: motivational, educational, and persuasive presentations

C. Design effective slides.
- Avoid the temptation to create "slideuments," slides that are so packed with information that they can be read as standalone documents.
- Use a key visual to organize related ideas in a clear and meaningful way.
- Write text content that will be readable from everywhere in the room.
- Write short, active, parallel phrases that support, not replace, your spoken message.
- Limit the amount of text so that your audience can focus on listening, not reading.
- Use color to emphasize important ideas, create contrast, isolate visual elements, and convey intended nonverbal signals.
- Limit color to a few compatible choices and use them consistently.

- Make sure your slide background doesn't compete with the foreground.
- Use decorative artwork sparingly and only to support your message.
- Emphasize functional artwork—photos, technical drawings, charts, and other visual elements containing information that is part of your message.
- Choose typefaces that are easy to read on-screen; limit the number of typefaces and use them consistently.
- Use slide masters to maintain consistency throughout your presentation.
- Use functional animation when it can support your message.
- Make sure slide transitions are subtle, if used at all.
- Use builds carefully to control the release of information.
- Use hyperlinks and action buttons to add flexibility to your presentation.
- Incorporate multimedia elements that can help engage your audience and deliver your message.

D. Complete slides and support materials.
- Review every slide carefully to ensure accuracy, consistency, and clarity.
- Make sure that all slides are fully operational.
- Use the slide sorter to verify and adjust the sequence of slides, if needed.
- Have a backup plan in case your electronic presentation plan fails.
- Create navigation and support slides.
- Create handouts to back up your presentation message.

Apply Your Knowledge

To review chapter content related to each question, refer to the indicated Learning Objective.

1. How do linear and nonlinear presentations differ? [LO-1]

2. You just gave an in-depth presentation on the company's new marketing programs, intended for the specialists in the marketing department. The marketing manager then asked you to give a shorter version of the presentation to the company's top executives. Generally speaking, how should you modify the scope of your presentation for this new audience? [LO-1]

 3. Is it ethical to use design elements and special effects to persuade an audience? Why or why not? [LO-3]

 4. Why is speaking from notes usually the best method of delivery? [LO-4]

Practice Your Skills

Messages for Analysis

5. **Message A: Improving a Presentation Slide**
To access this PowerPoint presentation, visit http://real-timeupdates.com/ebc12, click on Student Assignments, and select this chapter, Message 14.A. Revise the text on these slides to make them more effective for presentation use.

6. **Message: Analyzing Animation**
To access this PowerPoint presentation, visit http://real-timeupdates.com/ebc12, click on Student Assignments, and select this chapter, Message 14.B. Download and watch the presentation in slide show mode. After you've watched the presentation, identify at least three ways in which various animations, builds, and transitions either enhanced or impeded your understanding of the subject matter.

Exercises

Each activity is labeled according to the primary skill or skills you will need to use. To review relevant chapter content, you can refer to the indicated Learning Objective.

7. **Presentations: Planning a Presentation [LO-1]** Select one of the following topics, then research and prepare a brief presentation (5–10 minutes) to be given to your class:

a. What I expect to learn in this course

b. Past public speaking experiences: the good, the bad, and the ugly

c. I would be good at teaching _____

d. I am afraid of _____

e. It's easy for me to _____

f. I get angry when _____

g. I am happiest when I _____

h. People would be surprised if they knew that I _____

i. My favorite older person

j. My favorite charity

k. My favorite place

l. My favorite sport

m. My favorite store

n. My favorite television show

o. The town you live in suffers from a great deal of juvenile vandalism. Explain to a group of community members why juvenile recreational facilities should be built instead of a juvenile detention complex.

p. You are speaking to the Humane Society. Support or oppose the use of animals for medical research purposes.

q. You are talking to civic leaders of your community. Try to convince them to build an art gallery.

r. You are speaking to a first-grade class at an elementary school. Explain why they should brush their teeth after meals.

s. You are speaking to a group of traveling salespeople. Convince them that they should wear seat belts while driving.

t. You are speaking to a group of elderly people. Convince them to adopt an exercise program.

u. Energy issues (supply, conservation, alternative sources, national security, global warming, pollution, etc.)

v. Financial issues (banking, investing, family finances, etc.)

w. Government (domestic policy, foreign policy, Social Security taxes, welfare, etc.)

x. Interesting new technologies (virtual reality, geographic information systems, nanotechnology, bioengineering, etc.)

y. Politics (political parties, elections, legislative bodies and legislation, the presidency, etc.)

z. Sports (amateur and professional, baseball, football, golf, hang gliding, hockey, rock climbing, tennis, etc.)

8. **Presentations: Planning, Developing, and Delivering [LO-1], [LO-2], [LO-3]** Identify a company whose prospects look bright over the next few years because of highly competitive products, strong leadership, fundamental changes in the market, or any other significant reason. Prepare a five-minute speech, without visuals, explaining why you think this company is going to do well in the near future.

9. **Presentations: Developing a Presentation; Collaboration: Team Projects [LO-2]** You've been asked to give an informative 10-minute talk on vacation opportunities in your home state. Draft your introduction, which should last no more than 2 minutes. Then pair up with a classmate and analyze each other's

introductions. How well do these two introductions arouse the audience's interest, build credibility, and preview the presentation? Suggest how these introductions might be improved.

10. **Presentations: Developing a Presentation [LO-2]** Locate the transcript of a speech, either online or through your school library. A good source *Vital Speeches of the Day*; ask if your library has a subscription to the database.) Many corporate websites also have archives of executives' speeches; look in the "investor relations" section. Examine the introduction and the close of the speech you've chosen and then analyze how these two sections work together to emphasize the main idea. What action does the speaker want the audience to take? Next, identify the transitional sentences or phrases that clarify the speech's structure for the listener, especially those that help the speaker shift between supporting points. Using these transitions as clues, list the main message and supporting points; then indicate how each transitional phrase links the current supporting point to the succeeding one. Prepare a two- to three-minute presentation summarizing your analysis for your class.

11. **Presentations: Designing Presentation Visuals [LO-4]** Look through recent issues (print or online) of *Bloomberg Businessweek, Fortune,* or other business publications for articles discussing challenges that a specific company or industry is facing. Using the articles and the guidelines discussed in this chapter, create a short Prezi or three to five slides summarizing these issues.

12. **Presentations: Designing Presentation Visuals [LO-4]** Find a business-related slide presentation online and analyze the design. Do you consider it structured or free form? Does the design help the audience understand and remember the message? Why or why not? What improvements would you suggest to the design?

13. **Presentations: Mastering Delivery; Nonverbal Communication: Analyzing Nonverbal Signals [LO-5]** Observe and analyze the delivery of a speaker in a school, work, or other setting. What type of delivery did the speaker use? Was this delivery appropriate for the occasion? What nonverbal signals did the speaker use to emphasize key points? Were these signals effective? Which nonverbal signals would you suggest to further enhance the delivery of this oral presentation? Why?

14. **Presentations: Delivering a Presentation; Collaboration: Team Projects; Media Skills: Microblogging [LO-5]** In a team of six students, develop a 10-minute Prezi or slide presentation on any topic that interests you. Nominate one person to give the presentation; the other five will participate via a Twitter backchannel. Create a web page that holds at least one downloadable file that will be discussed during the presentation. Practice using the backchannel, including using a hashtag for the meeting and having the presenter ask for audience feedback during a "Twitter break." Be ready to discuss your experience with the entire class.

Expand Your Skills

Critique the Professionals

Visit the TED website at www.ted.com/talks and listen to any presentation that interests you. Compare the speaker's delivery and visual support materials with the concepts presented in this chapter. What works? What doesn't work? Using whatever medium your instructor requests, write a brief summary of your analysis.

Sharpen Your Career Skills Online

Bovée and Thill's Business Communication Web Search, at http://websearch.businesscommunicationnetwork.com, is a unique research tool designed specifically for business communication research. Use the Web Search function to find a website, video, PDF document, podcast, or presentation that offers advice on creating and delivering business presentations. Write a brief email message to your instructor or a post for your class blog, describing the item that you found and summarizing the career skills information you learned from it.

Improve Your Grammar, Mechanics, and Usage

The following exercises help you improve your knowledge of and power over English grammar, mechanics, and usage. Turn to the Handbook of Grammar, Mechanics, and Usage at the end of this text and review Capitalization, Underscores and Italics, and Abbreviations. Then indicate the preferred choice in the following groups of sentences.

15. a. Send this report to Mister H. K. Danforth, RR 1, Albany, NY 12885.
    b. Send this report to Mister H. K. Danforth, Rural Route 1, Albany, New York 12885.
    c. Send this report to Mr. H. K. Danforth, RR 1, Albany, NY 12885.
16. a. She received her MBA degree from the University of Michigan.
    b. She received her Master of Business Administration degree from the university of Michigan.
17. a. Sara O'Rourke (a reporter from The Wall Street Journal) will be here Thursday.
    b. Sara O'Rourke (a reporter from The Wall Street Journal) will be here Thursday.
    c. Sara O'Rourke (a reporter from the *Wall Street Journal*) will be here Thursday.
18. a. The building is located on the corner of Madison and Center streets.
    b. The building is located on the corner of Madison and Center Streets.
19. a. Call me at 8 a.m. tomorrow morning, PST, and I'll have the information you need.
    b. Call me at 8 tomorrow morning, PST, and I'll have the information you need.
    c. Call me tomorrow at 8 a.m. PST, and I'll have the information you need.

20. a. Whom do you think *Time* magazine will select as its Person of the Year?
  b. Whom do you think *Time magazine* will select as its *Person of the Year?*
  c. Whom do you think *Time magazine* will select as its Person of the Year?
21. a. The art department will begin work on Feb. 2, just one wk. from today.
  b. The art department will begin work on February 2, just one week from today.
  c. The art department will begin work on Feb. 2, just one week from today.
22. a. You are to meet him on friday at the UN building in NYC.
  b. You are to meet him on Friday at the UN building in NYC.

c. You are to meet him on Friday at the un building in New York city.
23. a. You must help her distinguish between i.e. (which means "that is") and e.g. (which means "for example").
  b. You must help her distinguish between i.e. (which means "that is") and *e.g.* (which means "for example").
  c. You must help her distinguish between *i.e.* (which means that is) and *e.g.* (which means for example).
24. a. We plan to establish a sales office on the West coast.
  b. We plan to establish a sales office on the west coast.
  c. We plan to establish a sales office on the West Coast.

Cases

Website links for selected companies mentioned in cases can be found in the Student Assignments section at http://real-time-updates.com/ebc12.

PRESENTATION SKILLS / PORTFOLIO BUILDER

25. Presentations: Planning a Presentation [LO-1]
Pecha-kucha is a style of presentation that might be the ultimate in creative constraint: The speaker is limited to 20 slides, each of which is displayed for exactly 20 seconds before automatically advancing. Pecha-kucha Nights, which are open to the public, are now put on in cities all over the world. Visit www.pecha-kucha.org for more information on these events or to view some archived presentations.

Your task: Select one of the subjects from Exercise 7 and develop a pecha-kucha style presentation with 20 slides, each designed to be displayed for 20 seconds. Use the slide-timing capabilities in your presentation software to control the timing. Make sure you practice before presenting to your class so that you can hit the precise timing requirements.[35]

PRESENTATION SKILLS / SOCIAL NETWORKING SKILLS

26. Presentations: Planning a Presentation [LO-1]
You know those times when you're craving Thai food or the perfect fruit smoothie, but you don't know where to go? Or when you're out shopping or clubbing and want to let your friends know where you are? Foursquare's location-based services connect you with friends and companies that offer products and services of interest.

Your task: Create a brief presentation explaining the Foursquare concept and its features and benefits. List two Foursquare competitors and give a brief assessment of which of the three you would recommend to your classmates.

PRESENTATION SKILLS

27. Planning, Designing, and Creating Presentation Slides [LO-1], [LO-2], [LO-3], [LO-4] Not long ago, snowboarding seemed to be on pace to pass skiing as the country's favorite way to zoom down snowy mountains, but the sport's growth has cooled off in recent years.[36]

Your task: Research and prepare a 10-minute presentation on participation trends in snowboarding and skiing, including explanations for the relative popularity of both sports. Include at least three quotations to emphasize key points in your presentation. Use either structured or free-form slides.

PRESENTATION SKILLS

28. Planning, Designing, and Creating Presentation Slides [LO-1], [LO-2], [LO-3], [LO-4] Many companies publish stories of their founding and early years. The computer company Hewlett-Packard (HP), for example, tells the story of how founders Bill Hewlett and Dave Packard started the company in a garage in Palo Alto, California, in 1938, doing anything they could to "bring in a nickel." That garage is now preserved as "the birthplace of Silicon Valley," which helps maintain HP's image as a technology pioneer.[37]

Your task: Choose a company that has been in business for at least two decades and prepare a 10-minute presentation on its history.

PRESENTATION SKILLS / TEAM SKILLS

29. Presentations: Planning a Presentation [LO-1] In your job as a business development researcher for a major corporation, you're asked to gather and process information on a wide variety of subjects. Management has gained confidence in your research and analysis skills and would now like you to begin making regular presentations at management retreats and other functions. Topics are likely to include the following:

- Offshoring of U.S. jobs
- Foreign ownership of U.S. firms
- Employment issues involving workers from other countries
- Tax breaks offered by local and state governments to attract new businesses
- Economic impact of environmental regulations

Your task: With a team assigned by your instructor, choose one of the topics from the list and conduct enough research to familiarize yourself with the topic. Identify at least three important issues that anyone involved with this topic should know about. Prepare a 10-minute presentation that introduces the topic, comments on its importance to the U.S. economy, and discusses the issues you've identified. Assume that your audience is a cross-section of business managers who don't have any particular experience in the topic you've chosen.

PRESENTATION SKILLS / PORTFOLIO BUILDER

30. Presentations: Designing Presentation Visuals [LO-4] Depending on the sequence your instructor chose for this course, you've probably covered a dozen chapters at this point and learned or improved many valuable skills. Think through your progress and identify five business communication skills that you've either learned for the first time or developed during this course.

Your task: Create a Prezi or slide presentation that describes

each of the five skills you've identified. Be sure to explain how each skill could help you in your career. Use any visual style that you feel is appropriate for the assignment.

PRESENTATION SKILLS / MOBILE SKILLS

31. Presentations: Designing Presentation Visuals; Mobile Media [LO-4] On SlideShare or any other source, find a business presentation on any topic that interests you.

Your task: Re-create the first five slides in the presentation in a manner that will make them more mobile-friendly. Create as many additional slides as you need.

PRESENTATION SKILLS / TEAM SKILLS

32. Planning, Designing, and Creating Presentation Slides; Collaboration: Team Projects [LO-1], [LO-2], [LO-3], [LO-4] Changing a nation's eating habits is a Herculean task, but the physical and financial health of the United States depends on it. You work for the USDA Center for Nutrition Policy and Promotion (www.cnpp.usda.gov), and it's your job to educate people on the dangers of unhealthy eating and the changes they can make to eat more balanced and healthful diets.

Your task: Visit http://real-timeupdates.com/ebc12, click on Student Assignments, and download this chapter Case (*Dietary Guidelines for Americans*). With a team assigned by your instructor, develop a 10- to 15-minute presentation that conveys the key points from the *Guidelines*, "Food and Food Components to Reduce." The objectives of your presentation are to alert people to the dangers of excessive consumption of the five components discussed in the chapter and to let them know what healthy levels of consumptions are. This chapter has a lot of information, but you don't need to pack it all into your presentation; you can assume that the chapter will be available as a handout to anyone who attends your presentation. Along with your presentation, draft speaking notes that someone outside your team could use to give the presentation. You can use images from the *Guidelines* PDF, the websites of the U.S. Department of Agriculture and the U.S. Department of Health and Human Services, or a nongovernment source such as Creative Commons. Cite all your image sources and make sure you follow the usage and attribution guidelines for any photos you find on nongovernment sites.

MyBCommLab

Go to the Assignments section of your MyLab to complete these writing exercises.

33. How can visually oriented free-form slides help keep an audience engaged in a presentation? [LO-3]

34. How does embracing the backchannel reflect the "you" attitude? [LO-5]

Endnotes

1. John Bowe, "Funny = Money," *New York Times,* 30 December 2010, www.nytimes.com; Stephanie Palmer Taxy, Good in a Room website, accessed 13 March 2011, www.goodinaroom.com; Mike Fleming, "A Banner Day for Two Former Assistants," *Deadline Hollywood,* 20 January 2011, www.deadline.com.

2. Nancy Duarte, *Slide:ology: The Art and Science of Creating Great Presentations* (Sebastopol, Calif.: O'Reilly Media, 2008), 13.

3. Amber Naslund, "Twebinar: GE's Tweetsquad," 4 August 2009, www.radian6.com/blog.

4. "Get Started with Prezi," *Prezi* website, accessed 2 May 2014, https://prezi.com.

5. Adam Noar, "PowerPoint vs. Prezi: What's the Difference?" Presentation Panda blog, 21 February 2012, http://presentationpanda.com.

6. Carmine Gallo, "How to Deliver a Presentation Under Pressure," *BusinessWeek* online, 18 September 2008, www.businessweek.com.

7. Sarah Lary and Karen Pruente, "Powerless Point: Common PowerPoint Mistakes to Avoid," *Public Relations Tactics,* February 2004, 28.

8. Garr Reynolds, *Presentation Zen: Simple Ideas on Presentation Design and Delivery* (Berkeley, Calif.: New Riders, 2008), 39–42.

9. Sherwyn P. Morreale and Courtland L. Bovée, *Excellence in Public Speaking* (Fort Worth, Tex.: Harcourt Brace College Publishers, 1998), 234–237.

10. John Windsor, "Presenting Smart: Keeping the Goal in Sight," *Presentations,* 6 March 2008, www.presentations.com.

11. Morreale and Bovée, *Excellence in Public Speaking,* 241–243.

12. "12 Most Engaging Presenter Behaviors … to Keep Your Audience Awake," Wilder Presentations, 12 August 2012, www.wilderpresentations.com; Sims Whyeth, "10 Ways Great Speakers Capture People's Attention," *Inc.,* 14 July 2015, www.inc.com; Jacquelyn Smith, "7 Excellent Ways to Start a Presentation and Capture Your Audience's Attention," *Financial Post,* 7 July 2014, http://business.financialpost.com.

13. Carmine Gallo, "Grab Your Audience Fast," *BusinessWeek,* 13 September 2006, 19.

14. Walter Kiechel III, "How to Give a Speech," *Fortune,* 8 June 1987, 180.

15. *Communication and Leadership Program* (Santa Ana, Calif.: Toastmasters International, 1980), 44, 45.

16. Reynolds, *Presentation Zen,* 10.

17. Cliff Atkinson, "The Cognitive Load of PowerPoint: Q&A with Richard E. Mayer," *Sociable Media,* accessed 15 August 2009, www.sociablemedia.com/articles_mayer.htm.

18. "The Power of Color in Presentations," *3M Meeting Network,* accessed 25 May 2007, www.3rd-force.org/meetingnetwork/readingroom/meetingguide_power_color.html.

19. Duarte, *Slide:ology: The Art and Science of Creating Great Presentations,* 152.

20. Lary and Pruente, "Powerless Point: Common PowerPoint Mistakes to Avoid," 28.

21. Greg Anderson, "Presefy Syncs and Controls Presentations over Your Phone," *Arctic Startup,* 14 March 2013, www.arcticstartup.com; Kanda Software website, accessed 2 May 2014, www.kandasoft.com; Heather Clancy, "Broadcast Your Mobile Presentations to Remote Attendees," *ZDNet,* 27 March 2013, www.zdnet.com.

22. Reynolds, *Presentation Zen,* 85.

23. Reynolds, *Presentation Zen,* 66.

24. Reynolds, *Presentation Zen,* 208.

25. Richard Zeoli, "The Seven Things You Must Know About Public Speaking," *Forbes,* 3 June 2009, www.forbes.com; Morreale and Bovée, *Excellence in Public Speaking,* 24–25.

26. Jennifer Rotondo and Mike Rotondo, Jr., *Presentation Skills for Managers* (New York: McGraw-Hill, 2002), 9.

27. Rick Gilbert, "Presentation Advice for Boardroom Success," *Financial Executive,* September 2005, 12.

28. Rotondo and Rotondo, *Presentation Skills for Managers,* 151.

29. Teresa Brady, "Fielding Abrasive Questions During Presentations," *Supervisory Management,* February 1993, 6.

30. Robert L. Montgomery, "Listening on Your Feet," *The Toastmaster,* July 1987, 14–15.

31. Cliff Atkinson, *The Backchannel* (Berkeley, Calif.: New Riders, 2010), 17.

32. Atkinson, *The Backchannel,* 51, 68–73.

33. Olivia Mitchell, "10 Tools for Presenting with Twitter," Speaking About Presenting blog, 3 November 2009, www.speakingaboutpresenting.com; Atkinson, *The Backchannel,* 51, 68–73, 99.

34. SlideShare website, accessed 2 July 2012, www.slideshare.net.

35. PechaKucha20x20 website, accessed 4 August 2010, www.pecha-kucha.org; Reynolds, *Presentation Zen,* 41.

36. Hugo Martin, "Snowboarding Craze Fades, Skiing Becomes Cool Again," *Seattle Times,* 7 February 2013, http://seattletimes.com.

37. HP website, accessed 11 February 2013, www.hp.com

Answer Key for "Learning Objectives Checkup"

1. linear, nonlinear
2. d
3. b
4. b
5. a
6. a
7. b
8. b
9. c
10. c
11. b
12. d
13. a
14. transitions, builds
15. c
16. d
17. b
18. d
19. d
20. d
21. b
22. c
23. d.
24. a

Answer Key for "Improve Your Grammar, Mechanics, and Usage" Exercises

15. c (3.1, 3.3)
16. a (3.1, 3.3)
17. c (3.2)
18. a (3.1)
19. c (3.3)
20. a (3.1, 3.2)
21. b (3.1, 3.3)
22. b (3.1, 3.3)
23. a (3.2)
24. c (3.1)

Collaboration, Interpersonal Communication, and Business Etiquette

Collaboration, Interpersonal Communication, and Business Etiquette

LEARNING OBJECTIVES

After studying this chapter, you will be able to

1. List the advantages and disadvantages of working in teams, describe the characteristics of effective teams, and highlight four key issues of group dynamics.

2. Offer guidelines for collaborative communication, identify major collaboration technologies, and explain how to give constructive feedback.

3. List the key steps needed to ensure productive team meetings.

4. Identify the major technologies used to enhance or replace in-person meetings.

5. Identify three major modes of listening, describe the listening process, and explain the problem of selective listening.

6. Explain the importance of nonverbal communication and identify six major categories of nonverbal expression.

7. Explain the importance of business etiquette, and identify four key areas in which good etiquette is essential.

ON THE JOB: COMMUNICATING AT
CEMEX

Social Communication "Makes a Big Company Look Like a Small Company"

You have probably been on a lab team or other project team that had trouble collaborating. Maybe you couldn't get everyone in the same room at the same time, or important messages got buried in long email threads, or good ideas were lost because the right information didn't get to the right people at the right time.

Imagine trying to collaborate when you have thousands of potential team members spread across dozens of countries. The Mexican company Cemex is one of the world's largest producers of concrete and its two primary components, cement and aggregates (crushed stone, sand, and gravel). Cemex faces teamwork challenges on a global scale, with 44,000 employees in more than 50 countries. After a period of worldwide expansion that began in the 1990s, the century-old company now operates quarries, cement plants, and other facilities on every continent except Antarctica.

Concrete and cement are two of the oldest products on earth and might not spring to mind when most people think of innovation. However, innovation is key to Cemex's long-term success, for several reasons. First, architects and builders continue to push the envelope by creating designs that require concrete with new performance and handling qualities. Second, Cemex's ability to operate profitably depends on running efficient

D. Hurst/Alamy

An innovative collaboration platform helps the global cement company Cemex operate with the agility and flexibility of a small company.

operations, from raw material extraction to processing to transportation. Third, the production and distribution of concrete-related products have significant environmental impacts, including the acquisition and consumption of heating fuels required by high-temperature cement kilns.

To stay competitive and profitable and to minimize the environmental effects of its operations, Cemex knew it needed to accelerate the pace of innovation. Company leaders figured the way to do that was to enable better collaboration, and the way to do *that* was to enable better communication.

The company's response to this multilayered challenge is a comprehensive online collaboration platform called *Shift*, which combines social networking, wikis, blogs, a Twitter-like microblogging system, social bookmarking, videoconferencing, a trend-spotting tool called *Shift Radar*, and more. A custom mobile app lets employees access the system wherever their work takes them.

By connecting people and information quickly and easily, Shift helps overcome the barriers of geography, time zones, and organizational boundaries. Employees and managers can tap into expertise anywhere in the company, workers with similar responsibilities can share ideas on improving operations, and

problems and opportunities can be identified and brought to management attention in much less time.

Technology is only part of the solution, however. Many companies that have implemented social platforms struggle to get employees to change ingrained behaviors and use the new tools. By getting top-level executives on board early, Cemex achieved nearly universal adoption, with 95 percent of employees using Shift and forming more than 500 online communities based on technical specialties and shared interests. That level of engagement is paying off in numerous ways, such as launching a new global brand of ready-mix concrete in one-third the expected time, nearly tripling the company's use of renewable energy, and reducing carbon dioxide emissions by almost 2 million metric tons.

Perhaps most impressive, Shift has lived up to its name by shifting the entrenched hierarchical culture of a large, old-school company to a more agile and responsive social business that is better prepared to face the future in its highly competitive markets. As Gilberto Garcia, Cemex's innovation director puts it, social collaboration "can make a big company look like a small company" by connecting people and ensuring the free exchange of ideas.[1]

WWW.CEMEX.COM

Communicating Effectively in Teams

The interactions among the employees at Cemex (profiled in the chapter-opening On the Job) represent one of the most essential elements of interpersonal communication. **Collaboration**—working together to meet complex challenges—is a prime skill expected in a wide range of professions. No matter what career path you pursue, it's a virtual guarantee that you will need to collaborate in at least some of your work activities. Your communication skills will pay off handsomely in these interactions because the productivity and quality of collaborative efforts depend heavily on the communication skills of the professionals involved.

A **team** is a unit of two or more people who share a mission and the responsibility for working to achieve a common goal.[2] **Problem-solving teams** and **task forces** assemble to resolve specific issues and then disband when their goals have been accomplished. Such teams are often *cross-functional*, pulling together people from a variety of departments who have different areas of expertise and responsibility. The diversity of opinions and experiences can lead to better decisions, but competing interests can lead to tensions that highlight the need for effective communication. **Committees** are formal teams that usually have a long life span and can become a permanent part of the organizational structure. Committees typically deal with regularly recurring tasks, such as an executive committee that meets monthly to plan strategies and review results.

ADVANTAGES AND DISADVANTAGES OF TEAMS

When teams are successful, they can improve productivity, creativity, employee involvement, and even job security.[3] Teams are often at the core of **participative management**, the effort to involve employees in the company's decision making. A successful team can provide a number of advantages:[4]

- **Increased information and knowledge.** By pooling the experience of several individuals, a team has access to more information.
- **Increased diversity of views.** Team members can bring a variety of perspectives to the decision-making process—as long as these diverse viewpoints are guided by a shared goal.[5]

1 LEARNING OBJECTIVE
List the advantages and disadvantages of working in teams, describe the characteristics of effective teams, and highlight four key issues of group dynamics.

Collaboration, working together to solve complex problems, is an essential skill for workers in nearly every profession.

Team members have a shared mission and are collectively responsible for their work.

Effective teams can pool knowledge, take advantage of diverse viewpoints, and increase acceptance of solutions the team proposes.

- **Increased acceptance of a solution.** Those who participate in making a decision are more likely to support it and encourage others to accept it.
- **Higher performance levels.** Working in teams can unleash new levels of creativity and energy in workers who share a sense of purpose and mutual accountability. Effective teams can be better than top-performing individuals at solving complex problems.[6]

Although teamwork has many advantages, it also has a number of potential disadvantages. At the worst, working in teams can be a frustrating waste of time. Teams need to be aware of and work to counter the following potential disadvantages:

Teams need to avoid the negative impact of groupthink, hidden agendas, and excessive costs.

- **Groupthink.** Like other social structures, business teams can generate tremendous pressures to conform with accepted norms of behavior. **Groupthink** occurs when peer pressures cause individual team members to withhold contrary or unpopular opinions. The result can be decisions that are worse than the choices the team members might have made individually.
- **Hidden agendas.** Some team members may have a **hidden agenda**—a private, counterproductive motive, such as a desire to take control of the group, to undermine someone else on the team, or to pursue a business goal that runs counter to the team's mission.
- **Cost.** Aligning schedules, arranging meetings, and coordinating individual parts of a project can eat up a lot of time and money.

CHARACTERISTICS OF EFFECTIVE TEAMS

Effective teams have a clear sense of purpose, open and honest communication, consensus-based decision making, creativity, and effective conflict resolution.

The most effective teams have a clear objective and shared sense of purpose, have a strong sense of trust, communicate openly and honestly, reach decisions by consensus, think creatively, and know how to resolve conflict.[7] Teams that have these attributes can focus their time and energy on their work, without being disrupted by destructive conflict.

In contrast, teams lacking one or more of these attributes can get bogged down in conflict or waste time and resources pursuing unclear goals. Two of the most common reasons cited for unsuccessful teamwork are lack of trust and poor communication. A lack of trust can result from team members being suspicious of one another's motives or ability to contribute.[8] Communication breakdowns are most likely to occur when teams operate across cultures, countries, or time zones.[9]

REAL-TIME UPDATES

LEARN MORE BY READING THIS ARTICLE

Three factors that distinguish smart teams

Common sense might tell you that smarter individuals make for a smarter team, but these researchers discovered otherwise. Go to http://real-timeupdates.com/ebc12 and click on Learn More in the Students section.

GROUP DYNAMICS

Group dynamics are the interactions and processes that take place in a team.

The interactions and processes that take place among the members of a team are called **group dynamics**. Productive teams tend to develop clear **norms**, informal standards of conduct that members share and that guide member behavior. Group dynamics are influenced by several factors: the roles team members assume, the current phase of team development, the team's success in resolving conflict, and the team's success in overcoming resistance.

Assuming Team Roles

Each member of a group plays a role that affects the outcome of the group's activities.

Members of a team can play various roles, which fall into three categories (see Table 1). Members who assume **self-oriented roles** are motivated mainly to fulfill personal needs, so they tend to be less productive than other members. "Dream teams" composed of multiple superstars often don't perform as well as one might expect because high-performing individuals can have trouble putting the team's needs ahead of their own.[10] In addition, highly skilled and experienced people with difficult personalities might not contribute, for the simple reason that other team members may avoid interacting with them.[11] Far more

TABLE 1 Team Roles—Functional and Dysfunctional		
Dysfunctional: Self-Oriented Roles	**Functional: Team-Maintenance Roles**	**Functional: Task-Oriented Roles**
Controlling: Dominating others by exhibiting superiority or authority	**Encouraging:** Drawing out other members by showing verbal and nonverbal support, praise, or agreement	**Initiating:** Getting the team started on a line of inquiry
Withdrawing: Retiring from the team either by becoming silent or by refusing to deal with a particular aspect of the team's work	**Harmonizing:** Reconciling differences among team members through mediation or by using humor to relieve tension	**Information giving or seeking:** Offering (or seeking) information relevant to questions facing the team
Attention seeking: Calling attention to oneself and demanding recognition from others	**Compromising:** Offering to yield on a point in the interest of reaching a mutually acceptable decision	**Coordinating:** Showing relationships among ideas, clarifying issues, summarizing what the team has done
Diverting: Focusing the team's discussion on topics of interest to the individual rather than on those relevant to the task		**Procedure setting:** Suggesting decision-making procedures that will move the team toward a goal

likely to contribute to team goals are members who assume **team-maintenance roles** to help everyone work well together and those who assume **task-oriented roles** to help the team reach its goals.[12]

Allowing for Team Evolution

Teams typically evolve through a number of phases on their way to becoming productive. A variety of models have been proposed to describe the evolution toward becoming a productive team. Figure 1 shows how one commonly used model identifies the phases a problem-solving team goes through as it evolves:[13]

1. **Orientation.** Team members socialize, establish their roles, and begin to define their task or purpose. Team-building exercises and activities can help teams break down barriers and develop a sense of shared purpose.[14] For geographically dispersed virtual teams, creating a "team operating agreement" that sets expectations for online meetings, communication processes, and decision making can help overcome the disadvantages of distance.[15]
2. **Conflict.** Team members begin to discuss their positions and become more assertive in establishing their roles. Disagreements and uncertainties are natural in this phase.
3. **Brainstorming.** Team members air all the options and fully discuss the pros and cons. At the end of this phase, members begin to settle on a single solution to the problem. Note that although group brainstorming remains a highly popular activity in today's companies, it may not always be the most productive way to generate new ideas. Some research indicates that having people brainstorm individually and then bring their ideas to a group meeting is more successful.[16]

> Teams typically evolve through a variety of phases, such as orientation, conflict, brainstorming, emergence, and reinforcement.

Figure 1   Phases of Group Development
Groups generally progress through several stages on their way to becoming productive and reaching their objectives.
Sources: B. Aubrey Fisher, *Small Group Decision Making: Communication and the Group Process*, 2nd ed. (New York: McGraw-Hill, 1980), 145–149; Stephen P. Robbins and David A. DeCenzo, *Fundamentals of Management*, 4th ed. (Upper Saddle River, N.J.: Prentice Hall, 2004), 334–335; Richard L. Daft, *Management*, 6th ed. (Cincinnati: Thomson South-Western, 2003), 602–603.

4. **Emergence.** Consensus is reached when the team finds a solution that all members are willing to support (even if they have reservations).

5. **Reinforcement.** The team clarifies and summarizes the agreed-on solution. Members receive their assignments for carrying out the group's decision, and they make arrangements for following up on those assignments.

You may also hear the process defined as *forming, storming, norming, performing,* and *adjourning,* the phases identified by researcher Bruce Tuckman when he proposed one of the earliest models of group development.[17] Regardless of the model you consider, these stages are a general framework for team development. Some teams may move forward and backward through several stages before they become productive, and other teams may be productive right away, even though some or all members are in a state of conflict.[18]

Resolving Conflict

Conflict in teams can be either constructive or destructive.

Conflict in team activities can arise for a number of reasons: competition for resources, disagreement over goals or responsibilities, poor communication, power struggles, or fundamental differences in values, attitudes, and personalities.[19] Although the term *conflict* sounds negative, conflict isn't necessarily bad. Conflict can be *constructive* if it forces important issues into the open, increases the involvement of team members, and generates creative ideas for solving a problem. Teamwork isn't necessarily about happiness and harmony; even teams that have some interpersonal friction can excel with effective leadership and team players committed to strong results. As teamwork experts Andy Boynton and Bill Fischer put it, "Virtuoso teams are not about getting polite results."[20]

Destructive conflict can lead to win-lose or lose-lose outcomes.

In contrast, conflict is *destructive* if it diverts energy from more important issues, destroys the morale of teams or individual team members, or polarizes or divides the team.[21] Destructive conflict can lead to *win-lose* or *lose-lose* outcomes, in which one or both sides lose, to the detriment of the entire team. If you approach conflict with the idea that both sides can satisfy their goals to at least some extent (a *win-win* strategy), you can minimize losses for everyone. For a win-win strategy to work, everybody must believe that (1) it's possible to find a solution that both parties can accept, (2) cooperation is better for the organization than competition, (3) the other party can be trusted, and (4) greater power or status doesn't entitle one party to impose a solution.

The following seven measures can help team members successfully resolve conflict:

- **Proactive behavior.** Deal with minor conflict before it becomes major conflict.
- **Communication.** Get those directly involved in a conflict to participate in resolving it.
- **Openness.** Get feelings out in the open before dealing with the main issues.
- **Research.** Seek factual reasons for a problem before seeking solutions.
- **Flexibility.** Don't let anyone lock into a position before considering other solutions.
- **Fair play.** Insist on fair outcomes and don't let anyone avoid a fair solution by hiding behind the rules.
- **Alliance.** Get opponents to fight together against an "outside force" instead of against each other.

Overcoming Resistance

One particular type of conflict that can affect team progress is resistance to change. Sometimes this resistance is clearly irrational, such as when people resist any kind of change, whether the change makes sense or not. Sometimes, however, resistance is perfectly logical. A change may require someone to relinquish authority or give up comfortable ways of doing things. If someone is resisting change, you can be persuasive with calm, reasonable communication:

When you encounter resistance or hostility, try to maintain your composure and address the other person's emotional needs.

- **Express understanding.** You might say, "I understand that this change might be difficult, and if I were in your position, I might be reluctant myself." Help the other person relax and talk about his or her anxiety so that you have a chance to offer reassurance.[22]

- **Bring resistance out into the open.** When people are noncommittal and silent, they may be tuning you out without even knowing why. Continuing with your argument is futile. Deal directly with the resistance, without accusing. You might say, "You seem to have reservations about this idea. Have I made some faulty assumptions?" Such questions force people to face and define their resistance.[23]
- **Evaluate others' objections fairly.** Use active listening to focus on what the other person is expressing, both the words and the feelings. Get the person to open up so that you can understand the basis for the resistance. Others' objections may raise legitimate points that you'll need to discuss, or they may reveal problems that you'll need to minimize.[24]

Hold your arguments until the other person is ready for them. Getting your point across depends as much on the other person's frame of mind as it does on your arguments. You can't assume that a strong argument will speak for itself. By becoming more audience centered, you will learn to address the other person's emotional needs first.

REAL-TIME UPDATES

LEARN MORE BY LISTENING TO THIS PODCAST

How to keep small battles from escalating into big ones

Use these insights to manage adversarial relationships in the workplace and keep them from getting destructive. Go to http://real-timeupdates.com/ebc12 and click on Learn More in the Students section.

Collaborating on Communication Efforts

When a team collaborates on reports, websites, presentations, and other communication projects, the collective energy and expertise of the various members can produce results that transcend what each individual could do alone.[25] However, collaborating on team messages requires special effort and planning.

2 LEARNING OBJECTIVE
Offer guidelines for collaborative communication, identify major collaboration technologies, and explain how to give constructive feedback.

GUIDELINES FOR COLLABORATIVE WRITING

In any collaborative effort, team members coming from different backgrounds may have different work habits or priorities: A technical expert may focus on accuracy and scientific standards, an editor may be more concerned about organization and coherence, and a manager may focus on schedules, cost, and corporate goals. In addition, team members differ in writing styles, work habits, and personality traits.

To collaborate effectively, everyone must be flexible and open to other opinions, focusing on team objectives rather than on individual priorities.[26] Successful writers know that most ideas can be expressed in many ways, so they avoid the "my way is best" attitude. The following guidelines will help you collaborate more successfully:[27]

MOBILE APP
Freedcamp is a free collaboration and project management system.

- **Select collaborators carefully.** Whenever possible, choose a combination of people who together have the experience, information, and talent needed for each project.
- **Agree on project goals before you start.** Starting without a clear idea of what the team hopes to accomplish inevitably leads to frustration and wasted time.
- **Give your team time to bond before diving in.** If people haven't had the opportunity to work together before, make sure they can get to know each other before being asked to collaborate.
- **Clarify individual responsibilities.** Because members will be depending on each other, make sure individual responsibilities are clear.
- **Establish clear processes.** Make sure everyone knows how the work will be managed from start to finish.
- **Avoid composing as a group.** The actual composition is the only part of developing team messages that does not usually benefit from group participation. Brainstorming the wording of short pieces of text, particularly headlines, slogans, and other high-visibility elements, can be an effective way to stimulate creative word choices. However, for longer projects, it is usually more efficient to plan, research, and outline together but assign the task of writing to one person or divide larger projects among multiple writers. If you divide the writing, try to have one person do a final revision pass to ensure a consistent style.

Successful collaboration on writing projects requires a number of steps, from selecting the right partners and agreeing on project goals to establishing clear processes and avoiding writing as a group.

- **Make sure tools and techniques are ready and compatible across the team.** Even minor details such as different versions of software can delay projects.
- **Check to see how things are going along the way.** Don't assume that everything is working just because you don't hear anything negative.

TECHNOLOGIES FOR COLLABORATIVE WRITING

A wide variety of collaboration tools now exist to help professionals work on reports, presentations, and other communication efforts.

A variety of tools and systems are available to help writers collaborate on everything from short documents to entire websites. The simplest tools are software features such as *commenting* (which lets colleagues write comments in a document without modifying the document text) and *change tracking* (which lets one or more writers propose changes to the text while keeping everyone's edits separate and reversible). The widely used Adobe Acrobat electronic document system (PDF files) also has group review and commenting features, including the option for live collaboration.

Collaboration Systems

Writing for websites often involves the use of a **content management system**, which organizes and controls website content and can include features that help team members work together on web pages and other documents. These tools range from simple blogging systems on up to *enterprise* systems that manage web content across an entire corporation. Many systems include *workflow* features that control how pages or documents can be created, edited, and published.

Wiki benefits include simple operation and the ability to post new or revised material instantly without a formal review process.

In contrast to the formal controls of a content management system, a **wiki**, from the Hawaiian word for *quick*, is a website that allows anyone with access to add new material and edit existing material. Public wikis (Wikipedia is the best known) allow any registered user to edit pages; private wikis are accessible only with permission. A key benefit of wikis is the freedom to post new or revised material without prior approval.

Teams and other work groups can also take advantage of a set of broader technologies often referred to as *groupware* or *collaboration platforms*. These technologies let people communicate, share files, review previous message threads, work on documents simultaneously, and connect using social networking tools. These systems help companies capture and share knowledge from multiple experts, bringing greater insights to bear on tough challenges.[28] Collaboration systems often take advantage of *cloud computing*, a somewhat vague term that refers to on-demand capabilities delivered over the Internet, rather than through conventional on-site software.[29]

Shared workspaces are online "virtual offices" that give everyone on a team access to the same set of resources and information (see Figure 2). You may see some of these workspaces referred to as *intranets* (restricted-access websites that are open to employees only) or *extranets* (restricted sites that are available to employees and to outside parties by invitation only). Many intranets have now evolved into social networking systems that include a variety of communication and collaboration tools, from microblogging to video clip libraries. For example, the performance troupe Blue Man Group uses a *social intranet* to help its 500 employees plan, stage, and promote shows all over the world.[30]

Social Networks and Virtual Communities

A *community of practice* links professionals with similar job interests; a key benefit is accumulating long-term organizational knowledge.

Internal social networks help companies assemble the best resources for a given task, regardless of where the employees are located.

Social networking technologies are redefining teamwork and team communication by helping erase the constraints of geographic and organization boundaries. Some companies use social networks to form *virtual communities* or *communities of practice* that link employees with similar professional interests throughout the company and sometimes with customers and suppliers as well.

The huge advantage that social networking brings to these team efforts is in identifying the best people to collaborate on each problem or project, no matter where they are around the world or what their official roles are in the organization. Such communities are similar to teams in many respects, but one major difference is in the responsibility for accumulating organizational knowledge over the long term. For example, the

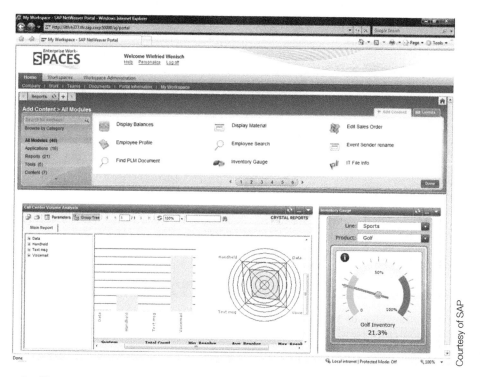

Courtesy of SAP

Figure 2 Shared Workspaces
Shared workspaces give employees instant access to the all the files they need, from company reports to website content.

pharmaceutical company Pfizer has a number of permanent product-safety communities that provide specialized advice on drug safety issues to researchers throughout the organization.[31]

Social networking can also help a company maintain a sense of community even as it grows beyond the size that normally permits a lot of daily interaction. At the online retailer Zappos, fostering a supportive work environment is the company's top priority. To encourage the sense of community among its expanding workforce, Zappos uses social networking tools to track employee connections and encourage workers to reach out and build relationships.[32]

Collaboration via Mobile Devices

Mobile devices add another layer of options for collaborative writing and other communication projects, particularly when used with cloud computing. Today's mobile systems can do virtually everything that fixed-web collaboration systems can do, from writing on virtual whiteboards to sharing photos, videos, and other multimedia files.[33] Mobility lets workers participate in online brainstorming sessions, seminars, and other formal or informal events from wherever they happen to be at the time (see Figure 3 on the next page). This flexibility can be particularly helpful during the review and production stages of major projects, when deadlines are looming and decisions and revisions need to be made quickly.

An important aspect of mobile collaboration and mobile communication in general is **unified communication**, which integrates such capabilities as voice and video calling, voice and video conferencing, instant messaging, and real-time collaboration software into a single system. By minimizing or eliminating the need to manage multiple communication systems and devices, unified communication promises to improve response times, productivity, and collaboration efforts.[34]

Collaboration apps for mobile devices support nearly all the features of computer-based platforms.

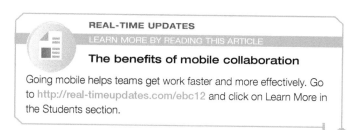

REAL-TIME UPDATES
LEARN MORE BY READING THIS ARTICLE

The benefits of mobile collaboration

Going mobile helps teams get work faster and more effectively. Go to http://real-timeupdates.com/ebc12 and click on Learn More in the Students section.

Figure 3 Collaboration on Mobile Devices
Mobile connectivity is transforming collaboration activities, helping teams and work groups stay connected no matter where their work takes them. For example, this team was able to discuss and edit a press release using their tablets in different locations.

GIVING—AND RESPONDING TO—CONSTRUCTIVE FEEDBACK

When you give writing feedback, make it constructive by focusing on how the material can be improved.

Aside from processes and tools, collaborative communication often involves giving and receiving feedback about writing efforts. **Constructive feedback**, sometimes called *constructive criticism*, focuses on the process and outcomes of communication, not on the people involved (see Table 2). In contrast, **destructive feedback** delivers criticism with no guidance to stimulate improvement.[35] For example, "This proposal is a confusing mess, and you failed to convince me of anything" is destructive feedback. The goal is to be more constructive: "Your proposal could be more effective with a clearer description of the manufacturing process and a well-organized explanation of why the positives outweigh the negatives." When giving feedback, avoid personal attacks and give the person clear guidelines for improvement.

TABLE 2 Giving Constructive Feedback

How to Be Constructive	Explanation
Think through your suggested changes carefully.	Many business documents must illustrate complex relationships between ideas and other information, so isolated and superficial edits can do more harm than good.
Discuss improvements rather than flaws.	Instead of saying "this is confusing," for instance, explain how the writing can be improved to make it clearer.
Focus on controllable behavior.	The writer may not have control over every variable that affected the quality of the message, so focus on those aspects the writer can control.
Be specific.	Comments such as "I don't get this" or "Make this clearer" don't give the writer much direction.
Keep feedback impersonal.	Focus comments on the message, not on the person who created it.
Verify understanding.	If in doubt, ask for confirmation from the recipient to make sure that the person understood your feedback.
Time your feedback carefully.	Respond in a timely fashion so that the writer will have sufficient time to implement the changes you suggest.
Highlight any limitations your feedback may have.	If you didn't have time to give the document a thorough edit, or if you're not an expert in some aspect of the content, let the writer know so that he or she can handle your comments appropriately.

When you receive constructive feedback, resist the understandable urge to defend your work or deny the validity of the feedback. Remaining open to criticism isn't easy when you've invested lots of time and energy in a project, but good feedback provides a valuable opportunity to learn and to improve the quality of your work.

Making Your Meetings More Productive

Much of your workplace communication will occur during in-person or online meetings, so to a large degree, your ability to contribute to the company—and to be recognized for your contributions—will depend on your meeting skills. Well-run meetings can help companies solve problems, develop ideas, and identify opportunities. Meetings can also be a great way to promote team building through the experience of social interaction.[36] As useful as meetings can be, though, they can be a waste of time if they aren't planned and managed well. You can help ensure productive meetings by preparing carefully, conducting meetings efficiently, and using meeting technologies wisely.

PREPARING FOR MEETINGS

The first step in preparing for a meeting is to make sure the meeting is really necessary. Meetings can consume hundreds or thousands of dollars of productive time while taking people away from other work, so don't hold a meeting if some other form of communication (such as a blog post) can serve the purpose as effectively.[37] If a meeting is truly necessary, proceed with these four planning tasks:

- **Define your purpose.** Meetings can focus on exchanging information, reaching decisions, or collaborating to solve problems or identify opportunities. Whatever your purpose, define the best possible result of the meeting (such as "we carefully evaluated all three product ideas and decided which one to invest in"). Use this hoped-for result to shape the direction and content of the meeting.[38]

- **Select participants for the meeting.** The rule here is simple: Invite everyone who really needs to be involved, and don't invite anyone who doesn't. For decision-making meetings, for example, invite only those people who are in a direct position to help the meeting reach its objective. The more people you have, the longer it will take to reach consensus. Meetings with more than 10 or 12 people can become unmanageable if everyone is expected to participate in the discussion and decision making.
- **Choose the venue and the time.** Online meetings are often the best way and sometimes the only way to connect people in multiple locations or to reach large audiences. For in-person meetings, review the facility and the seating arrangements. Is theater-style seating suitable, or do you need a conference table or some other arrangement? Pay attention to room temperature, lighting, ventilation, acoustics, and refreshments; these details can make or break a meeting. If you have control over the timing, morning meetings are often more productive because people are generally more alert and not yet engaged with the work of the day.
- **Set the agenda.** The success of a meeting depends on the preparation of the participants. Distribute a carefully written agenda to participants, giving them enough time to prepare as needed (see Figure 4 on the next page). A productive agenda answers three key questions: (1) What do we need to do in this meeting to accomplish our goals? (2) What issues will be of greatest importance to all participants? (3) What information must be available to discuss these issues?[39]

CONDUCTING AND CONTRIBUTING TO EFFICIENT MEETINGS

Everyone in a meeting shares the responsibility for making the meeting productive. If you're the leader, however, you have an extra degree of responsibility and accountability. The following guidelines will help leaders and participants contribute to more effective meetings:

The agenda title clearly identifies the scope of the meeting.

The clear and concise outline format identifies the topics that will be addressed and the order of discussion, which helps participants plan questions and suggestions.

Establishing a time limit for each section helps keep the meeting on track and ensures that time will be available for every topic.

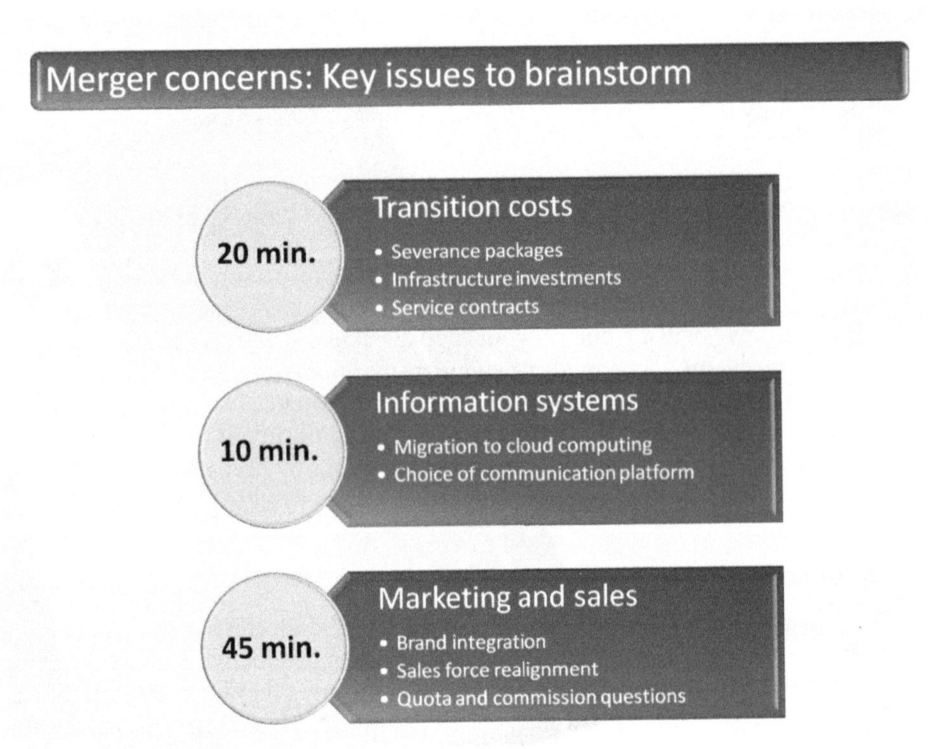

Merger concerns: Key issues to brainstorm

Transition costs
20 min.
- Severance packages
- Infrastructure investments
- Service contracts

Information systems
10 min.
- Migration to cloud computing
- Choice of communication platform

Marketing and sales
45 min.
- Brand integration
- Sales force realignment
- Quota and commission questions

Figure 4 Typical Meeting Agenda
Agenda formats vary widely, depending on the complexity of the meeting and the presentation technologies that will be used. One good approach is to first distribute a detailed planning agenda so that presenters know what they need to prepare, then create a simpler display agenda such as this PowerPoint slide to guide the progress of the meeting. Note how the agenda includes the time limit for each topic.

- **Keep the discussion on track.** A good meeting draws out the best ideas and information the group has to offer. Good leaders occasionally need to guide, mediate, probe, stimulate, summarize, and redirect discussions that have gotten off track.
- **Follow agreed-on rules.** The larger the meeting, the more formal you need to be to maintain order. Formal meetings use **parliamentary procedure**, a time-tested method for planning and running effective meetings. The best-known guide to this procedure is *Robert's Rules of Order.*
- **Encourage participation.** You may discover that some participants are too quiet and others are too talkative. Draw out nonparticipants by asking for their input. For the overly talkative, you can say that time is limited and others need to be heard.
- **Participate actively.** Make a point to contribute to the progress of the meeting and the smooth interaction of participants. Use your listening skills and powers of observation to size up the interpersonal dynamics of the group, then adapt your behavior to help the group achieve its goals. Speak up if you have something useful to say, but don't talk or ask questions just to demonstrate how much you know about the subject at hand.
- **Use mobile devices respectfully.** Tweeting key points from a convention speech or using your phone or tablet to jot down essential ideas and follow-up questions can be productive and respectful ways to use a device during a meeting. Checking Facebook or working on unrelated tasks is not. If you intend to use your device to take notes during a meeting, consider letting the meeting leader know that's what you're doing.[40]
- **Close effectively.** At the conclusion of the meeting, verify that the objectives have been met or arrange for follow-up work, if needed. Either summarize the general conclusion of the discussion or the actions to be taken. Make sure all participants have a chance to clear up any misunderstandings.

PUTTING MEETING RESULTS TO PRODUCTIVE USE

In most cases, the value of a meeting doesn't end when the meeting ends. For example, problems or opportunities brought up during a meeting need to be addressed, any action items assigned during the meeting need to be acted on, and key decisions and announcements should be distributed to anyone who is affected but was unable to attend. Having a written, audio, or video record of a meeting also gives the participants a chance to verify their impressions and conclusions.

The conventional method of recording meetings is through written **minutes**, a summary of the important information presented and the decisions made. One person is usually assigned to keep notes as the meeting progresses and then to share them afterward. The specific format of the minutes is less important than making sure you record all the key information, particularly regarding responsibilities that were assigned during the meeting. Typical elements include a list of those present and a list of those who were invited but didn't attend, followed by the times the meeting started and ended, all major decisions reached at the meeting, all assignments of tasks to meeting participants, and all subjects that were deferred to a later meeting. In addition, the minutes objectively summarize important discussions, noting the names of those who contributed major points. Any handouts, electronic slides, or supporting documents can be attached to the minutes when they are distributed.

Depending on the meeting technologies at your disposal, you may have software specifically designed to record, distribute, and store meeting minutes (see Figure 5). Some systems automatically forward action items to each employee, record audio discussions for future playback, and make all the relevant documents and files available in one convenient place.[41]

To review the tasks that contribute to productive meetings, refer to "Checklist: Improving Meeting Productivity" on the next page.

> Minutes are written summaries of important information presented and the decisions made in meetings.

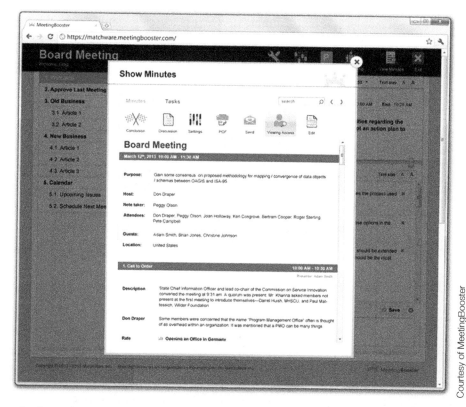

Courtesy of MeetingBooster

Figure 5 Capturing Key Decisions and Discoveries from a Meeting
Meeting technologies such as the MeetingBooster system help teams and other groups capture decisions and discoveries from meetings and put this information to productive use.

Improving Meeting Productivity

A. Prepare carefully.
- Make sure the meeting is necessary.
- Decide on your purpose.
- Select participants carefully.
- Choose the venue and the time.
- Establish and distribute a clear agenda.

B. Lead effectively and participate fully.
- Keep the meeting on track.
- Follow agreed-on rules.
- Encourage participation.
- Participate actively.
- Close effectively.

C. Put the results to effective use.
- Distribute meeting minutes to participants and other interested parties.
- Make sure task assignments are clearly communicated.

Using Meeting Technologies

4 LEARNING OBJECTIVE
Identify the major technologies used to enhance or replace in-person meetings.

Virtual meeting technologies connect people spread around the country or around the world.

MOBILE APP
WebEx Mobile gives you access to one of the world's most popular online meeting platforms.

Today's companies use a number of technologies to enhance or even replace traditional in-person meetings. Holding **virtual meetings** can dramatically reduce costs and resource usage, reduce wear and tear on employees, and give teams access to a wider pool of expertise (see Figure 6).

Instant messaging (IM) and teleconferencing are the simplest forms of virtual meetings. Videoconferencing lets participants see and hear each other, demonstrate products, and transmit other visual information. *Telepresence* (see Figure 7) enables realistic conferences in which participants thousands of miles apart almost seem to be in the same room.[42] The ability to convey nonverbal subtleties such as facial expressions and hand gestures makes these systems particularly good for negotiations, collaborative problem solving, and other complex discussions.[43]

The most sophisticated web-based meeting systems combine the best of real-time communication, shared workspaces, and videoconferencing with other tools, such as *virtual whiteboards*, that let teams collaborate in real time. Such systems are used for everything from spontaneous discussions among small groups to carefully planned formal events such as press conferences, training sessions, sales presentations, and *webinars* (web-based seminars).[44] One of the newest virtual tools is online brainstorming, in which a company can conduct "idea campaigns" to generate new ideas from people across the organization.

Courtesy of Cisco Systems, Inc. Unauthorized use not permitted

Figure 6 Virtual Meetings
With broadband wireless connections, virtual meetings are easy to conduct using smartphones or tablets

Figure 7   Telepresence
How many people are actually in this conference room in Chicago? Only the two people in the foreground are in the room; the other six are in Atlanta and London. Virtual meeting technologies such as this telepresence system connect people spread across the country or around the world.

Conducting successful virtual meetings requires extra planning beforehand and more diligence during the meeting. Recognizing the limitations of the virtual meeting format is a key to using it successfully.[45] Because virtual meetings offer less visual contact and non-verbal communication than in-person meetings, leaders need to make sure everyone stays engaged and has the opportunity to contribute. Paying attention during online meetings takes greater effort as well. Participants need to stay committed to the meeting and resist the temptation to work on unrelated tasks.[46]

> Conducting successful virtual meetings requires extra planning and more diligence during the meeting.

For the latest information on meeting technologies, visit http://real-timeupdates .com/ebc12 and click on this Chapter.

Improving Your Listening Skills

Your long-term career prospects are closely tied to your ability to listen effectively. In fact, some 80 percent of top executives say listening is the most important skill needed to get things done in the workplace.[47] Plus, today's younger employees place a high premium on being heard, so listening is becoming even more vital for managers.[48]

5 LEARNING OBJECTIVE
Identify three major modes of listening, describe the listening process, and explain the problem of selective listening.

Effective listening strengthens organizational relationships, alerts the organization to opportunities for innovation, and allows the organization to manage growing diversity both in the workforce and in the customers it serves.[49] Companies whose employees and managers listen effectively are able to stay informed, up to date, and out of trouble. Conversely, poor listening skills can cost companies millions of dollars per year as a result of lost opportunities, legal mistakes, and other errors. Effective listening is also vital to the process of building trust between organizations and between individuals.[50]

> Listening is one of the most important skills in the workplace.

RECOGNIZING VARIOUS TYPES OF LISTENING

Effective listeners adapt their listening approaches to different situations. The primary goal of **content listening** is to understand and retain the information in the speaker's message. Because you're not evaluating the information at this point, it doesn't matter whether you agree or disagree, approve or disapprove—only that you understand. Try to overlook the speaker's style and any limitations in the presentation; just focus on the information.[51]

> To be a good listener, adapt the way you listen to suit the situation.

The goal of **critical listening** is to understand and evaluate the meaning of the speaker's message on several levels: the logic of the argument, the strength of the evidence, the validity of the conclusions, the implications of the message, the speaker's intentions and motives, and the omission of any important or relevant points. If you're skeptical, ask questions to explore the speaker's point of view and credibility. Be on the lookout for bias that could color the way the information is presented, and be careful to separate opinions from facts.[52]

The goal of **empathic listening** is to understand the speaker's feelings, needs, and wants so that you can appreciate his or her point of view, regardless of whether you share that perspective. By listening with empathy, you help the individual vent the emotions that prevent a calm, clear-headed approach to the subject. Avoid the temptation to jump in with advice unless the person specifically asks for it. Also, don't judge the speaker's feelings, and don't try to tell people they shouldn't feel this or that emotion. Instead, let the speaker know that you appreciate his or her feelings and understand the situation. After you establish that connection, you can help the speaker move on to search for a solution.[53]

Listening actively means making the effort to turn off your internal "filters" and biases to truly hear and understand what the other person is saying.

No matter what mode they are using at any given time, effective listeners try to engage in **active listening**, making a conscious effort to turn off their own filters and biases to truly hear and understand what the other party is saying. They ask questions to verify key points and encourage the speaker through positive body language.[54]

UNDERSTANDING THE LISTENING PROCESS

Listening is a far more complex process than most people think—and most of us aren't very good at it. People typically listen at no better than a 25 percent efficiency rate, remember only about half of what's said during a 10-minute conversation, and forget half of that within 48 hours.[55] Furthermore, when questioned about material they've just heard, they are likely to get the facts mixed up.[56]

Why is such a seemingly simple activity so difficult? The reason is that listening is not a simple process, by any means. Listening follows the same sequence as the general communication process model, with the added challenge that it happens in real time. To listen effectively, you need to successfully complete five steps:[57]

Listening involves five steps: receiving, decoding, remembering, evaluating, and responding.

1. **Receiving.** You start by physically hearing the message and acknowledging it. Physical reception can be blocked by noise, impaired hearing, or inattention. Some experts also include nonverbal messages as part of this stage because these factors influence the listening process as well.
2. **Decoding.** Your next step is to assign meaning to sounds, which you do according to your own values, beliefs, ideas, expectations, roles, needs, and personal history.
3. **Remembering.** Before you can act on the information, you need to store it for future processing. Incoming messages must first be captured in short-term memory before being transferred to long-term memory for more permanent storage.
4. **Evaluating.** The next step is to evaluate the message by applying critical thinking skills to separate fact from opinion and evaluate the quality of the evidence.
5. **Responding.** After you've evaluated the speaker's message, you react. If you're communicating one-on-one or in a small group, the initial response generally takes the form of verbal feedback. If you're one of many in an audience, your initial response may take the form of applause, laughter, or silence. Later on, you may act on what you have heard.

If any one of these steps breaks down, the listening process becomes less effective or may even fail entirely. As both a sender and a receiver, you can reduce the failure rate by recognizing and overcoming a variety of physical and mental barriers to effective listening.

OVERCOMING BARRIERS TO EFFECTIVE LISTENING

Good listeners look for ways to overcome potential barriers throughout the listening process (see Table 3). You may not be able to control some factors, such as conference room acoustics or poor phone reception. However, you can control other factors, such as not interrupting speakers and not creating distractions that make it difficult for others to pay attention. And don't think you're not interrupting just because you're not talking. Such actions as texting or checking your watch can interrupt a speaker and lead to communication breakdowns.

Selective listening is one of the most common barriers to effective listening. If your mind wanders, you may stay tuned out until you hear a word or phrase that gets your attention again. But by that time, you're unable to recall what the speaker *actually* said; instead, you remember what you think the speaker *probably* said.[58]

One reason listeners' minds tend to wander is that people think faster than they speak. Most people speak at about 120 to 150 words per minute, but listeners can process audio information at up to 500 words per minute or more.[59] Consequently, your brain has a lot of free time whenever you're listening, and if left unsupervised, it will find a thousand other things to think about. Make the effort to focus on the speaker and use the extra time to analyze and paraphrase what you hear or to take relevant notes.

Overcoming interpretation barriers can be difficult because you may not even be aware of them. Selective perception leads listeners to mold messages to fit their own conceptual frameworks. Listeners sometimes make up their minds before fully hearing the speaker's message, or they engage in *defensive listening*—protecting their egos by tuning out anything that doesn't confirm their beliefs or their view of themselves.

Even when your intentions are good, you can still misinterpret incoming messages if you and the speaker don't share enough language or experience. When listening to a speaker whose native language or life experience is different from yours, try to paraphrase that person's ideas. Give the speaker a chance to confirm what you think you heard or to correct any misinterpretation.

If the information you hear will be important to use later, write it down or otherwise record it. Don't rely on your memory. If you do need to memorize, you can hold information in short-term memory by repeating it silently or organizing a long list of items into several shorter lists. To store information in long-term memory, four techniques can help: (1) associate new information with something closely related (such as the restaurant in

Good listeners actively try to overcome barriers to successful listening.

Your mind can process information much faster than most speakers talk, so you need to focus to listen effectively.

TABLE 3 What Makes an Effective Listener?

Effective Listeners	Ineffective Listeners
Listen actively.	Listen passively.
Take careful and complete notes, when applicable.	Take no notes or ineffective notes.
Make frequent eye contact with the speaker (depends on culture to some extent).	Make little or no eye contact—or inappropriate eye contact.
Stay focused on the speaker and the content.	Allow their minds to wander, are easily distracted, work on unrelated tasks.
Mentally paraphrase key points to maintain attention level and ensure comprehension.	Fail to paraphrase.
Adjust listening style to the situation.	Listen with the same style, regardless of the situation.
Give the speaker nonverbal cues (such as nodding to show agreement or raising eyebrows to show surprise or skepticism).	Fail to give the speaker nonverbal feedback.
Save questions or points of disagreement until an appropriate time.	Interrupt whenever they disagree or don't understand.
Overlook stylistic differences and focus on the speaker's message.	Are distracted by or unduly influenced by stylistic differences; are judgmental.
Make distinctions between main points and supporting details.	Are unable to distinguish main points from details.
Look for opportunities to learn.	Assume they already know everything that's important to know.

Sources: Adapted from Madelyn Burley-Allen, *Listening: The Forgotten Skill* (New York: Wiley, 1995), 70–71, 119–120; Judi Brownell, *Listening: Attitudes, Principles, and Skills* (Boston: Allyn & Bacon, 2002), 3, 9, 83, 89, 125; Larry Barker and Kittie Watson, *Listen Up* (New York: St. Martin's, 2000), 8, 9, 64.

> **CHECKLIST** ✔ Overcoming Barriers to Effective Listening
>
> - Lower barriers to physical reception whenever you can (such as avoiding interrupting speakers by asking questions or by exhibiting disruptive nonverbal behaviors).
> - Avoid selective listening by focusing on the speaker and carefully analyzing what you hear.
> - Keep an open mind by avoiding any prejudgment and by not listening defensively.
>
> - Don't count on your memory; write down or record important information.
> - Improve your short-term memory by repeating information or breaking it into shorter lists.
> - Improve your long-term memory by using association, categorization, visualization, and mnemonics.

which you met a new client), (2) categorize the new information into logical groups (such as alphabetizing a list of names), (3) visualize words and ideas as pictures, and (4) create mnemonics such as acronyms or rhymes.

For a reminder of the steps you can take to overcome listening barriers, see "Checklist: Overcoming Barriers to Effective Listening."

Improving Your Nonverbal Communication Skills

6 LEARNING OBJECTIVE
Explain the importance of nonverbal communication, and identify six major categories of nonverbal expression.

Nonverbal communication can supplement or even replace verbal messages (those that use words).

Nonverbal communication is the interpersonal process of sending and receiving information, both intentionally and unintentionally, without using written or spoken language. Nonverbal signals play a vital role in communication because they can strengthen a verbal message (when the nonverbal signals match the spoken words), weaken a verbal message (when nonverbal signals don't match the words), or replace words entirely. For example, you might tell a client that a project is coming along nicely, but your forced smile and nervous glances will send an entirely different message.

RECOGNIZING NONVERBAL COMMUNICATION

You've been tuned in to nonverbal communication since your first contact with other human beings. Paying special attention to nonverbal signals in the workplace will enhance your ability to communicate successfully. Moreover, as you work with a diverse range of people in the global marketplace, you'll also need to grasp the different meanings of common gestures, expressions, and other signals in various cultures. Six types of signals are particularly important:

Nonverbal signals include facial expression, gesture and posture, vocal characteristics, personal appearance, touch, and time and space.

- **Facial expression.** Your face is the primary vehicle for expressing your emotions; it reveals both the type and the intensity of your feelings.[60] Your eyes are especially effective for indicating attention and interest, influencing others, regulating interaction, and establishing dominance.[61]
- **Gesture and posture.** The way you position and move your body expresses both specific and general messages, some voluntary and some involuntary. Many gestures—a wave of the hand, for example—have specific and intentional meanings. Other types of body movement are unintentional and express more general messages. Slouching, leaning forward, fidgeting, and walking briskly are all unconscious signals that can reveal whether you feel confident or nervous, friendly or hostile, assertive or passive, powerful or powerless.
- **Vocal characteristics.** Voice carries both intentional and unintentional messages. A speaker can intentionally control pitch, pace, and stress to convey a specific message. For instance, compare "*What* are you doing?" and "What are *you* doing?" Unintentional vocal characteristics can convey happiness, surprise, fear, and other emotions (for example, fear often increases the pitch and pace of your speaking voice).

REAL-TIME UPDATES
LEARN MORE BY READING THIS ARTICLE

Improve your professional "curb appeal"

Send these nonverbal signals to build credibility in conversations. Go to http://real-timeupdates.com/ebc12 and click on Learn More in the Students section.

- **Personal appearance.** People respond to others on the basis of their physical appearance, sometimes fairly and other times unfairly. Although an individual's body type and facial features impose some limitations on appearance, you can control grooming, clothing, accessories, piercings, tattoos, and hairstyle. To make a good impression, adopt the style of the people you want to impress. Many employers also have guidelines concerning attire, body art, and other issues, so make sure you understand and follow them.[62]

- **Touch.** Touch is an important way to convey warmth, comfort, and reassurance—as well as control. Touch is so powerful, in fact, that it is governed by cultural customs that establish who can touch whom and how in various circumstances. Even within each culture's norms, however, individual attitudes toward touch vary widely. A manager might be comfortable using hugs to express support or congratulations, but his or her subordinates could interpret those hugs as a show of dominance or sexual interest.[63] Touch is a complex subject. The best advice: When in doubt, don't touch.

- **Time and space.** Like touch, time and space can be used to assert authority, imply intimacy, and send other nonverbal messages. For instance, some people try to demonstrate their own importance or disregard for others by making other people wait; others show respect by being on time. Similarly, taking care not to invade private space, such as standing too close when talking, is a way to show respect for others. Keep in mind that expectations regarding both time and space vary by culture.

USING NONVERBAL COMMUNICATION EFFECTIVELY

Paying attention to nonverbal cues will make you a better speaker and a better listener. When you're talking, be more conscious of the nonverbal cues you could be sending. Are they effective without being manipulative? Consider a situation in which an employee has come to you to talk about a raise. This situation is stressful for the employee, so don't say you're interested in what she has to tell you and then spend your time glancing at your computer or checking your watch. Conversely, if you already know you won't be able to give her the raise, be honest in your expression of emotions. Don't overcompensate for your own stress by smiling too broadly or shaking her hand too vigorously. Both nonverbal signals would raise her hopes without justification. In either case, match your nonverbal cues to the tone of the situation.

> Work to make sure your nonverbal signals match the tone and content of your spoken communication.

Also consider the nonverbal signals you send when you're not talking—the clothes you wear, the way you sit, the way you walk (see Figure 8). Are you talking like a serious

> What signals does your personal appearance send?

Radoslaw Korga/Shutterstock

Figure 8 Nonverbal Signals
The nonverbal signals you send in any business setting influence how others perceive you and your ideas.

CHECKLIST ✔ **Improving Nonverbal Communication Skills**

- Understand the roles that nonverbal signals play in communication, complementing verbal language by strengthening, weakening, or replacing words.
- Note that facial expressions (especially eye contact) reveal the type and intensity of a speaker's feelings.
- Watch for cues from gestures and posture.

- Listen for vocal characteristics that can signal the emotions underlying the speaker's words.
- Recognize that listeners are influenced by physical appearance.
- Be careful with physical contact; touch can convey positive attributes but can also be interpreted as dominance or sexual interest.
- Pay attention to the use of time and space.

business professional but dressing like you belong in a dance club or a frat house? Whether or not you think it is fair to be judged on superficial matters, the truth is that you are judged this way. Don't let careless choices or disrespectful habits undermine all the great work you're doing on the job.

When you listen, be sure to pay attention to the speaker's nonverbal cues. Do they amplify the spoken words or contradict them? Is the speaker intentionally using nonverbal signals to send you a message that he or she can't put into words? Be observant, but don't assume that you can "read someone like a book." Nonverbal signals are powerful, but they aren't infallible, particularly if you don't know a person's normal behavioral patterns.[64] For example, contrary to popular belief, avoiding eye contact and covering one's face while talking are not reliable clues that someone is lying. Even when telling the truth, most people don't make uninterrupted eye contact with the listeners, and various gestures such as touching one's face might be normal behavior for particular people.[65] Moreover, these and other behaviors may be influenced by culture (in some cultures, sustained eye contact can be interpreted as a sign of disrespect) or might just be ways of coping with stressful situations.[66]

If something doesn't feel right, ask the speaker an honest and respectful question; doing so may clear everything up, or it may uncover issues you need to explore further. See "Checklist: Improving Nonverbal Communication Skills" for a summary of key ideas regarding nonverbal skills.

Developing Your Business Etiquette

Etiquette is an essential element of every aspect of business communication.

You may have noticed a common thread running through the topics of successful teamwork, productive meetings, effective listening, and nonverbal communication: All these activities depend on mutual respect and consideration among all participants. Nobody wants to work with someone who is rude to colleagues or an embarrassment to the company. Moreover, shabby treatment of others in the workplace can be a huge drain on morale and productivity.[67] Poor etiquette can drive away customers, investors, and other critical audiences—and it can limit your career potential.

This section addresses some key etiquette points to remember when you're in the workplace, out in public, online, and using mobile devices. Long lists of etiquette rules can be difficult to remember, but you can get by in almost every situation by remembering to be aware of your effect on others, treating everyone with respect, and keeping in mind that the impressions you leave behind can have a lasting effect on you and your company. As etiquette expert Cindy Post Senning points out, "The principles of respect, consideration, and honesty are universal and timeless."[68]

BUSINESS ETIQUETTE IN THE WORKPLACE

Personal appearance can have considerable impact on your success in business.

Workplace etiquette includes a variety of behaviors, habits, and aspects of nonverbal communication. Although it isn't always thought of as an element of etiquette, your personal appearance in the workplace sends a strong signal to managers, colleagues, and customers (see Figure 9). Pay attention to the style of dress where you work and adjust your style

Figure 9 **Showing Respect for Organizational Culture**
Being aware of expectations for personal appearance in a business setting is not only a sign of respect, it will help keep you from making career-limiting mistakes.

Paul Bradbury/OJO Images Ltd/Alamy

to match. Expectations for specific jobs, companies, and industries can vary widely. The financial industries tend to be more formal than high-tech firms, for instance, and sales and executive positions usually involve more formal expectations than positions in engineering or manufacturing. Observe others, and don't be afraid to ask for advice. If you're not sure, dress modestly and simply—earn a reputation for what you can do, not for what you wear. Table 4 offers some general guidelines on assembling a business wardrobe that's cost-effective and flexible.

Grooming is as important as attire. Pay close attention to cleanliness, and avoid using products with powerful scents, such as perfumed soaps, colognes, shampoos, and after-shave lotions (many people are bothered by these products, and some are allergic to them).

TABLE 4   Assembling a Business Wardrobe

1 **Smooth and Finished (Start with This)**	2 **Elegant and Refined (To Column 1, Add This)**	3 **Crisp and Starched (To Column 2, Add This)**	4 **Up-to-the-Minute Trendy (To Column 3, Add This)**
• Choose well-tailored clothing that fits well; it doesn't have to be expensive, but it does have to fit and be appropriate for business. • Keep buttons, zippers, and hemlines in good repair. • Select shoes that are comfortable enough for long days but neither too casual nor too dressy for the office; keep shoes clean and in good condition. • Make sure the fabrics you wear are clean, are carefully pressed, and do not wrinkle easily. • Choose colors that flatter your height, weight, skin tone, and style; sales advisors in good clothing stores can help you choose.	• Choose form-fitting (but not skin-tight) clothing—not swinging or flowing fabrics, frills, or fussy trimmings. • Choose muted tones and soft colors or classics, such as a dark blue suit or a basic black dress. • If possible, select a few classic pieces of jewelry (such as a string of pearls or diamond cuff links) for formal occasions. • Wear jackets that complement an outfit and lend an air of formality to your appearance. Avoid jackets with more than two tones; one color should dominate.	• Wear blouses or shirts that are or appear starched. • Choose closed top-button shirts or button-down shirt collars, higher-neckline blouses, or long sleeves with French cuffs and cuff links. • Wear creased trousers or a longer skirt hemline.	• Supplement your foundation with pieces that reflect the latest styles. • Add a few pieces in bold colors but wear them sparingly to avoid a garish appearance. • Embellish your look with the latest jewelry and hairstyles but keep the overall effect looking professional.

Whose Skin Is This, Anyway?

Generational differences abound in the workplace, but few are quite as visible as body art: tattoos, piercings (other than ear lobes), and hair dyes in unconventional colors. According to survey data from the Pew Research Center, people younger than 40 are much more inclined than those older than 40 to display some form of body art. For example, people 26 to 40 years old are four times more likely to have tattoos than people who are 41 to 64 years old.

With such profound differences, it's no surprise that body art has become a contentious issue in many workplaces, between employees wanting to express themselves and employers wanting to maintain particular standards of professional appearance. As employment law attorney Danielle S. Urban notes, the issue gets even more complicated when religious symbolism is involved.

Who is likely to win this battle? Will the body art aficionados who continue to join the workforce and who are now rising up the managerial ranks force a change in what is considered acceptable appearance in the workplace? Or will they be forced to cover up to meet traditional standards?

So far, most companies appear to be relying on the judgment of their employees and managers, rather than enforcing strict guidelines. Many seem to accept that tastes and norms are changing and that body art has become a widespread form of self-expression rather than a mode of rebellion. Starbucks, which used to require employees to hide tattoos under long sleeves, recently revised its policy to allow employees to display tattoos everywhere except on their faces. The semiconductor giant Intel even featured photos of employee tattoos in its online technology newsletter.

Job seekers are still advised to be discreet, however, particularly with facial piercings and large, visible tattoos. The nonverbal signals you think you are sending might not be the signals a hiring manager receives—or wants to receive.

CAREER APPLICATIONS

1. Should companies have stricter standards of appearance for "customer-facing" employees than for employees who do not interact with customers? Why or why not?
2. Should companies allow their employees the same freedom of expression and appearance latitude as their customers exhibit? For example, if a firm's clientele tends to be heavily tattooed, should employees be allowed the same freedom? Why or why not?

Sources: Micah Solomon, "Starbucks to Allow Tattoos, Piercings: Wise or Risky Customer Service, HR Move?" *Forbes*, 17 October 2014, www.forbes.com; "Intel Tattoos Speak Volumes," 17 March 2011, *Intel Free Press*, www.intelfreepress.com; Rita Pyrillis, "Body of Work," *Workforce Management*, November 2010, www.workforce.com; Danielle S. Urban, "What to Do About 'Body Art' at Work," *Workforce Management*, March 2010, www.workforce.com; "36%—Tattooed Gen Nexters," Pew Research Center, http://pewresearch.org.

Your telephone skills will be vital to your business success.

IM and other text-based tools have taken over many exchanges that used to take place over the phone, but phone skills are still essential. Because phone calls lack the visual richness of face-to-face conversations, you have to rely on your attitude and tone of voice to convey confidence and professionalism. Here are some important tips for using phones at work:[69]

- **Be conscious of how your voice sounds.** Don't speak in a monotone; vary your pitch and inflections so people know you're interested. Slow down when conversing with people whose native language isn't the same as yours.

Basic courtesy on the phone makes communication more efficient and more pleasant for everyone involved.

- **Be courteous when you call someone.** Identify yourself and your organization, briefly describe why you're calling, and verify that you've called at a good time. Minimize the noise level in your environment as much as possible. For important or complicated conversations, plan what you want to say before calling.
- **Convey a positive, professional attitude when you answer the phone.** Answer promptly and with a smile so that you sound welcoming. Identify yourself and your company (some companies have specific instructions for what to say when you answer). Establish the needs of your caller by asking, "How may I help you?" If you know the caller's name, use it. If you can't answer the caller's questions, either forward the call to a colleague who can or advise the caller on how to get his or her questions resolved. If you do forward a call, put the caller on hold and call the next person yourself to verify that he or she is available.
- **End calls with courtesy and clarity.** Close in a friendly, positive manner and double-check all vital information such as meeting times and dates.
- **Use your own voicemail features to help callers.** Record a brief, professional-sounding outgoing message for regular use. When you will be away or unable to

answer the phone for an extended period, record a temporary greeting that tells callers when you will respond to their messages. If you don't check your messages regularly or at all, disable your voicemail. Letting messages pile up for days or weeks without answering them is extremely thoughtless.

- **Be considerate when leaving voicemail messages.** Retrieving voicemail messages can be a chore, so be thoughtful about leaving them. Unless voicemail is the best or only choice, consider leaving a message through other means, such as text messaging or email. If you do leave a voicemail message, make it as brief as possible. Leave your name, number (don't assume the recipient has caller ID), reason for calling, and times you can be reached. State your name and telephone number slowly so the other person can easily write them down; repeat both if the other person doesn't know you.

If you never or rarely check your voicemail, disable it or record an outgoing message advising callers to reach you another way.

BUSINESS ETIQUETTE IN SOCIAL SETTINGS

From business lunches to industry conferences, you may be asked to represent your company in public. Make sure your appearance and actions are appropriate to the situation. Get to know the customs of other cultures when it comes to meeting new people. For example, in North America, a firm handshake is expected when two people meet, whereas a respectful bow of the head is more appropriate in Japan. If you are expected to shake hands, be aware that the passive "dead fish" handshake creates an extremely negative impression. If you are physically able, always stand when shaking someone's hand.

When introducing yourself, include a brief description of your role in the company. When introducing two other people, speak their first and last names clearly and then try to offer some information (perhaps a shared professional interest) to help the two people ease into a conversation.[70] Generally speaking, the lower-ranking person is introduced to the senior-ranking person, without regard to gender.[71]

Business is often conducted over meals, and knowing the basics of dining etiquette will make you more effective in these situations.[72] Start by choosing foods that are easy to eat. Avoid alcoholic beverages in most instances, but if drinking one is appropriate, save it for the end of the meal. Leave business documents under your chair until entrée plates have been removed; the business aspect of the meal doesn't usually begin until then.

Remember that business meals are a forum for business. Don't discuss politics, religion, or any other topic that's likely to stir up emotions. Don't complain about work, don't ask deeply personal questions, avoid profanity, and be careful with humor—a joke that entertains some people could easily offend others.

Etiquette is particularly important when you represent your company out in public.

MOBILE APP
The Etiquette App helps you make appropriate choices in a variety of social and business situations.

BUSINESS ETIQUETTE ONLINE

Electronic media seem to be a breeding ground for poor etiquette. Learn the basics of professional online behavior to avoid mistakes that could hurt your company or your career. Here are some guidelines to follow whenever you are representing your company while using electronic media:[73]

- **Avoid personal attacks.** The anonymous and instantaneous nature of online communication can cause even level-headed people to strike out in blog postings, social networks, and other media.
- **Stay focused on the original topic.** If you want to change the subject of an email exchange, a forum discussion, or a blog comment thread, start a new message.
- **Don't present opinions as facts, and support facts with evidence.** This guideline applies to all communication, of course, but online venues in particular seem to tempt people into presenting their beliefs and opinions as unassailable truths.
- **Follow basic expectations of spelling, punctuation, and capitalization.** Sending careless, acronym-filled messages that look like you're texting your high school buddies makes you look like an amateur.
- **Use virus protection and keep it up to date.** Sending or posting a file that contains a computer virus puts others at risk.

When you represent your company online, you must adhere to a high standard of etiquette and respect for others.

Collaboration, Interpersonal Communication, and Business Etiquette

- **Use difficult-to-break passwords on email, Twitter, and other accounts.** If someone hacks your account, it can create spam headaches—or worse—for your contacts and followers.
- **Ask if this is a good time for an IM chat.** Don't assume that just because a person is showing as "available" on your IM system, he or she wants to chat at this moment.
- **Watch your language and keep your emotions under control.** A single indiscretion could haunt you forever.
- **Avoid multitasking while using IM and other tools.** You might think you're saving time by doing a dozen things at once, but you're probably making the other person wait while you bounce back and forth between IM and your other tasks.
- **Never assume privacy.** Assume that anything you type will be stored forever, could be forwarded to other people, and might be read by your boss or the company's security staff.
- **Don't use "Reply All" in email unless everyone can benefit from your reply.** If one or more recipients of an email message don't need the information in your reply, remove their addresses before you send.
- **Don't waste others' time with sloppy, confusing, or incomplete messages.** Doing so is disrespectful.
- **Respect boundaries of time and virtual space.** For instance, don't start using an employee's personal Facebook page for business messages unless you've discussed it beforehand, and don't assume people are available to discuss work matters around the clock, even if you do find them online in the middle of the night.
- **Be careful of online commenting mechanisms.** For example, many blogs and websites now use your Facebook login to let you comment on articles. If your Facebook profile includes your job title and company name, those could show up along with your comment.

Respect personal and professional boundaries when using Facebook and other social networking tools.

BUSINESS ETIQUETTE USING MOBILE DEVICES

Like every other aspect of communication, your mobile device habits say a lot about how much respect you have for the people around you. Selecting obnoxious ringtones, talking loudly in open offices or public places, using your phone right next to someone else, making excessive or unnecessary personal calls during work hours, invading someone's privacy by using your phone's camera without permission, taking or making calls in restrooms and other inappropriate places, texting during a meal or while someone is talking to you, allowing incoming calls to interrupt meetings or discussions—these are all disrespectful choices that will reflect negatively on you.[74] In general, older employees, managers, and customers are less tolerant of mobile device use than are younger people, so don't assume that your habits will be universally acceptable.[75]

Your mobile phone habits send a signal about the degree of respect you have for those around you.

MOBILE APP

Locale can "geofence" your smartphone, automatically changing settings based on your location—such as activating silent mode when you arrive at your office.

Virtual assistants and other mobile phone voice features can annoy and disrupt the workplace and social settings if not used with respect for others.

Virtual assistants, such as the Siri voice recognition system in Apple iPhones, raise another new etiquette dilemma. From doing simple web searches to dictating entire memos, these systems may be convenient for users, but they can create distractions and annoyances for other people.[76] As with other public behaviors, think about the effect you have on others before using these technologies.

Note that expectations and policies regarding mobile device use vary widely from company to company. At one extreme, venture capitalist Ben Horowitz fines his employees if they even look at a mobile device while an entrepreneur is making a business plan pitch, because he considers it disrespectful to people making presentations.[77] Not all bosses are quite so strict, but make sure you understand the situation in your workplace.

ON THE JOB: SOLVING COMMUNICATION DILEMMAS AT CEMEX

You work as a customer account manager in Cemex's Houston office, where you're an enthusiastic user of the Shift collaboration platform. Even in the best work environments, conflicts and misunderstandings can arise. Study these scenarios and decide how to respond, based on what you learned in this chapter.

1. You rely heavily on CEMEXpedia, the wiki that contains technical and business information about the company's operations. As you've become more experienced in your job, you have also become a frequent contributor to the wiki. Lately you've noticed one particular employee from the Cemex office in Madrid, Spain, keeps editing the pages you create on the wiki, often making changes that appear to add no value, as far as you can see. She doesn't seem to be editing other employees' pages nearly so often, so you are beginning to wonder if she has a personal grudge against you, even though you have never met her. You want to address this uncomfortable situation without dragging your boss into it. How should you handle it?
   a. Edit some of her pages needlessly to help her understand how annoying this behavior is.
   b. Use the private messaging tools on Shift to ask her if there is something about your writing style that she finds unclear. That will open a conversation in a nonthreatening way.
   c. Post a notice on the wiki, emphasizing that all edits should be useful and that unnecessary edits waste everybody's time.
   d. Ignore her behavior; confronting her will get you nowhere.

2. You've been asked to take over leadership of a group of customer account managers that once had a reputation for being a tight-knit, supportive team, but you quickly figure out that this team is in danger of becoming dysfunctional. For example, minor issues that healthy teams routinely handle, from helping each other with computer questions to covering the phones when someone has an outside appointment, frequently generate conflict within this group. What steps should you take to help your crew return to positive behavior?
   a. Give the team the task of healing itself, without getting directly involved. Explain the steps necessary in forming an effective team and then let them figure out how to make it happen.
   b. Lead the "team restoration" project yourself so that you can mediate whatever conflicts arise, at least until the team is able to function on its own in a more positive manner.
   c. Don't try to interfere; the negative behaviors were probably caused by an ineffective manager in the past, but now that you're in charge, the team will return to positive behavior under your enlightened guidance.

   d. Your professional reputation is on the line, so you don't have time for the niceties of team building. Sit down with the group and demand that the negative, unprofessional behavior stop immediately.

3. After a few weeks with the account management team, you notice that team meetings often degenerate into little more than complaint sessions. Workers seem to gripe about everything from difficult customers to the temperature in the office. Some of these complaints sound like valid business issues that might require additional training or other employee support efforts; others are superficial issues you suspect are simply by-products of the negative atmosphere. How should you handle complaints during the meetings?
   a. Try to defuse each complaint with humor; after awhile, employees will begin to lighten up and stop complaining so much.
   b. Ask employees to refrain from complaining during meetings; after all, these are important business meetings, not random social gatherings.
   c. Set up a whiteboard and write down each issue that is raised. After you've compiled a list over the course of a week or so, add a problem-solving segment to each meeting, in which you and the team tackle one issue per meeting to determine the scope of each problem and identify possible solutions.
   d. Whenever a complaint is raised, stop the meeting and confront the person who raised the issue. Challenge him or her to prove that the problem is a real business issue and not just a personal complaint. By doing this, you will not only identify the real problems that need to be fixed but also discourage people from raising petty complaints that shouldn't be aired in the workplace.

4. You're in charge of hiring a replacement for a customer account manager who recently retired. Four job candidates are waiting outside your office, and you have a few moments to observe them before inviting them in for an initial interview (you can see them through the glass wall but can't hear them). Based on the following descriptions, which of these people seems like the best fit for the firm? Why?
   a. **Candidate A:** A woman who is dressed perfectly for an interview at Cemex. Her appearance is contemporary but business appropriate, which suggests that she appreciates and shows respect for the situation she finds herself in. However, you are slightly troubled by the fact that she's listening to music on her phone and has kicked off her shoes and tucked her feet under her while she waits in the chair.
   b. **Candidate B:** A man who has also dressed the part, although this candidate's behavior is nothing like the relaxed, carefree attitude that Candidate A is showing.

Collaboration, Interpersonal Communication, and Business Etiquette

He seems to be juggling multiple tasks at once: checking notes on some sort of digital device, organizing a collection of papers he pulled from his briefcase, reattaching several sticky notes that keep falling loose, and fiddling with a mobile phone that he has answered at least twice in the few minutes you've been watching.

   c. Candidate C: A woman who closed the notebook she was scanning in order to help Candidate B with some problem he was having with his mobile phone. (If you had to guess, he was having trouble figuring out how to silence the ringer.) After their interaction, they shake hands and appear to be introducing themselves with

cordial smiles. Unfortunately, although the city is suffering through record high temperatures, her casual dress and sandals strike you as too informal for a job interview.

   d. Candidate D: A man wearing what appears to be a finely tailored, conservative suit. His appearance is more dignified and businesslike than the other three, and he knows how to dress for success—carefully knotted tie, starched shirt, perfect posture, the works. He keeps to himself and avoids bothering the other candidates, although his facial expressions make it clear that he disapproves of the noise Candidate B is making with his mobile phone.

Learning Objectives Checkup

Assess your understanding of the principles in this chapter by reading each learning objective and studying the accompanying exercises.

Objective 1: List the advantages and disadvantages of working in teams, describe the characteristics of effective teams, and highlight four key issues of group dynamics.

1. Teams can achieve a higher level of performance than individuals alone because
   a. They combine the intelligence and energy of multiple individuals
   b. They can foster motivation and creativity
   c. They involve more input and a greater diversity of views, which tends to result in better decisions
   d. They do all of the above
2. Which of the following is a potential disadvantage of working in teams?
   a. Teams always stamp out creativity by forcing people to conform to existing ideas and practices.
   b. Teams increase a company's clerical workload because of the additional government paperwork required for administering workplace insurance.
   c. Team members are never held accountable for their individual performance.
   d. Social pressure within the group can lead to groupthink, in which people go along with a bad idea or poor decision even though they may not really believe in it.
3. Conflict in team settings can be _____ if it forces important issues into the open, increases the involvement of team members, and generates creative ideas for solving a problem.

Objective 2: Offer guidelines for collaborative communication, identify major collaboration technologies, and explain how to give constructive feedback.

4. Which of the following is the best way for a team of people to write a report?
   a. Each member should plan, research, and write his or her individual version and then the group can select the strongest report.

   b. The team should divide and conquer, with one person doing the planning, one doing the research, one doing the writing, and so on.
   c. To ensure a true group effort, every task from planning through final production should be done as a team, preferably with everyone in the same room at the same time.
   d. Research and plan as a group but assign the actual writing to one person, or at least assign separate sections to individual writers and have one person edit them all to achieve a consistent style.
5. Which of the following steps should be completed before anyone from the team does any planning, researching, or writing?
   a. The team should agree on the project's goals.
   b. The team should agree on the report's title.
   c. To avoid compatibility problems, the team should agree on which word processor or other software will be used.
   d. The team should always step away from the work environment and enjoy some social time in order to bond effectively before starting work.
6. Which of the following is not a benefit of using social media for business communication?
   a. Social media are "out in the open," so messages are easier for managers to monitor and control.
   b. Social media help erase geographic and organization boundaries.
   c. Social media give customers an easy way to voice their opinions and concerns.
   d. Social media can help "faceless" companies adopt a more human, conversational tone.

Objective 3: List the key steps needed to ensure productive team meetings.

7. What are the three key steps to making sure meetings are productive?
   a. Planning, planning, and more planning
   b. Preparing carefully, conducting meetings efficiently, and putting meeting results to productive use
   c. Preparing carefully, conducting meetings using true democratic participation, and using meeting technologies wisely
   d. Preparing carefully, using meeting technologies wisely, and distributing in-depth minutes to everyone in the company
8. *Robert's Rules of Order* is a guide to _____ procedure.

Objective 2.4: Identify the major technologies used to enhance or replace in-person meetings.

9. _____ teams are teams whose members work in different locations and interact electronically.

10. _____ technologies enable realistic conferences in which participants thousands of miles apart almost seem to be in the same room.

Objective 2.5: Identify three major modes of listening, describe the listening process, and explain the problem of selective listening.

11. After receiving messages, listeners _____ what they've heard by assigning meaning to the sounds.

12. If you're giving an important presentation and notice that many of the audience members look away when you try to make momentary eye contact, which of the following is most likely going on?
    a. These audience members don't want to challenge your authority by making direct eye contact.
    b. You work with a lot of shy people.
    c. The information you're presenting is making your audience uncomfortable in some way.
    d. The audience is taking time to carefully think about the information you're presenting.

13. If you don't agree with something the speaker says in a large, formal meeting, the best response is to
    a. Signal your disagreement by folding your arms across your chest and staring defiantly back at the speaker.
    b. Use your mobile phone to begin sending text messages to other people in the room, explaining why the speaker is wrong.
    c. Immediately challenge the speaker so that the misinformation is caught and corrected.
    d. Quietly make a note of your objections and wait until a question-and-answer period to raise your hand.

Objective 6: Explain the importance of nonverbal communication, and identify six major categories of nonverbal expression.

14. Nonverbal signals can be more influential than spoken language because
    a. Body language is difficult to control and therefore difficult to fake, so listeners often put more trust in nonverbal cues than in the words a speaker uses.
    b. Nonverbal signals communicate faster than spoken language, and most people are impatient.
    c. Body language saves listeners from the trouble of paying attention to what a speaker is saying.

15. Which of the following is true about nonverbal signals?
    a. They can strengthen a spoken message.
    b. They can weaken a spoken message.
    c. They can replace spoken messages.
    d. All of the above are true.

Objective 7: Explain the importance of business etiquette, and identify four key areas in which good etiquette is essential.

16. Which of the following is the best characterization of etiquette in today's business environment?

    a. Business etiquette is impossible to generalize because every company has its own culture; you have to make it up as you go along.
    b. With ferocious international competition and constant financial pressure, etiquette is an old-fashioned luxury that businesses simply can't afford today.
    c. Ethical businesspeople don't need to worry directly about etiquette because ethical behavior automatically leads to good etiquette.
    d. Etiquette plays an important part in the process of forming and maintaining successful business relationships.

17. If you forgot to shut off your mobile phone before stepping into a business meeting and you receive a call during the meeting, the most appropriate thing to do is to
    a. Lower your voice to protect the privacy of your phone conversation.
    b. Answer the phone and then quickly hang it up to minimize the disruption to the meeting.
    c. Excuse yourself from the meeting and find a quiet place to talk.
    d. Continue to participate in the meeting while taking the call; this shows everyone that you're an effective multitasker.

18. Your company has established a designated "quiet time" from 1:00 to 3:00 every afternoon, during which office phones, IM, and email are disabled so that people can concentrate on planning, researching, writing, and other intensive tasks without being interrupted. However, a number of people continue to flout the guidelines by leaving their mobile phones on, saying their families and friends need to able to reach them. With all the various ringtones going off at random, the office is just as noisy as it was before. What is the best response?
    a. Agree to reactivate the office phone system if everyone will shut off their mobile phones, but have all incoming calls routed through a receptionist who will take messages for all routine calls and deliver a note if an employee truly is needed in an emergency.
    b. Give up on quiet time; with so many electronic gadgets in the workplace today, you'll never achieve peace and quiet.
    c. Get tough on the offenders by confiscating mobile phones whenever they ring during quiet time.
    d. Without telling anyone, simply install one of the available mobile phone jamming products that block incoming and outgoing mobile phone calls.

19. Constantly testing the limits of your company's dress and grooming standards sends a strong signal that you
    a. Don't understand or don't respect your company's culture.
    b. Are a strong advocate for worker's rights.
    c. Are a creative and independent thinker who is likely to generate lots of successful business ideas.
    d. Represent the leading edge of a new generation of enlightened workers who will redefine the workplace according to contemporary standards.

Quick Learning Guide

LEARNING OBJECTIVES

1. List the advantages and disadvantages of working in teams, describe the characteristics of effective teams, and highlight four key issues of group dynamics.

2. Offer guidelines for collaborative communication, identify major collaboration technologies, and explain how to give constructive feedback.

3. List the key steps needed to ensure productive team meetings.

4. Identify the major technologies used to enhance or replace in-person meetings.

5. Identify three major modes of listening, describe the listening process, and explain the problem of selective listening.

6. Explain the importance of nonverbal communication, and identify six major categories of nonverbal expression.

7. Explain the importance of business etiquette, and identify four key areas in which good etiquette is essential.

KEY TERMS

active listening Making a conscious effort to turn off filters and biases to truly hear and understand what someone is saying

collaboration Working together to meet complex challenges

committees Formal teams that usually have a long life span and can become a permanent part of the organizational structure

constructive feedback Focuses on the process and outcomes of communication, not on the people involved

content listening Listening to understand and retain the speaker's message

content management systems Computer systems that organize and control the content for websites

critical listening Listening to understand and evaluate the meaning of the speaker's message

destructive feedback Delivers criticism with no guidance to stimulate improvement

empathic listening Listening to understand the speaker's feelings, needs, and wants so that you can appreciate his or her point of view

group dynamics The interactions and processes that take place among the members of a team

groupthink Situation in which peer pressure causes individual team members to withhold contrary or unpopular opinions

hidden agenda Private, counterproductive motives, such as a desire to take control of the group

minutes Written summary of the important information presented and the decisions made during a meeting

nonverbal communication Sending and receiving information, both intentionally and unintentionally, without using written or spoken language

norms Informal standards of conduct that members share and that guide member behavior

parliamentary procedure A time-tested method for planning and running effective meetings; the best-known guide to this procedure is *Robert's Rules of Order*

participative management The effort to involve employees in the company's decision making

problem-solving teams Teams that assemble to resolve specific issues and then disband when their goals have been accomplished

selective listening Listening to only part of what a speaker is saying; ignoring the parts one doesn't agree with or find interesting

self-oriented roles Unproductive team roles in which people are motivated mainly to fulfill personal needs

shared workspaces Online "virtual offices" that give everyone on a team access to the same set of resources and information

task forces Another form of problem-solving teams, often with members from more than one organization

task-oriented roles Productive team roles directed toward helping the team reach its goals

team A unit of two or more people who share a mission and the responsibility for working to achieve a common goal

team-maintenance roles Productive team roles directed toward helping everyone work well together

unified communication Integrates voice and video calling, voice and video conferencing, instant messaging, real-time collaboration software, and other capabilities into a single system

virtual meetings Meetings that take place online rather than in person

wiki Special type of website that allows anyone with access to add new material and edit existing material

Apply Your Knowledge

To review chapter content related to each question, refer to the indicated Learning Objective.

⭐ 1. You head up the interdepartmental design review team for a manufacturer of high-performance motorcycles, and things are not going well at the moment. The design engineers and marketing strategists keep arguing about which should be a higher priority, performance or aesthetics, and the accountants say both groups are driving up the cost of the new model by adding too many new features. Everyone has valid points to make, but the team is bogging down in conflict. Explain how you could go about resolving the stalemate. [LO-1]

⭐ 2. You and another manager in your company disagree about whether employees should be encouraged to create online profiles on LinkedIn and other business-oriented social networking websites. You say these connections can be valuable to employees by helping them meet their peers throughout the industry and valuable to the company by identifying potential sales leads and business partners. The other manager says that encouraging employees to become better known in the industry will only make it easier for competitors to lure them away with enticing job offers. Write a brief email message that outlines your argument. (Make up any information you need about the company and its industry.) [LO-2]

3. How can nonverbal communication help you run a meeting? How can it help you call a meeting to order, emphasize important topics, show approval, express reservations, regulate the flow of conversation, and invite a colleague to continue with a comment? [LO-3], [LO-6]

⭐ 4. Why do you think people are more likely to engage in rude behaviors during online communication than during in-person communication? [LO-7]

⭐ 5. You're giving your first major presentation at your new job and you notice at least half the people in the small conference room are looking at their mobile devices more than they are looking at you. How should you handle the situation? [LO-7]

Practice Your Skills

Message for Analysis: Planning Meetings [LO-3]

A project leader has made notes about covering the following items at the quarterly budget meeting. Prepare a formal agenda by putting these items into a logical order and rewriting, where necessary, to give phrases a more consistent sound.

- Budget Committee Meeting to be held on December 12, 2016, at 9:30 a.m., and we have allotted one hour for the meeting
- I will call the meeting to order.
- Real estate director's report: A closer look at cost overruns on Greentree site. (10 minutes)
- The group will review and approve the minutes from last quarter's meeting. (5 minutes)
- I will ask the finance director to report on actual versus projected quarterly revenues and expenses. (15 minutes)
- I will distribute copies of the overall divisional budget and announce the date of the next budget meeting.
- Discussion: How can we do a better job of anticipating and preventing cost overruns? (20 minutes)
- Meeting will take place in Conference Room 3, with WebEx active for remote employees.
- What additional budget issues must be considered during this quarter?

Exercises

Each activity is labeled according to the primary skill or skills you will need to use. To review relevant chapter content, you can refer to the indicated Learning Objective.

6. **Collaboration: Working in Teams [LO-1], [LO-2]** In teams assigned by your instructor, prepare a 10-minute presentation on the potential disadvantages of using social media for business communication. When the presentation is ready, discuss how effective the team was using the criteria of (a) having a clear objective and a shared sense of purpose, (b) communicating openly and honestly, (c) reaching decisions by consensus, (d) thinking creatively, and (e) knowing how to resolve conflict. Be prepared to discuss your findings with the rest of the class.

7. **Negotiation and Conflict Resolution: Resolving Conflicts; Communication Ethics: Providing Ethical Leadership [LO-1]** During team meetings, one member constantly calls for votes or decisions before all the members have voiced their views. As the leader, you asked this member privately about his behavior. He replied that he is trying to move the team toward its goals, but you are concerned that he is really trying to take control. How can you deal with this situation without removing the member from the group?

8. **Collaboration: Collaborating on Writing Projects; Media Skills: Blogging [LO-2]** In this project, you will conduct research on your own and then merge your results with those of the rest of your team. Search Twitter for messages on the subject of workplace safety. (You can use Twitter's advanced search function or use the site "twitter.com" qualifier on a regular search engine.) Compile at least five general safety tips that apply to any office setting, and then meet with your team to select the five best tips from all those the team has collected. Collaborate on a blog post that lists the team's top five tips.

9. **Communication Etiquette: Etiquette in the Workplace, Participating in Meetings [LO-3], [LO-7]** In group meetings, some of your colleagues have a habit of interrupting and arguing with the speaker, taking credit for ideas that aren't theirs, and shooting down ideas they don't agree with. As the newest person in the group, you're not sure if

this is accepted behavior in this company, but it concerns you both personally and professionally. Should you go with the flow and adopt their behavior or stick with your own communication style, even though you might get lost in the noise? In a two-paragraph email message or post for your class blog, explain the pros and cons of both approaches.

10. **Collaboration: Participating in Meetings [LO-3]** With a classmate, attend a local community or campus meeting where you can observe a group discussion, vote, or take other group action. During the meeting, take notes individually and, afterward, work together to answer the following questions.

    a. What is your evaluation of this meeting? In your answer, consider (1) the leader's ability to articulate the meeting's goals clearly, (2) the leader's ability to engage members in a meaningful discussion, (3) the group's dynamics, and (4) the group's listening skills.

    b. How did group members make decisions? Did they vote? Did they reach decisions by consensus? Did those with dissenting opinions get an opportunity to voice their objections?

    c. How well did the individual participants listen? How could you tell?

    d. Did any participants change their expressed views or their votes during the meeting? Why might that have happened?

    e. Did you observe any communication barriers? Identify them.

    f. Compare the notes you took during the meeting with those of your classmate. What differences do you notice? How do you account for these differences?

11. **Collaboration: Leading Meetings [LO-3]** Every month, each employee in your department is expected to give a brief oral presentation on the status of his or her project. However, your department has recently hired an employee who has a severe speech impediment that prevents people from understanding most of what he has to say. As department manager, how will you resolve this dilemma? Please explain.

12. **Collaboration: Using Collaboration Technologies [LO-4]** In a team assigned by your instructor, use Zoho (free for personal use) or a comparable system to collaborate on a set of directions that out-of-town visitors could use to reach a specific point on your campus, such as a stadium or dorm. The team should choose the location and the mode(s) of transportation involved. Be creative—brainstorm the best ways to guide first-time visitors to the selected location using all the media at your disposal.

13. **Interpersonal Communication: Listening Actively [LO-5]** For the next several days, take notes on your listening performance during at least a half-dozen situations in class, during social activities, and at work, if applicable. Referring to the traits of effective listeners in Table 3, rate yourself using *always, frequently, occasionally,* or *never* on these positive listening habits. In a report no longer than one page, summarize your analysis and identify specific areas in which you can improve your listening skills.

14. **Nonverbal Communication: Analyzing Nonverbal Signals [LO-6]** Select a business letter and envelope you

have received at work or home. Analyze their appearance. What nonverbal messages do they send? Are these messages consistent with the content of the letter? If not, what could the sender have done to make the nonverbal communication consistent with the verbal communication? Summarize your findings in a post on your class blog or in an email message to your instructor.

15. **Communication Etiquette: Etiquette in the Workplace [LO-7]** As the regional manager of an international accounting firm, you place high priority on professional etiquette. Not only does it communicate respect to your clients, it also instills confidence in your firm by showing that you and your staff are aware of and able to meet the expectations of almost any audience. Earlier today, you took four recently hired college graduates to lunch with an important client. You've done this for years, and it's usually an upbeat experience for everyone, but today's lunch was a disaster. One of the new employees made not one, not two, but three calls on his mobile phone during lunch. Another interrupted the client several times and even got into a mild argument. The third employee kept making sarcastic jokes about politics, making everyone at the table uncomfortable. And the fourth showed up dressed like she was expecting to bale hay or work in a coal mine, not have a business lunch in a posh restaurant. You've already called the client to apologize, but now you need to coach these employees on proper business etiquette. Draft a brief memo to these employees, explaining why etiquette is so important to the company's success—and to their individual careers.

Expand Your Skills

Critique the Professionals

Celebrities can learn from successful businesses when it comes to managing their careers, but businesses can learn from successful celebrities, too—particularly when it comes to building communities online using social media. For instance, social media guru Dan Schawbel cites Vin Diesel, Ashton Kutcher, Lady Gaga, Lenny Kravitz, and Michael Phelps as celebrities who have used Facebook to build their personal brands.[78] Locate three celebrities (musicians, actors, authors, or athletes) who have sizable fan bases on Facebook and analyze how they use the social network. Using whatever medium your instructor requests, write a brief analysis (no more than one page) of the lessons, positive or negative, that a business could learn from these celebrities. Be sure to cite specific elements from the Facebook pages you've chosen, and if you think any of the celebrities have made mistakes in their use of Facebook, describe those as well.

Sharpening Your Career Skills Online

Bovée and Thill's Business Communication Web Search, at http://websearch.businesscommunicationnetwork.com, is a unique research tool designed specifically for business communication research. Use the Web Search function to find a website, video, PDF document, podcast, or presentation that offers advice on improving your active listening skills in business situations. Write a brief email message to your instructor, describing the item you found and summarizing the career skills information you learned from it.

Improve Your Grammar, Mechanics, and Usage

The following exercises help you improve your knowledge of and power over English grammar, mechanics, and usage. Turn to the Handbook of Grammar, Mechanics, and Usage at the end of this text and review Pronouns. Then look at the following 10 items. Underline the preferred choice within each set of parentheses.

16. The sales staff is preparing guidelines for (*their, its*) clients.

17. Few of the sales representatives turn in (*their, its*) reports on time.

18. The board of directors has chosen (*their, its*) officers.

19. Gomez and Archer have told (*his, their*) clients about the new program.

20. Each manager plans to expand (*his, their, his or her*) sphere of control next year.

21. Has everyone supplied (*his, their, his or her*) Social Security number?

22. After giving every employee (*his, their, a*) raise, George told (*them, they, all*) about the increased work load.

23. Bob and Tim have opposite ideas about how to achieve company goals. (*Who, Whom*) do you think will win the debate?

24. City Securities has just announced (*who, whom*) it will hire as CEO.

25. Either of the new products would readily find (*their, its*) niche in the marketplace.

MyBCommLab

Go to the Assignments section of your MyLab to complete these writing exercises.

26 As a team or department leader, what steps can you take to ensure that your meetings are successful and efficient? [LO-3]

27 Considering what you've learned about nonverbal communication, what are some of the ways in which communication might break down during an online meeting in which the participants can see video images of only the person presenting at any given time—and then only his or her head? [LO-6]

Endnotes

1. "Company Profile," Cemex website, accessed 8 February 2015, www.cemex.com; "What Is Shift," Cemex website, accessed 8 February 2015, www.cemex.com; *Cemex: Building the Future*, accessed 11 May 2013, www.cemex.com; Cemex Shift Twitter account, https://twitter.com/CX_Shift, accessed 11 May 2013; Dion Hinchcliffe, "Social Business Success: CEMEX," *ZDNet*, 1 February 2012, www.zdnet.com; "Cemex and Becoming a Social Business with IBM Software," video embedded in Jesus Gilberto Garcia, Miguel Angel Lozano Martinez, and Arturo San Vicente, "Shift Changes the Way Cemex Works," *Management Exchange*, 15 July 2011, www.managementexchange.com; Debra Donston-Miller, "Social Business Leader Cemex Keeps Ideas Flowing," *InformationWeek*, 6 November 2012, www.informationweek.co.uk.

2. Courtland L. Bovée and John V. Thill, *Business in Action*, 5th ed. (Upper Saddle River, N.J.: Pearson Prentice Hall, 2011), 172.

3. "Five Case Studies on Successful Teams," *HR Focus*, April 2002, 18+.

4. Stephen R. Robbins, *Essentials of Organizational Behavior*, 6th ed. (Upper Saddle River, N.J.: Prentice Hall, 2000), 98.

5. Max Landsberg and Madeline Pfau, "Developing Diversity: Lessons from Top Teams," *Strategy + Business*, Winter 2005, 10–12.

6. "Groups Best at Complex Problems," *Industrial Engineer*, June 2006, 14.

7. Nicola A. Nelson, "Leading Teams," *Defense AT&L*, July–August 2006, 26–29; Larry Cole and Michael Cole, "Why Is the Teamwork Buzz Word Not Working?" *Communication World*, February–March 1999, 29; Patricia Buhler, "Managing in the 90s: Creating Flexibility in Today's Workplace," *Supervision*, January 1997, 241; Allison W. Amason, Allen C. Hochwarter, Wayne A. Thompson, and Kenneth R. Harrison, "Conflict: An Important Dimension in Successful Management Teams," *Organizational Dynamics*, Autumn 1995, 201.

8. Geoffrey Colvin, "Why Dream Teams Fail," *Fortune*, 12 June 2006, 87–92.

9. Vijay Govindarajan and Anil K. Gupta, "Building an Effective Global Business Team," *MIT Sloan Management Review*, Summer 2001, 631.

10. Colvin, "Why Dream Teams Fail," 87–92.

11. Tiziana Casciaro and Miguel Sousa Lobo, "Competent Jerks, Lovable Fools, and the Formation of Social Networks," *Harvard Business Review*, June 2005, 92–99.

12. Stephen P. Robbins and David A. DeCenzo, *Fundamentals of Management*, 4th ed. (Upper Saddle River, N.J.: Prentice Hall, 2004), 266–267; Jerald Greenberg and Robert A. Baron, *Behavior in Organizations*, 8th ed. (Upper Saddle River, N.J.: Prentice Hall, 2003), 279–280.

13. B. Aubrey Fisher, *Small Group Decision Making: Communication and the Group Process*, 2nd ed. (New York: McGraw-Hill, 1980), 145–149; Robbins and De Cenzo, *Fundamentals of Management*, 334–335; Richard L. Daft, *Management*, 6th ed. (Cincinnati: Thomson South-Western, 2003), 602–603.

14. Michael Laff, "Effective Team Building: More Than Just Fun at Work," *Training + Development*, August 2006, 24–35.

15. Claire Sookman, "Building Your Virtual Team," *Network World*, 21 June 2004, 91.

16. Jared Sandberg, "Brainstorming Works Best if People Scramble for Ideas on Their Own," *Wall Street Journal*, 13 June 2006, B1.

17. Mark K. Smith, "Bruce W. Tuckman—Forming, Storming, Norming, and Performing in Groups," Infed.org, accessed 5 July 2005, www.infed.org.

18. Robbins and DeCenzo, *Fundamentals of Management*, 258–259.

19. Daft, *Management*, 609–612.

20. Andy Boynton and Bill Fischer, *Virtuoso Teams: Lessons from Teams That Changed Their Worlds* (Harrow, UK: FT Prentice Hall, 2005), 10.

21. Thomas K. Capozzoli, "Conflict Resolution—A Key Ingredient in Successful Teams," *Supervision*, November 1999, 14–16.

22. Jesse S. Nirenberg, *Getting Through to People* (Paramus, N.J.: Prentice Hall, 1973), 134–142.

23. Nirenberg, *Getting Through to People*, 134–142.

24. Nirenberg, *Getting Through to People*, 134–142.

25. Jon Hanke, "Presenting as a Team," *Presentations*, January 1998, 74–82.

26. William P. Galle Jr., Beverly H. Nelson, Donna W. Luse, and Maurice F. Villere, *Business Communication: A Technology-Based Approach* (Chicago: Irwin, 1996), 260.

27. Mary Beth Debs, "Recent Research on Collaborative Writing in Industry," *Technical Communication*, November 1991, 476–484.

28. Rob Koplowitz, "Building a Collaboration Strategy," *KM World*, November/December 2009, 14–15.

29. Eric Knorr and Galen Gruman, "What Cloud Computing Really Means," *InfoWorld*, 3 May 2012, www.infoworld.com; Lamont Wood, "Cloud Computing Poised to Transform Communication," *LiveScience*, 8 December 2009, www.livescience.com.

30. "How Blue Man Group Gets Creative with Its Social Intranet," Socialtext website, accessed 1 May 2012, www.socialtext.com.

31. Richard McDermott and Douglas Archibald, "Harnessing Your Staff's Informal Networks," *Harvard Business Review*, March 2010, 82–89.

32. Tony Hsieh, "Why I Sold Zappos," *Inc.*, 1 June 2010, www.inc.com.

33. "Adobe Connect Mobile," Adobe website, accessed 27 February 2014, www.adobe.com.

34. Parks Associates, "Mobile Collaborative Communications for Business," white paper, accessed 27 February 2014, www.parksassociates.com.

35. Chuck Williams, *Management*, 2nd ed. (Cincinnati: Thomson South-Western, 2002), 706–707.

36. Ron Ashkenas, "Why We Secretly Love Meetings," *Harvard Business Review* blogs, 5 October 2010, http://blogs.hbr.org.

37. Douglas Kimberly, "Ten Pitfalls of Pitiful Meetings," *Payroll Manager's Report*, January 2010, 1, 11; "Making the Most of Meetings," *Journal of Accountancy*, March 2009, 22.

38. Cyrus Farivar, "How to Run an Effective Meeting," BNET website, accessed 12 August 2008, www.bnet.com.

39. "Better Meetings Benefit Everyone: How to Make Yours More Productive," *Working Communicator Bonus Report*, July 1998, 1.

40. Janine Popick, "Business Meeting Etiquette: 8 Pet Peeves," *Inc.*, 9 April 2012, www.inc.com.

41. "Features Overview," MeetingSense website, accessed 11 May 2013, www.meetingsense.com.

42. Roger O. Crockett, "The 21st Century Meeting," *BusinessWeek*, 26 February 2007, 72–79.

43. Steve Lohr, "As Travel Costs Rise, More Meetings Go Virtual," *New York Times*, 22 July 2008, www.nytimes.com.

44. GoToMeeting website, accessed 3 May 2012, www.gotogmeeting.com; "Unlock the Full Power of the Web Conferencing," CEOworld.biz, 20 November 2007, www.ceoworld.biz.

45. Nick Morgan, "How to Conduct a Virtual Meeting," *Harvard Business Review* blogs, 1 March 2011, http://blogs.hbr.org.

46. "17 Tips for More Productive Conference Calls," AccuConference, accessed 30 January 2008, www.accuconference.com.

47. Judi Brownell, *Listening*, 2nd ed. (Boston: Allyn & Bacon, 2002), 9, 10.

48. Carmine Gallo, "Why Leadership Means Listening," *BusinessWeek*, 31 January 2007, www.businessweek.com.

49. Augusta M. Simon, "Effective Listening: Barriers to Listening in a Diverse Business Environment," *Bulletin of the Association for Business Communication* 54, no. 3 (September 1991): 73–74.

50. Robyn D. Clarke, "Do You Hear What I Hear?" *Black Enterprise*, May 1998, 129.

51. Dennis M. Kratz and Abby Robinson Kratz, *Effective Listening Skills* (New York: McGraw-Hill, 1995), 45–53; J. Michael Sproule, *Communication Today* (Glenview, Ill.: Scott Foresman, 1981), 69.

52. Brownell, *Listening*, 230–231.

53. Kratz and Kratz, *Effective Listening Skills*, 78–79; Sproule, *Communication Today*, 69.

54. Bill Brooks, "The Power of Active Listening," *American Salesman*, June 2003, 12; "Active Listening," Study Guides and Strategies website, accessed 5 February 2005, www.studygs.net.

55. Bob Lamons, "Good Listeners Are Better Communicators," *Marketing News*, 11 September 1995, 13+; Phillip Morgan and H. Kent Baker, "Building a Professional Image: Improving Listening Behavior," *Supervisory Management*, November 1985, 35–36.

56. Clarke, "Do You Hear What I Hear?"; Dot Yandle, "Listening to Understand," *Pryor Report Management Newsletter Supplement* 15, no. 8 (August 1998): 13.

57. Brownell, *Listening*, 14; Kratz and Kratz, *Effective Listening Skills*, 8–9; Sherwyn P. Morreale and Courtland L. Bovée, *Excellence in Public Speaking* (Orlando, Fla.: Harcourt Brace, 1998), 72–76; Lyman K. Steil, Larry L. Barker, and Kittie W. Watson, *Effective Listening: Key to Your Success* (Reading, Mass.: Addison Wesley, 1983), 21–22.

58. Patrick J. Collins, *Say It with Power and Confidence* (Upper Saddle River, N.J.: Prentice Hall, 1997), 40–45.

59. Morreale and Bovée, *Excellence in Public Speaking*, 296.

60. Dale G. Leathers, *Successful Nonverbal Communication: Principles and Applications* (New York: Macmillan, 1986), 19.

61. Gerald H. Graham, Jeanne Unrue, and Paul Jennings, "The Impact of Nonverbal Communication in Organizations: A Survey of Perceptions," *Journal of Business Communication* 28, no. 1 (Winter 1991): 45–62.

62. Danielle S. Urban, "What to Do About 'Body Art' at Work," *Workforce Management*, March 2010, www.workforce.com.

63. Virginia P. Richmond and James C. McCroskey, *Nonverbal Behavior in Interpersonal Relations* (Boston: Allyn & Bacon, 2000), 153–157.

64. Mary Ellen Slayter, "Pamela Meyer on the Science Behind 'Liespotting,'" SmartBlog on Workforce, 14 September 2010, http://smartblogs.com.

65. Slayter, "Pamela Meyer on the Science Behind 'Liespotting.'"

66. Joe Navarro, "Body Language Myths," *Psychology Today*, 25 October 2009, www.psychologytoday.com; Richmond and McCroskey, *Nonverbal Behavior in Interpersonal Relations*, 2–3.

67. John Hollon, "No Tolerance for Jerks," *Workforce Management*, 12 February 2007, 34.

68. Linton Weeks, "Please Read This Story, Thank You," NPR, 14 March 2012, www.npr.org.

69. Alan Cole, "Telephone Etiquette at Work," Work Etiquette website, 14 March 2012, www.worketiquette.co.uk; Alf Nucifora, "Voice Mail Demands Good Etiquette from Both Sides," *Puget Sound Business Journal*, 5–11 September 2003, 24; Ruth Davidhizar and Ruth Shearer, "The Effective Voice Mail Message," *Hospital Material Management Quarterly*, 45–49; "How to Get the Most Out of Voice Mail," *The CPA Journal*, February 2000, 11; Jo Ind, "Hanging on the Telephone," *Birmingham Post*, 28 July 1999, PS10; Larry Barker and Kittie Watson, *Listen Up* (New York: St. Martin's Press, 2000), 64–65; Lin Walker, *Telephone Techniques*, (New York: Amacom, 1998), 46–47; Dorothy Neal, *Telephone Techniques*, 2nd ed. (New York: Glencoe McGraw-Hill, 1998), 31; Jeannie Davis, *Beyond "Hello"* (Aurora, Col.: Now Hear This Inc., 2000), 2–3; "Ten Steps to Caller-Friendly Voice Mail," *Managing Office Technology*, January 1995, 25; Rhonda Finniss, "Voice Mail: Tips for a Positive Impression," *Administrative Assistant's Update*, August 2001, 5.

70. Dana May Casperson, *Power Etiquette: What You Don't Know Can Kill Your Career* (New York: AMACOM, 1999), 10–14; Ellyn Spragins, "Introducing Politeness," *Fortune Small Business*, November 2001, 30.

71. Tanya Mohn, "The Social Graces as a Business Tool," *New York Times*, 10 November 2002, sec. 3, 12.

72. Casperson, *Power Etiquette*, 44–46.

73. "Are You Practicing Proper Social Networking Etiquette?" *Forbes*, 9 October 2009, www.forbes.com; Pete Babb, "The Ten Commandments of Blog and Wiki Etiquette," *InfoWorld*, 28 May 2007, www.infoworld.com; Judith Kallos, "Instant Messaging Etiquette," NetM@nners blog, accessed 3 August 2008, www.netmanners.com; Michael S. Hyatt, "E-Mail Etiquette 101," From Where I Sit blog, 1 July 2007, www.michaelhyatt.com.

74. J. J. McCorvey, "How to Create a Cell Phone Policy," *Inc.*, 10 February 2010, www.inc.com.

75. Chad Brooks, "Poor Mobile Manners Not Lost on Bosses," Fox Business, 29 October 2013, http://smallbusiness.foxbusiness.com.

76. Nick Wingfield, "Oh, for the Good Old Days of Rude Cellphone Gabbers," *New York Times*, 2 December 2011, www.nytimes.com.

77. Cromwell Schubarth, "VC Ben Horowitz on What He Wants in a Startup and Why Rap Genius Is It," *Silicon Valley Business Journal*, 4 February 2014, www.bizjournals.com.

78. Dan Schawbel, "5 Lessons Celebrities Can Teach Us About Facebook Pages," Mashable, 15 May 2009, http://mashable.com.

Answer Key for "Learning Objectives Checkup"

1. d
2. d
3. constructive
4. d
5. a
6. a
7. b
8. parliamentary
9. virtual
10. telepresence
11. decode
12. c
13. d
14. a
15. d
16. d
17. c
18. a
19. a

Answer Key for "Improve Your Grammar, Mechanics, and Usage" Exercises

16. its (1.2.5)
17. their (1.2.5)
18. its (1.2.5)
19. their (1.2.1)
20. his or her (1.2.3)
21. his or her (1.2.3)
22. a, them (1.2.3, 1.2.4)
23. Who (1.2.4)
24. whom (1.2.4)
25. its (1.2.5)

Communication Challenges
in a Diverse, Global Marketplace

From Chapter 3 of *Excellence in Business Communication*, Twelfth Edition. John V. Thill, Courtland L. Bovée. Copyright © 2017 by Pearson Education, Inc. All rights reserved.

Communication Challenges in a Diverse, Global Marketplace

LEARNING OBJECTIVES

After studying this chapter, you will be able to

1 Discuss the opportunities and challenges of intercultural communication.

2 Define *culture*, explain how culture is learned, and define *ethnocentrism* and *stereotyping*.

3 Explain the importance of recognizing cultural variations, and list eight categories of cultural differences.

4 List four general guidelines for adapting to any business culture.

5 Identify seven steps you can take to improve your intercultural communication skills.

ON THE JOB: COMMUNICATING AT EY

Listening, Learning, and Leveraging the Power of Diversity

With 167,000 employees spread across 140 countries, the member firms of the global professional services organization EY have deep experience with the rewards and challenges of intercultural communication. With business operations in virtually every corner of the world, the organization's ability to communicate across cultures is vital to its success.

Working with colleagues and customers from diverse backgrounds and life experiences can present new communication challenges.

Huntstock/Disability Images/Alamy

As you'll read in this chapter, cultural background influences almost every aspect of communication, and cultural differences are among the most common barriers to successful communication. However, those differences can also enrich communication, decision making, and other aspects of business by bringing a broader range of perspectives and experiences to the table. Guiding the communication process in ways that minimize the barriers and maximize the benefits is one of the most important tasks for every business manager.

The keys are recognizing and appreciating the diversity of today's workforces and making sure all those diverse voices have the opportunity to be heard. Karyn Twaronite, Americas Inclusive Officer, who oversees the EY organization's diversity and inclusiveness strategies in North and South America, puts it this way: "Diversity and inclusiveness are not an appendage to our business strategy—both are central to the success of our people and our markets. All of our people bring diverse talents we can leverage, so we expect, reinforce, and reward inclusive leadership. Differences matter in our business and make us better."

EY has taken numerous steps to make its member firm leaders understand their diverse workforces and incorporate EY viewpoints into strategic planning and day-to-day business operations. Soon after she moved into her current role, for example, Twaronite went on a "listening tour" of EY member firm offices in nearly 20 cities, from São Paulo to Mexico City, to hear what made the EY employees feel included or excluded, how

their team leaders factored into their feelings, and if they felt they could bring their "whole selves" to work.

In addition to giving employees a voice, Ernst & Young LLP, the U.S. unit of the global EY organization, also encourages collaboration and support through a variety of professional networks throughout the company. These include networks for women; working parents; veterans; people with differing abilities; lesbian, gay, bisexual, and transgender (LGBT) professionals; and members of specific ethnic groups. In addition to offering employees a sense of belonging, the networks aid in mentoring, recruiting, and fostering positive relationships with various external stakeholder groups, as well as helping the U.S. firm's people connect with their colleagues, clients, and communities. And in the spirit of inclusiveness, these networks are open to any employee or manager with an interest in the needs and perspectives of a particular employee community.

EY's proactive approach to diversity and inclusiveness pays off in multiple ways, from bottom-line profits to high levels of employee satisfaction and engagement. For example, Ernst & Young LLP was among *Fortune* magazine's "100 Best Companies to Work For" for the 15th consecutive year in 2013, and *DiversityInc* ranked the firm fourth on the "2013 DiversityInc Top 50 Companies for Diversity" list, marking the fifth consecutive year the firm appeared in the top 10. *DiversityInc* also frequently spotlights Ernst & Young LLP as one of the best places to work for women, people with disabilities, and LGBT employees.[1]

WWW.EY.COM

Understanding the Opportunities and Challenges of Communication in a Diverse World

1 **LEARNING OBJECTIVE**
Discuss the opportunities and challenges of intercultural communication.

EY (profiled in the chapter-opening On the Job) illustrates the opportunities and the challenges for business professionals who know how to communicate with diverse audiences. Although the concept is often framed in terms of ethnic background, a broader and more useful definition of **diversity** includes "all the characteristics and experiences that define each of us as individuals."[2] As one example, the pharmaceutical company Merck identifies 19 separate dimensions of diversity, including race, age, military experience, parental status, marital status, and thinking style.[3] As you'll learn in this chapter, these characteristics and experiences can have a profound effect on the way businesspeople communicate.

Diversity includes all the characteristics that define people as individuals.

Intercultural communication is the process of sending and receiving messages between people whose cultural backgrounds could lead them to interpret verbal and nonverbal signs differently. Every attempt to send and receive messages is influenced by culture, so to communicate successfully, you need a basic grasp of the cultural differences you may encounter and how you should handle them. Your efforts to recognize and bridge cultural differences will open up business opportunities throughout the world and maximize the contributions of all the employees in a diverse workforce.

MOBILE APP
The Diversity Now app serves up the latest news and insights in the field of diversity.

THE OPPORTUNITIES IN A GLOBAL MARKETPLACE

Chances are good that you'll be working across international borders sometime in your career. Thanks to communication and transportation technologies, natural boundaries and national borders are no longer the impassable barriers they once were. Local markets

You will communicate with people from other cultures throughout your career.

are opening to worldwide competition as businesses of all sizes look for new growth opportunities outside their own countries. Thousands of U.S. businesses depend on exports for significant portions of their revenues. Every year, these companies export hundreds of billions of dollars worth of materials and merchandise, along with billions more in personal and professional services. If you work in one of these companies, you may well be called on to visit or at least communicate with a wide variety of people who speak languages other than English and who live in cultures quite different from what you're used to. Of the top 10 export markets for U.S. products, only Canada and Great Britain have English as an official language; Canada also has French as an official language.[4]

Not surprisingly, effective communication is important to cross-cultural and global business. In a recent survey, nearly 90 percent of executives said their companies' profits, revenue, and market share would all improve with better international communication skills. In addition, half of these executives said communication or collaboration breakdowns had affected major international business efforts in their companies.[5] The good news here is that improving your cultural communication skills could make you a more valuable job candidate at every stage of your career.

THE ADVANTAGES OF A DIVERSE WORKFORCE

The diversity of today's workforce brings distinct advantages to businesses:
- A broader range of views and ideas
- A better understanding of diverse, fragmented markets
- A broader pool of talent from which to recruit

Even if you never visit another country or transact business on a global scale, you will interact with colleagues from a variety of cultures, with a wide range of characteristics and life experiences. Over the past few decades, many innovative companies have changed the way they approach diversity, from seeing it as a legal requirement (providing equal opportunities for all) to seeing it as a strategic opportunity to connect with customers and take advantage of the broadest possible pool of talent.[6] Smart business leaders recognize the competitive advantages of a diverse workforce that offers a broader spectrum of viewpoints and ideas, helps businesses understand and identify with diverse markets, and enables companies to benefit from a wider range of employee talents. "It just makes good business sense," says Gord Nixon, CEO of Royal Bank of Canada.[7]

Diversity is simply a fact of life for all companies. The United States has been a nation of immigrants from the beginning, and that trend continues today. The western and northern Europeans who made up the bulk of immigrants during the nation's early years now share space with people from across Asia, Africa, Eastern Europe, and other parts of the world. Across the United States, the term *minority*, as it is traditionally applied to non-white residents, makes less and less sense every year. Caucasian Americans make up less than half the population in a growing number of cities and counties and in two or three decades will make up less than half of the overall U.S. population.[8]

REAL-TIME UPDATES

LEARN MORE BY VISITING THIS WEBSITE

Looking for jobs at diversity-minded companies?

DiversityWorking.com connects job searchers with companies that recognize the value of diverse workforces. Go to http://real-timeupdates.com/ebc12 and click on Learn More in the Students section.

However, you and your colleagues don't need to be recent immigrants to constitute a diverse workforce. Differences in everything from age and gender to religion and ethnic heritage to geography and military experience enrich the workplace. Immigration and workforce diversity create advantages—and challenges—for business communicators throughout the world.

THE CHALLENGES OF INTERCULTURAL COMMUNICATION

Today's increasingly diverse workforce encompasses a wide range of skills, traditions, backgrounds, experiences, outlooks, and attitudes toward work—all of which can affect communication in the workplace. Supervisors face the challenge of connecting with these diverse employees, motivating them, and fostering cooperation and harmony among them. Teams face the challenge of working together closely, and companies are challenged to coexist peacefully with business partners and with the community as a whole.

A company's cultural diversity affects how its business messages are conceived, composed, delivered, received, and interpreted.

The interaction of culture and communication is so pervasive that separating the two is virtually impossible. The way you communicate is deeply influenced by the culture in which you were raised. The meaning of words, the significance of gestures, the importance of time and space, the rules of human relationships—these and many other aspects of communication are defined by culture. To a large degree, your culture influences the way you think, which naturally affects the way you communicate as both a sender and a receiver.[9] Intercultural communication is much more complicated than simply matching language between sender and receiver; it goes beyond mere words to beliefs, values, and emotions.

Elements of human diversity can affect communication at every stage of the communication process, from the ideas a person deems important enough to share to the habits and expectations of giving feedback. In particular, your instinct is to encode your message using the assumptions of *your* culture. However, members of your audience decode your message according to the assumptions of *their* culture. The greater the difference between cultures, the greater the chance for misunderstanding.[10]

Throughout this chapter, you'll see examples of how communication styles and habits vary from one culture to another. These examples are intended to illustrate the major themes of intercultural communication, not to give an exhaustive list of styles and habits of any particular culture. With an understanding of these major themes, you'll be prepared to explore the specifics of any culture.

> Culture influences everything about communication, including
> - Language
> - Nonverbal signals
> - Word meaning
> - Time and space issues
> - Rules of human relationships

REAL-TIME UPDATES

LEARN MORE BY EXPLORING THIS INTERACTIVE WEBSITE

Take a closer look at how the United States is changing

The U.S. population is aging and becoming more diverse; dive into the details with this interactive presentation. Go to http://real-timeupdates.com/ebc12 and click on Learn More in the Students section.

Developing Cultural Competency

Cultural competency includes an appreciation for cultural differences that affect communication and the ability to adjust one's communication style to ensure that efforts to send and receive messages across cultural boundaries are successful. In other words, it requires a combination of attitude, knowledge, and skills.[11]

The good news is that you're already an expert in culture, at least in the culture in which you grew up. You understand how your society works, how people are expected to communicate, what common gestures and facial expressions mean, and so on. The bad news is that because you're such an expert in your own culture, your communication is largely automatic; that is, you rarely stop to think about the communication rules you're following. An important step toward successful intercultural communication is becoming more aware of these rules and of the way they influence your communication.

> **2 LEARNING OBJECTIVE**
> Define *culture*, explain how culture is learned, and define *ethnocentrism* and *stereotyping*.

> Cultural competency requires a combination of attitude, knowledge, and skills.

UNDERSTANDING THE CONCEPT OF CULTURE

Culture is a shared system of symbols, beliefs, attitudes, values, expectations, and norms for behavior. Your cultural background influences the way you prioritize what is important in life, helps define your attitude toward what is appropriate in a situation, and establishes rules of behavior.[12]

Actually, you belong to several cultures. In addition to the culture you share with all the people who live in your own country, you belong to other cultural groups, including an ethnic group, possibly a religious group, and perhaps a profession that has its own special language and customs. With its large population and long history of immigration, the United States is home to a vast array of cultures. As one indication of this diversity, the inhabitants of this country now speak more than 170 languages (see Figure 1 on the following page).[13] In contrast, Japan is much more homogeneous, having only a few distinct cultural groups.[14]

Members of a given culture tend to have similar assumptions about how people should think, behave, and communicate, and they all tend to act on those assumptions in much the same way. Cultures can vary in their rate of change, degree of complexity, and tolerance toward outsiders. These differences affect the level of trust and openness you can achieve when communicating with people of other cultures.

People learn culture directly and indirectly from other members of their group. As you grow up in a culture, you are taught by the group's members who you are and how best to function in that culture. Sometimes you are explicitly told which behaviors are acceptable;

> Culture is a shared system of symbols, beliefs, attitudes, values, expectations, and behavior norms.

> You belong to several cultures, each of which affects the way you communicate.

> You learn culture both directly (by being instructed) and indirectly (by observing others).

Communication Challenges in a Diverse, Global Marketplace

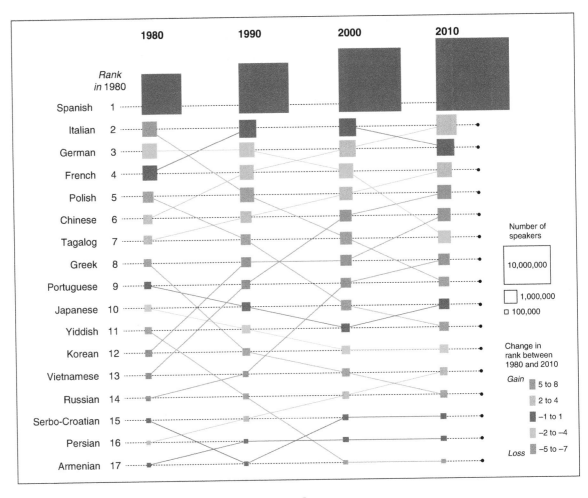

Figure 1 **Language Diversity in the United States**
Language is one of the distinguishing factors of population diversity. This chart shows the trend in relative ranking of languages other than English spoken in the United States since 1980.
Source: "Top Languages Other than English Spoken in 1980 and Changes in Relative Rank, 1990-2010," U.S. Census Bureau, accessed 17 March 2014, www.census.gov.

> Cultures tend to offer views of life that are both coherent (internally logical) and complete (able to answer all of life's big questions).

at other times you learn by observing which values work best in a particular group. In these ways, culture is passed on from person to person and from generation to generation.[15]

In addition to being automatic, culture tends to be *coherent*; that is, a culture appears to be fairly logical and consistent when viewed from the inside. Certain norms within a culture may not make sense to someone outside the culture, but they probably make sense to those inside. Such coherence generally helps a culture function more smoothly internally, but it can create disharmony between cultures that don't view the world in the same way.

Finally, cultures tend to be complete; that is, they provide their members with most of the answers to life's big questions. This idea of completeness dulls or even suppresses curiosity about life in other cultures. Not surprisingly, such completeness can complicate communication with other cultures.[16]

OVERCOMING ETHNOCENTRISM AND STEREOTYPING

> Ethnocentrism is the tendency to judge all other groups according to the standards, behaviors, and customs of one's own group.

Ethnocentrism is the tendency to judge other groups according to the standards, behaviors, and customs of one's own group. Given the automatic influence of one's own culture, when people compare their culture to others, they often conclude that their own is superior.[17] An even more extreme reaction is **xenophobia**, a fear of strangers and foreigners. Clearly, businesspeople who take these views are not likely to communicate successfully across cultures.

Distorted views of other cultures or groups also result from **stereotyping**, assigning a wide range of generalized attributes to an individual on the basis of membership in a particular culture or social group. For instance, assuming that an older colleague will be out of touch with the youth market or that a younger colleague can't be an inspiring leader would be stereotyping age groups.

Those who want to show respect for others and to communicate effectively in business need to adopt a more positive viewpoint, in the form of **cultural pluralism**—the practice of accepting multiple cultures on their own terms. When crossing cultural boundaries, you'll be even more effective if you move beyond simple acceptance and adapt your communication style to that of the new cultures you encounter—even integrating aspects of those cultures into your own.[18] A few simple habits can help:

- **Avoid assumptions.** Don't assume that others will act the same way you do, use language and symbols the same way you do, or even operate from the same values and beliefs. For instance, in a comparison of the 10 most important values in three cultures, people from the United States had *no* values in common with people from Japanese or Arab cultures.[19]
- **Avoid judgments.** When people act differently, don't conclude that they are in error or that their way is invalid or inferior.
- **Acknowledge distinctions.** Don't ignore the differences between another person's culture and your own.

Unfortunately, overcoming ethnocentrism and stereotyping is not a simple task, even for people who are highly motivated to do so. Moreover, research suggests that people often have beliefs and biases that they're not even aware of—and that may even conflict with the beliefs they *think* they have.[20]

Stereotyping is assigning generalized attributes to an individual on the basis of membership in a particular group.

Cultural pluralism is the acceptance of multiple cultures on their own terms.

You can avoid ethnocentrism and stereotyping by avoiding assumptions and judgments and by accepting differences.

Recognizing Variations in a Diverse World

You can begin to learn how people in other cultures want to be treated by recognizing and accommodating eight main types of cultural differences: contextual, legal and ethical, social, nonverbal, age, gender, religious, and ability.

3 LEARNING OBJECTIVE
Explain the importance of recognizing cultural variations, and list eight categories of cultural differences.

CONTEXTUAL DIFFERENCES

Every attempt at communication occurs within a **cultural context**, which is the pattern of physical cues, environmental stimuli, and implicit understanding that convey meaning between two members of the same culture. However, cultures around the world vary widely in the role that context plays in communication.

In a **high-context culture**, people rely less on verbal communication and more on the context of nonverbal actions and environmental setting to convey meaning. For instance, a Chinese speaker expects the receiver to discover the essence of a message and uses indirectness and metaphor to provide a web of meaning.[21] The indirect style can be a source of confusion during discussions with people from low-context cultures, who are more accustomed to receiving direct answers. Also, in high-context cultures, the rules of everyday life are rarely explicit; instead, as individuals grow up, they learn how to recognize situational cues (such as gestures and tone of voice) and how to respond as expected.[22] The primary role of communication in high-context cultures is building relationships, not exchanging information.[23]

In a **low-context culture** such as the United States, people rely more on verbal communication and less on circumstances and cues to convey meaning. In such cultures, rules and expectations are usually spelled out through explicit statements such as "Please wait until I'm finished" or "You're welcome to browse."[24] The primary task of communication in low-context cultures is exchanging information.[25]

Contextual differences are apparent in the way businesspeople approach situations such as decision making, problem solving, negotiating, interacting among levels in the organizational hierarchy, and socializing outside the workplace.[26] For instance, in low-context

Cultural context is the pattern of physical cues, environmental stimuli, and implicit understanding that conveys meaning between members of the same culture.

High-context cultures rely heavily on nonverbal actions and environmental setting to convey meaning; low-context cultures rely more on explicit verbal communication.

cultures, businesspeople tend to focus on the results of the decisions they face, a reflection of the cultural emphasis on logic and progress (for example, "Will this be good for our company? For my career?"). In comparison, higher-context cultures emphasize the means or the method by which a decision will be made. Building or protecting relationships can be as important as the facts and information used in making the decisions.[27] Consequently, negotiators working on business deals in such cultures may spend most of their time together building relationships rather than hammering out contractual details.

The distinctions between high and low context are generalizations, of course, but they are important to keep in mind as guidelines. Communication tactics that work well in a high-context culture may backfire in a low-context culture, and vice versa.

REAL-TIME UPDATES

LEARN MORE BY EXPLORING THIS INTERACTIVE WEBSITE

A business-focused model for identifying cultural differences

The Lewis model is designed to help business professional communicate across cultural boundaries. Go to http://real-timeupdates.com/ebc12 and click on Learn More in the Students section.

LEGAL AND ETHICAL DIFFERENCES

Cultural context influences legal and ethical behavior, which in turn can affect communication. For example, the meaning of business contracts can vary from culture to culture. Whereas a manager from a U.S. company would tend to view a signed contract as the end of the negotiating process, with all the details resolved, his or her counterpart in many Asian cultures might view the signed contract as an agreement to do business—and only then begin to negotiate the details of the deal.[28]

As you conduct business around the world, you'll find that both legal systems and ethical standards differ from culture to culture. Making ethical choices across cultures can seem complicated, but you can keep your messages ethical by applying four basic principles:[29]

Honesty and respect are cornerstones of ethical communication, regardless of culture.

- **Actively seek mutual ground.** To allow the clearest possible exchange of information, both parties must be flexible and avoid insisting that an interaction take place strictly in terms of one culture or another.
- **Send and receive messages without judgment.** To allow information to flow freely, both parties must recognize that values vary from culture to culture, and they must trust each other.
- **Send messages that are honest.** To ensure that information is true, both parties must see things as they are—not as they would like them to be. Both parties must be fully aware of their personal and cultural biases.
- **Show respect for cultural differences.** To protect the basic human rights of both parties, each must understand and acknowledge the other's needs and preserve each other's dignity by communicating without deception.

SOCIAL DIFFERENCES

Formal rules of etiquette are explicit and well defined, but informal rules are learned through observation and imitation.

The nature of social behavior varies among cultures, sometimes dramatically. Some behavioral rules are formal and specifically articulated (table manners are a good example), whereas others are informal and learned over time (such as the comfortable distance to stand from a colleague during a discussion). The combination of formal and informal rules influences the overall behavior of most people in a society most of the time. In addition to the factors already discussed, social norms can vary from culture to culture in the following areas:

- **Attitudes toward work and success.** In the United States, for instance, a widespread view is that material comfort earned by individual effort is a sign of superiority and that people who work hard are better than those who don't.
- **Roles and status.** Culture influences the roles people play, including who communicates with whom, what they communicate, and in what way. For example, in some

countries women still don't play a prominent role in business, so women executives who visit these countries may find they're not taken seriously as businesspeople.[30] Culture also dictates how people show respect and signify rank. For example, people in the United States show respect by addressing top managers as "Mr. Roberts" or "Ms. Gutierrez." However, people in China are addressed according to their official titles, such as "President" or "Manager."[31]

Respect and rank are reflected differently from culture to culture in the way people are addressed and in their working environment.

- **Use of manners.** What is polite in one culture may be considered rude in another. For instance, asking a colleague "How was your weekend?" is a common way of making small talk in the United States, but the question sounds intrusive to people in cultures in which business and private lives are seen as separate spheres.

The rules of polite behavior vary from country to country.

- **Concepts of time.** People in low-context cultures see time as a way to plan the business day efficiently, often focusing on only one task during each scheduled period and viewing time as a limited resource. However, executives from high-context cultures often see time as more flexible. Meeting a deadline is less important than building a business relationship.[32]

Attitudes toward time, such as strict adherence to meeting schedules, can vary throughout the world.

- **Future orientation.** Successful companies tend to have a strong *future orientation,* planning for and investing in the future, but national cultures around the world vary widely in this viewpoint. Some societies encourage a long-term outlook that emphasizes planning and investing—making sacrifices in the short term for the promise of better outcomes in the future. Others are oriented more toward the present, even to the point of viewing the future as hopelessly remote and not worth planning for.[33]

- **Openness and inclusiveness.** At the national level as well as within smaller groups, cultures vary on how open they are to accepting people from other cultures and people who don't necessarily fit the prevailing norms within the culture. An unwillingness to accommodate others can range from outright exclusion to subtle pressures to conform to majority expectations.

Cultures around the world exhibit varying degrees of openness toward both outsiders and people whose personal identities don't align with prevailing social norms.

- **Use of communication technologies.** Don't assume that colleagues and customers around the world use the same communication tools you use. For example, although mobile phone usage is high in most countries around the world, the percentage of users with smartphones and the broadband service required for communication services such as video varies widely.[34]

NONVERBAL DIFFERENCES

Nonverbal communication can be a helpful guide to determining the meaning of a message—but this situation holds true only if the sender and receiver assign the same meaning to nonverbal signals. For instance, the simplest hand gestures have different meanings in different cultures. A gesture that communicates good luck in Brazil is the equivalent of giving someone "the finger" in Colombia.[35] Don't assume that the gestures you grew up with will translate to another culture; doing so could lead to embarrassing mistakes.

The meaning of nonverbal signals can vary widely from culture to culture, so you can't rely on assumptions.

When you have the opportunity to interact with people in another culture, the best advice is to study the culture in advance and then observe the way people behave in the following areas:

- **Greetings.** Do people shake hands, bow, or kiss lightly (on one side of the face or both)? Do people shake hands only when first introduced or every time they say hello or goodbye?

- **Personal space.** When people are conversing, do they stand closer together or farther away than you are accustomed to?

- **Touching.** Do people touch each other on the arm to emphasize a point or slap each other on the back to show congratulations? Or do they refrain from touching altogether?

REAL-TIME UPDATES

LEARN MORE BY VIEWING THIS INFOGRAPHIC

Seven common hand gestures that will stir up trouble in other cultures

Find out what gestures that have positive meanings in the United States can have intensively negative meanings in other cultures. Go to http://real-timeupdates.com/ebc12 and click on Learn More in the Students section.

- **Facial expressions.** Do people shake their heads to indicate "no" and nod them to indicate "yes"? This is what people are accustomed to in the United States, but it is not universal.
- **Eye contact.** Do people make frequent eye contact or avoid it? Frequent eye contact is often taken as a sign of honesty and openness in the United States, but in other cultures it can be a sign of aggressiveness or disrespect.
- **Posture.** Do people slouch and relax in the office and in public, or do they sit up and stand up straight?
- **Formality.** In general, does the culture seem more or less formal than yours?

Following the lead of people who grew up in the culture is not only a great way to learn but a good way to show respect as well.

AGE DIFFERENCES

A culture's views on youth and aging affect how people communicate with one another.

In U.S. culture, youth is often associated with strength, energy, possibilities, and freedom, and age is sometimes associated with declining powers and the inability to keep pace. However, older workers can offer broader experience, the benefits of important business relationships nurtured over many years, and high degrees of "practical intelligence"—the ability to solve complex, poorly defined problems.[36]

In contrast, in cultures that value age and seniority, longevity earns respect and increasing power and freedom. For instance, in many Asian societies, the oldest employees hold the most powerful jobs, the most impressive titles, and the greatest degrees of freedom and decision-making authority. If a younger employee disagrees with one of these senior executives, the discussion is never conducted in public. The notion of "saving face"—avoiding public embarrassment—is too strong. Instead, if a senior person seems to be in error about something, other employees will find a quiet, private way to communicate whatever information they feel is necessary.[37]

The multiple generations within a culture present another dimension of diversity. Today's workplaces can have three or even four generations working side by side. Each has been shaped by dramatically different world events, social trends, and technological advances, so it is not surprising that they often have different values, expectations, and communication habits. For instance, Generation Y workers (see "Us Versus Them: Generational Conflict in the Workplace") have a strong preference for communicating via short electronic messages, but Baby Boomers and Generation Xers sometimes find these brief messages abrupt and impersonal.[38]

GENDER DIFFERENCES

Gender influences workplace communication in several important ways. First, the perception of men and women in business varies from culture to culture, and gender bias can range from overt discrimination to subtle and even unconscious beliefs.

Second, although the ratio of men and women in entry-level professional positions is roughly equal, the percentage of management roles held by men increases steadily the further one looks up the corporate ladder. This imbalance can significantly affect communication in such areas as mentoring, which is a vital development opportunity for lower and middle managers who want to move into senior positions. In one recent survey, for example, some men in executive positions expressed reluctance to mentor women, partly because they find it easier to bond with other men and partly out of concerns over developing relationships that might look inappropriate.[39]

Broadly speaking, men tend to emphasize content in their messages, whereas women tend to emphasize relationship maintenance.

Third, evidence suggests that men and women tend to have somewhat different communication styles. Broadly speaking, men emphasize content and outcomes in their communication efforts, whereas women place a higher premium on relationship maintenance.[40] As one example, men are more likely than women to try to negotiate a pay raise. Moreover, according to research by Linda Babcock of Carnegie Mellon University, both men and women tend to accept this disparity, viewing assertiveness as a positive quality in men but a negative quality in women. Changing these perceptions could go a long way toward improving communication and equity in the workplace.[41]

Us Versus Them: Generational Conflict in the Workplace

The way people view the world as adults is profoundly shaped by the social and technological trends they experienced while growing up, so it's no surprise that each generation entering the workforce has a different perspective than the generations already at work. Throw in the human tendencies to resist change and to assume that whatever way one is doing something must be the best way to do it, and you have a recipe for conflict. Moreover, generations in a workplace sometimes feel themselves competing for jobs, resources, influence, and control. The result can be tension, mistrust, and communication breakdowns.

Lumping people into generations is an imprecise science at best, but it helps to know the labels commonly applied to various age groups and to have some idea of their broad characteristics. These labels are not official, and there is no general agreement on when some generations start and end, but you will see and hear references to the following groups (approximate years of birth shown in parentheses):

- **The Radio Generation (1925 to 1945).** People in this group are beyond what was once considered the traditional retirement age of 65, but some want or need to continue working.
- **Baby Boomers (1946 to 1964).** This large segment of the workforce, which now occupies many mid- and upper-level managerial positions, got its name from the population boom in the years following World War II. The older members of this generation are now reaching retirement age, but many will continue to work beyond age 65—meaning that younger workers waiting for some of these management spots to open up might have to wait a while longer.
- **Generation X (1965 to 1980).** This relatively smaller "MTV generation" is responsible for many of the innovations that have shaped communication habits today but sometimes feels caught between the large mass of baby boomers ahead of them and the younger Generation Y employees entering the workforce. When Generation X does finally get the chance to take over starting in 2015 or 2020, it will be managing in a vastly different business

landscape, one in which virtual organizations and networks of independent contractors replace much of the hierarchy inherited from the baby boomers.
- **Generation Y (1981 to 1995).** Also known as *millennials*, this youngest generation currently in the workforce is noted for its entrepreneurial instincts and technological savvy. This generation's comfort level with social media and other communication technologies is helping to change business communication practices but is also a source of concern for managers worried about information leaks and employee productivity.
- **Generation Z (after 1996).** If you're a member of Generation Y, those footsteps you hear behind you are coming from Generation Z, also known as *Generation I* (for Internet) or the *Net Generation*. The first full generation to be born after the World Wide Web was invented will be entering the workforce soon.

These brief summaries can hardly do justice to entire generations of workers, but they give you some idea of the different generational perspectives and the potential for communication problems. As with all cultural conflicts, successful communication starts with recognizing and understanding these differences.

CAREER APPLICATIONS

1. How would you resolve a conflict between a Baby Boomer manager who worries about the privacy and productivity aspects of social networking and a Generation Y employee who wants to use these tools on the job?
2. Consider the range of labels from the Radio Generation to the Net Generation. What does this tell you about the possible influence of technology on business communication habits?

Sources: Anne Fisher, "When Gen X Runs the Show," *Time*, 14 May 2009, www .time.com; Deloitte, "Generation Y: Powerhouse of the Global Economy," research report, 2009, www.deloitte.com; "Generation Y," Nightly Business Report website, 30 June 2010, www.pbs.org; Sherry Posnick-Goodwin, "Meet Generation Z," *California Educator*, February 2010, www.cta.org; Ernie Stark, "Lost in a Time Warp," *People & Strategy* 32 no. 4 (2009): 58–64.

RELIGIOUS DIFFERENCES

As one of the most personal and influential aspects of life, religion brings potential for controversy and conflict in the workplace setting—as evidenced by a significant rise in the number of religious discrimination lawsuits in recent years.[42] Many employees believe they should be able to follow and express the tenets of their faith in the workplace. However, companies may need to accommodate employee behaviors that can conflict with each other and with the demands of operating the business. The situation is complicated, with no simple answers that apply to every situation. As more companies work to establish inclusive workplaces, you can expect to see this issue being discussed more often in the coming years.

U.S. law requires employers to accommodate employees' religious beliefs to a reasonable degree.

ABILITY DIFFERENCES

Colleagues and customers with disabilities that affect communication represent an important aspect of the diversity picture. People whose hearing, vision, cognitive ability, or physical ability to operate electronic devices is impaired can be at a significant disadvantage in today's workplace. As with other elements of diversity, success starts with respect for individuals and sensitivity to differences.

Employers can also invest in a variety of *assistive technologies* that help people with disabilities perform activities that might otherwise be difficult or impossible. These technologies include devices and systems that help workers communicate orally and visually, interact with computers and other equipment, and enjoy greater mobility in the workplace. For example, designers can emphasize *web accessibility*, taking steps to make websites more accessible to people whose vision is limited. Assistive technologies create a vital link for thousands of employees with disabilities, giving them opportunities to pursue a greater range of career paths and giving employers access to a broader base of talent.[43]

> Assistive technologies help employers create more inclusive workplaces and benefit from the contribution of people with physical or cognitive impairments.

Adapting to Other Business Cultures

4 LEARNING OBJECTIVE
List four general guidelines for adapting to any business culture.

Whether you're trying to work productively with members of another generation in your own office or with a business partner on the other side of the world, adapting your approach is essential to successful communication. This section offers general advice on adapting to any business culture and specific advice for professionals from other cultures on adapting to U.S. business culture.

GUIDELINES FOR ADAPTING TO ANY BUSINESS CULTURE

You'll find a variety of specific tips in "Improving Intercultural Communication Skills," but here are four general guidelines that can help all business communicators improve their cultural competency:

> An important step in understanding and adapting to other cultures is to recognize the influences that your own culture has on your communication habits.

- **Become aware of your own biases.** Successful intercultural communication requires more than just an understanding of the other party's culture; you need to understand your own culture and the way it shapes your communication habits.[44] For instance, knowing that you value independence and individual accomplishment will help you communicate more successfully in a culture that values consensus and group harmony.
- **Be careful about applying the "Golden Rule."** You probably heard this growing up: "Treat people the way you want to be treated." The problem with the Golden Rule is that other people don't always want to be treated the same way you want to be treated, particularly across cultural boundaries. The best approach: Treat people the way *they* want to be treated.
- **Exercise tolerance, flexibility, and respect.** As IBM's Ron Glover puts it, "To the greatest extent possible, we try to manage our people and our practices in ways that are respectful of the core principles of any given country or organization or culture."[45]
- **Practice patience and maintain a sense of humor.** Even the most committed and attuned business professionals can make mistakes in intercultural communication, so it is vital for all parties to be patient with one another. As business becomes ever more global, even people in the most tradition-bound cultures are learning to deal with outsiders more patiently and overlook occasional cultural blunders.[46] A sense of humor is a helpful asset as well, allowing people to move past awkward and embarrassing moments. When you make a mistake, simply apologize and, if appropriate, ask the other person to explain the accepted way; then move on.

REAL-TIME UPDATES
LEARN MORE BY WATCHING THESE VIDEOS

See what Google employees have to say about diversity

The search giant's YouTube channel features employees talking about their experiences working at Google. Go to http://real-timeupdates.com/ebc12 and click on Learn More in the Students section.

GUIDELINES FOR ADAPTING TO U.S. BUSINESS CULTURE

If you are a recent immigrant to the United States or grew up in a culture outside the U.S. mainstream, you can apply all the concepts and skills in this chapter to help adapt to U.S. business culture. Here are some key points to remember as you become accustomed to business communication in this country:[47]

- **Individualism,** In contrast to cultures that value group harmony and group success, U.S. culture generally expects individuals to succeed by their own efforts, and it rewards individual success. Even though teamwork is emphasized in many companies, competition between individuals is expected and even encouraged in many cases.

- **Equality.** Although the country's historical record on equality has not always been positive and some inequalities still exist, equality is considered a core American value. This principle applies to race, gender, social background, and even age. To a greater degree than people in many other cultures, Americans believe that every person should be given the opportunity to pursue whatever dreams and goals he or she has in life.

- **Privacy and personal space.** Although this appears to be changing somewhat with the popularity of social networking and other personal media, people in the United States are accustomed to a fair amount of privacy. That also applies to their "personal space" at work. For example, they expect you to knock before entering a closed office and to avoid asking questions about personal beliefs or activities until they get to know you well.

- **Time and schedules.** U.S. businesses value punctuality and the efficient use of time. For instance, meetings are expected to start and end at designated times.

- **Religion.** The United States does not have an official state religion. Many religions are practiced throughout the country, and people are expected to respect each other's beliefs.

- **Communication style.** Communication tends to be direct and focused more on content and transactions than on relationships or group harmony.

The values espoused by American culture include individualism, equality, and privacy.

As with all observations about culture, these are generalizations, of course. Any nation of more than 300 million people will exhibit a wide variety of behaviors. However, following these guidelines will help you succeed in most business communication situations.

Improving Intercultural Communication Skills

5 LEARNING OBJECTIVE
Identify seven steps you can take to improve your intercultural communication skills.

Communicating successfully between cultures requires a variety of skills (see Figure 2 on the next page). You can improve your intercultural skills throughout your career by studying other cultures and languages, respecting preferences for communication styles, learning to write and speak clearly, listening carefully, knowing when to use interpreters and translators, and helping others adapt to your culture.

STUDYING OTHER CULTURES

Effectively adapting your communication efforts to another culture requires not only knowledge about the culture but also the ability and motivation to change your personal habits as needed.[48] Fortunately, you don't need to learn about the whole world all at once. Many companies appoint specialists for countries or regions, giving employees a chance to focus on just one culture at a time. And if your employer conducts business internationally, it may offer training and support for employees who need to more about specific cultures.

REAL-TIME UPDATES
LEARN MORE BY EXPLORING THIS INTERACTIVE WEBSITE

How are your global travel skills?

Take this quiz to see if you have the knowledge to travel like a pro. Go to http://real-timeupdates.com/ebc12 and click on Learn More in the Students section.

Communication Challenges in a Diverse, Global Marketplace

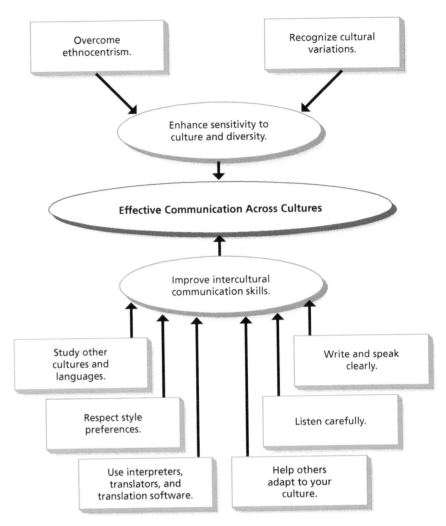

Figure 2 Components of Successful Intercultural Communication
Communicating in a diverse business environment is not always an easy task, but you can continue to improve your sensitivity and build your skills as you progress in your career.

Even a small amount of research and practice will help you get through many business situations. In addition, most people respond positively to honest effort and good intentions, and many business associates will help you along if you show an interest in learning more about their cultures. Don't be afraid to ask questions. People will respect your concern and curiosity. You will gradually accumulate considerable knowledge, which will help you feel comfortable and be effective in a wide range of business situations.

Numerous websites and books offer advice on traveling to and working in specific cultures. Also try to sample newspapers, magazines, and even the music and movies of another country. For instance, a movie can demonstrate nonverbal customs even if you don't grasp the language. (However, be careful not to rely solely on entertainment products. If people in other countries based their opinions of U.S. culture only on the silly teen flicks and violent action movies that the United States exports around the globe, what sort of impression do you imagine they'd get?) For some of the key issues to research before doing business in another country, refer to Table 1.

STUDYING OTHER LANGUAGES

Successful intercultural communication can require the modification of personal communication habits.

As commerce continues to become more globalized and many countries become more linguistically diverse, the demand for multilingual communicators continues to grow as

Communication Challenges in a Diverse, Global Marketplace

TABLE 1 Doing Business in Other Cultures

Action	Details to Consider
Understand social customs	• How do people react to strangers? Are they friendly? Hostile? Reserved? • How do people greet each other? Should you bow? Nod? Shake hands? • How do you express appreciation for an invitation to lunch, dinner, or someone's home? Should you bring a gift? Send flowers? Write a thank-you note? • Are any phrases, facial expressions, or hand gestures considered rude? • How do you attract the attention of a waiter? Do you tip the waiter? • When is it rude to refuse an invitation? How do you refuse politely? • What topics may or may not be discussed in a social setting? In a business setting? • How do social customs dictate interaction between men and women? Between younger people and older people?
Learn about clothing and food preferences	• What occasions require special attire? • What colors are associated with mourning? Love? Joy? • Are some types of clothing considered taboo for one gender or the other? • How many times a day do people eat? • How are hands or utensils used when eating? • Where is the seat of honor at a table?
Assess political patterns	• How stable is the political situation? • Does the political situation affect businesses in and out of the country? • Is it appropriate to talk politics in social or business situations?
Understand religious and social beliefs	• To which religious groups do people belong? • Which places, objects, actions, and events are sacred? • Do religious beliefs affect communication between men and women or between any other groups? • Is there a tolerance for minority religions? • How do religious holidays affect business and government activities? • Does religion require or prohibit eating specific foods? At specific times?
Learn about economic and business institutions	• Is the society homogeneous or heterogeneous? • What languages are spoken? • What are the primary resources and principal products? • Are businesses generally large? Family controlled? Government controlled? • What are the generally accepted working hours? • How do people view scheduled appointments? • Are people expected to socialize before conducting business?
Appraise the nature of ethics, values, and laws	• Is money or a gift expected in exchange for arranging business transactions? • Do people value competitiveness or cooperation? • What are the attitudes toward work? Toward money? • Is politeness more important than factual honesty?

well. The ability to communicate in more than one language can make you a more competitive job candidate and open up a wider variety of career opportunities.

Even if your colleagues or customers in another country speak your language, it's worth the time and energy to learn common phrases in theirs. Doing so not only helps you get through everyday business and social situations but also demonstrates your commitment to the business relationship. After all, the other person probably spent years learning your language.

Mobile devices can be a huge help in learning another language and in communicating with someone in another language. A wide variety of apps and websites are available that help with essentials words and phrases, grammar, pronunciation, text translation, and even real-time audio translation (see Figure 3 on the next page).

Finally, don't assume that people from two countries who speak the same language speak it the same way. The French spoken in Quebec and other parts of Canada is often noticeably different from the French spoken in France. Similarly, it's often said that the United States and the United Kingdom are two countries divided by a common language. For instance, *period* (punctuation), *elevator*, and *gasoline* in the United States are *full stop, lift,* and *petrol* in the United Kingdom.

Making an effort to learn about another person's culture is a sign of respect.

MOBILE APP
iTranslate translates more than 80 languages and features voice input and output.

English is the most prevalent language in international business, but don't assume that everyone understands it or speaks it the same way.

Figure 3   Mobile Language Tools
Translation apps are handy tools for working in multilingual business settings. Even if you don't speak a word of a particular language, you can get fast translations of essential phrases.

RESPECTING PREFERENCES FOR COMMUNICATION STYLE

Communication style—including the level of directness, the degree of formality, media preferences, and other factors—varies widely from culture to culture (see Figures 4a through 4d). Knowing what your communication partners expect can help you adapt to their particular style. Once again, watching and learning are the best ways to improve your skills. However, you can infer some generalities by learning more about the culture. For instance, U.S. workers typically prefer an open and direct communication style; they find other styles frustrating or suspect. Directness is also valued in Sweden as a sign of efficiency, but heated debates and confrontations are unusual. Italian, German, and French executives usually don't put colleagues at ease with praise before they criticize; doing so seems manipulative to them. Meanwhile, professionals from high-context cultures, such as Japan or China, tend to be less direct.[49] Finally, in general, business correspondence in other countries is often more formal than the style used by U.S. businesspeople.

UpdraftRC
4308 Preston Highway
Louisville, KY 40213
Toll Free: 1.800.FLY.RITE
Fax: (502) 555-1324
www.updraftrc.com

Zhejang Shan Tou Manufacturing Company, Ltd.
Guoliwei Industry Park
Libang Road, Longgang District
Shenzhen, Guangdong, China

Dear Mr. Li,

My company, Updraft RC, has designed a cool new line of radio-control toys that use smartphones as the controller. We are looking for a manufacturing partner, and your firm is one of the candidates we're having a look at.

Before we discuss technical details, I must say I have two sets of concerns about working with a foreign manufacturer. The first involves all the usual—transportation costs, delays, quality control, and risk of intellectual property theft. I'll need some assurances on how you address these issues to make sure they don't become problems in our relationship.

Second, companies here in the States that use foreign manufacturers often have to deal with heavy news coverage and activist publicity on such matters as workplace safety, worker rights, and environmentally sensitive manufacturing. Even though the U.S. company doesn't directly control what happens in the overseas contract manufacturer, the U.S. company takes the heat when the media uncovers abuse, neglect, pollution, etc. I know that Nike and other U.S. companies have spent millions and worked for years to promote positive conditions in overseas factories, but even these major corporations haven't been able to completely avoid problems and bad press. How can I be sure that a small company such as ours will? I do not want our product launch to get caught up in some scandal over "sweatshops."

I look forward to seeing your comprehensive response as soon as possible.

All the best,

Henry Gatlin

Henry Gatlin
Founder, CEO
Updraft RC

5 August 2016

Annotations (right margin):

Language such as "cool" and "having a look at" is too informal for external business communication, particularly for international correspondence.

The tone of this paragraph is too demanding.

"Here in the States" is too informal, and referring to the reader as "foreign" is potentially insulting.

Inflammatory language as *bad press, scandal,* and *sweatshops* will put the reader on the defensive and discourage a positive response.

The request for a response sounds too demanding, and it lacks a specific deadline.

The closing is too informal.

Figure 4a Intercultural Business Letter: Ineffective Original Draft
This letter (from a Kentucky company that designs radio-controlled airplanes) exhibits a number of problems that would create difficulties for its intended reader (the manager of a contract manufacturing company in China). Follow the changes in Figures 4b, 4c, and 4d to see how the letter was adapted and then translated for its target audience.

WRITING CLEARLY

Writing clearly is always important, of course, but it is essential when you are writing to people whose first language is not English. Follow these recommendations to make sure your message can be understood:[50]

- **Choose words carefully.** Use precise words that don't have the potential to confuse with multiple meanings. For instance, the word *right* has several dozen different meanings and usages, so look for a synonym that conveys the specific meaning you intend, such as *correct, appropriate, desirable, moral, authentic,* or *privilege*.[51]

Clarity and simplicity are essential when writing to or speaking with people who don't share your native language.

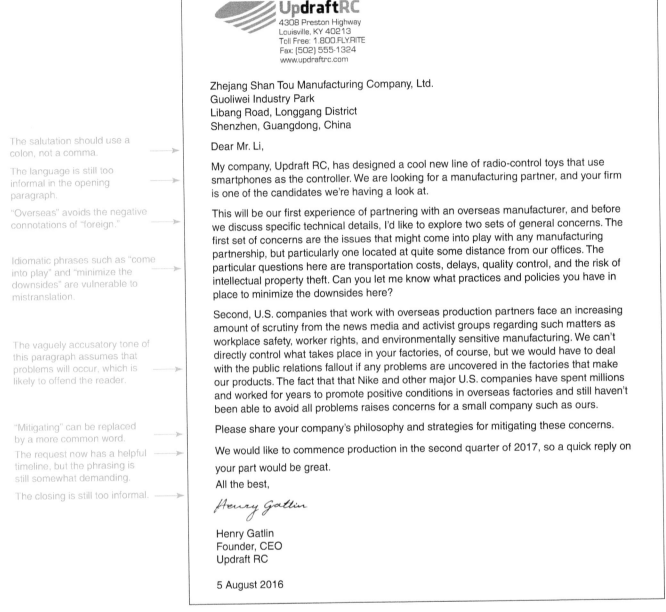

The salutation should use a colon, not a comma.

The language is still too informal in the opening paragraph.

"Overseas" avoids the negative connotations of "foreign."

Idiomatic phrases such as "come into play" and "minimize the downsides" are vulnerable to mistranslation.

The vaguely accusatory tone of this paragraph assumes that problems will occur, which is likely to offend the reader.

"Mitigating" can be replaced by a more common word.

The request now has a helpful timeline, but the phrasing is still somewhat demanding.

The closing is still too informal.

UpdraftRC
4308 Preston Highway
Louisville, KY 40213
Toll Free: 1.800.FLY.RITE
Fax: (502) 555-1324
www.updraftrc.com

Zhejiang Shan Tou Manufacturing Company, Ltd.
Guoliwei Industry Park
Libang Road, Longgang District
Shenzhen, Guangdong, China

Dear Mr. Li,

My company, Updraft RC, has designed a cool new line of radio-control toys that use smartphones as the controller. We are looking for a manufacturing partner, and your firm is one of the candidates we're having a look at.

This will be our first experience of partnering with an overseas manufacturer, and before we discuss specific technical details, I'd like to explore two sets of general concerns. The first set of concerns are the issues that might come into play with any manufacturing partnership, but particularly one located at quite some distance from our offices. The particular questions here are transportation costs, delays, quality control, and the risk of intellectual property theft. Can you let me know what practices and policies you have in place to minimize the downsides here?

Second, U.S. companies that work with overseas production partners face an increasing amount of scrutiny from the news media and activist groups regarding such matters as workplace safety, worker rights, and environmentally sensitive manufacturing. We can't directly control what takes place in your factories, of course, but we would have to deal with the public relations fallout if any problems are uncovered in the factories that make our products. The fact that that Nike and other major U.S. companies have spent millions and worked for years to promote positive conditions in overseas factories and still haven't been able to avoid all problems raises concerns for a small company such as ours.

Please share your company's philosophy and strategies for mitigating these concerns.

We would like to commence production in the second quarter of 2017, so a quick reply on your part would be great.

All the best,

Henry Gatlin

Henry Gatlin
Founder, CEO
Updraft RC

5 August 2016

Figure 4b   Intercultural Business Letter: First Revision
This version eliminates most of the problems with overly informal phrases and potentially offensive language. With these revisions, it would function well as a message between native speakers of English, but it still has some wording and formatting issues that could create difficulties for a Chinese reader. Compare with Figure 4c.

- **Be brief.** Use simple sentences and short paragraphs, breaking information into smaller chunks that are easier for readers to process.
- **Use plenty of transitions.** Help readers follow your train of thought by using transitional words and phrases. For example, tie related points together with expressions such as *in addition* and *first, second,* and *third.*
- **Cite numbers and dates carefully.** In the United States, 12-05-15 means December 5, 2015, but in many other countries, it means May 12, 2015. Dates in Japan and China are usually expressed with the year first, followed by the month and then the day; therefore, to write December 5, 2015, in Japan, write it as 2015-12-05. Similarly, in

UpdraftRC
4308 Preston Highway
Louisville, KY 40213
Toll Free: 1.800.FLY.RITE
Fax: (502) 555-1324
www.updraftrc.com

Dear Mr. Li:

With the widespread adoption of mobile phones, more and more accessories and associated products are being developed to meet new market demands. My company, Updraft RC, has designed a new line of radio-controlled toys that use smartphones as the controller. Our market tests show strong potential for demand among younger consumers, who are often eager to try new products. We are now looking for a manufacturing partner, and we are very willing to collaborate with you.

This will be our first experience of partnering with an overseas manufacturer, and before we discuss specific technical details, I would like you to know two of our general concerns. The first concern involves all the general challenges of a long-distance manufacturing partnership, including transportation costs, shipping delays, quality control, and the risk of intellectual property theft.

Second, U.S. companies that work with overseas production partners face an increasing amount of scrutiny from the news media and activist groups regarding such matters as workplace safety, worker rights, and environmentally sensitive manufacturing. Nike and other major U.S. companies have spent millions of dollars and worked for years to improve conditions in overseas factories, but even they have not be able to avoid all problems. As a small company with no ability to monitor factories, we are worried about any manufacturing-related problems that could affect our public image.

Please share your company's philosophy and strategies for minimizing these two concerns.

We would like to commence production in the second quarter of 2017, so we would like to hear your reply as soon as possible.

Thank you,

Henry Gatlin

Henry Gatlin
Founder, CEO
Updraft RC

5 August 2016

An inside address is typically not used in Chinese correspondence.

The salutation uses a colon rather than a comma.

The revised opening gives the reader some helpful context and the assurance that this is a meaningful business opportunity.

The phrase "we are very willing to collaborate with you" shows respect for the reader and suggests the interest in forming a partnership.

This paragraph has been shortened to eliminate the redundant request for information.

This revised paragraph still conveys the seriousness of the writer's concerns without offending the reader.

"Minimizing" is easier for a non-native speaker to understand than "mitigating."

"Thank you" is a simple and adequately formal closing.

Figure 4c   Intercultural Business Letter: Final Revision
Here is the final English version, revised to ensure more successful translation into Chinese and to conform to standard practices in Chinese business communication (including removing the inside address).

the United States and Great Britain, 1.000 means one with three decimal places, but it means one thousand in many European countries.

- **Avoid slang, idiomatic phrases, and business jargon.** Everyday speech and writing are full of slang and **idiomatic phrases**—phrases that mean more than the sum of their literal parts. Examples from U.S. English include "Knocked one out of the park" and "More bang for the buck." Your audience may have no idea what you're talking about when you use such phrases.

- **Avoid humor and references to popular culture.** Jokes and references to popular entertainment usually rely on culture-specific information that might be completely unknown to your audience.

Humor does not "travel well" because it usually relies on intimate knowledge of a particular culture.

4308 Preston Highway
Louisville, KY 40213
Toll Free: 1.800.FLY.RITE
Fax: (502) 555-1324
www.updraftrc.com

李华先生:

随着智能手机的普及，越来越多的配件和周边产品正在被研发以满足市场的需求。我们的公司，Updraft RC,已经设计了一种新型的用智能手机控制的遥控玩具。我们的市场测试表明年轻客户，一个愿意尝试新产品的群体，（对我们的产品）有巨大的潜在需求。我们现在正在寻找制造伙伴，所以我们非常愿意与你们合作。

这是我们第一次与海外制造伙伴合作，在我们讨论具细节之前，我非常愿意让你们知道我们的两个问题。第一个问题对远距制造商合作关系来说都是一个挑战，这个挑战包括运输费用，运输延迟，质量控制和知识产权盗窃。

第二，与大洋对岸合作的美国公司面临着越来越高的来自新媒体和活跃组织的审查。这些审查包括工作场所安全性，劳工权益和可能对环境产生损害的制造。耐克和其他主要的美国公司已经花费了数百万美元，工作了几十年用来提升海外工厂的情况，但是他们仍然不能避免所有的问题。对于没有能力监控（海外）工厂的小公司来说，我们比较当心与制造相关的一系列问题可能影响到我们公司的形象。

所以请让我们知道你们公司解决这两个问题的策略和方法。

我们计划在 2017 年的第二个季度投入产品的生产。所以我们希望尽快得到你们公司的回应。

亨利 加特林
创始人，首席执行官
2016年8月5日

Figure 4d Intercultural Business Letter: Translated Version
Here is the translated version, formatted in accordance with Chinese business communication practice.

Although some of these differences may seem trivial, meeting the expectations of an international audience illustrates both knowledge of and respect for the other cultures (see Figure 5).

SPEAKING AND LISTENING CAREFULLY

Languages vary considerably in the significance of tone, pitch, speed, and volume, which can create challenges for people trying to interpret the explicit meaning of words themselves as well as the overall nuance of a message. The English word *progress* can be a noun or a verb, depending on which syllable you emphasize. In Chinese, the meaning of the word *mà* changes depending on the speaker's tone; it can mean *mother, pileup, horse,* or *scold.* And routine Arabic speech can sound excited or angry to an English-speaking U.S. listener.[52]

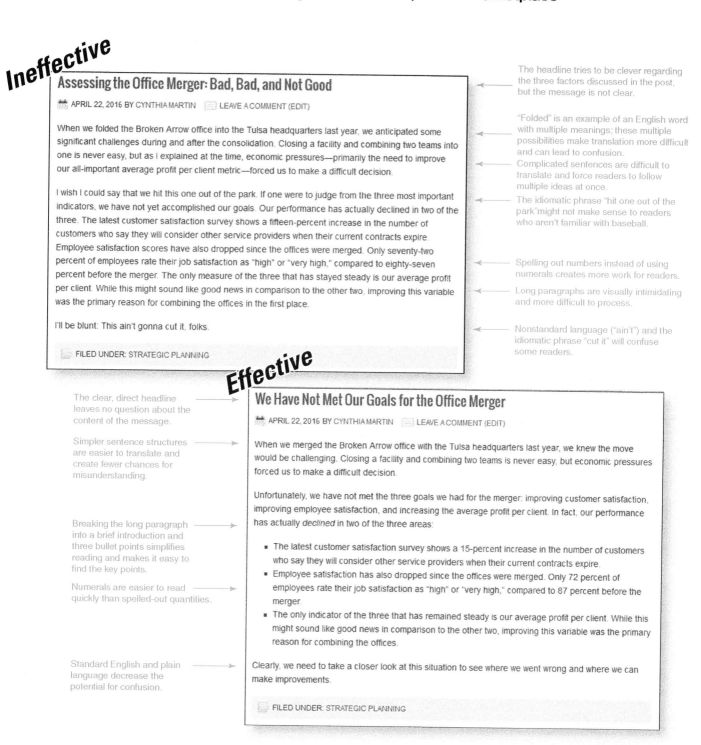

Ineffective

Assessing the Office Merger: Bad, Bad, and Not Good

APRIL 22, 2016 BY CYNTHIA MARTIN   LEAVE A COMMENT (EDIT)

When we folded the Broken Arrow office into the Tulsa headquarters last year, we anticipated some significant challenges during and after the consolidation. Closing a facility and combining two teams into one is never easy, but as I explained at the time, economic pressures—primarily the need to improve our all-important average profit per client metric—forced us to make a difficult decision.

I wish I could say that we hit this one out of the park. If one were to judge from the three most important indicators, we have not yet accomplished our goals. Our performance has actually declined in two of the three. The latest customer satisfaction survey shows a fifteen-percent increase in the number of customers who say they will consider other service providers when their current contracts expire. Employee satisfaction scores have also dropped since the offices were merged. Only seventy-two percent of employees rate their job satisfaction as "high" or "very high," compared to eighty-seven percent before the merger. The only measure of the three that has stayed steady is our average profit per client. While this might sound like good news in comparison to the other two, improving this variable was the primary reason for combining the offices in the first place.

I'll be blunt: This ain't gonna cut it, folks.

FILED UNDER: STRATEGIC PLANNING

The headline tries to be clever regarding the three factors discussed in the post, but the message is not clear.

"Folded" is an example of an English word with multiple meanings; these multiple possibilities make translation more difficult and can lead to confusion.

Complicated sentences are difficult to translate and force readers to follow multiple ideas at once.

The idiomatic phrase "hit one out of the park" might not make sense to readers who aren't familiar with baseball.

Spelling out numbers instead of using numerals creates more work for readers.

Long paragraphs are visually intimidating and more difficult to process.

Nonstandard language ("ain't") and the idiomatic phrase "cut it" will confuse some readers.

Effective

The clear, direct headline leaves no question about the content of the message.

Simpler sentence structures are easier to translate and create fewer chances for misunderstanding.

Breaking the long paragraph into a brief introduction and three bullet points simplifies reading and makes it easy to find the key points.

Numerals are easier to read quickly than spelled-out quantities.

Standard English and plain language decrease the potential for confusion.

We Have Not Met Our Goals for the Office Merger

APRIL 22, 2016 BY CYNTHIA MARTIN   LEAVE A COMMENT (EDIT)

When we merged the Broken Arrow office with the Tulsa headquarters last year, we knew the move would be challenging. Closing a facility and combining two teams is never easy, but economic pressures forced us to make a difficult decision.

Unfortunately, we have not met the three goals we had for the merger: improving customer satisfaction, improving employee satisfaction, and increasing the average profit per client. In fact, our performance has actually *declined* in two of the three areas:

- The latest customer satisfaction survey shows a 15-percent increase in the number of customers who say they will consider other service providers when their current contracts expire.
- Employee satisfaction has also dropped since the offices were merged. Only 72 percent of employees rate their job satisfaction as "high" or "very high," compared to 87 percent before the merger.
- The only indicator of the three that has remained steady is our average profit per client. While this might sound like good news in comparison to the other two, improving this variable was the primary reason for combining the offices.

Clearly, we need to take a closer look at this situation to see where we went wrong and where we can make improvements.

FILED UNDER: STRATEGIC PLANNING

Figure 5   Writing for Multilingual Audiences
In today's global and diversified work environment, chances are that many of your messages will be read by people whose native language is not English.

REAL-TIME UPDATES
LEARN MORE BY READING THIS ARTICLE

Study the seven habits of effective intercultural communicators

The willingness to take risks is a key habit; see what the other six are. Go to http://real-timeupdates.com/ebc12 and click on Learn More in the Students section.

To ensure successful conversations between parties who speak different native languages or even regional variations of the same language, speakers and listeners alike need to make accommodations.[53] Speakers should adjust the content of their messages and the style of their delivery to accommodate the needs of their listeners and the circumstances of the conversation. For example, if you are speaking in person or over an electronic connection that includes a video component, you can use hand gestures and other nonverbal signals to clarify your spoken message. However, when you don't have a visual connection, you must take extra care to convey your meaning through words and vocal characteristics alone. Conversely, listeners need to be tolerant of accents, vocabulary choices, gestures, and other factors that might distract them from hearing the meaning of a speaker's message.

When talking with people whose native language is different from yours, remember that the processing of even everyday conversations can be difficult. For instance, speakers from the United States sometimes string together multiple words into a single, mystifying pseudo-word, such as turning "Did you eat yet?" into "Jeetyet?" In spoken French, many word pairs are joined as a matter of rule, and the pronunciation can change depending on which words are next to one another. In these instances, non-native French speakers can have a hard time telling when one word ends and the next one begins.

To be more effective in intercultural conversations, remember these tips: (1) Speak slowly and clearly; (2) don't rephrase until it's obviously necessary (immediately rephrasing something you've just said doubles the translation workload for the listener); (3) look for and ask for feedback to make sure your message is getting through; (4) don't talk down to the other person by overenunciating words or oversimplifying sentences; and (5) at the end of the conversation, double-check to make sure you and the listener agree on what has been said and decided.

As a listener, you'll need some practice to get a sense of vocal patterns. The key is simply to accept what you hear first, without jumping to conclusions about meaning or motivation. Let other people finish what they have to say. If you interrupt, you may miss something important. You'll also show a lack of respect. If you do not understand a comment, ask the person to repeat it. Any momentary awkwardness you might feel in asking for extra help is less important than the risk of unsuccessful communication.

Speaking clearly and getting plenty of feedback are two of the keys to successful intercultural conversations.

To listen more effectively in intercultural situations, accept what you hear without judgment and let people finish what they have to say.

USING INTERPRETERS, TRANSLATORS, AND TRANSLATION SOFTWARE

You may encounter business situations that require using an *interpreter* (for spoken communication) or a *translator* (for written communication). Interpreters and translators can be expensive, but skilled professionals provide invaluable assistance for communicating in other cultural contexts.[54] Keeping up with current language usage in a given country or culture is also critical in order to avoid embarrassing blunders. Some companies use *back-translation* to ensure accuracy. Once a translator encodes a message into another language, a different translator retranslates the same message into the original language. This back-translation is then compared with the original message to discover any errors or discrepancies.

The time and cost required for professional translation has encouraged the development of computerized translation tools. Dedicated software tools, mobile apps, and online services such as WorldLingo offer various forms of automated translation. Major search engines let you request translated versions of the websites you find. Although none of these tools can translate as well as human translators, they are getting better all the time.

For important business communication, use a professional interpreter (for oral communication) or translator (for written communication).

HELPING OTHERS ADAPT TO YOUR CULTURE

Everyone can contribute to successful intercultural communication. Whether a younger person is unaccustomed to the formalities of a large corporation or a colleague from another country is working on a team with you, look for opportunities to help people fit in

Help others adapt to your culture; it will create a more productive workplace and teach you about their cultures as well.

CHECKLIST ✔ Improving Intercultural Communication Skills

- Understand your own culture so that you can recognize its influences on your communication habits.
- Study other cultures so that you can appreciate cultural variations.
- Study the languages of people with whom you communicate, even if you can learn only a few basic words and phrases.
- Help non-native speakers learn your language.
- Respect cultural preferences for communication style.
- Write clearly, using brief messages, simple language, generous transitions, and appropriate international conventions.

- Avoid slang, humor, and references to popular culture.
- Speak clearly and slowly, giving listeners time to translate your words.
- Ask for feedback to verify that communication was successful.
- Listen carefully and ask speakers to repeat anything you don't understand.
- Use interpreters and translators for important messages.

and adapt their communication style. For example, if a non-native English speaker is making mistakes that could hurt his or her credibility, you can offer advice on the appropriate words and phrases to use. Most language learners truly appreciate this sort of assistance, as long as it is offered in a respectful manner. Moreover, chances are that while you're helping, you'll learn something about the other person's culture and language, too.

You can also take steps to simplify the communication process. For instance, oral communication in a second language is usually more difficult than written forms of communication, so instead of asking a foreign colleague to provide information in a conference call, you could ask for a written response instead of or in addition to the live conversation.

For a brief summary of ideas to improve intercultural communication in the workplace, see "Checklist: Improving Intercultural Communication Skills."

ON THE JOB: SOLVING COMMUNICATION DILEMMAS AT EY

Karyn Twaronite is responsible for workforce diversity and inclusiveness across EY's Americas region, but every manager throughout the company is expected to foster a climate of inclusion and support for employees of every cultural background. As a team leader in one of EY's U.S. offices, you're learning to exercise sound business judgment and use good listening skills to help resolve situations that arise within your diverse group of employees. How would you address these challenges?

1. Joo Mi Kang, a recent immigrant from South Korea, is a brilliant analyst who continues to impress with her knowledge of international taxation. Unfortunately, she usually doesn't do a good job of explaining tax matters to your corporate clients. You suspect from seeing some of her emails that she has trouble writing in English. What should your first step be?
   a. Send her an email reminding her of the need to communicate with clients; attach a copy of her job description.
   b. Suggest that she find a tutor to help her develop her English skills.

   c. Visit her in her office and discuss the situation; ask if she understands the importance of communicating with clients and whether she has encountered any difficulty in doing so.
   d. Assign several other analysts the task of pitching in to take care of her communication chores.

2. Your employees are breaking into ethnically based cliques. Members of ethnic groups eat together, socialize together, and often chat in their native languages while they work. You appreciate how these groups give their members a sense of community, but you worry that these informal communication channels are alienating nonmembers and fragmenting the flow of information. How do you encourage a stronger sense of community and teamwork across your department?
   a. Ban the use of languages other than English at work.
   b. Do nothing. This is normal behavior, and any attempt to disrupt it will only generate resentment.
   c. Structure work assignments and other activities (such as volunteer projects) in ways that bring people from the

various cultural groups into regular contact with one another and make them more dependent on one another as well.

    d. Send all your employees to diversity training classes.

3. Fabio Silva joined your office after immigrating from Brazil three years ago. He is a competent business strategist, but he resists working with other employees, even in team settings where collaboration is expected. Given the importance that you place on teamwork, how should you handle the situation?

    a. Stay out of the way and let the situation resolve itself. Silva has to learn how to get along with the other team members.

    b. Tell the rest of the team to work harder at getting along with Silva.

    c. Tell Silva he must work with others or he will not progress in the company.

    d. Talk privately with Silva and help him understand the importance of working together as a team. During the conversation, try to uncover why he doesn't participate more in team efforts.

4. You've been surprised at the confusion that some of your memos and other written messages have generated lately. You suspect your casual and often humorous writing style might be the culprit and decide to "test drive" a different writing style. You've drafted four versions of a blog post that explains a new policy aimed at keeping client projects on schedule as they near completion. Which of these do you choose and why?

    a. "As each new project nears completion, I recognize how hard you all try to keep projects on schedule, even with the last-minute problems that are always part of client projects. To lighten your workload during the hectic final phase, you'll no longer be expected to attend routine department meetings or tend to other nonessential tasks during the final four weeks of each project."

    b. "As each new project races toward the finish line, I appreciate that all of you work like dogs to keep projects on schedule, even with the inevitable glitches and gremlins that always seem to attack projects at the last minute. Good news: During the last four weeks of every project, you'll be excused from nonessential tasks such as routine department meetings so that you can focus on your programming work (admit it—I know you hate coming to these meetings anyway!)."

    c. "As usual, the solution to all of life's problems can be found on television! While watching the Raiders–Chiefs game yesterday, I realized that we need to have our own version of the two-minute drill. To help avoid schedule slippage during the crazy final few weeks of each project, team members will be excused from routine meetings and other nonessential tasks not directly related to their project responsibilities."

    d. "As you should all be aware, numerous entities both internal and external to the corporation rely on us for timely project completion. While the inherent nature of complex consulting projects presents unexpected difficulties during the final stages of a project, it is incumbent upon us to employ every tactic possible to avoid significant completion delays. Henceforth, team members will be excused from nonessential tasks during the final four weeks of every development project."

Learning Objectives Checkup

Assess your understanding of the principles in this chapter by reading each learning objective and studying the accompanying exercises.

Objective 1: Discuss the opportunities and challenges of intercultural communication.

1. Which of the following factors is a significant reason U.S. business professionals often need to understand the cultures of other countries?

    a. Recent changes to government regulations require cultural education before companies are granted export licenses.

    b. The U.S. economy has been shrinking for the past 20 years, forcing companies to look overseas.

    c. Many countries require business executives to be fluent in at least two languages.

    d. Thousands of U.S. companies, including many of the largest corporations in the country, rely on markets in other countries for a significant portion of their sales.

2. Which of the following is a benefit of a multicultural workforce?

    a. Providing a broader range of viewpoints and ideas

    b. Giving companies a better understanding of diverse markets

    c. Enabling companies to recruit workers from the broadest possible pool of talent

    d. All of the above

3. A culturally rich workforce, composed of employees representing a wide range of ethnicities, religions, ages, physical abilities, languages, and other factors,

    a. Always slows down the decision-making process.

    b. Can be more challenging to manage but can pay off in a variety of important ways.

    c. Is easier to manage because so many new ideas are present.

    d. Is a concern only for companies that do business outside the United States.

Objective 2: Define *culture*, explain how culture is learned, and define *ethnocentrism* and *stereotyping*.

4. Culture is defined as

    a. A distinct group that exists within a country.

    b. A shared system of symbols, beliefs, attitudes, values, expectations, and norms for behavior.

    c. The pattern of cues and stimuli that convey meaning between two or more people.

    d. Serious art forms such as classical music, painting, sculpture, drama, and poetry.

5. Which of the following is *not* an example of a cultural group?

    a. Hindus

    b. Wrestling fans

  c. Television viewers
  d. Members of a fraternity
6. Culture is learned from
  a. Family members.
  b. Explicit teaching by others in the culture.
  c. Observations of the behavior of others in the culture.
  d. All of the above.
7. _____ is the tendency to judge all other groups according to the standards, behaviors, and customs of one's own group.
8. _____ is the mistake of assigning a wide range of generalized attributes to individuals on the basis of their membership in a particular culture or social group, without considering an individual's unique characteristics.
9. Which of the following is one of several techniques you can use to make sure you don't fall into the traps of ethnocentrism and stereotyping?
  a. Minimize interactions with people whose cultures you don't understand.
  b. Make sure that the people you work with clearly understand your culture.
  c. Insist that every employee who works for you strictly follows the company's guidelines for intercultural communication.
  d. Avoiding making assumptions about people in other cultures.

Objective 3: Explain the importance of recognizing cultural variations, and list eight categories of cultural differences.

10. In business, recognizing cultural differences is important because
  a. Doing so helps reduce the chances for misunderstanding.
  b. Someone from another culture may try to take advantage of your ignorance.
  c. If you don't, you'll be accused of being politically incorrect.
  d. Doing so helps you become more ethnocentric.
11. An example of low-context cultural communication would be
  a. Someone using metaphors to convey meaning.
  b. Someone insisting that the details of an agreement can be worked out later.
  c. Someone vigorously arguing his point of view in a problem-solving situation.
  d. Someone encouraging socializing before entering into official negotiations.
12. Which of the following is generally true about high-context cultures?
  a. Employees work shorter hours in such cultures because context allows them to communicate less often.
  b. People rely less on verbal communication and more on the context of nonverbal actions and environmental setting to convey meaning.
  c. People rely more on verbal communication and less on the context of nonverbal actions and environmental setting to convey meaning.
  d. The rules of everyday life are explicitly taught to all people within the culture.
13. Differing attitudes toward greeting gestures, personal space, touching, facial expression, eye contact, posture, and formality are common examples of _____ differences between cultures.

Objective 4: List four general guidelines for adapting to any business culture.

14. Why is understanding your own culture an important step in learning to relate well with other cultures?
  a. Understanding your own culture is important because it helps you recognize personal biases that shape your communication habits.
  b. Understanding your own culture is important because it helps you identify the ways that other cultures are inferior (or at least might be inferior) to your own.
  c. Understanding your own culture is important because it helps you identify the ways that other cultures are superior (or at least might be superior) to your own.
  d. Understanding your own culture is not important when you are trying to reach out to other cultures.

Objective 5: Identify seven steps you can take to improve your intercultural communication skills.

15. When communicating orally to those who speak English as a second language, you should make a habit to always
  a. Immediately rephrase every important point you make to give your listeners two options to choose from.
  b. Speak louder if listeners don't seem to understand you.
  c. Ignore the other person's body language.
  d. Rephrase your key points if you observe body language that suggests a lack of understanding.
16. Understanding the nuances of a culture can take years to learn, so the best approach when preparing to communicate with people in a culture that you don't know well is to
  a. Learn as much as you can from websites, travel guides, and other resources and not be afraid to ask for help while you are communicating in that new culture.
  b. Learn as much as you can from websites, travel guides, and other resources but never ask for help because doing so will only show everyone how ignorant you are.
  c. Learn as much as you can from television shows and movies that feature the other culture; the combination of spoken words, visuals, and music is the best way to learn a culture.
  d. Not worry about cultural variations; you'll never have time to understand them all, so your energy is better spent on other business issues.
17. When writing for audiences who don't speak the same native language as you speak, you can improve communication by
  a. Spelling out numbers rather than writing them as figures.
  b. Using simple sentences and careful word choices.
  c. Using long paragraphs to reduce the number of visual breaks on the page.
  d. Doing all of the above.
18. When you are writing for multilanguage audiences, humor
  a. Should be used often because it makes your audience feel welcome on a personal level.
  b. Should rarely, if ever, be used because humor is one of the most difficult elements of communication to encode or decode in a second language.
  c. Should never be used because movies and other entertainment products rarely cross over national boundaries.
  d. Should be used at least once per letter to show that you appreciate your audience as human beings.

Quick Learning Guide

LEARNING OBJECTIVES

1   Discuss the opportunities and challenges of intercultural communication.

2   Define *culture*, explain how culture is learned, and define *ethnocentrism* and *stereotyping*.

3   Explain the importance of recognizing cultural variations, and list eight categories of cultural differences.

4   List four general guidelines for adapting to any business culture.

5   Identify seven steps you can take to improve your intercultural communication skills.

KEY TERMS

cultural competency An appreciation for cultural differences that affect communication and the ability to adjust one's communication style to ensure that efforts to send and receive messages across cultural boundaries are successful

cultural context The pattern of physical cues, environmental stimuli, and implicit understanding that convey meaning between two members of the same culture

cultural pluralism The practice of accepting multiple cultures on their own terms

culture A shared system of symbols, beliefs, attitudes, values, expectations, and norms for behavior

diversity All the characteristics and experiences that define each of us as individuals

ethnocentrism The tendency to judge other groups according to the standards, behaviors, and customs of one's own group

high-context culture Culture in which people rely less on verbal communication

and more on the context of nonverbal actions and environmental setting to convey meaning

idiomatic phrases Phrases that mean more than the sum of their literal parts; such phrases can be difficult for nonnative speakers to understand

intercultural communication The process of sending and receiving messages between people whose cultural backgrounds could lead them to interpret verbal and nonverbal signs differently

low-context culture Culture in which people rely more on verbal communication and less on circumstances and nonverbal cues to convey meaning

stereotyping Assigning a wide range of generalized attributes to an individual on the basis of membership in a particular culture or social group

xenophobia Fear of strangers and foreigners

CHECKLIST ✓

Improving Intercultural Communication Skills

- Understand your own culture so that you can recognize its influences on your communication habits.
- Study other cultures so that you can appreciate cultural variations.
- Study the languages of people with whom you communicate, even if you can learn only a few basic words and phrases.
- Help non-native speakers learn your language.
- Respect cultural preferences for communication style.
- Write clearly, using brief messages, simple language, generous

transitions, and appropriate international conventions.
- Avoid slang, humor, and references to popular culture.
- Speak clearly and slowly, giving listeners time to translate your words.
- Ask for feedback to verify that communication was successful.
- Listen carefully and ask speakers to repeat anything you don't understand.
- Use interpreters and translators for important messages.

MyBCommLab®

To complete the problems with the ⭐, go to EOC Discussion Questions in the MyLab.

Apply Your Knowledge

To review chapter content related to each question, refer to the indicated Learning Objective.

1. Make a list of the top five priorities in your life (for example, fame, wealth, family, spirituality, peace of mind, individuality, artistic expression). Compare your list with the priorities that appear to be valued in the culture in which you are currently living. (You can be as broad or as narrow as you like in defining *culture* for this exercise, such as overall U.S. culture or the culture in your college or university.) [LO-2]

2. Do the priorities in your list align with the culture's priorities? If not, how might this disparity affect your communication with other members of the culture? [LO-2]

3. How does making an effort to avoid assumptions contribute to the practice of cultural pluralism? [LO-3]

4. Think about the last three movies or television shows set in the United States that you've watched. In what ways would these entertainment products be helpful or unhelpful for people from other countries trying to learn about U.S. culture? [LO-5]

⭐ 5. How can helping someone adapt to your culture help you gain a better understand of it yourself?

Practice Your Skills

Message for Analysis: Adapting to Cultural Differences [LO-5]

Your boss wants to send a brief email message welcoming employees recently transferred to your department from the company's Hong Kong branch. These employees, all of whom are Hong Kong natives, speak English, but your boss asks you to review his message for clarity. What would you suggest your boss change in the following email message, and why? Would you consider this message to be audience centered? Why or why not? (Hint: Do some quick research on Hong Kong to identify the style of English that people in Hong Kong are likely to speak.)

> I wanted to welcome you ASAP to our little family here in the States. It's high time we shook hands in person and not just across the sea. I'm pleased as punch about getting to know you all, and I for one will do my level best to sell you on America.

Exercises

Each activity is labeled according to the primary skill or skills you will need to use. To review relevant chapter content, you can refer to the indicated Learning Objective.

6. **Intercultural Communication: Recognizing Cultural Variations [LO-1], [LO-3], [LO-4]** Review the definitions of the generations. Based on your year of birth, in which generation do you belong? Do you feel a part of this generation? Why or why not? If you were born outside the United States, do the generational boundaries seem accurate to you? Now consider the biases that you might have regarding other generations. For example, if you are a member of Generation Y, what do you think about the baby boomers and their willingness to embrace new ideas? Identify several of your generational biases that could create friction in the workplace. Summarize your responses to these questions in a post on your class blog or an email message to your instructor.

7. **Intercultural Communication: Adapting to Cultural Variations [LO-2]** You are a new manager at K & J Brick, a masonry products company that is now run by the two sons of the man who founded it 50 years ago. For years, the co-owners have invited the management team to a wilderness lodge for a combination of outdoor sports and annual business planning meetings. You don't want to miss the event, but you know that the outdoor activities weren't designed for someone like you, whose physical impairments prevent participation in the sporting events. Draft a short email message to the rest of the management team, suggesting changes to the annual event that will allow all managers to participate.

8. **Intercultural Communication: Writing for Multiple-Language Audiences [LO-5]** Reading English-language content written by non-native speakers of English can be a good reminder of the challenges of communicating in another language. The writing can be confusing or even amusing at first glance, but the key to remember here is that your writing might sound just as confusing or amusing to someone else if your roles were reversed.

   Identify a company that is based in a non-English speaking country but that includes English-language text on its website. (The "advanced" search capabilities of your favorite search engine can help you locate websites from a particular country.) Study the language on this site. Does it sound as though it was written by someone adept at English? If the first site you've found does have writing that sounds natural to a native U.S. English speaker, find another company whose website doesn't. Select a section of text, at least several sentences long, and rewrite it to sound more "American." Submit the original text and your rewritten version to your instructor.

9. **Intercultural Communication: Writing for Multiple-Language Audiences; Collaboration: Team Projects [LO-5]** With a team assigned by your instructor, review the Facebook pages of five companies, looking for words and phrases that might be confusing to a non-native speaker of English. If you (or someone on the team) are a non-native speaker, explain to the team why those word choices could be confusing. Choose three sentences, headlines, company slogans, or other pieces of text that contain potentially confusing

words and rewrite them to minimize the chances of misinterpretation. As much as possible, try to retain the tone of the original—although you may find that this is impossible in some instances. Use Google Docs to compile the original selections and your revised versions, then email the documents to your instructor.

10. **Intercultural Communication: Speaking with Multiple-Language Audiences; Collaboration: Team Projects [LO-5]** Working with two other students, prepare a list of 10 examples of slang (in your own language) that might be misinterpreted or misunderstood during a business conversation with someone from another culture. Next to each example, suggest other words you might use to convey the same message. Do the alternatives mean *exactly* the same as the original slang or idiom? Submit your list of original words and suggested replacements, with an explanation of why each replacement is better than the original.

11. **Intercultural Communication: Writing for Multiple-Language Audiences [LO-5]** Explore the powers and limitations of free online translation services such as Google Translate. Enter a sentence from this chapter, such as "Local markets are opening to worldwide competition as businesses of all sizes look for new growth opportunities outside their own countries." First, translate the sentence from English to Spanish and click to complete the translation. Next, copy the Spanish version and paste it into the translation entry box and back-translate it from Spanish to English. Now repeat this test for German, French, Italian, or another language. Did the sentence survive the round trip? Does it still sound like normal business writing when translated back into English?

(1) What are the implications for the use of automated translation services for international correspondence? (2) Would you feel comfortable using an online tool such as this to translate an important business message? (3) How might you use this website to sharpen your intercultural communication skills? Summarize your findings in a brief report.

12. **Intercultural Communication: Speaking with Multiple-Language Audiences; Media Skills: Podcasting [LO-5]** Your company was one of the first to use podcasting as a business communication tool. Executives frequently record messages (such as monthly sales summaries) and post them on the company's intranet site; employees from the 14 offices in Europe, Asia, and North America then download the files to their music players or other devices and listen to the messages while riding the train to work, eating lunch at their desks, and so on. Your boss asks you to draft the opening statement for a podcast that will announce a revenue drop caused by intensive competitive pressure. She reviews your script and hands it back with a gentle explanation that it needs to be revised for international listeners. Improve the following statement in as many ways as you can:

Howdy, comrades. Shouldn't surprise anyone that we took a beating this year, given the insane pricing moves our knucklehead competitors have been making. I mean, how those clowns can keep turning a profit is beyond me, what with steel costs still going through the roof and labor costs heating up—even in countries where everybody goes to find cheap labor—and hazardous waste disposal regs adding to operating costs, too.

Expand Your Skills

Critique the Professionals

Find an online business document—such as a company webpage, blog post, Facebook Info tab, or LinkedIn profile—that you believe commits an intercultural communication blunder by failing to consider the needs of at least some of its target readers. For example, a website might use slang or idiomatic language that could confuse some readers, or it might use language that offends some readers. In a post on your class blog, share the text you found and explain why you think it does not succeed as effective intercultural communication. Be sure to include a link back to the original material.

Sharpening Your Career Skills Online

Bovée and Thill's Business Communication Web Search, at http://websearch.businesscommunicationnetwork.com, is a unique research tool designed specifically for business communication research. Use the Web Search function to find a website, video, PDF document, podcast, or presentation that offers advice on communicating with business contacts in another country or culture. Write a brief email message to your instructor, describing the item you found and summarizing the career skills information you learned from it.

Improve Your Grammar, Mechanics, and Usage

The following exercises help you improve your knowledge of and power over English grammar, mechanics, and usage. Turn to the Handbook of Grammar, Mechanics, and Usage at the end of this text and review all Verbs. Then look at the following 10 items. Indicate the letter of the preferred choice in the following groups of sentences.

13. Which sentence contains a verb in the present perfect form?
    a. I became the resident expert on repairing the copy machine.
    b. I have become the resident expert on repairing the copy machine.

14. Which sentence contains a verb in the simple past form?
    a. She knows how to conduct an audit when she came to work for us.
    b. She knew how to conduct an audit when she came to work for us.

15. Which sentence contains a verb in the simple future form?
    a. Next week, call John to tell him what you will do to help him set up the seminar.

b. Next week, call John to tell him what you will be doing to help him set up the seminar.

16. Which sentence is in the active voice?
    a. The report will be written by Leslie Cartwright.
    b. Leslie Cartwright will write the report.

17. Which sentence is in the passive voice?
    a. The failure to record the transaction was mine.
    b. I failed to record the transaction.

18. Which sentence contains the correct verb form?
    a. Everyone upstairs receives mail before we do.
    b. Everyone upstairs receive mail before we do.

19. Which sentence contains the correct verb form?
    a. Neither the main office nor the branches is blameless.
    b. Neither the main office nor the branches are blameless.

20. Which sentence contains the correct verb form?
    a. C&B Sales are listed in the directory.
    b. C&B Sales is listed in the directory.

21. Which sentence contains the correct verb form?
    a. When measuring shelves, 7 inches is significant.
    b. When measuring shelves, 7 inches are significant.

22. Which sentence contains the correct verb form?
    a. About 90 percent of the employees plans to come to the company picnic.
    b. About 90 percent of the employees plan to come to the company picnic.

MyBCommLab

Go to the Assignments section of your MyLab to complete these writing exercises.

23 How have market globalization and cultural diversity contributed to the increased importance of intercultural communication? [LO-1]

24 What four principles apply to ethical intercultural communication? [LO-3]

Endnotes

1. Karyn Twaronite LinkedIn profile, accessed 9 February 2015, www.linkedin.com; Ernst & Young website, accessed 9 February 2015, www.ey.com; "8 CEOs Whose Inclusive Styles Change Corporate Cultures," *DiversityInc*, accessed 21 January 2013, www.diversityinc.com; "E&Y's Karyn Twaronite Interviewed by HBA's Marianne Fray," Healthcare Businesswomen's Association, accessed 21 January 2013, www.youtube.com; "No. 6: Ernst & Young," *DiversityInc*, accessed 21 January 2013, www.diversityinc.com; "How Ernst & Young Improved Engagement, Innovation for 167,000 Employees," *DiversityInc*, accessed 21 January 2013, www.diversityinc.com; "HR & Communications: How Ernst &Young Gets Its Diversity Message to 50,000 Employees Every Day," *DiversityInc*, accessed 21 January 2013.

2. Michael R. Carrell, Everett E. Mann, and Tracey Honeycutt-Sigler, "Defining Workforce Diversity Programs and Practices in Organizations: A Longitudinal Study," *Labor Law Journal*, Spring 2006, 5–12.

3. "Dimensions of Diversity—Workforce," Merck website, accessed 4 January 2011, www.merck.com.

4. "Top Ten Countries with Which the U.S. Trades," U.S. Census Bureau website, accessed 29 December 2010, www.census.gov.

5. *Competing Across Borders: How Cultural and Communication Barriers Affect Business*, Economist Intelligence Unit Ltd., 2012, 4.

6. Nancy R. Lockwood, "Workplace Diversity: Leveraging the Power of Difference for Competitive Advantage," *HR Magazine*, June 2005, special section, 1–10.

7. Alan Kline, "The Business Case for Diversity," *USBanker*, May 2010, 10–11.

8. Paul Taylor, "The Next America," Pew Research Center, 10 April 2014, www.pewressarch.com; "More Than 300 Counties Now 'Majority–Minority,'" press release, U.S. Census Bureau website, 9 August 2007, www.census.gov; Robert Kreitner, *Management*, 9th ed. (Boston: Houghton Mifflin, 2004), 84.

9. Tracy Novinger, *Intercultural Communication, A Practical Guide* (Austin: University of Texas Press, 2001), 15.

10. Larry A. Samovar and Richard E. Porter, "Basic Principles of Intercultural Communication," in *Intercultural Communication: A Reader*, 6th ed., edited by Larry A. Samovar and Richard E. Porter (Belmont, Calif.: Wadsworth, 1991), 12.

11. Arthur Chin, "Understanding Cultural Competency," *New Zealand Business*, December 2010/January 2011, 34–35; Sanjeeta R. Gupta, "Achieve Cultural Competency," *Training*, February 2009, 16–17; Diane Shannon, "Cultural Competency in Health Care Organizations: Why and How," *Physician Executive*, September–October 2010, 15–22.

12. Linda Beamer and Iris Varner, *Intercultural Communication in the Workplace*, 2nd ed. (New York: McGraw-Hill Irwin, 2001), 3.

13. "Languages of the United States," Ethnologue website, accessed 29 December 2010, www.ethnologue.com.

14. Philip R. Harris and Robert T. Moran, *Managing Cultural Differences*, 3rd ed. (Houston: Gulf, 1991), 394–397, 429–430.

15. Lillian H. Chaney and Jeanette S. Martin, *Intercultural Business Communication*, 2nd ed. (Upper Saddle River, N.J.: Prentice Hall, 2000), 6.

16. Beamer and Varner, *Intercultural Communication in the Workplace*, 4.

17. Chaney and Martin, *Intercultural Business Communication*, 2nd ed., 9.

18. Richard L. Daft, *Management*, 6th ed. (Cincinnati: Thomson South-Western, 2003), 455.

19. Lillian H. Chaney and Jeanette S. Martin, *Intercultural Business Communication*, 4th ed. (Upper Saddle River, N.J.: Pearson Prentice Hall, 2007), 53.

20. Project Implicit website, accessed 29 December 2010, http://implicit.harvard.edu/implicit.

21. Linda Beamer, "Teaching English Business Writing to Chinese-Speaking Business Students," *Bulletin of the Association for Business Communication* 57, no. 1 (1994): 12–18.

22. Edward T. Hall, "Context and Meaning," in *Intercultural Communication*, 6th ed., edited by Larry A. Samovar and Richard E. Porter (Belmont, Calif.: Wadsworth, 1991), 46–55.

23. Daft, *Management*, 459.

24. Charley H. Dodd, *Dynamics of Intercultural Communication*, 3rd ed. (Dubuque, Ia.: Brown, 1991), 69–70.

25. Daft, *Management*, 459.

26. Hannah Seligson, "For American Workers in China, a Culture Clash," *New York Times*, 23 December 2009, www.nytimes.com.

27. Beamer and Varner, *Intercultural Communication in the Workplace*, 230–233.

28. Ed Marcum, "More U.S. Businesses Abandon Outsourcing Overseas," *Seattle Times*, 28 August 2010, www.seattletimes.com.

29. Guo-Ming Chen and William J. Starosta, *Foundations of Intercultural Communication* (Boston: Allyn & Bacon, 1998), 288–289.

30. Mary A. DeVries, *Internationally Yours* (New York: Houghton Mifflin, 1994), 194.

31. Robert O. Joy, "Cultural and Procedural Differences That Influence Business Strategies and Operations in the People's Republic of China," *SAM Advanced Management Journal*, Summer 1989, 29–33.

32. Chaney and Martin, *Intercultural Business Communication*, 2nd ed., 122–123.

33. Mansour Javidan, "Forward-Thinking Cultures," *Harvard Business Review*, July–August 2007, 20.

34. "The 100 Million Club 2013: The Top 14 Mobile Markets by Number of Mobile Subscriptions And 3G/4G Subscribers," *MobiThinking*, 26 November 2013, www.mobithinking.com.

35. Tracy Novinger, *Intercultural Communication, A Practical Guide* (Austin: University of Texas Press, 2001), 54.

36. Peter Coy, "Old. Smart. Productive." *BusinessWeek*, 27 June 2005, www.businessweek.com; Beamer and Varner, *Intercultural Communication in the Workplace*, 107–108.

37. Beamer and Varner, *Intercultural Communication in the Workplace*, 107–108.

38. Steff Gelston, "Gen Y, Gen X and the Baby Boomers: Workplace Generation Wars," *CIO*, 30 January 2008, www.cio.com.

39. Joanna Barsh and Lareina Yee, "Changing Companies' Minds About Women," *McKinsey Quarterly*, 2011, Issue 4, 48–59.

40. John Gray, *Mars and Venus in the Workplace* (New York: Harper Collins, 2002), 10, 25–27, 61–63.

41. Jennifer Luden, "Ask for a Raise? Most Women Hesitate," *NPR*, 14 February 2011, www.npr.org.

42. "Religious Bias a Growing Issue," *Business Insurance*, 13 February 2012, 8; Mark D. Downey, "Keeping the Faith," *HR Magazine*, January 2008, 85–88.

43. IBM Accessibility Center, accessed 24 August 2006, www.03.ibm.com/able; AssistiveTech.net, accessed 24 August 2006, www.assistivetech.net; Business Leadership Network website, accessed 24 August 2006, www.usbln.org; National Institute on Disability and Rehabilitation Research website, accessed 24 August 2006, www.ed.gov/about/offices/list/osers/nidrr; Rehabilitation Engineering & Assistive Technology Society of North America website, accessed 24 August 2006, www.resna.org.

44. Daphne A. Jameson, "Reconceptualizing Cultural Identity and Its Role in Intercultural Business Communication," *Journal of Business Communication*, July 2007, 199–235.

45. Leslie Knudson, "Diversity on a Global Scale," *HR Management*, accessed 17 August 2008, www.hrmreport.com.

46. Craig S. Smith, "Beware of Green Hats in China and Other Cross-Cultural Faux Pas," *New York Times*, 30 April 2002, C11.

47. Sana Reynolds and Deborah Valentine, *Guide for Internationals: Culture, Communication, and ESL* (Upper Saddle River, N.J.: Pearson Prentice Hall, 2006), 3–11, 14–19, 25.

48. P. Christopher Earley and Elaine Mosakowsi, "Cultural Intelligence," *Harvard Business Review*, October 2004, 139–146.

49. Bob Nelson, "Motivating Workers Worldwide," *Global Workforce*, November 1998, 25–27.

50. Mona Casady and Lynn Wasson, "Written Communication Skills of International Business Persons," *Bulletin of the Association for Business Communication* 57, no. 4 (1994): 36–40.

51. Lynn Gaertner-Johnston, "Found in Translation," Business Writing blog, 25 November 2005, www.businesswritingblog.com.

52. Myron W. Lustig and Jolene Koester, *Intercultural Competence*, 4th ed. (Boston: Allyn & Bacon, 2003), 196.

53. "'Can You Spell That for Us Nonnative Speakers?' Accommodation Strategies in International Business Meetings," Pamela Rogerson-Revell, *Journal of Business Communication* 47, no. 4 (October 2010): 432–454.

54. James Wilfong and Toni Seger, *Taking Your Business Global* (Franklin Lakes, N.J.: Career Press, 1997), 232.

Answer Key for "Learning Objectives Checkup"

1. d
2. d
3. b
4. b
5. c
6. d
7. ethnocentrism
8. stereotyping
9. d
10. a
11. c
12. b
13. nonverbal
14. a
15. d
16. a
17. b
18. b

Answer Key for "Improve Your Grammar, Mechanics, and Usage" Exercises

13. b (1.3.1)
14. b (1.3.1)
15. a (1.3.1)
16. b (1.3.5)
17. a (1.3.5)
18. a (1.3.4)
19. b (1.3.4)
20. b (1.3.4)
21. a (1.3.4)
22. b (1.3.4)

Planning Business Messages

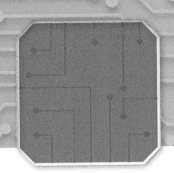

Planning Business Messages

LEARNING OBJECTIVES

After studying this chapter, you will be able to

1 Describe the three-step writing process.

2 Explain why it's important to analyze a communication situation in order to define your purpose and profile your audience before writing a message.

3 Discuss information-gathering options for simple messages, and identify three attributes of quality information.

4 List the factors to consider when choosing the most appropriate medium for a message.

5 Explain why good organization is important to both you and your audience, and list the tasks involved in organizing a message.

ON THE JOB: COMMUNICATING AT
H&R BLOCK

Adding Some Excitement to a Most Unexciting Task

Many taxpayers don't think about their taxes until they absolutely have to and even then they want to think about taxes as little as possible. Knowing this makes communicating about tax preparation products and services a challenge, but one H&R Block has addressed with creative use of new communication media.

H&R Block is the leading tax-preparation firm in the United States, with a range of options for taxpayers. Those who want assistance with tax preparation can hand the job over to one of the company's 90,000 tax professionals. Those who prefer to do the work themselves can choose from the company's do-it-yourself alternatives, which include PC software and online solutions.

Although tax preparation isn't typically considered exciting, H&R Block has developed a reputation for a fresh approach to communication and innovative social media efforts. Through partnerships with social influencers, video series, sweepstakes, bilingual social channels, and more, the company takes a straightforward and often lighthearted approach to an otherwise daunting topic.

In the spirit of the social communication model, H&R Block emphasizes a conversational, two-way approach, in which it listens as carefully as it speaks. During tax season, the company's social media team is available almost round-the-clock, interacting with clients across social

H&R Block makes extensive use of social media to connect with customers and simplify the chore of filing tax returns.

networks and providing information and resources. The team often refers clients to the Block Talk Blog, which has a wealth of tax-related resources in an easy-to-read format. They also regularly surprise clients who post positive comments and reviews with fun prizes such as gift cards and H&R Block bow ties as a "thank you" for the social media praise, further cementing the two-way relationship.

For a business that has been operating since 1955 in a somewhat stodgy field, this cutting-edge communication has helped H&R Block bring tax preparation into the 21st century and positioned the firm as an innovator in the eyes of today's digital natives.[1]

WWW.HRBLOCK.COM

Understanding the Three-Step Writing Process

1 LEARNING OBJECTIVE
Describe the three-step writing process.

The emphasis that H&R Block (profiled in the chapter-opening On the Job) puts on connecting with customers is a lesson that applies to business messages for all stakeholders. By following the process introduced in this chapter, you can create successful messages that meet audience needs and highlight your skills as a perceptive business professional.

The three-step writing process (see Figure 1) helps ensure that your messages are both *effective* (meeting your audience's needs and getting your points across) and *efficient* (making the best use of your time and your audience's time):

The three-step writing process consists of planning, writing, and completing your messages.

- **Step 1: Planning business messages.** To plan any message, first *analyze the situation* by defining your purpose and developing a profile of your audience. When you're sure what you need to accomplish with your message, *gather the information* that will meet your audience's needs. Next, *select the right medium* (oral, written, visual, or electronic) to deliver your message. Then *organize the information* by defining your main

1 Plan →	**2** Write →	**3** Complete
Analyze the Situation Define your purpose and develop an audience profile. **Gather Information** Determine audience needs and obtain the information necessary to satisfy those needs. **Choose Medium and Channel** Identify the best combination for the situation, message, and audience. **Organize the Information** Define your main idea, limit your scope, select a direct or an indirect approach, and outline your content.	**Adapt to Your Audience** Be sensitive to audience needs by using a "you" attitude, politeness, positive emphasis, and unbiased language. Build a strong relationship with your audience by establishing your credibility and projecting your company's preferred image. Control your style with a conversational tone, plain English, and appropriate voice. **Compose the Message** Choose strong words that will help you create effective sentences and coherent paragraphs.	**Revise the Message** Evaluate content and review readability, edit and rewrite for conciseness and clarity. **Produce the Message** Use effective design elements and suitable layout for a clean, professional appearance. **Proofread the Message** Review for errors in layout, spelling, and mechanics. **Distribute the Message** Deliver your message using the chosen medium; make sure all documents and all relevant files are distributed successfully.

Figure 1   The Three-Step Writing Process
This three-step process will help you create more effective messages in any medium. As you get more practice with the process, it will become easier and more automatic.
Sources: Kevin J. Harty and John Keenan, *Writing for Business and Industry: Process and Product* (New York: Macmillan Publishing Company, 1987), 3–4; Richard Hatch, *Business Writing* (Chicago: Science Research Associates, 1983), 88–89; Richard Hatch, *Business Communication Theory and Technique* (Chicago: Science Research Associates, 1983), 74–75; Center for Humanities, *Writing as a Process: A Step-by-Step Guide* (Mount Kisco, N.Y.: Center for Humanities, 1987); Michael L. Keene, *Effective Professional Writing* (New York: D. C. Heath, 1987), 28–34.

idea, limiting your scope, selecting the direct or indirect approach, and outlining your content. Planning messages is the focus of this chapter.

- **Step 2: Writing business messages.** After you've planned your message, *adapt to your audience* by using sensitivity, relationship skills, and an appropriate writing style. Then you're ready to *compose your message* by choosing strong words, creating effective sentences, and developing coherent paragraphs.

- **Step 3: Completing business messages.** After writing your first draft, *revise your message* by evaluating the content, reviewing readability, and editing and rewriting until your message comes across concisely and clearly, with correct grammar, proper punctuation, and effective format. Next, *produce your message.* Put it into the form that your audience will receive and review all design and layout decisions for an attractive, professional appearance. *Proofread* the final product to ensure high quality and then *distribute your message.*

Throughout this text, you'll learn how to apply these steps to a wide variety of business messages.

OPTIMIZING YOUR WRITING TIME

As a starting point, allot roughly half your available time for planning, one quarter for writing, and one quarter for completing a message.

The more you use the three-step writing process, the more intuitive and automatic it will become. You'll also get better at allotting time for each task during a writing project. Start by figuring out how much time you have to spend. Then, as a general rule, set aside roughly 50 percent of that time for planning, 25 percent for writing, and 25 percent for completing.

Reserving half your time for planning might seem excessive, but as the next section explains, careful planning usually saves time overall by focusing your writing and reducing rework. Of course, the ideal time allocation varies from project to project. Simpler and shorter messages require less planning than long reports, websites, and other complex projects. Also, the time required to produce and distribute messages can vary widely, depending on the media, the size of the audience, and other factors. However, start with the 50-25-25 split as a guideline, and use your best judgment for each project.

PLANNING EFFECTIVELY

For everything beyond brief and simple messages, resist the urge to skip the planning step.

As soon as the need to create a message appears, inexperienced communicators are often tempted to dive directly into writing. However, skipping or shortchanging the planning stage often creates extra work and stress later in the process. First, thoughtful planning is necessary to make sure you provide the right information in the right format to the right people. Taking the time to understand your audience members and their needs helps you find and assemble the facts they're looking for and deliver that information in a concise and compelling way. Second, with careful planning, the writing stage is faster, easier, and a lot less stressful. Third, planning can save you from embarrassing blunders that could hurt your company or your career.

2 LEARNING OBJECTIVE
Explain why it's important to analyze a communication situation in order to define your purpose and profile your audience before writing a message.

Analyzing the Situation

Every communication effort takes place in a particular situation, meaning you have a specific message to send to a specific audience under a specific set of circumstances. For example, describing your professional qualifications in an email message to an executive in your own company differs significantly from describing your qualifications in your LinkedIn profile. The email message is likely to be focused on a single goal, such as explaining why you would be a good choice to head up a major project, and you have the luxury of focusing on the needs of a single, personally identifiable reader. In contrast, your social networking profile could have multiple goals, such as connecting with your peers in other companies and presenting your qualifications to potential employers, and it might be viewed by hundreds or thousands of readers, each with his or her own needs.

The underlying information for these two messages could be roughly the same, but the level of detail to include, the tone of the writing, the specific word choices—these and other choices you need to make will differ from one situation to another. Making the right choices starts with defining your purpose clearly and understanding your audience's needs.

DEFINING YOUR PURPOSE

All business messages have a **general purpose**: to inform, to persuade, or to collaborate with the audience. This purpose helps define the overall approach you'll need to take, from gathering information to organizing your message. Within the scope of its general purpose, each message also has a **specific purpose**, which identifies what you hope to accomplish with your message and what your audience should do or think after receiving your message. For instance, is your goal simply to update your audience about some upcoming event, or do you want people to take immediate action? State your specific purpose as precisely as possible, even to the point of identifying which audience members should respond, how they should respond, and when.

> Business messages have both a general purpose and a specific purpose.

After you have defined your specific purpose, take a moment for a reality check. Decide whether that purpose merits the time and effort required for you to prepare and send the message—and for your audience to spend the time required to read it, view it, or listen to it. Test your purpose by asking these four questions:

> After defining your purpose, verify that the message will be worth the time and effort required to create, send, and receive it.

- **Will anything change as a result of your message?** Don't contribute to information overload by sending messages that won't change anything. For instance, if you don't like your company's latest advertising campaign but you're not in a position to influence it, sending a critical message to your colleagues won't change anything and won't benefit anyone.
- **Is your purpose realistic?** Recognizing whether a goal is realistic is an important part of having good business sense. For example, if you request a raise while the company is struggling, you might send the message that you're not tuned into the situation around you.
- **Is the time right?** People who are busy or distracted when they receive your message are less likely to pay attention to it. Many professions and departments have recurring cycles in their workloads, for instance, and messages sent during peak times may be ignored.
- **Is your purpose acceptable to your organization?** Your company's business objectives and policies, and even laws that apply to your particular industry, may dictate whether a particular purpose is acceptable.

When you are satisfied that you have a clear and meaningful purpose and that this is a smart time to proceed, your next step is to understand the members of your audience and their needs.

DEVELOPING AN AUDIENCE PROFILE

Before audience members will take the time to read or listen to your messages, they have to be interested in what you're saying. They need to know the message is relevant to their needs—even if they don't necessarily want to read or see it. The more you know about your audience members, their needs, and their expectations, the more effectively you'll be able to communicate with them. Follow these steps to conduct a thorough audience analysis (see Figure 2 on the next page):

> Ask yourself some key questions about your audience:
> - Who are they?
> - How many people do you need to reach?
> - How much do they already know about the subject?
> - What is their probable reaction to your message?

- **Identify your primary audience.** For some messages, certain audience members may be more important than others. Don't ignore the needs of less influential members, but make sure you address the concerns of the key decision makers.
- **Determine audience size and geographic distribution.** A message aimed at 10,000 people spread around the globe will probably require a different approach than one aimed at a dozen people down the hall.
- **Determine audience composition.** Look for similarities and differences in culture, language, age, education, organizational rank and status, attitudes, experience, motivations, biases, beliefs, and any other factors that might affect the success of your message (see Figure 3 on the next page).

> If audience members have different levels of understanding of the topic, aim your message at the most influential decision makers.

Planning Business Messages

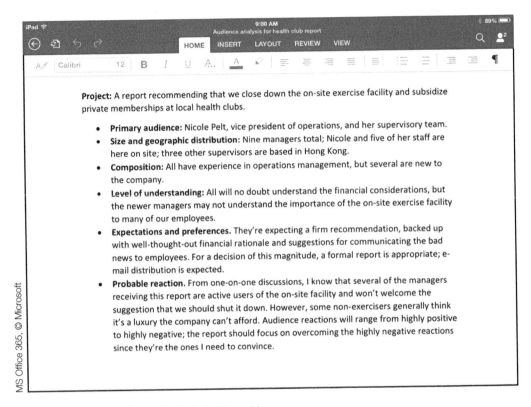

MS Office 365, © Microsoft

Figure 2   Using Audience Analysis to Plan a Message
For simple, routine messages, you usually don't need to analyze your audience in depth. However, for complex messages or messages for indifferent or hostile audiences, take the time to study their information needs and potential reactions to your message.

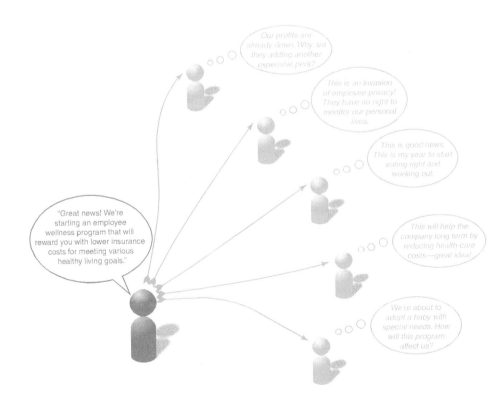

Figure 3   Predicting the Effects of Audience Composition
As just one example of why it's important to analyze the composition of your audience, the attitudes and beliefs of individual audience members can have a significant impact on the success of a message. In this scenario, for instance, a seemingly positive message about employee benefits can generate a wide range of responses from employees with different beliefs and concerns.

- **Gauge audience members' level of understanding.** If audience members share your general background, they'll probably understand your material without difficulty. If not, your message will need an element of education to help people understand your message.
- **Understand audience expectations and preferences.** For example, will members of your audience expect complete details or just a summary of the main points? In general, for internal communication, the higher up the organization your message goes, the fewer details people want to see.
- **Forecast probable audience reaction.** As you'll read later in the chapter, potential audience reaction affects message organization. If you expect a favorable response, you can state conclusions and recommendations up front and offer minimal supporting evidence. If you expect skepticism, you can introduce conclusions gradually and with more proof.

REAL-TIME UPDATES

LEARN MORE BY READING THIS PDF

Dig deep into audience needs with this planning tool

This in-depth tool can help you analyze audiences for even the most complex communication scenarios. Go to http://real-timeupdates .com/ebc12 and click on Learn More in the Students section.

Gathering Information

When you have a clear picture of your audience, your next step is to assemble the information to include in your message. For simple messages, you may already have all the information at hand, but for more complex messages, you may need to do considerable research and analysis before you're ready to begin writing. You can often use a variety of informal techniques to gather insights and guide your research efforts:

3 LEARNING OBJECTIVE
Discuss information-gathering options for simple messages, and identify three attributes of quality information.

If a project doesn't require formal research techniques, or you need answers in a hurry, you can use a variety of informal techniques to gather the information your audience needs.

- **Consider the audience's perspective.** Put yourself in the audience's position. What are these people thinking, feeling, or planning? What information do they need in order to move forward? If you are initiating a conversation in a social media context, what information will stimulate discussion in your target communities?
- **Listen to the community.** For almost any subject related to business these days, chances are there is a community of customers, product enthusiasts, or other people who engage in online discussions. Find them and listen to what they have to say.
- **Read reports and other company documents.** Annual reports, financial statements, news releases, blogs by industry experts, marketing reports, and customer surveys are just a few of the many potential sources. Find out whether your company has a *knowledge management system*, a centralized database that collects the experiences and insights of employees throughout the organization.
- **Talk with supervisors, colleagues, or customers.** Fellow workers and customers may have information you need, or they may have good insights into the needs of your target audience.
- **Ask your audience for input.** If you're unsure what audience members need from your message, ask them, if at all possible. Admitting you don't know but want to meet their needs will impress an audience more than guessing and getting it wrong.

MOBILE APP

The note-taking apps Evernote and Notebook help you collect, organize, and retrieve the information for planning writing projects.

UNCOVERING AUDIENCE NEEDS

In many situations, your audience's information needs will be obvious, or readers will be able to tell you what they need. In other situations, though, people may be unable to articulate exactly what they want. If someone makes a vague or broad request, ask questions to narrow the focus. If your boss says, "Find out everything you can about Interscope Records," narrow the investigation by asking which aspect of the company and its business is most important. Asking a question or two often forces the person to think through the request and define more precisely what is required.

In addition, try to think of relevant information needs that your audience may not have expressed. Suppose you've been asked to compare two health insurance plans for your firm's employees, but your research has uncovered a third alternative that might be even

Audience members might not be able to describe all the information they need, or you might not have the opportunity to ask them, so you may have to engage in some detective work.

better. You could then expand your report to include a brief explanation of why the third plan should be considered and compare it to the two original plans. Use judgment, however; in some situations you need to provide only what the audience expects and nothing more.

FINDING YOUR FOCUS

Use free writing and other discovery techniques if you need to the find the focus of a new writing project.

You may encounter situations in which the assignment or objective is so vague that you have no idea how to get started in determining what the audience needs to know. In such cases, you can use some *discovery techniques* to help generate ideas and uncover possible avenues to research. One popular technique is **free writing**, in which you write whatever comes to mind, without stopping to make any corrections, for a set period of time. The big advantage of free writing is that you silence your "inner critic" and just express ideas as they come to you. You might end up with a rambling mess by any conventional measure, but that's not important. Within that tangle of expressions, you might also find some useful ideas and angles that hadn't occurred to you yet—perhaps the crucial idea that will jumpstart the entire project.

The best discovery option in some cases might not be writing at all, but rather *sketching*. If you're unable to come up with any words, grab a sketchpad and start drawing. While you're thinking visually, your brain might release some great ideas that were trapped behind words.

The techniques listed under "Defining Your Main Idea" can also be helpful if you don't know where to start.

PROVIDING REQUIRED INFORMATION

The journalistic approach asks *who, what, when, where, why,* and *how.*

After you have defined your audience's information needs, your next step is to satisfy those needs completely. One good way to test the thoroughness of your message is to use the **journalistic approach**: Check to see whether your message answers *who, what, when, where, why,* and *how.* Using this method, you can quickly tell whether a message fails to deliver. For example, consider this message requesting information from employees:

> We are exploring ways to reduce our office space leasing costs and would like your input on a proposed plan in which employees who telecommute on alternate days could share offices. Please let me know what you think of this proposal.

The message fails to tell employees everything they need to know in order to provide meaningful responses. The *what* could be improved by identifying the specific information points the writer needs from employees (such as whether individual telecommuting patterns are predictable enough to allow scheduling of shared offices). The writer also doesn't specify *when* the responses are needed or *how* the employees should respond. By failing to address such points, the request is likely to generate a variety of responses, some possibly helpful but some probably not.

Be Sure the Information Is Accurate

You have a responsibility to provide quality information to your readers.

The *quality* of the information you provide is every bit as important as the *quantity.* Inaccurate information in business messages can cause a host of problems, from embarrassment and lost productivity to serious safety and legal issues. You may commit the organization to promises it can't keep—and the error could harm your reputation as a reliable businessperson. Thanks to the Internet, inaccurate information may persist for years after you distribute it.

You can minimize mistakes by double-checking every piece of information you collect. If you are consulting sources outside the organization, ask yourself whether the information is current and reliable. You must be particularly careful when using sources you find online. Be sure to review any mathematical or financial calculations. Check all dates and schedules and examine your own assumptions and conclusions to be certain they are valid.

Be Sure the Information Is Ethical

By working hard to ensure the accuracy of the information you gather, you'll also avoid many ethical problems in your messages. If you do make an honest mistake, such as delivering information you initially thought to be true but later found to be false, contact the recipients of the message immediately and correct the error. No one can reasonably fault you in such circumstances, and people will respect your honesty.

Messages can also be unethical if important information is omitted (see "Practicing Ethical Communication: How Much Information Is Enough?"). Of course, as a business professional, you may have legal or other sound business reasons for not including every detail about every matter. Just how much detail should you include? Make sure you include enough to avoid misleading your audience. If you're unsure how much information your audience needs, offer as much as you believe best fits your definition of complete and then offer to provide more upon request.

Omitting important information can be an unethical decision.

Be Sure the Information Is Pertinent

When gathering information for your message, remember that some points will be more important to your audience than others. Audience members will appreciate your efforts to prioritize the information they need and filter out the information they don't. Moreover, by focusing on the information that concerns your audience the most, you increase your chances of accomplishing your own communication goals.

Select the information you include based on how pertinent it is to your readers.

If you don't know your audience or if you're communicating with a large group of people who have diverse interests, use common sense to identify points of interest. Audience factors such as age, job, location, income, and education can give you clues. If you're trying to sell memberships in a health club, you might adjust your message for athletes, busy professionals, families, and people in different locations or in different income brackets. The comprehensive facilities and professional trainers would appeal to athletes, whereas the low monthly rates would appeal to college students on tight budgets.

Some messages necessarily reach audiences with a diverse mix of educational levels, subject awareness, and other variables. If possible, provide each audience segment with its own targeted information, such as by using sections in a brochure or links on a webpage.

PRACTICING ETHICAL COMMUNICATION

How Much Information Is Enough?

Your company, Furniture Formations, creates a variety of home furniture products, with extensive use of fine woods. To preserve the look and feel of the wood, your craftspeople use a linseed oil–based finish that you purchase from a local wholesaler. The workers apply the finish with rags, which are thrown away after each project. After a news report about spontaneous combustion of waste rags occurring in other furniture shops, you grow concerned enough to contact the wholesaler and ask for verification of the product's safety. The wholesaler knows you've been considering a nonflammable, water-based alternative from another source but tries to assure you with the following message:

> Seal the rags in an approved container and dispose of it according to local regulations. As you probably already know, county regulations require all commercial users of oil-based materials to dispose of leftover finishes at the county's hazardous waste facility.

You're still not satisfied. You visit the website of the oil's manufacturer and find the following cautionary statement about the product you're currently using:

Finishes that contain linseed oil or tung oil require specific safety precautions to minimize the risk of fire. Oil-soaked rags and other materials such as steel wool must be sealed in water-filled metal containers and then disposed of in accordance with local waste management regulations. Failure to do so can lead to spontaneous combustion that results from the heat-producing chemical reaction that takes place as the finish dries. In particular, DO NOT leave wet, oil-soaked rags in a pile or discard them with other waste.

CAREER APPLICATIONS

1. Was the wholesaler guilty of an ethical lapse in this case? If yes, explain what you think the lapse is and why you believe it is unethical. If no, explain why you think the statement qualifies as ethical.
2. Would the manufacturer's warning be as effective without the explanation of spontaneous combustion? Why or why not?

Selecting the Best Combination of Media and Channels

4 LEARNING OBJECTIVE
List the factors to consider when choosing the most appropriate medium for a message.

With the necessary information in hand, your next decision involves the best combination of media and channels to reach your target audience. The medium is the *form* a message takes and the channel is the *system* used to deliver the message. The distinction between the two isn't always crystal clear, and some people use the terms in different ways, but these definitions are a useful way to think about the possibilities for business communication.

Most media can be distributed through more than one channel, so whenever you have a choice, think through your options to select the optimum combination. For example, a brief written message could be distributed as a printed letter or memo, or it could be distributed through a variety of digital channels, from email to blogging to social networking.

THE MOST COMMON MEDIA AND CHANNEL OPTIONS

Media can be divided into *oral, written,* and *visual* forms, and all three can be distributed through *digital* and *nondigital* channels.

The simplest way to categorize media choices is to divide them into *oral* (spoken), *written,* and *visual.* Each of these media can be delivered through *digital* and *nondigital channels,* which creates six basic combinations, discussed in the following sections. Table 1 summarizes the general advantages and disadvantages of the six medium/channel combinations. Specific options within these categories have their own strengths and weaknesses to consider as well.

Oral Medium, In-Person Channel

The oral medium, in-person combo involves talking with people who are in the same location, whether it's a one-on-one conversation over lunch or a more formal speech or presentation. Being in the same physical space is a key distinction because it enables the nuances of nonverbal communication more than any other media-channel combo. These nonverbal signals can carry as much weight in the conversation as the words being spoken.

The nonverbal and interactive aspects of in-person communication are difficult to replicate in most other media/channel combinations.

By giving people the ability to see, hear, and react to each other, in-person communication is useful for encouraging people to ask questions, make comments, and work together to reach a consensus or decision. Face-to-face interaction is particularly helpful in complex, emotionally charged situations in which establishing or fostering a business relationship is important.[2] Managers who engage in frequent "walk-arounds," chatting with employees face-to-face, can get input, answer questions, and interpret important business events and trends.[3]

Oral Medium, Digital Channel

Oral media via digital channels include any transmission of voice via electronic means, both live and recorded, including telephone calls, podcasts, and voicemail messages. Live phone conversations offer the give-and-take of in-person conversations and can be the best alternative to talking in person. However, without a video component, they can't provide the nuances of nonverbal communication. Podcasts can be a good way to share lectures, commentary, and other spoken content.

Written Medium, Print Channel

Written, printed documents are the classic format of business communication. **Memos** are brief printed documents traditionally used for the routine, day-to-day exchange of information within an organization. **Letters** are brief written messages sent to customers and other recipients outside the organization. Reports and proposals are usually longer than memos and letters, although both can be created in memo or letter format. These documents come in a variety of lengths, ranging from a few pages to several hundred, and are usually fairly formal in tone.

Planning Business Messages

TABLE 1 Medium/Channel Combinations: Advantages and Disadvantages

Medium/ Channel	Advantages	Disadvantages
Oral, in-person	• Provide opportunity for immediate feedback • Easily resolve misunderstandings and negotiate meanings • Involve rich nonverbal cues (both physical gesture and vocal inflection) • Allow you to express the emotion behind your message	• Restrict participation to those physically present • Unless recorded, provide no permanent, verifiable record of the communication • Reduces communicator's control over the message
Oral, digital	• Can provide opportunity for immediate feedback (live phone or online conversations) • Not restricted to participants in the same location • Allow time-shifted consumption (e.g., podcasts)	• Lack nonverbal cues other than voice inflections • Can be tedious to listen to if not audience focused (recorded messages)
Written, printed	• Allow writers to plan and control their messages • Can reach geographically dispersed audiences • Offer a permanent, verifiable record • Minimize the distortion that can accompany oral messages • Can be used to avoid immediate interactions • Deemphasize any inappropriate emotional components • Give recipients time to process messages before responding (compared to oral communication)	• Offer limited opportunities for timely feedback • Lack the rich nonverbal cues provided by oral media • Often take more time and more resources to create and distribute • Can require special skills in preparation and production if document is elaborate
Written, digital	• Generally, all the advantages of written printed documents plus: • Fast delivery • Can reach geographically dispersed audiences • Flexibility of multiple formats and channels, from microblogs to wikis • Flexibility to structure messages in creative ways, such as writing a headline on Twitter and linking to the full message on a blog • Ability to link to related and more in-depth information • Can increase accessibility and openness in an organization through broader sharing • Enable audience interaction through social media features Ease of integrating with other media types, such as embedded videos or photos	• Can be limited in terms of reach and capability (e.g., on Twitter you can reach only those people who follow you or search for you) • Require Internet or mobile phone connectivity • Vulnerable to security and privacy problems • Are easy to overuse (sending too many messages to too many recipients) • Create privacy risks and concerns (exposing confidential data; employer monitoring; accidental forwarding) • Entail security risks (viruses, spyware; network breaches) • Create productivity concerns (frequent interruptions; nonbusiness usage)
Visual, printed	• Can convey complex ideas and relationships quickly • Often less intimidating than long blocks of text • Can reduce the burden on the audience to figure out how the pieces of a message or concept fit • Can be easy to create in spreadsheets and other software (simple charts and graphs), then integrate with reports	• Can require artistic skills to design • Require some technical skills to create • Can require more time to create than equivalent amount of text • Can be expensive to print
Visual, digital	• Generally, all the advantages of visual printed documents and all the advantages of written digital formats plus: • Can personalize and enhance the experience for audience members • Offer the persuasive power of multimedia formats, particularly video	• Potential time, cost, and skills needed to create • Can require large amounts of bandwidth

Although still a useful format, printed documents have been replaced by digital alternatives in many instances. However, here are several situations in which you should consider a printed message over electronic alternatives:

- When you want to make a formal impression
- When you are legally required to provide information in printed form
- When you want to stand out from the flood of electronic messages
- When you need a permanent, unchangeable, or secure record

Obviously, if you can't reach a particular audience electronically, you'll need to use a printed message.

Digital media/channel formats have replaced printed documents in many instances, but print is still the best choice for some messages and situations.

Written Medium, Digital Channel

Most of your business communication efforts will involve the combination of written medium and digital channel.

Most of your business communication efforts will involve written digital messages, with everything from 140-character tweets to website content to book-length reports distributed as portable document format (PDF) files (see Figure 4). Business uses of written, digital messages keeps evolving as companies look for ways to communicate more effectively. For example, email has been a primary business medium for the past decade or two, but it is being replaced in many cases by a variety of other digital formats.[4]

Visual Medium, Print Channel

Photographs and diagrams can be effective communication tools for conveying emotional content, spatial relationships, technical processes, and other content that can be difficult to describe using words alone. You may occasionally create visual, printed messages as stand-alone items, but most will be used as supporting material in printed documents.

Visual Medium, Digital Channel

The combination of the visual medium and a digital channel can be the most compelling and engaging choice for many messages, although it is not always the easiest or cheapest format.

Business messages can really come alive when conveyed by visual media in digital channels. Infographics, interactive diagrams, animation, and digital video have the potential to

Harley-Davidson
21 hours ago

Would you ride a 78 year old Harley across the United States? That's exactly what these riders are doing right now on the Motorcycle Cannonball - A 4,150-mile coast-to-coast ride from Daytona Beach, Florida to Tacoma, Washington for motorcycles older than 1937. Check out this shot from the start and find updates at http://bit.ly/1BnWFMY.

Like Comment Share

11,770 people like this.

563 Shares

Top Comments

Courtesy Harley-Davidson

Figure 4 Media and Channel Choices: Written + Digital
Harley-Davidson could've chosen a variety of media/channel combinations to share this information Harley fans taking a cross-country ride on vintage motorcycles. Facebook was an appealing choice because the company's huge fan base (more than 7 million people) and the ease of sharing the message on the social network.

engage audiences in ways that other formats can't, which is why the use of visual elements in business communication continues to grow.

Traditional business messages rely primarily on text, with occasional support from graphics such as charts, graphs, or diagrams to help illustrate points discussed in the text. However, many business communicators are discovering the power of messages in which the visual element is dominant and supported by small amounts of text. For the purposes of this discussion, you can think of visual media as formats in which one or more visual elements play a central role in conveying the message content.

Messages that combine powerful visuals with supporting text can be effective for a number of reasons. Today's audiences are pressed for time and bombarded with messages, so anything that communicates quickly is welcome. Visuals are also effective at describing complex ideas and processes because they can reduce the work required for an audience to identify the parts and relationships that make up the whole. Also, in a multilingual business world, diagrams, symbols, and other images can lower communication barriers by requiring less language processing. Finally, visual images can be easier to remember than purely textual descriptions or explanations.

The Unique Challenges of Communication on Mobile Devices

Mobile devices can be used to create and consume virtually every digital form of oral, written, and visual media. Thanks to the combination of portability and the flexibility enabled by a wide array of business-focused apps, mobile devices have become a primary tool in business communication. Consider these issues whenever your messages are likely to be viewed on mobile devices:

- **Screen size and resolution.** The screen resolution of phones and tablets has improved considerably in recent years, but the limited size of these screens still presents a challenge simply because many messages are significantly larger than the screens they will be viewed on. The result is a dilemma that pits clarity again context. Readers can zoom in to make text readable and visuals understandable, but particularly on phone screens, the inability to see an entire document page or visual at once can limit a reader's ability to grasp its full meaning. This can be particularly troublesome if you are collaborating on writing or presentation projects and team members need to review documents or slides.

- **Input technologies.** Even for accomplished texters, typing on mobile keyboards can be a challenge. Voice recognition is one way around the keyboard limitation, but anyone using it in public areas or shared offices runs the risk of sharing private message content and annoying anyone within earshot. In addition, even with a stylus, selecting items on a touch screen can be more difficult than doing so on a PC screen using a mouse. If your website content or other messages and materials require a significant amount of input activity from recipients, try to make it as easy as possible for them. Even simple steps such as increasing the size of buttons and text-entry fields can help.

- **Bandwidth, speed, and connectivity limitations.** The speed and quality of mobile connectivity varies widely by device, carrier, service plan, and geographic location. Even users with higher bandwidth service don't always enjoy the advertised transfer speeds they are paying for. Moreover, mobile users can lose connectivity while traveling, passing through network "dead spots," or during peak-demand hours or events (trade shows and conventions are notorious for this). Don't assume that your mobile recipients will be able to satisfactorily consume the content that you might be creating on a fast, reliable, in-office network.

- **Data usage and operational costs.** As the amount of video traffic in particular increases (video requires much higher bandwidth than text or audio), data consumption is becoming a key concern for mobile carriers and customers alike. Many mobile users do not have unlimited data-usage plans and have to manage their data consumption carefully to avoid excess fees. Some carriers offer unlimited data plans, but even those can come with restrictions such as bandwidth throttling that reduces the speed of a user's connection.[5] Given these factors, be careful about expecting or requiring mobile users to consume a lot of video or other data-intensive content.

The mobile digital channel has become significant in business communication of all types, but it presents some challenges that must be considered.

As the third major revolution in business communication in the past two decades (after the World Wide Web and social media), mobile communication has the potential to change nearly every aspect of business communication. Here is a small sample of the ways companies are putting mobile to work.

Training

In the face of changing markets, government regulations, and other forces in the business environment, developing and maintaining employee skill sets is an ongoing challenge for most companies. The challenge is made even more difficult when employees are constantly on the move or geographically dispersed. With training materials developed specifically for mobile devices, companies can deliver training content when and where it helps employees the most.[8]

Distributed Decision Making

A complementary aspect to managing remote workers via mobile apps is giving employees the authority to make decisions in the field, rather than relying on managers back in the office. In the oil and gas industry, for instance, specialized mobile apps include tools for data visualization, collaboration, and data collection to help on-site employees and supervisors communicate and coordinate their efforts. This capability can be particularly vital after accidents or other crisis events, because it lets employees who are on the scene choose the best course of action without delay.[9]

Mobile Glossary

In addition to terms defined elsewhere in this chapter, here are some helpful mobile terms.

3G, 4G, and 5G

Successive generations of mobile phone technology, although the generational boundaries are loosely defined and each generation includes a number of competing technologies; roughly speaking, we're in a transition from 3G to 4G now, and 5G (whatever it ends up being) won't arrive for at least several more years.

Android and iOS

The two major operating systems/platforms for mobile devices. Android devices are made by a wide variety of manufacturers, but iOS devices are made only by Apple.

Bandwidth

A measure of the data-carrying capacity of a mobile, Wi-Fi, or other network connection; streaming video and other demanding applications require a broadband connection, but there's no general agreement on exactly what constitutes broadband.

Cellular Versus Mobile

Two terms for the same concept; cellular (derived from the way phone networks are configured) is used mainly in the United States, whereas mobile is used more generally around the world and is also more descriptive.

Remote Workforce Management

Dispersed workforces also present a variety of supervision and management difficulties. Mobile workforce management apps can address many of these problems, from basic functions such as ensuring that workers show up on time at remote job sites to rescheduling customer appointments on the fly to collecting information to share with technical support staff. Sales managers can give just-in-time coaching and encouragement to representatives who are about to call on potential customers. Some systems can even embed information on best practices from experienced workers and deliver virtual coaching to less-experienced workers in the field.[10]

Ndoeljindoel/Shutterstock

Recruiting

With a target population that is often on the move, companies are responding by integrating mobile into their recruiting processes. These efforts include mobile-friendly job postings, mobile application and recruiting apps, and interviewing systems that let candidates and recruiters connect using their mobile devices.[11]

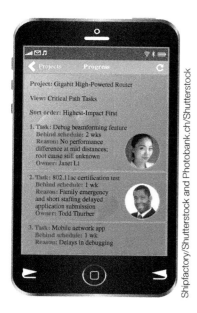

Shipfactory/Shutterstock and Photobank.ch/Shutterstock

Project Management

Work teams are often dispersed over wide geographic ranges and frequently on the move, so mobile communication is an essential element of contemporary project management. Instant access to task status and other vital information helps project managers stay on top of rapidly moving projects and helps team members communicate efficiently.

Miroslava Levina/Shutterstock

Context Awareness
A mobile device's ability to modify its operation based on knowledge of where it is; silencing the ringer when you arrive at your office is a simple example.

Geofencing
Using the location-sensing capabilities of mobile devices to remotely monitor and control the device and its user; delivery companies, for example, can monitor where their drivers are and make sure they stay within designated areas.

Over-the-Top (OTT) Application
A digital service that bypasses a traditional distribution network to provide similar capability, often by using cloud capabilities; an example is WhatsApp using Internet connections to create services traditionally provided by mobile phone carriers.[12]

Phablet
A rather ungainly name for mobile devices that are larger than phones but smaller than tablets.

Quick Response (QR) Codes and Near-Field Communication (NFC)
Two ways for a mobile device to access additional information; QR codes are square, phone-scannable barcodes that connect the phone to a website; NFC is a short-distance radio technology that enables a data link between a phone and tags that can be attached to products or other locations.

FACTORS TO CONSIDER WHEN CHOOSING MEDIA AND CHANNELS

You don't always have the option of choosing which medium or channel to use for a particular message. For example, many companies have internal IM or social networking systems that you are expected to use for certain types of communication, such as project updates. However, when you do have a choice, consider these factors:

Media vary widely in terms of *richness*, which encompasses the number of information cues, feedback mechanisms, and opportunities for personalization.

- **Richness.** *Richness* is a medium's ability to (1) convey a message through more than one informational cue (visual, verbal, vocal), (2) facilitate feedback, and (3) establish personal focus.[6] Face-to-face communication is a rich medium because it delivers information both verbally and nonverbally, it allows immediate feedback through both verbal and nonverbal responses, and it has the potential to be intimate and personal, at least in one-on-one and small-group settings. In contrast, lean media are limited in one or more of these three aspects. For example, texting and IM allow rapid feedback and can easily be personalized. However, they usually deliver information through only one informational cue (words), which can lead to misinterpretation. Emoticons, which attempt to add emotional nuances that might otherwise be convey through visual means such as facial expressions, are a response to the one-dimensional leanness of text-only messages. In general, use richer media to send nonroutine or complex messages, to humanize your presence throughout the organization, to communicate caring to employees, and to gain employee commitment to company goals. Use leaner media to send routine messages or to transfer information that doesn't require significant explanation.[7]
- **Formality.** Your media choice is a nonverbal signal that affects the style and tone of your message. For example, a printed memo or letter is likely to be perceived as a more formal gesture than an IM or email message.
- **Media and channel limitations.** Every medium and channel has limitations. For instance, IM is perfect for communicating simple, straightforward messages between two people, but it is less effective for complex messages or conversations that involve three or more people.

Many types of media/channel combinations offer instantaneous delivery, but take care not to interrupt people unnecessarily (e.g., with IM or phone calls) if you don't need an immediate answer.

- **Urgency.** Some media establish a connection with the audience faster than others, so choose wisely if your message is urgent. However, be sure to respect audience members' time and workloads. If a message isn't urgent and doesn't require immediate feedback, choose a medium such as email or blogging that allows people to respond at their convenience.
- **Cost.** Cost is both a real financial factor and a perceived nonverbal signal. For example, depending on the context, extravagant (and expensive) video or multimedia presentations can send a nonverbal signal of sophistication and professionalism—or careless disregard for company budgets.

Remember that media and channel choices can also send a nonverbal signal regarding costs; make sure your choices are financially appropriate.

- **Audience preferences.** If you know that your audience prefers a particular media and channel combination, use that format if it works well for the message and the situation. Otherwise you risk annoying the audience or having your message missed or ignored.

When choosing media and channels, don't forget to consider your audience's expectations and preferences.

- **Security and privacy.** Your company may have restrictions on the media and channels that can be used for certain types of messages, but even if it doesn't think carefully whenever your messages include sensitive information. Never assume that your email, IM, and other digital communications are private. Many companies monitor these channels, and there is always the risk that networks could get hacked or that messages will be forwarded beyond their original recipients.

5 LEARNING OBJECTIVE Explain why good organization is important to both you and your audience, and list the tasks involved in organizing a message.

Organizing Your Information

Organization can make the difference between success and failure. Good organization helps your readers or listeners in three key ways. First, it helps them understand your message. In a well-organized message, you make the main point clear at the outset, present additional points to support that main idea, and satisfy all the information needs of the audience. But if your message is poorly organized, your meaning can be obscured, and your audiences may form inaccurate conclusions about what you've written or said.

Second, good organization helps receivers accept your message. If your writing appears confused and disorganized, people will likely conclude that the *thinking* behind the writing is also confused and disorganized. Moreover, effective messages often require a bit more than simple, clear logic. A diplomatic approach helps receivers accept your message, even if it's not exactly what they want to hear. In contrast, a poorly organized message on an emotionally charged topic can alienate the audience before you have the chance to get your point across.

Third, good organization saves your audience time. Well-organized messages are efficient. They contain only relevant ideas, and they are brief. Moreover, each piece of information is located in a logical place in the overall flow; each section builds on the one before to create a coherent whole, without forcing people to look for missing pieces.

In addition to saving time and energy for your readers, good organization saves *you* time and consumes less of your creative energy. Writing moves more quickly because you don't waste time putting ideas in the wrong places or composing material that you don't need. You spend far less time rewriting, trying to extract sensible meaning from disorganized rambling. Last but far from least, organizational skills are good for your career because they help you develop a reputation as a clear thinker who cares about your readers.

Good organization benefits your audiences by helping them understand and accept your message in less time.

Good organization helps you by reducing the time and creative energy needed to create effective messages.

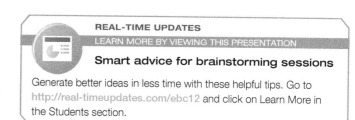

REAL-TIME UPDATES

LEARN MORE BY VIEWING THIS PRESENTATION

Smart advice for brainstorming sessions

Generate better ideas in less time with these helpful tips. Go to http://real-timeupdates.com/ebc12 and click on Learn More in the Students section.

DEFINING YOUR MAIN IDEA

The **topic** of your message is the overall subject, and your **main idea** is a specific statement about that topic (see Table 2). For example, if you believe that the current system of using paper forms for filing employee insurance claims is expensive and slow, you might craft a message in which the topic is employee insurance claims and the main idea is that a new web-based system would reduce costs for the company and reduce reimbursement delays for employees.

The topic is the broad subject; the main idea makes a statement about the topic.

In longer documents and presentations, you often need to unify a mass of material with a main idea that encompasses all the individual points you want to make. Finding a common thread through all these points can be a challenge. Sometimes you won't even be sure what your main idea is until you sort through the information. For tough assignments like these, consider a variety of techniques to generate creative ideas:

- **Brainstorming.** Working alone or with others, generate as many ideas and questions as you can, without stopping to criticize or organize. After you capture all these pieces, look for patterns and connections to help identify the main idea and the groups of supporting ideas. For example, if your main idea concerns whether

TABLE 2	Defining Topic and Main Idea		
General Purpose	**Example of Specific Purpose**	**Example of Topic**	**Example of Main Idea**
To inform	Teach customer service representatives how to edit and expand the technical support wiki	Technical support wiki	Careful, thorough edits and additions to the wiki help the entire department provide better customer support.
To persuade	Convince top managers to increase spending on research and development	Funding for research and development	Competitors spend more than we do on research and development, enabling them to create more innovative products.
To collaborate	Solicit ideas for a companywide incentive system that ties wages to profits	Incentive pay	Tying wages to profits motivates employees and reduces compensation costs in tough years.

to open a new restaurant in Denver, you'll probably find a group of ideas related to financial return, another related to competition, and so on. Identifying such groups helps you see the major issues that will lead you to a conclusion you can feel confident about.

- **Journalistic approach.** The journalistic approach asks *who, what, when, where, why,* and *how* questions to distill major ideas from unorganized information.
- **Question-and-answer chain.** Start with a key question, from the audience's perspective, and work back toward your message. In most cases, you'll find that each answer generates new questions until you identify the information that needs to be in your message.
- **Storyteller's tour.** Some writers find it best to talk through a communication challenge before they try to write. Record yourself as you describe what you intend to write. Then listen to the playback, identify ways to tighten and clarify the message, and repeat the process until you distill the main idea down to a single concise message.
- **Mind mapping.** You can generate and organize ideas using a graphic method called *mind mapping* (see Figure 5). Start with a main idea and then branch out to connect every other related idea that comes to mind. You can find a number of free mind-mapping tools online.

LIMITING YOUR SCOPE

Limit the scope of your message so that you can convey your main idea as briefly as possible.

The **scope** of your message is the range of information you present, the overall length, and the level of detail—all of which need to correspond to your main idea. The length of some business messages has a preset limit, whether from a boss's instructions, the technology you're using, or a time frame such as individual speaker slots during a seminar. Even if you don't have a preset length, it's vital to limit yourself to the scope needed to convey your main idea—and no more.

Whatever the length of your message, limit the number of major supporting points to half a dozen or so—and if you can get your idea across with fewer points, all the better. Listing 20 or 30 supporting points might feel as though you're being thorough, but your audience is likely to view such detail as rambling and mind numbing. Instead, group your supporting points under major headings, such as finance, customers, competitors, employees, or whatever is appropriate for your subject. Look for ways to combine your supporting points so that you have a smaller number with greater impact.

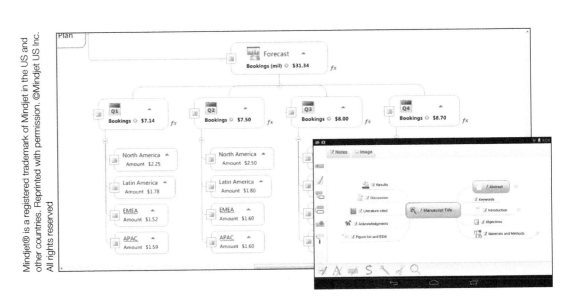

Figure 5   Mind Mapping
Mind-mapping tools such as Mindjet Map make it easy to explore the organization of your material, and mobile apps (see inset) bring this capability to tablets and other mobile devices.

The ideal length of a message depends on your topic, your audience members' familiarity with the material, their receptivity to your conclusions, and your credibility. You'll need fewer words to present routine information to a knowledgeable audience that already knows and respects you. You'll need more words to build a consensus about a complex and controversial subject, especially if the members of your audience are skeptical or hostile strangers.

CHOOSING BETWEEN DIRECT AND INDIRECT APPROACHES

After you've defined your main idea and supporting points, you're ready to decide on the sequence you will use to present your information. You have two basic options:

- The **direct approach** starts with the main idea (such as a recommendation, a conclusion, or a request) and follows that with supporting evidence.
- The **indirect approach** starts with the evidence and builds up to the main idea.

To choose between these two alternatives, analyze your audience's likely reaction to your purpose and message (see Figure 6). Bear in mind, however, that Figure 6 presents only general guidelines; always consider the unique circumstances of each message and audience situation. The following sections offer more insight on choosing the best approach for routine and positive messages, negative messages, and persuasive messages.

The type of message also influences the choice of the direct or indirect approach.

With the direct approach, you open with the main idea of your message and support it with reasoning, evidence, and examples.

With the indirect approach, you withhold the main idea until you have built up to it logically and persuasively with reasoning, evidence, and examples.

Outlining saves time and helps you create more effective messages.

Outliner is one of several apps that make it easy to create and modify writing outlines.

OUTLINING YOUR CONTENT

After you have chosen the best approach, it's time to figure out the most logical and effective way to present your major points and supporting details. Get into the habit of creating outlines when you're preparing business messages. You'll save time, get better results, and do a better job of navigating through complicated business situations. Even if you're just jotting down three or four key points, making an outline will help you organize your thoughts for

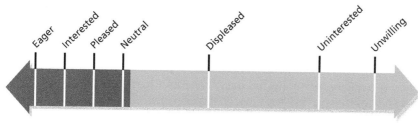

	Direct Approach	Indirect Approach	
Audience Reaction	Eager/interested/ pleased/neutral	Displeased	Uninterested/unwilling
Message Opening	Start with the main idea, the request, or the good news.	Start with a neutral statement that acts as a transition to the reasons for the bad news.	Start with a statement or question that captures attention.
Message Body	Provide necessary details.	Give reasons to justify a negative answer. State or imply the bad news, and make a positive suggestion.	Arouse the audience's interest in the subject. Build the audience's desire to comply.
Message Close	Close with a cordial comment, a reference to the good news, or a statement about the specific action desired.	Close cordially.	Request action.

Figure 6 Choosing Between the Direct and Indirect Approaches
Think about the way your audience is likely to respond before choosing your approach.

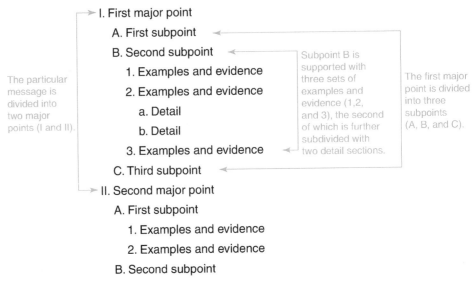

Figure 7 **Organizing Your Thoughts with a Clear Outline**
No matter what outlining format you use, think through your major supporting points and the examples and evidence that can support each point.

faster writing. When you're preparing a longer, more complex message, an outline is indispensable because it helps you visualize the relationships among the various parts.

You're no doubt familiar with the basic outline formats that identify each point with a number or letter and that indent certain points to show which ones are of equal status. A good outline divides a topic into at least two parts, restricts each subdivision to one category, and ensures that each subdivision is separate and distinct (see Figure 7).

Another way to visualize the outline of your message is to create an organization chart similar to the charts used to show a company's management structure. Put the main idea in the highest-level box to establish the big picture. The lower-level ideas, like lower-level employees, provide the details. All the ideas should be logically organized into divisions of thought, just as a company is organized into divisions and departments.[8] Using a visual chart instead of a traditional outline has many benefits. Charts help you (1) see the various levels of ideas and how the parts fit together, (2) develop new ideas, and (3) restructure your information flow. The mind-mapping technique used to generate ideas works in a similar way.

Whichever outlining or organizing scheme you use, start your message with the main idea, follow that with major supporting points, and then illustrate these points with evidence.

Start with the Main Idea

The main idea establishes what you want your readers to do or think and why they should do so.

The main idea helps you establish the goals and general strategy of the message, and it summarizes two vital considerations: (1) *what* you want your audience members to do or think and (2) *why* they should do so. Everything in your message should either support the main idea or explain its implications. As discussed earlier, the direct approach states the main idea quickly and directly, whereas the indirect approach delays the main idea until after the evidence is presented.

State the Major Points

Choose supporting points, evidence, and examples carefully; a few strong points will make your case better than a large collection of weaker points.

You need to support your main idea with major points that clarify and explain the main idea in concrete terms. If your purpose is to inform and the material is factual, your major points may be based on something physical or financial—something you can visualize or measure, such as activities to be performed, functional units, spatial or chronological relationships, or parts of a whole. When you're describing a process, the major points are almost inevitably steps in the process. When you're describing an object, the major points often correspond to the parts of the object. When you're giving a historical account, major points represent events in the chronological chain of events. If your purpose is to persuade or to collaborate, select major points that develop a line of reasoning or a logical argument that proves your central message and motivates your audience to act.

Provide Examples and Evidence

After you've defined the main idea and identified major supporting points, think about examples and evidence that can confirm, illuminate, or expand on your supporting points. Choose examples and evidence carefully so that these elements support your overall message without distracting or overwhelming your audience. One good example, particularly if it is conveyed through a compelling story (see the next section), is usually more powerful than several weaker examples. Similarly, a few strong points of evidence are usually more persuasive than a large collection of minor details. Keep in mind that you can back up your major supporting points in a variety of ways, depending on the subject material and the available examples and evidence (see Table 3).

If your schedule permits, put your outline aside for a day or two before you begin composing your first draft. Then review it with a fresh eye, looking for opportunities to improve the flow of ideas.

Figure 8 on the next page illustrates several of the key themes about organizing a message: helping readers get the information they need quickly, defining and conveying the main idea, limiting the scope of the message, choosing the approach, and outlining your information.

TABLE 3 **Six Types of Detail**

Type of Detail	Example	Comment
Facts and figures	Sales are strong this month. We have two new contracts worth $5 million and a good chance of winning another worth $2.5 million.	Enhances credibility more than any other type, but can become boring if used excessively.
Example or illustration	We've spent four months trying to hire recent accounting graduates, but so far, only one person has joined our firm. One candidate told me that she would love to work for us, but she can get $10,000 more a year elsewhere.	Adds life to a message, but one example does not prove a point. Idea must be supported by other evidence as well.
Description	Upscale hamburger restaurants target burger lovers who want more than the convenience and low prices of a McDonald's burger. These places feature wine and beer, half-pound burgers, and generous side dishes (nachos, potato skins). Atmosphere is key.	Helps audience visualize the subject by creating a sensory impression. Does not prove a point but clarifies it and makes it memorable. Begins with an overview of the function, defines its purpose, lists major parts, and explains how it operates.
Narration (storytelling)	When Rita Longworth took over as CEO, she faced a tough choice: shut down the tablet PC division entirely or outsource manufacturing as a way to lower costs while keeping the division alive. As her first step, she convened a meeting with all the managers in the division to get their input on the two options. (Story continues from there.)	Stimulates audience interest through the use of dramatic tension. In many instances, must be supplemented with statistical data in order to prove a point convincingly.
Reference to authority	I discussed this idea with Jackie Loman in the Chicago plant, and she was very supportive. As you know, Jackie has been in charge of that plant for the past six years. She is confident that we can speed up the number 2 line by 150 units an hour if we add another worker.	Bolsters a case while adding variety and credibility. Works only if authority is recognized and respected by audience.
Visual aids	Graphs, charts, tables, infographics, data visualization, photos, video	Helps audience grasp the key points about sets of data or visualize connections between ideas.

Planning Business Messages

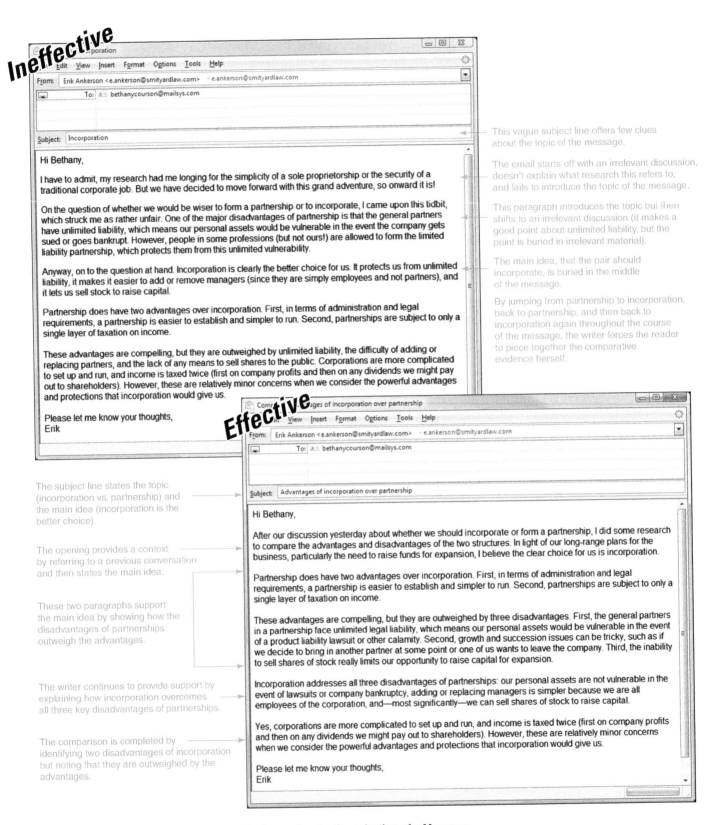

Ineffective

Subject: Incorporation

Hi Bethany,

I have to admit, my research had me longing for the simplicity of a sole proprietorship or the security of a traditional corporate job. But we have decided to move forward with this grand adventure, so onward it is!

On the question of whether we would be wiser to form a partnership or to incorporate, I came upon this tidbit, which struck me as rather unfair. One of the major disadvantages of partnership is that the general partners have unlimited liability, which means our personal assets would be vulnerable in the event the company gets sued or goes bankrupt. However, people in some professions (but not ours!) are allowed to form the limited liability partnership, which protects them from this unlimited vulnerability.

Anyway, on to the question at hand. Incorporation is clearly the better choice for us. It protects us from unlimited liability, it makes it easier to add or remove managers (since they are simply employees and not partners), and it lets us sell stock to raise capital.

Partnership does have two advantages over incorporation. First, in terms of administration and legal requirements, a partnership is easier to establish and simpler to run. Second, partnerships are subject to only a single layer of taxation on income.

These advantages are compelling, but they are outweighed by unlimited liability, the difficulty of adding or replacing partners, and the lack of any means to sell shares to the public. Corporations are more complicated to set up and run, and income is taxed twice (first on company profits and then on any dividends we might pay out to shareholders). However, these are relatively minor concerns when we consider the powerful advantages and protections that incorporation would give us.

Please let me know your thoughts,
Erik

This vague subject line offers few clues about the topic of the message.

The email starts off with an irrelevant discussion, doesn't explain what research this refers to, and fails to introduce the topic of the message.

This paragraph introduces the topic but then shifts to an irrelevant discussion (it makes a good point about unlimited liability, but the point is buried in irrelevant material).

The main idea, that the pair should incorporate, is buried in the middle of the message.

By jumping from partnership to incorporation, back to partnership, and then back to incorporation again throughout the course of the message, the writer forces the reader to piece together the comparative evidence herself.

Effective

Subject: Advantages of incorporation over partnership

Hi Bethany,

After our discussion yesterday about whether we should incorporate or form a partnership, I did some research to compare the advantages and disadvantages of the two structures. In light of our long-range plans for the business, particularly the need to raise funds for expansion, I believe the clear choice for us is incorporation.

Partnership does have two advantages over incorporation. First, in terms of administration and legal requirements, a partnership is easier to establish and simpler to run. Second, partnerships are subject to only a single layer of taxation on income.

These advantages are compelling, but they are outweighed by three disadvantages. First, the general partners in a partnership face unlimited legal liability, which means our personal assets would be vulnerable in the event of a product liability lawsuit or other calamity. Second, growth and succession issues can be tricky, such as if we decide to bring in another partner at some point or one of us wants to leave the company. Third, the inability to sell shares of stock really limits our opportunity to raise capital for expansion.

Incorporation addresses all three disadvantages of partnerships: our personal assets are not vulnerable in the event of lawsuits or company bankruptcy, adding or replacing managers is simpler because we are all employees of the corporation, and—most significantly—we can sell shares of stock to raise capital.

Yes, corporations are more complicated to set up and run, and income is taxed twice (first on company profits and then on any dividends we might pay out to shareholders). However, these are relatively minor concerns when we consider the powerful advantages and protections that incorporation would give us.

Please let me know your thoughts,
Erik

The subject line states the topic (incorporation vs. partnership) and the main idea (incorporation is the better choice).

The opening provides a context by referring to a previous conversation and then states the main idea.

These two paragraphs support the main idea by showing how the disadvantages of partnerships outweigh the advantages.

The writer continues to provide support by explaining how incorporation overcomes all three key disadvantages of partnerships.

The comparison is completed by identifying two disadvantages of incorporation but noting that they are outweighed by the advantages.

Figure 8 Improving the Organization of a Message
This writer is following up on a conversation from the previous day, in which he and the recipient discussed which of two forms of ownership, a partnership or a corporation, they should use for their new company. (*Partnership* has a specific legal meaning in this context.) That question is the topic of the message; the main idea is the recommendation that they incorporate, rather than form a partnership. Notice how the Improved version uses the direct approach to quickly get to the main idea and then supports that by comparing the advantages and disadvantages of both forms of ownership. In contrast, the Poor version contains irrelevant information, makes the comparison difficult to follow, and buries the main idea in the middle of the message.

BUILDING READER INTEREST
WITH STORYTELLING TECHNIQUES

Storytelling might seem like an odd subject for a business communication course, but narrative techniques can be an effective way to organize messages in a surprising number of business situations, from recruiting and training employees to enticing investors and customers. Storytelling is such a vital means of communicating that, in the words of management consultant Steve Tobak, "It's hard to imagine your career going anywhere if you can't tell a story."[9] Fortunately, you've been telling stories all your life, so narrative techniques already come naturally to you; now it's just a matter of adapting those techniques to business situations.

You've already been on the receiving end of thousands of business stories: Storytelling is one of the most common structures used in television commercials and other advertisements. People love to share stories about themselves and others, too, which makes social media ideal for storytelling.[10]

Career-related stories, such as how someone sought and found the opportunity to work on projects he or she is passionate about, can entice skilled employees to consider joining a firm. Entrepreneurs use stories to help investors see how their new ideas have the potential to affect people's lives (and therefore generate lots of sales). Stories can be cautionary tales as well, dramatizing the consequences of career blunders, ethical mistakes, and strategic missteps.

A key reason storytelling can be so effective is that stories help readers and listeners imagine themselves living through the experience of the person in the story. Chip Heath of Stanford University and his brother, Dan Heath of Duke University, have spent years exploring the question of why some ideas "stick" and others disappear. One of their conclusions is that ideas conveyed through storytelling tend to thrive because stories "put knowledge into a framework that is more lifelike, more true to our day-to-day existence."[11]

In addition, stories can demonstrate cause-and-effect relationships in a compelling fashion.[12] Imagine attending a new employee orientation and listening to the trainer read off a list of ethics rules and guidelines. Now imagine the trainer telling the story of someone who sounded a lot like you in the near future, fresh out of college, and full of energy and ambition. Desperate to hit demanding sales targets, the person in the story began entering transactions before customers had actually agreed to purchase, hoping the sales would eventually come through and no one would be the wiser. However, the scheme was exposed during a routine audit, and the rising star was booted out of the company with an ethical stain that would haunt him for years. You may not remember all the rules and guidelines, but chances are you will remember what happened to that person who sounded a lot like you. This ability to share organizational values is one of the major benefits of using storytelling in business communication, particularly across diverse workforces.[13]

A classic story has three basic parts. The beginning of the story presents someone whom the audience can identify with in some way, and this person has a dream to pursue or a problem to solve. (Think of how movies and novels often start by introducing a likable character who immediately gets into danger, for example.) The middle of the story shows this character taking action and making decisions as he or she pursues the goal or tries to solve the problem. The storyteller's objective here is to build the audience's interest by increasing the tension: Will the "hero" overcome the obstacles in his or her path and defeat whatever adversary is keeping him or her away from her goal?[14] The end of the story answers that question and usually offers a lesson to be learned about the outcome as well.

By the way, even though these are "stories," they must not be made-up tales. Telling stories that didn't happen to people who don't exist while presenting them as real-life events is a serious breach of ethics that damages a company's credibility.[15]

Consider adding an element of storytelling whenever your main idea involves the opportunity to inspire, to persuade, to teach, or to warn readers or listeners about the potential outcomes of a particular course of action.

For a quick refresher on message-planning tasks, see "Checklist: Planning Business Messages" on the next page.

Storytelling is an effective way to organize many business messages because it helps readers personalize the message and understand causes and consequences.

Organize stories in three parts: a beginning that introduces a sympathetic person with a dream or a challenge, a middle that shows the obstacles to be overcome, and an ending that resolves the situation and shows the moral or message of the story.

CHECKLIST ✔ Planning Business Messages

A. Analyze the situation.
- Determine whether the purpose of your message is to inform, persuade, or collaborate.
- Identify what you want your audience to think or do after receiving the message.
- Make sure your purpose is worthwhile and realistic.
- Make sure the time is right for your message.
- Make sure your purpose is acceptable to your organization.
- Identify the primary audience.
- Determine the size and composition of your audience.
- Estimate your audience's level of understanding and probable reaction to your message.

B. Gather information.
- Decide whether to use formal or informal techniques for gathering information.
- Find out what your audience needs to know.

- Provide all required information and make sure it's accurate, ethical, and pertinent.

C. Select the best combination of medium and channel for your message.
- Understand the advantages and disadvantages of oral, written, and visual medium distributed through both digital and nondigital channels.
- Consider media richness, formality, media limitations, urgency, cost, and audience preference.

D. Organize your information.
- Define your main idea.
- Limit your scope.
- Choose the direct or indirect approach.
- Outline content by starting with the main idea, adding major points, and illustrating with evidence.
- Look for opportunities to use storytelling to build audience interest.

ON THE JOB: SOLVING COMMUNICATION DILEMMAS AT H&R BLOCK

Robert Turtledove, H&R Block's chief marketing officer, was impressed enough with your communication skills and social media experience to add you to the team that markets H&R Block's digital tax-preparation solutions. Using the insights you gained in this chapter, address these internal and external communication challenges.

1. A carefully defined purpose is essential for every message, but particularly so with marketing messages. These persuasive messages can accomplish any number of different tasks, from changing perceptions about an overall category of products to encouraging shoppers to visit a retail store to enticing people to place an order for a specific product right away. Any confusion about purpose will result in a message that either doesn't know what it's trying to accomplish or tries to accomplish too much. Turtledove has asked you to plan a promotional campaign that encourages people who do their own taxes but have never used tax preparation software to at least consider these products. Which of the following statements does the best job of defining the specific purpose of this message?

   a. To persuade everyone who visits the H&R Block website to order a copy of H&R Block tax software within two hours of landing on the website.

   b. To persuade people who do their own taxes but have never used tax software to visit the H&R Block website and order a copy of H&R Block software.

   c. To persuade at least 75 percent of all visitors to the H&R Block website to learn more about the advantages of using software to prepare their taxes.

   d. To persuade people who do their own taxes but have never used tax software to visit the H&R Block website to learn more about the advantages of using software to prepare their taxes.

2. You've just learned that the company's software developers are going to redesign the H&R Block tax software to make it easier to use, and they have asked for feedback from Turtledove's department to help prioritize their work. Unfortunately, they actually made the request about a month ago, but the message fell through the cracks somehow and no one in marketing has prepared any information. The design team needs the information first thing tomorrow morning, and it's already 3:00 PM. You have a couple of hours to gather as much information as possible, then you can write a brief report this evening and email it to the development manager. Which of these is the best way to gather useful information?

   a. Interview the customer service manager to find out which features and functions have generated the most calls from frustrated customers.

   b. Use the software yourself for two hours, analyzing its usability and taking note of functions that are difficult to use.

   c. Do an extensive Internet search using several search engines. Look for negative reviews in software and financial magazines, negative comments from bloggers and Twitter users, and other feedback.

   d. Recruit a dozen people in your office for a panel discussion, asking them to share their own experiences with learning the software and to pass along any feedback they've heard from family, friends, and customers.

3. After submitting the emergency report on usability frustrations, you realize the company could benefit from a more systematic way of collecting feedback from customers. Which of the following media choices would you recommend and why?
   a. Publish the software development manager's email address and invite customers to write to that address whenever they get frustrated with any aspect of the software.
   b. Publish a toll-free telephone number that users can call whenever they are frustrated with the software. Operators can record the information and then email the results of each call to the software development manager.
   c. Build an Internet link into the software that gives users access to a feedback form whenever they get frustrated or confused. They can instantly record their grievances, and the information will then be transmitted to H&R Block and automatically fed into a searchable database.
   d. Create the same form and database described in choice (c) but put the form on the H&R Block website, rather than embedding it in the software.

4. You think you've spotted a potential business opportunity for H&R Block: a mobile app for personal financial planning. The company already has a mobile app for tax preparation, but a general-purpose financial app would let users track expenses, balance their checking accounts, and perform other routine tasks. You know that such a product would be a strategic departure for H&R Block, which has always been all about taxes, so your proposal will surely encounter some resistance and skepticism. Which of the following approaches should you take in organizing a proposal that recommends the company explore the possibility of creating this new app?
   a. Launching a new product is a serious business decision, so be direct. Come right out and say what you propose in the opening paragraph of your proposal and then back that up with details in the body of the message. Your readers will study the supporting details and then evaluate your idea on its merits alone.
   b. The fact that H&R Block doesn't already have a financial planning app is mystifying to you. After all, the company is one of the best-known firms in the financial services sector. Your proposal needs to be not only direct but also blunt: Without exactly saying so, you need to convey the message that only a fool would ignore an opportunity like this.
   c. Your proposal should take an indirect approach because your readers will initially be resistant to the idea. Moreover, it would be bad form to dictate precisely what the solution should be, so write only in general terms (such as "the opportunity for smartphone software apps is significant") and let the readers reach a conclusion on their own (as in, deciding specifically to create a personal finance manager for smartphones).
   d. If the proposal doesn't quickly address the audience's reservations regarding moving beyond tax preparation tools into general-purpose financial tools, audience members won't bother to read the details or consider the proposal. Consequently, an indirect approach is best. Start by announcing that you've identified a business opportunity that is ideal for H&R Block but needs to be acted on soon or a competitor will get there first. After you've captured the audience's attention with that intriguing opening, continue with your persuasive argument in favor of the financial planning app.

Learning Objectives Checkup

Assess your understanding of the principles in this chapter by reading each learning objective and studying the accompanying exercises.

Objective 1: Describe the three-step writing process.

1. The three major steps in the three-step writing process are
   a. Writing, editing, and producing.
   b. Planning, writing, and completing.
   c. Writing, editing, and distributing.
   d. Organizing, defining your purpose, and writing.
2. The first step of the three-step writing process is
   a. Writing the first draft.
   b. Organizing your information.
   c. Planning your message.
   d. Preparing an outline.
3. Which of the following tasks should you do when you're planning a writing project?
   a. Define your purpose.
   b. Revise carefully to make sure you haven't made any embarrassing mistakes.
   c. Choose words and sentences carefully to make sure the audience understands your main idea.
   d. Do all of the above.

Objective 2: Explain why it's important to analyze a communication situation in order to define your purpose and profile your audience before writing a message.

4. The _____ _____ of a message indicates whether you intend to use the message to inform, to persuade, or to collaborate.
5. If you were to write a letter to a manufacturer complaining about a defective product and asking for a refund, your general purpose would be
   a. To inform
   b. To persuade
   c. To collaborate
   d. To entertain
6. No matter what the message is or the audience you want to reach, you should always
   a. Determine the information your audience needs in order to grasp your main idea
   b. Learn the names of everyone in the target audience
   c. Estimate the percentage of audience members who are likely to agree with your message

d. Determine a complete demographic profile of your audience

7. If audience members will vary in terms of the amount of information they already know about your topic, your best approach is to
   a. Provide as much extra information as possible to make sure everyone gets every detail
   b. Provide just the basic information; if your audience needs to know more, they can find out for themselves
   c. Gear your coverage to your primary audience and provide the information most relevant to them
   d. Include lots of graphics

Objective 3: Discuss information-gathering options for simple messages, and identify three attributes of quality information.

8. To make sure you have provided all the necessary information, use the journalistic approach, which is to
   a. Interview your audience about its needs
   b. Check the accuracy of your information
   c. Verify whether your message answers the questions of *who, what, when, where, why,* and *how*
   d. Make sure your information is ethical

9. To determine whether the information you've gathered is good enough, verify that it is
   a. Accurate
   b. Ethical
   c. Pertinent to the audience's needs
   d. All of the above

10. If you realize you have given your audience incorrect information, the most ethical action would be to
    a. Say nothing and hope no one notices
    b. Wait until someone points out the error and then acknowledge the mistake
    c. Post a correction on your website
    d. Contact the audience immediately and correct the error

Objective 4: List the factors to consider when choosing the most appropriate medium for a message.

11. The media choices of oral, written, and visual can be delivered through ____ and ____ channels.

12. Which of the following choices would be best for communicating a complex policy change to employees in a company with offices all over the world?
    a. A teleconference followed by an email message
    b. Instant messaging
    c. A traditional typed memo sent via regular postal mail
    d. A posting on an internal website with an email message alerting employees to the change and directing them to the website for more information

13. Media richness is a measure of
    a. A medium's ability to use more than one informational cue, facilitate feedback, and establish personal focus
    b. A medium's ability to use more than one informational cue, limit destructive feedback, and establish personal focus
    c. How expensive the delivery options are likely to be, particularly for large or geographically dispersed audiences
    d. How much total employee cost is involved in creating messages using a particular medium

Objective 5: Explain why good organization is important to both you and your audience, and list the tasks involved in organizing a message.

14. Which of the following is an important benefit of taking time to organize your business messages?
    a. You can delay the actual writing.
    b. You save time and conserve creative energy because the writing process is quicker.
    c. Organizing your thoughts and information saves you the trouble of asking colleagues for input.
    d. In many cases, you can simply send a detailed outline and save the trouble of writing the document.

15. The purpose of limiting your scope when planning a writing project is to
    a. Make your job easier
    b. Reduce the number of things you need to think about
    c. Make sure your memos are never longer than one page
    d. Make sure that your message stays focused on the main idea and any necessary supporting details

16. Starting with the main idea and then offering supporting evidence is known as the ____ approach.

17. Starting with evidence first and building toward your main idea is known as the ____ approach.

18. When your audience is likely to have a skeptical or even hostile reaction to your main idea, you should generally use
    a. The indirect approach
    b. The direct approach
    c. The open-ended approach
    d. The closed approach

19. Which of the following is one of the reasons storytelling can be effective in business communication?
    a. Stories help readers and listeners imagine themselves living through the experience of the person in story.
    b. Stories are entertaining, so they offer some diversion from the daily grind of work.
    c. Readers and listeners are overloaded with data, so avoiding facts and figures is a proven way to get their attention.
    d. Stories are inherently funny, and people are more receptive to new ideas when they are in a good mood.

Quick Learning Guide

LEARNING OBJECTIVES

1 Describe the three-step writing process.

2 Explain why it's important to analyze a communication situation in order to define your purpose and profile your audience before writing a message.

3 Discuss information-gathering options for simple messages, and identify three attributes of quality information.

4 List the factors to consider when choosing the most appropriate medium for a message.

5 Explain why good organization is important to both you and your audience, and list the tasks involved in organizing a message.

KEY TERMS

direct approach Message organization that starts with the main idea (such as a recommendation, a conclusion, or a request) and follows that with your supporting evidence

free writing An exploratory technique in which you write whatever comes to mind, without stopping to make any corrections, for a set period of time

general purpose The broad intent of a message—to inform, to persuade, or to collaborate with the audience

indirect approach Message organization that starts with the evidence and builds your case before presenting the main idea

journalistic approach Verifying the completeness of a message by making sure it answers the *who, what, when, where, why,* and *how* questions

letters Brief written messages sent to customers and other recipients outside the organization

main idea A specific statement about the topic

memos Brief printed documents traditionally used for the routine, day-to-day exchange of information within an organization

scope The range of information presented in a message, its overall length, and the level of detail provided

specific purpose Identifies what you hope to accomplish with your message and what your audience should do or think after receiving your message

topic The overall subject of a message

CHECKLIST ✓

Planning Business Messages

A. Analyze the situation.
- Determine whether the purpose of your message is to inform, persuade, or collaborate.
- Identify what you want your audience to think or do after receiving the message.
- Make sure your purpose is worthwhile and realistic.
- Make sure the time is right for your message.
- Make sure your purpose is acceptable to your organization.
- Identify the primary audience.
- Determine the size and composition of your audience.
- Estimate your audience's level of understanding and probable reaction to your message.

B. Gather information.
- Decide whether to use formal or informal techniques for gathering information.
- Find out what your audience needs to know.
- Provide all required information and make sure it's accurate, ethical, and pertinent.

C. Select the best combination of medium and channel for your message.
- Understand the advantages and disadvantages of oral, written, and visual medium distributed through both digital and nondigital channels.
- Consider media richness, formality, media limitations, urgency, cost, and audience preference.

D. Organize your information.
- Define your main idea.
- Limit your scope.
- Choose the direct or indirect approach.
- Outline content by starting with the main idea, adding major points, and illustrating with evidence.
- Look for opportunities to use storytelling to build audience interest.

Apply Your Knowledge

To review chapter content related to each question, refer to the indicated Learning Objective.

⭐ 1. Some writers argue that planning messages wastes time because they inevitably change their plans as they proceed. How would you respond to this argument? Briefly explain. [LO-1]

⭐ 2. A day after sending an email to all 1,800 employees in your company regarding income tax implications of the company's retirement plan, you discover that one of the sources you relied on for your information plagiarized from other sources. You quickly double-check all the information in your message and confirm that it is accurate. However, you are concerned about using plagiarized information, even though you did nothing wrong. Write a brief email message to your instructor, explaining how you would handle the situation. [LO-3]

⭐ 3. You are organizing an exploratory in-person meeting with engineering representatives from a dozen manufacturers around the world to discuss updates to a technical standard that all the companies' products must adhere to. The representatives have a wide range of firmly held opinions on the subject, because the changes could help some companies and hurt others. They can't even agree on what should be addressed in the first meeting, so you need to develop a minimum level of consensus on what should be on the agenda. Which combination of media and channels would you use to move the conversation forward and finalize the agenda? Each company has one representative, and any discussions need to be kept confidential. [LO-4]

4. How might the inability to view an entire document at once on a mobile screen hinder a reader's ability to grasp the full meaning of the message? [LO-4]

5. You have been invited to speak at an annual industry conference. After preparing the outline for your presentation, you see that you've identified 14 different points to support your main idea. Should you move ahead with creating the slides for your presentation or move back and rethink your outline? Why? [LO-5]

Practice Your Skills

Message for Analysis: Outlining Your Content [LO-5]

A writer is working on an insurance information brochure and is having trouble grouping the ideas logically into an outline. Using the following information, prepare the outline, paying attention to the appropriate hierarchy of ideas. If necessary, rewrite phrases to make them all consistent.

Accident Protection Insurance Plan

- Coverage is only pennies a day
- Benefit is $100,000 for accidental death on common carrier

- Benefit is $100 a day for hospitalization as result of motor vehicle or common carrier accident
- Benefit is $20,000 for accidental death in motor vehicle accident
- Individual coverage is only $17.85 per quarter; family coverage is just $26.85 per quarter
- No physical exam or health questions
- Convenient payment—billed quarterly
- Guaranteed acceptance for all applicants
- No individual rate increases
- Free, no-obligation examination period
- Cash paid in addition to any other insurance carried
- Covers accidental death when riding as fare-paying passenger on public transportation, including buses, trains, jets, ships, trolleys, subways, or any other common carrier
- Covers accidental death in motor vehicle accidents occurring while driving or riding in or on automobile, truck, camper, motor home, or nonmotorized bicycle

Exercises

Each activity is labeled according to the primary skill or skills you will need to use. To review relevant chapter content, you can refer to the indicated Learning Objective.

6. **Planning: Identifying Your Purpose [LO-2]** For each of the following communication tasks, state a specific purpose (if you have trouble, try beginning with "I want to …").

a. A report to your boss, the store manager, about the outdated items in the warehouse

b. A memo to clients about your booth at the upcoming trade show

c. A letter to a customer who hasn't made a payment for three months

d. A memo to employees about the department's high phone bills

e. A phone call to a supplier, checking on an overdue parts shipment

f. A report to future users of the computer program you have chosen to handle the company's mailing list

7. **Planning: Assessing Audience Needs [LO-2]** For each communication task that follows, write brief answers to three questions: Who is the audience? What is the audience's general attitude toward my subject? What does the audience need to know?

- A final-notice collection letter from an appliance manufacturer to an appliance dealer that is 3 months behind on payments, sent 10 days before initiating legal collection procedures
- An advertisement for smartphones
- A proposal to top management, suggesting that the four sales regions in the United States be combined into just two regions
- Fliers to be attached to doorknobs in the neighborhood, announcing reduced rates for chimney cleaning or repairs
- A cover letter sent along with your résumé to a potential employer

- A website that describes the services offered by a consulting firm that helps accounting managers comply with government regulations

8. **Planning: Assessing Audience Needs [LO-2]** Choose a fairly simple electronic device (such as a digital music player) that you know how to operate well. Write two sets of instructions for operating the device: one set for a reader who has never used that type of device and one set for someone who is generally familiar with that type of machine but has never operated the specific model. Briefly explain how your two audiences affect your instructions.

9. **Planning: Analyzing the Situation; Collaboration: Planning Meetings [LO-2]** How can the material discussed in this chapter also apply to meetings? Outline your ideas in a brief presentation or a post for your class blog.

10. **Planning: Creating an Audience Profile; Collaboration: Team Projects [LO-2], [LO-3]** With a team assigned by your instructor, compare the Facebook pages of three companies in the same industry. Analyze the content on all the available tabs. What can you surmise about the intended audience for each company? Which of the three does the best job of presenting the information its target audience is likely to need? Prepare a brief presentation, including slides that show samples of the Facebook content from each company.

11. **Planning: Analyzing the Situation, Selecting Media; Media Skills: Email [LO-2], [LO-4]** You are the head of public relations for a cruise line that operates out of Miami. You are shocked to read a letter in a local newspaper from a disgruntled passenger, complaining about the service and entertainment on a recent cruise. You need to respond to these publicized criticisms in some way. What audiences will you need to consider in your response? What medium or media should you choose? If the letter had been published in a travel publication widely read by travel agents and cruise travelers, how might your course of action have differed? In an email message to your instructor, explain how you will respond.

12. **Planning: Assessing Audience Needs; Media Skills: Blogging; Communication Ethics: Making Ethical Choices [LO-3]** Your supervisor has asked you to withhold important information that you think should be included in a report you are preparing. Disobeying him could be disastrous for your working relationship and your career. Obeying him could violate your personal code of ethics. What should you do? Would you consider this situation to be an ethical dilemma or an ethical lapse? Explain your analysis in a brief email message to your instructor.

13. **Planning: Limiting Your Scope [LO-5]** Suppose you are preparing to recommend that top management install a new heating system that uses the cogeneration process. The following information is in your files. Eliminate topics that aren't essential and then arrange the other topics so that your report will give top managers a clear understanding of the heating system and a balanced, concise justification for installing it.

- History of the development of the cogeneration heating process
- Scientific credentials of the developers of the process
- Risks assumed in using this process
- Your plan for installing the equipment in the headquarters building
- Stories about the successful use of cogeneration technology in comparable facilities
- Specifications of the equipment that would be installed
- Plans for disposing of the old heating equipment
- Costs of installing and running the new equipment
- Advantages and disadvantages of using the new process
- Detailed 10-year cost projections
- Estimates of the time needed to phase in the new system
- Alternative systems that management might want to consider

14. **Planning: Choosing the Direct or Indirect Approach [LO-5]** Indicate whether the direct or indirect approach would be best in each of the following situations and briefly explain why. Would any of these messages be inappropriate for email? Explain.
- A message to the owner of an automobile dealership, complaining about poor service work
- A message from a recent college graduate, requesting a letter of recommendation from a former instructor
- A message turning down a job applicant
- A message announcing that because of high air-conditioning costs, the plant temperature will be held at 78° F during the summer
- A message from an advertising agency to a troublesome long-term client, explaining that the agency will no longer be able to work on the client's account

15. **Planning: Using Storytelling Techniques; Communication Ethics: Providing Ethical Leadership; Media Skills: Podcasting [LO-5]** Research recent incidents of ethical lapses by a business professional or executive in any industry. Choose one example that has a clear story "arc" from beginning to end. Outline a cautionary tale that explains the context of the ethical lapse, the choice the person made, and the consequences of the ethical lapse. Script a podcast (aim for roughly 3 to 5 minutes) that tells the story. If your instructor directs, record your podcast and post to your class blog.

Expand Your Skills

Critique the Professionals

Locate an example of professional communication in any medium-channel that you think would work equally well—or perhaps better—in another medium. Using the information in this chapter and your understanding of the communication process, write a brief analysis (no more than one page) of the company's media-channel choice and explain why your choice would be at least as effective. Use whatever medium your instructor requests for your report and be sure to cite specific elements from the piece and support from the chapter.

Bovée and Thill's Business Communication Web Search, at http://websearch.businesscommunicationnetwork.com, is a unique research tool designed specifically for business communication research. Use the Web Search function to find a website, video, PDF document, podcast, or presentation that offers advice on planning a report, speech, or other business message. Write a brief email message to your instructor, describing the item you found and summarizing the career skills information you learned from it.

Improve Your Grammar, Mechanics, and Usage

The following exercises help you improve your knowledge of and power over English grammar, mechanics, and usage. Then look at the following 10 items and identify the preferred choice within each set of parentheses.

16. Of the two products, this one has the (*greater, greatest*) potential.
17. The (*most perfect, perfect*) solution is *d*.
18. Here is the (*interesting, most interesting*) of all the ideas I have heard so far.
19. The (*hardest, harder*) part of my job is firing people.
20. A (*highly placed, highly-placed*) source revealed Dotson's (*last ditch, last-ditch*) efforts to cover up the mistake.
21. A (*top secret, top-secret*) document was taken from the president's office last night.
22. A (*30 year old, 30-year-old*) person should know better.
23. The two companies are engaged in an (*all-out no-holds-barred; all-out, no-holds-barred*) struggle for dominance.
24. A (*tiny metal; tiny, metal*) shaving is responsible for the problem.
25. You'll receive our (*usual cheerful prompt; usual, cheerful, prompt; usual cheerful, prompt*) service.

For additional exercises focusing on adjectives, visit MyB CommLab.

MyBCommLab

Go to the Assignments section of your MyLab to complete these writing exercises.

26. Email lacks both the visual element and the instantaneous connection of some other media. Could these supposed shortcomings actually help some employees communicate more comfortably and effectively? Explain your answer. [LO-5]

27. Would you use the direct or indirect approach to ask employees to work overtime to meet an important deadline? Please explain. [LO-5]

Endnotes

1. H&R Block website, accessed 10 February 2015, www.hrblock.com; Paula Drum, "I Got People (Online): How H&R Block Connects by Using Social Media," presentation at BlogWell conference, 22 January 2009, www.socialmedia.org; Shel Israel, "Twitterville Notebook: H&R Block's Paula Drum," Global Neighbourhoods blog, 22 December 2008, http://redcouch.typepad.com/weblog; "H&R Block's Paula Drum Talks Up Value of Online 'Presence,'" The Deal website, video interview, 6 June 2008, www.thedeal.com; Shel Israel, "SAP Global Survey: H&R Block's Paula Drum," Global Neighbourhoods blog, 4 April 2008, http://redcouch.typepad.com/weblog; "Tango in Plain English," video, accessed 27 August 2008, www.youtube.com; "H&R Block, Inc.," Hoovers, accessed 27 August 2008, www.hoovers.com; Linda Zimmer, "H&R Block Tangoes into Second Life," Business Communicators of Second Life blog, 17 March 2007, http://freshtakes.typepad.com/sl_communicators; "H&R Block Launches First Virtual Tax Experience in Second Life," press release, 27 August 2008, www.hrblock.com.
2. Carol Kinsey Gorman, "What's So Great About Face-to-Face?" Communication World, May–June 2011, 38–39.
3. Linda Duyle, "Get Out of Your Office," HR Magazine, July 2006, 99–101.
4. Caroline McCarthy, "The Future of Web Apps Will See the Death of Email," Webware blog, 29 February 2008, http://news.cnet.com; Kris Maher, "The Jungle," Wall Street Journal, 5 October 2004, B10; Kevin Maney, "Surge in Text Messaging Makes Cell Operators," USA Today, 28 July 2005, B1–B2.
5. Roger Cheng, "Verizon CEO: Unlimited Data Plans Just Aren't Sustainable," CNET, 24 September 2013, http://news.cnet.com; Brian Bennet, "Sprint Officially Outs New Unlimited Plans," CNET, 11 July 2013, http://reviews.cnet.com; footnotes on Sprint website, accessed 2 March 2014, http://shop.sprint.com.
6. Laurey Berk and Phillip G. Clampitt, "Finding the Right Path in the Communication Maze," IABC Communication World, October 1991, 28–32.
7. Samantha R. Murray and Joseph Peyrefitte, "Knowledge Type and Communication Media Choice in the Knowledge Transfer Process," Journal of Managerial Issues, Spring 2007, 111–133.
8. Holly Weeks, "The Best Memo You'll Ever Write," Harvard Management Communication Letter, Spring 2005, 3–5.
9. Steve Tobak, "How to Be a Great Storyteller and Win Over Any Audience," BNET, 12 January 2011, www.bnet.com.
10. Debra Askanase, "10 Trends in Sustainable Social Media," Community Organizer 2.0 blog, 13 May 2010, www.communityorganizer20.com.
11. Chip Heath and Dan Heath, Made to Stick: Why Some Ideas Survive and Others Die (New York: Random House, 2008), 214.
12. Heath and Heath, Made to Stick, 206, 214.
13. Randolph T. Barker and Kim Gower, "Strategic Application of Storytelling in Organizations," Journal of Business Communication 47, no. 3 (July 2010): 295–312.
14. David Meerman Scott, "Effective Storytelling for Business," WebInkNow blog, 18 February 2013, www.webinknow.com.
15. Jennifer Aaker and Andy Smith, "7 Deadly Sins of Business Storytelling," American Express Open Forum, accessed 21 March 2011, www.openforum.com.

Answer Key for "Learning Objectives Checkup"

1. b
2. c
3. a
4. general purpose
5. b
6. a
7. c
8. c
9. d
10. d
11. digital, nondigital
12. d
13. a
14. b
15. d
16. direct
17. indirect
18. a
19. a

Answer Key for "Improve Your Grammar, Mechanics, and Usage" Exercises

16. greater (1.4.1)
17. perfect (1.4.1)
18. most interesting (1.4.1)
19. hardest (1.4.1)
20. highly placed, last-ditch (1.4.2)
21. top-secret (1.4.2)
22. 30.year-old (1.4.2)
23. all-out, no-holds-barred struggle (1.4)
24. tiny metal (1.4)
25. usual cheerful, prompt service (1.4)

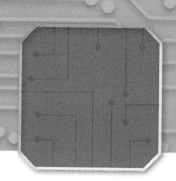

Writing Business Messages

LEARNING OBJECTIVES

After studying this chapter, you will be able to

1 Identify the four aspects of being sensitive to audience needs when writing business messages.

2 Explain how establishing your credibility and projecting your company's image are vital aspects of building strong relationships with your audience.

3 Explain how to achieve a tone that is conversational but businesslike, explain the value of using plain language, and define active and passive voice.

4 Describe how to select words that are both correct and effective.

5 Define the four types of sentences, and explain how sentence style affects emphasis within a message.

6 Define the three key elements of a paragraph, and list five ways to develop unified, coherent paragraphs.

7 List five techniques for writing effective messages for mobile readers.

ON THE JOB: COMMUNICATING AT
SHE TAKES ON THE WORLD

Natalie MacNeil Writes Her Way to a Better World

Natalie MacNeil is not a dreamer of small dreams. Here's how she introduces herself on one of her online profiles: "My name is Natalie MacNeil, and I want to change the world." For MacNeil, that change means inspiring and helping women launch their own businesses and take more control over their careers. As she puts it, "I want to see more women leading companies, organizations, and countries."

MacNeil knows a thing or two about launching a business. She started her first when she was 18 and by her mid-20s had founded or cofounded a small portfolio of companies, including an Emmy-winning digital media production company, a collaborative workspace for entrepreneurs in the early startup phase, and She Takes on the World, which MacNeil describes as "a training platform and community for women entrepreneurs."

Communication is at the heart of MacNeil's world-changing quest. On the She Takes on the World site and in a book by the same name, MacNeil shares firsthand knowledge on everything from finding investors to expanding a company internationally. Her writing has appeared in a variety of other popular forums as well, including AllBusiness, American Express OPEN Forum, Mashable, *Forbes*, Entrepreneur.com, and *The Wall Street Journal*.

Image by Ashley Wessel

Women who run or aspire to run their own businesses are the target audience for Natalie MacNeil's She Takes on the World, a training and community platform that offers advice on all aspects of launching and managing a company.

From Chapter 5 of *Excellence in Business Communication*, Twelfth Edition. John V. Thill, Courtland L. Bovée. Copyright © 2017 by Pearson Education, Inc. All rights reserved.

Plenty of entrepreneurs, executives, and other experts offer advice on launching businesses, so what sets MacNeil apart? One key element is a clear idea of who her audience is and the type of information these readers are likely to need. When promoting her book, for example, she emphasizes that no business book can appeal to every reader, and she lists the specific types of readers who can benefit from her book. She also does something that many business "how-to" writers don't: She addresses the personal side of being a successful entrepreneur.

Another key element is her positive writing style. The editor of *ForbesWoman* calls MacNeil's blog and book "smart, upbeat, inspirational, and full of practical advice for women who want to own their dream careers." As someone who came of age in the postdigital economy, MacNeil is also tuned into the new world of work, where individuals must manage their personal brands and take control of their careers. In fact, one of her target audiences is college students who might want to create their own companies right out of college, without ever pursuing traditional employment.

The content and style of her messages is clearly connecting with readers. She Takes on the World has grown to include several dozen bloggers who cover every aspect of managing an entrepreneurial career in the new economy. The site was named one of *Forbes* magazine's top 10 entrepreneurial websites for women, among numerous other awards and recognitions it has received. MacNeil shows no signs of slowing down, either, with new investors behind her and ambitious expansion plans.[1]

HTTP://SHETAKESONTHEWORLD.COM/

Adapting to Your Audience: Being Sensitive to Audience Needs

1 LEARNING OBJECTIVE
Identify the four aspects of being sensitive to audience needs when writing business messages.

Natalie MacNeil (profiled in the chapter-opening On the Job) knows it takes more than just a great idea to change the way people think. Expressing ideas clearly and persuasively starts with adapting to one's audience.

Whether consciously or not, audiences greet most incoming messages with a selfish question: "What's in this for me?" If your readers or listeners don't think you understand or care about their needs, they won't pay attention, plain and simple. You can improve your audience sensitivity by adopting the "you" attitude, maintaining good standards of etiquette, emphasizing the positive, and using bias-free language.

Readers and listeners are more likely to respond positively when they believe messages address their concerns.

USING THE "YOU" ATTITUDE

Adopting the "you" attitude means speaking and writing in terms of your audience's wishes, interests, hopes, and preferences.

The "you attitude is speaking and writing in terms of your audience's wishes, interests, hopes, and preferences. On the simplest level, you can adopt the "you" attitude by replacing terms such as *I, me, mine, we, us,* and *ours* with *you* and *yours:*

Instead of This	Write This
Tuesday is the only day that we can promise quick response to purchase order requests; we are swamped the rest of the week.	If you need a quick response, please submit your purchase order requests on Tuesday.
We offer MP3 players with 50, 75, or 100 gigabytes of storage capacity.	You can choose an MP3 player with 50, 75, or 100 gigabytes of storage.

However, the "you" attitude is more than simply using particular pronouns. It's a matter of demonstrating genuine interest in your readers and concern for their needs (see Figure 1). You can use *you* 25 times in a single page and still offend your audience or ignore readers' true concerns. If you're writing to a retailer, try to think like a retailer; if you're dealing with a production supervisor, put yourself in that position; if you're writing to a dissatisfied customer, imagine how you would feel at the other end of the transaction.

Be aware that on some occasions, it's better to avoid using *you,* particularly if doing so will sound overly authoritative or accusing:

Avoid using *you* and *your* when doing so
- Makes you sound dictatorial
- Makes someone else feel guilty
- Goes against your organization's style

Instead of This	Write This
You failed to deliver the customer's order on time.	The customer didn't receive the order on time.
You must correct all five copies by noon.	All five copies must be corrected by noon.

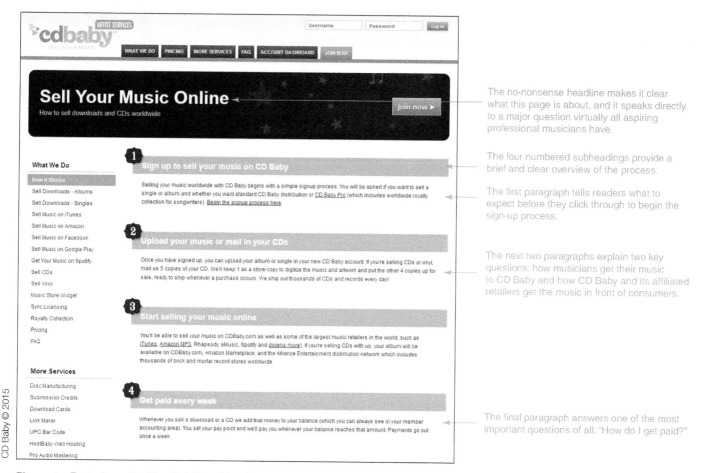

Figure 1 Fostering a Positive Relationship with an Audience
CD Baby, the world's largest retailer of independent music, uses clear, positive language to help musicians understand the process of selling their music through the company and its affiliates. By making the effort to communicate clearly and succinctly, the company encourages a positive response from its target readers.

As you practice using the "you" attitude, be sure to consider the attitudes of other cultures and the policies of your organization. In some cultures, it is improper to single out one person's achievements, because the whole team is responsible for the outcome; in that case, using the pronoun *we* or *our* (when you and your audience are part of the same team) would be more appropriate. Similarly, some companies have a tradition of avoiding references to *you* and *I* in most messages and reports.

MAINTAINING STANDARDS OF ETIQUETTE

Good etiquette not only indicates respect for your audience but also helps foster a more successful environment for communication by minimizing negative emotional reaction:

Even if a situation calls for you to be brutally honest, express the facts of the matter in a kind and thoughtful manner.

Instead of This	Write This
Once again, you've managed to bring down the entire website through your incompetent programming.	Let's review the last website update to explore ways to improve the process.
You've been sitting on our order for two weeks, and we need it now!	Our production schedules depend on timely delivery of parts and supplies, but we have not yet received the order you promised to deliver two weeks ago. Please respond today with a firm delivery commitment.

Writing Business Messages

Use extra tact when communicating with people higher up the organization chart or outside the company.

Of course, some situations require more diplomacy than others. If you know your audience well, a less formal approach may be more appropriate. However, when you are communicating with people who outrank you or with people outside your organization, an added measure of courtesy is usually needed.

Written communication and most forms of digital communication generally require more tact than oral communication does. When you're speaking, your words are softened by your tone of voice and facial expression. Plus, you can adjust your approach according to the feedback you get. If you inadvertently offend someone in writing or in a podcast, for example, you don't usually get the immediate feedback you would need in order to resolve the situation. In fact, you may never know that you offended your audience.

EMPHASIZING THE POSITIVE

You can communicate negative news without being negative.

During your career, you will have many occasions in which you need to communicate bad news. However, there is a big difference between *delivering* negative news and *being* negative. When the tone of your message is negative, you put unnecessary strain on business relationships. Never try to hide negative news, but always be on the lookout for positive points that will foster a good relationship with your audience:[2]

Instead of This	Write This
It is impossible to repair your laptop today.	Your computer can be ready by Tuesday. Would you like a loaner until then?
We wasted $300,000 advertising in that magazine.	Our $300,000 advertising investment did not pay off. Let's analyze the experience and apply the insights to future campaigns.

If you find it necessary to criticize or correct, don't dwell on the other person's mistakes. Avoid referring to failures, problems, or shortcomings. Focus instead on what the audience members can do to improve the situation:

Instead of This	Write This
The problem with this department is a failure to control costs.	The performance of this department can be improved by tightening cost controls.
You failed to provide all the necessary information on the previous screen.	Please review the items marked in red on the previous screen so that we can process your order as quickly as possible.

Show audience members how they will benefit by responding to your message.

If you're trying to persuade audience members to buy a product, pay a bill, or perform a service for you, emphasize what's in it for them. When people recognize the benefits of doing so, they are more likely to respond positively to your appeal:

Instead of This	Write This
We will notify all three credit reporting agencies if you do not pay your overdue bill within 10 days.	Paying your overdue bill within 10 days will prevent a negative entry on your credit record.
I am tired of seeing so many errors in the customer service blog.	Proofreading your blog postings will help you avoid embarrassing mistakes that generate more customer service complaints.

Euphemisms are milder synonyms that can express an idea while triggering fewer negative connotations, but they should never be used to obscure the truth.

In general, try to state your message without using words that may hurt or offend your audience. Look for appropriate opportunities to use **euphemisms**—words or phrases that express a thought in milder terms—that convey your meaning without carrying negative or unpleasant connotations. For example, one common euphemism is referring to people beyond a certain age as "senior citizens" rather than "old people." *Senior* conveys respect in a way that *old* doesn't.

Euphemisms can bring a tone of civility to unpleasant communication, but they must be used with great care because they are so easy—and so tempting—to misuse. Euphemisms can be annoying if they force readers to "read between the lines" to get the message, and they can be unethical if they obscure the truth. For instance, one of the toughest messages a manager ever has to write is an internal memo or email announcing layoffs. This is a difficult situation for everyone involved, and managers can be tempted to resort to euphemisms such as *streamlining, restructuring, improving efficiency, reducing layers,* or *eliminating redundancies* to avoid using the word *layoff*.[3] Doing so might ease the emotional burden on the writer and promote the illusion that the message isn't as negative as it really is. However, these euphemisms can fail the "you" attitude test, as well as the standards of ethical information, by failing to answer the question every reader in these situations has, which is simply: *Am I going to lose my job?*

If you are considering using a euphemism, ask yourself this question: Are you trying to protect the reader's feelings or your own feelings? Even if it is unpleasant, people generally respond better to an honest message delivered with integrity than they do to a sugar-coated message that obscures the truth.

USING BIAS-FREE LANGUAGE

Bias-free language avoids words and phrases that unfairly and even unethically categorize or stigmatize people in ways related to gender, race, ethnicity, age, disability, or other personal characteristics (See Table 1). Contrary to what some may think, biased language

> Bias-free language avoids words and phrases that unfairly and even unethically categorize or stigmatize people.

TABLE 1   Overcoming Bias in Language

Examples	Unacceptable	Preferable
Gender Bias		
Using words containing *man*	Man-made	Artificial, synthetic, manufactured, constructed, human-made
	Mankind	Humanity, human beings, human race, people
	Manpower	Workers, workforce
	Businessman	Executive, manager, businessperson, professional
	Salesman	Sales representative, salesperson
	Foreman	Supervisor
Using female-gender words	Actress, stewardess	Actor, flight attendant
Using special designations	Woman doctor, male nurse	Doctor, nurse
Using *he* to refer to "everyone"	The average worker . . . he	The average worker . . . he or she *OR* Average workers . . . they
Identifying roles with gender	The typical executive spends four hours of his day in meetings.	Most executives spend four hours a day in meetings.
	the consumer . . . she	consumers . . . they
	the nurse/teacher . . . she	nurses/teachers . . . they
Identifying women by marital status	Mrs. Norm Lindstrom	Maria Lindstrom *OR* Ms. Maria Lindstrom
	Norm Lindstrom and Ms. Drake	Norm Lindstrom and Maria Drake *OR* Mr. Lindstrom and Ms. Drake
Racial and Ethnic Bias		
Assigning stereotypes	Not surprisingly, Shing-Tung Yau excels in mathematics.	Shing-Tung Yau excels in mathematics.
Identifying people by race or ethnicity	Mario M. Cuomo, Italian American politician and ex-governor of New York	Mario M. Cuomo, politician and ex-governor of New York
Age Bias		
Including age when irrelevant	Mary Kirazy, 58, has just joined our trust department.	Mary Kirazy has just joined our trust department.
Disability Bias		
Putting the disability before the person	Disabled workers face many barriers on the job.	Workers with physical disabilities face many barriers on the job.
	An epileptic, Tracy has no trouble doing her job.	Tracy's epilepsy has no effect on her job performance.

REAL-TIME UPDATES

LEARN MORE BY READING THIS PDF

Get detailed advice on using bias-free language

This in-depth guide offers practical tips for avoiding many types of cultural bias in your writing and speaking. Go to http://real-timeupdates.com/ebc12 and click on Learn More in the Students section.

is not simply about "labels." To a significant degree, language reflects the way we think and what we believe, and biased language may well perpetuate the underlying stereotypes and prejudices it represents.[4] Moreover, because communication is all about perception, simply *being* fair and objective isn't enough. To establish a good relationship with your audience, you must also *appear* to be fair.[5] Good communicators make every effort to change biased language. Bias can come in a variety of forms:

- **Gender bias.** Avoid sexist language by using the same labels for everyone, regardless of gender. Don't refer to a woman as *chairperson* and then to a man as *chairman*. Use chair, chairperson, or chairman consistently. (Note that it is not uncommon to use chairman when referring to a woman who heads a board of directors. Archer Daniels Midland's Patricia Woertz and Xerox's Ursula Burns, for example, both refer to themselves as "chairman."[6]) Reword sentences to use *they* or to use no pronoun at all rather than refer to all individuals as *he*. Note that the preferred title for women in business is *Ms.* unless the individual asks to be addressed as *Miss* or *Mrs.* or has some other title, such as *Dr.*

- **Racial and ethnic bias.** Avoid identifying people by race or ethnic origin unless such a label is relevant to the matter at hand—and it rarely is.

- **Age bias.** Mention the age of a person only when it is relevant. Moreover, be careful of the context in which you use words that refer to age; such words carry a variety of positive and negative connotations. For example, *young* can imply energy, youthfulness, inexperience, or even immaturity, depending on how it's used.

- **Disability bias.** Physical, mental, sensory, or emotional impairments should never be mentioned in business messages unless those conditions are directly relevant to the subject. If you must refer to someone's disability, put the person first and the disability second.[7] For example, by saying "employees with physical handicaps," not "handicapped employees," you focus on the whole person, not the disability. Finally, never use outdated terminology such as *crippled* or *retarded*.

2 **LEARNING OBJECTIVE**

Explain how establishing your credibility and projecting your company's image are vital aspects of building strong relationships with your audience.

Adapting to Your Audience: Building Strong Relationships

Successful communication relies on a positive relationship between sender and receiver. Establishing your credibility and projecting your company's image are two vital steps in building and fostering positive business relationships.

ESTABLISHING YOUR CREDIBILITY

People are more likely to react positively to your message when they have confidence in you.

Audience responses to your messages depend heavily on your **credibility**, a measure of your believability based on how reliable you are and how much trust you evoke in others. With audiences who don't know you and trust you already, you need to establish credibility before they'll accept your messages (see Figure 2). On the other hand, when you do establish credibility, communication becomes much easier because you no longer have to spend time and energy convincing people that you are a trustworthy source of information and ideas. To build, maintain, or repair your credibility, emphasize the following characteristics:

To enhance your credibility, emphasize such factors as honesty, objectivity, and awareness of audience needs.

- **Honesty.** Demonstrating honesty and integrity will earn you the respect of your audiences, even if they don't always agree with or welcome your messages.

- **Objectivity.** Show that you can distance yourself from emotional situations and look at all sides of an issue.

- **Awareness of audience needs.** Directly or indirectly, let your audience members know that you understand what's important to them.

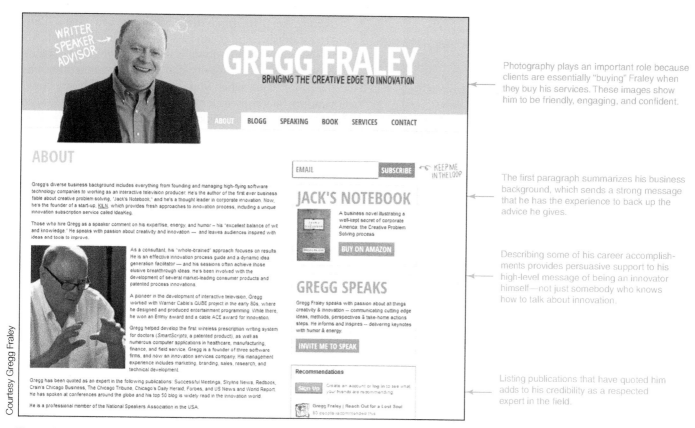

Photography plays an important role because clients are essentially "buying" Fraley when they buy his services. These images show him to be friendly, engaging, and confident.

The first paragraph summarizes his business background, which sends a strong message that he has the experience to back up the advice he gives.

Describing some of his career accomplishments provides persuasive support to his high-level message of being an innovator himself—not just somebody who knows how to talk about innovation.

Listing publications that have quoted him adds to his credibility as a respected expert in the field.

Courtesy Gregg Fraley

Figure 2 Building Credibility
Gregg Fraley is a highly regarded expert in the field of creativity and business innovation, but because his services are intangible, potential clients can't "test drive" those services before making a purchase decision. He therefore takes special care to build credibility as part of his communication efforts.

- **Credentials, knowledge, and expertise.** Audiences need to know that you have whatever it takes to back up your message, whether it's education, professional certification, special training, past successes, or simply the fact that you've done your research.
- **Endorsements.** An *endorsement* is a statement on your behalf by someone who is accepted by your audience as an expert.
- **Performance.** Demonstrating impressive communication skills is not enough; people need to know they can count on you to get the job done.
- **Sincerity.** When you offer praise, don't use *hyperbole*, such as "you are the most fantastic employee I could ever imagine." Instead, point out specific qualities that warrant praise.

In addition, audiences need to know that you believe in yourself and your message. If you lack faith in yourself, you're likely to communicate an uncertain attitude that undermines your credibility. In contrast, if you are convinced that your message is sound, you can state your case with authority. Look out for phrases containing words such as *hope* and *trust*, which can drain the audience's confidence in your message:

Instead of This	Write This
We hope this recommendation will be helpful.	We're pleased to make this recommendation.
We trust that you'll want to extend your service contract.	By extending your service contract, you can continue to enjoy top-notch performance from your equipment.

Finally, keep in mind that credibility can take a long time to establish—and it can be wiped out in an instant. An occasional mistake or letdown is usually forgiven, but major lapses in honesty or integrity can destroy your reputation. On the other hand, when you do establish credibility, communication becomes much easier because you no longer have to spend time and energy convincing people that you are a trustworthy source of information and ideas.

PROJECTING YOUR COMPANY'S IMAGE

Your company's interests and reputation take precedence over your personal views and communication style.

When you communicate with anyone outside your organization, it is more than a conversation between two individuals. You represent your company and therefore play a vital role in helping the company build and maintain positive relationships with all its stakeholders. Most successful companies work hard to foster a specific public image, and your external communication efforts need to project that image. As part of this responsibility, the interests and preferred communication style of your company must take precedence over your own views and personal communication style.

Many organizations have specific communication guidelines that show everything from the correct use of the company name to preferred abbreviations and other grammatical details. Specifying a desired style of communication is more difficult, however. Observe more experienced colleagues, and never hesitate to ask for editorial help to make sure you're conveying the appropriate tone. For instance, with clients entrusting thousands or millions of dollars to it, an investment firm communicates in a style quite different from that of a clothing retailer. And a clothing retailer specializing in high-quality business attire communicates in a different style than a store catering to the latest trends in casual wear.

Adapting to Your Audience: Controlling Your Style and Tone

Your communication **style** involves the choices you make to express yourself: the words you select, the manner in which you use those words in sentences, and the way you build paragraphs from individual sentences. Your style creates a certain **tone**, or overall

---

Being Dependable and Accountable

By any definition, a "pro" is somebody who gets the job done. Develop a reputation as somebody people can count on. This means meeting your commitments, including keeping on schedule and staying within budgets. These are skills that take some time to develop as you discover how much time and money are required to accomplish various tasks and projects. With experience, you'll learn to be conservative with your commitments. You don't want to be known as someone who overpromises and underdelivers.

If you can't confidently predict how long a project will take or how much it will cost, be sure to let your client, colleagues, or supervisor know that. And if changing circumstances threaten your ability to meet a previous commitment, be sure to share that information with anyone who might be affected by your performance.

Being accountable also means owning up to your mistakes and learning from failure so that you can continue to improve. Pros don't make excuses or blame others. When they make mistakes—and everybody does—they face the situation head on, make amends, and move on.

CAREER APPLICATIONS

1. What steps could you take to make realistic commitments on tasks and projects in which you have little or no experience?
2. Does being accountable mean you never make mistakes? Explain your answer.

impression, in your messages. The right tone depends on the nature of your message and your relationship with the reader.

CREATING A CONVERSATIONAL TONE

The tone of your business messages can range from informal to conversational to formal. When you're communicating with your superiors or with customers, your tone may tend to be more formal and respectful.[8] However, that formal tone might sound distant and cold if used with close colleagues.

Most business messages aim for a conversational style that is warm but businesslike.

Compare the three versions of the message in Table 2. The first is too formal and stuffy for today's audiences, whereas the third is inappropriately casual for business. The second message demonstrates the **conversational tone** used in most business communication—plain language that sounds businesslike without being stuffy at one extreme or too laid-back and informal at the other extreme. You can achieve a tone that is conversational but still businesslike by following these guidelines:

- **Understand the difference between texting and writing.** Texting can be an efficient way to communicate quickly, particularly on mobile devices with cramped keyboards. However, it's best to view texting as a mode of *conversation*, rather than as a mode of *writing*—and to keep the two modes clear in your mind when you are writing. Communication effectiveness and your personal credibility can suffer if you let texting habits (such as using sentence fragments, sloppy punctuation, and lots of acronyms) creep into your business writing.

TABLE 2   Finding the Right Tone

Tone	Example
Stuffy: too formal for today's audiences	Dear Ms. Navarro: Enclosed please find the information that was requested during our telephone communication of May 14. As was mentioned at that time, Midville Hospital has significantly more doctors of exceptional quality than any other health facility in the state. As you were also informed, our organization has quite an impressive network of doctors and other health-care professionals with offices located throughout the state. In the event that you should need a specialist, our professionals will be able to make an appropriate recommendation. In the event that you have questions or would like additional information, you may certainly contact me during regular business hours. Most sincerely yours, Samuel G. Berenz
Conversational: just right for most business communication	Dear Ms. Navarro: Here's the information you requested during our phone conversation on Friday. As I mentioned, Midville Hospital has the highest-rated doctors and more of them than any other hospital in the state. In addition, we have a vast network of doctors and other health professionals with offices throughout the state. If you need a specialist, they can refer you to the right one. If you would like more information, please call any time between 9:00 and 5:00, Monday through Friday. Sincerely, Samuel G. Berenz
Unprofessional: too casual for business communication	Here's the 411 you requested. IMHO, we have more and better doctors than any other hospital in the state. FYI, we also have a large group of doctors and other health professionals w/offices close to U at work/home. If U need a specialist, they'll refer U to the right one. Any ? just ring or msg. L8R, S

- **Avoid stale and pompous language.** Most companies now shy away from such dated phrases as "attached please find" and "please be advised that." Similarly, avoid using obscure words, stale or clichéd expressions, and overly complicated sentences designed only to impress others (see Table 3).
- **Avoid preaching and bragging.** Readers tend to get irritated by know-it-alls who like to preach or brag. However, if you need to remind your audience of something that should be obvious, try to work in the information casually, perhaps in the middle of a paragraph, where it will sound like a secondary comment rather than a major revelation.
- **Be careful with intimacy.** Business messages should generally avoid intimacy, such as sharing personal details or adopting a casual, unprofessional tone. However, when you have a close relationship with audience members, such as among the members of a close-knit team, a more intimate tone is sometimes appropriate and even expected.
- **Be careful with humor.** Humor can easily backfire and divert attention from your message. If you don't know your audience well or you're not skilled at using humor in a business setting, don't use it at all. Avoid humor in formal messages and when you're communicating across cultural boundaries.

USING PLAIN LANGUAGE

Audiences can understand and act on plain language without reading it over and over.

An important aspect of creating a conversational tone is using *plain language* (or *plain English* specifically when English is involved). Plain language presents information in a simple, unadorned style that allows your audience to easily grasp your meaning—language that recipients "can read, understand and act upon the first time they read it."[9] You can see how this definition supports using the "you" attitude and shows respect for your audience. In addition, plain language can make companies more productive and more profitable because people spend less time trying to figure out messages that are confusing or aren't written to meet their needs.[10] Finally, plain language helps nonnative speakers read your messages.

Creative Commons, a not-for-profit organization that provides content creators with an alternative to traditional copyright law, offers a great example of adapting

REAL-TIME UPDATES

LEARN MORE BY READING THIS ARTICLE

Take your communication skills from good to great

These seven tips can help you transform your business writing from merely ordinary to powerful and persuasive. Go to http://real-timeupdates.com/ebc12 and click on Learn More in the Students section.

TABLE 3 Weeding Out Obsolete Phrases	
Obsolete Phrase	**Up-to-Date Replacement**
we are in receipt of	we received
kindly advise	please let me/us know
attached please find	enclosed is or I/we have enclosed
it has come to my attention	I have just learned or [someone] has just informed me
the undersigned	I/we
in due course	(specify a time or date)
permit me to say that	(omit; just say whatever you need to say)
pursuant to	(omit; just say whatever you need to say)
in closing, I'd like to say	(omit; just say whatever you need to say)
we wish to inform you that	(omit; just say whatever you need to say)
please be advised that	(omit; just say whatever you need to say)

The introductory sentence expresses the main idea, that the licenses are built in three layers (note that "use" would be a simpler alternative to "incorporate").

Three "Layers" Of Licenses

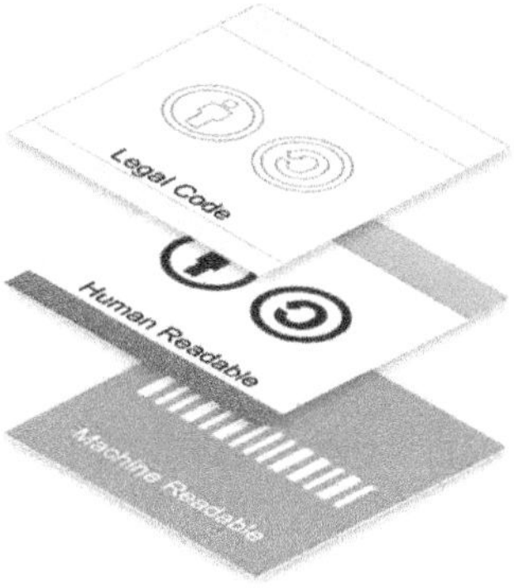

Our public copyright licenses incorporate a unique and innovative "three-layer" design. Each license begins as a traditional legal tool, in the kind of language and text formats that most lawyers know and love. We call this the Legal Code layer of each license.

But since most creators, educators, and scientists are not in fact lawyers, we also make the licenses available in a format that normal people can read — the Commons Deed (also known as the "human readable" version of the license). The Commons Deed is a handy reference for licensors and licensees, summarizing and expressing some of the most important terms and conditions. Think of the Commons Deed as a user-friendly interface to the Legal Code beneath, although the Deed itself is not a license, and its contents are not part of the Legal Code itself.

The final layer of the license design recognizes that software, from search engines to office productivity to music editing, plays an enormous role in the creation, copying, discovery, and distribution of works. In order to make it easy for the Web to know when a work is available under a Creative Commons license, we provide a "machine readable" version of the license — a summary of the key freedoms and obligations written into a format that software systems, search engines, and other kinds of technology can understand. We developed a standardized way to describe licenses that software can understand called CC Rights Expression Language (CC REL) to accomplish this.

Searching for open content is an important function enabled by our approach. You can use Google to search for Creative Commons content, look for pictures at Flickr, albums at Jamendo, and general media at spinxpress. The Wikimedia Commons, the multimedia repository of Wikipedia, is a core user of our licenses as well.

Taken together, these three layers of licenses ensure that the spectrum of rights isn't just a legal concept. It's something that the creators of works can understand, their users can understand, and even the Web itself can understand.

The notion of three layers is carried through the text and reinforced with the diagram.

The paragraph on the "human readable" version explains why it exists and whom it benefits.

The purpose and function of the "machine readable" version are less obvious than in the other two versions, so this paragraph offers a more extensive explanation.

Figure 3 Plain Language at Creative Commons
Creative Commons uses this diagram and text to explain the differences among its three versions of content licenses.
Source: Creative Commons, Inc.

to readers with plain language. Its licensing terms are available in three versions: a complete "legal code" document that spells out contractual details in specific legal terms that meet the needs of legal professionals, a "human readable" version that explains the licensing terms in nontechnical language that anyone can understand, and a "machine readable" version fine-tuned for search engines and other systems (see Figure 3).[11]

SELECTING THE ACTIVE OR PASSIVE VOICE

Your choice of the active or passive voice affects the tone of your message. In **active voice**, the subject performs the action and the object receives the action: "Jodi sent the email message." In **passive voice**, the subject receives the action: "The email message was sent by Jodi." As you can see, the passive voice combines the helping verb *to be* with a form of the verb that is usually similar to the past tense.

Using the active voice helps make your writing more direct, livelier, and easier to read (see Table 4 on the next page). In contrast, the passive voice is often cumbersome, can be unnecessarily vague, and can make sentences overly long. In most cases, the active voice is your best choice.[12] Nevertheless, using the passive voice can help you demonstrate the "you" attitude in some situations:

Active sentences are usually stronger than passive ones.

- When you want to be diplomatic about pointing out a problem or an error of some kind (the passive version seems less like an accusation)
- When you want to point out what's being done without taking or attributing either the credit or the blame (the passive version shifts the spotlight away from the person or persons involved)
- When you want to avoid personal pronouns in order to create an objective tone (the passive version may be used in a formal report, for example)

Use passive sentences to soften bad news, to put yourself in the background, or to create an impersonal tone when needed.

The second half of Table 4 illustrates several other situations in which the passive voice helps you focus your message on your audience.

TABLE 4	Choosing Active or Passive Voice

In general, avoid passive voice in order to make your writing lively and direct.

Dull and Indirect in Passive Voice	Lively and Direct in Active Voice
The new procedure was developed by the operations team.	The operations team developed the new procedure.
Legal problems are created by this contract.	This contract creates legal problems.
Reception preparations have been undertaken by our PR people for the new CEO's arrival.	Our PR people have begun planning a reception for the new CEO.

However, passive voice is helpful when you need to be diplomatic or want to focus attention on problems or solutions rather than on people.

Accusatory or Self-Congratulatory in Active Voice	More Diplomatic in Passive Voice
You lost the shipment.	The shipment was lost.
I recruited seven engineers last month.	Seven engineers were recruited last month.
We are investigating the high rate of failures on the final assembly line.	The high rate of failures on the final assembly line is being investigated.

Composing Your Message: Choosing Powerful Words

4 LEARNING OBJECTIVE
Describe how to select words that are both correct and effective.

After you have decided how to adapt to your audience, you're ready to begin composing your message. As you write your first draft, let your creativity flow. Don't try to write and edit at the same time or worry about getting everything perfect. Make up words if you can't think of the right word, draw pictures, talk out loud—do whatever it takes to get the ideas out of your head and onto screen or paper. If you've scheduled carefully, you should have time to revise and refine the material later. In fact, many writers find it helpful to establish a personal rule of never showing a first draft to anyone. By working in this "safe zone," away from the critical eyes of others, your mind will stay free to think clearly and creatively.

If you get stuck and feel unable to write, try to overcome writer's block by jogging your brain in creative ways. The introduction is often the hardest part to write, so put it aside and work on whichever parts of the document you're most comfortable with at any given moment. In most cases, you don't need to write the sections in any particular order.[13] Work on nontext elements such as graphics or your cover page. Revisit your purpose and confirm your intent in writing the message. Give yourself a mental break by switching to a different project. Sometimes all you need to do is start writing without worrying about the words you're using or how they will sound to the audience. Words will start flowing, your mind will engage, and the writing will come easier.

Correctness is the first consideration when choosing words.

You may find it helpful to hone your craft by viewing your writing at three levels: strong words, effective sentences, and coherent paragraphs. Starting at the word level, successful writers pay close attention to the correct use of words.[14] If you make errors of grammar or usage, you lose credibility with your audience—even if your message is otherwise correct. Poor grammar suggests to readers that you're unprofessional, and they may choose not to trust you as a result. Moreover, poor grammar may imply that you don't respect your audience enough to get things right.

The rules of grammar and usage can be a source of worry for writers because some of them are complex and some evolve over time. Even professional editors and grammarians occasionally have questions about correct usage, and they may disagree about the answers. For example, the word *data* is the plural form of *datum*, yet some experts now

MOBILE APP

Dragon Dictation uses voice recognition to convert speech to text at up to five times faster than typing.

REAL-TIME UPDATES
LEARN MORE BY EXPLORING THIS INTERACTIVE WEBSITE
Grammar questions? Click here for help

This comprehensive online guide can help you out of just about any grammar dilemma. Go to http://real-timeupdates.com/ebc12 and click on Learn More in the Students section.

prefer to treat *data* as a singular noun when it's used in nonscientific material to refer to a body of facts or figures.

With practice, you'll become more skilled in making correct choices over time. If you have doubts about what is correct, you have many ways to find the answer. Check the Handbook of Grammar, Mechanics, and Usage at the end of this text, or consult the many special reference books and resources available in libraries, in bookstores, and on the Internet.

In addition to using words correctly, successful writers and speakers take care to use the most effective words and phrases. Selecting and using words effectively is often more challenging than using words correctly because doing so is a matter of judgment and experience. Careful writers continue to work at their craft to find words that communicate with power (see Figure 4).

Effectiveness is the second consideration when choosing words.

In many cases, global is an absolute term and doesn't benefit from a modifier such as truly. However, economic globalization is occurring in stages, so truly here suggests the point at which globalization is nearly complete.

Two Sides of the Story

Growing interest in the global acceptance of a single set of robust accounting standards comes from all participants in the capital markets. Many multinational companies and national regulators and users support it because they believe that the use of common standards in the preparation of public company financial statements will make it easier to compare the financial results of reporting entities from different countries. They believe it will help investors understand opportunities better. Large public companies with subsidiaries in multiple jurisdictions would be able to use one accounting language company-wide and present their financial statements in the same language as their competitors.

Robust goes beyond simply strong to suggest resilient and comprehensive as well.

Another benefit some believe is that in a truly global economy, financial professionals including CPAs will be more mobile, and companies will more easily be able to respond to the human capital needs of their subsidiaries around the world.

Gold standard (a term borrowed from economics) refers to something against which all similar entities are compared, an unsurpassed model of excellence.

Nevertheless, many people also believe that U.S. GAAP is the gold standard, and something will be lost with full acceptance of IFRS. However, recent SEC actions and global trends have increased awareness of the need to address possible adoption. According to a survey conducted in the first half of 2008 by Deloitte & Touche among chief financial officers and other financial professionals, U.S. companies have an interest in adopting IFRS and this interest is steadily growing. Thirty percent would consider adopting IFRS now, another 28 percent are unsure or do not have sufficient knowledge to decide, while 42 percent said they would not. Still, an AICPA survey conducted in Fall 2008 among its CPA members shows a significant and positive shift in the number of firms and companies that are starting to prepare for eventual adoption of IFRS. A 55 percent majority of CPAs at firms and companies nationwide said they are preparing in a variety of ways for IFRS adoption, an increase of 14 percentage points over the 41 percent who were preparing for change, according to an April 2008 AICPA survey.

In the context of a survey significant means more than just important; it indicates a statistical observation that is large enough to be more than mere chance. Positive indicates the direction of the change and suggests affirmation and progress.

Claim is a powerful word here because it suggests a strong element of doubt.

Another concern is that worldwide many countries that claim to be converging to international standards may never get 100 percent compliance. Most reserve the right to carve out selectively or modify standards they do not consider in their national interest, an action that could lead to incompatibility—the very issue that IFRS seek to address.

Carve out is much stronger than remove because it could suggest surgical precision if done well or perhaps violent destruction if not done with finesse. In this context, carve out is meant to express a concern about countries weakening the international financial standards by modifying them to meet their own needs.

GAAP and IFRS, Still Differences

The diplomatic use of passive voice keeps the focus on the issue at hand, rather than on the organizations that are involved.

Great strides have been made by the FASB and the IASB to converge the content of IFRS and U.S. GAAP. The goal is that by the time the SEC allows or mandates the use of IFRS for U.S. publicly traded companies, most or all of the key differences will have been resolved.

Because of these ongoing convergence projects, the extent of the specific differences between IFRS and U.S. GAAP is shrinking. Yet significant differences do remain. For example:

- IFRS does not permit Last In First Out (LIFO) as an inventory costing method.
- IFRS uses a single-step method for impairment write-downs rather than the two-step method used in U.S. GAAP, making write-downs more likely.
- IFRS has a different probability threshold and measurement objective for contingencies.
- IFRS does not permit curing debt covenant violations after year-end.
- IFRS guidance regarding revenue recognition is less extensive than GAAP and contains relatively little industry-specific instructions.

5

Figure 4 Choosing Powerful Words

Notice how careful word choices help this excerpt from a report published by the American Institute of Certified Public Accountants make a number of important points. The tone is formal, which is appropriate for a report with global, public readership. (GAAP refers to accounting standards currently used in the United States; IFRS refers to international standards.)

Source: Ignite Social Media—The Original Social Media Agency®; www.@lgnitesocialmedia.com

UNDERSTANDING DENOTATION AND CONNOTATION

A word may have both a denotative and a connotative meaning. The **denotative meaning** is the literal, or dictionary, meaning. The **connotative meaning** includes all the associations and feelings evoked by the word.

The denotative meaning of *desk* is "a piece of furniture with a flat work surface and various drawers for storage." The connotative meaning of desk may include thoughts associated with work or study, but the word *desk* has fairly neutral connotations—neither strong nor emotional. However, some words have much stronger connotations than others and should be used with care. For example, the connotations of the word *fail* are negative and can have a dramatic emotional impact. If you say the sales department *failed* to meet its annual quota, the connotative meaning suggests that the group is inferior, incompetent, or below some standard of performance. However, the reason for not achieving 100 percent might be an inferior product, incorrect pricing, or some other factor outside the control of the sales department. In contrast, by saying the sales department achieved 85 percent of its quota, you clearly communicate that the results were less than expected without triggering all the negative emotions associated with *failure*.

BALANCING ABSTRACT AND CONCRETE WORDS

The more abstract a word is, the more it is removed from the tangible, objective world of things that can be perceived with the senses.

Words vary dramatically in their degree of abstraction or concreteness. An **abstract word** expresses a concept, quality, or characteristic. Abstractions are usually broad, encompassing a category of ideas, and they are often intellectual, academic, or philosophical. *Love, honor, progress, tradition,* and *beauty* are abstractions, as are such important business concepts as *productivity, profits, quality,* and *motivation*. In contrast, a **concrete word** stands for something you can touch, see, or visualize. Most concrete terms are anchored in the tangible, material world. *Chair, table, horse, rose, kick, kiss, red, green,* and *two* are concrete words; they are direct, clear, and exact. Incidentally, technology continues to generate new words and new meanings that describe things that don't have a physical presence but are nonetheless concrete: *software, database,* and *website* are all concrete terms as well.

As you can imagine, abstractions tend to cause more trouble for writers and readers than concrete words. Abstractions tend to be "fuzzy" and can be interpreted differently, depending on the audience and the circumstances. The best way to minimize such problems is to blend abstract terms with concrete ones, the general with the specific. State the concept, and then pin it down with details expressed in more concrete terms. Save the abstractions for ideas that cannot be expressed any other way. In addition, abstract words such as *small, numerous, sizable, near, soon, good,* and *fine* are imprecise, so try to replace them with terms that are more accurate. Instead of referring to a sizable loss, give an exact number.

FINDING WORDS THAT COMMUNICATE WELL

Try to use words that are powerful and familiar.

By practicing your writing, learning from experienced writers and editors, and reading extensively, you'll find it easier to choose words that communicate exactly what you want to say. When you compose your business messages, think carefully to find the most powerful words for each situation and to avoid obscure words, clichés, and buzzwords that are turning into clichés (see Table 5):

- **Choose strong, precise words.** Choose words that express your thoughts clearly, specifically, and dynamically. If you find yourself using a lot of adjectives and adverbs, you're probably trying to compensate for weak nouns and verbs. Saying that *sales plummeted* is stronger and more efficient than saying sales *dropped dramatically* or sales *experienced a dramatic drop*.
- **Choose familiar words.** You'll communicate best with words that are familiar to both you and your readers. Efforts to improve a situation certainly can be *ameliorative*, but saying they are *helpful* is a lot more effective. Moreover, trying to use an unfamiliar word for the first time in an important document can lead to embarrassing mistakes.

Avoid clichés, be extremely careful with trendy buzzwords, and use jargon only when your audience is completely familiar with it.

- **Avoid clichés and be careful with buzzwords.** Although familiar words are generally the best choice, avoid *clichés*—terms and phrases so common that they have lost some of their power to communicate. *Buzzwords*, newly coined terms often associated

TABLE 5   Selected Examples of Finding Powerful Words

Potentially Weak Words and Phrases	Stronger Alternatives (Effective Usage Depends on the Situation)
Increase (as a verb)	Accelerate, amplify, augment, enlarge, escalate, expand, extend, magnify, multiply, soar, swell
Decrease (as a verb)	Curb, cut back, depreciate, dwindle, shrink, slacken
Large, small	(Use a specific number, such as $100 million)
Good	Admirable, beneficial, desirable, flawless, pleasant, sound, superior, worthy
Bad	Abysmal, corrupt, deficient, flawed, inadequate, inferior, poor, substandard, worthless
We are committed to providing. . .	We provide . . .
It is in our best interest to. . .	We should . . .
Unfamiliar Words	**Familiar Words**
Ascertain	Find out, learn
Consummate	Close, bring about
Peruse	Read, study
Circumvent	Avoid
Unequivocal	Certain
Clichés and Buzzwords	**Plain Language**
An uphill battle	A challenge
Writing on the wall	Prediction
Call the shots	Lead
Take by storm	Attack
Costs an arm and a leg	Expensive
A new ball game	Fresh start
Fall through the cracks	Be overlooked
Think outside the box	Be creative
Run it up the flagpole	Find out what people think about it
Eat our own dog food	Use our own products
Mission-critical	Vital
Disintermediate	Get rid of
Green light (as a verb)	Approve
Architect (as a verb)	Design
Space (as in, "we compete in the XYZ space")	Market or industry
Blocking and tackling	Basic skills
Trying to boil the ocean	Working frantically but without focus
Human capital	People, employees, workforce
Low-hanging fruit	Tasks that are easy to complete or sales that are easy to close
Pushback	Resistance

with technology, business, or cultural changes, are slightly more difficult to handle than clichés, but in small doses and in the right situation, they can be useful. The careful use of a buzzword can signal that you're an insider, someone in the know.[15] However, buzzwords quickly become clichés, and using them too late in their "life cycle" can mark you as an outsider desperately trying to look like an insider. When people use clichés and overuse buzzwords, they often sound as though they don't know how to express themselves otherwise and don't invest the energy required for original writing.[16]

- **Use jargon carefully.** *Jargon*, the specialized language of a particular profession or industry, has a bad reputation, but it's not always bad. Using jargon is usually an efficient way to communicate within the specific groups that understand these terms. After all, that's how jargon develops in the first place, as people with similar interests devise ways to communicate complex ideas quickly. For instance, when a recording engineer wants to communicate that a particular piece of music is devoid of reverberation and other sound effects, it's a lot easier to simply describe the track as "dry." Of course, to people who aren't familiar with such insider terms, jargon is meaningless and intimidating— one more reason it's important to understand your audience before you start writing.

MOBILE APP
The Advanced English Dictionary and Thesaurus helps you find the right word by organizing words according to their relationship with other words.

5 LEARNING OBJECTIVE
Define the four types of sentences, and explain how sentence style affects emphasis within a message.

Composing Your Message: Creating Effective Sentences

Arranging your carefully chosen words in effective sentences is the next step in creating powerful messages. Start by selecting the best type of sentence to communicate each point you want to make.

CHOOSING FROM THE FOUR TYPES OF SENTENCES

Sentences come in four basic varieties: simple, compound, complex, and compound-complex. A **simple sentence** has one main *clause* (a single subject and a single predicate), although it may be expanded by nouns and pronouns that serve as objects of the action and by modifying phrases. Here's an example with the subject noun underlined once and the predicate verb underlined twice:

A simple sentence has one main clause.

<u>Profits</u> <u>increased</u> in the past year.

A compound sentence has two main clauses.

A **compound sentence** has two main clauses that express two or more independent but related thoughts of equal importance, usually joined by *and, but,* or *or*. In effect, a compound sentence is a merger of two or more simple sentences (independent clauses) that are related. For example:

Wage <u>rates</u> <u>have declined</u> by 5 percent, and employee <u>turnover</u> <u>has been</u> high.

The independent clauses in a compound sentence are always separated by a comma or by a semicolon (in which case the conjunction—*and, but, or*—is dropped).

A complex sentence has one main clause and one subordinate clause.

A **complex sentence** expresses one main thought (the independent clause) and one or more subordinate, related thoughts (dependent clauses that cannot stand alone as valid sentences). Independent and dependent clauses are usually separated by a comma. In this example, "Although you may question Gerald's conclusions" is a subordinate thought expressed in a dependent clause:

Although you may question Gerald's conclusions, <u>you</u> <u>must admit</u> that his research is thorough.

A compound-complex sentence has two main clauses and at least one dependent clause.

A **compound-complex sentence** has two main clauses, at least one of which contains a subordinate clause:

<u>Profits</u> <u>increased</u> 35 percent in the past year, so although the company faces long-term challenges, <u>I</u> <u>agree</u> that its short-term prospects look quite positive.

154

When constructing sentences, choose the form that matches the relationship of the ideas you want to express. If you have two ideas of equal importance, express them as two simple sentences or as one compound sentence. However, if one of the ideas is less important than the other, place it in a dependent clause to form a complex sentence. For example, although the following compound sentence uses a conjunction to join two ideas, they aren't truly equal:

REAL-TIME UPDATES

LEARN MORE BY READING THIS ARTICLE

Practical tips for more-effective sentences

The Writer's Handbook from the University of Wisconsin offers tips on writing clear, concise sentences. Go to http://real-timeupdates .com/ebc12 and click on Learn More in the Students section.

> The chemical products division is the strongest in the company, and its management techniques should be adopted by the other divisions.

By making the first thought subordinate to the second, you establish a cause-and-effect relationship and emphasize the more important idea (that the other divisions should adopt the chemical division's management techniques):

> Because the chemical products division is the strongest in the company, its management techniques should be adopted by the other divisions.

In addition to selecting the best type for each thought you want to express, using a variety of sentence types throughout a document can make your writing more interesting and effective. For example, if you use too many simple sentences in a row, you may struggle to properly express the relationships among your ideas, and your writing will sound choppy and abrupt. At the other extreme, a long series of compound, complex, or compound-complex sentences can be tiring to read.

Maintain some variety among the four sentence types to keep your writing from getting choppy (too many short, simple sentences) or exhausting (too many long sentences).

USING SENTENCE STYLE TO EMPHASIZE KEY THOUGHTS

In every message of any length, some ideas are more important than others. You can emphasize these key ideas through your sentence style. One obvious technique is to give important points the most space. When you want to call attention to a thought, use extra words to describe it. Consider this sentence:

Emphasize specific parts of sentences by
- Devoting more words to them
- Putting them at the beginning or at the end of the sentence
- Making them the subject of the sentence

> The chairperson called for a vote of the shareholders.

To emphasize the importance of the chairperson, you might describe her more fully:

> Having considerable experience in corporate takeover battles, the chairperson called for a vote of the shareholders.

You can increase the emphasis even more by adding a separate, short sentence to augment the first:

> The chairperson called for a vote of the shareholders. She has considerable experience in corporate takeover battles.

You can also call attention to a thought by making it the subject of the sentence. In the following example, the emphasis is on the person:

> I can write letters much more quickly by using voice dictation.

However, by changing the subject, the voice dictation capability takes center stage:

Using voice dictation enables me to write letters much more quickly.

Another way to emphasize an idea (in this instance, the idea of stimulating demand) is to place it either at the beginning or at the end of a sentence:

Less emphatic: We are cutting the price to stimulate demand.
More emphatic: To stimulate demand, we are cutting the price.

In complex sentences, the placement of the dependent clause hinges on the relationship between the ideas expressed. If you want to emphasize the subordinate idea, put the dependent clause at the end of the sentence (the most emphatic position) or at the beginning (the second most emphatic position). If you want to downplay the idea, put the dependent clause within the sentence:

Most emphatic: The electronic parts are manufactured in Mexico, <u>which has lower wage rates than the United States</u>.
Emphatic: <u>Because wage rates are lower in Mexico than in the United States</u>, the electronic parts are manufactured there.
Least emphatic: Mexico, <u>which has lower wage rates than the United States</u>, was selected as the production site for the electronic parts.

Techniques such as these give you a great deal of control over the way your audience interprets what you have to say.

The best placement of the dependent clause depends on the relationship between the ideas in the sentence.

Composing Your Message: Crafting Unified, Coherent Paragraphs

6 LEARNING OBJECTIVE Define the three key elements of a paragraph, and list five ways to develop unified, coherent paragraphs.

MOBILE APP
Pages is a full-featured word processing app for iOS devices.

Most paragraphs consist of
- A topic sentence that reveals the subject of the paragraph
- Related sentences that support and expand the topic
- Transitions that help readers move between sentences and paragraphs

Paragraphs organize sentences related to the same general topic. Readers expect every paragraph to be *unified*—focusing on a single topic—and *coherent*—presenting ideas in a logically connected way. By carefully arranging the elements of each paragraph, you help your readers grasp the main idea of your document and understand how the specific pieces of support material back up that idea.

CREATING THE ELEMENTS OF A PARAGRAPH

Paragraphs vary widely in length and form, but a typical paragraph contains three basic elements: a topic sentence, support sentences that develop the topic, and transitional words and phrases.

Topic Sentence

An effective paragraph deals with a single topic, and the sentence that introduces that topic is called the **topic sentence** (see Figure 5). In informal and creative writing, the topic sentence may be implied rather than stated. In business writing, the topic sentence is generally explicit and is often the first sentence in the paragraph. The topic sentence gives

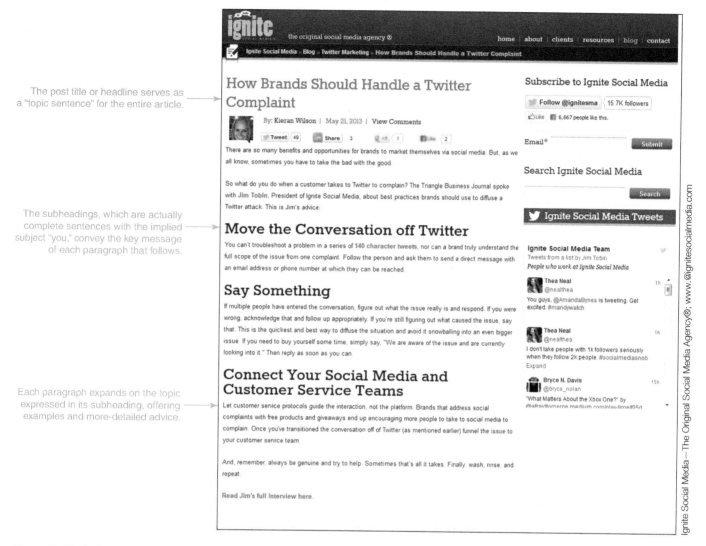

The post title or headline serves as a "topic sentence" for the entire article.

The subheadings, which are actually complete sentences with the implied subject "you," convey the key message of each paragraph that follows.

Each paragraph expands on the topic expressed in its subheading, offering examples and more-detailed advice.

Figure 5 Topic Sentences
In this blog post, informative subheadings function as topic sentences for the paragraphs that follow.

readers a summary of the general idea that will be covered in the rest of the paragraph. The following examples show how a topic sentence can introduce the subject and suggest the way the subject will be developed:

> The medical products division has been troubled for many years by public relations problems. [In the rest of the paragraph, readers will learn the details of the problems.]
>
> To get a refund, please supply us with the following information. [The details of the necessary information will be described in the rest of the paragraph.]

In addition to helping your readers, topic sentences help you as a writer because they remind you of the purpose of each paragraph and thereby encourage you to stay focused. In fact, a good way to test the effectiveness of your writing is to prepare a summary version that consists of only the first sentences of all your paragraphs. If this summary communicates the essence of your message in a sensible, compelling way, you've probably done a good job of presenting your information.[17]

Support Sentences

In most paragraphs, the topic sentence needs to be explained, justified, or extended with one or more support sentences. These related sentences must all have a bearing on the general subject and must provide enough specific details to make the topic clear:

The medical products division has been troubled for many years by public relations problems. Since 2014, the local newspaper has published 15 articles that portray the division in a negative light. We have been accused of everything from mistreating laboratory animals to polluting the local groundwater. Our facility has been described as a health hazard. Our scientists are referred to as "Frankensteins," and our profits are considered "obscene."

The support sentences are all more specific than the topic sentence. Each one provides another piece of evidence to demonstrate the general truth of the main thought. Also, each sentence is clearly related to the general idea being developed, which gives the paragraph unity. A paragraph is well developed if it contains enough information to make the topic sentence understood and convincing, and if it doesn't contain any extraneous, unrelated sentences.

Transitions

Transitions connect ideas by showing how one thought is related to another. They also help alert the reader to what lies ahead so that shifts and changes don't cause confusion. In addition to helping readers understand the connections you're trying to make, transitions give your writing a smooth, even flow.

Depending on the specific need within a document, transitional elements can range in length from a single word to an entire paragraph or more. You can establish transitions in a variety of ways:

Transitional elements include
- *Connecting words (conjunctions)*
- *Repeated words or phrases*
- *Pronouns*
- *Words that are frequently paired*

- **Use connecting words.** Use conjunctions such as *and, but, or, nevertheless, however, in addition,* and so on.
- **Echo a word or phrase from a previous paragraph or sentence.** "A system should be established for monitoring inventory levels. *This system* will provide . . ."
- **Use a pronoun that refers to a noun used previously.** "Ms. Arthur is the leading candidate for the president's position. *She* has excellent qualifications."
- **Use words that are frequently paired.** "The machine has a *minimum* output of . . . Its *maximum* output is . . ."

Some transitions serve as mood changers, alerting the reader to a change in mood from the previous material. Some announce a total contrast with what's gone on before, some announce a causal relationship, and some signal a change in time. Here is a list of transitions frequently used to move readers smoothly between clauses, sentences, and paragraphs:

Additional detail: moreover, furthermore, in addition, besides, first, second, third, finally
Cause-and-effect relationship: therefore, because, accordingly, thus, consequently, hence, as a result, so
Comparison: similarly, here again, likewise, in comparison, still
Contrast: yet, conversely, whereas, nevertheless, on the other hand, however, but, nonetheless
Condition: although, if
Illustration: for example, in particular, in this case, for instance
Time sequence: formerly, after, when, meanwhile, sometimes
Intensification: indeed, in fact, in any event
Summary: in brief, in short, to sum up
Repetition: that is, in other words, as mentioned previously

Consider using a transition whenever it could help the reader understand your ideas and follow you from point to point. You can use transitions inside paragraphs to tie related points together and between paragraphs to ease the shift from one distinct thought to another. In longer reports, a transition that links major sections or chapters may be a complete paragraph that serves as a mini-introduction to the next section or as a summary of the ideas presented in the section just ending. Here's an example:

> Given the nature of this product, our alternatives are limited. As the previous section indicates, we can stop making it altogether, improve it, or continue with the current model. Each of these alternatives has advantages and disadvantages, which are discussed in the following section.

This paragraph makes it clear to the reader that the analysis of the problem (offered in the previous section) is now over and that the document is making a transition to an analysis of the possible solutions (to be offered in the next section).

CHOOSING THE BEST WAY TO DEVELOP EACH PARAGRAPH

You have a variety of options for developing paragraphs, each of which can convey a specific type of idea. Five of the most common approaches are illustration, comparison or contrast, cause and effect, classification, and problem and solution (see Table 6).

In some instances, combining approaches in a single paragraph is an effective strategy. Notice how the example provided for "Problem and solution" in Table 6 also includes an element of illustration by listing some of the unique products that could be part of the proposed solution. However, when combining approaches, do so carefully so that you don't lose readers partway through the paragraph.

In addition, before settling for the first approach that comes to mind, consider the alternatives. Think through various methods before committing yourself, or even write several test paragraphs to see which method works best. By avoiding the easy habit of repeating the same old paragraph pattern time after time, you can keep your writing fresh and interesting.

Five ways to develop paragraphs:
- Illustration
- Comparison or contrast
- Cause and effect
- Classification
- Problem and solution

TABLE 6 Five Techniques for Developing Paragraphs

Technique	Description	Example
Illustration	Giving examples that demonstrate the general idea	Some of our most popular products are available through local distributors. For example, Everett & Lemmings carries our frozen soups and entrees. The J. B. Green Company carries our complete line of seasonings, as well as the frozen soups. Wilmont Foods, also a major distributor, now carries our new line of frozen desserts.
Comparison or contrast	Using similarities or differences to develop the topic	When the company was small, the recruiting function could be handled informally. The need for new employees was limited, and each manager could comfortably screen and hire her or his own staff. However, our successful bid on the Owens contract means that we will be doubling our labor force over the next six months. To hire that many people without disrupting our ongoing activities, we will create a separate recruiting group within the human resources department.
Cause and effect	Focusing on the reasons for something	The heavy-duty fabric of your Wanderer tent probably broke down for one of two reasons: (1) a sharp object punctured the fabric, and without reinforcement, the hole was enlarged by the stress of pitching the tent daily for a week or (2) the fibers gradually rotted because the tent was folded and stored while still wet.
Classification	Showing how a general idea is broken into specific categories	Successful candidates for our supervisor trainee program generally come from one of several groups. The largest group by far consists of recent graduates of accredited business management programs. The next largest group comes from within our own company, as we try to promote promising staff workers to positions of greater responsibility. Finally, we occasionally accept candidates with outstanding supervisory experience in related industries.
Problem and solution	Presenting a problem and then discussing the solution	Selling handmade toys online is a challenge because consumers are accustomed to buying heavily advertised toys from major chain stores or well-known websites such as Amazon. However, if we develop an appealing website, we can compete on the basis of product novelty and quality. In addition, we can provide unusual crafts at a competitive price: a rocking horse of birch, with a hand-knit tail and mane; a music box with the child's name painted on the top; and a real teepee, made by Native American artisans.

Writing Messages for Mobile Devices

7 LEARNING OBJECTIVE
List five techniques for writing effective messages for mobile readers.

One obvious adaptation to make for audiences using mobile devices is to modify the design and layout of your messages to fit smaller screen sizes and different user interface features. However, modifying your approach to writing is also an important step. Reading is more difficult on small screens, and consequently users' ability to comprehend what they read on mobile devices is lower than it is on larger screens.[18] In fact, research shows that comprehension can drop by 50 percent when users move from reading on a full-size screen to reading on a smartphone, and they can scroll right past vital information without noticing it.[19] Use these five techniques to make your mobile messages more effective:

To write effectively for mobile devices
- Use a linear organization
- Prioritize information
- Write short, focused messages
- Use short subject lines and headings
- Use short paragraphs

- **Use a linear organization.** In a printed document or on a larger screen, readers can easily take in multiple elements on a page, such as preview or summary boxes, tables and other supporting visuals, and sidebars with related information. All these elements are in view at the same time, so readers can jump around the page to read various parts without feeling lost. However, with small mobile device screens, a complicated organization requires readers to zoom in and out and pan around to see all these elements at readable text sizes. This makes reading slower and raises the odds that readers will get disoriented and lose the thread of the message because they can't see the big picture. In addition, using a touch screen momentarily obscures some of the information, so the more users have to hunt and scroll, the more likely they will miss something.[20] To simplify reading, organize with a linear flow from the top to the bottom of the message or article.

- **Prioritize information.** Small screens make it difficult for readers to scan the page to find the information they want most. Prioritize the information based on what you know about their needs and put that information first.[21] Use the *inverted pyramid* style favored by journalists, in which you reveal the most important information briefly at first and then provide successive layers of detail that readers can consume if they want. Note that you may need to avoid using the indirect approach if your message is complicated, because it will be more difficult for readers to follow your chain of reasoning.

- **Write shorter and more-focused messages and documents.** Mobile users often lack the patience or opportunity to read lengthy messages or documents, so keep it short.[22] In some cases, this could require you to write two documents, a shorter *executive summary* for mobile use and a longer supporting document that readers can access with their PCs if they want more details.

- **Use shorter subject lines and headings.** Mobile devices, particularly phones, can't display as many characters in a single line of text as the typical computer screen can. Depending on the app or website, email subject lines and page headings will be truncated or will wrap around to take up multiple lines. Both formats make reading more difficult. A good rule of thumb is to keep subject lines and headlines to around 25 characters.[23] This doesn't give you much text to work with, so make every word count and make sure you start with the key words so readers can instantly see what the subject line or heading is about.[24]

- **Use shorter paragraphs.** In addition to structuring a message according to discrete blocks of information, paragraphs have a visual role in written communication as well. Shorter paragraphs are less intimidating and let readers take frequent "micro rests" as they move through a document. Because far less text is displayed at once on a mobile screen, keep paragraphs as short as possible so readers don't have to swipe through screen after screen before getting to paragraph breaks.

REAL-TIME UPDATES
LEARN MORE BY VISITING THIS WEBSITE
Expert advice on making technologies usable
Usability experts at Nielsen Norman Group offer dozens of research-based articles on effective communication using mobile devices and other technologies. Go to http://real-timeupdates.com/ebc12 and click on Learn More in the Students section.

Compare the two messages in Figure 6 to get a sense of how to write reader-friendly mobile content.

For a reminder of the tasks involved in writing messages, see "Checklist: Writing Business Messages".

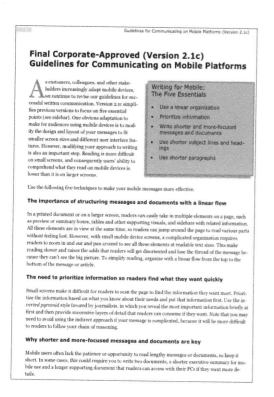

The text from this conventional report page is too small to read on a phone screen.

However, zooming in to read forces the reader to lose context and repeatedly move around to find all the pieces of the page.

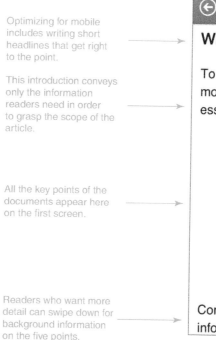

Optimizing for mobile includes writing short headlines that get right to the point.

This introduction conveys only the information readers need in order to grasp the scope of the article.

All the key points of the documents appear here on the first screen.

Readers who want more detail can swipe down for background information on the five points.

Figure 6 Writing for Mobile Devices

Messages and documents created for printed pages and full-sized screen can be difficult and frustrating on mobile devices (Figures 6a and 6b). For mobile audiences, rewrite with short headlines and concise, linear content (Figure 6c).

CHECKLIST: ✔ Writing Business Messages

A. Adapt to your audience.
- Use the "you" attitude.
- Maintain good etiquette through polite communication.
- Emphasize the positive whenever possible.
- Use bias-free language.
- Establish credibility in the eyes of your audience.
- Project your company's preferred image.
- Use a conversational but still professional and respectful tone.
- Use plain language for clarity.

B. Compose your message.
- Choose strong words that communicate efficiently.
- Pay attention to the connotative meaning of your words.

- Balance abstract and concrete terms to convey your meaning accurately.
- Avoid clichés and trendy buzzwords.
- Use jargon only when your audience understands it and prefers it.
- Vary your sentence structure for impact and interest.
- Develop coherent, unified paragraphs.
- Use transitions generously to help your audience follow your message.
- As needed adapt your writing for the limitations of mobile devices.

ON THE JOB: SOLVING COMMUNICATION DILEMMAS AT SHE TAKES ON THE WORLD

Natalie MacNeil recently hired you as an assistant editor at She Takes on the World. One of your responsibilities is to review the work of guest bloggers and suggest improvements. Use what you've learned in this chapter to address these writing challenges.

1. You're reviewing a draft that encourages college students who are about to graduate to consider starting a business rather than applying for conventional jobs. The writer has two main reasons for making this suggestion. First, the current job market is tough in many professions, and some graduates will be forced to take jobs that are outside their intended fields and perhaps below the level of their qualifications. Second, the nature of employment is changing in many professions and industries, and many companies now engage independent contractors (also known as freelancers) for short durations, rather than hiring employees for the long term. Which of these statements is the most sensitive to the audience's needs as they relate to this specific topic?
   a. The job market remains slow in many industries and professions, so you should seriously consider creating your own job by starting a small company and setting up shop as an independent contractor.
   b. The job market remains slow in many industries and professions, and many of those jobs aren't coming back even when the economy fully recovers. Chances are you'll end up working as an independent contractor at some point anyway, so you might as well do it now.
   c. What could be more fun than creating your own job the minute you graduate?
   d. Chances are you'll be facing a tough job market when you graduate, and many traditional jobs are converting to contract work. Why not convert a challenge into opportunity and create your own job?

2. For a blog post on the risks of going into business with friends or family members, which of these sentences has the most appropriate tone and demonstrates the best use of plain language?
   a. The attraction of entering into strategic partnerships with known personalities notwithstanding, one must exercise great caution when considering working with friends and family members.
   b. Going into business with friends or family members can sound appealing, but just because a relationship works on a personal level doesn't automatically mean it will work on a business level.
   c. Going into business with friends or family members can sound appealing, but you need to remember that managing a business is not the same as interacting with people in a social or personal sphere.
   d. Think about how even your best friends can drive you nuts sometimes—do you really want that kind of crazy in your business, too?

3. In a post about pitching a business plan to investors, a guest blogger wants to give entrepreneurs a realistic expectation about getting funding from venture capitalists. Which of the following sentence structures conveys this idea most effectively?
   a. Venture capitalists can provide valuable management expertise and industry connections in addition to startup funds, but they fund only a tiny percentage of all new companies.
   b. Venture capitalists, who fund only a tiny percentage of all new companies, can provide valuable management expertise and industry connections in addition to start-up funds.

c. Venture capitalists can provide valuable management expertise and industry connections in addition to start-up funds. However, they fund only a tiny percentage of all new companies.

d. They fund only a tiny percentage of all new companies, but venture capitalists can provide valuable management expertise and industry connections in addition to start-up funds.

4. The following paragraphs all have the same topic sentence; which has the most effective set of support sentences?

a. First-line supervisors, those on the lowest rung of the managerial ladder, face several unique challenges. As the interface between management and nonmanagerial employees, they have the most immediate responsibility for ensuring that necessary work is done according to agreed-on performance standards. They must also deal directly with any friction that exists between labor and

management. Supervisors are also deeply involved in recruiting, hiring, and training of employees.

b. First-line supervisors, those on the lowest rung of the managerial ladder, face several unique challenges. These managers have a good feel for the concerns and activities of employees, given their close day-to-day contact with them. Plus, when supervisors are newly promoted into management, the experience of being an employee is still fresh in their minds—a perspective that is often lost as managers move higher up the corporate ladder.

c. First-line supervisors, those on the lowest rung of the managerial ladder, face several unique challenges. As the interface between management and nonmanagerial employees, they are the ones who must deal with any friction that exists between labor and management. Even if they are sympathetic to employees' concerns or complaints, they represent management and so must take management's side in any disputes.

Learning Objectives Checkup

Assess your understanding of the principles in this chapter by reading each learning objective and studying the accompanying exercises. You can check your responses against the answer key.

Objective 1: Identify the four aspects of being sensitive to audience needs when writing business messages.

1. Why should you take the time to adapt your messages to your audience?
   a. People are more inclined to read and respond to messages that they believe apply to them and their concerns.
   b. Adapting messages to audiences is corporate policy in nearly all large companies.
   c. Adapting your message saves time during planning and writing.
   d. You can manipulate audience responses more easily by adapting your messages.
2. How is your audience likely to respond to a message that doesn't seem to be about their concerns or that is written in language they don't understand?
   a. They will ignore the message.
   b. If they read the message, they will be less inclined to respond in a positive way.
   c. They will assume the writer doesn't respect them enough to adapt the message.
   d. All of the above could occur.

Objective 2: Explain how establishing your credibility and projecting your company's image are vital aspects of building strong relationships with your audience.

3. Credibility is a measure of
   a. Your power within the organization
   b. The length of time the audience has known you
   c. Your confidence
   d. The audience's perception of your believability

4. If you have developed a reputation for missing deadlines on projects you manage, which of the following statements would do the best job of helping to rebuild your credibility? (You have previously committed to a project completion date of April 1.)
   a. No April foolin' this time; we'll be finished by April 1.
   b. After analyzing past projects, I now realize that a failure to clarify project objectives up front created significant delays down the line. In order to meet the April 1 deadline, I will make sure to clarify the objective as soon as the team assembles.
   c. I plan to work extra hard this time to make sure we will be finished by April 1.
   d. I hope that we will be finished by April 1.

Objective 3: Explain how to achieve a tone that is conversational but businesslike, explain the value of using plain language, and define active and passive voice.

5. A good way to achieve a businesslike tone in your messages is to
   a. Use formal business terminology, such as "In re your letter of the 18th"
   b. Brag about your company
   c. Use a conversational style that is not intimate or chatty
   d. Use plenty of humor
6. Plain English is
   a. Never recommended when speaking with people for whom English is a second language
   b. A movement toward using "English only" in U.S. businesses
   c. A way of writing and arranging content to make it more readily understandable
   d. An attempt to keep writing at a fourth- or fifth-grade level
7. If you want to avoid attributing blame or otherwise calling attention to a specific person, the _____ voice is a more diplomatic approach.

8. The ____ voice usually makes sentences shorter, more direct, and livelier.

Objective 4: Describe how to select words that are both correct and effective.

9. Which of the following defines the connotative meaning of the word *flag*?
   a. A flag is a piece of material with a symbol of some kind sewn on it.
   b. A flag is a symbol of everything that a nation stands for.
   c. A flag is fabric on a pole used to mark a geographic spot.
   d. A flag is an object used to draw attention.

10. Which of the following is a concrete word?
    a. Little
    b. Mouse
    c. Species
    d. Kingdom

11. If you're not sure about the meaning of a word you'd like to use, which of the following is the most appropriate way to handle the situation?
    a. Your readers probably have instant access to online dictionaries these days, so go ahead and use the word.
    b. Use the word but include a humorous comment in parentheses saying that you're not really sure what this big, important word means.
    c. Either verify the meaning of the word or rewrite the sentence so that you don't need to use it.
    d. Find a synonym in a thesaurus and use that word instead.

12. Using jargon is
    a. Often a good idea when discussing complex subjects with people who are intimately familiar with the subject and common jargon relating to it
    b. Never a good idea
    c. A good way to build credibility, no matter what the purpose of the message
    d. A sign of being an "insider"

Objective 5: Define the four types of sentences and explain how sentence style affects emphasis within a message.

13. Where is the most emphatic place to put a dependent clause?
    a. At the end of the sentence
    b. At the beginning of the sentence
    c. In the middle of the sentence
    d. Anywhere in the sentence

14. Devoting a lot of words to a particular idea shows your audience that
    a. The idea is complicated
    b. The idea is the topic sentence
    c. The idea is important
    d. The idea is new and therefore requires more explanation

Objective 6: Define the three key elements of a paragraph and list five ways to develop unified, coherent paragraphs.

15. When developing a paragraph, keep in mind
    a. That you should stick to one method of development within a single paragraph
    b. That once you use one method of development, you should use that same method for all the paragraphs in a section
    c. That your choice of technique should take into account your subject, your intended audience, and your purpose
    d. All of the above

16. To develop a paragraph by illustration, give your audience enough ____ to help them grasp the main idea.

17. Paragraphs organized by comparison and contrast point out the ____ or ____ between two or more items.

18. To explain the reasons something happened, which of these paragraph designs should you use?
    a. Cause-effect
    b. Opposition and argument
    c. Classification
    d. Prioritization

Objective 7: List five techniques for writing effective messages for mobile readers.

19. What is meant by using a linear organization to craft messages for mobile devices?
    a. Using only ethically proven information
    b. Organizing all the information in a single topical thread from start to finish
    c. Putting each paragraph on its own line
    d. Using line art to convey key message points

20. The _____ _____ style recommended for mobile messages means you reveal the most important information briefly at first and then provide successive layers of detail that readers can consume if they want.

21. What is a good rule of thumb for the length of subject lines and headlines intended for mobile readers?
    a. Two words, three at a most
    b. As long as the device's screen is wide in landscape mode
    c. Around 25 characters
    d. Around 25 words

Quick Learning Guide

CHAPTER OUTLINE

LEARNING OBJECTIVES

1 Identify the four aspects of being sensitive to audience needs when writing business messages.

2 Explain how establishing your credibility and projecting your company's image are vital aspects of building strong relationships with your audience.

3 Explain how to achieve a tone that is conversational but businesslike, explain the value of using plain language, and define active and passive voice.

4 Describe how to select words that are both correct and effective.

5 Define the four types of sentences, and explain how sentence style affects emphasis within a message.

6 Define the three key elements of a paragraph, and list five ways to develop unified, coherent paragraphs.

7 List five techniques for writing effective messages for mobile readers.

KEY TERMS

abstract word Word that expresses a concept, quality, or characteristic; abstractions are usually broad

active voice Sentence structure in which the subject performs the action and the object receives the action

bias-free language Language that avoids words and phrases that categorize or stigmatize people in ways related to gender, race, ethnicity, age, or disability

complex sentence Sentence that expresses one main thought (the independent clause) and one or more subordinate, related thoughts (dependent clauses that cannot stand alone as valid sentences)

compound sentence Sentence with two main clauses that express two or more independent but related thoughts of equal importance, usually joined by *and, but,* or *or*

compound-complex sentence Sentence with two main clauses, at least one of which contains a subordinate clause

concrete word Word that represents something you can touch, see, or visualize; most concrete terms related to the tangible, material world

connotative meaning All the associations and feelings evoked by a word

conversational tone The tone used in most business communication; it uses plain language that sounds businesslike without being stuffy at one extreme or too laid-back and informal at the other extreme

credibility A measure of your believability, based on how reliable you are and how much trust you evoke in others

denotative meaning The literal, or dictionary, meaning of a word

euphemisms Words or phrases that express a thought in milder terms

passive voice Sentence structure in which the subject receives the action

simple sentence Sentence with one main clause (a single subject and a single predicate)

style The choices you make to express yourself: the words you select, the manner in which you use those words in sentences, and the way you build paragraphs from individual sentences

tone The overall impression in your messages, created by the style you use

topic sentence Sentence that introduces that topic of a paragraph

transitions Words or phrases that tie together ideas by showing how one thought is related to another

CHECKLIST: ✔

Writing Business Messages

A. Adapt to your audience.
- Use the "you" attitude.
- Maintain good etiquette through polite communication.
- Emphasize the positive whenever possible.
- Use bias-free language.
- Establish credibility in the eyes of your audience.
- Project your company's preferred image.
- Use a conversational but still professional and respectful tone.
- Use plain language for clarity.

B. Compose your message.
- Choose strong words that communicate efficiently.
- Pay attention to the connotative meaning of your words.
- Balance abstract and concrete terms to convey your meaning accurately.
- Avoid clichés and trendy buzzwords.
- Use jargon only when your audience understands it and prefers it.
- Vary your sentence structure for impact and interest.
- Develop coherent, unified paragraphs.
- Use transitions generously to help your audience follow your message.
- As needed adapt your writing for the limitations of mobile devices.

Apply Your Knowledge

To review chapter content related to each question, refer to the indicated Learning Objective.

⭐ 1. Millions of people in the United States are allergic to one or more food ingredients. Each year, thousands of these people end up in the emergency room after suffering allergic reactions, and hundreds of them die. Many of these tragic events are tied to poorly written food labels that either fail to identify dangerous allergens or use scientific terms that most consumers don't recognize.[25] Do food manufacturers have a responsibility to ensure that consumers read, understand, and follow warnings on food products? Explain your answer. [LO-1]

⭐ 2. When composing business messages, how can you communicate with an authentic voice and project your company's image at the same time? [LO-2]

3. Does using plain language make you come across as less of an expert? Explain your answer. [LO-3]

⭐ 4. Should you bother using transitions if the logical sequence of your message is obvious? Why or why not? [LO-6]

5. Why can it be difficult to use the indirect approach for a complex message that will be read on mobile devices? [LO-7]

Practice Your Skills

Messages for Analysis: Creating a Businesslike Tone [LO-1], [LO-3]

Read the following email draft and then (a) analyze the strengths and weaknesses of each sentence and (b) revise the document so that it follows this chapter's guidelines. The message was written by the marketing manager of an online retailer of baby-related products in the hope of becoming a retail outlet for Inglesina strollers and high chairs. As a manufacturer of stylish, top-quality products, Inglesina (based in Italy) is extremely selective about the retail outlets through which it allows its products to be sold.

> Our e-tailing site, www.BestBabyGear.com, specializes in only the very best products for parents of newborns, infants, and toddlers. We constantly scour the world looking for products that are good enough and well-built enough and classy enough—good enough to take their place alongside the hundreds of other carefully selected products that adorn the pages of our award-winning website, www.bestbabygear .com. We aim for the fences every time we select a product to join this portfolio; we don't want to waste our time with onesey-twosey products that might sell a half dozen units per annum—no, we want every product to be a top-drawer success, selling at least one hundred units per specific model per year in order to justify our expense and hassle factor in adding it to the above mentioned portfolio. After careful consideration, we thusly concluded that your Inglesina lines meet our needs and would therefore like to add it.

Exercises

Each activity is labeled according to the primary skill or skills you will need to use. To review relevant chapter content, you can refer to the indicated Learning Objective.

Writing: Communicating with Sensitivity and Tact [LO-1]
Substitute a better phrase for each of the following:

6. You claim that
7. You must update
8. It is not our policy to
9. You neglected to
10. In which you assert
11. We are sorry you are dissatisfied
12. You failed to enclose
13. We request that you send us
14. Apparently you overlooked our terms
15. We have been very patient
16. We are at a loss to understand

Writing: Demonstrating the "You" Attitude [LO-1] Rewrite these sentences to reflect your audience's viewpoint:

17. Your email order cannot be processed; we request that you use the order form on our website instead.
18. We insist that you always bring your credit card to the store.
19. We want to get rid of all our 15-inch LCD screens to make room in our warehouse for the new 19-, 23-, and 35-inch monitors. Thus, we are offering a 25 percent discount on all sales of 15-inch models this week.
20. I am applying for the position of bookkeeper in your office. I feel my grades prove that I am bright and capable, and I think I can do a good job for you.
21. As requested, we are sending the refund for $25.
22. If you cared about doing a good job, you would've made the extra effort required to learn how to use the machinery properly.
23. Your strategy presentation this morning absolutely blew me away; there's no way we can fail with all the brilliant ideas you've pulled together—I'm so glad you're running the company now!
24. Regarding your email message from September 28 regarding the slow payment of your invoice, it's important for you to realize that we've just undergone a massive upgrade of our accounts payable system and payments have been delayed for everybody, not just you.
25. I know I'm late with the asset valuation report, but I haven't been feeling well and I just haven't had the energy needed to work through the numbers yet.
26. With all the online news sources available today, I can't believe you didn't know that MyTravel and Thomas Cook were in merger talks—I mean, you don't even have to get up from your computer to learn this!

Writing: Emphasizing the Positive [LO-1] Revise these sentences to be positive rather than negative:

27. To avoid damage to your credit rating, please remit payment within 10 days.
28. We don't offer refunds on returned merchandise that is soiled.
29. Because we are temporarily out of Baby Cry dolls, we won't be able to ship your order for 10 days.

30. You failed to specify the color of the blouse that you ordered.
31. You should have realized that waterbeds will freeze in unheated houses during winter. Therefore, our guarantee does not cover the valve damage, and you must pay the **$9.50** valve-replacement fee (plus postage).

Writing: Using Unbiased Language [LO-1] Rewrite each of the following to eliminate bias:

32. For an Indian, Maggie certainly is outgoing.
33. He needs a wheelchair, but he doesn't let his handicap affect his job performance.
34. A pilot must have the ability to stay calm under pressure, and then he must be trained to cope with any problem that arises.
35. Renata Parsons, married and the mother of a teenager, is a top candidate for CEO.
36. Even at his age, Sam Nugent is still an active salesman.
37. **Writing: Establishing Your Credibility; Microblogging Skills [LO-2]** Search LinkedIn for the profile of an expert in any industry or profession. Now imagine that you are going to introduce this person as a speaker at a convention. You will make an in-person introduction at the time of the speech, but you decide to introduce him or her the day before on Twitter. Write four tweets: one that introduces the expert and three that cover three key supporting points that will enhance the speaker's credibility in the minds of potential listeners. Make up any information you need to complete this assignment, and then email the text of your proposed tweets to your instructor.
38. **Writing: Using Plain Language; Communication Ethics: Making Ethical Choices [LO-3]** Your company has been a major employer in the local community for years, but shifts in the global marketplace have forced some changes in the company's long-term direction. In fact, the company plans to reduce local staffing by as much as 50 percent over the next 5 to 10 years, starting with a small layoff next month. The size and timing of future layoffs have not been decided, although there is little doubt that more layoffs will happen at some point. In the first draft of a letter aimed at community leaders, you write that "this first layoff is part of a continuing series of staff reductions anticipated over the next several years." However, your boss is concerned about the vagueness and negative tone of the language and asks you to rewrite that sentence to read "this layoff is part of the company's ongoing efforts to continually align its resources with global market conditions." Do you think this suggested wording is ethical, given the company's economic influence in the community? Explain your answer in an email message to your instructor.
39. **Writing: Creating Effective Sentences: Media Skills: Social Networking [LO-4]** If you are interested in business, chances are you've had an idea or two for starting a company. If you haven't yet, go ahead and dream up an idea now. Make it something you are passionate about, something you could really throw yourself into. Now write a four-sentence summary that could appear on the Info tab on a Facebook profile. Make sure the first sentence

is a solid topic sentence, and make sure the next three sentences offer relevant evidence and examples. Feel free to make up any details you need. Email your summary to your instructor or post it on your class blog.

Writing: Choosing Powerful Words [LO-4] Write a concrete phrase for each of these vague phrases:

40. Sometime this spring
41. A substantial savings
42. A large number attended
43. Increased efficiency
44. Expanded the work area
45. Flatten the website structure

Writing: Choosing Powerful Words [LO-4] List terms that are stronger than the following:

46. Ran after
47. Seasonal ups and downs
48. Bright
49. Suddenly rises
50. Moves forward

Writing: Choosing Powerful Words [LO-4] As you rewrite these sentences, replace the clichés and buzzwords with plain language (for any terms you don't recognize, you can find definitions online):

51. Being a jack-of-all-trades, Dave worked well in his new general manager job.
52. Moving Leslie into the accounting department, where she was literally a fish out of water, was like putting a square peg into a round hole, if you get my drift.
53. My only takeaway from the offsite was that Laird threw his entire department under the bus for missing the deadline.
54. I'd love to help with that project, but I'm bandwidth-constrained.
55. The board green-lighted our initiative to repurpose our consumer products for the commercial space.

Writing: Choosing Powerful Words [LO-4] Suggest short, simple words to replace each of the following:

56. Inaugurate
57. Terminate
58. Utilize
59. Anticipate
60. Assistance
61. Endeavor
62. Ascertain
63. Procure
64. Consummate
65. Advise
66. Alteration
67. Forwarded
68. Fabricate
69. Nevertheless
70. Substantial

Writing: Choosing Powerful Words [LO-4] Write up-to-date, less-stuffy versions of these phrases; write "none" if you think there is no appropriate substitute or "delete" if the phrase should simply be deleted:

71. As per your instructions
72. Attached herewith
73. In lieu of

74. In reply I wish to state
75. Please be advised that

Writing: Creating Effective Sentences [LO-5] Rewrite each sentence so that it is active rather than passive:

76. The raw data are entered into the customer relationship management system by the sales representative each Friday.
77. High profits are publicized by management.
78. The policies announced in the directive were implemented by the staff.
79. Our computers are serviced by the Santee Company.
80. The employees were represented by Janet Hogan.
81. **Writing: Crafting Unified, Coherent Paragraphs; Collaboration: Evaluating the Work of Others [LO-6]** Working with four other students, divide the following five topics among yourselves and each write one paragraph on your selected topic. Be sure each student uses a different technique when writing his or her paragraph: One student should use the illustration technique, one the comparison or contrast technique, one a discussion of cause and effect, one the classification technique, and one a discussion of problem and solution. Then exchange paragraphs within the team and pick out the main idea and general purpose of the paragraph one of your teammates wrote. Was everyone able to correctly identify the main idea and purpose? If not, suggest how the paragraph could be rewritten for clarity.

    - Types of *phablets* available for sale
    - Advantages and disadvantages of eating at fast-food restaurants
    - Finding that first full-time job
    - Good qualities of my car (or house, or apartment, or neighborhood)
    - How to make a dessert (or barbecue a steak or make coffee)

Writing: Using Transitions [LO-6] Add transitional elements to the following sentences to improve the flow of ideas. (Note: You may need to eliminate or add some words to smooth out your sentences.)

82. Facing some of the toughest competitors in the world, Harley-Davidson had to make some changes. The company introduced new products. Harley's management team set out to rebuild the company's production process. New products were coming to market and the company was turning a profit. Harley's quality standards were not on par with those of its foreign competitors. Harley's costs were still among the highest in the industry. Harley made a U-turn and restructured the company's organizational structure. Harley's efforts have paid off.
83. Whether you're indulging in a doughnut in New York or California, Krispy Kreme wants you to enjoy the same delicious taste with every bite. The company maintains consistent product quality by carefully controlling every step of the production process. Krispy Kreme tests all raw ingredients against established quality standards. Every delivery of wheat flour is sampled and measured for its moisture content and protein levels. Krispy Kreme blends the ingredients. Krispy Kreme tests the doughnut mix for quality. Krispy Kreme delivers the mix to its stores. Financial critics are not as kind to the company as food critics have been. Allegations of improper financial reporting have left the company's future in doubt.
84. **Media Skills: Writing for Mobile Devices [LO-7]** Find an interesting website article on any business topic. Write a three-paragraph summary that would be easy to read on a phone screen.

Expand Your Skills

Critique the Professionals

Locate an example of professional communication from a reputable online source. Choose a paragraph that has at least three sentences. Evaluate the effectiveness of this paragraph at three levels, starting with the paragraph structure. Is the paragraph unified and cohesive? Does it have a clear topic sentence and sufficient support to clarify and expand on that topic? Second, evaluate each sentence. Are the sentences easy to read and easy to understand? Did the writer vary the types and lengths of sentences to produce a smooth flow and rhythm? Is the most important idea presented prominently in each sentence? Third, evaluate at least six word choices. Did the writer use these words correctly and effectively? Using whatever medium your instructor requests, write a brief analysis of the piece (no more than one page), citing specific elements from the piece and support from the chapter.

Sharpening Your Career Skills Online

Bovée and Thill's Business Communication Web Search, at http://websearch.businesscommunicationnetwork.com, is a unique research tool designed specifically for business communication research. Use the Web Search function to find a website, video, PDF document, podcast, or presentation that offers advice on writing effective sentences. Write a brief email message to your instructor, describing the item that you found and summarizing the career skills information you learned from it.

Improve Your Grammar, Mechanics, and Usage

The following exercises help you improve your knowledge of and power over English grammar, mechanics, and usage. Turn to the Handbook of Grammar, Mechanics, and Usage at the end of this text and review Adverbs. Then look at the following 10 items and indicate the preferred choice within each set of parentheses.

85. Their performance has been (*good, well*).
86. I (*sure, surely*) do not know how to help you.
87. He feels (*sick, sickly*) again today.
88. Customs dogs are chosen because they smell (*good, well*).
89. The redecorated offices look (*good, well*).
90. Which of the two programs computes (*more fast, faster*)?
91. Of the two we have in stock, this model is the (*best, better*) designed.

92. He doesn't seem to have (*any, none*).

93. That machine is scarcely (*never, ever*) used.

94. They (*can, can't*) hardly get replacement parts for this equipment (*any, no*) more.

MyBCommLab

Go to the Assignments section of your MyLab to complete these writing exercises.

95 Why are email, texting, and other forms of digital communication so prone to inadvertent etiquette breakdowns, in which even well-intentioned writers insult or confuse readers? [LO-1]

96 What steps can you take to make abstract concepts such as opportunity feel more concrete in your messages? [LO-4]

Endnotes

1. Personal communication, Natalie MacNeil, 10 February 2015; She Takes on the World website, accessed 11 February 2015, http://shetakesontheworld.com; Prashanth Gopalan, "Natalie MacNeil Vs. the World," *TechVibes*, 29 September 2010, www.techvibes.com; Natalie MacNeil website, accessed 9 June 2013, http://nataliemacneil.com; product page for *She Takes on the World: A Guide to Being Your Own Boss, Working Happy, and Living on Purpose*, accessed 9 June 2013, www.amazon.com; Natalie MacNeil bio, *Huffington Post*, accessed 9 June 2013, http://www.huffingtonpost.com/natalie-macneil.

2. Annette N. Shelby and N. Lamar Reinsch Jr., "Positive Emphasis and You Attitude: An Empirical Study," *Journal of Business Communication* 32, no. 4 (1995): 303–322.

3. Quinn Warnick, "A Close Textual Analysis of Corporate Layoff Memos," *Business Communication Quarterly* 73, no. 3 (September 2010): 322–326.

4. Sherryl Kleinman, "Why Sexist Language Matters," *Qualitative Sociology* 25, no. 2 (Summer 2002): 299–304.

5. Judy E. Pickens, "Terms of Equality: A Guide to Bias-Free Language," *Personnel Journal*, August 1985, 24.

6. Xerox website, accessed 12 March 2014, www.xerox.com; ADM website, accessed 12 March 2014, www.adm.com.

7. Lisa Taylor, "Communicating About People with Disabilities: Does the Language We Use Make a Difference?" *Bulletin of the Association for Business Communication* 53, no. 3 (September 1990): 65–67.

8. Susan Benjamin, *Words at Work* (Reading, Mass.: Addison Wesley, 1997), 136–137.

9. Plain English Campaign website, accessed 28 June 2010, www.plainenglish.co.uk.

10. Plain Language website; Irene Etzkorn, "Amazingly Simple Stuff," presentation 7 November 2008, www.slideshare.net.

11. Creative Commons website, accessed 16 January 2011, www.creativecommons.org.

12. Susan Jaderstrom and Joanne Miller, "Active Writing," *Office Pro*, November/December 2003, 29.

13. Mary Munter, *Guide to Managerial Communication*, 7th ed. (Upper Saddle River, N.J.: Pearson Prentice Hall, 2006), 41.

14. Portions of this section are adapted from Courtland L. Bovée, *Techniques of Writing Business Letters, Memos, and Reports* (Sherman Oaks, Calif.: Banner Books International, 1978), 13–90.

15. Catherine Quinn, "Lose the Office Jargon; It May Sunset Your Career," *The Age* (Australia), 1 September 2007, www.theage.com.au.

16. Robert Hartwell Fiske, *The Dimwit's Dictionary* (Oak Park, Ill.: Marion Street Press, 2002), 16–20.

17. Beverly Ballaro and Christina Bielaszka-DuVernay, "Building a Bridge over the River Boredom," *Harvard Management Communication Letter*, Winter 2005, 3–5.

18. Jakob Nielsen, "Mobile Content Is Twice as Difficult," NN/g, 28 February 2011, www.nngroup.com.

19. Jakob Nielsen and Raluca Budiu, *Mobile Usability*, (Berkeley: New Riders, 2013), 10, 102.

20. Nielsen and Budiu, *Mobile Usability*, 23.

21. "Mobile Web Best Practices," W3C website, accessed 12 March 2014, www.w3.org.

22. "Mobile Message Mayhem," Verne Ordman & Associates, accessed 12 March 2014, www.businesswriting.biz.

23. "Mobile Message Mayhem."

24. Marieke McCloskey, "Writing Hyperlinks: Salient, Descriptive, Start with Keyword," NN/g, 9 March 2014, www.nngroup.com.

25. Food Allergy Initiative website, accessed 5 September 2008, www.foodallergyinitiative.org; Diana Keough, "Snacks That Can Kill; Schools Take Steps to Protect Kids Who Have Severe Allergies to Nuts," *Plain Dealer*, 15 July 2003, E1; "Dawdling over Food Labels," *New York Times*, 2 June 2003, A16; Sheila McNulty, "A Matter of Life and Death," *Financial Times*, 10 September 2003, 14.

Answer Key for "Learning Objectives Checkup"

1. a
2. d
3. d
4. b
5. c
6. c
7. passive
8. active
9. b
10. b
11. c
12. a
13. a
14. c
15. c
16. examples
17. differences, similarities
18. a
19. b
20. inverted pyramid
21. c

Answer Key for "Improve Your Grammar, Mechanics, and Usage" Exercises

85. good (1.5)
86. surely (1.5)
87. sick (1.5)
88. well (1.5)
89. good (1.5)
90. faster (1.5.2)
91. better (1.5.2)
92. any (1.5.1)
93. ever (1.5.1)
94. can, any (1.5.1)

Completing Business Messages

From Chapter 6 of *Excellence in Business Communication*, Twelfth Edition. John V. Thill, Courtland L. Bovée. Copyright © 2017 by Pearson Education, Inc. All rights reserved.

Completing Business Messages

LEARNING OBJECTIVES

After studying this chapter, you will be able to

1 Discuss the value of careful revision, and describe the tasks involved in evaluating your first drafts and the work of other writers.

2 List four techniques you can use to improve the readability of your messages.

3 Describe eight steps you can take to improve the clarity of your writing, and give four tips on making your writing more concise.

4 List four principles of effective design, and explain the role of major design elements in document readability.

5 Explain the importance of proofreading, and give eight tips for successful proofreading.

6 Discuss the most important issues to consider when distributing your messages.

ON THE JOB: COMMUNICATING AT
JEFFERSON RABB WEB DESIGN

Using Leading-Edge Digital Media to Reach Today's Book Audience

As a composer, game designer, photographer, programmer, and website developer, Jefferson Rabb epitomizes the "multi" in multimedia. For all the technical and creative skills he brings, however, Rabb's work never loses sight of audiences and their desire to be informed and entertained when they visit a website.

Rabb's career history includes stints at MTV.com and Sephora.com, but most of his current work as an independent designer involves projects in the publishing industry. The best-selling authors he has helped bring to the web include Dan Brown, Gary Shteyngart, Jhumpa Lahiri, Laura Hillenbrand, and Anita Shreve.

Kathy deWitt/Alamy

Authors such as Monica Ali still rely on personal contact with readers to promote books, but websites and other digital media have become an increasingly important element in book promotion.

For every project, Rabb starts his design work with an in-depth analysis of the audience. The questions he asks about site visitors include their familiarity with the author's work, the range of their reading interests, and their general demographics. He also wants to know whether a site needs to serve book reviewers, bookstore buyers, and other industry professionals in addition to readers.

With some insight into who the target visitors are, Rabb puts himself in their place and imagines the knowledge and experiences they hope to gain during their visits. These needs can vary from biographical information about the author to multimedia exhibits (such as video interviews and photographs depicting locations mentioned in a book) to complex games that extend a novel's storylines. Rabb makes a point of finding compelling visual connections between a book and a website, too, such as basing the design of the site for Shteyngart's *Super Sad True Love Story* on the portable communication device featured in the story. Completing the multimedia experience, he often composes music to create a specific mood that reflects the themes of a book.[1]

Your business communication efforts may not always be as elaborate as Rabb's, but you can always apply his strategy of combining methodical analysis with creative design and implementation. This chapter addresses the third step in the three-step writing process, completing your messages—which includes the important tasks of revising, producing, proofreading, and distributing your messages.

WWW.JEFFERSONRABB.COM

Revising Your Message: Evaluating the First Draft

1 LEARNING OBJECTIVE
Discuss the value of careful revision, and describe the tasks involved in evaluating your first drafts and the work of other writers.

Successful communicators like Jefferson Rabb (profiled in the chapter opening On the Job) recognize that the first draft is rarely as tight, clear, and compelling as it needs to be. Careful revision can mean the difference between a rambling, unfocused message and a lively, direct message that gets results.

The revision task can vary somewhat, depending on the medium and the nature of your message. For informal messages to internal audiences, particularly when using instant messaging, text messaging, email, or blogging, the revision process is often as simple as quickly looking over your message to correct any mistakes before sending or posting it. However, don't fall into the common trap of thinking that you don't need to worry about grammar, spelling, clarity, and other fundamentals of good writing when you use such media. These qualities can be *especially* important in digital media, particularly if these messages are the only contact your audience has with you. Audiences are likely to equate the quality of your writing with the quality of your thinking. Poor-quality messages create an impression of poor-quality thinking and can cause confusion, frustration, and costly delays.

With more complex messages, try to put your draft aside for a day or two before you begin the revision process so that you can approach the material with a fresh eye. Then start with the "big picture," making sure that the document accomplishes your overall goals before moving to finer points, such as readability, clarity, and conciseness. Compare the letters in Figures 1 and 2 on the next two pages for an example of how careful revision improves a customer letter.

For important messages, schedule time to put your draft aside for a day or two before you begin the revision process.

EVALUATING YOUR CONTENT, ORGANIZATION, STYLE, AND TONE

When you begin the revision process, focus your attention on content, organization, style, and tone. To evaluate the content of your message, answer these questions:

- Is the information accurate?
- Is the information relevant to the audience?
- Is there enough information to satisfy the readers' needs?
- Is there a good balance between general information (giving readers enough background information to appreciate the message) and specific information (giving readers the details they need to understand the message)?

Completing Business Messages

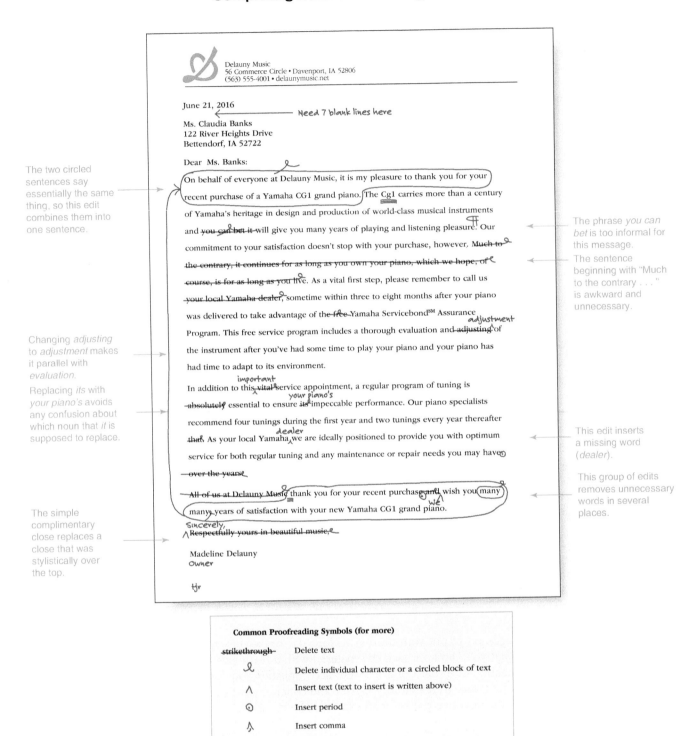

The two circled sentences say essentially the same thing, so this edit combines them into one sentence.

The phrase *you can bet* is too informal for this message.

The sentence beginning with "Much to the contrary . . ." is awkward and unnecessary.

Changing *adjusting* to *adjustment* makes it parallel with *evaluation*.

Replacing *its* with *your piano's* avoids any confusion about which noun that *it* is supposed to replace.

This edit inserts a missing word (*dealer*).

This group of edits removes unnecessary words in several places.

The simple complimentary close replaces a close that was stylistically over the top.

Figure 1 Improving a Customer Letter Through Careful Revision

Careful revision makes this draft shorter, clearer, and more focused. The proofreading symbols you see here are still widely used whenever printed documents are edited and revised. Note that many business documents are now "marked up" using such technological tools as revision marks in Microsoft Word and comments in Adobe Acrobat. No matter what the medium, however, careful revision is key to more effective messages.

Delauny Music
56 Commerce Circle• Davenport, IA 52806
(563) 555-4001 • delaunymusic.net

June 21, 2016

Ms. Claudia Banks
122 River Heights Drive
Bettendorf, IA 52722

Dear Ms. Banks:

Thank you for your recent purchase. We wish you many years of satisfaction with your new Yamaha CG1 grand piano. The CG1 carries more than a century of Yamaha's heritage in design and production of world-class musical instruments and will give you many years of playing and listening pleasure.

Our commitment to your satisfaction doesn't stop with your purchase, however. As a vital first step, please remember to call us sometime within three to eight months after your piano was delivered to take advantage of the Yamaha Servicebond℠ Assurance Program. This free service program includes a thorough evaluation and adjustment of the instrument after you've had some time to play your piano and your piano has had time to adapt to its environment.

In addition to this important service appointment, a regular program of tuning is essential to ensure your piano's impeccable performance. Our piano specialists recommend four tunings during the first year and two tunings every year thereafter. As your local Yamaha dealer, we are ideally positioned to provide you with optimum service for both regular tuning and any maintenance or repair needs you may have.

Sincerely,

Madeline Delauny

Madeline Delauny
Owner

tjr

The letter is now properly formatted.

The content is now organized in three coherent paragraphs, each with a distinct message.

The tone is friendly and engaging without being flowery.

Figure 2 Professional Business Letter
Here is the revised and finished version of the edited letter from Figure 1. Note that the *block format* used here is just one of several layout options.

When you are satisfied with the content of your message, you can review its organization. Answer another set of questions:

- Are all the points covered in the most logical order?
- Do the most important ideas receive the most space, and are they placed in the most prominent positions?
- Would the message be more convincing if it were arranged in a different sequence?
- Are any points repeated unnecessarily?
- Are details grouped together logically, or are some still scattered through the document?

Next, consider whether you have achieved the right tone for your audience. Is your writing formal enough to meet the audience's expectations without being too formal or academic? Is it too casual for a serious subject?

Spend a few extra moments on the beginning and end of your message; these sections usually have the greatest impact on the audience. Be sure that the opening is relevant, interesting, and geared to the reader's probable reaction. In longer messages, ensure that the first few paragraphs establish the subject, purpose, and organization of the material. Review the conclusion to be sure that it summarizes the main idea and leaves the audience with a positive impression.

EVALUATING, EDITING, AND REVISING THE WORK OF OTHERS

When you evaluate, edit, or revise someone else's work, remember that your job is to help that person succeed, not to impose your own style.

At many points in your career, you will be asked to evaluate, edit, or revise the work of others. Whether you're suggesting improvements or actually making the improvements yourself (as you might on a wiki site, for example), you can make a contribution by using all the skills you are learning.

Before you dive into someone else's work, recognize the dual responsibility that doing so entails. First, unless you've been specifically asked to rewrite something in your own style or to change the emphasis of the message, remember that your job is to help the other writer succeed at his or her task, not to impose your writing style or pursue your own agenda. In other words, make sure your input focuses on making the piece more effective, not on making it more like something you would've written. Second, make sure you understand the writer's intent before you begin suggesting or making changes. If you try to edit or revise without knowing what the writer hoped to accomplish, you run the risk of making the piece less effective, not more. With those thoughts in mind, answer the following questions as you evaluate someone else's writing:

- What is the purpose of this document or message?
- Who is the target audience?
- What information does the audience need?
- Does the document provide this information in a well-organized way?
- Does the writing demonstrate the "you" attitude toward the audience?
- Is the tone of the writing appropriate for the audience?
- Can the readability be improved?
- Is the writing clear? If not, how can it be improved?
- Is the writing as concise as it could be?
- Does the design support the intended message?

2 LEARNING OBJECTIVE
List four techniques you can use to improve the readability of your messages.

Revising to Improve Readability

After confirming the content, organization, style, and tone of your message, make a second pass to improve *readability*. Most professionals are inundated with more reading material than they can ever hope to consume, and they'll appreciate your efforts to make your documents easier to read. You'll benefit from this effort, too: If you earn a reputation for creating well-crafted documents that respect the audience's time, people will pay more attention to your work.

You may be familiar with one of the many indexes that have been developed over the years in an attempt to measure readability. For example, the Flesch-Kincaid Grade Level score computes reading difficulty relative to grade-level achievement, with, for instance, a score of 10 suggesting that a document can be read and understood by the average 10th grader. Most business documents score in the 8–11 range. Technical documents often score in the 12–14 range. A similar scoring system, the Flesch Reading Ease score, ranks documents on a 100-point scale; the higher the score, the easier the document is to read. If these measurements aren't built into your word processing software, you can find a number of calculators for various indexes online.

Readability indexes offer a useful reference point, but they are limited by what they are able to measure: word length, number of syllables, sentence length, and paragraph length. They can't measure any of the other factors that affect readability, such as document design, the "you" attitude, clear sentence structure, smooth transitions, and proper word usage. Compare these two paragraphs:

> Readability indexes offer a useful reference point, but they are all limited by what they are able to measure: word length, number of syllables, sentence length, and paragraph length. They can't measure any of the other factors that affect readability, from "you" orientation to writing clarity to document design.

> Readability indexes can help. But they don't measure everything. They don't measure whether your writing clarity is good. They don't measure whether your document design is good or not. Reading indexes are based on word length, syllables, sentences, and paragraphs.

The second paragraph scores much better on both grade level and reading ease, but it is choppy, unsophisticated, and poorly organized. As a general rule, then, don't assume that a piece of text is readable if it scores well on a readability index—or that it is difficult to read if it doesn't score well.

Beyond using shorter words and simpler sentences, you can improve the readability of a message by making the document interesting and easy to skim. Most business audiences—particularly influential senior managers—tend to skim documents, looking for key ideas, conclusions, and recommendations. If they determine that a document contains valuable information or requires a response, they will read it more carefully when time permits. Four techniques will make your message easier to read and easier to skim: varying sentence length, using shorter paragraphs, using lists and bullets instead of narrative, and adding effective headings and subheadings.

VARYING YOUR SENTENCE LENGTH

Varying the length of your sentences is a creative way to make your messages interesting and readable. By choosing words and sentence structure with care, you can create a rhythm that emphasizes important points, enlivens your writing style, and makes information more appealing to your reader. For example, a short sentence that highlights a conclusion at the end of a substantial paragraph of evidence makes your key message stand out. Try for a mixture of sentences that are short (up to 15 words or so), medium (15–25 words), and long (more than 25 words).

Each sentence length has its advantages. Short sentences can be processed quickly and are easier for nonnative speakers and translators to interpret. Medium-length sentences are useful for showing the relationships among ideas. Long sentences are often the best for conveying complex ideas, listing multiple related points, or summarizing or previewing information.

Of course, each sentence length also has disadvantages. Too many short sentences in a row can make your writing choppy. Medium sentences can lack the punch of short sentences and the informative power of longer sentences. Long sentences can be difficult to understand because they contain more information and usually have a more complicated structure. Because readers can absorb only a few words per glance, longer sentences are also more difficult to skim. By choosing the best sentence length for each communication need and remembering to mix sentence lengths for variety, you'll get your points across while keeping your messages lively and interesting.

To keep readers' interest, look for ways to combine a variety of short, medium, and long sentences.

KEEPING YOUR PARAGRAPHS SHORT

Large blocks of text can be visually daunting, particularly on screen, so the optimum paragraph length is short to medium in most cases. Unless you break up your thoughts somehow, you'll end up with lengthy paragraphs that are guaranteed to intimidate

Short paragraphs have the major advantage of being easy to read.

even the most dedicated reader. Short paragraphs, generally 100 words or fewer (this paragraph has 84 words), are easier to read than long ones, and they make your writing look inviting. You can also emphasize ideas by isolating them in short, forceful paragraphs.

However, don't go overboard with short paragraphs. In particular, be careful to use one-sentence paragraphs only occasionally and only for emphasis. Also, if you need to divide a subject into several pieces to keep paragraphs short, be sure to help your readers keep the ideas connected by guiding them with plenty of transitional elements.

USING LISTS TO CLARIFY AND EMPHASIZE

Lists are effective tools for highlighting and simplifying material.

An effective alternative to using conventional sentences is to set off important ideas in a list—a series of words, names, or other items. Lists can show the sequence of your ideas, heighten their impact visually, and increase the likelihood that a reader will find key points. In addition, lists help simplify complex subjects, highlight main points, break up a page or screen visually, ease the skimming process for busy readers, and give readers a breather. Compare these two treatments of the same information:

Narrative	List
Owning your own business has many potential advantages. One is the opportunity to pursue your own personal passion. Another advantage is the satisfaction of working for yourself. As a sole proprietor, you also have the advantage of privacy because you do not have to reveal your financial information or plans to anyone.	Owning your own business has three advantages: • Opportunity to pursue personal passion • Satisfaction of working for yourself • Financial privacy

You can separate list items with numbers, letters, or bullets (a general term for any kind of graphical element that precedes each item). Bullets are generally preferred over numbers, unless the list is in some logical sequence or ranking or you need to refer to specific list items elsewhere in the document.

Lists are easier to locate and read if the entire numbered or bulleted section is set off by a blank line before and after, as the preceding examples demonstrate. Furthermore, make sure to introduce lists clearly so that people know what they're about to read. One way to introduce lists is to make them a part of the introductory sentence:

The board of directors met to discuss the revised annual budget. To keep expenses in line with declining sales, the directors voted to

- Cut everyone's salary by 10 percent
- Close the employee cafeteria
- Reduce travel expenses

Another way to introduce a list is to precede it with a complete introductory sentence, followed by a colon:

The decline in company profit is attributable to four factors:

- Slower holiday sales
- Increased transportation and fuel costs
- Higher employee wages
- Slower inventory turnover

Method	Example
TABLE 1	**Achieving Parallelism**
Parallel words	The letter was approved by Clausen, Whittaker, Merlin, and Carlucci.
Parallel phrases	We are gaining market share in supermarkets, in department stores, and in specialty stores.
Parallel clauses	I'd like to discuss the issue after Vicki gives her presentation but before Marvin shows his slides.
Parallel sentences	In 2014 we exported 30 percent of our production. In 2015 we exported 50 percent.

Regardless of the format you choose, the items in a list should be parallel; that is, they should all use the same grammatical pattern. For example, if one list item begins with a verb, every item should begin with a verb. If one item is a noun phrase, every one should be a noun phrase:

Nonparallel List Items (a mix of verb and noun phrases)

- Improve our bottom line
- Identification of new foreign markets for our products
- Global market strategies
- Issues regarding pricing and packaging size

Parallel List Items (all verb phrases)

- Improving our bottom line
- Identifying new foreign markets for our products
- Developing our global market strategies
- Resolving pricing and packaging issues

Parallel forms are easier to read and skim. You can create parallelism by repeating the pattern in words, phrases, clauses, or entire sentences (see Table 1).

ADDING HEADINGS AND SUBHEADINGS

A **heading** is a brief title that tells readers about the content of the section that follows. **Subheadings** are subordinate to headings, indicating subsections with a major section. Headings and subheadings serve these important functions:

Use headings to grab the reader's attention and organize material into short sections.

- **Organization.** Headings show your reader at a glance how the document is organized. They act as labels to group related paragraphs and organize lengthy material into shorter sections.
- **Attention.** Informative, inviting, and in some cases intriguing headings grab the reader's attention, make the text easier to read, and help the reader find the parts he or she needs to read—or skip.
- **Connection.** Using headings and subheadings together helps readers see the relationship between main ideas and subordinate ones so that they can understand your message more easily. Moreover, headings and subheadings visually indicate shifts from one idea to the next.

Headings and subheadings fall into two categories. **Descriptive headings**, such as "Cost Considerations," identify a topic but do little more. **Informative headings**, such as "Redesigning Material Flow to Cut Production Costs," guide readers to think in a certain way about the topic. They are also helpful in guiding your work as a writer, especially if cast as questions you plan to address in your document. Well-written informative headings are self-contained, which means readers can read just the headings and subheadings and understand them without reading the rest of the document. For example, "Introduction" conveys little information, whereas the heading "Staffing Shortages Cost the Company $150,000 Last Year" provides a key piece of information and captures the reader's attention. Whatever types of headings you choose, keep them brief and use parallel construction throughout the document.

Informative headings are generally more helpful than descriptive ones.

Editing for Clarity and Conciseness

After you've reviewed and revised your message for readability, your next step is to make sure your message is as clear and as concise as possible.

EDITING FOR CLARITY

Clarity is essential to getting your message across accurately and efficiently.

Make sure every sentence conveys the message you intend and that readers can extract that meaning without needing to read it more than once. To ensure clarity, look closely at your paragraph organization, sentence structure, and word choices. Can readers make sense of the related sentences in a paragraph? Is the meaning of each sentence easy to grasp? Is each word clear and unambiguous (meaning it doesn't have any risk of being interpreted in more than one way)?

See Table 2 for examples of the following tips:

- **Break up overly long sentences.** If you find yourself stuck in a long sentence, you're probably trying to make the sentence do more than it can reasonably do, such

TABLE 2   Revising for Clarity

Issues to Review	Ineffective	Effective
Overly Long Sentences Taking compound sentences too far	The magazine will be published January 1, and I'd better meet the deadline if I want my article included because we want the article to appear before the trade show.	The magazine will be published January 1. I'd better meet the deadline because we want the article to appear before the trade show.
Hedging Sentences Overqualifying sentences	I believe that Mr. Johnson's employment record seems to show that he may be capable of handling the position.	Mr. Johnson's employment record shows that he is capable of handling the position.
Unparallel Sentences Using dissimilar construction for similar ideas	Mr. Simms had been drenched with rain, bombarded with telephone calls, and his boss shouted at him. To waste time and missing deadlines are bad habits.	Mr. Sims had been drenched with rain, bombarded with telephone calls, and shouted at by his boss. Wasting time and missing deadlines are bad habits.
Dangling Modifiers Placing modifiers close to the wrong nouns and verbs	Walking to the office, a red sports car passed her. [suggests that the car was walking to the office] Reduced by 25 percent, Europe had its lowest semiconductor output in a decade. [suggests that Europe shrank by 25 percent]	A red sports car passed her while she was walking to the office. Europe reduced semiconductor output by 25 percent, its lowest output in a decade.
Long Noun Sequences Stringing too many nouns together	The window sash installation company will give us an estimate on Friday.	The company that installs window sashes will give us an estimate on Friday.
Camouflaged Verbs Changing verbs into nouns	The manager undertook implementation of the rules. Verification of the shipments occurs weekly. reach a conclusion about give consideration to	The manager implemented the rules. We verify shipment weekly. conclude consider
Sentence Structure Separating subject and predicate	A 10% decline in market share, which resulted from quality problems and an aggressive sales campaign by Armitage, the market leader in the Northeast, was the major problem in 2010.	The major problem in 2010 was a 10% loss of market share, which resulted from quality problems and an aggressive sales campaign by Armitage, the market leader in the Northeast.
Separating adjectives, adverbs, or prepositional phrases from the words they modify	Our antique desk lends an air of strength and substance with thick legs and large drawers.	With its thick legs and large drawers, our antique desk lends an air of strength and substance.
Awkward References	The Law Office and the Accounting Office distribute computer supplies for legal secretaries and beginning accountants, respectively.	The Law Office distributes computer supplies for legal secretaries; the Accounting Office distributes those for beginning accountants.

as expressing two dissimilar thoughts or peppering the reader with too many pieces of supporting evidence at once. (Did you notice how difficult this long sentence was to read?)

- **Rewrite hedging sentences.** *Hedging* means pulling back from making a confident, definitive statement about a topic. Granted, sometimes you have to write *may* or *seems* to avoid stating a judgment or prediction as a fact. However, when you hedge too often or without good reason, you come across as being unsure of what you're saying.

    Hedging is appropriate when you can't be absolutely sure of a statement, but excessive hedging undermines your authority.

- **Impose parallelism.** When you have two or more similar ideas to express, make them parallel by using the same grammatical construction. Parallelism shows that the ideas are related, of similar importance, and on the same level of generality.

    When you use parallel grammatical patterns to express two or more ideas, you show that they are comparable thoughts.

- **Correct dangling modifiers.** Sometimes a modifier is not just an adjective or an adverb but an entire phrase modifying a noun or a verb. Be careful not to leave this type of modifier *dangling*, with no connection to the subject of the sentence.

- **Reword long noun sequences.** When multiple nouns are strung together as modifiers, the resulting sentence can be hard to read. See if a single well-chosen word will do the job. If the nouns are all necessary, consider moving one or more to a modifying phrase, as shown in Table 2.

- **Replace camouflaged verbs.** Watch for words that end in *-ion*, *-tion*, *-ing*, *-ment*, *-ant*, *-ent*, *-ence*, *-ance*, and *-ency*. These endings often change verbs into nouns and adjectives, requiring you to add a verb to get your point across.

    Subject and predicate should be placed as close together as possible, as should modifiers and the words they modify.

- **Clarify sentence structure.** Keep the subject and predicate of a sentence as close together as possible. When the subject and predicate are far apart, readers may need

---

Help! I'm Drowning in Social Media!

Anyone who has sampled today's social media offerings has probably experienced this situation: You find a few fascinating blogs, a few interesting people to follow on Twitter, a couple of podcast channels with helpful business tips, and then *wham*—within a few hours of signing up, your computer is overflowing with updates. Even if every new item is useful (which is unlikely), you receive so many that you can't stay ahead of the incoming flood. With Twitter, newsfeeds, email, instant messaging, and social networks—not to mention a desk phone and a mobile phone—today's business professionals could easily spend their entire days just trying to keep up with incoming messages and never get any work done.

To keep social media from turning into a source of stress and information anxiety, consider these tips:

- **Understand what information you really need in order to excel in your current projects and along your intended career path.** Unfortunately, taking this advice is even trickier than it sounds because you can't always know what you need to know, so you can't always predict which sources will be helpful. However, don't gather information simply because it is interesting or entertaining; collect information that is useful or at least potentially useful.

- **Face the fact that you cannot possibly handle every update from every potentially interesting and helpful source.** You have to set priorities and make tough choices to protect yourself from information overload.

- **Add new information sources slowly.** Give yourself a chance to adjust to the flow and judge the usefulness of each new source.

- **Prune your sources vigorously and frequently.** Bloggers run out of things to say; your needs and interests change; higher-priority sources appear.

- **Remember that information is an enabler, a means to an end.** Collecting vast amounts of information won't get you a sweet promotion with a big raise. *Using* information creatively and intelligently will.

CAREER APPLICATIONS

1. How can you determine whether a social media source is worth paying attention to?

2. Should you allow any information source to interrupt your work flow during the day (even just to signal that a new message is available)? Why or why not?

to read the sentence twice to figure out who did what. Similarly, adjectives, adverbs, and prepositional phrases usually make the most sense when they're placed as close as possible to the words they modify.

- **Clarify awkward references.** If you want readers to refer to a specific point in a document, avoid vague references such as the *above-mentioned, as mentioned above, the aforementioned, the former, the latter,* and *respectively.*

EDITING FOR CONCISENESS

Many of the changes you make to improve clarity also shorten your message by removing unnecessary words. The next step is to examine the text with the specific goal of reducing the number of words. Readers appreciate conciseness and are more likely to read your documents if you have a reputation for efficient writing. See Table 3 for examples of the following tips:

Make your documents tighter by removing unnecessary words, phrases, and sentences.

- **Delete unnecessary words and phrases.** To test whether a word or phrase is essential, try the sentence without it. If the meaning doesn't change, leave it out.
- **Shorten long words and phrases.** Short words and phrases are generally more vivid and easier to read than long ones. Also, by using infinitives (the "to" form of a verb) in place of some phrases, you can often shorten sentences while making them clearer.
- **Eliminate redundancies.** In some word combinations, the words say the same thing. For instance, "visible to the eye" is redundant because *visible* is enough without further clarification; "to the eye" adds nothing.
- **Rewrite "It is/There are" starters.** If you start a sentence with an indefinite pronoun such as *it* or *there,* chances are the sentence could be shorter and more active. For instance, "We believe..." is a stronger opening than "It is believed that..." because it is shorter and because it identifies who is doing the believing.

As you rewrite, concentrate on how each word contributes to an effective sentence and on how each sentence helps build a coherent paragraph. For a reminder of the tasks involved in revision, see "Checklist: Revising Business Messages."

CHECKLIST ✔ Revising Business Messages

A. Evaluate content, organization, style, and tone.
- Make sure the information is accurate, relevant, and sufficient.
- Check that all necessary points appear in logical order.
- Verify that you present enough support to make the main idea convincing and compelling.
- Be sure the beginning and ending of the message are effective.
- Make sure you've achieved the right tone for the audience and the situation.

B. Review for readability.
- Consider using a readability index, but be sure to interpret the answer carefully.
- Use a mix of short, medium, and long sentences.
- Keep paragraphs short.

- Use bulleted and numbered lists to emphasize key points.
- Make the document easy to skim with headings and subheadings.

C. Edit for clarity.
- Break up overly long sentences and rewrite hedging sentences.
- Impose parallelism to simplify reading.
- Correct dangling modifiers.
- Reword long noun sequences and replace camouflaged verbs.
- Clarify sentence structure and awkward references.

D. Edit for conciseness.
- Delete unnecessary words and phrases.
- Shorten long words and phrases.
- Eliminate redundancies.
- Rewrite sentences that start with "It is" or "There are."

Completing Business Messages

TABLE 3 Revising for Conciseness

Issues to Review	Ineffective	Effective
Unnecessary Words and Phrases		
Using wordy phrases	for the sum of	for
	in the event that	if
	prior to the start of	before
	in the near future	soon
	at this point in time	now
	due to the fact that	because
	in view of the fact that	because
	until such time as	when
	with reference to	about
Using too many relative pronouns	Cars that are sold after January will not have a six-month warranty.	Cars sold after January will not have a six-month warranty.
	Employees who are driving to work should park in the underground garage.	Employees driving to work should park in the underground garage. OR Employees should park in the underground garage.
Using too few relative pronouns	The project manager told the engineers last week the specifications were changed.	The project manager told the engineers last week that the specifications were changed. The project manager told the engineers that last week the specifications were changed.
Long Words and Phrases		
Using overly long words	During the preceding year, the company accelerated productive operations.	Last year the company sped up operations.
	The action was predicated on the assumption that the company was operating at a financial deficit.	The action was based on the belief that the company was losing money.
Using wordy phrases rather than infinitives	If you want success as a writer, you must work hard.	To succeed as a writer, you must work hard.
	He went to the library for the purpose of studying.	He went to the library to study.
	The employer increased salaries so that she could improve morale.	The employer increased salaries to improve morale.
Redundancies		
Repeating meanings	absolutely complete	complete
	basic fundamentals	fundamentals
	follows after	follows
	free and clear	free
	refer back	refer
	repeat again	repeat
	collect together	collect
	future plans	plans
	return back	return
	important essentials	essentials
	end result	result
	actual truth	truth
	final outcome	outcome
	uniquely unusual	unique
	surrounded on all sides	surrounded
Using double modifiers	modern, up-to-date equipment	modern equipment
It Is/There Are Starters	It would be appreciated if you would sign the lease today.	Please sign the lease today.
Starting sentences with _It_ or _There_	There are five employees in this division who were late to work today.	Five employees in this division were late to work today.

Producing Your Message

Now it's time to put your hard work on display. The *production quality* of your message—the total effect of page or screen design, graphical elements, typography, and so on—plays an important role in the effectiveness of your message. A polished, inviting design not only makes your material easier to read but also conveys a sense of professionalism and importance.[2]

DESIGNING FOR READABILITY

Design affects readability in two important ways. First, if used carefully, design elements can improve the effectiveness of your message. In contrast, poor design decisions, such as using distracting background images behind text, pointless animations, or tiny typefaces, act as barriers to communication. Second, the visual design sends a nonverbal message to your readers, influencing their perceptions of the communication before they read a single word.

Effective design helps you establish the tone of your document and helps guide your readers through your message (see Figure 3). To achieve an effective design, pay careful attention to the following design elements:

- **Consistency.** Throughout each message, be consistent in your use of margins, typeface, type size, and space. Also be consistent when using recurring design elements, such as vertical lines, columns, and borders. In many cases, you'll want to be consistent from message to message as well; that way, audiences who receive multiple messages from you recognize your documents and know what to expect.
- **Balance.** Balance is an important but subjective issue. One document may have a formal, rigid design in which the various elements are placed in a grid pattern, whereas another may have a less formal design in which elements flow more freely across the page—and both could be in balance. Like the tone of your language, visual balance can be too formal, just right, or too informal for a given message.
- **Restraint.** Strive for simplicity in design. Don't clutter your message with too many design elements, too many typeface treatments, too many colors, or too many decorative touches. Let "simpler" and "fewer" be your guiding concepts.
- **Detail.** Pay attention to details that affect your design and thus your message. For instance, extremely wide columns of text can be difficult to read; in many cases a better solution is to split the text into two narrower columns.

Even without special training in graphic design, you can make your printed and electronic messages more effective by understanding the use of white space, margins and line justification, typefaces, and type styles.

White Space

Any space that doesn't contain text or artwork, both in print and online, is considered **white space**. (Note that "white space" isn't necessarily white; it is simply blank.) These unused areas provide visual contrast and important resting points for your readers. White space includes the open area surrounding headings, margins, paragraph indents, space around images, vertical space between columns, and horizontal space between paragraphs or lines of text. To increase the chance that readers will read your messages, be generous with white space; it makes pages and screens feel less intimidating and easier to read.[3]

Margins and Justification

Margins define the space around text and between text columns. In addition to their width, the look and feel of margins is influenced by the way you arrange lines of text, which can be set (1) *justified* (which means they are *flush*, or aligned vertically, on both the left and the right), (2) flush left with a *ragged-right* margin, (3) flush right with a *ragged-left* margin, or (4) centered. This paragraph is justified, whereas the paragraphs in Figure 2 are flush left with a ragged-right margin.

The quality of your document design, both on paper and on screen, affects readability and audience perceptions.

Good design enhances the readability of your material.

For effective design, pay attention to
- Consistency
- Balance
- Restraint
- Detail

White space separates elements in a document and helps guide the reader's eye.

Most business documents use a flush left margin and a ragged right margin.

The layout is *statically balanced*, with equal visual weight on either side of the vertical centerline.

The picture of the anvil (a device used by blacksmiths to shape pieces of iron) plays off the company name and provides visual interest without overwhelming the page.

These three concise labels are the "subheadings" of the website, directing readers to each of the major sections of content.

These introductory paragraphs offer succinct summaries of the three content areas. The centered paragraphs promote the look of calm balance, and in these small sections the centered text is easy to read.

When a reader clicks on any of the three sections above, this area presents the next level of detail.

Readers can "drill down" through layers of information without getting overwhelmed by large amounts of text or distracting visual elements.

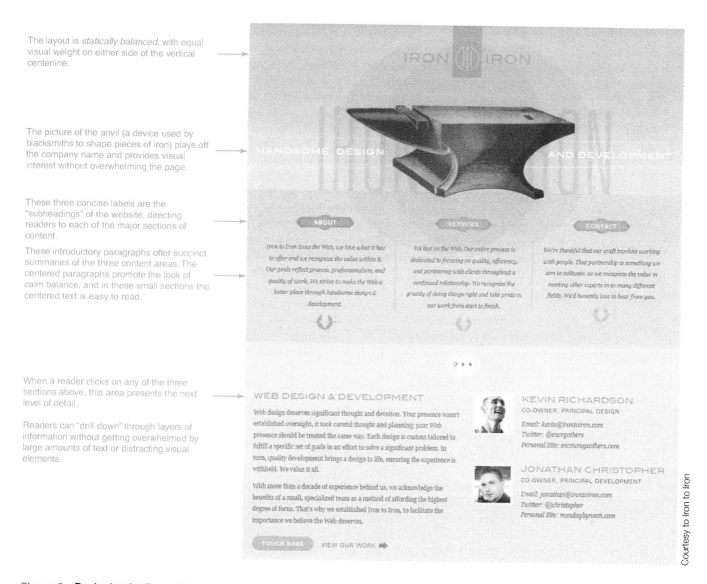

Courtesy to Iron to Iron

Figure 3   Designing for Readability
The website of the web development firm Iron to Iron is a model of elegant design that promotes easy reading.

Magazines, newspapers, and books often use justified type because it can accommodate more text in a given space. However, justified type needs to be used with care. First, it creates a denser look because the uniform line lengths decrease the amount of white space along the right margin. Second, it produces a more formal and less personalized look. Third, unless it is used with some skill and attention, justified type can be more difficult to read because it can produce large gaps between words and excessive hyphenation at the ends of lines. The publishing specialists who create magazines, newspapers, and books have the time and skill needed to carefully adjust character and word spacing to eliminate these problems. (In some cases, sentences are even rewritten in order to improve the appearance of the printed page.) Because most business communicators don't have that time or skill, it's best to avoid justified type in routine business documents.

In contrast to justified type, flush-left, ragged-right type creates a more open appearance on the page, producing a less formal and more contemporary look. Spacing between words is consistent, and only long words that fall at the ends of lines are hyphenated.

Centered type is rarely used for text paragraphs but is commonly used for headings and subheadings. Flush-right, ragged-left type is rarely used in business documents.

Typefaces

The classic style of document design uses a sans serif typeface for headings and a serif typeface for regular paragraph text; however, many contemporary documents and webpages now use all sans serif.

Typeface refers to the physical design of letters, numbers, and other text characters. (*Font* and *typeface* are often used interchangeably, although strictly speaking, a font is a set of characters in a given typeface.) Typeface influences the tone of your message, making it look authoritative or friendly, businesslike or casual, classic or modern, and so on (see Table 4). Be sure to choose fonts that are appropriate for your message; many of the fonts on your computer are not appropriate for business use.

Serif typefaces have small crosslines (called serifs) at the ends of each letter stroke. **Sans serif typefaces**, in contrast, lack these serifs. For years, the conventional wisdom in typography was that serif faces were easier to read in long blocks of text, because the serifs made it easier for the eye to pick out individual letters. Accordingly, the standard advice was to use serif faces for the body of a document and sans serif for headings and subheadings.

However, the research behind the conventional wisdom is not as conclusive as once thought.[4] In fact, many sans serif typefaces work as well or better for body text than some serif typefaces. This seems to be particularly true on screens, which often have lower resolution than printed text. Many contemporary documents and webpages now use sans serif for body text.

REAL-TIME UPDATES

LEARN MORE BY READING THIS ARTICLE

Improve your document designs by learning the fundamentals of typography

Knowing the basics of type usage will help you create more effective page and screen layouts. Go to http://real-timeupdates .com/ebc12 and click on Learn More in the Students section.

For most documents, you shouldn't need more than two typefaces, although if you want to make captions or other text elements stand out, you can use another font.[5] Using more typefaces can clutter a document and produce an amateurish look.

Type Styles

Avoid using any type style that inhibits your audience's ability to read your messages.

Type style refers to any modification that lends contrast or emphasis to type, including boldface, italic, underlining, color, and other highlighting and decorative styles. Using boldface type for subheads breaks up long expanses of text. You can also boldface individual words or phrases to draw more attention to them. For example, the key terms in this chapter are set in bold. Italic type also creates emphasis, although not as pronounced as boldface. Italic type has specific uses as well, such as highlighting quotations and indicating foreign words, irony, humor, book and movie titles, and unconventional usage.

As a general rule, avoid using any style in a way that slows your audience's progress through the message. For instance, underlining or using all-uppercase letters can interfere with a reader's ability to recognize the shapes of words, and shadowed or outlined type can seriously hinder legibility. Also, avoid overusing any type style. For example, putting too many words in boldface dilutes the impact of the special treatment by creating too many focal points in the paragraph.

TABLE 4 Typeface Personalities: Serious to Casual to Playful		
Serif Typefaces	**Sans Serif Typefaces**	**Specialty Typefaces (rarely used for routine business communication)**
Bookman Old Style	Arial	Bauhaus
Century Schoolbook	Calibri	Broadway
Courier	Eras Bold	Harrington
Garamond	Franklin Gothic Book	Zapfino
Georgia	Gill Sans	Magneto
Times New Roman	Verdana	STENCIL

Type size is an important consideration as well. For most printed business messages, use a size of 10 to 12 points for regular text and 12 to 18 points for headings and subheadings (1 point is approximately 1/72 inch). Resist the temptation to reduce type size too much in order to squeeze in extra text or to enlarge it to fill up space. Type that is too small is hard to read, whereas extra-large type looks unprofessional. Be particularly careful with small type online. Small type that looks fine on a medium-resolution screen can be hard to read on both low-resolution screens (because these displays can make letters look jagged or fuzzy) and high-resolution screens (because these monitors reduce the apparent size of the type even further).

REAL-TIME UPDATES

LEARN MORE BY VISITING THIS WEBSITE

See the newest designs from some of the brightest minds in typography

Type design is a fascinating and dynamic field; this portfolio shows dozens of innovative new typefaces. Go to http://real-timeupdates.com/ebc12 and click on Learn More in the Students section.

FORMATTING FORMAL LETTERS AND MEMOS

Formal business letters usually follow certain design conventions, as the letter in Figure 2 illustrates. Most business letters are printed on *letterhead stationery*, which includes the company's name, address, and other contact information. The first element to appear after the letterhead is the date, followed by the inside address, which identifies the person receiving the letter. Next is the salutation, usually in the form of *Dear Mr. or Ms. Last Name*. The message comes next, followed by the complimentary close, usually *Sincerely* or *Cordially*. And last comes the signature block: space for the signature, followed by the sender's printed name and title. Your company will probably have a standard format to follow for letters, possibly along with a template in Microsoft Word or whatever word processor is standard in the organization.

Like letters, business memos usually follow a preset design. Memos have largely been replaced by electronic media in many companies, but if they are still in use at the firm you join, the company may have a standard format or template for you to use. Most memos begin with a title such as *Memo, Memorandum,* or *Interoffice Correspondence.* Following that are usually four headings: *Date, To, From,* and *Subject.* (*Re:,* short for *Regarding,* is sometimes used instead of *Subject.*) Memos usually don't use a salutation, complimentary close, or signature, although signing your initials next to your name on the *From* line is standard practice in most companies. Bear in mind that memos are often distributed without sealed envelopes, so they are less private than most other message formats.

DESIGNING MESSAGES FOR MOBILE DEVICES

You can follow these steps to format that content for mobile devices:

- **Think in small chunks.** Remember that mobile users consume information one screen at a time, so try to divide your message into independent, easy-to-consume bites. If readers have to scroll through a dozen screens to piece together your message, they might miss your point or just give up entirely.
- **Make generous use of white space.** White space is always helpful, but it's critical on small screens because readers are trying to get the point of every message as quickly as possible. Keep your paragraphs short (4–6 lines), and separate them with blank lines so the reader's eyes can easily jump from one point to the next.[6]
- **Format simply.** Avoid anything that is likely to get in the way of fast, easy reading, including busy typefaces, complex graphics, and complicated layouts.
- **Consider horizontal and vertical layouts.** Most phones and tablets can automatically rotate their screen content from horizontal to vertical as the user rotates the device. A layout that doesn't work well with the narrow vertical perspective might be acceptable at the wider horizontal perspective.

Compare the two messages in Figure 4 on the next page; notice how much more difficult the screen in Figure 4a is to read.

Figure 4   Designing Messages for Mobile Devices
Even simple changes such as revising with shorter paragraphs, choosing cleaner typefaces, and making generous use of white space in and around the text can dramatically improve readability on mobile screens.
Source: MS Office Word 2013, © Microsoft.

5   LEARNING OBJECTIVE
Explain the importance of proofreading, and give eight tips for successful proofreading.

Your credibility is affected by your attention to the details of mechanics and form.

The types of details to look for when proofreading include language errors, missing material, design errors, and typographical errors.

MOBILE APP

NounPlus puts a grammar checker, spell checker, and pronunciation guide on your phone, so you're never without tips and advice.

Proofreading Your Message

Proofreading is the quality inspection stage for your documents, your last chance to make sure that your document is ready to carry your message—and your reputation—to the intended audience. Even a small mistake can doom your efforts, so take proofreading seriously.

Look for two types of problems: (1) undetected mistakes from the writing, design, and layout stages and (2) mistakes that crept in during production. Brush up on writing basics with the Handbook of Grammar, Mechanics, and Usage at the end of this text. The second category can include anything from computer glitches such as missing fonts to broken web links to problems with the ink used in printing. Be particularly vigilant with complex documents and complex production processes that involve multiple colleagues and multiple computers. Strange things can happen as files move from computer to computer, especially when lots of fonts and multimedia elements are involved.

Resist the temptation to treat proofreading as a casual scan up and down the page or screen. Instead, approach it as a methodical procedure in which you look for specific problems that may occur. Use these techniques from professional proofreaders to help ensure high-quality output:

- **Make multiple passes.** Go through the document several times, focusing on a different aspect each time. For instance, look for content errors the first time and layout errors the second time.
- **Use perceptual tricks.** You've probably experienced the frustration of reading over something a dozen times and still missing an obvious error. This happens because your brain has developed a wonderful skill of subconsciously supplying missing

---

CHECKLIST ✔ Proofing Business Messages

A. Look for writing errors.
- Typographical mistakes
- Misspelled words
- Grammatical errors
- Punctuation mistakes

B. Look for missing elements.
- Missing text sections
- Missing exhibits (drawings, tables, photographs, charts, graphs, online images, and so on)
- Missing source notes, copyright notices, or other reference items

C. Look for design, formatting, and programming mistakes.
- Incorrect or inconsistent font selections
- Problems with column sizing, spacing, and alignment
- Incorrect margins
- Incorrect special characters
- Clumsy line and page breaks
- Problems with page numbers
- Problems with page headers and footers
- Lack of adherence to company standards
- Inactive or incorrect links
- Missing files

---

pieces and correcting mistakes when it knows what is *supposed* to be on the page. To keep your brain from tricking you, you need to trick it by changing the way you process the visual information. Try (1) reading each page backward, from the bottom to the top, (2) placing your finger under each word and reading it silently, (3) making a slit in a sheet of paper that reveals only one line of type at a time, and (4) reading the document aloud and pronouncing each word carefully.

- **Double-check high-priority items.** Double-check the spelling of names and the accuracy of dates, addresses, and any number that could cause grief if incorrect (such as telling a potential employer that you'd be happy to work for $5,000 a year when you meant to say $50,000).
- **Give yourself some distance.** If possible, don't proofread immediately after finishing a document; let your mind wander off to new topics and then come back fresh later on.
- **Be vigilant.** Avoid reading large amounts of material in one sitting and try not to proofread when you're tired.
- **Stay focused.** Concentrate on what you're doing. Try to block out distractions and focus as completely as possible on your proofreading task.
- **Review complex electronic documents on paper.** Some people have trouble proofreading webpages, online reports, and other electronic documents on screen. If you have trouble, try to print the materials so you can review them on paper.
- **Take your time.** Quick proofreading is not careful proofreading.

The amount of time you need to spend on proofing depends on the length and complexity of the document and the situation. A typo in an email message to your team may not be a big deal, but a typo in a financial report, a contract, or a medical file certainly could be serious. See "Checklist: Proofing Business Messages" for a handy list of items to review during proofing.

REAL-TIME UPDATES

LEARN MORE BY LISTENING TO THIS PODCAST

Tips for proofing your papers

This advice for class assignments will help you on the job, too. Go to http://real-timeupdates.com/bce7 and click on Learn More in the Students section.

Distributing Your Message

With the production finished, you're ready to distribute your message. As with every other aspect of business communication, your options for distribution multiply with every advance in technology. In some cases, the choice is obvious: Just click the Send button in your email program or the *Publish* button on your blog. In other cases, such as when you have a 100-page report with full-color graphics or a massive multimedia file, you need to plan the distribution carefully so that your message is received by

6 LEARNING OBJECTIVE
Discuss the most important issues to consider when distributing your messages.

Completing Business Messages

everyone who needs it. When choosing a means to distribute messages, consider the following factors:

Consider cost, convenience, time, security, and privacy when choosing a distribution method.

- **Cost.** Cost isn't a concern for most messages, but for lengthy reports or multimedia productions, it may well be. Printing, binding, and delivering reports can be expensive, so weigh the cost versus the benefits. Be sure to consider the nonverbal message you send regarding cost as well. Overnight delivery of a printed report could look responsive in one situation but wasteful in another, for example.
- **Convenience.** How much work is involved for you and your audience? For instance, if you use a file-compression utility to shrink the size of email attachments, make sure your recipients have the means to expand the files on arrival. For extremely large files, consider recordable media such as DVDs or one of the many free or low-cost file-hosting sites now available.
- **Time.** How soon does the message need to reach the audience? Don't waste money on overnight delivery if the recipient won't read the report for a week. And speaking of time, don't mark any messages, printed or electronic, as "urgent" if they aren't truly urgent.
- **Security and privacy.** The convenience offered by electronic communication needs to be weighed against security and privacy concerns. For the most sensitive messages, your company will probably restrict both the people who can receive the messages and the means you can use to distribute them. In addition, most computer users are wary of opening attachments these days. Instead of sending word processor files, you can use Adobe Acrobat or an equivalent product to convert your documents to PDF files (which are more immune to viruses).

MOBILE APP

SignEasy solves the problem of signing digital documents such as contracts; you can sign right on your phone screen.

ON THE JOB: SOLVING COMMUNICATION DILEMMAS AT JEFFERSON RABB WEB DESIGN

Jefferson Rabb's web business is doing so well that he has hired you to help with a variety of writing and design tasks. Use what you've learned in this chapter about revising messages, designing for readability, and distributing messages to address the following challenges.[7]

1. You received some draft copy for an author website that contains the following rather long sentence:

   Alexander McCall Smith was born in what is now Zimbabwe and was educated there and in Scotland before becoming a law professor in Scotland and later returning to Africa to help set up a new law school at the University of Botswana.

   Which of these four alternatives does the best job of revising the material to improve its readability without losing any of the original information or introducing any new information?

   a. A native of what is now Zimbabwe, Alexander McCall Smith was educated in what is now Zimbabwe as well as Scotland. He became a law professor in Scotland and later returned to Africa to help set up a law school at the University of Botswana.
   b. Alexander McCall Smith was educated in Zimbabwe and Scotland, where he became a law professor. He

   later returned to Africa to help set up a law school at the University of Botswana.
   c. Returning to Africa to help set up a law school at the University of Botswana must've felt like a homecoming of sorts for Zimbabwe native Alexander McCall Smith, who was educated in both Zimbabwe and Scotland.
   d. Alexander McCall Smith was born in what is now Zimbabwe and was educated there and in Scotland. He became a law professor in Scotland and later returned to Africa to help set up a law school at the University of Botswana.

2. Like many popular authors, Anita Shreve offers guides that help reading groups or book groups explore and discuss her novels. A typical reading guide might contain a dozen or so questions that relate to events or themes from a novel. Groups can use these questions to structure their discussions of a novel. Which of the following navigational link titles would be the most effective to use on Shreve's website?
   a. Guides for Book Groups
   b. Reading Guides
   c. Discuss Shreve's Novels
   d. Explore Anita's Work

3. The following sentence appears on the website for Tom Vanderbilt's *Traffic*, a study of the technical and social

evolution of traffic and the never-ending attempts to making driving less dangerous and more efficient:

> Based on exhaustive research and interviews with driving experts and traffic officials around the globe, *Traffic* gets under the hood of the everyday activity of driving to uncover the surprisingly complex web of physical, psychological, and technical factors that explain how traffic works, why we drive the way we do, and what our driving says about us. [57 words]

Which of the following does the best job of reducing the length and complexity of this sentence without significantly altering its meaning?

a. *Traffic* explores the surprisingly complex web of physical, psychological, and technical factors that explain how traffic works, why we drive the way we do, and what our driving says about us. [31 words]

b. *Traffic* relies on extensive global research to explore the surprisingly complex web of physical, psychological, and technical factors that explain how traffic works, why we drive the way we do, and what our driving says about us. [37 words]

c. How traffic works, why we drive the way we do, and what our driving says about us—these are the questions addressed and answers in the exhaustively researched book *Traffic*. [30 words]

d. *Traffic* gets under the hood of the everyday activity of driving to uncover the surprisingly complex web of physical, psychological, and technical factors that explain how traffic works, why we drive the way we do, and what our driving says about us. [42words]

4. A number of authors reach out to their reader bases by offering to participate in book group discussions via Skype. If you wanted to get the word out that a new author was available to talk with book groups via Skype, which of the following distribution methods would you choose? (For this exercise, assume that you can choose only one of these.)

a. Posters in book stores

b. A message printed somewhere on the cover of the book

c. A Twitter update from the author

d. An update on the author's Facebook page

Learning Objectives Checkup

Assess your understanding of the principles in this chapter by reading each learning objective and study the accompanying exercises. You can check your responses against the answer key.

Objective 1: Discuss the value of careful revision and describe the tasks involved in evaluating your first drafts and the work of other writers.

1. Which of these is the most important reason you should take care to revise messages before sending them?
a. Revising shows your audience how hard you work.
b. Revising lowers the word count.
c. Revising makes it cheaper to email messages.
d. Revising can usually make your messages more successful.

2. Which of the following is not one of the main tasks involved in completing a business message?
a. Drafting the message
b. Revising the message
c. Producing the message
d. Proofreading the message

Objective 2: List four techniques you can use to improve the readability of your messages.

3. Regarding sentence length, the best approach for business messages is to
a. Keep all sentences as short as possible
b. Make most of your sentences long since you will usually have complex information to impart
c. Vary the length of your sentences
d. Aim for an average sentence length of 35 words

4. Regarding paragraph length, the best approach for business messages is to
a. Keep paragraphs short
b. Make most of your paragraphs long since that is standard practice in business writing
c. Make most of your paragraphs one sentence in length
d. Aim for an average paragraph length of 200 words

5. Regarding the use of lists, the best approach for business messages is to
a. Avoid using lists except where absolutely necessary
b. Make sure listed items are in parallel form
c. Use numbered lists rather than bulleted ones
d. Do all of the above

6. Which of the following is not an informative heading?
a. Why We Need a New Distributor
b. Five Challenges Facing Today's Distributors
c. Distributors Are a Better Choice for Us Than Wholesalers
d. Distributor Choices

Objective 3: Describe eight steps you can take to improve the clarity of your writing and give four tips on making your writing more concise.

7. Which of the following sentences contains hedging words?
a. It appears that we may have a problem completing the project by May 20.
b. There is a possibility that the project might be done by May 20.
c. It seems that the project could possibly miss its completion date of May 20.
d. All of the above contain hedging words.

8. Which of the following sentences lacks parallelism?
a. Consumers can download stock research, electronically file their tax returns, create a portfolio, or choose from an array of recommended mutual funds.

b. Consumers can download stock research, can electronically file their tax returns, create a portfolio, or they can choose from an array of recommended mutual funds.

c. Consumers can download stock research, can electronically file their tax returns, can create a portfolio, or can choose from an array of recommended mutual funds.

d. Consumers can download stock research, they can electronically file their tax returns, they can create a portfolio, or they can choose from an array of recommended mutual funds.

9. Which of the following sentences does not have a dangling modifier?

   a. Lacking brand recognition, some consumers are wary of using Internet-only banks.

   b. Because Internet-only banks lack brand recognition, some consumers are wary of using them.

   c. Because of a lack of brand recognition, some consumers are wary of using Internet-only banks.

   d. All have dangling modifiers.

10. When editing for conciseness, you should look for

    a. Unnecessary words and phrases

    b. Dangling modifiers

    c. Lack of parallelism

    d. Awkward references

11. Which of the following is not an example of a redundancy?

    a. Visible to the eye

    b. Free gift

    c. Very useful

    d. Repeat again

Objective 4: List four principles of effective design and explain the role of major design elements in document readability.

12. A well-designed document

    a. Includes a wide variety of typefaces

    b. Balances the space devoted to text, artwork, and white space

    c. Fills as much of the available space as possible with text and art

    d. Does all of the above

13. Any blank areas in a document are referred to as _____ _____.

14. Type that is justified is

    a. Flush on the left and ragged on the right

    b. Flush on the right and ragged on the left

    c. Flush on both the left and the right

    d. Centered

15. Why is it a good idea to think in small chunks when writing for mobile audiences?

    a. Mobile users consume information one screen at a time.

    b. More than 50 percent of mobile users refuse to scroll past the first screen.

    c. Many smartphones don't offer scrolling.

    d. Graphics are easier to create on mobile devices.

Objective 5: Explain the importance of proofreading and give eight tips for successful proofreading.

16. The best time to proofread is

    a. As you are writing

    b. Immediately after you finish the first draft, while the information is still fresh in your mind

    c. A day or so after you finish the first draft

    d. After you distribute the document

17. When proofreading, you should look for errors in

    a. Spelling and punctuation

    b. Grammar and usage

    c. Typography and format

    d. All of the above

Objective 6: Discuss the most important issues to consider when distributing your messages.

18. As a general rule, the cost of distributing a business message should be balanced against

    a. The importance and urgency of the message

    b. The length of the message

    c. Your career goals as they relate to the message

    d. The number of recipients

19. Which of the following concerns is the most important to consider when distributing messages through digital media such as email?

    a. The difficulty of reading on screen

    b. Privacy and security

    c. Differences between flat-panel and CRT monitors

    d. The difficulty of keeping email addresses current

Quick Learning Guide

CHAPTER OUTLINE

LEARNING OBJECTIVES

1 Discuss the value of careful revision, and describe the tasks involved in evaluating your first drafts and the work of other writers.

2 List four techniques you can use to improve the readability of your messages.

3 Describe eight steps you can take to improve the clarity of your writing, and give four tips on making your writing more concise.

4 List four principles of effective design, and explain the role of major design elements in document readability.

5 Explain the importance of proofreading, and give eight tips for successful proofreading.

6 Discuss the most important issues to consider when distributing your messages.

KEY TERMS

descriptive headings Headings that simply identify a topic

heading A brief title that tells readers about the content of the section that follows

informative headings Headings that guide readers to think in a certain way about the topic

sans serif typefaces Typefaces whose letters lack serifs

serif typefaces Typefaces with small crosslines (called *serifs*) at the ends of letter strokes

subheadings Titles that are subordinate to headings, indicating subsections within a major section

type style Any modification that lends contrast or emphasis to type, including boldface, italic, underlining, color, and other highlighting and decorative styles

typeface The physical design of letters, numbers, and other text characters (*font* and *typeface* are often used interchangeably, although strictly speaking, a font is a set of characters in a given typeface)

white space Space (of any color) in a document or screen that doesn't contain any text or artwork

CHECKLIST ✔ Proofing Business Messages

A. Look for writing errors.
- Typographical mistakes
- Misspelled words
- Grammatical errors
- Punctuation mistakes

B. Look for missing elements.
- Missing text sections
- Missing exhibits (drawings, tables, photographs, charts, graphs, online images, and so on)
- Missing source notes, copyright notices, or other reference items

C. Look for design, formatting, and programming mistakes.
- Incorrect or inconsistent font selections
- Problems with column sizing, spacing, and alignment
- Incorrect margins
- Incorrect special characters
- Clumsy line and page breaks
- Problems with page numbers
- Problems with page headers and footers
- Lack of adherence to company standards
- Inactive or incorrect links
- Missing files

CHECKLIST ✔ Revising Business Messages

A. Evaluate content, organization, style, and tone.
- Make sure the information is accurate, relevant, and sufficient.
- Check that all necessary points appear in logical order.
- Verify that you present enough support to make the main idea convincing and compelling.
- Be sure the beginning and ending of the message are effective.
- Make sure you've achieved the right tone for the audience and the situation.

B. Review for readability.
- Consider using a readability index, but be sure to interpret the answer carefully.
- Use a mix of short, medium, and long sentences.
- Keep paragraphs short.
- Use bulleted and numbered lists to emphasize key points.
- Make the document easy to skim with headings and subheadings.

C. Edit for clarity.
- Break up overly long sentences and rewrite hedging sentences.
- Impose parallelism to simplify reading.
- Correct dangling modifiers.
- Reword long noun sequences and replace camouflaged verbs.
- Clarify sentence structure and awkward references.

D. Edit for conciseness.
- Delete unnecessary words and phrases.
- Shorten long words and phrases.
- Eliminate redundancies.
- Rewrite sentences that start with "It is" or "There are."

Apply Your Knowledge

To review chapter content related to each question, refer to the indicated Learning Objective.

1. How does careful revision reflect the "you" attitude? [LO-1]
2. Why should you limit the number of typefaces and type styles in most business documents? [LO-4]
3. Why is white space particularly critical when designing documents for mobile devices? [LO-4]
4. How can you demonstrate good business sense in the choices you make regarding message distribution? [LO-6]

Practice Your Skills

Message for Analysis 6.A: Revising to Improve Readability [LO-2]

Analyze the strengths and weaknesses of this message, then revise it so that it follows the guidelines presented in this chapter:

As an organization, the North American Personal Motorsports Marketing Association has committed ourselves to helping our members—a diverse group comprising of dealers of motorcycles, all-terrain vehicles, Snowmobiles, and personal watercraft— achieve their business objectives. Consequently, our organization, which usually goes under the initials NAPMMA, has the following aims, goals, and objectives. Firstly, we endeavor to aid or assist our members in reaching their business objectives. Second, NAPMMA communicates ("lobbying" in slang terms) with local, state, and national governmental agencies and leaders on issues of importance to our members. And lastly, we educate the motorsports public, that being current motorsports vehicle owners, and prospective owners of said vehicles, on the safe and enjoyable operation of they're vehicles.

Message for Analysis 6.B: Designing for Readability [LO-4]

To access this message, visit http://real-timeupdates.com/ebc12, click on Student Assignments, select this chapter, Message 6.B. Download and open the document. Using the various page, paragraph, and font formatting options available in your word processor, modify the formatting of the document so that its visual tone matches the tone of the message.

Message for Analysis 6.C: Evaluating the Work of Another Writer [LO-1]

To access this message, visit http://real-timeupdates.com/ebc12, click on Student Assignments, select this chapter, Message 6.C. Download and open the document. Using your knowledge of effective writing and the tips for evaluating the work of other writers, evaluate this message. After you set Microsoft Word to

track changes, make any necessary corrections. Insert comments, as needed, to explain your changes to the author.

Each activity is labeled according to the primary skill or skills you will need to use. To review relevant chapter content, you can refer to the indicated Learning Objective.

5. **Evaluating the Work of Other Writers [LO-1]** Find a blog post (at least three paragraphs long) on any business-related topic. Evaluate it using the questions. Email your analysis to your instructor, along with a permalink (a permanent link to this specific post, rather than to the blog overall) to the blog post.

6. **Revising for Readability (Sentence and Paragraph Length [LO-2])** Rewrite the following paragraph to vary the length of the sentences and to shorten the paragraph so it looks more inviting to readers:

Although major league baseball remains popular, more people are attending minor league baseball games because they can spend less on admission, snacks, and parking and still enjoy the excitement of America's pastime. Connecticut, for example, has three AA minor league teams, including the New Haven Ravens, who are affiliated with the St. Louis Cardinals; the Norwich Navigators, who are affiliated with the New York Yankees; and the New Britain Rock Cats, who are affiliated with the Minnesota Twins. These teams play in relatively small stadiums, so fans are close enough to see and hear everything, from the swing of the bat connecting with the ball to the thud of the ball landing in the outfielder's glove. Best of all, the cost of a family outing to see rising stars play in a local minor league game is just a fraction of what the family would spend to attend a major league game in a much larger, more crowded stadium.

7. **Revising for Readability (Sentence Length) [LO-2]** Break the following sentences into shorter ones by adding more periods and revise as needed for smooth flow:
   a. The next time you write something, check your average sentence length in a 100-word passage, and if your sentences average more than 16 to 20 words, see whether you can break up some of the sentences.
   b. Don't do what the village blacksmith did when he instructed his apprentice as follows: "When I take the shoe out of the fire, I'll lay it on the anvil, and when I nod my head, you hit it with the hammer." The apprentice did just as he was told, and now he's the village blacksmith.
   c. Unfortunately, no gadget will produce excellent writing, but using a yardstick like the Fog Index gives us some guideposts to follow for making writing easier to read because its two factors remind us to use short sentences and simple words.
   d. Know the flexibility of the written word and its power to convey an idea, and know how to make your words behave so that your readers will understand.

e. Words mean different things to different people, and a word such as *block* may mean city block, butcher block, engine block, auction block, or several other things.

8. Editing for Conciseness (Unnecessary Words) [LO-3] Cross out unnecessary words in the following phrases:
  a. Consensus of opinion
  b. New innovations
  c. Long period of time
  d. At a price of $50
  e. Still remains

9. Editing for Conciseness (Long Words) [LO-3] Revise the following sentences, using shorter, simpler words:
  a. The antiquated calculator is ineffectual for solving sophisticated problems.
  b. It is imperative that the pay increments be terminated before an inordinate deficit is accumulated.
  c. There was unanimity among the executives that Ms. Jackson's idiosyncrasies were cause for a mandatory meeting with the company's personnel director.
  d. The impending liquidation of the company's assets was cause for jubilation among the company's competitors.
  e. The expectations of the president for a stock dividend were accentuated by the preponderance of evidence that the company was in good financial condition.

10. Editing for Conciseness (Lengthy Phrases) [LO-3] Use infinitives as substitutes for the overly long phrases in these sentences:
  a. For living, I require money.
  b. They did not find sufficient evidence for believing in the future.
  c. Bringing about the destruction of a dream is tragic.

11. Editing for Conciseness (Lengthy Phrases) [LO-3] Rephrase the following in fewer words:
  a. In the near future
  b. In the event that
  c. In order that
  d. For the purpose of
  e. With regard to
  f. It may be that
  g. In very few cases
  h. With reference to
  i. At the present time
  j. There is no doubt that

12. Editing for Conciseness (Lengthy Phrases) [LO-3] Revise to condense these sentences to as few words as possible:
  a. We are of the conviction that writing is important.
  b. In all probability, we're likely to have a price increase.
  c. Our goals include making a determination about that in the near future.
  d. When all is said and done at the conclusion of this experiment, I'd like to summarize the final windup.
  e. After a trial period of three weeks, during which time she worked for a total of 15 full working days, we found her work was sufficiently satisfactory so that we offered her full-time work.

13. Editing for Conciseness (Unnecessary Modifiers) [LO-3] Remove all the unnecessary modifiers from these sentences:
  a. Tremendously high pay increases were given to the extraordinarily skilled and extremely conscientious employees.
  b. The union's proposals were highly inflationary, extremely demanding, and exceptionally bold.

14. Editing for Clarity (Hedging) [LO-3] Rewrite these sentences so that they no longer contain any hedging:
  a. It would appear that someone apparently entered illegally.
  b. It may be possible that sometime in the near future the situation is likely to improve.
  c. Your report seems to suggest that we might be losing money.
  d. I believe Nancy apparently has somewhat greater influence over employees in the e-marketing department.
  e. It seems as if this letter of resignation means you might be leaving us.

15. Editing for Clarity (Indefinite Starters) [LO-3] Rewrite these sentences to eliminate the indefinite starters:
  a. There are several examples here to show that Elaine can't hold a position very long.
  b. It would be greatly appreciated if every employee would make a generous contribution to Mildred Cook's retirement party.
  c. It has been learned in Washington today from generally reliable sources that an important announcement will be made shortly by the White House.
  d. There is a rule that states that we cannot work overtime without permission.
  e. It would be great if you could work late for the next three Saturdays.

16. Editing for Clarity (Parallelism) [LO-3] Revise these sentences to present the ideas in parallel form:
  a. Mr. Hill is expected to lecture three days a week, to counsel two days a week, and must write for publication in his spare time.
  b. She knows not only accounting, but she also reads Latin.
  c. Both applicants had families, college degrees, and were in their thirties, with considerable accounting experience but few social connections.
  d. This book was exciting, well written, and held my interest.
  e. Don is both a hard worker and he knows bookkeeping.

17. Editing for Clarity (Awkward References) [LO-3] Revise the following sentences to delete the awkward references:
  a. The vice president in charge of sales and the production manager are responsible for the keys to 34A and 35A, respectively.
  b. The keys to 34A and 35A are in executive hands, with the former belonging to the vice president in charge of sales and the latter belonging to the production manager.

c. The keys to 34A and 35A have been given to the production manager, with the aforementioned keys being gold embossed.

d. A laser printer and an inkjet printer were delivered to John and Megan, respectively.

e. The walnut desk is more expensive than the oak desk, the former costing $300 more than the latter.

18. **Editing for Clarity (Dangling Modifiers) [LO-3]** Rewrite these sentences to clarify the dangling modifiers:

   a. Full of trash and ripped-up newspapers, we left Dallas on a plane that apparently hadn't been cleaned in days.

   b. Lying on the shelf, Ruby found the operations manual.

   c. With leaking plumbing and outdated wiring, I don't think we should buy that property.

   d. Being cluttered and filthy, Sandy took the whole afternoon to clean up her desk.

   e. After proofreading every word, the letter was ready to be signed.

19. **Editing for Clarity (Noun Sequences) [LO-3]** Rewrite the following sentences to eliminate the long strings of nouns:

   a. The focus of the meeting was a discussion of the bank interest rate deregulation issue.

   b. Following the government task force report recommendations, we are revising our job applicant evaluation procedures.

   c. The production department quality assurance program components include employee training, supplier cooperation, and computerized detection equipment.

   d. The supermarket warehouse inventory reduction plan will be implemented next month.

   e. The State University business school graduate placement program is one of the best in the country.

20. **Editing for Clarity (Sentence Structure) [LO-3]** Rearrange the following sentences to bring the subjects closer to their verbs:

   a. Trudy, when she first saw the bull pawing the ground, ran.

   b. It was Terri who, according to Ted, who is probably the worst gossip in the office (Tom excepted), mailed the wrong order.

   c. William Oberstreet, in his book Investment Capital Reconsidered, writes of the mistakes that bankers through the decades have made.

   d. Judy Schimmel, after passing up several sensible investment opportunities, despite the warnings of her friends and family, invested her inheritance in a jojoba plantation.

   e. The president of U-Stor-It, which was on the brink of bankruptcy after the warehouse fire, the worst tragedy in the history of the company, prepared a press announcement.

21. **Editing for Clarity (Camouflaged Verbs) [LO-3]** Rewrite each sentence so that the verbs are no longer camouflaged:

   a. Adaptation to the new rules was performed easily by the employees.

   b. The assessor will make a determination of the tax due.

   c. Verification of the identity of the employees must be made daily.

   d. The board of directors made a recommendation that Mr. Ronson be assigned to a new division.

22. The auditing procedure on the books was performed by the vice president.

23. **Completing: Designing for Readability; Media Skills: Blogging [LO-4]** Compare the home pages of Bloomberg (www.bloomberg.com) and MarketWatch (www.marketwatch.com), two websites that cover financial markets. What are your first impressions of these two sites? How do their overall designs compare in terms of information delivery and overall user experience? Choose three pieces of information that a visitor to these sites would be likely to look for, such as a current stock price, news from international markets, and commentary from market experts. Which site makes it easier to find this information? Why? Present your analysis in a post for your class blog.

24. **Communication Ethics: Making Ethical Choices; Media Skills: Blogging [LO-3]** The time and energy required for careful revision can often benefit you or your company directly, such as by increasing the probability that website visitors will buy your products. But what about situations in which the quality of your writing and revision work really doesn't stand to benefit you directly? For instance, assume that you are putting a notice on your website, informing the local community about some upcoming construction to your manufacturing plant. The work will disrupt traffic for nearly a year and generate a significant amount of noise and air pollution, but knowing the specific dates and times of various construction activities will allow people to adjust their commutes and other activities to minimize the negative impact on their daily lives. However, your company does not sell products in the local area, so the people affected by all this are not potential customers. Moreover, providing accurate information to the surrounding community and updating it as the project progresses will take time away from your other job responsibilities. Do you have an ethical obligation to keep the local community informed with accurate, up-to-date information? Why or why not?

25. **Proofreading [LO-5]** Proofread the following email message, and revise it to correct any problems you find:

   Our final company orrientation of the year will be held on Dec. 20. In preparation for this sesssion, please order 20 copies of the Policy handbook, the confindentiality agreenemt, the employee benefits Manual, please let me know if you anticipate any delays in obtaining these materials.

Expand Your Skills

Critique the Professionals

Identify a company website that in your opinion violates one or more of the principles of good design. Using whatever medium your instructor requests, write a brief analysis of the site (no more than one page), citing specific elements from the piece and support from the chapter.

Sharpening Your Career Skills Online

Bovée and Thill's Business Communication Web Search, at http://websearch.businesscommunicationnetwork.com, is a unique research tool designed specifically for business communication research. Use the Web Search function to find a website, video, PDF document, podcast, or presentation that offers advice on effective proofreading. Write a brief email message to your instructor, describing the item you found and summarizing the career skills information you learned from it.

Improve Your Grammar, Mechanics, and Usage

The following exercises help you improve your knowledge of and power over English grammar, mechanics, and usage. Turn to the Handbook of Grammar, Mechanics, and Usage at the end of this text and review Prepositions. Then look at the following 10 items. Underline the preferred choice within each set of parentheses.

26. Where was your argument (*leading to, leading*)?
27. I wish he would get (*off, off of*) the phone.
28. U.S. Mercantile must become (*aware, aware of*) and sensitive to its customers' concerns.
29. Dr. Namaguchi will be talking (*with, to*) the marketing class, but she has no time for questions.
30. Matters like this are decided after thorough discussion (*among, between*) all seven department managers.
31. We can't wait (*on, for*) their decision much longer.
32. Their computer is similar (*to, with*) ours.
33. This model is different (*than, from*) the one we ordered.
34. She is active (*in not only, not only in*) a civic group but also in an athletic organization.
35. Carolyn told Jorge not to put the used inkjet cartridges (*in, into*) the trash can.

MyBCommLab

Go to the Assignments section of your MyLab to complete these writing exercises.

36 Why is it helpful to put your first draft aside for a while before you begin the editing process? [LO-1]

37 How do your typeface selections help determine the personality of your documents and messages? [LO-4]

Endnotes

1. Jefferson Rabb website, accessed 21 January 2013, www .jeffersonrabb.com; Joshua Bodwell, "Artful Author Web Sites," *Poets & Writers*, January/February 2011, 79–84; Super Sad True Love Story website, accessed 22 January 2011, http://supersadtruelove story.com; Beat the Reaper website, accessed 22 January 2011, www.beatthereaper.com.
2. Deborah Gunn, "Looking Good on Paper," *Office Pro*, March 2004, 10–11.
3. Jacci Howard Bear, "Desktop Publishing Rules of Page Layout," About.com, accessed 22 August 2005, www.about.com.
4. Kas Thomas, "The Serif Readability Myth," assertTrue blog, 18 January 2013, asserttrue.blogspot.com; Ole Lund, "Knowledge Construction in Typography: The Case of Legibility Research and the Legibility of Sans Serif Typefaces," doctoral dissertation, University of Reading, October 1999.
5. Jacci Howard Bear, "Desktop Publishing Rules for How Many Fonts to Use," About.com, accessed 22 August 2005, www.about.com.
6. "Mobile Message Mayhem," Verne Ordman & Associates, accessed 12 March 2014, www.businesswriting.biz.
7. The writing samples in this exercise were taken or adapted from the Alexander McCall Smith website, accessed 2 June 2011, www .alexandermccallsmith.com; Anita Shreve website, accessed 2 June 2011, www.anitashreve.com; *Traffic* website, accessed 2 June 2011, http://tomvanderbilt.com/traffic.

Answer Key for "Learning Objectives Checkup"

1. d
2. a
3. c
4. a
5. b
6. c
7. d
8. b
9. b
10. a

11. c
12. b
13. white space
14. c
15. a
16. c
17. d
18. a
19. b

Answer Key for "Improve Your Grammar, Mechanics, and Usage" Exercises

26. leading (1.6.1)
27. off (1.6.1)
28. aware of (1.6.1)
29. to (1.6.1)
30. among (1.6.1)

31. for (1.6.1)
32. to (1.6.1)
33. from (1.6.1)
34. not only in (1.6.1)
35. into (1.6.1)

Crafting Messages for Digital Channels

Crafting Messages for Digital Channels

LEARNING OBJECTIVES

After studying this chapter, you will be able to

1 Identify the major digital channels used for brief business messages, and describe the nine compositional modes needed for digital media.

2 Describe the use of social networks in business communication.

3 Explain how companies and business professionals can use information and content sharing websites.

4 Describe the evolving role of email in business communication, and explain how to adapt the three-step writing process to email messages.

5 Describe the business benefits of instant messaging (IM), and identify guidelines for effective IM in the workplace.

6 Describe the use of blogging and microblogging in business communication, and briefly explain how to adapt the three-step process to blogging.

7 Explain how to adapt the three-step writing process for podcasts.

ON THE JOB: COMMUNICATING AT GOPRO

Building a Brand Through Social Engagement

If you've watched a daredevil video on YouTube in the past few years, chances are the video was shot with a GoPro camera. GoPro's digital cameras have captured everything from extreme snowboarders to Felix Baumgartner's epic 24-mile freefall leap from the edge of space. The "adrenaline market" is at the core of the GoPro brand, but the growing population of GoPro users also includes filmmakers, sports and wildlife photographers, oceanographers, atmospheric researchers, and others who need high-quality video footage from a small, rugged, and relatively inexpensive digital camera.

Not surprisingly, for its own business communication needs, GoPro makes extensive use of video. Like many companies, it uses video to showcase new products and provide how-to advice for customers. However, GoPro has gone far beyond what many companies do with video by harnessing the amplifying power of social media. The company has taken user-generated content to the extreme, using a variety of recognition and reward mechanisms to encourage GoPro customers to submit video clips. For example, GoPro runs a nonstop contest that recognizes several customers every day

Viewer interest in extreme sports and other eye-catching events and phenomena has created a huge market for GoPro's video cameras. The company, led by founder and CEO Nick Woodman, has capitalized on this visceral appeal with an extensive social media presence centered around online video.

for the best footage shot on GoPro cameras. These clips are then highlighted on the company's website and all across the major social media platforms, including YouTube, Facebook, Twitter, Google+, and Instagram. In addition, a daily sweepstakes awards one lucky participant with one of every product the company makes, which maintains a high level of interest among people who don't yet own a GoPro camera.

The company's strategy of building a global video community has been a huge success. When Google (which owns YouTube) announced its first-ever monthly ranking of the highest-performing branded channels on YouTube, it determined that GoPro had the most engaged fan base. To measure engagement, Google factors in such variables as the amount of

time visitors spending watching videos, the number of repeat visitors, and the number of times people "like" a video or leave a comment. When you consider that virtually every video on GoPro's YouTube channel functions as an advertisement for the company's cameras, you get an idea of the immense promotional power that this high level of engagement represents.

Even if your job doesn't involve snowboarding off cliffs or parachuting from space, GoPro offers a great example of how creative companies can build connections in today's digital, social business environment.[1]

HTTP://GOPRO.COM

Digital Channels for Business Communication

1 LEARNING OBJECTIVE
Identify the major digital channels used for brief business messages, and describe the nine compositional modes needed for digital media.

GoPro's choice of social media for customer communication may seem like an obvious move, but the use of social media represents a fundamental shift in business communication. The shift is still taking place, as more consumers adopt social and mobile media and as businesses experiment with the best ways to integrate these media and adapt them to their internal and external communication practices.

Social media such as Facebook are digital media/channel combinations that empower stakeholders as participants in the communication process by allowing them to share content, revise content, respond to content, or contribute new content. For instance, many people now rely heavily on content sharing through social media tools to get information of personal and professional interest. Additionally, many consumers and professionals frequently engage in "content snacking," consuming large numbers of small pieces of information and bypassing larger documents that might require more than a few minutes or even a few seconds to read.[2] Moreover, the amount of content accessed from mobile devices (with the challenges they present in terms of screen size and input mechanisms) continues to rise.[3] Faced with such behavior, communicators need to be more careful than ever to create audience-focused messages and to consider restructuring messages using more *teasers, orientations,* and *summaries.*

With all these changes taking place, the field of business communication is a lot more interesting—but also a lot more complicated—than it was just a few years ago. For example, newer and smaller firms have a better opportunity to compete against big companies with big communication budgets because the quality of the message and the credibility of the sender carry more weight in this new environment. Empowered stakeholders can use the reach of social media to help companies that appear to be acting in stakeholders' best interests and harm companies that are not. Social media also have the potential to increase transparency, with more eyes and ears to monitor business activities and to use the crowd's voice to demand accountability and change.

Although social media have reduced the amount of control businesses have over the content and process of communication,[4] today's smart companies are learning how to adapt their communication efforts to this new media landscape and to welcome customers' participation. Social media are also revolutionizing internal communication, breaking down traditional barriers in the organizational hierarchy, promoting the flow of information and ideas, and enabling networks of individuals and organizations to collaborate on a global scale.[5]

Increasingly, employees expect the leaders in their organizations to be active in social media. In one recent study, more than 80 percent of U.S. employees agreed that "CEOs who engage in social media are better equipped than their peers to lead companies in a

The range of options for short business messages continues to grow with innovations in digital and social media.

Social media reduce a communicator's control over messages.

Web 2.0 world." Moreover, roughly the same percentage are more likely to trust companies whose leadership teams engage with stakeholders via social media, and they would prefer to work for such companies as well.[6]

MEDIA CHOICES FOR BRIEF MESSAGES

Social media are not the only options available for business communication, of course. Individuals and companies have a broad range of options for sending brief messages (from one or two sentences up to several pages long), including the following:

- Social networks
- Information and content sharing sites
- Email
- Instant messaging (IM)
- Text messaging
- Blogging and microblogging
- Podcasting

This chapter covers all of these media.

As this list suggests, businesses use many of the same tools you use for personal communication. Generally speaking, companies are quick to jump on any communication platform where consumers are likely to congregate or that promise more-efficient internal or external communication.

Although most of your business communication is likely to be via digital means, don't automatically dismiss the benefits of printed messages. Here are several situations in which you should use a printed message over digital alternatives:

- When you want to make a formal impression
- When you are legally required to provide information in printed form
- When you want to stand out from the flood of digital messages
- When you need a permanent, unchangeable, or secure record

Even with the widespread use of digital formats, printed memos and letters still play an important role in business communication.

Obviously, if you can't reach a particular audience through digital channels, you'll also need to use a printed message.

COMPOSITIONAL MODES FOR DIGITAL MEDIA

As you practice using digital media in this course, focus on the principles of social media communication and the fundamentals of planning, writing, and completing messages, rather than on the specific details of any one medium or system.[7] Fortunately, the basic communication skills required usually transfer from one system to another. You can succeed with written communication in virtually all digital media by using one of nine *compositional modes*:

Communicating successfully with digital media requires a wide range of writing approaches.

- **Conversations.** IM is a great example of a written medium that mimics spoken conversation. And just as you wouldn't read a report to someone sitting in your office, you wouldn't use conversational modes to exchange large volumes of information or to communicate with more than a few people at once.
- **Comments and critiques.** One of the most powerful aspects of social media is the opportunity for interested parties to express opinions and provide feedback, whether it's leaving comments on a blog post or reviewing products on an e-commerce site. Sharing helpful tips and insightful commentary is also a great way to build your personal brand. To be an effective commenter, focus on short chunks of information that a broad spectrum of other site visitors will find helpful. Rants, insults, jokes, and blatant self-promotion are usually of little benefit to other visitors.

REAL-TIME UPDATES
LEARN MORE BY READING THIS ARTICLE

Should you email, text, or pick up the phone?

These tips will help you make the best choice in various business situations. Go to http://real-timeupdates.com/ebc12 and click on Learn More in the Students section.

- **Orientations.** The ability to help people find their way through an unfamiliar system or subject is a valuable writing skill and a talent that readers greatly appreciate. Unlike summaries (see next item), orientations don't give away the key points in the collection of information, but rather tell readers where to find those points. Writing effective orientations can be a delicate balancing act because you need to know the material well enough to guide others through it while being able to step back and view it from the inexperienced perspective of a "newbie."

- **Summaries.** At the beginning of an article or webpage, a summary functions as a miniature version of the document, giving readers all the key points while skipping over details. At the end of an article or webpage, a summary functions as a review, reminding readers of the key points they've just read. A series of key points extracted from an article or webpage can also serve as a summary (see the discussion of *tweetables*).

- **Reference materials.** One of the greatest benefits of the Internet is the access it can provide to vast quantities of reference materials—numerical or textual information that people typically don't read in a linear way but rather search through to find particular data points, trends, or other details. One of the challenges of writing reference material is that you can't always know how readers will want to access it. Making the information accessible via search engines is an important step. However, readers don't always know which search terms will yield the best results, so consider an orientation and organize the material in logical ways with clear headings that promote skimming.

- **Narratives.** The storytelling techniques can be effective in a wide variety of situations, from company histories to product reviews and demonstrations. Narratives work best when they have an intriguing beginning that piques readers' curiosity, a middle section that moves quickly through the challenges that an individual or company faced, and an inspiring or instructive ending that gives readers information they can apply in their own lives and jobs.

- **Teasers.** Teasers intentionally withhold key pieces of information as a way to pull readers or listeners into a story or other document. Teasers are widely used in marketing and sales messages, such as a bit of copy on the outside of an envelope that promises important information on the inside. In digital media, the space limitations and URL linking capabilities of Twitter and other microblogging systems make them a natural tool for the teaser approach. Be sure that the *payoff*, the information a teaser links to, is valuable and legitimate. You'll quickly lose credibility if readers think they are being tricked into clicking through to information they don't really want. (*Tweetables* are Twitter-ready bites of information extracted from a blog post or other messages. They often serve as teasers, although a series of them can make an effective summary as well.)

> With Twitter and other super-short messaging systems, the ability to write a compelling *teaser* is an important skill.

- **Status updates and announcements.** If you use social media frequently, much of your writing will involve status updates and announcements. However, don't post trivial information that only you are likely to find interesting. Post only those updates that readers will find useful, and include only the information they need (see Figure 1 on the next page).

- **Tutorials.** Given the community nature of social media, the purpose of many messages is to share how-to advice. Becoming known as a reliable expert is a great way to build customer loyalty for your company while enhancing your own personal value.

CREATING CONTENT FOR SOCIAL MEDIA

No matter what media or compositional mode you are using for a particular message, writing for social media requires a different approach than for traditional media. Whether you're writing a blog or posting a product demonstration video to YouTube, consider these tips for creating successful content for social media:[8]

REAL-TIME UPDATES

LEARN MORE BY READING THIS ARTICLE

Telling compelling stories on social media

Storytelling is an effective business communication strategy, and social media can be the idea platform for it. Go to http://real-timeupdates.com/ebc12 and click on Learn More in the Students section.

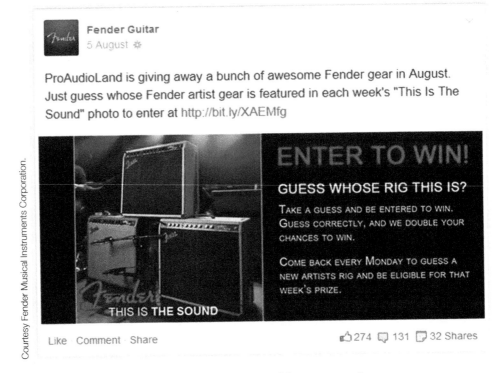

Figure 1 Compositional Modes: Status Updates and Announcements
Contests, such as this one feature Fender musical equipment, are a popular message form on Facebook and other social media.

Writing for social media requires a different approach than writing for traditional media.

- **Remember that it's a conversation, not a lecture or a sales pitch.** One of the great appeals of social media is the feeling of conversation, of people talking *with* one another instead of one person talking *at* everyone else. As more and more people gain a voice in the marketplace, companies that try to maintain the old "we talk, you listen" mindset are likely to be ignored in the social media landscape.

- **Write informally but not carelessly.** Write as a human being with a unique, personal voice. However, don't take this as a license to get sloppy; no one wants to slog through misspelled words and half-baked sentences to find your message.

- **Create concise, specific, and informative headlines.** Given the importance of headlines in the face of content snacking and information overload, headlines are extremely important in social media. Avoid the temptation to engage in clever wordplay when writing headlines and teasers. This advice applies to all forms of business communication, of course, but it is essential for social media. Readers don't want to spend time figuring out what your witty headlines mean. Search engines won't know what they mean either, so fewer people will find your content.

- **Get involved and stay involved.** Social media make some businesspeople nervous because they don't permit a high level of control over messages. However, don't hide from criticism. Take the opportunity to correct misinformation or explain how mistakes will be fixed.

- **Be transparent and honest.** Honesty is always essential, of course, but the social media environment is unforgiving. Attempts to twist the truth, withhold information, or hide behind a virtual barricade only invite attack in the "public square" of social media.

A momentary lapse of concentration or judgment while using social media can cause tremendous damage to your career.

- **Think before you post!** Because of careless messages, individuals and companies have been sued because of Twitter updates, employees have been fired for Facebook wall postings, vital company secrets have been leaked, and business and personal relationships have been strained. Remember that you share the responsibility of keeping your company's and your customers' data private and secure. Assume that every message you send in any digital medium will be stored forever and might be read by people far beyond your original audience. Ask yourself two questions: First, "Would I say this to my audience face to face?" And second, "Am I comfortable with this message becoming a permanent part of my personal and professional communication history?"

OPTIMIZING CONTENT FOR MOBILE DEVICES

While keeping the limitations of small screens and alternative input methods in mind, look for opportunities to take advantage of mobile-specific capabilities via apps and mobile-friendly websites. Mobile expands your options as a content creator, and it gives your audience members a wider range of more-engaging ways to consume your content:

- **Location-based services.** *Location-based social networking* links the virtual world of online social networking with the physical world of retail stores and other locations. As mobile web use in general continues to grow, location-based networking promises to become an important business communication medium because mobile consumers are a significant economic force—through the purchases they make directly and through their ability to influence other consumers.[9]

Mobile offers a range of exciting ways to enhance the audience experience.

- **Gamification.** The addition of game-playing aspects to apps and web services, known as *gamification,* can increase audience engagement and encourage repeat use. Examples include Foursquare's "check-in" competitions and Bunchball's Nitro competitions for sales teams.[10]
- **Augmented reality.** Superimposing data on live camera images can help mobile consumers learn about companies and services in the immediate vicinity, for example. Another potential business use is on-the-job training, in which training content is provided as workers are learning or performing various tasks.

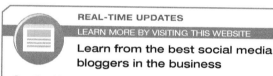

- **Wearable technology.** From virtual-reality goggles to smartwatches to body-movement sensors, wearable technology pushes the radical connectivity of mobile to the next level. Some of these work as auxiliary screens and controls for other mobile devices, but others are meant for independent use. One of the key promises of wearable technology is simplifying and enhancing everyday tasks for consumers and employees alike.[11]
- **Mobile blogging.** Smartphones and tablets are idea for mobile blogs, sometimes referred to as *moblogs.* The mobile capability is great for workers whose jobs keep them on the move and for special-event coverage such as live-blogging trade shows and industry conventions.
- **Mobile podcasting.** Similarly, smartphone-based podcasting tools make it easy to record audio on the go and post finished podcasts to your blog or website.
- **Cloud-based services.** Mobile communication is ideal for cloud-based services—digital services that rely on resources stored in the cloud.

MOBILE APP

Mobile Podcaster lets you record audio podcasts on your mobile devices and instantly post them on your WordPress blog.

Social Networks

Social networks—online services that help people and organizations form connections and share information—have become a major force in both internal and external business communication in recent years. In addition to Facebook, a variety of public and private social networks are used by businesses and professionals. They can be grouped into three categories:

2 LEARNING OBJECTIVE
Describe the use of social networks in business communication.

- **Public, general-purpose networks.** Facebook is the largest such network, and Google+ has also attracted many companies and brands. Additionally, regionally focused networks have significant user bases in some countries, such as China's Renren and Kaixin001.[12]

- **Public, specialized networks.** Whereas Facebook and Google+ serve a wide variety of personal and professional needs, other networks focus on a particular function or a particular audience. The most widely known of these is LinkedIn, with its emphasis on career- and sales-related networking. Other networks address the needs of entrepreneurs, small-business owners, specific professions, product enthusiasts, and other narrower audiences.

- **Private networks.** Some companies have built private social networks for internal use. For example, the defense contractor Lockheed Martin created its Unity network, complete with a variety of social media applications, to meet the expectations of younger employees accustomed to social media and to capture the expert knowledge of older employees nearing retirement.[13]

Regardless of the purpose and audience, social networks are most beneficial when all participants give and receive information, advice, support, and introductions—just as in offline social interaction. The following two sections describe how social networks are used in business communication and offer advice on using these platforms successfully.

Business communicators make use of a wide range of specialized and private social networks, in addition to public networks such as Facebook and Google+.

BUSINESS COMMUNICATION USES OF SOCIAL NETWORKS

With their ability to reach virtually unlimited numbers of people through a variety of digital formats, social networks are a great fit for many business communication needs. Here are some of the key applications of social networks for internal and external business communication:

- **Integrating company workforces.** Just as public networks can bring friends and family together, internal social networks can help companies grow closer, including

---

DIGITAL + SOCIAL + MOBILE: TODAY'S COMMUNICATION ENVIRONMENT

Community Manager: One of the Hottest New Jobs in Business

With the rise in social media over the past few years and its transformative effect on business, *community manager* is one of the hottest new jobs in business. In the narrowest sense, a community manager is the social media interface between a company and its external stakeholders. More broadly, some community managers also plan and manage corporate events and oversee customer support operations. In smaller firms, the community manager might be the sole voice in a company's social media presence (running its Twitter account and Facebook pages, for example). In larger firms, the job often entails supervising a team of people who carry out a broad range of audience-engagement activities.

Not surprisingly, communications skills are essential for community managers. These skills include not only handling the nuts and bolts of using social media effectively but also fostering a sense of community and inspiring people to be passionate about a company and its brands. In addition, community management is a data-intensive job in many companies, with managers expected to make full use of analytical tools to measure the effects of social interaction and to use those answers to plan new initiatives. Community managers also have to be well-versed in their company's product and service offerings.

On a personal level, the job requires high energy, resilience, a thick skin for handling negative comments, and a willingness to be connected far beyond the limits of a 40-hour week. You are "the face of brand," as Adobe's community manager Rachael King describes it, and when major events hit, social managers are expected to respond in real time.

If the attractions and challenges of this job sound appealing to you, be sure to add community manager to the list of career paths you explore as you get closer to graduation.

CAREER APPLICATIONS

1. Would someone with limited work experience but a long personal history of using social media be a good candidate for a community manager position? Why or why not?
2. What are the risks of having a single person be the voice of a company, and how should companies address this risk?

Sources: Don Power, "In Their Own Words: What Community Managers Do Every Day," *SproutSocial,* 7 March 2013, sproutsocial.com; Ryan Lytle, "10 Qualities of an Effective Community Manager," *Mashable,* 27 January 2013, http://mashable.com; Jennifer Grayeb, "The 4 Pillars of Community Management," *Forbes,* 25 December 2013, www.forbes.com; Tim McDonald, "Community Manager: Key to the Future of Business," *Huffington Post,* 27 January 2014, www.huffingtonpost.com.

helping new employees navigate their way through the organization, finding experts, mentors, and other important contacts; encouraging workforces to "gel" after reorganizations or mergers; and overcoming structural barriers in communication channels, bypassing the formal communication system to deliver information where it is needed in a timely fashion.

- **Fostering collaboration.** Networks can play a major role in collaboration by identifying the best people, both inside the company and in other companies, to collaborate on projects; finding pockets of knowledge and expertise within the organization; giving meeting or seminar participants a way to meet before an event and to maintain relationships after an event; accelerating the development of teams by helping members get to know one another and to identify individual areas of expertise; and sharing information throughout the organization.

- **Building communities.** Social networks are a natural tool for bringing together *communities of practice*, people who engage in similar work, and *communities of interest*, people who share enthusiasm for a particular product or activity. Large and geographically dispersed companies can benefit greatly from communities of practice that connect experts who may work in different divisions or different countries. Communities of interest that form around a specific product are sometimes called **brand communities**, and nurturing these communities can be a vital business communication task. A majority of consumers now trust their peers more than any other source of product information, so formal and informal brand communities are becoming an essential information source in consumer buying decisions.[14]

- **Socializing brands and companies.** According to one recent survey of company executives, *socialization* now accounts for more than half of a company or brand's global reputation.[15] **Brand socialization** is a measure of how effectively a company engages with its various online stakeholders in a mutually beneficial exchange of information.

  Socializing a brand is becoming an increasingly important element of marketing and public relations strategies.

- **Understanding target markets.** With hundreds of millions of people expressing themselves via social media, you can be sure that smart companies are listening. When asked about the value of having millions of Facebook fans, Coca-Cola CEO Muhtar Kent replied, "The value is you can talk with them. They tell you things that are important for your business and brands."[16] In addition, a number of tools now exist to gather market intelligence from social media more or less automatically. For example, *sentiment analysis* is an intriguing research technique in which companies track social networks and other media with automated language-analysis software that tries to take the pulse of public opinion and identify influential opinion makers.[17]

  Social networks are vital tools for distributing information as well as gathering information about the business environment.

- **Recruiting employees and business partners.** Companies use social networks to find potential employees, short-term contractors, subject-matter experts, product and service suppliers, and business partners. A key advantage here is that these introductions are made via trusted connections in a professional network. On LinkedIn, for example, members can recommend each other based on current or past business relationships, which helps remove the uncertainty of initiating business relationships with complete strangers.

- **Connecting with sales prospects.** Salespeople on networks such as LinkedIn can use their network connections to identify potential buyers and then to ask for introductions through those shared connections. Sales networking can reduce *cold calling*, telephoning potential customers out of the blue—a practice that few people on either end of the conversation find pleasant.

- **Supporting customers.** Customer service is another one of the fundamental areas of business communication that have been revolutionized by social media. *Social customer service* involves using social networks and other social media tools to give customers a more convenient way to get help from the company and to help each other.

- **Extending the organization.** Social networking is also fueling the growth of *networked organizations*, sometimes known as *virtual organizations*, where companies supplement the talents of their employees with services from one or more external partners, such as a design lab, a manufacturing firm, or a sales and distribution company.

STRATEGIES FOR BUSINESS COMMUNICATION ON SOCIAL NETWORKS

Social networks offer lots of business communication potential, but with those opportunities comes a certain degree of complexity. Moreover, the norms and practices of business social networking continue to evolve. Follow these guidelines to make the most of social networks for both personal branding and company communication:[18]

- **Choose the best compositional mode for each message, purpose, and network.** As you visit various social networks, take some time to observe the variety of message types you see in different parts of each website. For example, the informal status update mode works well for Facebook Wall posts but would be less effective for company overviews and mission statements.
- **Offer valuable content to members of your online communities.** People don't join social networks to be sales targets, of course. They join looking for connections and information. *Content marketing* is the practice of providing free information that is valuable to community members but that also helps a company build closer ties with current and potential customers.[19]

- **Join existing conversations.** Search for online conversations that are already taking place. Answer questions, solve problems, and respond to rumors and misinformation.
- **Anchor your online presence in your hub.** Although it's important to join those conversations and be visible where your stakeholders are active, it's equally important to anchor your presence at your own central *hub*—a web presence you own and control. This can be a combination of a conventional website, a blog, and a company-sponsored online community, for example.[20] Use the hub to connect the various pieces of your online "self" (as an individual or a company) to make it easier for people to find and follow you. For example, you can link to your blog from your LinkedIn profile or automatically post your blog entries into the Notes tab on your Facebook page.
- **Facilitate community building.** Make it easy for customers and other audiences to connect with the company and with each other. For example, you can use the group feature on Facebook, LinkedIn, and other social networks to create and foster special-interest groups within your networks. Groups are a great way to connect people who are interested in specific topics, such as owners of a particular product (see Figure 2).

- **Restrict conventional promotional efforts to the right time and right place.** Persuasive communication efforts are still valid for specific communication tasks, such as regular advertising and the product information pages on a website, but efforts to inject blatant "salespeak" into social networking conversations will usually be rejected by the audience.
- **Maintain a consistent personality.** Each social network is a unique environment with particular norms of communication.[21] For example, as a strictly business-oriented network, LinkedIn has a more formal "vibe" than Facebook and Google+, which cater to both consumers and businesses. However, while adapting to the expectations of each network, be sure to maintain a consistent personality across all the networks in which you are active.[22]

MOBILE APP
The social media management app Social Oomph lets you monitor multiple social media sites, schedule updates, and perform other time-saving tasks.

Product promotion can be done on social networks, but it needs to be done in a low-key, indirect way.

3 LEARNING OBJECTIVE
Explain how companies and business professionals can use information and content sharing websites.

Information and Content Sharing Sites

Social networks allow members to share information and media items as part of the networking experience, but a variety of systems have been designed specifically for sharing content. The field is diverse and still evolving, but the possibilities can be divided into user-generated content sites, content curation sites, and community Q&A sites.

Figure 2 **Community Building via Social Media**
Customer-affiliation groups can be an effective way to build stakeholder support for a company and its products. Indian Motorcycles used this Google⁺ post to spur interest in its rider groups.

USER-GENERATED CONTENT SITES

YouTube, Flickr, Yelp, and other **user-generated content (UGC) sites**, in which users rather than website owners contribute most or all of the content, have become serious business tools. On YouTube, for example, companies post everything from product demonstrations and TV commercials to company profiles and technical support explanations.

As with other social media, the keys to effective UGC are making it valuable and making it easy. First, provide content that people want to see and share with colleagues. A video clip that explains how to use a product more effectively will be more popular than a clip that talks about how amazing the company behind the product is. Also, keep videos short, generally no longer than three to five minutes, if possible.[23]

Second, make material easy to find, consume, and share. For example, a *branded channel* on YouTube lets a company organize all its videos in one place, making it easy for visitors to browse the selection or subscribe to get automatic updates of future videos. Sharing features let fans share videos through email or their accounts on Twitter, Facebook, and other platforms.

> YouTube and other user-generated content sites are now important business communication channels.

CONTENT CURATION SITES

Newsfeeds from blogs and other online publishers can be a great way to stay on top of developments in any field. However, anyone who has signed up for more than a few RSS feeds has probably experienced the "firehose effect" of getting so many feeds so quickly that it becomes impossible to stay on top of them. Moreover, when a highly active publisher feeds every new article, from the essential to the trivial, the reader is left to sort it all out every day.

> Content curation is the process of collecting and presenting information on a particular topic in a way that makes it convenient for target readers.

Companies in virtually every industry use social media and continue to experiment with new ways to connect with customers and other stakeholders. From offering helpful tips on using products to helping customers meet each other, these companies show the enormous range of possibilities that new media continue to bring to business communication.[14]

Recruiting and Business-Focused Social Networks

Marketo, a developer of digital marketing software, maintains a profile on LinkedIn, as do hundreds of its employees.

Tweetups

A powerful capability of online social media is bringing people with similar interests together offline. *Tweetups,* for example, are in-person meetings planned and organized over Twitter.

Value-Added Content via Social Networks

Thousands of companies are on social networking platforms, but blatantly promotional posts are not always welcome by fans and followers. Instead, companies such as Whole Foods use social networks to share information of interest, such as recipes and nutritional advice.

Value-Added Content via Blogging

One of the best ways to become a valued member of a network is to provide content that is useful to others in the network. The Quizzle personal finance blog offers a steady stream of articles and advice that help people manage their finances.

Value-Added Content via Online Video

Lie-Nielsen Toolworks of Warren, Maine, uses its YouTube channel to offer valuable information on choosing and using premium woodworking tools. By offering sought-after information for both current and potential customers free of charge, these videos help Lie-Nielsen foster relationships with the worldwide woodworking community and solidify its position as one of the leaders in this market. Animal Planet, Best Western, and Taco Bell are among the many other companies that make effective use of branded channels on YouTube.

Employee Recruiting

Zappos is one of the many companies now using Twitter as a recruiting tool. The company's @InsideZappos account gives potential employees an insider's look at the company's offbeat and upbeat culture.

An intriguing alternative to newsfeeds is **content curation**, in which someone with expertise or interest in a particular field collects and republishes material on a particular topic. The authors' Business Communication Headline News (http://bchn .businesscommunicationnetwork.com), for instance, was one of the earliest examples of content curation in the field of business communication.

New curation tools, including Pinterest and Scoop.it, make it easy to assemble attractive online magazines or portfolios on specific topics. Although it raises important issues regarding content ownership and message control,[24] curation has the potential to bring the power of community and shared expertise to a lot of different fields; ultimately, it could reshape audience behavior and therefore the practice of business communication.

COMMUNITY Q&A SITES

Community Q&A sites, on which visitors answer questions posted by other visitors, are a contemporary twist on the early ethos of computer networking, which was people helping each other. (Groups of like-minded people connected online long before the World Wide Web was even created.) Community Q&A sites include dedicated customer support communities such as those hosted on Get Satisfaction and public sites such as Quora and Yahoo! Answers.

Community Q&A sites offer great opportunities for building your personal brand.

Responding to questions on Q&A sites can be a great way to build your personal brand, demonstrate your company's commitment to customer service, and counter misinformation about your company and its products. Keep in mind that when you respond to an individual query on a community Q&A site, you are also "responding in advance" to every person in the future who comes to the site with the same question. In other words, you are writing a type of reference material in addition to corresponding with the original questioner, so keep the long time frame and wider audience in mind.

Email

Email has been an important communication tool for many companies for several decades, and in the beginning it offered a huge advantage in speed and efficiency over the media it usually replaced (printed and faxed messages). Over the years, email began to be used for many communication tasks simply because it was the only widely available digital format for written messages and millions of users were comfortable with it. However, newer tools—such as instant messaging, blogs, microblogs, social networks, and shared workspaces—are taking over specific tasks for which they are better suited.[25] For example, email is not usually the best choice for conversational communication (IM is better) or project management discussions and updates (blogs, wikis, and various purpose-built systems are often preferable).

Email remains a primary format for companies, but better alternatives now exist for many types of communication.

In addition to the widespread availability of better alternatives for many communication purposes, the indiscriminate use of email has lowered its appeal in the eyes of many professionals. In a sense, email is too easy to use—with a couple of mouse clicks you can send low-value messages to multiple recipients or trigger long message chains that become impossible to follow as people chime in along the way. In fact, frustration with email is so high in some companies that managers are making changes to reduce or even eliminate its use for internal communication.[26]

Email can seem a bit "old school" in comparison to social networks and other technologies, but it is still one of the more important business communication media.

However, email still has compelling advantages that will keep it in steady use in many companies. First, email is universal. Anybody with an email address can reach anybody else with an email address, no matter which systems the senders and receivers are on. Second, email is still the best medium for many private, short- to medium-length messages, particularly when the exchange is limited to two people. Unlike with microblogs or IM, for instance, midsize messages are easy to compose and easy to read on email. Third, email's noninstantaneous nature is an advantage when used properly. Email lets senders compose substantial messages in private and on their own schedule, and it lets recipients read those messages at their leisure.

PLANNING EMAIL MESSAGES

The solution to email overload starts in the planning step, by making sure every message has a useful, business-related purpose. Also, be aware that many companies now have formal email policies that specify how employees can use email, including restrictions against using company email service for personal messages, sending confidential information, or sending material that might be deemed objectionable. In addition, many employers now monitor email, either automatically with software programmed to look for sensitive content or manually via security staff actually reading selected email messages. Regardless of formal policies, though, every email user has a responsibility to avoid actions that could cause trouble, from opening virus-infected attachments to sending inappropriate photographs.

Even with fairly short messages, spend a moment or two on the message-planning tasks: analyzing the situation, gathering necessary information for your readers, and organizing your message. You'll save time in the long run because you will craft a more effective message on the first attempt. Your readers will get the information they need and won't have to generate follow-up messages asking for clarification or additional information.

Do your part to stem the flood of email by making sure you don't send unnecessary messages or cc people who don't really need to see particular messages.

WRITING EMAIL MESSAGES

When you approach email writing on the job, recognize that business email is a more formal medium than you are probably accustomed to with email for personal communication (see Figure 3 on the next page). The expectations of writing quality for business email are higher than for personal email, and the consequences of bad writing or poor judgment can be much more serious. For example, email messages and other digital documents have the same legal weight as printed documents, and they are often used as evidence in lawsuits and criminal investigations.[27]

Business email messages are more formal than the email messages you send to family and friends.

The email subject line might seem like a small detail, but it is actually one of the most important parts of an email message because it helps recipients decide which messages to read and when to read them. To capture your audience's attention, make your subject lines informative and compelling. Go beyond simply describing or classifying your message; use the opportunity to build interest with keywords, quotations, directions, or questions.[28] For example, "July sales results" may accurately describe the content of a message, but "July sales results: good news and bad news" is more intriguing. Readers will want to know why some news is good and some is bad.

A poorly written subject line could lead to a message being deleted or ignored.

In addition, many email programs display the first few words or lines of incoming messages, even before the recipient opens them. In the words of social media public relations expert Steve Rubel, you can "tweetify" the opening lines of your email messages to make them stand out. In other words, choose the first few words carefully to grab your reader's attention.[29] Think of the first sentence as an extension of your subject line.

Attitudes about emoticons in business communication are changing; you'll have to use your best judgment in every case.

As a lean medium, email can present challenges when you need to express particular emotional nuances, whether positive or negative. For years, users of email (as well as IM and text messaging) have used a variety of *emoticons* to express emotions in casual communication. For example, to express sympathy as a way to take some of the sting out of negative news, one might use a "frowny face," either the :(character string or a graphical emoticon such as or one of the colorful and sometimes animated characters available in some systems.

In the past, the use of emoticons was widely regarded as unprofessional and therefore advised against in business communication. Recently, though, an increasing number of professionals seem to be using them, particularly for communication with close colleagues, even as other professionals continue to view them as evidence of lazy or immature writing.[30] In the face of these conflicting perspectives, the best advice is to use caution. Avoid emoticons for nearly all types of external communication and for formal internal communication, and avoid those bright yellow graphical emoticons (and particularly animated emoticons) in all business communication.

Crafting Messages for Digital Channels

Figure 3 Email for Business Communication
In this response to an email query from a colleague, Elaine Burgman takes advantage of her email system's features to create an efficient and effective message.

COMPLETING EMAIL MESSAGES

Particularly for important messages, taking a few moments to revise and proofread might save you hours of headaches and damage control. Also, favor simplicity when it comes to producing your email messages. A clean, easily readable font, in black on a white background, is sufficient for nearly all email messages. Take advantage of your email system's ability to include an **email signature**, a small file that automatically includes such items as your full name, title, company, and contact information at the end of your messages.

When you're ready to distribute your message, pause to verify what you're doing before you click on Send. Make sure you've included everyone necessary—and no one else. Did you click on Reply All when you meant to click on only Reply? The difference could be embarrassing or even career threatening. Don't include people in the cc (courtesy copy) or bcc (blind courtesy copy) fields unless you know how these features work. (Everyone who receives the message can see who is on the cc line but not who is on the bcc line.) Also, don't set the message priority to "high" or "urgent" unless your message is truly urgent. And if you intend to include an attachment, be sure that it is indeed attached.

Think twice before clicking on Send. A simple mistake in your content or distribution can cause major headaches.

Will Emoticons Give Your Career a Frowny Face?

Your project team has just been reprimanded by the boss for missing a deadline. Your colleagues left the meeting grumbling about being criticized in public after working nights and weekends, and you fear that morale will slip.

You could craft an inspirational message to soothe the bruised egos and get the team's energy turned around in a positive direction. However, writing such a message could be risky, because world-weary teammates might just brush it off as happytalk and resent you for trying to be a cheerleader.

Alternatively, you could suggest that your colleagues lighten up and stay focused on the ultimate goal of the project. However, you already know that telling grumpy people to cheer up is a surefire way to make most of them even grumpier.

Instead, you opt for a quick bit of gentle sarcasm, designed to help release the negative emotions in a collegial way. When you get back to your desk, you write the following instant message:

Well, let's pick up the pieces of our shattered lives and move on ;-)

The over-the-top phrasing is a subtle way to remind everyone that the criticism wasn't all *that* traumatic, and that winking emoticon tells everyone to lighten up without actually saying so. The apparent sarcasm connects with people who are marinating in their negative emotions, but it's really a pep talk disguised as sarcasm.

Then you worry that the emoticon will seem unprofessional, so you replace it with a simple period:

Well, let's pick up the pieces of our shattered lives and move on.

Oops. That one minor change to make the message more professional turned it into a statement of resigned sadness. You search your keyboard for any acceptable symbol that might help:

Well, let's pick up the pieces of our shattered lives and move on!

Great, now you've managed to sound bitter and demanding at the same time.

Given the difficulty of communicating emotional nuance in lean media such as IM and email, are emoticons really all that bad? The answer depends on the situation, your relationship with your audience, and the company culture. Until emoticons become more widely accepted in business communication, it's wise to err on the side of caution.

CAREER APPLICATIONS

1. As a manager, what reaction would you have to job applicants who use emoticons in their email messages?
2. Are emoticons just a generational difference in perspective, or is there more to the issue? Explain your answer.

To review the tips and techniques for successful email, see Table 1 on the next page and "Checklist: Creating Effective Email Messages" below.

CHECKLIST ✔ CREATING EFFECTIVE EMAIL MESSAGES

A. Planning email messages
- Make sure every email message you send is necessary.
- Don't cc or bcc anyone who doesn't really need to see the message.
- Follow company email policy; understand the restrictions your company places on email usage.
- Practice good email hygiene by not opening suspicious messages, keeping virus protection up to date, and following other company guidelines.
- Follow the chain of command.

B. Writing email messages
- Remember that business email is more formal than personal email.
- Recognize that email messages carry the same legal weight as other business documents.
- Pay attention to the quality of your writing and use correct grammar, spelling, and punctuation.
- Make your subject lines informative by clearly identifying the purpose of your message.
- Make your subject lines compelling by wording them in a way that intrigues your audiences.
- Use the first few words of the email body to catch the reader's attention.

C. Completing email messages
- Revise and proofread carefully to avoid embarrassing mistakes.
- Keep the layout of your messages simple and clean, particularly for mobile recipients.
- Use an email signature file to give recipients your contact information.
- Double-check your recipient list before sending.
- Don't mark messages as "urgent" unless they truly are urgent.

Crafting Messages for Digital Channels

TABLE 1 Tips for Effective Email Messages

Tip	Why It's Important
When you request information or action, make it clear what you're asking for, why it's important, and how soon you need it; don't make your reader write back for details.	People will be tempted to ignore your messages if they're not clear about what you want or how soon you want it.
When responding to a request, either paraphrase the request or include enough of the original message to remind the reader what you're replying to.	Some businesspeople get hundreds of email messages a day and may need reminding what your specific response is about.
If possible, avoid sending long, complex messages via email.	Long messages are easier to read as attached reports or web content.
Adjust the level of formality to the message and the audience.	Overly formal messages to colleagues can be perceived as stuffy and distant; overly informal messages to customers or top executives can be perceived as disrespectful.
Activate a signature file, which automatically pastes your contact information into every message you create.	A signature saves you the trouble of retyping vital information and ensures that recipients know how to reach you through other means.
Don't let unread messages pile up in your in-basket.	You'll miss important information and create the impression that you're ignoring other people.
Never type in all caps.	ALL CAPS ARE INTERPRETED AS SCREAMING.
Don't overformat your messages with background colors, multicolored type, unusual fonts, and so on.	Such messages can be difficult and annoying to read on screen.
Remember that messages can be forwarded anywhere and saved forever.	Don't let a moment of anger or poor judgment haunt you for the rest of your career.
Use the "return receipt requested" feature only for the most critical messages.	This feature triggers a message back to you whenever someone receives or opens your message; some consider this an invasion of privacy.
Make sure your computer has up-to-date virus protection.	One of the worst breaches of netiquette is infecting other computers because you haven't bothered to protect your own system.
Pay attention to grammar, spelling, and capitalization.	Some people don't think email needs formal rules, but careless messages make you look unprofessional and can annoy readers.
Use acronyms sparingly.	Shorthand such as IMHO (in my humble opinion) and LOL (laughing out loud) can be useful in informal correspondence with colleagues, but avoid using them in more formal messages.
Be careful with the use of emoticons.	Many people view the use of these symbols as unprofessional.
Assume that recipients may read your messages on small mobile screens.	Email is more difficult to read on small screens, so don't burden recipients with long, complicated messages.

Instant Messaging and Text Messaging

5 LEARNING OBJECTIVE
Describe the business benefits of instant messaging (IM), and identify guidelines for effective IM in the workplace.

IM is taking the place of email and voicemail for routine communication in many companies.

Phone-based text messaging is being integrated into a variety of digital communication systems.

Computer-based **instant messaging (IM)**, in which users' messages appear on each other's screens instantly, is used extensively for internal and external communication. IM is available in both stand-alone systems and as a function embedded in online meeting systems, collaboration systems, social networks, and other platforms. For conversational exchanges, it's hard to top the advantages of IM, and the technology is replacing both email and voicemail in many situations.[31] Business-grade IM systems offer a range of capabilities, including basic chat, *presence awareness* (the ability to quickly see which people are at their desks and available to IM), remote display of documents, video capabilities, remote control of other computers, automated newsfeeds from blogs and websites, and automated *bot* (derived from the word *robot*) capabilities in which a computer can carry on simple conversations.[32]

Text messaging has a number of applications in business as well, including marketing (alerting customers about new sale prices, for example), customer service (such as airline flight status, package tracking, and appointment reminders), security (for example, authenticating mobile banking transactions), crisis management (such as updating all employees working at a disaster scene), and process monitoring (alerting computer technicians to system failures, for example).[33] As it becomes more tightly integrated with other communication media, text messaging is likely to find even more widespread use in business communication. For instance, texting is now integrated into systems such as Facebook Messages and Gmail, and branded "StarStar numbers" can deliver web-based content such as videos, software apps, and digital coupons to mobile phones.[34]

The following sections focus on IM, but many of the benefits, risks, and guidelines pertain to text messaging as well.

UNDERSTANDING THE BENEFITS AND RISKS OF IM

The benefits of IM include its capability for rapid response to urgent messages, lower cost than phone calls and email, ability to mimic conversation more closely than email, and availability on a wide range of devices.[35] In addition, because it more closely resembles one-on-one conversation, IM doesn't get misused as a one-to-many broadcast method as often as email does.[36]

The potential drawbacks of IM include security problems (computer viruses, network infiltration, and the possibility that sensitive messages might be intercepted by outsiders), the need for *user authentication* (making sure that online correspondents are really who they appear to be), the challenge of logging messages for later review and archiving (a legal requirement in some industries), incompatibility between competing IM systems, and *spim* (unsolicited commercial messages, similar to email spam). Fortunately, with the growth of *enterprise instant messaging (EIM)*, or IM systems designed for large-scale corporate use, many of these problems are being overcome.

IM offers many benefits:
- Rapid response
- Low cost
- Ability to mimic conversation
- Wide availability

When using IM, be aware of the potential for constant interruptions and wasted time.

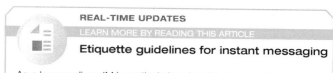

REAL-TIME UPDATES
LEARN MORE BY READING THIS ARTICLE
Etiquette guidelines for instant messaging

As a lean medium, IM is particularly vulnerable to misunderstandings; learn how to avoid them. Go to http://real-timeupdates.com/ebc12 and click on Learn More in the Students section.

ADAPTING THE THREE-STEP PROCESS FOR SUCCESSFUL IM

Although instant messages are often conceived, written, and sent within a matter of seconds, the principles of the three-step process still apply, particularly when communicating with customers and other important audiences:

- **Planning instant messages.** Except for simple exchanges, take a moment to plan IM "conversations" in much the same way you would plan an important oral conversation. A few seconds of planning can help you deliver information in a coherent, complete way that minimizes the number of individual messages required.
- **Writing instant messages.** As with email, the appropriate writing style for business IM is more formal than the style you may be accustomed to with personal IM or text messaging (see Figure 4 on the next page). Your company might discourage the use of IM acronyms (such as FWIW for "for what it's worth" or HTH for "hope that helps"), particularly for IM with external audiences.
- **Completing instant messages.** The only task in the completing stage is to send your message. Just quickly scan it before sending, to make sure you don't have any missing or misspelled words and verify that your message is clear and complete.

Although you don't plan individual instant messages the same way you do longer messages, view important IM exchanges as conversations with specific goals in mind.

To use IM effectively, keep in mind some important behavioral issues when relying on this medium: the potential for constant interruptions, the ease of accidentally mixing personal and business messages, the risk of being out of the loop (if a hot discussion or an impromptu meeting flares up when you're away from your PC or other IM device), and the frustration of being at the mercy of other people's typing abilities.[37]

Regardless of the system you're using, you can make IM more efficient and effective by heeding these tips:[38]

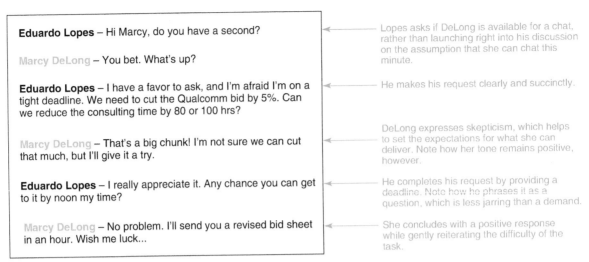

Figure 4   Instant Messaging for Business Communication
To use IM effectively in the workplace, adopt a casual but still professional tone, particularly when communicating with people outside the organization.

Understand the guidelines for successful business IM before you begin to use it.

- Be courteous; if you don't need an answer instantly, you can avoid interrupting someone by sending an email or other type of message instead.
- Unless a meeting is scheduled or you're expected to be available for other reasons, make yourself unavailable when you need to focus on other work.
- If you're not on a secure system, don't send confidential information using IM.
- Be extremely careful about sending personal messages; they have a tendency to pop up on other people's computers at embarrassing moments.
- Don't use IM for important but impromptu meetings if you can't verify that everyone concerned will be available.
- Don't use IM for lengthy, complex messages.
- Try to avoid carrying on multiple IM conversations at one time, to minimize the chance of sending messages to the wrong people or making one person wait while you tend to another conversation.
- Follow all security guidelines designed to keep your company's information and systems safe from attack.

To review the advice for effective IM in the workplace, see "Checklist: Using IM Productively".

CHECKLIST ✔ **USING IM PRODUCTIVELY**

- Pay attention to security and privacy issues and be sure to follow all company guidelines.
- Treat IM as a professional communication medium, not an informal, personal tool; avoid using IM slang with all but close colleagues.
- Maintain good etiquette, even during simple exchanges.
- Protect your own productivity by making yourself unavailable when you need to focus.
- In most instances, don't use IM for confidential messages, complex messages, or personal messages.

---

6 LEARNING OBJECTIVE
Describe the use of blogging and microblogging in business communication, and briefly explain how to adapt the three-step process to blogging.

Blogging and Microblogging

Blogs, online journals that are easier to personalize and update than conventional websites, have become a major force in business communication. Millions of business-oriented blogs are now in operation, and blogs have become an important source of information for consumers and professionals alike.[39] Good business blogs and microblogs pay close attention to several important elements:

- **Communicating with personal style and an authentic voice.** Most business messages designed for large audiences are carefully scripted and written in a "corporate voice" that is impersonal and objective. In contrast, successful business blogs are written by individuals and exhibit their personal style. Audiences relate to this fresh approach and often build closer emotional bonds with the blogger's organization as a result.

- **Delivering new information quickly.** Blogging tools let you post new material as soon as you create it or find it. This feature not only allows you to respond quickly when needed—such as during a corporate crisis—but also lets your audiences know that active communication is taking place. Blogs that don't offer a continuous stream of new and interesting content are quickly ignored in today's online environment.
- **Choosing topics of peak interest to audiences.** Successful blogs cover topics that readers care about.
- **Encouraging audiences to join the conversation.** Not all blogs invite comments, although most do, and many bloggers consider comments to be an essential feature. Blog comments can be a valuable source of news, information, and insights. In addition, the informal nature of blogging seems to make it easier for companies to let their guard down and converse with their audiences. To protect against comments that are not helpful or appropriate, many bloggers review all comments and post only the most helpful or interesting ones.

Writing in a personal, authentic voice is key to attracting and keeping blog readers.

REAL-TIME UPDATES

LEARN MORE BY READING THIS ARTICLE

Ten years later, are business blogs still a good investment?

Mainstream business blogging had been around for about a decade; is it still a good way to connect with audiences? Go to http://real-timeupdates.com/ebc12 and click on Learn More in the Students section.

UNDERSTANDING THE BUSINESS APPLICATIONS OF BLOGGING

Blogs are a potential solution whenever you have a continuing stream of information to share with an online audience—and particularly when you want the audience to have the opportunity to respond. Here are some of the many ways businesses are using blogs for internal and external communication:[40]

- **Anchoring the social media presence.** The multiple threads of any social media program should be anchored in a central hub the company or individual owns and controls. Blogs make an ideal social media hub.
- **Project management and team communication.** Using blogs is a good way to keep project teams up to date, particularly when team members are geographically dispersed. For instance, the trip reports that employees file after visiting customers or other external parties can be enhanced vividly with mobile blogs.
- **Company news.** Companies can use blogs to keep employees informed about general business matters, from facility news to benefit updates. Blogs also serve as online community forums, giving everyone in the company a chance to raise questions and voice concerns.
- **Customer support.** Customer support blogs answer questions, offer tips and advice, and inform customers about new products. Also, many companies monitor the *blogosphere* (and *Twittersphere*), looking for complaints and responding with offers to help dissatisfied customers.[41]
- **Public relations and media relations.** Many company employees and executives now share company news with both the general public and journalists via their blogs.
- **Recruiting.** Using a blog is a great way to let potential employees know more about your company, the people who work there, and the nature of the company culture. In the other direction, employers often find and evaluate the blogs and microblogs of prospective employees, making blogging is a great way to build a name for yourself within your industry or profession.
- **Policy and issue discussions.** Executive blogs in particular provide a public forum for discussing legislation, regulations, and other broad issues of interest to an organization.

The business applications of blogs include a wide range of internal and external communication tasks.

- **Crisis communication.** Using blogs is a convenient way to provide up-to-the-minute information during emergencies, correct misinformation, or respond to rumors.
- **Market research.** Blogs can be a clever mechanism for soliciting feedback from customers and experts in the marketplace. In addition to using their own blogs to solicit feedback, today's companies should monitor blogs that are likely to discuss them, their executives, and their products.
- **Brainstorming.** Online brainstorming via blogs offers a way for people to toss around ideas and build on each other's contributions.
- **Employee engagement.** Blogs can enhance communication across all levels of a company, giving lower-level employees a voice that they might not otherwise have and giving senior executives better access to timely information.
- **Customer education.** Blogs are a great way to help current and potential customers understand and use your products and services. This function can improve sales and support productivity as well, by reducing the need for one-on-one communication.
- **Word-of-mouth marketing.** Bloggers often make a point of providing links to other blogs and websites that interest them, giving marketers a great opportunity to have their messages spread by enthusiasts. (Online word-of mouth marketing is often called *viral marketing* in reference to the way biological viruses are transmitted from person to person. However, viral marketing is not really an accurate metaphor. As author Brian Solis puts it, "There is no such thing as viral marketing."[42] Real viruses spread from host to host on their own, whereas word-of-mouth marketing spreads *voluntarily* from person to person. The distinction is critical, because you need to give people a good reason—good content, in other words—to pass along your message.)
- **Influencing traditional media news coverage.** According to social media consultant Tamar Weinberg, "the more prolific bloggers who provide valuable and consistent content are often considered experts in their subject matter" and are often called on when journalists need insights into various topics.[43]
- **Community building.** Blogging is a great way to connect people with similar interests, and popular bloggers often attract a community of readers who connect with one another through the commenting function.

The uses of blogs are limited only by your creativity, so be on the lookout for new ways you can use them to foster positive relationships with colleagues, customers, and other important audiences (see Figure 5).

ADAPTING THE THREE-STEP PROCESS FOR SUCCESSFUL BLOGGING

The three-step writing process is easy to adapt to blogging tasks. The planning step is particularly important when you're launching a blog because you're planning an entire communication channel, not just a single message. Pay close attention to your audience, your purpose, and your scope:

- **Audience.** Except with team blogs and other efforts that have an obvious and well-defined audience, defining the target audience for a blog can be challenging. You want an audience large enough to justify the time you'll be investing but narrow enough that you can provide a clear focus for the blog. For instance, if you work for a firm that develops computer games, would you focus your blog on "hardcore" players, the types who spend thousands of dollars on super-fast PCs optimized for video games, or would you broaden the reach to include all video gamers? The decision often comes down to business strategy.
- **Purpose.** A business blog needs to have a business-related purpose that is important to your company and to your chosen audience. Moreover, the purpose has to "have legs"—that is, it needs to be something that can drive the blog's content for months or years—rather than focus on a single event or an issue of only temporary

Blogs are an ideal medium for *word-of-mouth marketing*, the spread of promotional messages from one audience member to another.

Before you launch a blog, make sure you have a clear understanding of your target audience, the purpose of your blog, and the scope of subjects you plan to cover.

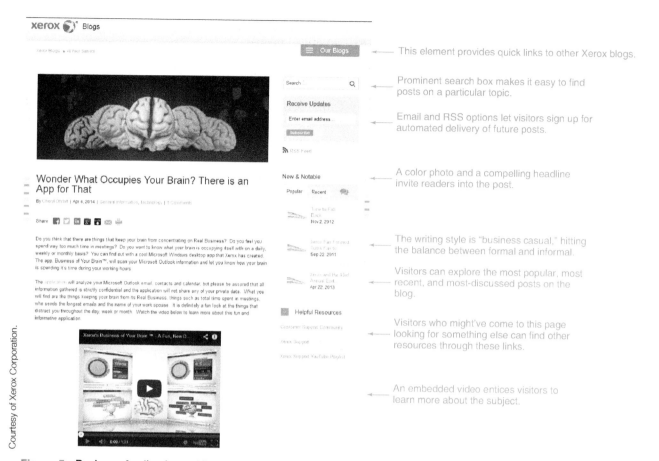

Figure 5 Business Applications of Blogging
This Xerox blog illustrates the content, writing style, and features that make an effective, reader-friendly company blog.

interest. For instance, if you're a technical expert, you might create a blog to give the audience tips and techniques for using your company's products more effectively—a never-ending subject that's important to both you and your audience. This would be the general purpose of your blog; each posting would have a specific purpose within the context of that general purpose. Finally, if you are not writing an official company blog but rather blogging as an individual employee, make sure you understand your employer's blogging guidelines. IBM, for example, gives its employees 12 specific social computing guidelines, such as identifying their role as IBM employees if they are discussing matters related to the company and respecting intellectual property laws.[44]

- **Scope.** Defining the scope of your blog can be a bit tricky. You want to cover a subject area that is broad enough to offer discussion possibilities for months or years but narrow enough to have an identifiable focus.

After you begin writing your blog, careful planning needs to continue with each message. Unless you're posting to a restricted-access blog, such as an internal blog on a company intranet, you can never be sure who might see your posts. Other bloggers might link to them months or years later.

Use a comfortable, personal writing style. Blog audiences don't want to hear from your company; they want to hear from *you*. Bear in mind, though, that comfortable does not mean careless. Sloppy writing damages your credibility. Successful blog content also needs to be interesting, valuable to readers, and as brief as possible.[45] In addition, although audiences expect you to be knowledgeable in the subject area your blog covers, you don't need to know everything about a topic. If you don't have all the information yourself, provide links to other blogs and websites that supply relevant information. In fact, content curation is one of the most valuable aspects of blogging. Just be sure the content you

Write blog postings in a comfortable—but not careless—style.

REAL-TIME UPDATES

LEARN MORE BY READING THIS INFOGRAPHIC

Grab readers' attention with your blog posts

Follow these tips to make sure your posts get noticed and get read. Go to http://real-timeupdates.com/ebc12 and click on Learn More in the Students section.

share is relevant to your readers and compatible with your communication goals.

Completing messages for your blog is usually quite easy. Evaluate the content and readability of your message, proofread to correct any errors, and post using your blogging system's tools. If you're using any contemporary blogging system, it should offer a *newsfeed* option so that your audience can automatically receive headlines and summaries of new blog posts. Really Simple Syndication (RSS) is the most common type of newsfeed.

Finally, make your material easier to find by **tagging** it with descriptive words. Your readers can then click on these "content labels" to find additional posts on those topics. Tags are usually displayed with each post, and they can also be groups in a *tag cloud* display, which shows all the tags in use on your blog.

Table 2 offers a variety of tips for successful blogging, and "Checklist: Blogging for Business" summarizes some of the key points to remember when creating and writing a business blog.

TABLE 2 Tips for Effective Business Blogging

Tip	Why It's Important
Don't blog without a clear plan.	Without a clear plan, your blog is likely to wander from topic to topic and fail to build a sense of community with your audience.
Post frequently; the whole point of a blog is fresh material.	If you won't have a constant supply of new information or new links, create a traditional website instead.
Make it about your audience and the issues important to them.	Readers want to know how your blog will help them, entertain them, or give them a chance to communicate with others who have similar interests.
Write in an authentic voice; never create an artificial character who supposedly writes a blog.	Flogs, or fake blogs, violate the spirit of blogging, show disrespect for your audience, and will turn audiences against you as soon as they uncover the truth. Fake blogs used to promote products are now illegal in some countries.
Link generously—but carefully.	Providing interesting links to other blogs and websites is a fundamental aspect of blogging, but make sure the links will be of value to your readers and don't point to inappropriate material.
Keep it brief.	Most online readers don't have the patience to read lengthy reports. Rather than writing long, report-style posts, you can write brief posts that link to in-depth reports.
Don't post anything you wouldn't want the entire world to see.	Future employers, government regulators, competitors, journalists, and community critics are just a few of the people who might eventually see what you've written.
Minimize marketing and sales messages.	Readers want information about them and their needs.
Take time to write compelling, specific headlines for your postings.	Readers usually decide within a couple of seconds whether to read your postings; boring or vague headlines will turn them away instantly.
Pay attention to spelling, grammar, and mechanics.	No matter how smart or experienced you are, poor-quality writing undermines your credibility with intelligent audiences.
Respond to criticism openly and honestly.	Hiding sends the message that you don't have a valid response to the criticism. If your critics are wrong, patiently explain why you think they're wrong. If they are right, explain how you'll fix the situation.
Listen and learn.	If you don't take the time to analyze the comments people leave on your blog or the comments other bloggers make about you, you're missing out on one of the most valuable aspects of blogging.
Respect intellectual property.	Improperly using material you don't own is not only unethical but can be illegal as well.
Be scrupulously honest and careful with facts.	Honesty is an absolute requirement for every ethical business communicator, of course, but you need to be extra careful online because inaccuracies (both intentional and unintentional) are likely to be discovered quickly and shared widely.
If you review products on your blog, disclose any beneficial relationships you have with the companies that make those products.	Bloggers who receive free products or other compensation from companies whose products they write about are now required to disclose the nature of these relationships.

CHECKLIST ✔ **BLOGGING FOR BUSINESS**

- Consider creating a blog or microblog account whenever you have a continuing stream of information to share with an online audience.
- Identify an audience that is broad enough to justify the effort but narrow enough to have common interests.
- Identify a purpose that is comprehensive enough to provide ideas for a continuing stream of posts.
- Consider the scope of your blog carefully; make it broad enough to attract an audience but narrow enough to keep you focused.

- Communicate with a personal style and an authentic voice, but don't write carelessly.
- Deliver new information quickly.
- Choose topics of peak interest to your audience.
- Encourage audiences to join the conversation.
- Consider using Twitter or other microblog updates to alert readers to new posts on your regular blog.

MICROBLOGGING

A **microblog** is a variation on blogging in which messages are sharply restricted to specific character counts. Twitter is the best known of these systems, but many others exist. Some companies have private microblogging systems for internal use only; these systems are sometimes referred to as *enterprise microblogging* or *internal micromessaging*.[46]

Many of the concepts of regular blogging apply to microblogging as well, although the severe length limitations call for a different approach to composition. Microblog messages often involve short summaries or teasers that provide links to more information. In addition, microblogs tend to have a stronger social aspect that makes it easier for writers and readers to forward messages and for communities to form around individual writers.[47]

Like regular blogging, microblogging quickly caught on with business users and is now a mainstream business medium. Microblogs are used for virtually all of the blog applications mentioned previously. In addition, microblogs are often used for interacting with customers (see Figure 6 on the next page), providing company updates, offering coupons and notice of sales, presenting tips on product usage, sharing relevant and interesting information from experts, announcing headlines of new blog posts, and serving as the *backchannel* in meetings and presentations. By following top names in your field, you can customize Twitter as your own real-time news source.[48] Customer service is becoming a popular use for Twitter as well, thanks to its ease, speed, and the option of switching between public tweets and private direct messages as the situation warrants.[49] The social networking aspect of Twitter and other microblogs also makes them good for *crowdsourcing* research questions, asking ones' followers for input or advice.[50] Finally, the ease of *retweeting*, the practice of forwarding messages from other Twitter users, is the microblogging equivalent of sharing other content from other bloggers via content curation.

In addition to its usefulness as a stand-alone system, Twitter is also integrated with other social media systems and a variety of publishing and reading tools and services. Many of these system use the informal Twitter feature known as the *hashtag* (the # symbol followed by a word or phrase), which makes it easy for people to label and search for topics of interest and to monitor ongoing Twitter conversations about particular topics.

MOBILE APP
The mobile app for Twitter helps you stay connected with your followers and the accounts you follow.

The business communication uses of microblogging extend beyond the publication of brief updates.

REAL-TIME UPDATES

LEARN MORE BY READING THIS ARTICLE

Twitter tips for beginners

An experienced user shares tips for getting the most from Twitter. Go to http://real-timeupdates.com/ebc12 and click on Learn More in the Students section.

REAL-TIME UPDATES

LEARN MORE BY READING THIS ARTICLE

Managing multiple Twitter accounts at Walmart

See how Walmart's social media team interacts with followers across seven Twitter accounts. Go to http://real-timeupdates .com/ebc12 and click on Learn More in the Students section.

Courtesy of Mathews Archery, Inc.

Figure 6   Business Applications of Microblogging
Mathews, a small manufacturer of archery products, uses Twitter to foster relationships with customers and other interested parties. Notice how every tweet in this time line is part of a conversation.

Don't let the speed and simplicity of microblogging lull you into making careless mistakes; every message should support your business communication objectives.

Although microblogs are designed to encourage spontaneous communication, when you're using the medium for business communication, don't just tweet out whatever pops into your head. Make sure messages are part of your overall communication strategy. Twitter followers consider tweets that are entertaining, surprising, informative, or engaging (such as asking followers for advice) as the most valuable. In contrast, the least-valuable tweets tend to be complaints, conversations between the Twitter account owner and a specific follower, and relatively pointless messages such as saying "good morning."[51]

Podcasting

7 LEARNING OBJECTIVE
Explain how to adapt the three-step writing process for podcasts.

Podcasting is the process of recording audio or video files and distributing them online via RSS subscriptions, in the same way that blog posts are automatically fed to subscribers. Podcasting combines the media richness of voice or visual communication with the convenience of portability. Audiences can listen or watch podcasts on a blog or website, or they can download them to phones or portable music players to consume on the go. Particularly with audio podcasts, the hands-off, eyes-off aspect makes them great for listening to while driving or exercising.

Podcasting can be used to deliver a wide range of audio and video messages.

The most obvious use of podcasting is to replace existing audio and video messages, such as one-way teleconferences in which a speaker provides information without expecting to engage in conversation with the listeners. Training is another good use of podcasting; you may have already taken a college course via podcasts. Podcasting is also a great way to offer free previews of seminars and training classes.[52] Many business writers and consultants use podcasting to build their personal brands and to enhance their other product and service offerings. You can find a wide selection on iTunes, many of which are free (go to the Podcasting section and select the Business category).

Although it might not seem obvious at first, the three-step writing process adapts quite nicely to podcasting. First, focus the planning step on analyzing the situation, gathering the information you'll need, and organizing your material. One vital planning step depends on whether you intend to create podcasts for limited use and distribution (such as a weekly audio update to your virtual team) or to create a **podcasting channel** with regular recordings on a consistent theme, designed for a wider public audience. As with planning a blog, if you intend to create a podcasting channel, be sure to think through the range of topics you want to address over time to verify that you have a sustainable purpose. If you bounce from one theme to another, you risk losing your audience.[53] Maintaining a consistent schedule is also important; listeners will stop paying attention if they can't count on regular updates.[54]

As you organize the content for a podcast, pay close attention to previews, transitions, and reviews. These steering devices are especially vital in audio recordings because audio lacks the "street signs" (such as headings) that audiences rely on in print media. Moreover, scanning back and forth to find specific parts of an audio or video message is much more difficult than with textual messages, so you need to do everything possible to make sure your audience successfully receives and interprets your message on the first try.

One of the attractions of podcasting is the conversational, person-to-person feel of the recordings, so unless you need to capture exact wording, speaking from an outline and notes rather than a prepared script is often the best choice. However, no one wants to listen to rambling podcasts that take several minutes to get to the topic or struggle to make a point, so don't try to make up your content on the fly. Effective podcasts, like effective stories, have a clear beginning, middle, and end.

The completing step is where podcasting differs most dramatically from written communication, for the obvious reason that you are recording and distributing audio or video files. Particularly for more formal podcasts, start by revising your script or thinking through your speaking notes before you begin to record. The closer you can get to recording your podcasts in one take, the more productive you'll be.

Most personal computers, smartphones, and other devices now have basic audio recording capability, including built-in microphones, and free editing software such as Audacity is available online (see Figure 7 on the next page). These tools can be sufficient for creating informal podcasts for internal use, but to achieve the higher production quality expected in formal or public podcasts, you'll need additional pieces of hardware and software. These can include an audio processor (to filter out extraneous noise and otherwise improve the audio signal), a mixer (to combine multiple audio or video signals), a better microphone, more sophisticated recording and editing software, and perhaps some physical changes in your recording location to improve the acoustics.

Podcasts can be distributed in several ways, including through media stores such as iTunes, by dedicated podcast hosting services, or on a blog with content that supports the podcast channel. If you distribute your podcast on a blog, you can provide additional information and use the commenting feature of the blog to encourage feedback from your audience.[55]

The three-step process adapts quite well to podcasting.

Steering devices such as transitions, previews, and reviews are vital in podcasts.

Plan your podcast content carefully; editing is more difficult with podcasts than with textual messages.

For basic podcasts, your computer and perhaps even your smartphone might have most of the hardware you already need, and you can download recording software.

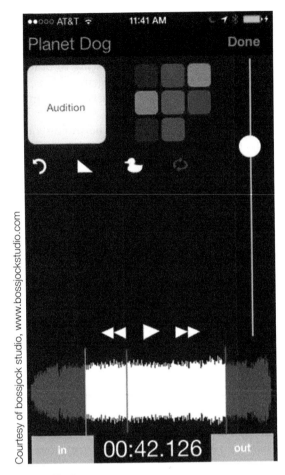

Courtesy of bossjock studio, www.bossjockstudio.com

Figure 7 Mobile Podcasting Tools
Mobile podcasting apps make it easy to record podcasts on location.

ON THE JOB: SOLVING COMMUNICATION DILEMMAS AT GOPRO

You've joined GoPro's community engagement team, and your job involves a variety of communication tasks across multiple channels. Use what you've learned in the course so far to solve these communication dilemmas.

1. You've written a blog post for a competition called "Catch Something Amazing," in which GoPro users can submit "unplanned and unrehearsed" footage of events, performances, or other bits of action they just happen to stumble across while out and about with the GoPro cameras. Which of the following tweets is the best teaser to encourage people to click through to the blog post to read more about the competition?

   a. You've just caught something amazing on camera—don't hoard it; share it!
   b. We're not interested in the same old boring stuff. If you caught something amazing, we want to see it.
   c. Did you catch something amazing with your GoPro? Enter to win $500 worth of equipment accessories.
   d. Enter to win. Competition limited to GoPro users only (any model).

2. One member of the customer engagement team is retiring, and you've been asked to recruit her replacement with someone whose primary responsibility will be blogging. Your plan is to send an email message to everyone in the company, providing a brief reminder of the blog's purpose, describing the writing style you're looking for, and inviting interested writers to submit sample blog entries for evaluation. Which of the following paragraphs is the best way to describe the preferred writing style for the blog? (This message is for employees only; it won't be seen by the public.)

   a. Our best social content connects with thousands of readers because the writing is *engaging* (people want to read and respond), *personal* (readers want to get to know real, live human beings, not a faceless corporation), *honest* (we don't sugar-coat anything or hide from criticism), and *friendly* (our readers want to enjoy the experience).
   b. What kind of writing are we looking for? Well, let me tell you exactly what we need. We need writing that is above all (a) engaging—it makes people *want* to read and

become involved in the conversation. Plus, (b), the writing must be *personal*; we don't need anybody to repeat "the company line" here; we want *your unique* thoughts and opinions. However, (c), we, of course (!), need writing that is consistent with GoPro's culture.

c. You should be able to produce copy that meets the following criteria: Your writing must be engaging, personal, honest, and friendly. Writing that does not meet these criteria, no matter how well written in other respects, will not be accepted for online publication.

d. I'll be short and to the point: the writing we want for this blog must be engaging, personal, honest, and friendly.

3. Which of the following would be the best subject line for the email message to recruit a new blogger for the customer engagement team?

a. Opening for a blogger on the customer engagement team
b. Job opening: customer engagement team
c. Calling all bloggers
d. Would you like to join the GoPro social media conversation?

4. Which of the following would be the most effective headline for a Facebook post that announces a new version of the free GoPro Studio software?

a. The easiest way to edit and share your GoPro videos is now easier than ever
b. No geek cred? No prob; even you can edit videos with this software!
c. Creating exciting, pro-quality videos is now as easy as dropping your footage into a GoPro template that's complete with music and special effects.
d. Forgot those expensive, complicated video editing programs.

Learning Objectives Checkup

Assess your understanding of the principles in this chapter by reading each learning objective and studying the accompanying exercises. You can check your responses against the answer key.

Objective 1: Identify the major digital media used for brief business messages and describe the nine compositional modes needed for digital and social media.

1. How has content sharing through social media changed the information gathering habits of many consumers and professionals?
   a. They frequently "snack" on large numbers of small pieces of information and bypass larger documents that would take more time to read.
   b. Everyone above a certain level in the organization has content readers who "pre-read" documents and messages to select the most important.
   c. All major business decisions now rely on the "hive mind," the collective input of a professional's business network.
   d. Information that doesn't have a catchy teaser is routinely ignored.

2. To express sympathy to the family of one of your employees who recently died in a traffic accident, which of these media would you choose and why?
   a. Facebook post
   b. Printed letter
   c. Email message
   d. Instant message

3. Which of the following is not listed in the chapter as one of the compositional modes for digital media?
   a. Conversations
   b. Redacting

c. Comments and critiques
d. Narratives

4. Which of these descriptions best captures the preferred style of writing for social media in business?
   a. Businesslike and message-driven
   b. Unplanned, unrehearsed, and super casual
   c. Conversational, supportive, and engaged
   d. Funny, quirky, and intriguing

Objective 2: Describe the use of social networks in business communication.

5. A/an _____ _____ is a group of people united by their interest in and ownership or use of a particular product.

6. Which of these best describes the role of a *hub* in a company's social media strategy?
   a. An open-plan office in which all the company's social media users can congregate in order to ensure a coordinated public presence
   b. The company's Facebook page or its Facebook page and Twitter account
   c. A company-owned web property that serves as the anchor of its online presence
   d. An online brand community

7. _____ _____ is a measure of how effectively a company engages with its various online stakeholders in a mutually beneficial exchange of information.

Objective 3: Explain how companies and business professionals can use information and content sharing websites.

8. YouTube, Flickr, and Yelp are examples of
   a. Consumer-only websites
   b. User-generated content sites
   c. Social interactivity blogs
   d. Content exchanges

9. When someone with expertise or interest in a particular field collects and republishes material on a particular topic, the practice is known as
   a. Content curation
   b. Media consolidation
   c. Blog linking
   d. Tagging and pinning

Objective 4: Describe the evolving role of email in business communication and explain how to adapt the three-step writing process to email messages.

10. Which of the following is one reason many companies are trying to reduce email usage?
    a. To reduce the number of messages that can be used as legal evidence
    b. To reduce costs, because email hosting has doubled in price in the last decade
    c. To lower the processing demands on company servers
    d. To reduce the number of low-value messages employees have to contend with

11. Which of the following is true of email subject lines?
    a. Only "newbies" bother to use them anymore.
    b. Subject lines should never give away the content of the message because no one will bother to read it if they already know what the message is about.
    c. They can make the difference between a message being read right away, skipped over for later attention, or ignored entirely.
    d. They should always be in all caps to get the audience's attention.

12. Which of the following is the most effective email subject line?
    a. Production line: wiring issues
    b. Wiring errors in production: let's analyze the problem and explore solutions
    c. Wiring errors on the production line MUST STOP NOW!
    d. Careless employees => unhappy customers => fewer customers => fewer employees

13. You work in a customer service department, answering emails from customers. This morning you received an angry message from a customer who has a legitimate complaint about your company's warranty policies. After responding to the message as best you can, which of the following steps should you take?
    a. Forward the message to your immediate supervisor and suggest that the company might want to reconsider its warranty policies.
    b. Forward the message to the CEO and suggest that the company might want to reconsider its warranty policies.
    c. Forward the message to everyone in the department so they are aware of the problem with the warranty policy.
    d. Delete the customer's message; you can't fix the warranty policy.

Objective 5: Describe the business benefits of instant messaging (IM) and identify guidelines for effective IM in the workplace.

14. Which of the following reasons helps explain why IM usage is overtaking email in some companies?

a. People don't have to be so formal when they use IM; it saves time to use acronyms and emoticons and to avoid using capitalization, punctuation, and other time wasters.
b. IM works better as a broadcast mechanism than email.
c. IM is faster than email and mimics human conversation better than email, so many people find it a more natural way to communicate.
d. IM systems let you communicate using different colors of text, which is vital for highlighting key points and conveying nonverbal aspects that are impossible to communicate in email.

15. Which of these statements best describes how the three-step writing process applies to IM?
    a. Because there is no planning step and no completing step in IM, the three-step process does not apply.
    b. The real beauty of IM in the business world is that people don't have to spend so much time composing; they just zap out whatever is on their minds and get back to work.
    c. The three-step process for IM works exactly the same way as it does with letters, memos, and reports. Every message requires audience analysis, information gathering, and outlining.
    d. IM exchanges should be planned the same way conversations are planned to minimize confusion and the number of messages required. And instant messages don't have to be great works of literature, but they do need to be efficient and effective, so some degree of care in writing and revising is important.

16. Which of the following types of messages are most appropriate for IM?
    a. Long, complex messages
    b. Brief conversational messages
    c. Confidential or highly personal messages
    d. All of the above

Objective 6: Describe the role of blogging and microblogging in business communication, and briefly explain how to adapt the three-step writing process to blogging.

17. Which of the following is a good strategy for using blogs to promote products and services?
    a. Write in a style that is personal and conversational; minimize direct promotion of your products and services. Focus instead on topics your customers and potential customers find helpful and interesting.
    b. To cut through the noise in the blogosphere, promote your products and services constantly. If you don't, your competitors will drown you out.
    c. Make sure the blog matches all other corporate communications in both style and content; customers get confused when a company communicates in more than one style.
    d. Blogs should never be used for marketing and selling.

18. Which of the following best describes the idea of an "authentic voice" in blogging?
    a. A writing style that is scrupulously precise and free from technical and grammatical errors
    b. The voice of a real, living, breathing human being, communicating to other human beings on a personal level

c. Writing that is always highly emotional so as to counteract the dehumanizing logic and linear thinking that dominates business today

d. A detached, professional voice that is careful not to take sides, voice opinions, or otherwise inject elements into the conversation that could disturb or disappoint audiences

19. Which of the following best describes the optimum audience of a blog?

a. Always the largest audience possible

b. Only people who are experts in the subject matter so that comments and discussions aren't pulled off track by "newbies" who don't know what they are talking about

c. An audience large enough to justify the time required to maintain the blog but narrow enough to ensure a clear focus

d. Whatever audience happens to find the blog on the web

20. Which of the following is *not* a good general purpose for a blog?

a. Sharing news from the racing circuit, describing how the racers we sponsor are faring and how they use our products

b. Commenting on economic and social policy decisions that affect the national and international business environment

c. Explaining to the local community why we've decided not to expand employment at the Nampa facility

d. Describing the work going on in our research and development labs

21. Which of the following would be a good use of retweeting for an independent consulting engineer who uses Twitter to build relationships with potential clients?

a. Avoiding retweeting under any circumstances, because it is tantamount to plagiarizing

b. Retweeting every tweet he or she receives so that clients know how well-rounded and well-read she is

c. Retweeting fun and interesting messages on nonbusiness topics as a way to build an emotional bond with potential clients

d. Retweeting selectively, sharing only messages that meet two strict criteria: providing information that followers can use in their work and portraying the consultant as an expert who is up on the latest developments in her field

Objective 7: Explain how to adapt the three-step writing process for podcasts.

22. If one of the attractions of podcasting is its spontaneous, conversational feel, why should podcasters take the time to plan their recordings?

a. Individual podcasts that aren't well thought out can end up being rambling, confusing, and repetitive.

b. Podcasts are more difficult to edit than textual messages, so it's important to do enough planning to help avoid major mistakes.

c. If you don't plan ahead, you could run out of ideas and therefore have no reason to continue podcasting.

d. All of the above are reasons to plan podcasts.

23. A/an ____ ____ is an ongoing series of podcasts on the same general topic.

Quick Learning Guide

LEARNING OBJECTIVES

1 Identify the major digital channels used for brief business messages, and describe the nine compositional modes needed for digital media.

2 Describe the use of social networks in business communication.

3 Explain how companies and business professionals can use information and content sharing websites.

4 Describe the evolving role of email in business communication, and explain how to adapt the three-step writing process to email messages.

5 Describe the business benefits of instant messaging (IM), and identify guidelines for effective IM in the workplace.

6 Describe the use of blogging and microblogging in business communication, and briefly explain how to adapt the three-step process to blogging.

7 Explain how to adapt the three-step writing process for podcasts.

KEY TERMS

blogs Online journals that are easier to personalize and update than conventional websites

brand communities Communities of interest that form around a specific product

brand socialization A measure of how effectively a company engages with its various online stakeholders in a mutually beneficial exchange of information

community Q&A sites Sites on which visitors answer questions posted by other visitors,

content curation Practice in which someone with expertise or interest in a particular field collects and republishes material on a particular topic

email signature A small file that automatically includes such items as your full name, title, company, and contact information at the end of your messages

instant messaging (IM) Computer-based in which users' messages appear on each other's screens instantly

microblog A variation on blogging in which messages are sharply restricted to specific character counts

podcasting The process of recording audio or video files and distributing them online via RSS subscriptions

podcasting channel Series of podcasts on a consistent theme

social media Digital media-channel combinations that empower stakeholders as participants in the communication process by allowing them to share content, revise content, respond to content, or contribute new content

tagging Assigning descriptive words to social media content to simplify searching

text messaging Transmission of short text-only messages using phones

user-generated content (UGC) sites Sites in which users rather than website owners contribute most or all of the content

CHECKLIST ✔
Using IM Productively

- Pay attention to security and privacy issues and be sure to follow all company guidelines.
- Treat IM as a professional communication medium, not an informal, personal tool; avoid using IM slang with all but close colleagues.
- Maintain good etiquette, even during simple exchanges.
- Protect your own productivity by making yourself unavailable when you need to focus.
- In most instances, don't use IM for confidential messages, complex messages, or personal messages.

CHECKLIST ✔
Blogging for Business

- Consider creating a blog or microblog account whenever you have a continuing stream of information to share with an online audience.
- Identify an audience that is broad enough to justify the effort but narrow enough to have common interests.
- Identify a purpose that is comprehensive enough to provide ideas for a continuing stream of posts.
- Consider the scope of your blog carefully; make it broad enough to attract an audience but narrow enough to keep you focused.
- Communicate with a personal style and an authentic voice, but don't write carelessly.
- Deliver new information quickly.
- Choose topics of peak interest to your audience.
- Encourage audiences to join the conversation.
- Consider using Twitter or other microblog updates to alert readers to new posts on your regular blog.

MyBCommLab

To complete the problems with the ⭐, go to EOC Discussion Questions in the MyLab.

Apply Your Knowledge

To review chapter content related to each question, refer to the indicated Learning Objective.

⭐ 1. Given the strict limits on length, should all your microblogging messages function as teasers that link to more detailed information on a blog or website? Why or why not? [LO-1]

2. Can your company stay in control of it messages if its stay off social media? Why or why not? [LO-2]

⭐ 3. Is leveraging your connections on social networks for business purposes ethical? Why or why not? [LO-3]

⭐ 4. If one of the benefits of blogging is the personal, intimate style of writing, is it a good idea to limit your creativity by adhering to conventional rules of grammar, spelling, and mechanics? Why or why not? [LO-6]

5. What are some ways the president of a hiking equipment company could use Twitter to engage potential customers without being overtly promotional? [LO-6]

Practice Your Skills

6. **Message 7.A: Media Skills: IM; Creating a Business-like Tone [LO-5]** Review the following IM exchange and explain how the customer service agent could have handled the situation more effectively.

AGENT:	Thanks for contacting Home Exercise Equipment. What's up?
CUSTOMER:	I'm having trouble assembling my home gym.
AGENT:	I hear that a lot! LOL
CUSTOMER:	So is it me or the gym?
AGENT:	Well, let's see <g>. Where are you stuck?
CUSTOMER:	The crossbar that connects the vertical pillars doesn't fit.
AGENT:	What do you mean doesn't fit?
CUSTOMER:	It doesn't fit. It's not long enough to reach across the pillars.
AGENT:	Maybe you assembled the pillars in the wrong place. Or maybe we sent the wrong crossbar.
CUSTOMER:	How do I tell?
AGENT:	The parts aren't labeled so could be tough. Do you have a measuring tape? Tell me how long your crossbar is.

7. **Message 7.B: Media Skills: Blogging, Creating a Businesslike Tone [LO-6]** Read the following blog post and (a) analyze the strengths and weaknesses of each sentence and (b) revise it so that it follows the guidelines in this chapter.

We're DOOMED!!!!!

I was at the Sikorsky plant in Stratford yesterday, just checking to see how things were going with the assembly line retrofit we did for them last year. I think I saw the future, and it ain't pretty. They were demo'ing a prototype robot from Motoman that absolutely blows our stuff out of the water. They

wouldn't let me really see it, but based on the 10-second glimpse I got, it's smaller, faster, and more maneuverable than any of our units. And when I asked about the price, the guy just grinned. And it wasn't the sort of grin designed to make me feel good.

I've been saying for years that we need to pay more attention to size, speed, and maneuverability instead of just relying on our historical strengths of accuracy and payload capacity, and you'd have to be blind not to agree that this experience proves me right. If we can't at least show a design for a better unit within two or three months, Motoman is going to lock up the market and leave us utterly in the dust.

Believe me, being able to say "I told you so" right now is not nearly as satisfying as you might think!!

8. **Message 7.C: Media Skills: Podcasting [LO-7]** To access this podcast exercise, visit http://real-time updates.com/ebc12, click on Student Assignments, and select this chapter-, Message 7.C, and listen to this podcast. Identify at least three ways in which the podcast could be improved, and draft a brief email message you could send to the podcaster with your suggestions for improvement.

Exercises

Each activity is labeled according to the primary skill or skills you will need to use. To review relevant chapter content, you can refer to the indicated Learning Objective.

9. **Collaboration: Working in Teams; Planning: Selecting Media [LO-1]** Working with at least two other students, identify the best medium to use for each of the following messages. For each of these message needs, choose a medium that you think would work effectively and explain your choice. (More than one medium could work in some cases; just be able to support your particular choice.)

   a. A technical support service for people trying to use their digital music players

   b. A message of condolence to the family of an employee who passed away recently

   c. A collection of infographics from a variety of sources on the state of the consumer electronics industry

   d. A series of observations on the state of the industry

   e. A series of messages, questions, and answers surrounding the work of a project team on a confidential company project

10. **Media Skills: Social Networking [LO-2]** Pick a company in any industry that interests you. Imagine you are doing strategic planning for this firm, and identify one of your company's key competitors. (Hint: You can use the free listings on www.hoovers.com to find several top competitors for most medium and large companies in the United States.) Now search through social media sources to find three strategically relevant pieces of information about this competitor, such as the hiring of a new executive, the launch of a major new product, or a significant problem of some kind. In a post on your class blog, identify the information you found and the

sources you used. (If you can't find useful information, pick another firm or try another industry.)

11. **Media Skills: Writing Email Subject Lines [LO-4]** Using your imagination to make up whatever details you need, revise the following email subject lines to make them more informative:
   a. New budget figures
   b. Marketing brochure—your opinion
   c. Production schedule

12. **Media Skills: Email [LO-4]** The following email message contains numerous errors related to what you've learned about planning and writing business messages. First, list the flaws you find in this version. Then use the following steps to plan and write a better memo.

TO: Felicia August <b_august@evertrust.com>

SUBJECT: Compliance with new break procedure

Some of you may not like the rules about break times; however, we determined that keeping track of employees while they took breaks at times they determined rather than regular breaks at prescribed times was not working as well as we would have liked it to work. The new rules are not going to be an option. If you do not follow the new rules, you could be docked from your pay for hours when you turned up missing, since your direct supervisor will not be able to tell whether you were on a "break" or not and will assume that you have walked away from your job. We cannot be responsible for any errors that result from your inattentiveness to the new rules. I have already heard complaints from some of you and I hope this memo will end this issue once and for all. The decision has already been made.

Starting Monday, January 1, you will all be required to take a regular 15-minute break in the morning and again in the afternoon, and a regular thirty-minute lunch at the times specified by your supervisor, NOT when you think you need a break or when you "get around to it."

There will be no exceptions to this new rule!

Felicia August

Manager

Billing and accounting

First, describe the flaws you discovered in this email message. Next, develop a plan for rewriting the message. Use the following steps to organize your efforts before you begin writing:

- Determine the purpose.
- Identify and analyze your audience.
- Define the main idea.
- Outline the major supporting points.
- Choose between the direct and indirect approaches.

Now rewrite the email message. Don't forget to leave ample time for revision of your own work before you turn it in.

13. **Media Skills: Blogging [LO-6]** The members of the project team of which you are the leader have enthusiastically embraced blogging as a communication medium. Unfortunately, as emotions heat up during the project, some of the blog postings are getting too casual, too personal, and even sloppy. Because your boss and other managers around the company also read this project blog, you don't want the team to look unprofessional in anyone's eyes. Revise the following blog posting so that it communicates in a more businesslike manner while retaining the informal, conversational tone of a blog (be sure to correct any spelling and punctuation mistakes you find as well).

Well, to the profound surprise of absolutely nobody, we are not going to be able meet the June 1 commitment to ship 100 operating tables to Southeast Surgical Supply. (For those of you who have been living in a cave the past six months, we have been fighting to get our hands on enough high-grade chromium steel to meet our production schedule.) Sure enough, we got news, this morning that we will only get enough for 30 tables. Yes, we look lik fools for not being able to follow through on promises we made to the customer, but no, this didn't have to happpen. Six month's ago, purchasing warned us about shrinking supplies and suggested we advance-buy as much as we would need for the next 12 months, or so. We naturally tried to followed their advice, but just as naturally were shot down by the bean counters at corporate who trotted out the policy about never buying more than three months worth of materials in advance. Of course, it'll be us–not the bean counters who'll take the flak when everybody starts asking why revenues are down next quarter and why Southeast is talking to our friends at Crighton Manuf!!! Maybe, some day this company will get its head out of the sand and realize that we need to have some financial flexibility in order to compete.

14. **Media Skills: Blogging [LO-5]** From what you've learned about planning and writing business messages, you should be able to identify numerous errors made by the writer of the following blog post. List them below and then plan and write a better post, following the guidelines given.

Get Ready!

We are hoping to be back at work soon, with everything running smoothly, same production schedule and no late projects or missed deadlines. So you need to clean out your desk, put your stuff in boxes, and clean off the walls. You can put the items you had up on your walls in boxes, also.

We have provided boxes. The move will happen this weekend. We'll be in our new offices when you arrive on Monday.

We will not be responsible for personal belongings during the move.

First, describe the flaws you discovered in this blog post. Next, develop a plan for rewriting the post. Use the following steps to organize your efforts before you begin writing:
- Determine the purpose.
- Identify and analyze your audience.
- Define the main idea.
- Outline the major supporting points.
- Choose between the direct and indirect approaches.
Now rewrite the post. Don't forget to leave ample time for revision of your own work before you turn it in.

15. **Media Skills: Microblogging [LO-6]** Busy knitters can go through a lot of yarn in a hurry, so most keep a sharp eye out for sales. You're on the marketing staff of Knitting-Warehouse, and you like to keep your loyal shoppers up

to date with the latest deals. Visit the Knitting-Warehouse website at www.knitting-warehouse.com, select any on-sale product that catches your eye, and write a Twitter update that describes the product and the sale. Be sure to include a link back to the website so your Twitter followers can learn more. (Unless you are working on a private Twitter account that is accessible only by your instructor and your classmates, don't actually send this Twitter update. Email it to your instructor instead.)

16. **Media Skills: Podcasting [LO-7]** You've recently begun recording a weekly podcast to share information with your large and far-flung staff. After a month, you ask for feedback from several of your subordinates, and you're disappointed to learn that some people stopped listening to the podcast after the first couple weeks. Someone eventually admits that many staffers feel that the recordings are too long and rambling and that the information they contain isn't valuable enough to justify the time it takes to listen. You aren't pleased, but you want to improve. An assistant transcribes the introduction to last week's podcast so you can review it. You immediately see two problems. Revise the introduction based on what you've learned in this chapter.

So there I am, having lunch with Selma Gill, who just joined and took over the Northeast sales region from Jackson Stroud. In walks our beloved CEO with Selma's old boss at Uni-Plex; turns out they were finalizing a deal to co-brand our products and theirs and to set up a joint distribution program in all four domestic regions. Pretty funny, huh? Selma left Uni-Plex because she wanted sell our products instead, and now she's back selling her old stuff, too. Anyway, try to chat with her when you can; she knows the biz inside and out and probably can offer insight into just about any sales challenge you might be running up against. We'll post more info on the co-brand deal next week; should be a boost for all of us. Other than those two news items, the other big news this week is the change in commission reporting. I'll go into the details in minute, but when you log onto the intranet, you'll now see your sales results split out by product line and industry sector. Hope this helps you see where you're doing well and where you might beef things up a bit. Oh yeah, I almost forgot the most important bit. Speaking of our beloved CEO, Thomas is going to be our guest of honor, so to speak, at the quarterly sales meeting next week and wants an update on how petroleum prices are affecting customer behavior. Each district manager should be ready with a brief report. After I go through the commission reporting scheme, I'll outline what you need to prepare.

Expand Your Skills

Critique the Professionals

Locate the YouTube channel page of any company you find interesting and assess its social networking presence using the criteria for effective communication discussed in this chapter and your own experience using social media. What does this company do well with its YouTube channel? How might it improve? Using whatever medium your instructor requests, write a brief analysis of the company's YouTube presence (no more than one page), citing specific elements from the piece and support from the chapter.

Sharpen Your Career Skills Online

Bovée and Thill's Business Communication Web Search, at http://websearch.businesscommunicationnetwork.com, is a unique research tool designed specifically for business communication research. Use the Web Search function to find a website, video, PDF document, podcast, or presentation that offers advice on using social media in business. Write a brief email message to your instructor or a post for your class blog, describing the item that you found and summarizing the career skills information you learned from it.

Improve Your Grammar, Mechanics, and Usage

The following exercises help you improve your knowledge of and power over English grammar, mechanics, and usage. Turn to the Handbook of Grammar, Mechanics, and Usage at the end of this text and review Prepositions, Conjunctions, and Articles and Interjections. Then look at the following 10 items and indicate the preferred choice in the following groups of sentences.

17.   **a.** The response was not only inappropriate but it was also rude.
   b. The response was not only inappropriate but also rude.

18.   **a.** Be sure to look the spelling up in the dictionary.
   b. Be sure to look up the spelling in the dictionary.

19.   **a.** We didn't get the contract because our proposal didn't comply with the request for proposals (RFP).
   b. We didn't get the contract because our proposals didn't comply to the RFP.

20.   **a.** Marissa should of known not to send that email to the CEO.
   b. Marissa should have known not to send that email to the CEO.

21.   **a.** The Phalanx 1000 has been favorably compared to the Mac iBook.
   b. The Phalanx 1000 has been favorably compared with the Mac iBook.

22.   **a.** What are you looking for?
   b. For what are you looking?

23.   **a.** Have you filed an SEC application?
   b. Have you filed a SEC application?

24.   **a.** The project turned out neither to be easy nor simple.
   b. The project turned out to be neither easy nor simple.

25.   **a.** If you hire me, you will not regret your decision!
   b. If you hire me, you will not regret your decision.

26.   **a.** This is truly an historic event.
   b. This is truly a historic event.

Cases

Website links for selected companies mentioned in cases can be found in the Student Assignments section at http://real-timeupdates.com/ebc12.

SOCIAL NETWORKING SKILLS

27. Media Skills: Social Networking; Media Skills: Microblogging [LO-2] [LO-6] Foursquare is one of the leading providers of location-based social networking services. Millions of people use Foursquare for social engagement and friendly competition, and many business owners are starting to recognize the marketing potential of having people who are on the move in local areas broadcasting their locations and sharing information about stores, restaurants, clubs, and other merchants.

Your task: Review the information on Foursquare's Merchant Platform at http://business.foursquare.com. Now write four brief messages, no more than 140 characters long (including spaces). The first should summarize the benefits to stores, restaurants, and other brick-and-mortar businesses of participating in Foursquare, and the next three messages should convey three compelling points that support that overall benefit statement. If your class is set up with private Twitter accounts, use your private account to send your messages. Otherwise, email your four messages to your instructor or post them on your class blog, as your instructor directs.

SOCIAL NETWORKING SKILLS

28. Media Skills: Social Networking; Online Etiquette [LO-2] Employees who take pride in their work are a practically priceless resource for any business. However, pride can sometimes manifest itself in negative ways when employees come under criticism, and public criticism is a fact of life in social media. Imagine that your company has recently experienced a rash of product quality problems, and these problems have generated some unpleasant and occasionally unfair criticism on a variety of social media sites. Someone even set up a Facebook page specifically to give customers a place to vent their frustrations.

You and your public relations team jumped into action, responding to complaints with offers to provide replacement products and help customers who have been affected by the quality problems. Everything seemed to be going as well as could be expected, when you were checking a few industry blogs one evening and discovered that two engineers in your company's product design lab have been responding to complaints on their own. They identified themselves as company employees and defended their product design, blaming the company's production department and even criticizing several customers for lacking the skills needed to use such a sophisticated product. Within a matter of minutes, you see their harsh comments being retweeted and reposted on multiple sites, only fueling the fire of negative feedback against your firm. Needless to say, you are horrified.

Your task: You manage to reach the engineers by private message and tell them to stop posting messages, but you realize you have a serious training issue on your hands. Write a post for the internal company blog that advises employees on how to respond appropriately when they are representing the company online. Use your imagination to make up any details you need.

SOCIAL NETWORKING SKILLS

29. Media Skills: Social Networking [LO-2] Social media can be a great way to, well, socialize during your college years, but employers are increasingly checking up on the online activities of potential hires to avoid bringing in employees who may reflect poorly on the company.

Your task: Team up with another student and review each other's public presence on Facebook, Twitter, Flickr, blogs, and any other website that an employer might check during the interview and recruiting process. Identify any photos, videos, messages, or other material that could raise a red flag when an employer is evaluating a job candidate. Write your teammate an email message that lists any risky material.

EMAIL SKILLS / PORTFOLIO BUILDER

30. Media Skills: Email [LO-4] One-quarter of all motor vehicle accidents that involve children under age 12 are side-impact crashes, and these crashes result in higher rates of injuries and fatalities than those with front or rear impacts.

Your task: You work in the consumer information department at Britax, a leading manufacturer of car seats. Your manager has asked you to prepare an email message that can be sent out whenever parents request information about side-impact crashes and the safety features of Britax seats. Start by researching side-impact crashes on the Britax website (www.britax.com). Write a three-paragraph message that explains the seriousness of side-impact crashes, describes how injuries and fatalities can be minimized in these crashes, and describes how Britax's car seats are designed to help protect children in side-impact crashes.[56]

EMAIL SKILLS / PORTFOLIO BUILDER

31. Media Skills: Email; Message Strategies: Negative Messages [LO-4] Many companies operate on the principle that the customer is always right, even when the customer isn't right. They take any steps necessary to ensure happy customers, lots of repeat sales, and a positive reputation among potential buyers. Overall, this is a smart and successful approach to business. However, most companies eventually encounter a nightmare customer who drains so much time, energy, and profits that the only sensible option is to refuse the customer's business. For example, the nightmare customer might be someone who constantly berates you and your employees, repeatedly makes outlandish demands for refunds and discounts, or simply requires so much help that you not only lose money on this person but also no longer have enough time to help your other customers. "Firing" a customer is an unpleasant step that should be taken only in the most extreme cases and only after other remedies have been attempted (such as talking with the customer about the problem), but it is sometimes necessary for the well-being of your employees and your company.

Your task: If you are currently working or have held a job in the recent past, imagine that you've encountered just such a customer. If you don't have job experience to call on, imagine that you work in a retail location somewhere around campus or in your neighborhood. Identify the type of behavior this imaginary customer exhibits and the reasons the behavior can no longer be accepted. Write a brief email message to the customer to explain that you will no longer be able to accommodate him or her as a customer. Calmly explain why you have had to reach this difficult decision. Maintain a professional tone and keep your emotions in check.

EMAIL SKILLS / PORTFOLIO BUILDER

32. Media Skills: Email; Collaboration: Team Projects [LO-2] For the first time in history (aside from special situations such as major wars), more than half of all U.S. adult women now live without a spouse. (In other words, they live alone, with roommates, or as part of an unmarried couple.) Twenty-five percent have never married, and 26 percent are divorced, widowed, or married but living apart from their spouses. In the 1950s and into the 1960s, only 40 percent of women lived without a spouse, but every decade since, the percentage has increased. In your work as a consumer trend specialist for Seymour Powell, a product design firm based in London that specializes in the home, personal, leisure, and transportation sectors, it's your business to recognize and respond to demographic shifts such as this.

Your task: With a small team of classmates, brainstorm possible product opportunities that respond to this trend. In an email message to be sent to the management team at Seymour Powell, list your ideas for new or modified products that might sell well in a society in which more than half of all adult women live without a spouse. For each idea, provide a one-sentence explanation of why you think the product has potential.[57]

EMAIL SKILLS / MOBILE SKILLS

33. Media Skills: Email [LO-5] The size limitations of smartphone screens call for a different approach to writing and formatting documents.

Your task: On the website of any company that interests you, find a news release (some companies refer to them as press releases) that announces the launch of a new product. Using Pages or any other writing app at your disposal, revise and format the material in a way that would be effective on smartphone screens.

IM SKILLS

34. Media Skills: IM; Compositional Modes: Tutorials [LO-1] [LO-5] High-definition television can be a joy to watch—but, oh, what a pain to buy. The field is cluttered with compet-

ing technologies and arcane terminology that is meaningless to most consumers. Moreover, it's nearly impossible to define one technical term without invoking two or three others, leaving consumers swimming in an alphanumeric soup of confusion. As a sales support manager for Crutchfield, a leading online retailer of audio and video systems, you understand the frustration buyers feel; your staff is deluged daily by their questions.

Your task: To help your staff respond quickly to consumers who ask questions via Crutchfield's online IM chat service, you are developing a set of "canned" responses to common questions. When a consumer asks one of these questions, a sales adviser can simply click on the ready-made answer. Research the "Research and DIY" section on the Crutchfield website, then write concise, consumer-friendly definitions of the following terms: *1080p, HDMI, 4K,* and *3D TV.*

BLOGGING SKILLS

35. Media Skills: Blogging; Compositional Modes: Tutorials [LO-6] Tumblr has become a popular "short-form" blogging platform by combining the simplicity of Twitter with the ability to share photos and other media easily.

Your task: Write a 300- to 400-word post for your class blog that explains how to set up an account on Tumblr and get involved in the Tumblr community. The help pages on Tumblr are a good place to get more information about the service.

BLOGGING SKILLS

36. Media Skills: Blogging [LO-6] Credit card debt can be a crippling financial burden with myriad side effects, from higher insurance rates to more-expensive loans to difficulty getting a job or a promotion. Unfortunately, credit debt is also frighteningly easy to fall into, particularly for young people trying to get started in life with limited cash flow.

Your task: Write a three- to five-paragraph blog post that warns college students about the dangers of credit card debt. Be sure to credit the sources you find in your research.

BLOGGING SKILLS

37. Media Skills: Blogging; Compositional Modes: Tutorials [LO-6] Studying abroad for a semester or a year can be a rewarding experience in many ways—improving your language skills, experiencing another culture, making contacts in the international business arena, and building your self-confidence.

Your task: Write a post for your class blog that describes your college's study abroad program and summarizes the steps involved in applying for international study. If your school doesn't offer study-abroad opportunities, base your post on the program offered at another institution in your state.

MICROBLOGGING SKILLS

38. Media Skills: Microblogging; Compositional Modes: Summaries [LO-1] [LO-6] A carefully constructed series of tweets can serve as a summary of a blog post, video, or other message or document.

Your task: Find any article, podcast, video, or webpage on a business topic that interests you. Write four to six tweetables that summarize the content of the piece. Restrict the first tweetable to 120 characters to allow for a URL. Email the series to your instructor or publish them on Twitter if your instructor directs. If you quote phrases from the original directly, be sure to put them in quotation marks.

MICROBLOGGING SKILLS

39. Media Skills: Microblogging; Compositional Modes: Updates and Announcements [LO-5] JetBlue is known for its innovations in customer service and customer communication, including its pioneering use of Twitter. Nearly two million JetBlue fans and customers follow the company on Twitter to get updates on flight status during weather disruptions, facility upgrades, and other news.[58]

Your task: Write a message of no more than 120 characters that announces the cancellation of all flights into and out of Boston's Logan International from 6:00 a.m. on February 20 to 4:00 p.m. on February 21.

MICROBLOGGING SKILLS

40. Media Skills: Microblogging; Compositional Modes: Teasers [LO-1] Twitter updates are a great way to alert people to helpful articles, videos, and other online resources.

Your task: Find an online resource (it can be a website quiz, a YouTube video, a PowerPoint presentation, a newspaper article, or anything else appropriate) that offers some great tips to help college students prepare for job interviews. Write a teaser of no more than 120 characters that hints at the benefits other students can get from this resource. If your class is set up with private Twitter accounts, use your private account to send your message. Otherwise, email it to your instructor. Be sure to include the URL; if you're using a Twitter account, the system should shorten it to 20 characters to keep you within the 140-character limit.

PODCASTING SKILLS / PORTFOLIO BUILDER

41. Media Skills: Podcasting [LO-7] While writing the many messages that are part of the job search process, you find yourself wishing you could just talk to some of these companies so your personality could shine through. Well, you've just gotten that opportunity. One of the companies you've applied to has emailed you back, asking you to submit a two-minute podcast introducing yourself and explaining why you would be a good person to hire.

Your task: Identify a company you'd like to work for after graduation and select a job that would be a good match for your skills and interests. Write a script for a two-minute podcast (two minutes represents roughly 250 words for most speakers). Introduce yourself and the position you're applying for, describe your background, and explain why you think you're a good candidate for the job. Make up any details you need. If your instructor asks you to do so, record the podcast and submit the audio file.

PODCASTING SKILLS

42. Media Skills: Podcasting [LO-7] Between this chapter and your own experience as a user of social media, you know enough about social media to offer some insights to other business communicators.

Your task: Write a script for a two- to three-minute podcast (roughly 250 to 400 words) on any social media topic that you find compelling. Be sure to introduce your topic clearly in the introduction and provide helpful transitions along the way. If your instructor asks you to do so, record the podcast and submit the file.

PODCASTING SKILLS / PORTFOLIO BUILDER

43. Media Skills: Podcasting; Message Strategies: Marketing and Sales Messages [LO-5] With any purchase decision, from a restaurant meal to a college education, recommendations from satisfied customers are often the strongest promotional messages.

Your task: Write a script for a one- to two-minute podcast (roughly 150 to 250 words), explaining why your college or university is a good place to get an education. Your audience is high school juniors and seniors. You can choose to craft a general message, something that would be useful to all prospective students, or you can focus on a specific academic discipline, the athletic program, or some other important aspect of your college experience. Either way, make sure your introductory comments make it clear whether you are offering a general recommendation or a specific recommendation. If your instructor asks you to do so, record the podcast and submit the file electronically.

MyBCommLab

Go to the Assignments section of your MyLab to complete these writing exercises.

44. How can businesses make use of social networks such as Facebook for business communication? [LO-2]

45. Why does a personal style of writing on blogs and other social media channels help build stronger relationships with audiences? [LO-6]

Endnotes

1. GoPro website, accessed 19 February 2015, www.gopro.com; Garett Sloan, "The 10 Best Brand Channels on YouTube," *Adweek*, 2 April 2014, www.adweek.com; Christopher Ratcliff, "A Look Inside GoPro's Dazzling YouTube Strategy," Econsultancy website, 20 February 2014, http://econsultancy.com; GoPro channel on YouTube, accessed 26 April 2014, www.youtube.com/user/GoProCamera; "YouTube Brand Channel Leaderboard January–March 2014," *Google Think Insights*, 31 March 2014, www.thinkwithgoogle.com; Saya Weissman, "GoPro Might Have the Best Brand Content Around," *Digiday*, 6 February 2014, http://digiday.com; Shorty Industry Awards website, accessed 26 April 2014, http://industry.shortyawards.com; Anderson Cooper, "GoPro's Video Revolution," *60 Minutes*, 10 November 2013, www.cbsnews.com.

2. Angelo Fernando, "Content Snacking—and What You Can Do About It," *Communication World*, January–February 2011, 8–10.

3. Jennifer Van Grove, "Social Networking on Mobile Devices Skyrockets," *Mashable*, 20 October 2011, http://mashable.com.

4. Angelo Fernando, "Social Media Change the Rules," *Communication World*, January–February 2007, 9–10; Geoff Livingston and Brian Solis, *Now Is Gone: A Primer on New Media for Executives and Entrepreneurs* (Laurel, Md.: Bartleby Press, 2007), 60.

5. Don Tapscott and Anthony D. Williams, Wikinomics, *How Mass Collaboration Changes Everything* (London: Portfolio, 2006), 216–217; Dan Schawbel, "Why Social Media Makes It Possible for Gen-Y to Succeed," Personal Branding Blog, 12 December 2007, http://personalbrandingblog.wordpress.com.

6. 2012 CEO, Social Media & Leadership Survey, Brandfog, www.brandfog.com.

7. Richard Edelman, "Teaching Social Media: What Skills Do Communicators Need?" in "Engaging the New Influencers; Third Annual Social Media Academic Summit" (white paper), accessed 7 June 2010, www.newmediaacademicsummit.com.

8. Catherine Toole, "My 7 Deadly Sins of Writing for Social Media— Am I Right?" Econsultancy blog, 19 June 2007, www.econsultancy.com; Muhammad Saleem, "How to Write a Social Media Press Release," *Copyblogger*, accessed 16 September 2008, www.copyblogger.com; Melanie McBride, "5 Tips for (Better) Social Media Writing," Melanie McBride Online, 11 June 2008, http://melaniemcbride.net.

9. Samantha Murphy, "Why Mobile Commerce Is on the Rise," *Mashable*, 7 March 2012, http://mashable.com.

10. Christopher Swan, "Gamification: A New Way to Shape Behavior," *Communication World*, May–June 2012, 13–14.

11. "Wearables," AllThingsCK, accessed 6 April 2014, allthingsck.com.

12. Jon Russell, "Why 'Going Global' Makes No Sense for China's Social Networks—for Now," *The Next Web*, 14 May 2012, http://thenextweb.com.

13. Todd Henneman, "At Lockheed Martin, Social Networking Fills Key Workforce Needs While Improving Efficiency and Lowering Costs," *Workforce Management*, March 2010, www.workforce.com.

14. Patrick Hanlon and Josh Hawkins, "Expand Your Brand Community Online," *Advertising Age*, 7 January 2008, 14–15.

15. Todd Wasserman, "What Drives Brand Socialability?" *Mashable*, 12 October 2011.

16. Coca-Cola Facebook page, accessed 4 April 2014, www.facebook.com/cocacola; "Shaking Things Up at Coca-Cola," *Harvard Business Review*, October 2011, 94–99.

17. Alex Wright, "Mining the Web for Feelings, Not Facts," *New York Times*, 23 August 2009, www.nytimes.com.

18. Christian Pieter Hoffmann, "Holding Sway," *Communication World*, November–December 2011, 26–29; Josh Bernoff, "Social Strategy for Exciting (and Not So Exciting) Brands," *Marketing News*, 15 May 2009, 18; Larry Weber, *Marketing to the Social Web* (Hoboken, N.J.: Wiley, 2007), 12–14; David Meerman Scott, *The New Rules of Marketing and PR* (Hoboken, N.J.: Wiley, 2007), 62.

19. Sonia Simone, "What's the Difference Between Content Marketing and Copywriting?" *Copyblogger*, accessed 4 June 2012, www.copyblogger.com.

20. Matt Rhodes, "Build Your Own Community or Go Where People Are? Do Both," FreshNetworks blog, 12 May 2009, www.freshnetworks.com.

21. Brian Solis, *Engage!* (Hoboken, N.J.: Wiley, 2010), 13.

22. Zachary Sniderman, "5 Ways to Clean Up Your Social Media Identity," 7 July 2010, *Mashable*, http://mashable.com.

23. Tamar Weinberg, *The New Community Rules: Marketing on the Social Web* (Sebastopol, Calif.: O'Reilly Media, 2009), 288.

24. Rohit Bhargava, "How Curation Could Save the Internet (and Your Brand)," *Communication World*, January–February 2012, 20–23.

25. Reid Goldborough, "More Trends for 2009: What to Expect with Personal Technology," *Public Relations Tactics*, February 2009, 9.

26. Michelle V. Rafter, "If Tim Fry Has His Way, He'll Eradicate Email for Good," *Workforce Management*, 24 April 2012, www.workforce.com.

27. Hilary Potkewitz and Rachel Brown, "Spread of Email Has Altered Communication Habits at Work," *Los Angeles Business Journal*, 18 April 2005, www.findarticles.com; Nancy Flynn, *Instant Messaging Rules* (New York: AMACOM, 2004), 47–54.

28. Mary Munter, Priscilla S. Rogers, and Jone Rymer, "Business Email: Guidelines for Users," *Business Communication Quarterly*, March 2003, 26+; Renee B. Horowitz and Marian G. Barchilon, "Stylistic Guidelines for Email," *IEEE Transactions on Professional Communication* 37, no. 4 (December 1994): 207–212.

29. Steve Rubel, "Tip: Tweetify the Lead of Your Emails," The Steve Rubel Stream blog, 20 July 2010, www.steverubel.com.

30. Judith Newman, "If You're Happy and You Know It, Must I Know, Too?" *New York Times*, 21 October 2011, www.nytimes.com.

31. Michal Lev-Ram, "IBM: Instant Messaging Has Replaced Voicemail," *CNNMoney*, 31 May 2011, http://tech.fortune.cnn.com;

Robert J. Holland, "Connected—More or Less," *Richmond.com*, 8 August 2006, www.richmond.com.

32. Vayusphere website, accessed 22 January 2006, www.vayusphere.com; Christa C. Ayer, "Presence Awareness: Instant Messaging's Killer App," *Mobile Business Advisor*, 1 July 2004, www.highbeam.com; Jefferson Graham, "Instant Messaging Programs Are No Longer Just for Messages," *USA Today*, 20 October 2003, 5D; Todd R. Weiss, "Microsoft Targets Corporate Instant Messaging Customers," *Computerworld*, 18 November 2002, 12; "Banks Adopt Instant Messaging to Create a Global Business Network," *Computer Weekly*, 25 April 2002, 40; Michael D. Osterman, "Instant Messaging in the Enterprise," *Business Communications Review*, January 2003, 59–62; John Pallato, "Instant Messaging Unites Work Groups and Inspires Collaboration," *Internet World*, December 2002, 14.

33. Paul Mah, "Using Text Messaging in Business," Mobile Enterprise blog, 4 February 2008, http://blogs.techrepublic.com/wireless; Paul Kedrosky, "Why We Don't Get the (Text) Message," *Business 2.0*, 2 October 2006, www.business2.com; Dave Carpenter, "Companies Discover Marketing Power of Text Messaging," *Seattle Times*, 25 September 2006, www.seattletimes.com.

34. "About StarStar," Zoove website, accessed 6 June 2012, www.zoove.com.

35. Mark Gibbs, "Racing to Instant Messaging," *NetworkWorld*, 17 February 2003, 74.

36. "Email Is So Five Minutes Ago," *BusinessWeek*, 28 November 2005, www.businessweek.com.

37. Clint Boulton, "IDC: IM Use Is Booming in Business," *InstantMessagingPlanet.com*, 5 October 2005, www.instantmessagingplanet.com; Jenny Goodbody, "Critical Success Factors for Global Virtual Teams," *Strategic Communication Management*, February/March 2005, 18–21; Ann Majchrzak, Arvind Malhotra, Jeffrey Stamps, and Jessica Lipnack, "Can Absence Make a Team Grow Stronger?" *Harvard Business Review*, May 2004, 131–137; Christine Y. Chen, "The IM Invasion," *Fortune*, 26 May 2003, 135–138; Yudhijit Bhattacharjee, "A Swarm of Little Notes," *Time*, 16 September 2002, A3–A8; Mark Bruno, "Taming the Wild Frontiers of Instant Messaging," *Bank Technology News*, December 2002, 30–31; Richard Grigonis, "Enterprise-Strength Instant Messaging," *Convergence.com*, 10–15, accessed 15 March 2003, www.convergence.com.

38. Leo Babauta, "17 Tips to Be Productive with Instant Messaging," *Web Worker Daily*, 14 November 2007, http://webworkerdaily.com; Pallato, "Instant Messaging Unites Work Groups and Inspires Collaboration."

39. "State of the Blogosphere 2011," *Technorati*, 4 November 2011, http://technorati.com.

40. Marcus Sheridan, "5 Reasons Your Business Should Be Blogging," *Social Media Examiner*, 2 December 2011, www.socialmediaexaminer.com; Stephen Baker, "The Inside Story on Company Blogs," *BusinessWeek*, 14 February 2006, www.businessweek.com; Jeremy Wright, *Blog Marketing* (New York: McGraw-Hill, 2006), 45–56; Paul Chaney, "Blogs: Beyond the Hype!" 26 May 2005, http://radiantmarketinggroup.com.

41. Solis, *Engage!*, 314.

42. Solis, *Engage!*, 86.

43. Weinberg, "The New Community Rules: Marketing on the Social Web," 89.

44. "IBM Social Computing Guidelines," IBM website, accessed 5 June 2012, www.ibm.com.

45. Joel Falconer, "Six Rules for Writing Great Web Content," *Blog News Watch*, 9 November 2007, www.blognewswatch.com.

46. Dion Hinchcliffe, "Twitter on Your Intranet: 17 Microblogging Tools for Business," *ZDNet*, 1 June 2009, www.zdnet.com.

47. Hinchcliffe, "Twitter on Your Intranet: 17 Microblogging Tools for Business."

48. B. L. Ochman, "Why Twitter Is a Better Brand Platform Than Facebook," *Ad Age*, 1 June 2012, http://adage.com.

49. Leon Widrich, "4 Ways to Use Twitter for Customer Service and Support," *Social Media Examiner*, 12 April 2012, www.socialmediaexaminer.com.

50. Paul André, Michael Bernstein, and Kurt Luther, "What Makes a Great Tweet," *Harvard Business Review*, May 2012, 36–37.

51. André et al., "What Makes a Great Tweet."

52. Interview with Cliff Ravenscraft in Michael Stelzner, "Podcasting for Business: What You Need to Know," *Social Media Examiner*, 23 December 2011, www.socialmediaexaminer.com.

53. "Set Up Your Podcast for Success," *FeedForAll* website, accessed 4 October 2006, www.feedforall.com.

54. Nathan Hangen, "4 Steps to Podcasting Success," *Social Media Examiner*, 14 February 2011, www.socialmediaexaminer.com.

55. Shel Holtz, "Ten Guidelines for B2B Podcasts," *Webpronews.com*, 12 October 2005, www.webpronews.com.

56. "Side Impact Protection Revealed," Britax website, accessed 6 June 2012, www.britaxusa.com.

57. Seymour Powell website, accessed 16 January 2007, www.seymourpowell.com; Sam Roberts, "51% of Women Now Living Without a Spouse," *New York Times*, 16 January 2007, www.nytimes.com.

58. JetBlue Twitter page, accessed 19 February 2015, http://twitter.com/JetBlue.

Answer Key for "Learning Objectives Checkup"

1. a
2. b
3. b
4. c
5. brand community
6. c
7. brand socialization
8. b
9. a
10. d
11. c
12. b
13. a
14. c
15. d
16. b
17. a
18. b
19. c
20. c
21. d
22. d
23. podcast channel

Answer Key for "Improve Your Grammar, Mechanics, and Usage" Exercises

17. b (1.6.2)
18. b (1.6.1)
19. a (1.6.1)
20. b (1.6.1)
21. b (1.6.1)
22. a (1.6.1)
23. a (1.6.3)
24. b (1.6.2)
25. b (1.6.3)
26. b (1.6.3)

Writing Routine and Positive Messages

LEARNING OBJECTIVES

After studying this chapter, you will be able to

1 Outline an effective strategy for writing routine business requests.

2 Describe three common types of routine requests.

3 Outline an effective strategy for writing routine replies and positive messages.

4 Describe six common types of routine replies and positive messages.

ON THE JOB: COMMUNICATING AT
GET SATISFACTION

Using New Media Concepts to Solve an Age-Old Problem

For about as long as online communication has been possible, frustrated customers have been going online to complain about faulty products, confusing instructions, and poor service. When social media tools appeared, giving even nontechnical consumers a ready voice, the stream of "I need help!" messages turned into a full-time flood. On product review and shopping websites, enthusiast blogs, and various "complaint sites," consumers can vent their frustrations and ask for help when they feel they aren't getting satisfaction from the companies they do business with.

These various websites can occasionally provide answers, but they suffer from four fundamental drawbacks. First, they are randomly scattered all over the Web, so many consumers are never quite sure where to look for help. Second, the right experts from the right companies often aren't involved, meaning that customers often have to rely on each other—which sometimes works but sometimes doesn't. Third, even companies that make a valiant effort to keep their customers satisfied know that everyone can benefit if customers can share ideas, learn from one another, and participate in ongoing conversation.

Get Satisfaction is using social media to help companies that are overwhelmed by support requests and customers who are frustrated by poor service.

Fourth, companies often find that multiple customers have the same routine questions, but communicating with every customer individually can be time-consuming and expensive.

The San Francisco–based company Get Satisfaction is working to address all these issues with social networking technologies designed specifically for community-based customer support. Consumers can post questions or complaints and request notification whenever a response is posted. If someone else has already posted the same complaint, all a visitor needs do is ask to be notified when the issue is resolved, saving time for the people asking and answering questions. Consumers can also suggest ideas for new products and services or improvements to existing offerings.

On the other side of the relationship, employees from companies that sell products and services can register as official representatives to answer questions, solve problems, and solicit feedback. As both knowledgeable consumers and company representatives provide answers and solutions, the responses voted most useful rise to the top, ensuring that visitors always get the most helpful information available. Companies that use Get Satisfaction's services can deploy customer service capabilities in a variety of ways—including via Facebook, Twitter, and their own company blogs—to try to capture as many customer service conversations as possible.

The idea certainly seems to be catching on, with thousands of companies now using Get Satisfaction's "social helpdesk" approach to help millions of customers get satisfaction from the products and services they buy.[1]

HTTP://GETSATISFACTION.COM

Strategy for Routine Requests

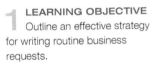

LEARNING OBJECTIVE

1 Outline an effective strategy for writing routine business requests.

Get Satisfaction (profiled in the chapter-opening On the Job) knows that much of the vital communication between a company and its customers is about routine matters, from product operation hints and technical support to refunds and order glitches. These messages fall into two groups: routine requests, in which you ask for information or action from another party, and a variety of routine and positive messages.

Making requests is a routine part of business. In most cases, your audience will be prepared to comply—as long as you're not being unreasonable or asking people to do something they would expect you to do yourself. By applying a clear strategy and tailoring your approach to each situation, you'll be able to generate effective requests quickly.

For routine requests and positive messages
- State the request or main idea
- Give necessary details
- Close with a cordial request for specific action

Like all other business messages, a routine request has three parts: an opening, a body, and a close. Using the direct approach, open with your main idea, which is a clear statement of your request. Use the body to give details and justify your request. Finally, close by requesting specific action.

STATING YOUR REQUEST UP FRONT

With routine requests, you can make your request at the beginning of the message. Of course, getting right to the point should not be interpreted as license to be abrupt or tactless:

Take care that your direct approach doesn't come across as abrupt or tactless.

- **Pay attention to tone.** Instead of demanding action ("Send me the latest version of the budget spreadsheet"), show respect by using words such as *please* and *I would appreciate.*
- **Assume that your audience will comply.** Because the request is routine, you can generally assume that your readers will comply when they clearly understand the reason for your request.
- **Be specific.** State precisely what you want. For example, if you request the latest market data from your research department, be sure to say whether you want a 1-page summary or 100 pages of raw data.

REAL-TIME UPDATES

LEARN MORE BY VISITING THIS WEBSITE

Insight into mobile strategies for routine communication

ClickSoftware's MobileFever blog discusses a range of topics on mobile business communication. Go to http://real-timeupdates .com/ebc12 and click on Learn More in the Students section.

EXPLAINING AND JUSTIFYING YOUR REQUEST

Use the body of your message to explain your request, as needed. Make the explanation a smooth and logical outgrowth of your opening remarks. If complying with the request could

CHECKLIST ✔ Writing Routine Requests

A. State your request up front.
- Write in a polite, undemanding, personal tone.
- Use the direct approach because your audience will probably respond favorably to your request.
- Be specific and precise in your request.

B. Explain and justify your request.
- Justify the request or explain its importance.
- Explain any potential benefits of responding.

- Ask the most important questions first.
- Break complex requests into individual questions that are limited to only one topic each.

C. Request specific action in a courteous close.
- Make it easy to comply by including appropriate contact information.
- Express your gratitude.
- Clearly state any important deadlines for the request.

benefit the reader, be sure to mention that. If you have multiple requests or questions, ask the most important questions first and deal with only one topic per question. If you have an unusual or complex request, break it down into specific, individual questions so that the reader can address each one separately. This consideration not only shows respect for your audience's time but also gets you a more accurate answer in less time.

If you have multiple requests or questions, start with the most important one.

REQUESTING SPECIFIC ACTION IN A COURTEOUS CLOSE

Close your message with three important elements: (1) a specific request that includes any relevant deadlines, (2) information about how you can be reached (if it isn't obvious), and (3) an expression of appreciation or goodwill. When you ask readers to perform a specific action, ask for a response by a specific date or time, if appropriate (for example, "Please send the figures by May 5 so that I can return first-quarter results to you before the May 20 conference."). Conclude your message with a sincere thanks. However, don't thank the reader "in advance" for cooperating; many people find that presumptuous. If the reader's reply warrants a word of thanks, send it after you've received the reply. To review, see "Checklist: Writing Routine Requests."

Close request messages with
- A request for some specific action
- Information about how you can be reached
- An expression of appreciation

Common Examples of Routine Requests

The most common types of routine messages are asking for information or action, asking for recommendations, and making claims and requesting adjustments.

2 LEARNING OBJECTIVE
Describe three common types of routine requests.

ASKING FOR INFORMATION AND ACTION

Most simple requests can be handled with three message points:

- What you want to know or what you want your readers to do
- Why you're making the request (not required in all cases)
- Why it may be in your readers' interest to help you (not applicable in all cases)

For simple requests, using the direct approach gets the job done with a minimum of fuss. In more complex situations, you may need to provide more extensive reasons and justification for your request. If applicable, point out any benefits to the reader of complying with your request. Naturally, be sure to adapt your request to your audience and the situation (see Figure 1 on the next page).

Routine requests can be handled with simple, straightforward messages, but more complicated requests can require additional justification and explanation.

ASKING FOR RECOMMENDATIONS

The need to inquire about people arises often in business. For example, before extending credit or awarding contracts, jobs, promotions, or scholarships, companies often ask applicants to supply references. Companies ask applicants to list people who can vouch for their ability, skills, integrity, character, and fitness for the job. Before you volunteer someone's name as a reference, ask permission. Some people don't want you to use their

Always ask for permission before using someone as a reference.

Writing Routine and Positive Messages

1 Plan →

Analyze the Situation
Verify that the purpose is to request information from company managers.

Gather Information
Gather accurate, complete information about local competitive threats.

Choose Medium and Channel
Email is effective for this internal message, and it allows the attachment of a Word document to collect the information.

Organize the Information
Clarify that the main idea is collecting information that will lead to a better competitive strategy, which will in turn help the various district managers.

2 Write →

Adapt to Your Audience
Show sensitivity to audience needs with a "you"attitude, politeness, positive emphasis, and bias-free language. The writer already has credibility, as manager of the department.

Compose the Message
Maintain a style that is conversational but still business like, using plain English and appropriate voice.

3 Complete

Revise the Message
Evaluate content and review readability; avoid unnecessary details.

Produce the Message
Simple email format is all the design this message needs.

Proofread the Message
Review for errors in layout, spelling, and mechanics.

Distribute the Message
Deliver the message via the company's email system.

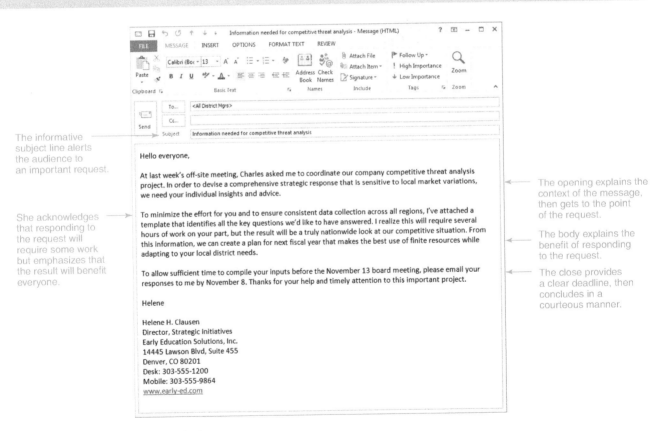

The informative subject line alerts the audience to an important request.

She acknowledges that responding to the request will require some work but emphasizes that the result will benefit everyone.

The opening explains the context of the message, then gets to the point of the request.

The body explains the benefit of responding to the request.

The close provides a clear deadline, then concludes in a courteous manner.

Email content:

To... <All District Mgrs>

Subject: Information needed for competitive threat analysis

Hello everyone,

At last week's off-site meeting, Charles asked me to coordinate our company competitive threat analysis project. In order to devise a comprehensive strategic response that is sensitive to local market variations, we need your individual insights and advice.

To minimize the effort for you and to ensure consistent data collection across all regions, I've attached a template that identifies all the key questions we'd like to have answered. I realize this will require several hours of work on your part, but the result will be a truly nationwide look at our competitive situation. From this information, we can create a plan for next fiscal year that makes the best use of finite resources while adapting to your local district needs.

To allow sufficient time to compile your inputs before the November 13 board meeting, please email your responses to me by November 8. Thanks for your help and timely attention to this important project.

Helene

Helene H. Clausen
Director, Strategic Initiatives
Early Education Solutions, Inc.
14445 Lawson Blvd, Suite 455
Denver, CO 80201
Desk: 303-555-1200
Mobile: 303-555-9864
www.early-ed.com

Figure 1   Routine Message Requesting Action
In this email request to district managers across the country, Helene Clausen asks them to fill out an attached information collection form. Although the request is not unusual and responding to it is part of the managers' responsibility, Clausen asks for their help in a courteous manner and points out the benefits of responding.
Source: MS Outlook 2013, © Microsoft.

CHECKLIST ✔ **Making Claims and Requesting Adjustments**

- Maintain a professional tone, even if you're extremely frustrated.
- Open with a straightforward statement of the problem.
- Provide specific details in the body.
- Present facts honestly and clearly.

- Politely summarize the desired action in the closing.
- Clearly state what you expect as a fair settlement or ask the reader to propose a fair adjustment.
- Explain the benefits of complying with the request, such as your continued patronage.

---

names, perhaps because they don't know enough about you to feel comfortable writing a letter or because they or their employers have a policy of not providing recommendations.

Requests for recommendations and references are routine, so you can organize your inquiry using the direct approach. Open your message by clearly stating why the recommendation is required (if it's not for a job, be sure to explain its purpose) and that you would like your reader to write the letter. If you haven't had contact with the person for some time, use the opening to trigger the reader's memory of the relationship you had, the dates of association, and any special events or accomplishments that might bring a clear and favorable picture of you to mind.

> Refresh the memory of any potential reference you haven't been in touch with for a while.

Close your message with an expression of appreciation and the full name and address of the person to whom the letter should be sent. When asking for an immediate recommendation, you should also mention the deadline. Always be sure to enclose a stamped, preaddressed envelope as a convenience to the other party. Figure 2 on the next page provides an example of a request that follows these guidelines.

REAL-TIME UPDATES

LEARN MORE BY VISITING THIS WEBSITE

Asking for recommendations on LinkedIn

Follow LinkedIn's advice for requesting a recommendation. Go to http://real-timeupdates.com/ebc12 and click on Learn More in the Students section.

MAKING CLAIMS AND REQUESTING ADJUSTMENTS

If you're dissatisfied with a company's product or service, you can opt to make a **claim** (a formal complaint) or request an **adjustment** (a settlement of a claim). In either case, it's important to maintain a professional tone in all your communication, no matter how angry or frustrated you are. Keeping your cool will help you get the situation resolved sooner.

> When writing a claim or requesting an adjustment
> - Explain the problem and give details
> - Provide backup information
> - Request specific action

Open with a clear and calm statement of the problem along with your request. In the body, give a complete, specific explanation of the details. Provide any information the recipient needs to verify your complaint. In your close, politely request specific action or convey a sincere desire to find a solution. And, if appropriate, suggest that the business relationship will continue if the problem is solved satisfactorily. Be prepared to back up your claim with invoices, sales receipts, canceled checks, dated correspondence, and any other relevant documents. Send copies and keep the originals for your files.

> Be prepared to document any claims you make with a company. Send copies and keep the original documents.

If the remedy is obvious, tell your reader exactly what you expect to be done, such as exchanging incorrectly shipped merchandise for the right item or issuing a refund if the item is out of stock. However, if you're uncertain about the precise nature of the trouble, you could ask the company to assess the situation and then advise you on how the situation could be fixed. Supply your full contact information so that the company can discuss the situation with you, if necessary. Compare the ineffective and effective versions in Figure 3 for an example of making a claim. To review the tasks involved in making claims and requesting adjustments, see "Checklist: Making Claims and Requesting Adjustments."

Strategy for Routine and Positive Messages

> **3 LEARNING OBJECTIVE**
> Outline an effective strategy for writing routine replies and positive messages.

Just as you'll make numerous requests for information and action throughout your career, you'll also respond to similar requests from other people. When you are responding positively to a request, sending routine announcements, or sending a positive or

Writing Routine and Positive Messages

1 Plan →

Analyze the Situation
Verify that the purpose is to request a recommendation letter from a college professor.

Gather Information
Gather information on classes and dates to help the reader recall you and to clarify the position you seek.

Choose Medium and Channel
The letter format gives this message an appropriate level of formality, although many professors prefer to be contacted by email.

Organize the Information
Messages like this are common and expected, so a direct approach is fine.

2 Write →

Adapt to Your Audience
Show sensitivity to audience needs with a "you" attitude, politeness, positive emphasis, and bias-free language.

Compose the Message
Style is respectful and business like, while still using plain English and appropriate voice.

3 Complete

Revise the Message
Evaluate content and review readability; avoid unnecessary details.

Produce the Message
Simple letter format is all the design this message needs.

Proofread the Message
Review for errors in layout, spelling, and mechanics.

Distribute the Message
Deliver the message via postal mail or email if you have the professor's email address.

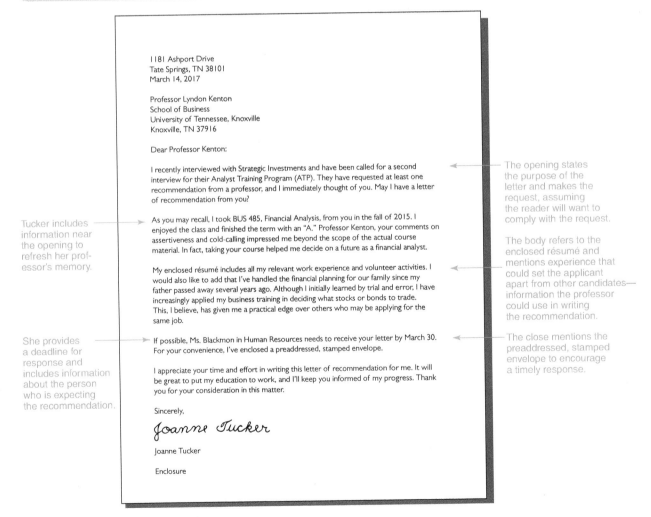

1181 Ashport Drive
Tate Springs, TN 38101
March 14, 2017

Professor Lyndon Kenton
School of Business
University of Tennessee, Knoxville
Knoxville, TN 37916

Dear Professor Kenton:

I recently interviewed with Strategic Investments and have been called for a second interview for their Analyst Training Program (ATP). They have requested at least one recommendation from a professor, and I immediately thought of you. May I have a letter of recommendation from you?

As you may recall, I took BUS 485, Financial Analysis, from you in the fall of 2015. I enjoyed the class and finished the term with an "A." Professor Kenton, your comments on assertiveness and cold-calling impressed me beyond the scope of the actual course material. In fact, taking your course helped me decide on a future as a financial analyst.

My enclosed résumé includes all my relevant work experience and volunteer activities. I would also like to add that I've handled the financial planning for our family since my father passed away several years ago. Although I initially learned by trial and error, I have increasingly applied my business training in deciding what stocks or bonds to trade. This, I believe, has given me a practical edge over others who may be applying for the same job.

If possible, Ms. Blackmon in Human Resources needs to receive your letter by March 30. For your convenience, I've enclosed a preaddressed, stamped envelope.

I appreciate your time and effort in writing this letter of recommendation for me. It will be great to put my education to work, and I'll keep you informed of my progress. Thank you for your consideration in this matter.

Sincerely,

Joanne Tucker

Joanne Tucker

Enclosure

Tucker includes information near the opening to refresh her professor's memory.

She provides a deadline for response and includes information about the person who is expecting the recommendation.

The opening states the purpose of the letter and makes the request, assuming the reader will want to comply with the request.

The body refers to the enclosed résumé and mentions experience that could set the applicant apart from other candidates—information the professor could use in writing the recommendation.

The close mentions the preaddressed, stamped envelope to encourage a timely response.

Figure 2 Effective Request for a Recommendation
This writer uses a direct approach when asking for a recommendation from a former professor. Note how she takes care to refresh the professor's memory because she took the class a year and a half ago. She also indicates the date by which the letter is needed and points to the enclosure of a stamped, preaddressed envelope.

Figure 3   Ineffective and Effective Versions of a Claim
Note the difference in both tone and information content in these two versions. The poor version is emotional and unprofessional, whereas the improved version communicates calmly and clearly.
Source: MS Outlook 2013, © Microsoft.

goodwill message, you have several goals: to communicate the information or the good news, answer all questions, provide all required details, and leave your reader with a good impression of you and your firm.

Readers receiving routine replies and positive messages will generally be interested in what you have to say, so use the direct approach. Place your main idea (the positive reply or the good news) in the opening. Use the body to explain all the relevant details, and close cordially, perhaps highlighting a benefit to your reader.

Use a direct approach for routine replies and positive messages.

STARTING WITH THE MAIN IDEA

By opening routine and positive messages with the main idea or good news, you're preparing your audience for the details that follow. Make your opening clear and concise. Although the following introductory statements make the same point, one is cluttered with unnecessary information that buries the purpose, whereas the other is brief and to the point:

With the direct approach, open with a clear and concise expression of the main idea or good news.

Instead of This	Write This
I am pleased to inform you that after careful consideration of a diverse and talented pool of applicants, each of whom did a thorough job of analyzing Trask Horton Pharmaceuticals's training needs, we have selected your bid.	Trask Horton Pharmaceuticals has accepted your bid to provide public speaking and presentation training to the sales staff.

The best way to write a clear opening is to have a clear idea of what you want to say. Ask yourself, "What is the single most important message I have for the audience?"

PROVIDING NECESSARY DETAILS AND EXPLANATION

Use the body to explain your point completely so that your audience won't be confused or doubtful about your meaning. As you provide the details, maintain the supportive tone established in the opening. This tone is easy to continue when your message is entirely positive, as in this example:

MOBILE APP

If your email service doesn't allow huge file attachments, Hightail lets you post the file on its servers and send your recipients a link instead.

> Your educational background and internship have impressed us, and we believe you would be a valuable addition to Green Valley Properties. As discussed during your interview, your salary will be $4,300 per month, plus benefits. Please plan to meet with our benefits manager, Paula Sanchez, at 8 A.M. on Monday, March 21. She will assist you with all the paperwork necessary to tailor our benefit package to your family situation. She will also arrange various orientation activities to help you acclimate to our company.

However, if your routine message is mixed and must convey mildly disappointing information, put the negative portion of your message into as favorable a context as possible:

Try to embed any negative information in a positive context.

Instead of This	Write This
No, we no longer carry the Sportsgirl line of sweaters.	The new Olympic line has replaced the Sportsgirl sweaters that you asked about. Olympic features a wider range of colors and sizes and more contemporary styling.

In this example, the more complete description is less negative and emphasizes how the recipient can benefit from the change. Be careful, though: You can use negative information in this type of message *only* if you're reasonably sure the audience will respond positively. Otherwise, use the indirect approach.

If you are communicating with a customer, you might also want to use the body of your message to assure the person of the wisdom of his or her purchase selection

---

CHECKLIST ✔ Writing Routine Replies and Positive Messages

A. Start with the main idea.
- Be clear and concise.
- Identify the single most important message before you start writing.

B. Provide necessary details and explanation.
- Explain your point completely to eliminate any confusion or lingering doubts.
- Maintain a supportive tone throughout.
- Embed negative statements in positive contexts or balance them with positive alternatives.

- Talk favorably about the choices the customer has made.

C. End with a courteous close.
- Let your readers know you have their personal well-being in mind.
- If further action is required, tell readers how to proceed and encourage them to act promptly.

(without being condescending or self-congratulatory). Using such favorable comments, often known as *resale*, is a good way to build customer relationships. These comments are commonly included in acknowledgments of orders and other routine announcements to customers, and they are most effective when they are short and specific:

> The KitchenAid mixer you ordered is our best-selling model. It should meet your cooking needs for many years.

ENDING WITH A COURTEOUS CLOSE

The close of routine replies and positive messages is usually short and simple because you're leaving things on a neutral or positive note and not usually asking for the reader to do anything. Often, a simple thank you is all you need. However, if follow-up action is required or expected, use the close to identify who will do what and when that action will take place. For a quick reminder of the steps involved in writing routine replies and positive messages, see "Checklist: Writing Routine Replies and Positive Messages."

In the close, make sure audience members understand what to do next and how that action will benefit them (if applicable).

Common Examples of Routine and Positive Messages

Most routine and positive messages fall into six main categories: answers to requests for information and action, grants of claims and requests for adjustment, recommendations, routine information, good-news announcements, and goodwill messages.

4 LEARNING OBJECTIVE
Describe six common types of routine replies and positive messages.

ANSWERING REQUESTS FOR INFORMATION AND ACTION

Every professional answers requests for information and action from time to time. If the response is a simple yes or some other straightforward information, the direct approach is appropriate. A prompt, gracious, and thorough response will positively influence how people think about you and the organization you represent.

When you're answering requests and a potential sale is involved, you have three main goals: (1) to respond to the inquiry and answer all questions, (2) to leave your reader with a good impression of you and your firm, and (3) to encourage the future sale.

GRANTING CLAIMS AND REQUESTS FOR ADJUSTMENT

Even the best-run companies make mistakes, and each of these events represents a turning point in your relationship with your customer. If you handle the situation well, your customer is likely to be even more loyal than before because you've proven that you're

Responding to mistakes in a courteous, reader-focused way helps repair important business relationships.

serious about customer satisfaction. However, if a customer believes that you mishandled a complaint, you'll make the situation even worse. Dissatisfied customers often take their business elsewhere without notice and tell numerous friends and colleagues about the negative experience. A transaction that might be worth only a few dollars by itself could cost you many times that amount in lost business. In other words, every mistake is an opportunity to improve a relationship.

Your specific response to a customer complaint depends on your company's policies for resolving such issues and your assessment of whether the company, the customer, or some third party is at fault. In general, take the following steps:

- Acknowledge receipt of the customer's claim or complaint.
- Sympathize with the customer's inconvenience or frustration.
- Take (or assign) personal responsibility for setting matters straight.
- Explain precisely how you have resolved, or plan to resolve, the situation.
- Take steps to repair the relationship.
- Follow up to verify that your response was correct.

In addition to taking these positive steps, maintain a professional demeanor. Don't blame colleagues by name; don't make exaggerated, insincere apologies; don't imply that the customer is at fault; and don't promise more than you can deliver.

> To grant a claim when the customer is at fault, try to discourage future mistakes without insulting the customer.

Communication about a claim is a delicate matter when the customer is clearly at fault. If you choose to grant the claim, open with that good news. However, the body needs special attention because you want to discourage similar claims in the future. Close in a courteous manner that expresses your appreciation for the customer's business (see Figure 4).

See "Checklist: Granting Claims and Adjustment Requests" to review the tasks involved in these kinds of business messages.

PROVIDING RECOMMENDATIONS AND REFERENCES

> Recommendation letters are vulnerable to legal complications, so consult your company's legal department before writing one.

People who need endorsements from employers or colleagues (when applying for a job, for example) often request letters of recommendation. These messages used to be a fairly routine matter, but employment recommendations and references have raised some complex legal issues in recent years. Employees have sued employers and individual managers for providing negative information or refusing to provide letters of recommendation, and employers have sued other employers for failing to disclose negative information about job candidates. Before you write a letter of recommendation for a former employee or provide information in response to another employer's background check, make sure you understand your company's policies. Your company may refuse to provide anything more than dates of employment and other basic details, for example.[2]

CHECKLIST ✔ **Granting Claims and Adjustment Requests**

A. Responding when your company is at fault.
- Be aware of your company's policies in such cases before you respond.
- For serious situations, refer to the company's crisis management plan.
- Start by acknowledging receipt of the claim or complaint.
- Take or assign personal responsibility for resolving the situation.
- Sympathize with the customer's frustration.
- Explain how you have resolved the situation (or plan to).
- Take steps to repair the customer relationship.
- Verify your response with the customer, and keep the lines of communication open.

B. Responding when the customer is at fault.
- Weigh the cost of complying with or refusing the request.
- If you choose to comply, open with the good news.
- Use the body of the message to respectfully educate the customer about steps needed to avoid a similar outcome in the future.
- Close with an appreciation for the customer's business.

C. Responding when a third party is at fault.
- Evaluate the situation and review your company's policies before responding.
- Avoid placing blame; focus on the solution.
- Regardless of who is responsible for resolving the situation, let the customer know what will happen to resolve the problem.

Writing Routine and Positive Messages

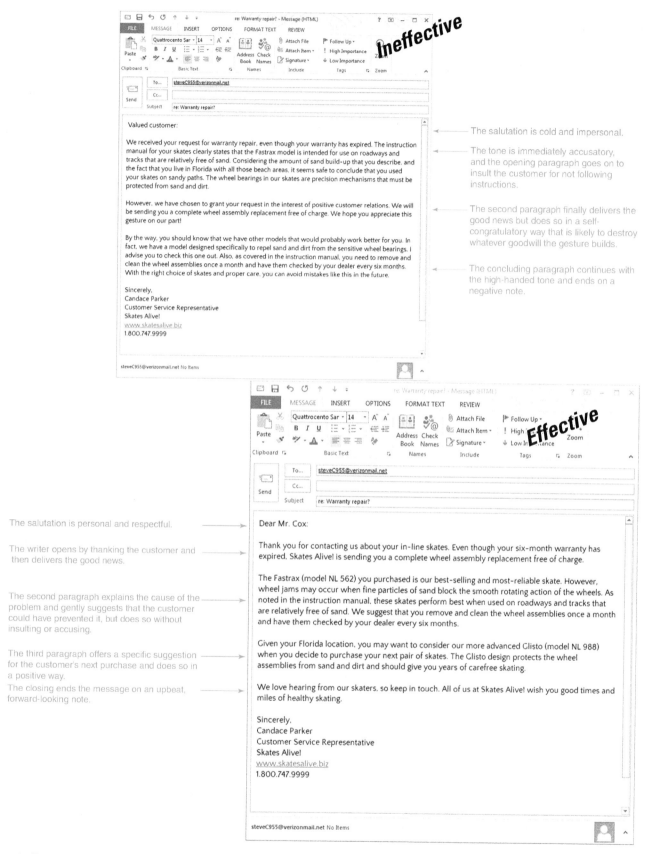

Figure 4   Responding to a Claim When the Buyer Is at Fault

Responding to a claim when the buyer is at fault is a positive gesture, so the content and tone of the message need to reflect that. After all, there's no point in fostering a positive relationship through actions but then undermining that through negative communication. Notice how the ineffective version sounds like a crabby parent who gives in to a child's demand but sends a mixed message by being highly critical anyway. The effective version is much more subtle, letting the customer know how to take care of his skates, without blaming or insulting him.
Source: MS Outlook 2013, © Microsoft.

If you decide to write a letter of recommendation or respond to a request for information about a job candidate, your goal is to convince readers that the person being recommended has the characteristics necessary for the job, assignment, or other objective the person is seeking. A successful recommendation letter contains a number of relevant details (see Figure 5):

- The candidate's full name
- The position or other objective the candidate is seeking
- The nature of your relationship with the candidate
- Facts and evidence relevant to the candidate and the opportunity
- A comparison of this candidate's potential with that of peers, if available (for example, "Ms. Jonasson consistently ranked in the top 10 percent of our national salesforce.")
- Your overall evaluation of the candidate's suitability for the opportunity

Keep in mind that every time you write a recommendation, you're putting your own reputation on the line. If the person's shortcomings are so pronounced

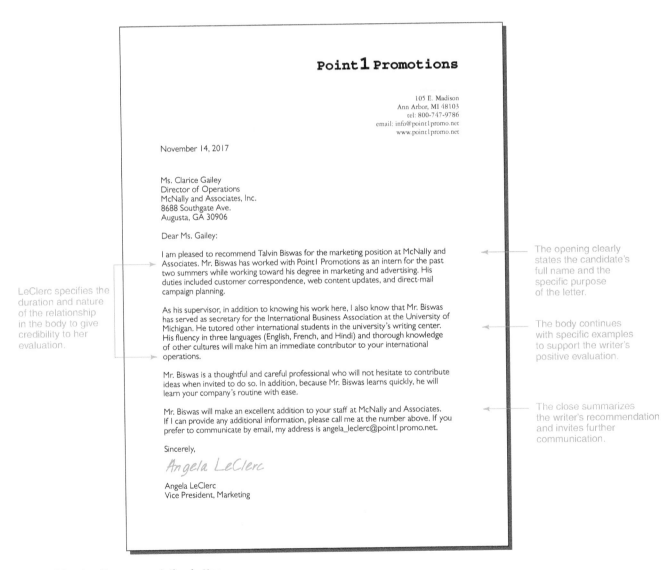

LeClerc specifies the duration and nature of the relationship in the body to give credibility to her evaluation.

The opening clearly states the candidate's full name and the specific purpose of the letter.

The body continues with specific examples to support the writer's positive evaluation.

The close summarizes the writer's recommendation and invites further communication.

Figure 5 Effective Recommendation Letter
This letter clearly states the nature of the writer's relationship to the candidate and provides specific examples to support the writer's endorsements.

Timeline Photos

Back to Album · JetBlue Airways's photos · JetBlue Airways's Page

Previous · Next

JetBlue Airways
Our first flight from Boston to Detroit just landed! We want to hear from those Detroiters in the know. What are your top stops in our newest Blue City? #DepictTheD
10 March

Album: Timeline Photos
Shared with: Public

Open Photo Viewer

Courtesy JetBlue Airways Corporation.

Figure 6   Announcing Good News
Encouraging online conversations is an important element of brand socialization. In this Facebook post celebrating its inaugural flight from Boston to Detroit, JetBlue asked residents of Detroit to recommend their favorite places around the city.

that you don't think he or she is a good fit for the job, the only choice is to not write the letter at all. Unless your relationship with the person warrants an explanation, simply suggest that someone else might be in a better position to provide a recommendation.

SHARING ROUTINE INFORMATION

Many messages involve sharing routine information, such as project updates and order status notifications. Use the opening of these routine messages to state the purpose and briefly mention the nature of the information you are providing. Give the necessary details in the body, and end your message with a courteous close.

Most routine communications are neutral, so you don't have to take special steps in anticipation of emotional reactions from readers. However, some routine informative messages may require additional care. For instance, policy statements or procedural changes may be good news for a company, perhaps by saving money. However, it may not be obvious to employees that such savings may make additional employee resources available or even lead to pay raises. In instances in which the reader may not initially view the information positively, use the body of the message to highlight the potential benefits from the reader's perspective.

> When sharing routine information
> - State the purpose at the beginning and briefly mention the nature of the information you are providing.
> - Provide the necessary details.
> - End with a courteous close.

ANNOUNCING GOOD NEWS

To develop and maintain good relationships, smart companies recognize that it's good business to spread the word about positive developments. Such developments can include opening new facilities, hiring a new executive, introducing new products or services, or sponsoring community events (see Figure 6). Because good news is always welcome, use the direct approach.

External good-news announcements are often communicated in a **news release**, also known as a *press release*, a specialized document used to share relevant information with the news media. (News releases are also used to announce negative news, such as plant closings.) In most companies, news releases are usually prepared or at least supervised by

> A news release or press release is a message (usually routine, but not always) designed to share information with the news media, although many are now written with customers and other stakeholders in mind as well.

specially trained writers in the public relations department. The content follows the customary pattern for a positive message: good news followed by details and a positive close. However, traditional news releases have a critical difference: You're not writing directly to the ultimate audience (such as the readers of a newspaper); you're trying to interest an editor or a reporter in a story, and that person will then write the material that is eventually read by the larger audience.

Until recently, news releases were crafted in a way to provide information to reporters, who would then write their own articles if the subject matter was interesting to their readers. Thanks to the Internet and social media, however, the nature of the news release is changing. Many companies now view it as a general-purpose tool for communicating directly with customers and other audiences, creating *direct-to-consumer news releases*.[3] Many of these are considered *social media releases* because they include social networking links, "Tweetables" (Twitter-ready statements that can be shared on Twitter at the click of a button), and other sharable content.

> The social media release includes share-ready content that is easy to reuse in blog posts, tweets, and other social media formats.

FOSTERING GOODWILL

> Goodwill is the positive feeling that encourages people to maintain a business relationship.

All business messages should be written with an eye toward fostering positive relationships with audiences, but some messages are written specifically to build goodwill. You can use these messages to enhance your relationships with customers, colleagues, and other businesspeople by sending friendly, even unexpected, notes with no direct business purpose (see Figure 7). Whether you're thanking an employee for a job well done or congratulating a colleague for a personal or professional achievement, the small effort to send a goodwill message can have a positive and lasting effect on the people around you.

> Many routine messages can be adapted to foster goodwill, either by sharing helpful information or providing an element of entertainment.

In addition to creating messages for a specific goodwill reason, you can craft almost any routine message in a way to build goodwill. Two ways to do so are by providing information that your readers might find helpful and by maintaining a positive tone throughout your message.

Sending Congratulations

> Taking note of significant events in someone's personal life helps foster the business relationship.

One prime opportunity for sending goodwill messages is to congratulate individuals or companies for significant business achievements. Other reasons for sending congratulations include highlights in people's personal lives, such as weddings, births, graduations,

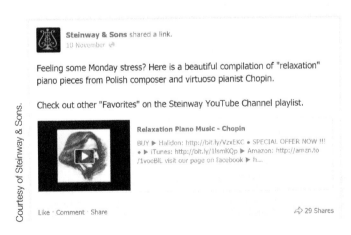

Courtesy of Steinway & Sons.

Figure 7 Goodwill Messages
Goodwill messages serve a variety of business functions. Fans who follow Steinway on Facebook love great pianos and great piano music. In this post, the company offers its fan community something of value—a playlist of relaxing piano music as a Monday mood booster. The post doesn't attempt to sell anything (the "Buy" link shown in the video capture is for the album itself and isn't part of Steinway's message). It's just a way of fostering goodwill among fellow music lovers.

and success in nonbusiness competitions. You may congratulate business acquaintances on their own achievements or on the accomplishments of a spouse or child. You may also take note of personal events, even if you don't know the reader well. If you're already friendly with the reader, a more personal tone is appropriate.

Sending Messages of Appreciation

An important leadership quality is the ability to recognize the contributions of employees, colleagues, suppliers, and other associates. Your praise does more than just make the person feel good; it encourages further excellence. Moreover, a message of appreciation may become an important part of someone's personnel file. So when you write a message of appreciation, try to specifically mention the person or people you want to praise. The brief message that follows expresses gratitude and reveals the happy result:

An effective message of appreciation documents a person's contributions.

> Thank you and everyone on your team for the heroic efforts you took to bring our servers back up after last Friday's flood. We were able to restore business right on schedule first thing Monday morning. You went far beyond the level of contractual service in restoring our data center within 16 hours. I would especially like to highlight the contribution of networking specialist Julienne Marks, who worked for 12 straight hours to reconnect our Internet service. If I can serve as a reference in your future sales activities, please do not hesitate to ask.

Hearing a sincere thank you can do wonders for morale.[4] Moreover, in today's electronic media environment, a handwritten thank-you note can be a particularly welcome acknowledgment.[5]

Offering Condolences

Condolence letters are brief personal messages written to comfort someone after the death of a loved one. You may have occasion to offer condolences to employees or other business associates (when the person has lost a family member) or to the family of an employee or business associate (when that person has died).

These messages can feel intimidating to write, but they don't need to be. Follow these three principles: short, simple, and sincere. You don't need to produce a work of literary art; the fact that you are writing sends a message that is as meaningful as anything you can say.

Timing and media choice are important considerations with condolence letters. The sooner your message is received, the more comforting it will be, so don't delay. And unless circumstances absolutely leave you no choice, do not use electronic media. A brief, handwritten note on quality stationery is the way to go.

Open a condolence message with a simple expression of sympathy, such as "I am deeply sorry to hear of your loss" or "I am sorry for your loss." How you continue from there depends on the circumstances and your relationships with the deceased and the person to whom you are writing. For example, if you are writing to the husband of a colleague who recently died and you have never met him, you might continue with "Having worked with Janice for more than a decade, I know what a kind and caring person she was." Such a statement accomplishes two goals: explaining why you in particular are writing and letting the recipient know that his loved one was appreciated in the workplace.

The primary purpose of condolence messages is to let the audience know that you and the organization you represent care about the person's loss.

Conversely, if you are writing to a colleague who recently lost a loved one, you might continue with "After meeting Warren at last year's company picnic and hearing your stories about his involvement with your son's soccer league and the many other ways he contributed to his community, I know what a special person he was." Sharing brief and positive memories like this adds meaning and depth to your expression of sympathy.

You can conclude with a simple statement such as "My thoughts are with you during this difficult time." If appropriate for the situation and your relationship, you might also include an offer of assistance. "Please call if there is anything I do for you."

As you decide what to include in the message, keep two points in mind. First, make it a personal expression of sympathy, but don't make the whole message about you and your sense of loss. You might be grieving as well, but unless you, the deceased, and the reader were all personally close, don't say things like "I was so devastated to hear the news about Mollie."

Second, don't offer "life advice," and don't include trite sayings that you may have heard or read. At this point, soon after the loss, the recipient doesn't want your advice, only your sympathy. Also, don't bring religion into the discussion unless you have a close personal relationship with the recipient and religion is already a part of your relationship. Otherwise, you risk offending with unwelcome or inappropriate sentiments.

Condolence letters are the most personal business messages you may ever have to write, so they require the utmost in care and respect for your reader. By keeping the messages simple, short, and sincere, you will be able to achieve the right tone.

To review the tasks involved in writing goodwill messages, see "Checklist: Sending Goodwill Messages." For the latest information on writing routine and positive messages, visit http://real-timeupdates.com/ebc12.

> Keep your condolence message focused on the recipient, not on your own emotions, and don't offer "life advice" or trite sayings.

CHECKLIST ✔ **Sending Goodwill Messages**

- Be sincere and honest.
- Don't exaggerate or use vague, grandiose language; support positive statements with specific evidence.
- Use congratulatory messages to build goodwill with clients and colleagues.

- Send messages of appreciation to emphasize how much you value the work of others.
- When sending condolence messages, open with a brief statement of sympathy, then adapt your message based on the circumstances and your relationship with the recipient.

ON THE JOB: SOLVING COMMUNICATION DILEMMAS AT GET SATISFACTION

After reading the many helpful responses you, as a representative of your company, posted on the Get Satisfaction website, Rahul Sachdev invited you to join the Get Satisfaction team as a customer service specialist; your job is to communicate with the companies that use Get Satisfaction's online services. Take what you've learned in this chapter and put it to good use as you address the following challenges. (Search for a few companies or product names on the Get Satisfaction website at http://getsatis faction.com to get a feel for how the system works.)

1. When people are frustrated with a problem and are trying to discuss it via a lean medium such as online postings, emotions can sometimes boil over. You've been monitoring a conversation between a representative for one of the companies that uses Get Satisfaction and one of its customers. Over the past couple of days, their online conversation has turned into an ugly argument, with accusations of incompetence and even dishonesty flying back and forth. Although the situation doesn't involve Get Satisfaction directly, you think it reflects poorly on your company because the dispute is taking place in full public view on your website—and it certainly isn't doing anybody any good to let this "flame war" keep raging. What is the best way to handle this situation?

a. Email the company representative privately and offer to mediate the dispute.

b. Post a public message offering to mediate the dispute.

c. Post a public message reminding both sides to be civil.

d. Ignore the dispute; it's between the company and its customer.

2. Web-based businesses occasionally suffer from page-loading problems, when a particular web page a visitor requests will not display, even when the rest of a website seems to be working normally. Get Satisfaction recently had a spate of these problems. Which of these is the best way to respond to queries while the company is working to fix the situation?

a. Yes, we've noticed this problem ourselves, but we hope to have everything stabilized soon.

b. We are soooooo sorry! We're working to resolve the situation as soon as possible.

c. Don't you just hate computers sometimes? We're working to resolve the situation as soon as possible.

d. We're having some problems with our host, which seems to be resulting in a lot of these errors. We're working on it now and hope to have everything stabilized soon.

3. Get Satisfaction recently released a new version of its software. Which of the following is the best one-sentence summary of this major milestone?

a. Version 4.0 is a major update that unleashes the full value of customer community to answer questions, solve problems, and collect ideas for developing the next generation of your products and services.

b. Version 4.0 rocks in every way imaginable.

c. Version 4.0 is our best work yet. It clearly shows how far we've come as a company and how much we've learned in the last two years.

d. Version 4.0 is a major update, incorporating multiple new features, expanded customizability, and a vastly improved and simplified user interface.

4. Get Satisfaction recently announced an *enterprise* version of its customer support software that companies can customize as part of their own information systems. The software is available in *beta release* form, a free pre-release version that software companies often release to encourage people to use as a way to see if anything needs to be changed or fixed before the official product is released. Get Satisfaction hasn't yet announced how much the software will cost when it is officially released, so not surprisingly, more than a few interested customers have written questions about the anticipated price. Small business owners in particular want to know if a less-expensive version will be available to small companies. The company is working on a pricing structure that would charge by the volume of usage, meaning that small companies would probably pay less than large companies. Which of the following responses is the most effective response to this question?

a. The pricing structure will be announced when the product is ready for formal release.

b. We can't specify exact pricing yet, because we're still working on those details.

c. We can't specify exact pricing yet, because we're still working on those details. We will make sure that the pricing structure does in fact work both for small companies and large ones, and that if there is a tiered structure, that it scales according to a reliable set of figures/metrics that reflect those size differences.

d. We can't specify exact pricing yet, because we're still working on those details. However, we are trying to figure out a tiered pricing structure that would be fair to both large and small companies.

Learning Objectives Checkup

Assess your understanding of the principles in this chapter by reading each learning objective and studying the accompanying exercises. You can check your responses against the answer key.

Objective 1: Outline an effective strategy for writing routine business requests.

1. When it comes to routine messages, you can
   a. Skip the planning stage
   b. Keep the planning stage brief
   c. Begin by gathering all the information you'll need
   d. Begin by choosing the channel and medium

2. When writing routine messages, you
   a. Can assume that your readers will be interested or neutral
   b. Should open with an "attention getter"
   c. Should use the indirect approach with most audiences
   d. Need not allow much time for revision, production, or proofreading

3. When writing a routine request, the best approach is to begin
   a. With a personal introduction, such as "My name is Lee Marrs, and I am…"
   b. With a vague reference to what you are writing about, such as "I have something to ask you."
   c. With a strong demand for action
   d. By politely stating your request

4. What should you do when asking questions in a routine request?
   a. Begin with the least important question and work your way up to the most important question.
   b. Include all possible questions about the topic, even if the list gets long.
   c. Deal with only one topic per question.
   d. Do all of the above.

5. Which of the following should you do when closing a routine request?
   a. Be sure to thank the reader "in advance" for complying with the request.
   b. Ask the reader to respond by a specific and appropriate time.
   c. Ask any remaining questions you have.
   d. Do all of the above.
6. A courteous close contains
   a. A specific request
   b. Information about how you can be reached (if it isn't obvious)
   c. An expression of appreciation or goodwill
   d. All of the above

Objective 2: Describe three common types of routine requests.

7. Which of the following would be an inappropriate goal for a routine, simple request?
   a. Explaining what you want to know or what you want the reader to do
   b. Explaining why you're making the request
   c. Explaining how you can use your position in the company to force the reader to comply
   d. Explaining why it may be in your reader's interest to help you
8. Requests for recommendations and references are routine messages, so you can organize your inquiry using the _____ approach.
9. If you are requesting an adjustment from a company but you're not sure what the best solution would be, which of the following tactics would be best?
   a. Ask the company to assess the situation and offer advice on solving the problem.
   b. Don't ask for a solution, because doing so could lead to a suboptimal outcome for you.
   c. Subtly hint that legal action could light a fire under the company.
   d. Demand that the company solve the problem immediately; after all, it's the right thing to do.

Objective 3: Outline an effective strategy for writing routine replies and positive messages.

10. If you are making a routine reply to a customer, it's a good idea to
    a. Leave out any negative information
    b. Include resale information to assure the customer of the wisdom of his or her purchase
    c. Leave out sales promotion material, which would be tacky to include
    d. Do all of the above
11. A positive message should open with a clear and concise statement of the _____ _____ or _____ _____.
12. If a message has both positive and negative elements, you should

a. Always start with the bad news to get it out of the way first
b. Write two separate messages; never mix good and bad news
c. Put the bad news in a postscript (p.s.) at the bottom of the letter
d. Try to put the negative news in a positive context

Objective 4: Describe six common types of routine replies and positive messages.

13. Which of the following is not among the recommended elements to include in your message if you are responding to a claim or complaint when your company is at fault?
    a. An acknowledgement that you received the customer's claim or complaint
    b. An expression of sympathy for the inconvenience or loss the customer has experienced
    c. An explanation of how you will resolve the situation
    d. Complete contact information for your corporate legal staff
14. If a customer who is clearly at fault requests an adjustment, you should
    a. Ignore the request; the customer is clearly wasting your time
    b. Carefully weigh the cost of complying with the request against the cost of denying it and then decide how to respond based on the overall impact on your company
    c. Always agree to such requests because unhappy customers spread bad publicity about a company
    d. Suggest in a firm but professional tone that the customer take his or her business elsewhere in the future
15. If a third party (such as a shipping company) is at fault when one of your customers makes a claim or requests an adjustment, the best response is to
    a. Follow the terms of whatever customer service agreement your company has with the third party
    b. Explain to the customer that your company is not at fault
    c. Always grant the request; after all, it's your customer, and the customer holds you responsible
    d. Forward the message to the third party as quickly as possible
16. The purpose of goodwill messages is to
    a. Generate sales
    b. Impress others
    c. Make yourself feel better
    d. Enhance relationships with customers, colleagues, and other businesspeople
17. The most effective goodwill messages
    a. Always try to find an "angle" that benefits the sender in addition to the receiver
    b. Avoid details and focus on the emotions of the situation
    c. Are sincere and honest
    d. Do all of the above

Quick Learning Guide

LEARNING OBJECTIVES

1 Outline an effective strategy for writing routine business requests.

2 Describe three common types of routine requests.

3 Outline an effective strategy for writing routine replies and positive messages.

4 Describe six common types of routine replies and positive messages.

KEY TERMS

adjustment The settlement of a claim
claim A formal complaint made in response to dissatisfaction over a product or service
condolence letters Brief personal messages written to comfort someone after the death of a loved one

news release Also known as a *press release*, a specialized document traditionally used to share relevant information with the local or national news media; today, many companies issue news releases directly to the public as well

---

CHECKLIST

Writing Routine Requests

A. State your request up front.
- Write in a polite, undemanding, personal tone.
- Use the direct approach because your audience will probably respond favorably to your request.
- Be specific and precise in your request.

B. Explain and justify your request.
- Justify the request or explain its importance.
- Explain any potential benefits of responding.
- Ask the most important questions first.
- Break complex requests into individual questions that are limited to only one topic each.

C. Request specific action in a courteous close.
- Make it easy to comply by including appropriate contact information.
- Express your gratitude.
- Clearly state any important deadlines for the request.

CHECKLIST ✔

Making Claims and Requesting Adjustments

- Maintain a professional tone, even if you're extremely frustrated.
- Open with a straightforward statement of the problem.
- Provide specific details in the body.
- Present facts honestly and clearly.
- Politely summarize the desired action in the closing.
- Clearly state what you expect as a fair settlement or ask the reader to propose a fair adjustment.
- Explain the benefits of complying with the request, such as your continued patronage.

CHECKLIST ✔

Writing Routine Replies and Positive Messages

A. Start with the main idea.
- Be clear and concise.
- Identify the single most important message before you start writing.

B. Provide necessary details and explanation.
- Explain your point completely to eliminate any confusion or lingering doubts.
- Maintain a supportive tone throughout.
- Embed negative statements in positive contexts or balance them with positive alternatives.
- Talk favorably about the choices the customer has made.

C. End with a courteous close.
- Let your readers know you have their personal well-being in mind.
- If further action is required, tell readers how to proceed and encourage them to act promptly.

CHECKLIST

Sending Goodwill Messages

- Be sincere and honest.
- Don't exaggerate or use vague, grandiose language; support positive statements with specific evidence.
- Use congratulatory messages to build goodwill with clients and colleagues.
- Send messages of appreciation to emphasize how much you value the work of others.
- When sending condolence messages, open with a brief statement of sympathy, then adapt your message based on the circumstances and your relationship with the recipient.

Apply Your Knowledge

To review chapter content related to each question, refer to the indicated Learning Objective.

1. You have a complaint against one of your suppliers, but you have no documentation to back it up. Should you request an adjustment anyway? Why or why not? [LO-2]

⭐ 2. The latest issue of a local business newspaper names 10 area executives who have exhibited excellent leadership skills in the past year. You are currently searching for a job, and a friend suggests that you write each executive a congratulatory letter and mention in passing that you are looking for new career opportunities and would appreciate the opportunity for an interview. Is this a smart strategy? Why or why not? [LO-4]

⭐ 3. You've been asked to write a letter of recommendation for an employee who worked for you some years ago. You recall that the employee did an admirable job, but you can't remember any specific information at this point. Should you write the letter anyway? Explain. [LO-4]

4. Your company's error cost an important business customer a new client; you know it, and your customer knows it. Do you apologize, or do you refer to the incident in a positive light without admitting any responsibility? Briefly explain. [LO-4]

Practice Your Skills

Messages for Analysis

Read the following messages and then (1) analyze the strengths and weaknesses of each sentence and (2) revise each document so that it follows this chapter's guidelines.

5. **Message 8.A: Message Strategies: Routine Requests [LO-2]**

   I'm fed up with the mistakes that our current accounting firm makes. I run a small construction company, and I don't have time to double-check every bookkeeping entry and call the accountants a dozen times when they won't return my messages. Please explain how your firm would do a better job than my current accountants. You have a good reputation among homebuilders, but before I consider hiring you to take over my accounting, I need to know that you care about quality work and good customer service.

6. **Message 8.B: Message Strategies: Responding to Claims and Requests for Adjustments [LO-4]**

   We read your letter, requesting your deposit refund. We couldn't figure out why you hadn't received it, so we talked to our maintenance engineer, as you suggested. He said you had left one of the doors off the hinges in your apartment in order to get a large sofa through the door. He also confirmed that you had paid him $5.00 to replace the door since you had to turn in the U-Haul trailer and were in a big hurry.

   This entire situation really was caused by a lack of communication between our housekeeping inspector and the maintenance engineer. All we knew was that the door was off the hinges when it was inspected by Sally Tarnley. You know that our policy states that if anything is wrong with the apartment, we keep the deposit. We had no way of knowing that George just hadn't gotten around to replacing the door.

   But we have good news. We approved the deposit refund, which will be mailed to you from our home office in Teaneck, New Jersey. I'm not sure how long that will take, however. If you don't receive the check by the end of next month, give me a call.

   Next time, it's really a good idea to stay with your apartment until it's inspected, as stipulated in your lease agreement. That way, you'll be sure to receive your refund when you expect it. Hope you have a good summer.

7. **Message 8.C: Message Strategies: Providing Recommendations [LO-4]**

   Your letter to Kunitake Ando, president of Sony, was forwarded to me because I am the human resources director. In my job as head of HR, I have access to performance reviews for all of the Sony employees in the United States. This means, of course, that I would be the person best qualified to answer your request for information on Nick Oshinski.

   In your letter of the 15th, you asked about Nick Oshinski's employment record with us because he has applied to work for your company. Mr. Oshinski was employed with us from January 5, 2001, until March 1, 2011. During that time, Mr. Oshinski received ratings ranging from 2.5 up to 9.6, with 10 being the top score. As you can see, he must have done better reporting to some managers than to others. In addition, he took all vacation days, which is a bit unusual. Although I did not know Mr. Oshinski personally, I know that our best workers seldom use all the vacation time they earn. I do not know if that applies in this case.

   In summary, Nick Oshinski performed his tasks well depending on who managed him.

Exercises

Each activity is labeled according to the primary skill or skills you will need to use. To review relevant chapter content, you can refer to the indicated Learning Objective.

Message Strategies: Routine Requests; Revising for Conciseness [LO-1] Critique the following closing paragraphs. How would you rewrite each to be concise, courteous, and specific?

8. I need your response sometime soon so I can order the parts in time for your service appointment. Otherwise, your air-conditioning system may not be in tip-top condition for the start of the summer season.

9. Thank you in advance for sending me as much information as you can about your products. I look forward to receiving your package in the very near future.

10. To schedule an appointment with one of our knowledgeable mortgage specialists in your area, you can always call our hotline at 1-800-555-8765. This is also the number to call if you have more questions about mortgage rates, closing procedures, or any other aspect of the mortgage process. Remember, we're here to make the home-buying experience as painless as possible.

Message Strategies: Routine Responses; Media Skills: Email [LO-3] Revise the following short email messages so they are more direct and concise; develop a subject line for each revised message.

11. I'm contacting you about your recent email request for technical support on your cable Internet service. Part of the problem we have in tech support is trying to figure out exactly what each customer's specific problem is so that we can troubleshoot quickly and get you back in business as quickly as possible. You may have noticed that in the online support request form, there are a number of fields to enter your type of computer, operating system, memory, and so on. While you did tell us you were experiencing slow download speeds during certain times of the day, you didn't tell us which times specifically, nor did you complete all the fields telling us about your computer. Please return to our support website and resubmit your request, being sure to provide all the necessary information; then we'll be able to help you.

12. Thank you for contacting us about the difficulty you had collecting your luggage at Denver International Airport. We are very sorry for the inconvenience this has caused you. As you know, traveling can create problems of this sort regardless of how careful the airline personnel might be. To receive compensation, please send us a detailed list of the items that you lost and complete the following questionnaire. You can email it back to us.

13. Sorry it took us so long to get back to you. We were flooded with résumés. Anyway, your résumé made the final 10, and after meeting three hours yesterday, we've decided we'd like to meet with you. What is your schedule like for next week? Can you come in for an interview on June 15 at 3:00 p.m.? Please get back to us by the end of this workweek and let us know if you will be able to attend. As you can imagine, this is our busy season.

14. We're letting you know that because we use over a ton of paper a year and because so much of that paper goes into the wastebasket to become so much more environmental waste, starting Monday, we're placing white plastic bins outside the elevators on every floor to recycle that paper and in the process, minimize pollution.

Message Strategies: Routine and Positive Messages; Revising for Conciseness [LO-3] Rewrite the following sentences so that they are direct and concise. If necessary, break your answer into two sentences.

15. We wanted to invite you to our special 40% off by-invitation-only sale; the sale is taking place on November 9.

16. We wanted to let you know that we are giving a tote bag and a voucher for five iTunes downloads with every $50 donation you make to our radio station.

17. The director planned to go to the meeting that will be held on Monday at a little before 11 a.m.

18. In today's meeting, we were happy to have the opportunity to welcome Paul Eccelson, who reviewed the shopping cart function on our website and offered some great advice; if you have any questions about these new forms, feel free to call him at his office.

19. **Message Strategies: Responding to Claims and Requests for Adjustments [LO-4]** Your company markets a line of automotive accessories for people who like to "tune" their cars for maximum performance. A customer has just written a furious email, claiming that a supercharger he purchased from your website didn't deliver the extra engine power he expected. Your company has a standard refund process to handle situations such as this, and you have the information you need to inform the customer about that. You also have information that could help the customer find a more compatible supercharger from one of your competitors, but the customer's email message is so abusive that you don't feel obligated to help. Is this an appropriate response? Why or why not?

20. **Message Strategies: Writing Positive Messages; Media Skills: Microblogging [LO-4]** Locate an online announcement for a new product you find interesting or useful. Read enough about the product to be able to describe it to someone else in your own words and then writer four Twitter tweets: one to introduce the product to your followers and three follow-on tweets that describe three particularly compelling features or benefits of the product.

21. **Message Strategies: Writing Goodwill Messages [LO-4]** Identify someone in your life who has recently accomplished a significant achievement, such as graduating from high school or college, completing a major project, or winning an important professional award. Write a brief congratulatory message using the guidelines presented in the chapter.

Expand Your Skills

Critique the Professionals

Locate an online example of a news release in which a company announces good news, such as a new product, a notable executive hire, an expansion, strong financial results, or an industry award. Analyze the release using the guidance provided in the chapter. In what ways did the writer excel? What aspects of the release could be improved? Does the release provide social media-friendly content and features? Using whatever medium your instructor requests, write a brief analysis of the piece (no more than one page), citing specific elements from the piece and support from the chapter.

Sharpening Your Career Skills Online

Bovée and Thill's Business Communication Web Search, at http://websearch.businesscommunicationnetwork.com, is a unique research tool designed specifically for business communication research. Use the Web Search function to find a website, video, PDF document, podcast, or PowerPoint presentation that offers advice on writing goodwill messages such as thank-you notes or congratulatory letters. Write a brief email message to your instructor, describing the item that you found and summarizing the career skills information you learned from it.

Improve Your Grammar, Mechanics, and Usage

The following exercises help you improve your knowledge of and power over English grammar, mechanics, and usage. Turn to the Handbook of Grammar, Mechanics, and Usage at the end of this text and review Sentences. Then look at the following 10 items. Circle the letter of the preferred choice within each group of sentences.

22. a. Joan Ellingsworth attends every stockholder meeting. Because she is one of the few board members eligible to vote.

b. Joan Ellingsworth attends every stockholder meeting. She is one of the few board members eligible to vote.

23 a. The executive director, along with his team members, is working quickly to determine the cause of the problem.

b. The executive director, along with his team members, are working quickly to determine the cause of the problem.

24 a. Listening on the extension, details of the embezzlement plot were overheard by the security chief.

b. Listening on the extension, the chief overheard details of the embezzlement plot.

25 a. First the human resources department interviewed dozens of people. Then it hired a placement service.

b. First the human resources department interviewed dozens of people then it hired a placement service.

26 a. Andrews won the sales contest, however he was able to sign up only two new accounts.

b. Andrews won the sales contest; however, he was able to sign up only two new accounts.

27 a. To find the missing file, the whole office was turned inside out.

b. The whole office was turned inside out to find the missing file.

28 a. Having finally gotten his transfer, he is taking his assistant right along with him.

b. Having finally gotten his transfer, his assistant is going right along with him.

29 a. Irving was recruiting team members for her project, she promised supporters unprecedented bonuses.

b. Because Irving was recruiting team members for her project, she promised supporters unprecedented bonuses.

30 a. He left the office unlocked overnight. This was an unconscionable act, considering the high crime rate in this area lately.

b. He left the office unlocked overnight. An unconscionable act, considering the high crime rate in this area lately.

31 a. When it comes to safety issues, the abandoned mine, with its collapsing tunnels, are cause for great concern.

b. When it comes to safety issues, the abandoned mine, with its collapsing tunnels, is cause for great concern.

Cases

Website links for selected companies mentioned in cases can be found in the Student Assignments section at http://real-time updates.com/ebc12.

Routine Requests

BLOGGING SKILLS

32. Message Strategies: Requesting Information [LO-2] You are writing a book about the advantages and potential pitfalls of using online collaboration systems for virtual team projects. You would like to include several dozen real-life examples from people in a variety of industries. Fortunately, you publish a highly respected blog on the subject, with several thousand regular readers.

Your task: Write a post for your blog that asks readers to submit brief descriptions of their experiences using collaboration tools for team projects. Ask them to email stories of how well a specific system or approach worked for them. Explain that they will receive an autographed copy of the book as thanks and that they will need to sign a release form if their stories are used. In addition, emphasize that you would like to use real names—of people, companies, and software—but you can keep the anecdotes anonymous if readers require. To stay on schedule, you need to have these stories by May 20.

EMAIL SKILLS

33. Message Strategies: Requesting a Recommendation [LO-2] One of your colleagues, Katina Vander, was recently promoted to department manager and now serves on the company's strategic planning committee. At its monthly meeting next week, the committee will choose an employee to lead an important market research project that will help define the company's product portfolio for the next five years.

You worked side by side with Vander for five years, so she knows your abilities well and has complimented your business insights on many occasions. You know that because she has only recently been promoted to manager, she needs to build credibility among her peers and will therefore be cautious about making such an important recommendation. On the other hand, making a stellar recommendation for such an important project would show that she has a good eye for talent—an essential leadership trait.

Your task: Write an email message to Vander, telling her that you are definitely interested in leading the project and asking her to put in a good word for you with the committee. Mention four attributes that you believe would serve you well in the role: a dozen years of experience in the industry, an engineering degree that helps you understand the technologies involved in product design, a consistent record of excellent or exceptional ratings in annual employee evaluations, and the three years you spent working in the company's customer support group, which gave you a firsthand look at customer satisfaction and quality issues. Make up any additional details you need to write the message.

EMAIL SKILLS

34. Message Strategies: Requesting a Recommendation [LO-2]
After five years of work in the human resources department at Cell Genesys (a company that is developing cancer treatment drugs), you were laid off in a round of cost-cutting moves that rippled through the biotech industry in recent years. The good news is that you found stable employment in the grocery distribution industry. The bad news is that in the three years since you left Cell Genesys, you have truly missed working in the exciting biotechnology field and having the opportunity to be a part of something as important as helping people recover from life-threatening diseases. You know careers in biotech are uncertain, but you have a few dollars in the bank now, and you're willing to ride that rollercoaster again.

Your task: Draft an email to Calvin Morris, your old boss at Cell Genesys, reminding him of the time you worked together and asking him to write a letter of recommendation for you.[6]

IM SKILLS

35. Message Strategies: Requesting Information [LO-2]
Many companies now provide presales and postsales customer support through some form of instant messaging or online chat function. As a consumer looking for information, you'll get better service if you can frame your requests clearly and succinctly.

Your task: Imagine that you need to replace your old laptop computer, but you're not sure whether to go with another laptop or switch to a tablet or perhaps one of the new tablet/laptop hybrids. Think through the various ways you will use this new device, from researching and note-taking during class to watching movies and interacting with friends on social media. Now imagine you're in a chat session with a sales representative from a computer company, and this person has asked how he or she can help you. Draft a message (no more than 100 words) that summarizes your computing and media requirements and asks the representative to recommend the right type of device for you.

TEXT MESSAGING SKILLS

26. Message Strategies: Requesting Information [LO-2]
The vast Consumer Electronics Show (CES) is the premier promotional event in the industry. More than 150,000 industry insiders from all over the world come to see the exciting new products on display from nearly 1,500 companies—everything from video-game gadgets to Internet-enabled refrigerators with built-in computer screens.[7] You've just stumbled on a video game controller that has a built-in webcam to allow networked gamers to see and hear each other while they play. Your company also makes game controllers, and you're worried that your customers will flock to this new controller-cam. You need to know how much buzz is circulating around the show: Have people seen it? What are they saying about it? Are they excited about it?

Your task: Compose a text message to your colleagues at the show, alerting them to the new controller-cam and asking them to listen for any buzz it might be generating among the attendees at the Las Vegas Convention Center and the several surrounding hotels where the show takes place. Here's the catch: Your text-messaging service limits messages to 160 characters, including spaces and punctuation, so your message can't be any longer than this.

EMAIL SKILLS

37. Message Strategies: Requesting an Adjustment [LO-2]
Love at first listen is the only way to describe the way you felt when you discovered the music streaming service Song-Throng. You enjoy dozens of styles of music, from Afrobeat and Tropicalia to mainstream pop and the occasional blast of industrial metal, and SongThrong has them all for only $9.99 a month. You can explore every genre imaginable, listening to as many tracks as you like for a fixed monthly fee. The service sounded too good to be true—and sadly, it was. The service was so unreliable that you began keeping note of when it was unavailable. Last month, it was down for all or part of 12 days—well over a third of the month. As much as you like it, you've had enough.

Your task: Write an email to support@songthrong.com, requesting a full refund. To get the $9.99 monthly rate, you prepaid for an entire year ($119.88), and you've been a subscriber for two months now. You know the service has been out for at least part of the time on 12 separate days last month, and while you didn't track outages during the first month, you believe it was about the same number of days.

LETTER WRITING SKILLS

38. Message Strategies: Requesting an Adjustment [LO-2]
As a consumer, you've probably bought something that didn't work right or paid for a service that did not turn out the way you expected. Maybe it was a pair of jeans with a rip in a seam that you didn't find until you got home or a watch that broke a week after you bought it. Or maybe your family hired a lawn service to do some yardwork and no one from the company showed up on the day promised, and when the gardeners finally appeared, they did not do what they'd been hired for but instead did other things that wound up damaging valuable plants.

Your task: Choose an incident from your own experience and write a claim letter, asking for a refund, repair, replacement, or other adjustment. You'll need to include all the details of the transaction, plus your contact address and phone number. If you can't think of such an experience, make up details for an imaginary situation. If your experience is real, you might want to mail the letter. The reply you receive will provide a good test of your claim-writing skills.

EMAIL SKILLS

39. Message Strategies: Requesting Action [LO-2] You head up the corporate marketing department for a nationwide chain of clothing stores. The company has decided to launch a new store-within-a-store concept, in which a small section of each store will showcase "business casual" clothing. To ensure a successful launch of this new strategy, you want to get input from the best retailing minds in the company. You also know it's important to get regional insights from around the country, because a merchandising strategy that works in one area might not succeed in another.

Your task: Write an email message to all 87 store managers, asking them to each nominate one person to serve on an advisory team (managers can nominate themselves if they are local market experts). Explain that you want to find people with at least five years of retailing experience, a good understanding of the local business climate, and thorough knowledge of the local retail competition. In addition, the best candidates will be good team players who are comfortable collaborating long distance, using virtual meeting technologies. Also, explain that while you are asking each of the 87 stores to nominate someone, the team will be limited to no more than eight people. You've met many of the store managers, but not all of them, so be sure to introduce yourself at the beginning of the message.

Routine Messages

EMAIL SKILLS

40. Message Strategies: Granting Claims [LO-4] Your company sells flower arrangements and gift baskets. Holidays are always a rush, and the overworked staff makes the occasional mistake. Last week, somebody made a big one. As a furious email message from a customer named Anders Ellison explains, he ordered a Valentine's Day bouquet for his wife, but the company sent a bereavement arrangement instead.

Your task: Respond to Ellison's email message, apologizing for the error, promising to refund all costs that Ellison incurred, informing him that the correct arrangement will arrive tomorrow (and he won't be charged anything for it), and offering Ellison his choice of any floral arrangement or gift basket for free on his wife's birthday.

EMAIL SKILLS

41. Message Strategies: Granting Claims [LO-4] Like many of the staff at Razer, you are an avid game player. You can therefore sympathize with a customer who got so excited during a hotly contested game that he slammed his Razer Anansi keyboard against his chair in celebration. Razer products are built for serious action, but no keyboard can withstand a blow like that. However, in the interest of building goodwill among the online gaming community, your manager has approved a free

replacement. This sort of damage is rare enough that the company isn't worried about unleashing a flood of similar requests.

Your task: Respond to Louis Hapsberg's email request for a replacement, in which he admitted to inflicting some abuse on this keyboard. Explain, tongue in cheek, that the company is "rewarding" him with a free keyboard in honor of his massive gaming win, but gently remind him that even the most robust electronic equipment needs to be used with care.

PODCASTING SKILLS / **PORTFOLIO BUILDER**

42. Message Strategies: Providing Routine Information; Media Skills: Podcasting [LO-4] As a training specialist in Winnebago Industry's human resources department, you're always on the lookout for new ways to help employees learn vital job skills. While watching a production worker page through a training manual while learning how to assemble a new recreational vehicle, you get what seems to be a great idea: Record the assembly instructions as audio files that workers can listen to while performing the necessary steps. With audio instructions, they wouldn't need to keep shifting their eyes between the product and the manual—and constantly losing their place. They could focus on the product and listen for each instruction. Plus, the new system wouldn't cost much at all; any computer can record the audio files, and you'd simply make them available on an intranet site for download into smartphones, tablets, and digital music players.

Your task: You immediately run your new idea past your boss, who has heard about podcasting but doesn't think it has any place in business. He asks you to prove the viability of the idea by recording a demonstration. Choose a process you engage in yourself—anything from replacing the strings on a guitar to sewing a quilt to changing the oil in a car—and write a brief (one page or less) description of the process that could be recorded as an audio file. Think carefully about the limitations of the audio format as a replacement for printed text (for instance, do you need to tell people to pause the audio while they perform a time-consuming task?). If directed by your instructor, record your instructions as a podcast.

BLOGGING SKILLS / **PORTFOLIO BUILDER**

43. Message Strategies: Providing Routine Information [LO-4] You are normally an easygoing manager who gives your employees a lot of leeway in using their own personal communication styles. However, the weekly staff meeting this morning pushed you over the edge. People were interrupting one another, asking questions that had already been answered, sending text messages during presentations, and exhibiting just about every other poor listening habit imaginable.

Your task: Review the advice on good listening skills, and then write a post for the internal company blog. Emphasize the importance of effective listening, and list at least five steps your employees can take to become better listeners.

Routine Replies

EMAIL SKILLS

44. Message Strategies: Routine Responses [LO-4] As administrative assistant to Walmart's director of marketing, you have just received a request from the company's webmaster to analyze Walmart's website from a consumer's point of view.

Your task: Visit www.walmart.com and browse through the site, considering the language, layout, graphics, and overall ease of use. In particular, look for aspects of the site that might be confusing or frustrating—annoyances that could prompt shoppers to abandon their quests and head to a competitor such as Target or Amazon. Summarize your findings and recommendations in an email message that could be sent to the webmaster.

MICROBLOGGING SKILLS

45. Message Strategies: Routine Announcements [LO-4]
As a way to give back to the communities in which it does business, your company supports the efforts of the United Way, a global organization that works to improve lives through education, income stability, and healthy living choices.[8] Each year, your company runs a fundraising campaign in which employees are encouraged to donate money to their local United Way agencies, and it also grants employees up to three paid days off to volunteer their time for the United Way. This year, you are in charge of the company's campaign.

Your task: Compose a four-message sequence to be posted on the company's internal microblogging system (a private version of Twitter, essentially). The messages are limited to 200 characters, including spaces and punctuation. The first message will announce the company's annual United Way volunteering and fundraising campaign (make up any details you need), and the other three messages will explain the United Way's efforts in the areas of education, income stability, and healthy living. Visit the United Way to learn more about these three areas.

LETTER WRITING SKILLS / TEAM SKILLS

46. Message Strategies: Providing Recommendations [LO-4] As a project manager at Expedia, one of the largest online travel services in the world, you've seen plenty of college interns in action. However, few have impressed you as much as Maxine "Max" Chenault. For one thing, she learned how to navigate the company's content management system virtually overnight and always used it properly, whereas other interns sometimes left things in a hopeless mess. She asked lots of intelligent questions about the business. You've been teaching her blogging and website design principles, and she's picked them up rapidly. Moreover, she is always on time, professional, and eager to assist. Also, she didn't mind doing mundane tasks.

On the downside, Chenault is a popular student. Early on, you often found her busy on the phone planning her many social activities when you needed her help. However, after you had a brief talk with her, this problem vanished.

You'll be sorry to see Chenault leave when she returns to school in the fall, but you're pleased to respond when she asks you for a letter of recommendation. She's not sure where she'll apply for work after graduation or what career path she'll choose, so she asks you to keep the letter fairly general.

Your task: Working with a team of your classmates, discuss what should and should not be in the letter. Prepare an outline based on your discussion and then draft the letter.

SOCIAL NETWORKING SKILLS

47. Message Strategies: Writing Routine Informative Messages; Composition Modes: Summarizing [LO-4]
As energy costs trend ever upward and more people become attuned to the environmental and geopolitical complexities of petroleum-based energy, interest in solar, wind, and other alternative energy sources continues to grow. In locations with high *insolation*, a measure of cumulative sunlight, solar panels can be cost-effective solutions over the long term. However, the upfront costs are still daunting for most homeowners. To help lower the entry barrier, the Foster City, California–based firm SolarCity now leases solar panels to homeowners for monthly payments that are less than their current electricity bills.[9]

Your task: Visit the Solar City website, click on Residential, and then click SolarLease to read about the leasing program. Next, study SolarCity's presence on Facebook to get a feel for how the company presents itself in a social networking environment. Now assume that you have been assigned the task of writing a brief summary of the SolarLease program that will appear on the Notes tab of SolarCity's Facebook page. In your own language and in 200 words or less, write an introduction to the SolarLease program and email it to your instructor.

Positive Messages

WEB WRITING SKILLS

48. Message Strategies: Good News Messages [LO-4]
Amateur and professional golfers in search of lower scores want to find clubs that are optimized for their individual swings. This process of *club fitting* has gone decidedly high tech in recent years, with fitters using Doppler radar, motion-capture video, and other tools to evaluate golfers' swing and ball flight characteristics. Hot Stix Golf is a leader in this industry, having fitted more than 200 professionals and thousands of amateurs.[10]

Your task: Imagine that you are the communications director at the Indian Wells Golf Resort in Indian Wells, California. Your operation has just signed a deal with Hot Stix to open a fitting center on site. Write a three-paragraph article that could be posted on the resort website. The first paragraph should announce the news that the Hot Stix center will open in six months, the second should summarize the benefits of club fitting, and the third should offer a brief overview of the services that will be available at the Indian Wells Hot Stix Center. Information on club fitting can be found on the Hot Stix website at www.hotstixgolf.com; make up any additional information you need to complete the article.

BLOGGING SKILLS / PORTFOLIO BUILDER

49. Message Strategies: Good-News Messages [LO-4]
Most people have heard of the Emmy, Grammy, Oscar, and Tony awards for television, music, movies, and theater performances, but fewer know what the Webby award is all about. Sponsored by the International Academy of Digital Arts and Sciences, the Webbys shine a spotlight on the best in website design, interactive media, and online film and video.[11]

Your task: Visit the Webby Awards website at www.webby awards.com, click on Winners, and choose one of the companies listed a winner in the Websites or Interactive Advertising categories. Now imagine you are the chief online strategist for this company, and you've just been informed your company won a Webby. Winning this award is a nice validation of the work your team has put in during the last year, and you want to share their success with the entire company. Write a brief post for the internal company blog, describing what the Webby awards are, explaining why they are a significant measure of accomplishment in the online industry, and congratulating the employees in your department who contributed to the successful web effort.

SOCIAL NETWORKING SKILLS

50. Message Strategies: Goodwill Messages [LO-4] As the largest employer in Loganville, your construction company provides jobs, purchasing activity, and tax receipts that make up a vital part of the city's economy. In your role as CEO, however, you realize that the relationship between your company and the community is mutually beneficial, and the company could not survive without the efforts of its employees, the business opportunities offered by a growing marketplace, and the physical and legal infrastructure that the government provides.

The company's dependence on the community was demonstrated in a moving and immediate way last weekend, when a powerful storm pushed the Logan River past flood stage and threatened to inundate your company's office and warehouse facilities. More than 200 volunteers worked alongside your

employees through the night to fill and stack sandbags to protect your buildings, and the city council authorized the deployment of heavy equipment and additional staff to help in the emergency effort. As you watched the water rise nearly 10 feet high behind the makeshift dike, you realized that the community came together to save your company.

Your task: Write a post for your company's Facebook page, thanking the citizens and government officials of Loganville for their help in protecting the company's facilities during the storm. Use your creativity to make up any details you need to write a 100- to 200-word message.

LETTER WRITING SKILLS

51. Message Strategies: Goodwill Messages [LO-4] Shari Willison worked as a geologist in your civil engineer firm for 20 years before succumbing to leukemia. With only a few dozen employees, the company has always been a tight-knit group, and you feel like you've lost a good friend in addition to a valued employee.

Your task: Write a letter of condolence to Willison's husband, Arthur, and the couple's teenaged children, Jordan and Amy. You have known all three socially through a variety of company holiday parties and events over the years. Make up any details you need.

MyBCommLab

Go to the Assignments section of your MyLab to complete these writing exercises.

52. Should you use the direct or indirect approach for most routine messages? Why? [LO-1]

53. Why is it good practice to explain why replying to a request could benefit the reader? [LO-1]

Endnotes

1. Get Satisfaction website, accessed 20 February 2015, http://get satisfaction.com; Dan Fost, "On the Internet, Everyone Can Hear You Complain," *New York Times*, 25 February 2008, www.nytimes.com; Ray Wang, "Executive Profiles: Disruptive Tech Leaders in Social Business—Wendy Lea, Get Satisfaction," *Forbes*, 8 June 2011, www.forbes.com.

2. "How to Write Reference Letters," National Association of Colleges and Employers website, accessed 5 July 2010, www.naceweb.org; "Five (or More) Ways You Can Be Sued for Writing (or Not Writing) Reference Letters," *Fair Employment Practices Guidelines*, July 2006, 1, 3.

3. David Meerman Scott, *The New Rules of Marketing and PR* (Hoboken, N.J.: Wiley, 2007), 62.

4. Pat Cataldo, "Op-Ed: Saying 'Thank You' Can Open More Doors Than You Think," Penn State University Smeal College of Business website, accessed 19 February 2008, www.smeal.psu.edu.

5. Jackie Huba, "Five Must-Haves for Thank-You Notes," Church of the Customer Blog, 16 November 2007, www.churchofthecustomer.com.

6. Tom Abate, "Need to Preserve Cash Generates Wave of Layoffs in Biotech Industry," *San Francisco Chronicle*, 10 February 2003, www.sfgate.com.

7. CES website, accessed 11 June 2012, www.cesweb.org; Darren Murph, "CES 2012 Sets All-Time Records for Attendance, Exhibitors and Claimed Floor Space," *Engadget*, 13 January 2012, www.engadget.com.

8. United Way website, accessed 30 January 2013, www.unitedway.org.

9. SolarCity website, accessed 7 July 2010, www.solarcity.com.

10. Adapted from Hot Stix Golf website, accessed 8 February 2011, www.hotstixgolf.com.

11. The Webby Awards website, accessed 30 January 2013, www.webbyawards.com.

Answer Key for "Learning Objectives Checkup"

1. b
2. a
3. d
4. c
5. b
6. d
7. c
8. direct
9. a
10. b
11. good news *or* positive news
12. d
13. d
14. b
15. a
16. d
17. c

Answer Key for "Improve Your Grammar, Mechanics, and Usage" Exercises

22. b (1.7.3)
23. a (1.7.2)
24. b (1.7.6)
25. a (1.7.4)
26. b (1.7.4)
27. b (1.7.6)
28. a (1.7.6)
29. b (1.7.4)
30. a (1.7.3)
31. b (1.7.2)

Professional Communication
in a Digital, Social, Mobile World

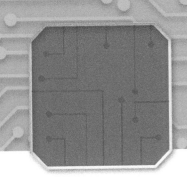

Professional Communication in a Digital, Social, Mobile World

LEARNING OBJECTIVES

After studying this chapter, you will be able to

1 Explain the importance of effective communication to your career and to the companies where you will work.

2 Explain what it means to communicate as a professional in a business context.

3 Describe the communication process model and the ways social media are changing the nature of business communication.

4 Outline the challenges and opportunities of mobile communication in business.

5 List four general guidelines for using communication technology effectively.

6 Define *ethics*, explain the difference between an ethical dilemma and an ethical lapse, and list six guidelines for making ethical communication choices.

ON THE JOB: COMMUNICATING AT
JETBLUE

Socializing the Customer Service Experience

If you have ever worked in retail, customer service, or a similar job, you know what a challenge it can be to make sure each customer has a great experience with your company. Imagine the challenge of keeping 25 million customers happy. That's how many passengers JetBlue carries every year—an average of roughly 70,000 customers per day.

As a relatively new airline, taking its first flight in 2000, JetBlue has always tried to differentiate itself from the older carriers in the business. A great example is its pioneering use of Twitter as a customer service platform. JetBlue joined Twitter in 2007, only a year after the microblogging service launched and well before most companies were aware of its potential for business communication. The company views its website as the central hub of its online presence, but social media (the company is quite active on Facebook as well) provide a vital connection between customers and the website. In fact, digital communication of all forms is so important that the company considers itself a digital brand.

The airline was also one of the first companies to truly get the *social* part of social media—that Twitter and other systems were about more than just pushing information outward. Morgan Johnstone, the JetBlue communications staffer who got the

JetBlue's use of social media for customer support coincides perfectly with air travelers' use of mobile devices.

company started on Twitter, recognized early on the power of listening via social media. He wanted to hear what people were saying about the company, whether it was plea for help during travel, a compliment for a company employee, or even an unpleasant criticism. This interaction became so valuable to the company that it now has more than two dozen Twitter agents all ready to interact in real time with the nearly 2 million travelers who follow the company. They answer questions, resolve problems and complaints, and even rebook flights on the spot if needed. Travelers who need assistance don't have time to wait, and JetBlue boasts the fastest Twitter response time in the industry.

For a company that is all about moving people from point A to point B, it's no surprise that mobile communication has become an essential part of JetBlue's connection with its customers. Customers who ask for help or who post complaints on Twitter often do so on their mobile devices, whether they're on their way to catch a flight, stuck in an airport trying to rebook on a different flight, or even on board an aircraft waiting to take off. Mobile is now a core element in the company's communication strategy, with a mobile-friendly website and JetBlue smartphone apps. The company is considering adding such nifty features as augmented reality, which would let travelers hold up their smartphones in airports to see where restrooms, coffee shops, gates, and other vital facilities are located. However the company innovates as it moves forward, its focus will be on using digital, social, and mobile communication to make sure customers have the best possible experience.[1]

TWITTER.COM/JETBLUE

Understanding Why Communication Matters

Whether it's as simple as a smile or as ambitious as a social media customer support program (see the chapter opener on JetBlue), **communication** is the process of transferring information and meaning between *senders* and *receivers*, using one or more written, oral, visual, or electronic media. The essence of communication is sharing—providing data, information, insights, and inspiration in an exchange that benefits both you and the people with whom you are communicating.[2] As Figure 1 on the next page indicates, this sharing can happen in a variety of ways, including simple and successful transfers of information, negotiations in which the sender and receiver arrive at an agreed-on meaning, and unsuccessful attempts in which the receiver creates a different message than the one the sender intended.

You will invest a lot of time and energy in this course developing your communication skills, so it's fair to ask whether the effort will be worthwhile. This section outlines the many ways in which good communication skills are critical for your career and for any company you join.

COMMUNICATION IS IMPORTANT TO YOUR CAREER

You can have the greatest ideas in the world, but they're no good to your company or your career if you can't express them clearly and persuasively. Some jobs, such as sales and customer support, are primarily about communicating. In fields such as engineering or finance, you often need to share complex ideas with executives, customers, and colleagues, and your ability to connect with people outside your field can be as important as your technical expertise. If you have the entrepreneurial urge, you will need to communicate with a wide range of audiences—from investors, bankers, and government regulators to employees, customers, and business partners.

The changing nature of employment is putting new pressure on communication skills, too. Many companies now supplement their permanent workforces with independent contractors who are brought on for a short period or even just a single project. Chances are you will spend some of your career as one of these independent freelancers, working without the support network that an established company environment provides. You will have to "sell yourself" into each new contract, communicate successfully in a wide range of work situations, and take full responsibility for your career growth and success.

> **1 LEARNING OBJECTIVE**
> Explain the importance of effective communication to your career and to the companies where you will work.

Communication is the process of transferring information and meaning between senders and receivers.

Ambition and great ideas aren't enough; you need to be able to communicate with people in order to succeed in business.

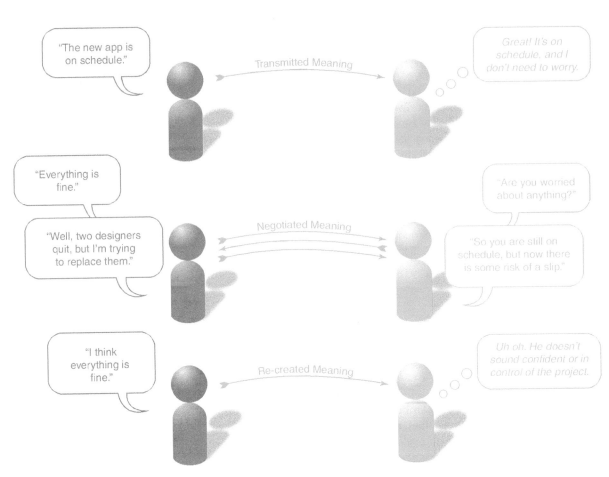

Figure 1 Sharing Information

These three exchanges between a software project manager (*left*) and his boss (*right*) illustrate the variety of ways in which information is shared between senders and receivers. In the top exchange, the sender's meaning is transmitted intact to the receiver, who accepts what the sender says at face value. In the middle exchange, the sender and receiver negotiate the meaning by discussing the situation. The negotiated meaning is that everything is fine so far, but the risk of a schedule slip is now higher than it was before. In the bottom exchange, the receiver has a negative emotional reaction to the word *think* and as a result creates her own meaning—that everything probably is not fine, despite what the sender says.

If you launch a company or move into an executive role in an existing organization, you can expect communication to consume the majority of your time. Top executives spend most of their workdays communicating, and businesspeople who can't communicate well don't stand much chance of reaching the top.

In fact, improving your communication skills may be the single most important step you can take in your career. The world is full of good marketing strategists, good accountants, good engineers, and good attorneys—but it is not full of good communicators. View this as an opportunity to stand out from your competition in the job market.

Employers sometimes express frustration at the poor communication skills of many employees—particularly recent college graduates who haven't yet learned how to adapt their communication styles to a professional business environment.[3] If you learn to write well, speak well, listen well, and recognize the appropriate way to communicate in any situation, you'll gain a major advantage that will serve you throughout your career.[4]

Strong communication skills give you an advantage in the job market.

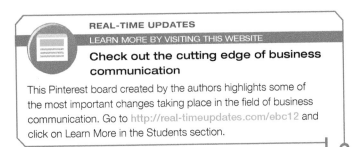

REAL-TIME UPDATES

LEARN MORE BY VISITING THIS WEBSITE

Check out the cutting edge of business communication

This Pinterest board created by the authors highlights some of the most important changes taking place in the field of business communication. Go to http://real-timeupdates.com/ebc12 and click on Learn More in the Students section.

COMMUNICATION IS IMPORTANT TO YOUR COMPANY

Aside from the personal benefits, communication should be important to you because it is important to your company. Effective communication helps businesses in numerous ways. It provides[5]

- Closer ties with important communities in the marketplace
- Opportunities to influence conversations, perceptions, and trends
- Increased productivity and faster problem solving
- Better financial results and higher return for investors
- Earlier warning of potential problems, from rising business costs to critical safety issues
- Stronger decision making based on timely, reliable information
- Clearer and more persuasive marketing messages
- Greater employee engagement with their work, leading to higher employee satisfaction and lower employee turnover

Effective communication yields numerous business benefits.

WHAT MAKES BUSINESS COMMUNICATION EFFECTIVE?

Effective communication strengthens the connections between a company and all of its **stakeholders**—those groups affected in some way by the company's actions: customers, employees, shareholders, suppliers, neighbors, the community, the nation, and the world as a whole.[6] To make your communication efforts as effective as possible, focus on making them practical, factual, concise, clear, and persuasive:

- **Provide practical information.** Give recipients useful information, whether it's to help them perform a desired action or understand a new company policy.
- **Give facts rather than vague impressions.** Use concrete language, specific detail, and information that is clear, convincing, accurate, and ethical. Even when an opinion is called for, present compelling evidence to support your conclusion.
- **Present information in a concise, efficient manner.** Concise messages show respect for people's time, and they increase the chances of a positive response.
- **Clarify expectations and responsibilities.** Craft messages to generate a specific response from a specific audience. When appropriate, clearly state what you expect from audience members or what you can do for them.
- **Offer compelling, persuasive arguments and recommendations.** Show your readers precisely how they will benefit by responding the way you want them to respond to your message.

Effective messages are practical, factual, concise, clear, and persuasive.

Keep these five important characteristics in mind as you compare the ineffective and effective versions of the message in Figure 2 on the next page.

Communicating as a Professional

You've been communicating your entire life, of course, but if you don't have a lot of work experience yet, meeting the expectations of a professional environment might require some adjustment. A good place to start is to consider what it means to be a professional. **Professionalism** is the quality of performing at a high level and conducting oneself with purpose and pride. It means doing more than putting in the hours and collecting a paycheck: True professionals go beyond minimum expectations and commit to making meaningful contributions. Professionalism can be broken down into six distinct traits: striving to excel, being dependable and accountable, being a team player, demonstrating a sense of etiquette, making ethical decisions, and maintaining a positive outlook (see Figure 3).

A key message to glean from Figure 3 is how much these elements of professionalism depend on effective communication. For example, to be a team player, you have to be able to collaborate, resolve conflicts, and interact with a wide variety of personalities. Without strong communication skills, you won't be able to perform to your potential, and others won't recognize you as the professional you'd like to be.

2 LEARNING OBJECTIVE Explain what it means to communicate as a professional in a business context.

Communication is an essential part of being a successful professional.

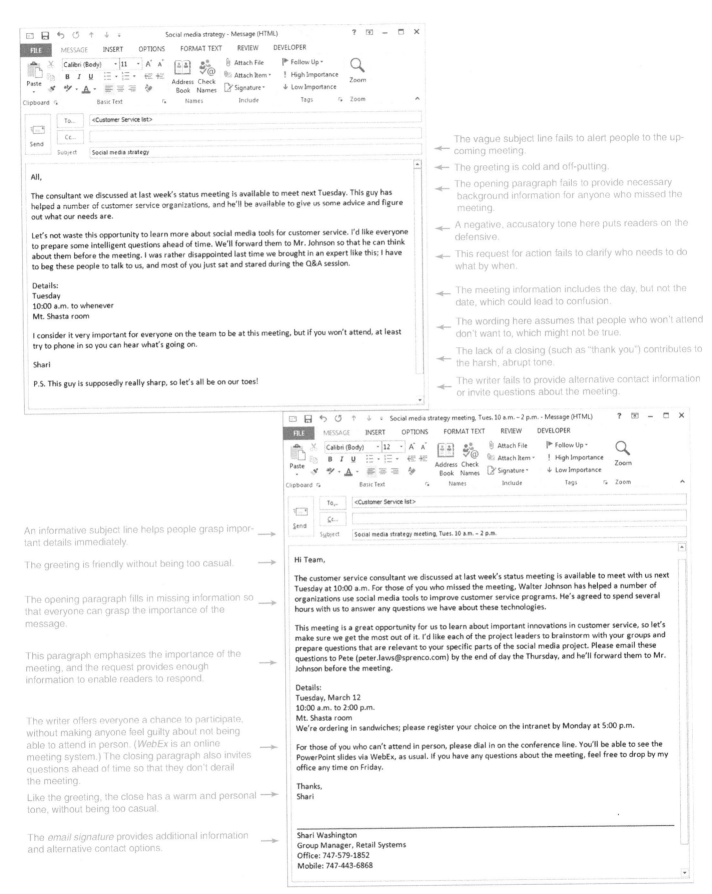

Figure 2 Effective Professional Communication
At first glance, this email message looks like a reasonable attempt at communicating with the members of a project team. However, review the blue annotations to see just how many problems the message really has.

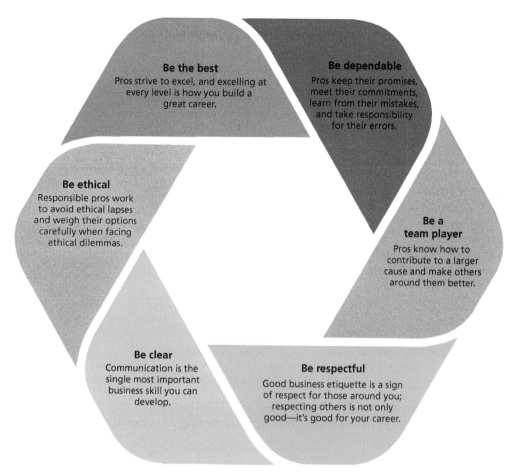

Figure 3 Elements of Professionalism
To be respected as a true professional, develop these six qualities.

This section offers a brief look at the skills employers will expect you to have, the nature of communication in an organizational environment, and the importance of adopting an audience-centered approach.

UNDERSTANDING WHAT EMPLOYERS EXPECT FROM YOU

Today's employers expect you to be competent at a wide range of communication tasks. Fortunately, the skills employers expect from you are the same skills that will help you advance in your career:[7]

- Recognizing information needs, using efficient search techniques to locate reliable sources of information, particularly from online sources, and using gathered information ethically; this collection of skills is often referred to as *digital information fluency*[8]
- Organizing ideas and information logically and completely
- Expressing ideas and information coherently and persuasively
- Actively listening to others
- Communicating effectively with people from diverse backgrounds and experiences
- Using communication technologies effectively and efficiently
- Following accepted standards of grammar, spelling, and other aspects of high-quality writing and speaking
- Communicating in a civilized manner that reflects contemporary expectations of business etiquette, even when dealing with indifferent or hostile audiences
- Communicating ethically, even when choices aren't crystal clear

Employers expect you to possess a wide range of communication skills.

Maintaining a Confident, Positive Outlook

Spend a few minutes around successful people in any field, and chances are you'll notice how optimistic they are. They believe in what they're doing, and they believe in themselves and their ability to solve problems and overcome obstacles.

Being positive doesn't mean displaying mindless optimism or spewing happy talk all the time. It means acknowledging that things may be difficult but then buckling down and getting the job done anyway. It means no whining and no slacking off, even when the going gets tough. We live in an imperfect world, no question; jobs can be boring or difficult, customers can be unpleasant, and bosses can be unreasonable. But when you're a pro, you find a way to power through.

Your energy, positive or negative, is contagious. Both in person and online, you'll spend as much time with your colleagues as you spend with family and friends. Personal demeanor is, therefore, a vital element of workplace harmony. No one expects (or wants) you to be artificially upbeat and bubbly every second of the day, but one negative personality can make an entire office miserable and unproductive. Every person in a company has a responsibility to contribute to a positive, energetic work environment.

CAREER APPLICATIONS

1. Do you have an ethical obligation to maintain a positive outlook on the job? Why or why not?
2. How can you lift your spirits when work is dragging you down?

- Managing your time wisely and using resources efficiently
- Using **critical thinking**, which is the ability to evaluate evidence completely and objectively in order to form logical conclusions and make sound recommendations

You'll have the opportunity to practice these skills throughout this course, but don't stop there. Successful professionals continue to hone communication skills throughout their careers.

COMMUNICATING IN AN ORGANIZATIONAL CONTEXT

The formal communication network mirrors the company's organizational structure.

In addition to having the proper skills, you need to learn how to apply those skills in the business environment, which can be quite different from the social and scholastic environments you are accustomed to. Every organization has a **formal communication network**, in which ideas and information flow along the lines of command (the hierarchical levels) in the company's organization structure (see Figure 4). Throughout the formal network, information flows in three directions. *Downward communication* flows from executives to employees, conveying executive decisions and providing information that helps employees do their jobs. *Upward communication* flows from employees to executives, providing insight into problems, trends, opportunities, grievances, and performance, thus allowing executives to solve problems and make intelligent decisions. *Horizontal communication* flows between departments to help employees share information, coordinate tasks, and solve complex problems.[9]

Every organization also has an **informal communication network**, often referred to as the *grapevine* or the *rumor mill*, which encompasses all communication that occurs outside the formal network. Some of this informal communication takes place naturally as a result of employee interaction on the job and in social settings, and some of it takes place when the formal network doesn't provide information that employees want. In fact, the inherent limitations of formal communication networks helped spur the growth of social media in the business environment.

ADOPTING AN AUDIENCE-CENTERED APPROACH

An audience-centered approach involves understanding, respecting, and meeting the needs of your audience members.

An **audience-centered approach** involves understanding and respecting the members of your audience and making every effort to get your message across in a way that is meaningful to them. This approach is also known as adopting the **"you" attitude**, in contrast to messages that are about "me." Learn as much as possible about the biases, education, age, status, style, and personal and professional concerns of your receivers. If you're

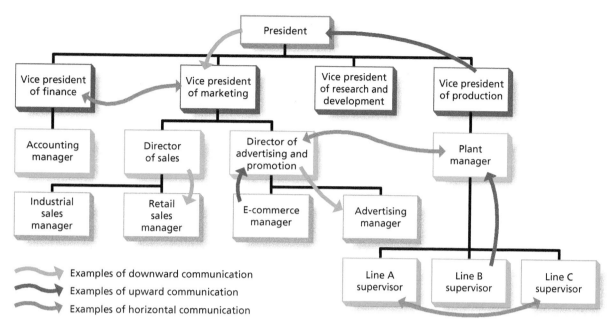

Figure 4 Formal Communication Network
The formal communication network is defined by the relationships between the various job positions in the organization. Messages can flow upward (from a lower-level employee to a higher-level employee), downward (from a higher-level employee to a lower-level employee), and horizontally (across the organization, between employees at the same or similar levels).

addressing people you don't know and you're unable to find out more about them, try to project yourself into their position by using common sense and imagination. This ability to relate to the needs of others is a key part of *emotional intelligence*, which is widely considered to be a vital characteristic of successful managers and leaders.[10] The more you know about the people you're communicating with, the easier it will be to concentrate on their needs—which, in turn, will make it easier for them to hear your message, understand it, and respond positively.

A vital element of audience-centered communication is **etiquette**, the expected norms of behavior in any particular situation. In today's hectic, competitive world, etiquette might seem a quaint and outdated notion. However, the way you conduct yourself and interact with others can have a profound influence on your company's success and your career. When executives hire and promote you, they expect your behavior to protect the company's reputation. The more you understand such expectations, the better chance you have of avoiding career-damaging mistakes.

Etiquette, the expected norms of behavior in any particular situation, can have a profound influence on your company's success and your career.

Exploring the Communication Process

Even with the best intentions, communication efforts can fail. Messages can get lost or simply ignored. The receiver of a message can interpret it in ways the sender never imagined. In fact, two people receiving the same information can reach different conclusions about what it means.

Fortunately, by understanding communication as a process with distinct steps, you can improve the odds that your messages will reach their intended audiences and produce their intended effects. This section explores the communication process in two stages: first by following a message from one sender to one receiver in the basic communication model and then by expanding on that approach with multiple messages and participants in the social communication model.

3 LEARNING OBJECTIVE
Describe the communication process model and the ways social media are changing the nature of business communication.

THE BASIC COMMUNICATION MODEL

Viewing communication as a process helps you identify steps you can take to improve your success as a communicator.

By viewing communication as a process (Figure 5), you can identify and improve the skills you need to be more successful. Many variations on this process model exist, but these eight steps provide a practical overview:

- **The sender has an idea.** Whether a communication effort will ultimately be effective starts right here and depends on the nature of the idea and the motivation for sending it. For example, if your motivation is to offer a solution to a problem, you have a better chance of crafting a meaningful message than if your motivation is merely to complain about a problem.
- **The sender encodes the idea as a message.** When someone puts an idea into a **message**—which you can think of as the "container" for an idea—he or she is **encoding** it, or expressing it in words or images. Much of the focus of this course is on developing the skills needed to successfully encode your ideas into effective messages.
- **The sender produces the message in a transmittable medium.** With the appropriate message to express an idea, the sender now needs a **communication medium** to present that message to the intended audience. To update your boss on the status of a project, for instance, you might have a dozen or more media choices, from a phone call to an instant message to a slideshow presentation.

The medium is the *form* a message takes and the *channel* is the system used to deliver the message.

- **The sender transmits the message through a channel.** Just as technology continues to increase the number of media options at your disposal, it continues to provide new **communication channels** you can use to transmit your messages. The distinction between medium and channel can get a bit murky, but think of the medium as the *form* a message takes (such as a Twitter update) and the channel as the system used to *deliver* the message (such as a mobile phone).
- **The audience receives the message.** If the channel functions properly, the message reaches its intended audience. However, mere arrival at the destination is no guarantee that the message will be noticed or understood correctly. As "How Audiences Receive Messages" explains, many messages are either ignored or misinterpreted as noise.
- **The audience decodes the message.** After a message is received, the receiver needs to extract the idea from the message, a step known as **decoding**. "How Audiences Decode Messages" takes a closer look at this complex and subtle step in the process.
- **The audience responds to the message.** By crafting messages in ways that show the benefits of responding, senders can increase the chances that recipients will respond in positive ways. However, as "How Audiences Respond to Messages" points out, whether a receiver responds as the sender hopes depends on the receiver (a) *remembering* the message long enough to act on it, (b) being *able* to act on it, and (c) being *motivated* to respond.

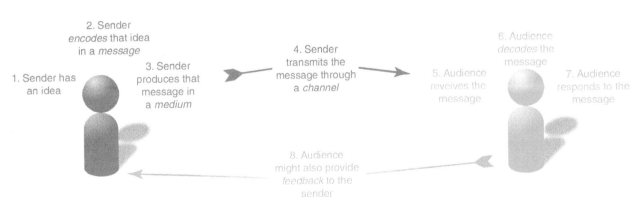

Figure 5 The Basic Communication Process
This eight-step model is a simplified view of how communication works in real life; understanding this basic model is vital to improving your communication skills.

- **The audience provides feedback to the sender.** In addition to responding (or not responding) to the message, audience members may give **feedback** that helps the sender evaluate the effectiveness of the communication effort. Feedback can be verbal (using written or spoken words), nonverbal (using gestures, facial expressions, or other signals), or both. Just like the original message, however, this feedback from the receiver also needs to be decoded carefully. A smile, for example, can have many meanings.

Considering the complexity of this process—and the barriers and distractions that often stand between sender and receiver—it should come as no surprise that communication efforts often fail to achieve the sender's objective. Fortunately, the better you understand the process, the more successful you'll be.

The following sections take a closer look at two important aspects of the process: environmental barriers that can block or distort messages and the steps audiences take to receive, decode, and respond to messages.

Barriers in the Communication Environment

Within any communication environment, messages can be disrupted by a variety of **communication barriers**. These barriers include noise and distractions, competing messages, filters, and channel breakdowns:

- **Noise and distractions.** External distractions range from uncomfortable meeting rooms to computer screens cluttered with instant messages and reminders popping up all over the place. Internal distractions are thoughts and emotions that prevent audiences from focusing on incoming messages. The common habit of *multitasking*—attempting more than one task at a time—is practically guaranteed to create communication distractions. Moreover, research suggests that "chronic multitasking" can reduce productivity and increase errors.[11] As more communication takes place on mobile devices, the need to insulate yourself from noise and distractions is going to keep growing.

  A number of barriers can block or distort messages before they reach the intended audience.

- **Competing messages.** Having your audience's undivided attention is a rare luxury. In most cases, you must compete with other messages that are trying to reach your audience at the same time.
- **Filters.** Messages can be blocked or distorted by *filters*, any human or technological interventions between the sender and the receiver. Filtering can be both intentional (such as automatically filing incoming messages based on sender or content) or unintentional (such as an overly aggressive spam filter that deletes legitimate emails). As mentioned previously, the structure and culture of an organization can also inhibit the flow of vital messages. And, in some cases, the people or companies you rely on to deliver your message can distort it or filter it to meet their own needs.
- **Channel breakdowns.** Sometimes the channel simply breaks down and fails to deliver your message at all. A colleague you were counting on to deliver a message to your boss might have forgotten to do so, or a computer server might have crashed and prevented your blog from updating.

Everyone in an organization can help minimize barriers and distractions. As a communicator, try to be aware of any barriers that could prevent your messages from reaching their intended audiences. As a manager, keep an eye out for any organizational barriers that could be inhibiting the flow of information. In any situation, a small dose of common sense and courtesy goes a long way. Turn off that mobile phone before you step into a meeting. Don't talk across the tops of other people's cubicles. Be sensitive to personal differences, too; for instance, some people enjoy working with music on, but music is a huge distraction for others.[12]

Minimizing barriers and distractions in the communication environment is everyone's responsibility.

Finally, take steps to insulate yourself from distractions. Don't let messages interrupt you every minute of the day. Instead, set aside time to attend to messages all at once so that you can focus the rest of the time.

Inside the Mind of Your Audience

After a message works its way through the communication channel and reaches the intended audience, it encounters a whole new set of challenges. Understanding how audiences receive, decode, and respond to messages will help you create more effective messages.

To actually receive a message, audience members need to sense it, select it, then perceive it as a message.

How Audiences Receive Messages For an audience member to receive a message, three events need to occur: The receiver has to *sense* the presence of a message, *select* it from all the other messages clamoring for attention, and *perceive* it as an actual message (as opposed to random, pointless noise).[13] You can appreciate the magnitude of this challenge by driving down any busy street in a commercial section of town. You'll encounter hundreds of messages—billboards, posters, store window displays, car stereos, pedestrians waving or talking on mobile phones, car horns, street signs, traffic lights, and so on. However, you'll sense, select, and perceive only a small fraction of these messages.

Today's business audiences are much like drivers on busy streets. They are inundated with so many messages and so much noise that they can miss or ignore many of the messages intended for them. Through this course, you will learn a variety of techniques to craft messages that get noticed. In general, follow these five principles to increase your chances of success:

To improve the odds that your messages will be successfully perceived by your audience, pay close attention to expectations, ease of use, familiarity, empathy, and technical compatibility.

- **Consider audience expectations.** Deliver messages using the media and channels that the audience expects. If colleagues expect meeting notices to be delivered by email, don't suddenly switch gears and start delivering the notices via blog postings without telling anyone. Of course, sometimes going *against* expectations can stimulate audience attention, which is why advertisers sometimes do wacky and creative things to get noticed. However, for most business communication efforts, following the expectations of your audience is the most efficient way to get your message across.
- **Ensure ease of use.** Even if audiences are actively looking for your messages, they probably won't see the messages if you make them hard to find, hard to navigate, or hard to read.
- **Emphasize familiarity.** Use words, images, and designs that are familiar to your audience. For example, most visitors to company websites expect to see information about the company on a page called "About" or "About Us."
- **Practice empathy.** Make sure your messages speak to the audience by clearly addressing *their* wants and needs—not yours. People are inclined to notice messages that relate to their individual concerns.[14]
- **Design for compatibility.** For the many messages delivered electronically these days, be sure to verify technological compatibility with your audience. For instance, if your website requires visitors to have a particular video capability in their browsers, you won't reach those audience members who don't have that software installed or updated.

Decoding is a complex process; receivers often extract different meanings from messages than senders attempt to encode in their messages.

How Audiences Decode Messages A received message doesn't "mean" anything until the recipient decodes it and assigns meaning to it, and there is no guarantee the receiver will assign the same meaning the sender intended. Even well-crafted, well-intentioned communication efforts can fail at this stage because assigning meaning through decoding is a highly personal process that is influenced by culture, individual experience, learning and thinking styles, hopes, fears, and even temporary moods. Moreover, audiences tend to extract the meaning they expect to get from a message, even if it's the opposite of what the sender intended.[15] In fact, rather than "extract" your meaning, it's more accurate to say that your audience members re-create their own meaning—or meanings—from the message.

Cultural and personal beliefs and biases influence the meaning audiences get from messages. For instance, the human brain organizes incoming sensations into a mental "map" that represents the person's individual **perception** of reality. If an incoming detail doesn't fit into that perception, a message recipient may simply distort the information to make it fit rather than rearrange his or her mental map—a phenomenon known as **selective perception**.[16] For example, an executive who has staked her reputation on a particular business strategy might distort or ignore evidence that suggests the strategy is failing.

Selective perception occurs when people ignore or distort incoming information to fit their preconceived notions of reality.

Differences in language and usage also influence received meaning. If you ask an employee to send you a report on sales figures "as soon as possible," does that mean within 10 seconds, 10 minutes, or 10 days? By clarifying expectations and resolving potential ambiguities in your messages, you can minimize such uncertainties. In general, the

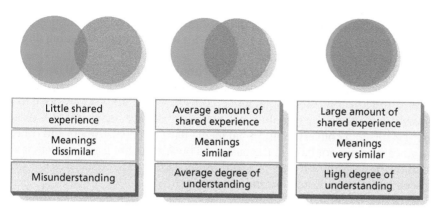

Little shared experience	Average amount of shared experience	Large amount of shared experience
Meanings dissimilar	Meanings similar	Meanings very similar
Misunderstanding	Average degree of understanding	High degree of understanding

Figure 6 How Shared Experience Affects Understanding
The more two people or two groups of people share experiences—personal, professional, and cultural—the more likely it is that receivers will extract the intended meanings senders encode into the messages.

more experiences you share with another person, the more likely you are to share perception and thus share meaning (see Figure 6).

Individual thinking styles are another important factor in message decoding. For example, someone who places a high value on objective analysis and clear logic might interpret a message differently than someone who values emotion or intuition (reaching conclusions without using rational processes).

How Audiences Respond to Messages Your message has been delivered, received, and correctly decoded. Now what? Will audience members respond in the way you'd like them to? Only if three events occur.

First, the recipient has to *remember* the message long enough to act on it. Simplifying greatly, memory works in several stages: *Sensory memory* momentarily captures incoming data from the senses; then, whatever the recipient pays attention to is transferred to *short-term memory*. Information in short-term memory will quickly disappear if it isn't transferred to *long-term memory*, which can be done either actively (such as when a person memorizes a list of items) or passively (such as when a new piece of information connects with something else the recipient already has stored in long-term memory). Finally, the information needs to be *retrieved* when the recipient wants to act on it.[17] In general, people find it easier to remember and retrieve information that is important to them personally or professionally. Consequently, by communicating in ways that are sensitive to your audience's wants and needs, you greatly increase the chance that your messages will be remembered and retrieved.

Second, the recipient has to be *able* to respond as you wish. Obviously, if recipients simply cannot do what you want them to do, they will not respond according to your plan. By understanding your audience, you can work to minimize these unsuccessful outcomes.

Third, the recipient has to be *motivated* to respond. You'll encounter many situations in which your audience has the option of responding but isn't required to. For instance, a record company may or may not offer your band a contract, or your boss may or may not respond to your request for a raise. Throughout this course, you'll learn techniques for crafting messages that can help motivate readers to respond positively to your messages.

Audiences will likely respond to a message if they remember it, if they're able to respond, and if they're properly motivated to respond.

By explaining how audiences will benefit by responding positively to your messages, you'll increase their motivation to respond.

THE SOCIAL COMMUNICATION MODEL

The basic model presented in Figure 5 illustrates how a single idea moves from one sender to one receiver. In a larger sense, it also helps represent the traditional nature of much business communication, which was primarily defined by a *publishing* or *broadcasting* mindset. Externally, a company issued carefully scripted messages to a mass audience that often had few options for responding to those messages or initiating messages of their own. Customers and other interested parties had few ways to connect with one another

The conversational and interactive social communication model is revolutionizing business communication.

to ask questions, share information, or offer support. Internally, communication tended to follow the same "we talk, you listen" model, with upper managers issuing directives to lower-level supervisors and employees.

However, in recent years, a variety of technologies have enabled and inspired a new approach to business communication. In contrast to the publishing mindset, this **social communication model** is interactive, conversational, and usually open to all who wish to participate. Audience members are no longer passive recipients of messages but active participants in a conversation. Social media have given customers and other stakeholders a voice they did not have in the past. And businesses are listening to that voice. In fact, one of the most common uses of social media among U.S. businesses is monitoring online discussions about a company and its brands.[18]

The social communication model can increase the speed of communication, lower cost, improve access to expertise, and boost employee satisfaction.

Instead of transmitting a fixed message, a sender in a social media environment initiates a conversation by asking a question or sharing valuable information. Information shared this way is often revised and reshaped by the web of participants as they forward it and comment on it. People can add to it or take pieces from it, depending on their needs and interests. Figure 7 lists some of the significant differences between the traditional and social models of business communication.

For all their advantages, social media tools also present a number of communication challenges.

The social communication model offers many advantages, but it has a number of disadvantages as well. Potential problems include information overload, fragmented attention, information security risks, distractions that hurt productivity, the need to monitor and respond to numerous conversational threads, and blurring of the line between personal and professional lives, which can make it difficult for people to disconnect from work.[19]

Of course, no company, no matter how enthusiastically it embraces the social communication model, is going to be run as a club in which everyone has a say in every business matter. Instead, a hybrid approach is emerging in which some communications (such as strategic plans and policy documents) follow the traditional approach, whereas others (such as project management updates and customer support messages) follow the social model.

Conventional Promotion: "We Talk, You Listen"

Tendencies
Publication, broadcast
Lecture
Intrusion
Unidirectinal
One to many; mass audience
Control
Low message frequency
Few channels
Information hoarding
Static
Hierarchical
Structured
Isolated
Planned
Resistive

The Social Model: "Let's Have a Conversation"

Tendencies
Converstion
Discussion
Permission
Bidirectional, multidirectional
One to one; many to many
Influence
High message frequency
Many channels
Information sharing
Dynamic
Egalitarian
Amorphous
Collaborative
Reactive
Responsive

Figure 7 The Social Communication Model
The social communication model differs from conventional communication strategies and practices in a number of significant ways. You're probably already an accomplished user of many new-media tools, and this experience will help you on the job.

The Mobile Revolution

As much of a game-changer as social media have been, some experts predict that mobile communication will change the nature of business and business communication even more. Venture capitalist Joe Schoendorf says that "mobile is the most disruptive technology that I have seen in 48 years in Silicon Valley."[20] Researcher Maribel Lopez calls mobile "the biggest technology shift since the Internet."[21]

Companies recognize the value of integrating mobile technology, from communication platforms to banking to retail. Mobile apps and communication systems can boost employee productivity, help companies form closer relationships with customers and business partners, and spur innovation in products and services (see Figure 8). Given the advantages and the rising expectations of employees and customers, firms on the leading edge of the mobile revolution are working to integrate mobile technology throughout their organizations.[22]

This section offers a high-level view of the mobile revolution, and you'll see coverage of specific topics integrated throughout the text, in everything from collaborative writing and research to presentations and job search strategies.

4 LEARNING OBJECTIVE
Outline the challenges and opportunities of mobile communication in business.

REAL-TIME UPDATES

LEARN MORE BY WATCHING THIS VIDEO

The mobile business advantage

See how leading-edge companies are adapting to take advantage of mobile communication. Go to http://real-timeupdates.com/ebc12 and click on Learn More in the Students section.

THE RISE OF MOBILE AS A COMMUNICATION PLATFORM

Whether it's emailing, social networking, watching videos, or doing research, the percentage of communication and media consumption performed on mobile devices continues to grow. For millions of people around the world, a mobile device is their primary way, if not their only way, to access the Internet. Globally, roughly 80 percent of Internet users access the web at least some of the time with a mobile device.[23]

Mobile has become the primary communication tool for many business professionals, including a majority of executives under age 40.[24] Email and web browsing rank first and second in terms of the most common nonvoice uses of smartphones, and more

Mobile devices are rapidly taking over as the primary communication platform for many business professionals.

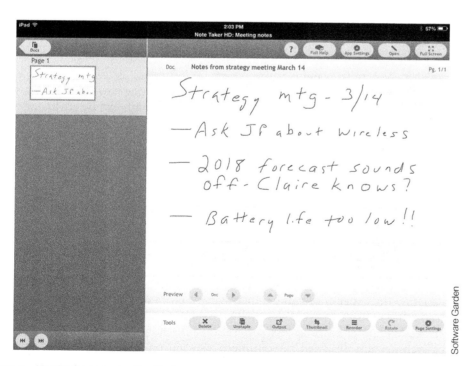

Software Garden

Figure 8   Mobile Communication Tools

Mobile technologies offer multiple ways to improve communication and other key business processes. For example, note-taking apps such as Note Taker HD offer an easy and unobtrusive way to take notes during meetings, site visits, and other business functions.

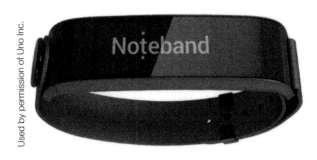

Used by permission of Uno Inc.

Figure 9 Wearable Technology
Smartwatches and other wearable mobile devices offer intriguing possibilities for business communication. The Uno Noteband incorporates Spritz speed-reading technology that makes it easier to read message content quickly.

REAL-TIME UPDATES
LEARN MORE BY VISITING THIS WEBSITE
The mobile revolution by the numbers

Explore dozens of statistical measures that show the impact of mobile communication. Go to http://real-timeupdates.com/ebc12 and click on Learn More in the Students section.

REAL-TIME UPDATES
LEARN MORE BY WATCHING THESE PRESENTATIONS
Exploring the potential of wearable technologies

Will wearable technologies influence business and business communication? These presentations explore the potential. Go to http://real-timeupdates.com/ebc12 and click on Learn More in the Students section.

email messages are now opened on mobile devices than on PCs.[25] Roughly half of U.S. consumers use a mobile device exclusively for their online search needs, and many online activities that eventually migrate to a PC screen start out on a mobile screen.[26] For many people, the fact that a smartphone can make phone calls is practically a secondary consideration; data traffic from mobile devices far outstrips voice traffic.[27]

Moreover, mobile phones—particularly smartphones—have become intensely personal devices in ways that PCs never did. For many users, the connection is so close they can feel a sense of panic when they don't have frequent access to their phones.[28] When people are closely attached to their phones, day and night, they are more closely connected to all the information sources, conversations, and networks that those phones can connect to. As a result, mobile connectivity can start to resemble a continuous stream of conversations that never quite end, which influences the way businesses need to interact with their stakeholders. If *wearable technologies* become mainstream devices, they will contribute even more to this shift in behaviors (see Figure 9).

The parallels between social media and mobile communication are striking: Both sets of technologies change the nature of communication, alter the relationships between senders and receivers, create opportunities as well as challenges, and force business professionals to hone new skills. In fact, much of the rise in social communication can be attributed to the connectivity made possible by mobile devices. Companies that work to understand and embrace mobile, both internally and externally, stand the best chance of capitalizing on this monumental shift in the way people communicate.

HOW MOBILE TECHNOLOGIES ARE CHANGING BUSINESS COMMUNICATION

The rise of mobile communication has some obvious implications, such as the need for websites to be mobile friendly. If you've ever tried to browse a conventional website on a tiny screen or fill in complicated online forms using the keypad on your phone, you know how frustrating the experience can be. Increasingly, users expect websites to be mobile friendly, and they're likely to avoid sites that aren't optimized for mobile.[29] As mobile access overtakes computer-based access, some companies now take a *mobile-first* approach, in which websites are designed for optimum viewing on smartphones and tablets.[30] Another successful approach is creating mobile apps that offer a more interactive and mobile-friendly experience than a conventional website can offer.

However, device size and portability are only the most obvious changes. Just as with social media, the changes brought about by mobile go far deeper than the technology itself. Mobile changes the way people communicate, which has profound implications for virtually every aspect of business communication.

Social media pioneer Nicco Mele coined the term *radical connectivity* to describe "the breathtaking ability to send vast amounts of data instantly, constantly, and globally."[31] Mobile plays a major and ever-expanding role in this phenomenon by keeping people connected 24/7, wherever they may be. People who've grown up with mobile communication technology expect to have immediate access to information and the ability to stay connected to their various social and business networks.[32]

Here are the most significant ways mobile technology is changing the practice of business communication:

- Constant connectivity is a mixed blessing. As with social media, mobile connectivity can blur the boundaries between personal and professional time and space, preventing people from fully disengaging from work during personal and family time. On the other hand, it can give employees more flexibility to meet their personal and professional obligations.[33] In this regard, mobile plays an important role in efforts to reduce operating costs through telecommuting and other nontraditional work models.[34]
- Small mobile displays and sometimes-awkward input technologies present challenges for creating and consuming content, whether it's typing an email message or watching a video. Email messages need to be written and formatted differently to make them easier to read on mobile devices.
- Mobile users are often multitasking—roughly half of mobile phone usage happens while people are walking, for instance—so they can't give full attention to the information on their screens.[35] Moreover, mobile use often occurs in environments with multiple distractions and barriers to successful communication.
- Mobile communication, particularly text messaging, has put pressure on traditional standards of grammar, punctuation, and writing in general.
- Mobile devices can serve as sensory and cognitive extensions.[36] For example, they can help people experience more of their environment (such as augmented reality apps that superimpose information on a live camera view) and have instant access to information without relying on faulty and limited human memory. The addition of *location-aware content*, such as facility maps and property information, enhances the mobile experience.
- Mobile devices create a host of security and privacy concerns, for end users and corporate technology managers alike.[37] Companies are wrestling with the "bring your own device" or "BYOD" phenomenon, in which employees want to be able to access company networks and files with their personal smartphones and tablets, both in the office and away from it. However, these devices don't always have the rigorous security controls that corporate networks need, and users don't always use the devices in secure ways.
- Mobile tools can enhance productivity and collaboration by making it easier for employees to stay connected and giving them access to information and work tasks during forced gaps in the workday or while traveling.[38]
- Mobile apps can assist in a wide variety of business tasks, from research to presentations (see Figure 10).[39]
- Mobile connectivity can accelerate decision making and problem solving by putting the right information in the hands of the right people at the right time. For example, if the people in a decision-making meeting need more information, they can do the necessary research on the spot.[40] Mobile communication also makes it easier to quickly tap into pockets of expertise within a company.[41] Customer service can be improved by making sure technicians and

People who grew up with mobile phones often expect to have the same level of connectivity as customers and as employees.

Constant connectivity is a mixed blessing; you can work from anywhere at any time, but it's more difficult to disconnect from work and recharge yourself.

Collaboration and problem solving are two key areas where mobile connectivity can boost productivity by enabling real-time interaction and access to vital information.

Figure 10   Mobile Communication: Opportunities and Challenges
From 24/7 connectivity to business-oriented apps that let professionals perform work tasks on the go (such as making notes for a presentation, as shown here on the mobile version of PowerPoint), mobile technology is revolutionizing business communication.

MS Powerpoint by Microsoft Corporation

other workers always have the information they need right at hand.[42] Companies can also respond and communicate faster during crises.[43]

- With interactivity designed to take advantage of the capabilities of mobile devices (including cameras, accelerometers, compasses, and GPS), companies can create more engaging experiences for customers and other users.[44]

The mobile revolution complicates business communication in some ways, but it can enhance communication in many ways if done thoughtfully.

Using Technology to Improve Business Communication

Today's businesses rely heavily on technology to enhance communication. In fact, many of the technologies you might use in your personal life, from microblogs to video games, are also used in business. You will find technology discussed extensively throughout this text, with specific advice on using both common and emerging tools. The four-page photo essay "Powerful Tools for Communicating Efficiently" provides an overview of the technologies that connect people in offices, factories, and other business settings.

However, anyone who has used advanced technology knows the benefits are not automatic. Poorly designed or inappropriately used technology can hinder communication more than help. To communicate effectively, learn to keep technology in perspective, guard against information overload and information addiction, use technological tools productively, and disengage from the computer frequently to communicate in person.

KEEPING TECHNOLOGY IN PERSPECTIVE

Perhaps the single most important point to remember about technology is that it is simply a tool, a means by which you can accomplish certain tasks. Technology is an aid to interpersonal communication, not a replacement for it. Technology can't think for you or communicate for you, and if you lack some essential skills, technology can't fill in the gaps. Throughout the text, you'll see advice on keeping the focus on your messages and your audiences, and using technology to enhance the communication process.

GUARDING AGAINST INFORMATION OVERLOAD

The overuse or misuse of communication technology can lead to **information overload**, in which people receive more information than they can effectively process. Information overload makes it difficult to discriminate between useful and useless information, lowers productivity, and amplifies employee stress both on the job and at home, even to the point of causing health and relationship problems.[45]

You often have some level of control over the number and types of messages you choose to receive. Use the filtering features of your communication systems to isolate high-priority messages that deserve your attention. Also, be wary of subscribing to too many Twitter streams and other sources. Focus on the information you truly need in order to do your job.

As a sender, you can help reduce information overload by making sure you don't send unnecessary messages. In addition, when you send messages that aren't urgent or crucial, let people know so they can prioritize. Also, most communication systems let you mark messages as urgent; however, use this feature only when it is truly needed. Its overuse leads to annoyance and anxiety, not action.

USING TECHNOLOGICAL TOOLS PRODUCTIVELY

Facebook, Twitter, YouTube, and other technologies are key parts of what has been called the *information technology paradox*, in which information tools can waste as much time as they save. Concerns over inappropriate use of social networking sites, for example, have led many companies to ban employees from accessing them during work hours.[46]

DIGITAL + SOCIAL + MOBILE: TODAY'S COMMUNICATION ENVIRONMENT

It's All Fun and Games—and Effective Business Communication

The fact that millions of people spend billions of hours playing games on their mobile devices is not lost on companies looking for ways to enhance communication with employees and customers. Whether they feature skill, chance, or compelling storylines, successful games try to engage users intellectually and emotionally—just as successful business communicators try to do.

Gamification is the addition of game-playing aspects to an activity or a process with the goal of increasing user engagement, and it's a natural for social media and mobile devices. Foursquare's check-in competitions, in which the person who "checks in" using Foursquare the most times during a 60-day window is crowned the "mayor" of that location, are one of the best-known uses of gamification. Foursquare wasn't invented as a way for people to become imaginary mayors of places they shop or eat, of course. It is an advertising platform that relies on user activity and user-generated content, and the game element encourages people to use the app more frequently.

Foursquare is a simple example of gamification, but other companies are pushing the concept in new ways to engage and motivate employees and other stakeholders. For example, Bunchball's Nitro software applies gamification concepts to a number of business communication platforms. On a customer-service system, the software rewards employees for increasing their productivity, meeting their service commitments to customers, and sharing knowledge with their colleagues. On several collaboration and brainstorming systems, gamification encourages people to make more connections, share ideas, and boost their influence within a community.

Gamification is also a key strategy for many companies trying to improve customer loyalty. Badgeville's Reputation Mechanics system, for example, boosts the profile of knowledgeable customers who share expertise on social media sites and other online forums. By rewarding their *product champions* this way, companies encourage them to keep contributing their expertise, thereby helping other customers be successful and satisfied.

Incidentally, if you are in the Millennial generation, those born between 1981 and 1995, you're a special target of gamification in the workplace and the marketplace, given your generation's enthusiasm for video games. Don't be surprised to find more gamified apps and systems on the job and everywhere you turn as a consumer.

CAREER APPLICATIONS

1. Gamification is about influencing employee and customer behaviors in ways that benefit a company. Is this ethical? Explain your answer.
2. Assume a company provides a job-search game app that helps you navigate your way through applying for a job, explore various job openings, and understand what it would be like to work there. Would the app make you feel more positively about the company, or would you find that using a game for this purpose would trivialize something as important as your job search? Explain your answer.

Sources: Bunchball website, accessed 23 February 2014, www.bunchball.com; Badgeville website, accessed 23 February 2014, http://badgeville.com; Foursquare for Business website, accessed 23 February 2014, http://business.foursquare.com; Christopher Swan, "Gamification: A New Way to Shape Behavior," *Communication World*, May–June 2012, 13–14.

Inappropriate web use not only distracts employees from work responsibilities, it can leave employers open to lawsuits for sexual harassment if inappropriate images are displayed in or transmitted around the company.[47] Social media have created another set of managerial challenges, given the risk that employee blogs or social networking pages can expose confidential information or damage a firm's reputation in the marketplace. With all these technologies, the best solution lies in developing clear policies that are enforced evenly for all employees.[48]

Managers need to guide their employees in productive use of information tools because the speed and simplicity of these tools are also among their greatest weaknesses. The flood of messages from an expanding array of electronic sources can significantly affect employees' ability to focus on their work. In one study, workers exposed to a constant barrage of email, instant messages, and phone calls experienced an average 10-point drop in their functioning intelligence quotient (IQ).[49]

In addition to using your tools appropriately, knowing how to use them efficiently can make a big difference in your productivity. You don't have to become an expert in most cases, but you do need to be familiar with the basic features and functions of the tools you are expected to use on the job. As a manager, you also need to ensure that your employees have sufficient training to productively use the tools you expect them to use.

MOBILE APP

WhatsApp lets you send and receive messages, videos, and other content via your phone's Internet connection.

Communicating in today's business environment requires at least a basic level of technical competence.

REAL-TIME UPDATES
LEARN MORE BY VISITING THIS WIKI

Get the latest news on gamification

The Gamification Wiki offers information on gamification concepts and examples across a variety of industries. Go to http://real-timeupdates.com/ebc12 and click on Learn More in the Students section.

Powerful Tools for Communicating Effectively

The tools of business communication evolve with every advance in digital technology. The 20 technologies highlighted on the next four pages help businesses redefine the office, collaborate and share information, connect with stakeholders, and build communities of people with shared interests and needs. For more examples of business uses of social media tools in particular.

Shared Online Workspaces

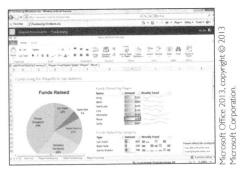

Microsoft Office 2013, copyright © 2013 Microsoft Corporation.

Online workspaces help teams work productively, even if they are on the move or spread out across the country. In addition to providing controlled access to shared files and other digital resources, some systems include such features as project management tools and real-time document sharing (letting two or more team members view and edit a document on screen at the same time).

Web-Based Meetings

Andresr/Shutterstock

Web-based meetings allow team members from all over the world to interact in real time. Meetings can also be recorded for later playback and review. Various systems support instant messaging, video, collaborative editing tools, and more.

Videoconferencing and Telepresence

.shock/Fotolia

Videoconferencing provides many of the benefits of in-person meetings at a fraction of the cost. Advanced systems feature *telepresence*, in which the video images of meeting participants are life-sized and extremely realistic.

Antun Hirsman/Shutterstock

Voice Technologies

Fancy/Alamy

Speech recognition (converting human speech to computer commands) and *speech synthesis* (converting computer commands to human speech) can enhance communication in many ways, including simplifying mobile computing, assisting workers who are unwilling or unable to use keyboards, and allowing "one-sided" conversations with information systems. *Speech analytics software* can evaluate conversations to improve customer service and other interactions. *Mobile VoIP* lets people make voice calls on WiFi networks to save connection and roaming charges.

Mobile Business Apps

As the range of business software applications on smartphones and tablet computers continues to expand, almost anything that can be accomplished on a regular computer can be done on a mobile device (although not always as efficiently or with the same feature sets).

Instant Messaging

Instant messaging (IM) is one of the most widely used digital communication tools in the business world, replacing many conversations and exchanges that once took place via email or phone calls. *Enterprise IM systems* are similar to consumer IM systems in many respects but have additional security and collaboration features.

Wikis

Wikis promote collaboration by simplifying the process of creating and editing online content. Anyone with access (some wikis are private; some are public) can add and modify pages as new information becomes available.

Data Visualization

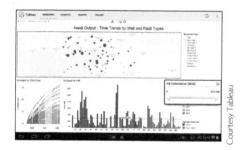

Data visualization is a powerful tool for presenting and exploring sets of data that are very large, complex, or dynamic. As more companies rely on "big data" to identify and capitalize on market opportunities, the ability to extract insights from these large data sets can be an important competitive advantage.

COLLABORATING AND SHARING INFORMATION

The need to work with and share information quickly and easily is a constant in business. A wide variety of tools have been developed to facilitate collaboration and sharing, from general purpose systems such as instant messaging to more specialized capabilities such as data visualization.

Crowdsourcing Platforms

Crowdsourcing, inviting input from groups of people inside or outside the organization, can give companies access to a much wider range of ideas, solutions to problems, and insights into market trends.

Collaboration Platforms

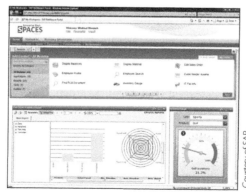

From general-purpose communication systems to task-specific apps and programs, collaboration platforms help teams and business partners coordinate their work on projects.

CONNECTING WITH STAKEHOLDERS

Electronic media and social media in particular have redefined the relationships businesses have with internal and external stakeholders. Any groups affected by a company's decisions now have tools to give voice to their opinions and needs, and companies have many more conversational threads that need to be monitored and managed.

Content Curation

Bovee and Thill, LLC website

Content curation, selecting videos and other items of interest to followers of a website or blog, has become one of the most popular ways to connect with stakeholders. Pinterest and Scoop.it are among the leading technologies in this area.

Applicant Tracking Systems

Screenshot from Recruit by ZOHO Corporation. Copyright © by Mason Hering. Used by permission of Mason Hering.

Applicant tracking systems now play a huge role in employment-related communications. At virtually all large companies and many medium and small companies, your résumé and application information will be entered into one of these systems. Recruiters use various tools to identify promising candidates and manage the interview and selection process. After hiring, some firms use *talent management systems* to track employee development through workers' entire careers at the company.

Blogging

Courtesy of Xerox Corporation

Blogs let companies connect with customers and other audiences in a fast and informal way. Commenting features let readers participate in the conversation, too.

Podcasting

LearningStockImages/Alamy

With the portability and convenience of downloadable audio and video recordings, podcasts have become a popular means of delivering everything from college lectures to marketing messages. Podcasts are also used for internal communication, replacing conference calls, newsletters, and other media.

Online Video

Google and the Google logo are registered trademarks of Google Inc., used with permission.

The combination of low-cost digital video cameras and video-sharing websites such as YouTube has spurred a revolution in business video. Product demonstrations, company overviews, promotional presentations, and training seminars are among the most popular applications of business video. *Branded channels* allow companies to present their videos as an integrated collection in a customized user interface.

User-Generated Content Sites

User-generated content sites let businesses host photos, videos, software programs, technical solutions, and other valuable content for their customer communities.

Microblogging

Microblogging services (of which Twitter is by far the best known) are a great way to share ideas, solicit feedback, monitor market trends, and announce special deals and events.

BUILDING COMMUNITIES

One of the most significant benefits of new communication technologies is the ease with which companies can foster a sense of community among customers, enthusiasts, and other groups. In some instances, the company establishes and manages the online community, while in others the community is driven by *product champions* or other enthusiasts.

Gaming Technologies

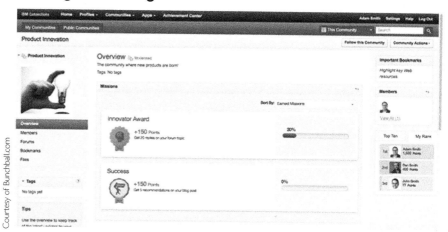

Encouraging people to play games, even games as simple as "checking in" at various retail locations, can build interest in a company and its brands.

Social Networking

Community Q&A Sites

Many companies now rely heavily on communities of customers to help each other with product questions and other routine matters.

Businesses use a variety of social networks as specialized channels to engage customers, find new employees, attract investors, and share ideas and challenges with peers.

RECONNECTING WITH PEOPLE

No matter how much technology is involved, communication is still about people connecting with people.

Even the best technologies can hinder communication if they are overused. For instance, a common complaint among employees is that managers rely too heavily on email and don't communicate face to face often enough.[50] Speaking with people over the phone or in person can take more time and effort and can sometimes force you to confront unpleasant situations directly, but it is often essential for solving tough problems and maintaining productive relationships.[51]

Moreover, even the best communication technologies can't show people who you really are. Remember to step out from behind the technology frequently to learn more about the people you work with and to let them learn more about you.

Committing to Ethical and Legal Communication

6 LEARNING OBJECTIVE
Define *ethics*, explain the difference between an ethical dilemma and an ethical lapse, and list six guidelines for making ethical communication choices.

Ethics are the accepted principles of conduct that govern behavior within a society. Ethical behavior is a companywide concern, but because communication efforts are the public face of a company, they are subjected to particularly rigorous scrutiny from regulators, legislators, investors, consumer groups, environmental groups, labor organizations, and anyone else affected by business activities. **Ethical communication** includes all relevant information, is true in every sense, and is not deceptive in any way. In contrast, unethical communication can distort the truth or manipulate audiences in a variety of ways:[52]

Any time you try to mislead your audience, the result is unethical communication.

- **Plagiarizing.** Plagiarism is presenting someone else's words or other creative product as your own. Note that plagiarism can be illegal if it violates a **copyright**, which is a form of legal protection for the expression of creative ideas.[53]
- **Omitting essential information.** Information is essential if your audience needs it to make an intelligent, objective decision.
- **Selective misquoting.** Distorting or hiding the true intent of someone else's words is unethical.
- **Misrepresenting numbers.** Statistics and other data can be unethically manipulated by increasing or decreasing numbers, exaggerating, altering statistics, or omitting numeric data.
- **Distorting visuals.** Images can be manipulated in unethical ways, such as altering photos in order to deceive audiences or changing the scale of graphs and charts to exaggerate or conceal differences.
- **Failing to respect privacy or information security needs.** Failing to respect the privacy of others or failing to adequately protect information entrusted to your care can also be considered unethical (and is sometimes illegal).

Transparency gives audience members access to all the information they need in order to process messages accurately.

The widespread adoption of social media has increased the attention given to the issue of **transparency**, which in this context refers to a sense of openness, of giving all participants in a conversation access to the information they need in order to accurately process the messages they are receiving. In addition to the information itself, audiences deserve to know when they are being marketed to and who is behind the messages they read or hear. For example, with *stealth marketing*, companies recruit people to promote products to friends and other contacts in exchange for free samples or other rewards, without requiring them to disclose the true nature of the communication. Critics, including the Federal Trade Commission (FTC), assert that such techniques are deceptive because they don't give targets the opportunity to raise their instinctive defenses against the persuasive powers of marketing messages.[54]

Aside from ethical concerns, trying to fool the public is simply bad for business. As LaSalle University communication professor Michael Smith puts it, "The public backlash can be long, deep, and damaging to a company's reputation."[55]

DISTINGUISHING ETHICAL DILEMMAS FROM ETHICAL LAPSES

Some ethical questions are easy to recognize and resolve, but others are not. Deciding what is ethical can be a considerable challenge in complex business situations. An **ethical dilemma** involves choosing among alternatives that aren't clear-cut. Perhaps two conflicting alternatives are both ethical and valid, or perhaps the alternatives lie somewhere in the gray area between clearly right and clearly wrong. Every company has responsibilities to multiple groups of people inside and outside the firm, and those groups often have competing interests. For instance, employees naturally want higher wages and more benefits, but investors who have risked their money in the company want management to keep costs low so that profits are strong enough to drive up the stock price. Both sides have a valid ethical position.

> An ethical dilemma is a choice between alternatives that may all be ethical and valid.

In contrast, an **ethical lapse** is a clearly unethical choice. With both internal and external communication efforts, the pressure to produce results or justify decisions can make unethical communication a tempting choice. Telling a potential customer you can complete a project by a certain date when you know you can't is simply dishonest, even if you need the contract to save your career or your company. There is no ethical dilemma here.

> An ethical lapse is making a choice you know to be unethical.

Compare the messages in Figures 11 and 12 for examples of how business messages can be unethically manipulated.

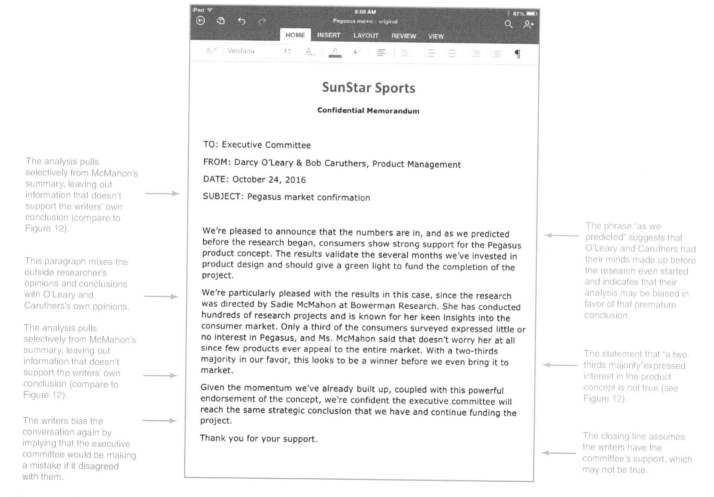

The analysis pulls selectively from McMahon's summary, leaving out information that doesn't support the writers' own conclusion (compare to Figure 12).

This paragraph mixes the outside researcher's opinions and conclusions with O'Leary and Caruthers's own opinions.

The analysis pulls selectively from McMahon's summary, leaving out information that doesn't support the writers' own conclusion (compare to Figure 12).

The writers bias the conversation again by implying that the executive committee would be making a mistake if it disagreed with them.

The phrase "as we predicted" suggests that O'Leary and Caruthers had their minds made up before the research even started and indicates that their analysis may be biased in favor of that premature conclusion.

The statement that "a two-thirds majority" expressed interest in the product concept is not true (see Figure 12).

The closing line assumes the writers have the committee's support, which may not be true.

SunStar Sports

Confidential Memorandum

TO: Executive Committee

FROM: Darcy O'Leary & Bob Caruthers, Product Management

DATE: October 24, 2016

SUBJECT: Pegasus market confirmation

We're pleased to announce that the numbers are in, and as we predicted before the research began, consumers show strong support for the Pegasus product concept. The results validate the several months we've invested in product design and should give a green light to fund the completion of the project.

We're particularly pleased with the results in this case, since the research was directed by Sadie McMahon at Bowerman Research. She has conducted hundreds of research projects and is known for her keen insights into the consumer market. Only a third of the consumers surveyed expressed little or no interest in Pegasus, and Ms. McMahon said that doesn't worry her at all since few products ever appeal to the entire market. With a two-thirds majority in our favor, this looks to be a winner before we even bring it to market.

Given the momentum we've already built up, coupled with this powerful endorsement of the concept, we're confident the executive committee will reach the same strategic conclusion that we have and continue funding the project.

Thank you for your support.

Figure 11 Unethical Communication
The writers of this memo clearly want the company to continue funding their pet project, even though the marketing research doesn't support such a decision. By comparing this memo with the version shown in Figure 12, you can see how the writers twisted the truth and omitted evidence in order to put a positive "spin" on the research.
Source: Screen shot reprinted with permission from Apple Inc.

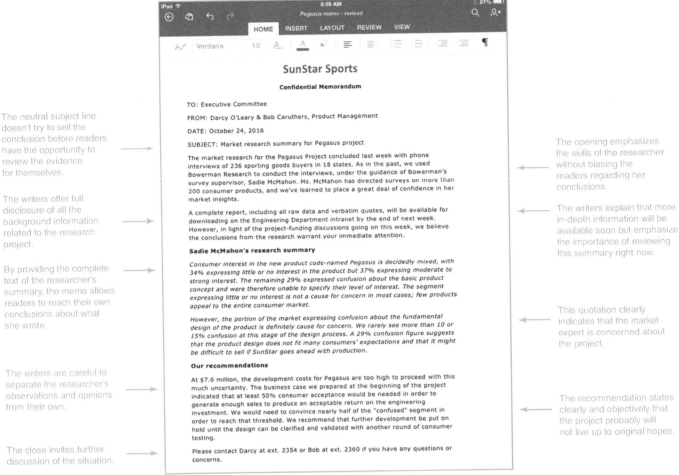

The neutral subject line doesn't try to sell the conclusion before readers have the opportunity to review the evidence for themselves.

The writers offer full disclosure of all the background information related to the research project.

By providing the complete text of the researcher's summary, the memo allows readers to reach their own conclusions about what she wrote.

The writers are careful to separate the researcher's observations and opinions from their own.

The close invites further discussion of the situation.

The opening emphasizes the skills of the researcher without biasing the readers regarding her conclusions.

The writers explain that more in-depth information will be available soon but emphasize the importance of reviewing this summary right now.

This quotation clearly indicates that the market expert is concerned about the project.

The recommendation states clearly and objectively that the project probably will not live up to original hopes.

Figure 12 Ethical Communication
This version of the memo from Figure 11 presents the evidence in a more honest and ethical manner.
Source: Screen shot reprinted with permission from Apple Inc.

ENSURING ETHICAL COMMUNICATION

Ensuring ethical business communication requires three elements: ethical individuals, ethical company leadership, and the appropriate policies and structures to support employees' efforts to make ethical choices.[56] Moreover, these three elements need to work in harmony. If employees see company executives making unethical decisions and flouting company guidelines, they might conclude that the guidelines are meaningless and emulate their bosses' unethical behavior.

Responsible employers establish clear ethical guidelines for their employees to follow.

Employers have a responsibility to establish clear guidelines for ethical behavior, including ethical business communication. Many companies establish an explicit ethics policy by using a written **code of ethics** to help employees determine what is acceptable. A code is often part of a larger program of employee training and communication channels that allow employees to ask questions and report instances of questionable ethics. To ensure ongoing compliance with their codes of ethics, many companies also conduct **ethics audits** to monitor ethical progress and to point out any weaknesses that need to be addressed.

However, whether or not formal guidelines are in place, every employee has a responsibility to communicate in an ethical manner. In the absence of clear guidelines, ask yourself the following questions about your business communications:[57]

If you can't decide whether a choice is ethical, picture yourself explaining your decision to someone whose opinion you value.

- Have you defined the situation fairly and accurately?
- What is your intention in communicating this message?
- What impact will this message have on the people who receive it or who might be affected by it?

- Will the message achieve the greatest possible good while doing the least possible harm?
- Will the assumptions you've made change over time? That is, will a decision that seems ethical now seem unethical in the future?
- Are you comfortable with your decision? Would you be embarrassed if it were printed in tomorrow's newspaper or spread across the Internet? Think about a person whom you admire and ask yourself what he or she would think of your decision.

ENSURING LEGAL COMMUNICATION

In addition to ethical guidelines, business communication is also bound by a wide variety of laws and regulations, including the following areas:

- **Promotional communication.** Marketing specialists need to be aware of the many laws that govern truth and accuracy in advertising. These laws address such issues as product reviews written by bloggers who receive compensation from the companies involved, false and deceptive advertising, misleading or inaccurate labels on product packages, and bait-and-switch tactics in which a store advertises a lower-priced product to lure consumers into a store but then tries to sell them a more expensive item.[58]

Business communication is governed by a wide variety of laws designed to ensure accurate, complete messages.

- **Contracts.** A **contract** is a legally binding promise between two parties in which one party makes a specified offer and the other party accepts. Contracts are fundamental to virtually every aspect of business, from product sales to property rental to credit cards and loans to professional service agreements.[59]

- **Employment communication.** A variety of local, state, and federal laws govern communication between employers and both potential and current employees. For example, job descriptions must be written in a way that doesn't intentionally or unintentionally discriminate against women, minorities, or people with disabilities.[60]

- **Intellectual property.** In an age when instant global connectivity makes copying and retransmitting electronic files effortless, the protection of intellectual property has become a widespread concern. **Intellectual property (IP)** includes patents, copyrighted materials, trade secrets, and even Internet domain names.[61] Bloggers in particular need to be careful about IP protection, given the carefree way that some post the work of others without offering proper credit.

REAL-TIME UPDATES
LEARN MORE BY VISITING THIS WEBSITE

Guidelines for trouble-free blogging

The Electronic Frontier Foundation offers a free *Legal Guide for Bloggers*. Go to http://real-timeupdates.com/ebc12 and click on Learn More in the Students section.

- **Financial reporting.** Finance and accounting professionals who work for publicly traded companies (those that sell stock to the public) must adhere to stringent reporting laws. For instance, a number of corporations have recently been targets of both government investigations and shareholder lawsuits for offering misleading descriptions of financial results and revenue forecasts.

- **Defamation.** Negative comments about another party raise the possibility of **defamation**, the intentional communication of false statements that damage character or reputation.[62] (Written defamation is called *libel*; spoken defamation is called *slander*.) Someone suing for defamation must prove (1) that the statement is false, (2) that the language is injurious to the person's reputation, and (3) that the statement has been published.

- **Transparency requirements.** Governments around the world are taking steps to help ensure that consumers and other parties know who is behind the information they receive, particularly when it appears online. The European Union, for instance, outlaws a number of online marketing tactics, including "flogs," short for "fake blogs," in which an employee or a paid agent posing as an independent consumer posts positive stories about a company's products.[63] In the United States, the FTC requires product-review bloggers to disclose any relationship—such as receiving payments or free goods—they have with the companies whose products they discuss in their blogs.[64]

If you have any doubts about the legality of a message you intend to distribute, ask for advice from your company's legal department. A small dose of caution can prevent huge legal headaches and protect your company's reputation in the marketplace.

For the latest information on ethical and legal issues in business communication, visit http://real-timeupdates.com/ebc12 and click on this Chapter.

Applying What You've Learned

At the beginning of this chapter, you read about JetBlue's experiences using social media to communicate with passengers. As you read through this chapter and become familiar with the concepts presented, imagine how they might apply to the company highlighted in the vignette.

At the end of this chapter, you'll take part in an innovative simulation called "On the Job: Solving Communication Dilemmas." You'll play the role of a person working in the highlighted organization, and you'll face situations you'd encounter on the job. You will be presented with several communication scenarios, each with several possible courses of action. It's up to you to recommend one course of action from each scenario as homework, as teamwork, as material for in-class discussion, or in a host of other ways. These scenarios let you explore various communication ideas and apply the concepts and techniques from the chapter.

Now you're ready for the first simulation. As you tackle each problem, think about the material you covered in this chapter and consider your own experience as a communicator. You'll probably be surprised to discover how much you already know about business communication.

ON THE JOB: SOLVING COMMUNICATION DILEMMAS AT JETBLUE

Imagine that you've joined the Twitter team at JetBlue, one of the more than two dozen communication specialists tasked with monitoring conversations about the company in the Twittersphere and responding to questions, requests, and complaints from passengers. Use what you've learned in this chapter to address the following challenges.

1. JetBlue emphasizes a friendly, open style of communication with its customers, even those occasional customers who make unrealistic demands or expect special treatment. Unfortunately, you've learned that some of the company's customer service representatives have been letting their emotions get in the way when dealing with these difficult customers. Several customers have complained about rude treatment. You're sensitive to the situation because you know customer service can be a difficult job, particularly in a social media environment where consumers are empowered to broadcast any disappointment they may feel. However, having a reputation for hostile customer service could spell doom for the company, so you need to communicate your concerns immediately. Which of the following sentences would be the best way to begin an email message to the customer service staff?

   a. "We must all work harder at serving customers in an efficient, timely manner."

   b. "The growing problem of abusive customers communications must stop immediately—after all,

without customers, we have no revenue; without revenue, you have no jobs."

   c. "Positive customer support is one of our most important competitive advantages, but it has come to management's attention that some of you are ruining the company's reputation by mistreating customers."

   d. "Thank you for your continued efforts at supporting our customers; I know this can be a challenging task at times."

2. The culture in your office is conscientious and professional but with a generally informal "vibe." However, as with any company, individual employees vary in how closely their own styles and personalities fit the corporate culture. For example, the new accounting manager in your organization tends to communicate in a formal, distant style that some company old-timers find off-putting and impersonal. Several of these people have expressed concerns that the new manager "doesn't fit in," even though she's doing a great job otherwise. How should you respond?

   a. Tell these people to stop complaining; the accounting manager is doing her job well, and that's what counts.

   b. In a private conversation with the accounting manager, explain the importance of fitting into the corporate culture and give her a four-week deadline to change her style.

   c. In a private conversation with the accounting manager, explain the reasoning behind the company's informal culture and its contribution to the company's success;

suggest that she might find her work here more enjoyable if she modifies her approach somewhat.

   d. Allow the accounting manager to continue communicating in the same style; after all, that's her personal style, and it's not up to the company to change it.

3. A false rumor has begun circulating among JetBlue employees that the company plans to replace its social media team with an automated "bot" system that will answer tweets and email messages using artificial intelligence. Members of the social media team are worried about their jobs, and other employees are worried that customers will miss the human touch if customer service representatives are replaced by a computer. How should you respond to the rumor?

   a. Try to spread a counter-rumor so that the employees who are worried about their jobs will get the right message the same way they got the wrong one.

   b. Immediately schedule an in-person meeting to set the record straight, emphasizing to everyone in the company that JetBlue has no plans to replace its social media team with bots.

   c. Post a message on an internal blog, setting the record straight and assuring the workforce that the social media jobs are safe; employees are accustomed to getting timely and essential information from this blog.

   d. Ignore the rumor. Like all other false rumors, it will eventually die out.

4. A passenger whose luggage didn't arrive on his flight from Boston to San Francisco is sending a string of angry tweets from the baggage claim at the San Francisco airport, accusing JetBlue of everything from lying to stealing his luggage. He is including the @JetBlue handle in every tweet, so his rants are showing up in the timelines of the company's followers on Twitter—all 1.9 million of them. How should you respond?

   a. Respond to every one of his tweets with a message that JetBlue is an honest company that would never steal luggage or lie to a passenger. In a situation like this, you have to fight fire with fire.

   b. Ignore the passenger's rants; every time you respond, you increase the chance that more of your Twitter followers will see his complaints. He will eventually get tired of complaining, and the storm will blow over.

   c. Get in touch with Twitter and ask the company to suspend the man's account. No one should be allowed to spread misinformation like that on social media.

   d. Reply to one of his tweets with an apology for the trouble he was encountered and an offer to switch to direct messaging to work out a solution to his problem. As soon as you send this tweet, telephone your colleagues in San Francisco. Explain the situation, ask them to figure out which baggage carousel the man is likely to be near (based on his flight info), and ask them try to locate the man and talk to him in person. People are more prone to be abusive on social media than in person, and the employee in San Francisco might be able to convince him to stop tweeting and help reconnect him with his luggage.

Learning Objectives Checkup

Assess your understanding of the principles in this chapter by reading each learning objective and studying the accompanying exercises. You can check your responses against the answer key.

Objective 1: Explain the importance of effective communication to your career and to the companies where you will work.

1. Which of the following is the most accurate description of the role that communication will play in your career?

   a. Ideas matter more than anything, so as long as you are creative and have strong business sense, you can hire people to take care of communication tasks.

   b. No matter what other skills, connections, and attributes you have, your prospects will be limited if you don't have good communication skills.

   c. In today's tough business world, performance is the most important differentiator; everything else is a distant second.

   d. As a "soft skill," communication is important in some careers, such as sales and human resources, but not in technical, financial, or administrative careers.

2. Effective business messages are

   a. Entertaining, blunt, direct, opinionated, and persuasive

   b. Practical, objective, concise, clear, and persuasive

   c. Personal, clear, short, catchy, and challenging

3. Why is it important for a business message to clearly state expectations regarding who is responsible for doing what in response to the message?

   a. To make sure other employees don't avoid their responsibilities

   b. To make sure the person who sent the message isn't criticized if important tasks don't get completed

   c. To eliminate confusion by letting each affected person know his or her specific responsibilities

Objective 2: Explain what it means to communicate as a professional in a business context.

4. Which of the following is not a skill employers will expect you to have?

   a. Communicating effectively with people from diverse backgrounds and experiences

   b. Using communication technologies effectively and efficiently

   c. Managing your time wisely and using resources efficiently

   d. Commanding employees to follow orders

5. Which of the following is not one of the six traits of professionalism identified in the chapter?

   a. Striving to excel

   b. Being dependable

c. Being ethical

d. Being loyal to the company no matter what

6. An audience-centered approach to communication

    a. Starts with the assumption that the audience is always right

    b. Improves the effectiveness of communication by focusing on the information needs of the audience

    c. Is generally a waste of time because it doesn't accommodate the needs of the sender

    d. Always simplifies the tasks involved in planning and creating messages

7. Sensitivity to business etiquette

    a. Reduces the chance of interpersonal blunders that might negatively affect communication

    b. Is considered by most companies to be a waste of time in today's fast-paced markets

    c. Is now legally required in all 50 states

    d. Always increases the cost of business communication

Objective 3: Describe the communication process model and the ways that social media are changing the nature of business communication.

8. Communication style using the social communication model is best described as

    a. Conversational

    b. Multilingual

    c. Technical

    d. Playful

9. Which of the following pairs of attributes best describes the social communication model?

    a. Interactive and conversational

    b. Technical and instantaneous

    c. Electronic and print

    d. Relaxed and unrestricted

10. For audience members to successfully receive messages, they must first _____ the presence of the message, then _____ it from other sensory input, and then _____ it as a message.

11. For the receiver of a message to respond in the manner desired by the sender, the receiver needs to

    a. Remember the message

    b. Be able to respond to the message

    c. Have the motivation to respond to the message

    d. Do all of the above

Objective 4: Outline the challenges and opportunities of mobile communication in business.

12. Which of these is a potential disadvantage of the constant connectivity enabled by mobile communication devices?

    a. Blurring the lines between personal and professional time

    b. Losing contact with key business markets around the globe

    c. Making unethical choices more tempting

    d. Reducing employee access to corporate data

13. Which of these is not one of the advantages of mobile communication discussed in the chapter?

    a. Giving employees more flexibility to meet their personal and professional obligations

    b. Guaranteeing ethical treatment of message recipients

    c. Enhancing productivity and collaboration

    d. Creating more engaging experiences for customers and other users

Objective 5: List four general guidelines for using communication technology effectively.

14. Communication technology has value only if it helps deliver the right _____ to the right _____ at the right time.

15. The information technology paradox means that

    a. Communication tools can sometimes waste more time than they save

    b. Computers lose as much information as they save

    c. People are no longer needed to create messages

    d. Technology isn't as expensive as it used to be

16. Reconnecting frequently with colleagues and customers in person

    a. Is widely considered an inappropriate use of time, given all the electronic options now available

    b. Is frowned on by successful managers

    c. Is critical because it helps ensure that technology doesn't hinder human interaction

Objective 6: Define ethics, explain the difference between an ethical dilemma and an ethical lapse, and list six guidelines for making ethical communication choices

17. Ethical communication

    a. Is the same thing as legal communication

    b. Costs more because there are so many rules to consider

    c. Is important only for companies that sell to consumers rather than to other businesses

    d. Includes all relevant information, is true in every sense, and is not deceptive in any way

18. An ethical _____ exists when a person is faced with two conflicting but ethical choices or alternatives that are neither entirely right nor entirely wrong; an ethical _____ occurs when a person makes an unethical choice.

Quick Learning Guide

LEARNING OBJECTIVES

1 Explain the importance of effective communication to your career and to the companies where you will work.

2 Explain what it means to communicate as a professional in a business context.

3 Describe the communication process model and the ways social media are changing the nature of business communication.

4 Outline the challenges and opportunities of mobile communication in business.

5 List four general guidelines for using communication technology effectively.

6 Define *ethics*, explain the difference between an ethical dilemma and an ethical lapse, and list six guidelines for making ethical communication choices.

KEY TERMS

audience-centered approach Understanding and respecting the members of your audience and making every effort to get your message across in a way that is meaningful to them

code of ethics A written set of ethical guidelines that companies expect their employees to follow

communication The process of transferring information and meaning using one or more written, oral, visual, or electronic media

communication barriers Forces or events that can disrupt communication, including noise and distractions, competing messages, filters, and channel breakdowns

communication channels Systems used to deliver messages

communication medium The form in which a message is presented; the four categories of media are oral, written, visual, and electronic

contract A legally binding promise between two parties, in which one party makes a specified offer and the other party accepts

copyright A form of legal protection for the expression of creative ideas

critical thinking The ability to evaluate evidence completely and objectively in order to form logical conclusions and make sound recommendations

decoding Extracting the idea from a message

defamation The intentional communication of false statements that damage character or reputation

encoding Putting an idea into a message (words, images, or a combination of both)

ethical communication Communication that includes all relevant information, is true in every sense, and is not deceptive in any way

ethical dilemma Situation that involves making a choice when the alternatives aren't completely wrong or completely right

ethical lapse A clearly unethical choice

ethics The accepted principles of conduct that govern behavior within a society

ethics audits Ongoing efforts to monitor ethical progress and to point out any weaknesses that need to be addressed

etiquette The expected norms of behavior in any particular situation

feedback Information from receivers regarding the quality and effectiveness of a message

formal communication network Communication channels that flow along the lines of command

informal communication network All communication that takes place outside the formal network; often referred to as the *grapevine* or the *rumor mill*

information overload Condition in which people receive more information than they can effectively process

intellectual property Assets including patents, copyrighted materials, trade secrets, and even Internet domain names

message The "container" for an idea to be transmitted from a sender to a receiver

perception A person's awareness or view of reality; also, the process of detecting incoming messages

professionalism The quality of performing at a high level and conducting oneself with purpose and pride

selective perception The inclination to distort or ignore incoming information rather than change one's beliefs

social communication model An interactive, conversational approach to communication in which formerly passive audience members are empowered to participate fully

stakeholders Groups affected by a company's actions: customers, employees, shareholders, suppliers, neighbors, the community, and the world at large

transparency Giving all participants in a conversation access to the information they need to accurately process the messages they are receiving

"you" attitude Communicating with an audience-centered approach; creating messages that are about "you," the receiver, rather than "me," the sender

MyBCommLab

To complete the problems with the ⭐, go to
EOC Discussion Questions in the MyLab.

Apply Your Knowledge

To review chapter content related to each question, refer to the indicated Learning Objective.

⭐ 1. Why do you think communication is vital to the success of every business organization? Explain briefly. [LO-1]

⭐ 2. How does the presence of a reader comments feature on a corporate blog reflect audience-centered communication? [LO-2]

3. What changes would you make to your email messages if you know your recipients are typically walking or riding on mass transit when they read your messages? [LO-4]

4. Is it possible for companies to be too dependent on communication technology? Explain briefly. [LO-5]

⭐ 5. You're the CEO of a company whose sales are declining, and there is a 50/50 chance you will need to lay off some of your employees sometime in the next two to three months. You have to decide whether to tell them now so they can look for new jobs as soon as possible, even though you're not yet sure layoffs will be necessary, or wait until you are sure layoffs will occur. Explain why this is an ethical dilemma. Be sure to consider the effect a sudden exodus of valuable employees could have on the company's prospects. [LO-6]

Practice Your Skills

Message for Analysis: Analyzing Communication Effectiveness [LO-1]

Read the following blog posting, and then (a) analyze whether the message is effective or ineffective (be sure to explain why) and (b) revise the message so that it follows this chapter's guidelines.

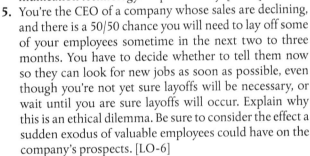

It has come to my attention that many of you are lying on your time cards. If you come in late, you should not put 8:00 on your card. If you take a long lunch, you should not put 1:00 on your time card. I will not stand for this type of cheating. I simply have no choice but to institute an employee monitoring system. Beginning next Monday, video cameras will be installed at all entrances to the building, and your entry and exit times will be logged each time you use electronic key cards to enter or leave.

Anyone who is late for work or late coming back from lunch more than three times will have to answer to me. I don't care if you had to take a nap or if you girls had to shop. This is a place of business, and we do not want to be taken advantage of by slackers who are cheaters to boot.

It is too bad that a few bad apples always have to spoil things for everyone.

Exercises

Each activity is labeled according to the primary skill or skills you will need to use. To review relevant chapter content, you can refer to the indicated Learning Objective. In some instances, supporting information will be found in another chapter, as indicated.

6. **Writing: Compositional Modes: Summaries [LO-1]** Write a paragraph introducing yourself to your instructor and your class. Address such areas as your background, interests, achievements, and goals. Submit your paragraph using email, blog, or social network, as indicated by your instructor.

7. **Media Skills: Microblogging, [LO-1]** Write four effective messages of no more than 140 characters each (short enough to work as Twitter tweets, in other words) to persuade other college students to take the business communication course. Think of the first message as the "headline" of an advertisement that makes a bold promise regarding the value this course offers every aspiring business professional. The next three messages should be support points that provide evidence to back up the promise made in the first message.[65]

8. **Fundamentals: Analyzing Communication Effectiveness [LO-1]** Identify a video clip (on YouTube or another online source) that you believe represents an example of effective communication. It can be in any context, business or otherwise, but make sure it is something appropriate to discuss in class. Post a link to the video on your class blog, along with a brief written summary of why you think this example shows effective communication in action.

9. **Planning: Assessing Audience Needs [LO-2]** Choose a business career that sounds interesting to you and imagine that you are getting ready to apply for jobs in that field. Naturally, you want to create a compelling, audience-focused résumé that answers the key questions a hiring manager is most likely to have. Identify three personal or professional qualities you have that would be important for someone in this career field. Write a brief statement (one or two sentences) regarding each quality, describing in audience-focused terms how you can contribute to a company in this respect. Submit your statements via email or class blog.

10. **Communication Etiquette: Communicating with Sensitivity and Tact [LO-2]** Potential customers frequently visit your production facility before making purchase decisions. You and the people who report to you in the sales department have received extensive training in etiquette issues because you deal with high-profile clients so often. However, the rest of the workforce has not received such training, and you worry that someone might inadvertently say or do something that would offend one of these potential customers. In a two-paragraph email, explain to the general manager why you think anyone who might come in contact with customers should receive basic etiquette training.

11. **Collaboration: Team Projects; Planning: Assessing Audience Needs [LO-2]** Your boss has asked your work group to research and report on corporate child-care facilities. Of course, you'll want

to know who (besides your boss) will be reading your report. Working with two team members, list four or five other things you'll want to know about the situation and about your audience before starting your research. Briefly explain why each of the items on your list is important.

12. **Planning: Constructing a Persuasive Argument, [LO-2]** Blogging has become a popular way for employees to communicate with customers and other parties outside the company. In some cases, employee blogs have been quite beneficial for both companies and their customers by providing helpful information and "putting a human face" on other formal and imposing corporations. However, in some other cases, employees have been fired for posting information that their employers said was inappropriate. One particular area of concern is criticism of the company or individual managers. Should employees be allowed to criticize their employers in a public forum such as a blog? In a brief email message, argue for or against company policies that prohibit critical information in employee blogs.

13. **Fundamentals: Analyzing Communication Effectiveness [LO-3]** Use the eight phases of the communication process to analyze a miscommunication you've recently had with a coworker, supervisor, classmate, teacher, friend, or family member. What idea were you trying to share? How did you encode and transmit it? Did the receiver get the message? Did the receiver correctly decode the message? How do you know? Based on your analysis, identify and explain the barriers that prevented your successful communication in this instance.

14. **Fundamentals: Analyzing Communication Effectiveness [LO-4]** Using a mobile device, visit the websites of five companies that make products or provide services you buy or might buy in the future. Which of the websites is the most user friendly? How does it differ from the other sites? Do any of the companies offer a mobile shopping app for your device?

15. **Technology: Using Communication Tools [LO-5]** Find a free online communication service that you have no experience using as a content creator or contributor. Services to consider include blogging (such as Blogger), microblogging (such as Twitter), community Q&A sites (such as Yahoo! Answers), and user-generated content sites (such as Flickr). Perform a basic task such as opening an account or setting up a blog. Was the task easy to perform? Were the instructions clear? Could you find help online if you needed it? Is there anything about the experience that could be improved? Summarize your conclusions in a brief email message to your instructor.

16. **Communication Ethics: Distinguishing Ethical Dilemmas and Ethical Lapses [LO-6]** Knowing that you have numerous friends throughout the company, your boss relies on you for feedback concerning employee morale and other issues affecting the staff. She recently asked you to start reporting any behavior that might violate company policies, from taking office

supplies home to making personal long-distance calls. List the issues you'd like to discuss with her before you respond to her request.

17. **Communication Ethics: Distinguishing Ethical Dilemmas and Ethical Lapses [LO-6]** In less than a page, explain why you think each of the following is or is not ethical.

    a. Keeping quiet about a possible environmental hazard you've just discovered in your company's processing plant

    b. Overselling the benefits of instant messaging to your company's managers; they never seem to understand the benefits of technology, so you believe it's the only way to convince them to make the right choice

    c. Telling an associate and close friend that she needs to pay more attention to her work responsibilities, or management will fire her

    d. Recommending the purchase of equipment your department doesn't really need in order to use up your allocated funds before the end of the fiscal year so that your budget won't be cut next year, when you might have a real need for the money

18. **Communication Ethics: Providing Ethical Leadership [LO-6]** Cisco, a leading manufacturer of equipment for the Internet and corporate networks, has developed a code of ethics that it expects employees to abide by. Visit the company's website and find its *code of conduct*. In a brief paragraph, describe three specific examples of things you could do that would violate these provisions; then list at least three opportunities that Cisco provides its employees to report ethics violations or ask questions regarding ethical dilemmas.

Expand Your Skills

Critique the Professionals

Locate an example of professional communication from a reputable online source. It can reflect any aspect of business communication, from an advertisement or a press release to a company blog or website. Evaluate this communication effort in light of any aspect of this chapter that is relevant to the sample and interesting to you. For example, is the piece effective? Audience-centered? Ethical? Using whatever medium your instructor requests, write a brief analysis of the piece (no more than one page), citing specific elements from the piece and support from the chapter.

Sharpening Your Career Skills Online

Bovée and Thill's Business Communication Web Search, at http://websearch.businesscommunicationnetwork.com, is a unique research tool designed specifically for business communication research. Use the Web Search function to find an online video, a presentation, a website, or an article that describes an innovative use of mobile technology in business communication. Write a brief email message to your instructor or a post for your class blog, describing the item that you found and summarizing the information you found.

Improve Your Grammar, Mechanics, and Usage

The following exercises help you improve your knowledge of and power over English grammar, mechanics, and usage. Turn to the Handbook of Grammar, Mechanics, and Usage at the end of this text and review all of Section 1 (Nouns). Then look at the following 10 items. Underline the preferred choice within each set of parentheses.

19. She remembered placing that report on her (*bosses, boss's*) desk.

20. We mustn't follow their investment advice like a lot of (*sheep, sheeps*).

21. Jones founded the company back in the early (*1990's, 1990s*).

22. Please send the (*Joneses, Jones'*) a dozen of the following: (*stopwatchs, stopwatches*), canteens, and headbands.

23. Our (*attorneys, attornies*) will talk to the group about incorporation.

24. Make sure that all (*copys, copies*) include the new addresses.

25. Ask Jennings to collect all (*employee's, employees'*) donations for the Red Cross drive.

26. Charlie now has two (*sons-in-law, son-in-laws*) to help him with his two online (*business's, businesses*).

27. Avoid using too many (*parentheses, parenthesis*) when writing your reports.

28. Follow President (*Nesses, Ness's*) rules about what constitutes a (*weeks, week's*) work.

For additional exercises focusing on nouns, visit MyBCommLab. Click on this Chapter, click on Additional Exercises to Improve Your Grammar, Mechanics, and Usage, and then click on 1. Possessive nouns or 2. Antecedents.

MyBCommLab

Go to the Assignments section of your MyLab to complete these writing exercises.

29. How does the social communication model differ from traditional business communication practices? [LO-3]

30. How is mobile technology changing the practice of business communication? [LO-4]

Endnotes

1. JetBlue website, accessed 23 February 2014, www.jetblue.com; "5 Social Media All-Stars," *CNNMoney*, 29 August 2013, http://money.cnn.com; JetBlue Twitter account, accessed 22 February 2014, https://twitter.com/JetBlue; Todd Wasserman, "How JetBlue's Social Media Strategy Took Flight," *Mashable*, 1 June 2011, http://mashable.com; "A Day In The Life: Social Media," BlueTales blog, 19 January 2012, http://blog.jetblue.com, Chantal Tode, "JetBlue Exec: Mobile Is Discovery Piece for Travelers," *Mobile Marketer*, 22 January 2013, www.mobilemarketer.com.

2. Richard L. Daft, *Management*, 6th ed. (Cincinnati: Thomson South-Western, 2003), 580.

3. "Employers: 13 Common Complaints About Recent Grads," Youturn, 2 October 2012, www.youturn.com.

4. Julie Connelly, "Youthful Attitudes, Sobering Realities," *New York Times*, 28 October 2003, E1, E6; Nigel Andrews and Laura D'Andrea Tyson, "The Upwardly Global MBA," *Strategy + Business 36* (Fall 2004): 60–69; Jim McKay, "Communication Skills Found Lacking," *Pittsburgh Post-Gazette*, 28 February 2005, www.delawareonline.com.

5. Brian Solis, *Engage!* (Hoboken, N.J.: John Wiley & Sons, 2010), 11–12; "Majority of Global Companies Face an Engagement Gap," Internal Comms Hub website, 23 October 2007, www.internalcommshub.com; Gary L. Neilson, Karla L. Martin, and Elizabeth Powers, "The Secrets to Successful Strategy Execution," *Harvard Business Review*, June 2008, 61–70; Nicholas Carr, "Lessons in Corporate Blogging," *BusinessWeek*, 18 July 2006, 9; Susan Meisinger, "To Keep Employees, Talk—and Listen—to Them!" *HR Magazine*, August 2006, 10.

6. Daft, *Management*, 147.

7. "CEOs to Communicators: 'Stick to Common Sense,'" Internal Comms Hub website, 23 October 2007, www.internalcommshub.com; "A Writing Competency Model for Business," BizCom101.com, 14 December 2007, www.business-writing-courses.com; Sue Dewhurst and Liam FitzPatrick, "What Should Be the Competency of Your IC Team?" white paper, 2007, http://competentcommunicators.com.

8. "Digital Information Fluency Model," 21cif.com, accessed 11 February 2014, http://21cif.com.

9. Philip C. Kolin, *Successful Writing at Work*, 6th ed. (Boston: Houghton Mifflin, 2001), 17–23.

10. Laura L. Myers and Mary L. Tucker, "Increasing Awareness of Emotional Intelligence in a Business Curriculum," *Business Communication Quarterly*, March 2005, 44–51.

11. Pete Cashmore, "10 Web Trends to Watch in 2010," CNN Tech, 3 December 2009, www.cnn.com.

12. Stephanie Armour, "Music Hath Charms for Some Workers—Others It Really Annoys," *USA Today*, 24 March 2006, B1–B2.

13. Paul Martin Lester, *Visual Communication: Images with Messages* (Belmont, Calif.: Thomson South-Western, 2006), 6–8.

14. Michael R. Solomon, *Consumer Behavior: Buying, Having, and Being*, 6th ed. (Upper Saddle River, N.J.: Pearson Prentice Hall, 2004), 65.

15. Anne Field, "What You Say, What They Hear," *Harvard Management Communication Letter*, Winter 2005, 3–5.

16. Chuck Williams, *Management*, 2nd ed. (Cincinnati: Thomson South-Western, 2002), 690.

17. Charles G. Morris and Albert A. Maisto, *Psychology: An Introduction*, 12th ed. (Upper Saddle River, N.J.: Pearson Prentice Hall, 2005),

226–239; Saundra K. Ciccarelli and Glenn E. Meyer, *Psychology* (Upper Saddle River, N.J.: Prentice Hall, 2006), 210–229; Mark H. Ashcraft, *Cognition*, 4th ed. (Upper Saddle River, N.J.: Prentice Hall, 2006), 44–54.

18. Ben Hanna, *2009 Business Social Media Benchmarking Study* (published by Business.com), 2 November 2009, 11.

19. Michael Killian, "The Communication Revolution—'Deep Impact' About to Strike," Avaya Insights blog, 4 December 2009, www.avayablog.com.

20. "The Mobile Revolution Is Just Beginning," press release, World Economic Forum, 13 September 2013, www.weforum.org.

21. Maribel Lopez, "Three Trends That Change Business: Mobile, Social and Cloud," *Forbes*, 28 January 2012, www.forbes.com.

22. Kevin Custis, "Three Ways Business Can Be Successful on Mobile," *Forbes*, 15 November 2013, www.forbes.com; "IBM Survey: Speed and Analytics Key Drivers in Mobile Adoption for Organizations," press release, IBM, 19 November 2013, www.ibm.com.

23. "More Than Nine in 10 Internet Users Will Go Online via Phone," eMarketer, 6 January 2014, www.emarketer.com.

24. Christina "CK" Kerley, *The Mobile Revolution & B2B*, white paper, 2011, www.b2bmobilerevolution.com.

25. Jordie can Rijn, "The Ultimate Mobile Email Statistics Overview," Emailmonday.com, accessed 9 February 2014, www.emailmonday.com.

26. Jessica Lee, "46% of Searchers Now Use Mobile Exclusively to Research [Study]," Search Engine Watch, 1 May 2013, http://searchenginewatch.com.

27. Dennis McCafferty, "10 Awesome Facts About the Mobile Revolution," *CIO Insight*, 6 December 2013, www.cioinsight.com.

28. Yun-Sen Chan, "Smartphones Are Changing Person-to-Person Communication," Modern Media Mix, 23 April 2013, http://modernmediamix.com.

29. "Mobile Facts and Market Stats," Mocapay, accessed 10 February 2014, www.mocapay.com.

30. *Mobile Revolution*, ebook, Extron, 2011.

31. Nicco Mele, *The End of Big: How the Internet Makes David the New Goliath* (New York: St. Martin's Press: 2013), 1–2.

32. "JWT's 13 Mobile Trends for 2013 and Beyond," J. Walter Thompson website, 2 April 2013, www.jwt.com.

33. *The Changing Role of Mobile Communications in the Workplace*, white paper, Frost & Sullivan, accessed 8 February 2014, www.frost.com.

34. *Top 10 Ways Successful Small Businesses Use Mobile Tech*, white paper, T-Mobile, 2012.

35. Armen Ghazarian, "How Do Users Interact with Mobile Devices," Medium.com, 29 November 2013, http://medium.com.

36. "JWT's 13 Mobile Trends for 2013 and Beyond."

37. "Bring Your Own Device: BYOD Is Here and You Can't Stop It," Garner, accessed 9 February 2014, www.garner.com.

38. Jessica Twentyman, "Deploying Smartphones, Tables, and Apps for a New Employee Communication Era," *SCM*, January/February 2013, 28–29; *The Changing Role of Mobile Communications in the Workplace*, Frost & Sullivan.

39. Aaref Hilaly, "The Biggest Opportunity in Mobile That No One Is Talking About," LinkedIn, 17 December 2013, www.linkedin.com.

40. Michael Saylor, *The Mobile Wave: How Mobile Intelligence Will Change Everything* (New York: Vanguard Press, 2012), 10.

41. *The Changing Role of Mobile Communications in the Workplace*, Frost & Sullivan.

42. *Top 10 Ways Successful Small Businesses Use Mobile Tech*, T-Mobile.

43. Milton Kazmeyer, "The Impact of Wireless Communication in the Workplace," *Houston Chronicle*, accessed 10 February 2014, http://smallbusiness.chron.com.

44. Gregg Hano, "The Power of Corporate Communications on Mobile Apps," Mag+, 1 August 2013, www.magplus.com.

45. Tara Craig, "How to Avoid Information Overload," *Personnel Today*, 10 June 2008, 31; Jeff Davidson, "Fighting Information Overload," *Canadian Manager*, Spring 2005, 16+.

46. "The Top Ten Ways Workers Waste Time Online," 24/7 Wall St., 30 September 2010, http://247wallst.com.

47. Eric J. Sinrod, "Perspective: It's My Internet—I Can Do What I Want," News.com, 29 March 2006, www.news.com.

48. Eric J. Sinrod, "Time to Crack Down on Tech at Work?" News.com, 14 June 2006, www.news.com.

49. Jack Trout, "Beware of 'Infomania,'" *Forbes*, 11 August 2006, www.forbes.com.

50. "Many Senior Managers Communicate Badly, Survey Says," Internal Comms Hub, 6 August 2007, www.internalcommshub.com.

51. Mike Schaffner, "Step Away from the Computer," *Forbes*, 7 August 2009, www.forbes.com.

52. Philip C. Kolin, *Successful Writing at Work*, 6th ed. (Boston: Houghton Mifflin, 2001), 24–30.

53. Nancy K. Kubasek, Bartley A. Brennan, and M. Neil Browne, *The Legal Environment of Business*, 3rd ed. (Upper Saddle River, N.J.: Prentice Hall, 2003), 172.

54. Word of Mouth Marketing Association, "WOM 101," accessed 2 June 2010, http://womma.org; Nate Anderson, "FTC Says Stealth Marketing Unethical," *Ars Technica*, 13 December 2006, http://-arstechnica.com; "Undercover Marketing Uncovered," CBSnews.com, 25 July 2004, www.cbsnews.com; Stephanie Dunnewind, "Teen Recruits Create Word-of-Mouth 'Buzz' to Hook Peers on Products," *Seattle Times*, 20 November 2004, www.seattletimes.com.

55. Linda Pophal, "Tweet Ethics: Trust and Transparency in a Web 2.0 World," *CW Bulletin*, September 2009.

56. Daft, *Management*, 155.

57. Based in part on Robert Kreitner, *Management*, 9th ed. (Boston: Houghton Mifflin, 2004), 163.

58. Henry R. Cheeseman, *Contemporary Business and E-Commerce Law*, 4th ed. (Upper Saddle River, N.J.: Prentice Hall, 2003), 841–843.

59. Cheeseman, *Contemporary Business and E-Commerce Law*, 201.

60. John Jude Moran, *Employment Law: New Challenges in the Business Environment*, 2nd ed. (Upper Saddle River, N.J.: Prentice Hall, 2002), 186–187; Kubasek et al., *The Legal Environment of Business*, 562.

61. Cheeseman, *Contemporary Business and E-Commerce Law*, 325.

62. Kubasek et al., *The Legal Environment of Business*, 306.

63. Robert Plummer, "Will Fake Business Blogs Crash and Burn?" *BBC News*, 22 May 2008, http://news.bbc.co.uk.

64. Tim Arango, "Soon, Bloggers Must Give Full Disclosure," *New York Times*, 5 October 2009, www.nytimes.com.

65. The concept of a four-tweet summary is from Cliff Atkinson, *The Backchannel* (Berkeley, Calif.: New Riders, 2010), 120–121.

Answer Key for "Learning Objectives Checkup"

1. b
2. b
3. c
4. d
5. d
6. b
7. a
8. a
9. a
10. sense, select, perceive
11. d
12. a
13. b
14. information, people
15. a
16. c
17. d
18. dilemma, lapse

Answer Key for "Improve Your Grammar, Mechanics, and Usage" Exercises

19. boss's (1.1.4)
20. sheep (1.1.3)
21. 1990s (1.1.3)
22. Joneses, stopwatches (1.1.3)
23. attorneys (1.1.3)
24. copies (1.1.3)
25. employees' (1.1.4)
26. sons-in-law, businesses (1.1.3, 1.1.4)
27. parentheses (1.1.3)
28. Ness's, week's (1.1.4)

Building Careers and Writing Résumés

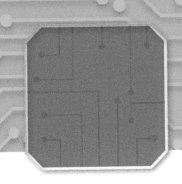

Building Careers and Writing Résumés

LEARNING OBJECTIVES

After studying this chapter, you will be able to

1 List eight key steps to finding the ideal opportunity in today's job market.

2 Explain the process of planning your résumé, including how to choose the best résumé organization.

3 Describe the tasks involved in writing your résumé, and list the major sections of a traditional résumé.

4 Characterize the completing step for résumés, including the six most common formats in which you can produce a résumé.

ON THE JOB: COMMUNICATING AT
VMWARE

Software Maker's Early Experiment with Social Media Recruiting Pays Off

Innovative businesspeople are always on the lookout for better ways to work and for any developments in the business environment that can give their companies a competitive edge. Back in 2009, James Malloy, a recruiting manager at VMWare, picked up on the early buzz surrounding *social recruiting* and wanted to know if his company might benefit from the growth of LinkedIn, Facebook, and other social platforms.

Social networking wasn't a new technology at that point, but most companies were still feeling their way through this new world and trying to figure out if or how to use all these new tools. In addition, corporate recruiters already had well-established systems for finding, evaluating, and recruiting new talent, and few companies knew if social media could add value to such a vital business process.

Moreover, even though social media were taking off with consumers and many consumer-oriented companies, VMWare is about as far from the frontlines of consumer activity as a company can get. Its specialty is *virtualization*, a software technique that lets a single computer act like multiple, independent machines. Virtualization is a critical technology behind cloud computing and much of today's information technology (IT)

James Molloy's hunch that social media might benefit VMWare's employee recruiting set off a revolution in how the company finds, evaluates, and recruits top talent.

Kristoffer Tripplaar/Alamy

infrastructure, but it's not exactly the sort of trendy topic that blows up on Twitter or prompts a million "you have to see this" shares on Facebook.

However, Malloy was intrigued by social recruiting and decided to conduct a low-risk experiment on Facebook to see if there was any potential. He set up a page and began posting job openings to it—and the effort caught on quickly as interested candidates found the openings. Importantly, the Facebook presence brought VMWare in touch with talented people that it hadn't been in contact with before.

Technology companies compete fiercely with one another to attract the best software designers and other specialists, so anything that gives recruiters an advantage is going to get attention. Malloy's simple Facebook experiment was so successful that VMWare's top management decided to realign its entire recruiting strategy around social networking.

Recruiting isn't the only aspect of company operations that adopted social media with gusto. The company is social through and through, with hundreds of official social media accounts and

groups focused on specific technical or business issues, including nearly a hundred Twitter accounts alone. Four of those Twitter accounts are dedicated to careers and recruiting, including @VMWareU, the account for the VMWare University Recruiting Team. Through this account, the company announces job openings targeted at recent graduates, internship opportunities, and news of interest to potential employees.

The company's social recruiting strategy goes far beyond simple announcements, however. Molloy and his colleagues use these channels to build relationships with potential hires, to share videos and other media that showcase the VMWare corporate culture, and to brand VMWare as an exciting, supportive place to work. The social recruiting effort has been so successful that the company continues to expand it. Moving the forward, it is focusing on expanding its use of mobile recruiting apps and in helping employees become effective "brand advocates" for the company in their own social networks.[1]

WWW.VMWARE.COM

Finding the Ideal Opportunity in Today's Job Market

1 LEARNING OBJECTIVE
List eight key steps to finding the ideal opportunity in today's job market.

The social recruiting efforts made by VMWare (profiled in the chapter-opening On the Job) show the importance that top companies place on finding the right employees and the investments these companies are willing to make in both personnel and technology to attract and keep valuable talent. Whether you'll be looking for your first professional job on graduation or you're already in mid-career, you need to put as much thought and care into finding the right job as employers put into finding the right employees.

Identifying and landing a job can be a long and challenging process. Fortunately, the skills you're developing in this course will give you a competitive advantage. This section offers a general job-search strategy with advice that applies to just about any career path you might want to pursue. As you craft your personal strategy, keep these three guidelines in mind:

- **Get organized.** Your job search could last many months and involve multiple contacts with dozens of companies. You need to keep all the details straight to ensure that you don't miss opportunities or make mistakes such as losing someone's email address or forgetting an appointment.
- **Start now and stick to it.** Even if you are a year or more away from graduation, now is not too early to get started with some of the essential research and planning tasks. If you wait until the last minute, you will miss opportunities and you won't be as prepared as other candidates.
- **Look for stepping-stone opportunities.** Particularly in today's tough job market, you might not find the opportunity you're looking for right away. You might need to take a job that doesn't meet your expectations while you keep looking to get on the right track. But view every job as an opportunity to learn workplace skills, observe effective and ineffective business practices, and fine-tune your sense of how you'd like to spend your career.

If you haven't already, read the Prologue, "Building a Career with Your Communication Skills," before studying this chapter.

WRITING THE STORY OF YOU

Writing or updating your résumé is a great opportunity to step back and think about where you've been and where you'd like to go. Do you like the path you're on, or is it time for a change? Are you focused on a particular field, or do you need some time to explore?

What's your story? Thinking about where you've been and where you want to go will help focus your job search.

My Story

Where I Have Been

- Honor student and all around big shot in high school (but discovered that college is full of big shots!)
- Have worked several part-time jobs; only thing that really appealed to me in any of them was making improvements, making things work better

Where I Am Now

- Junior; on track to graduate in 2017
- Enjoy designing creative solutions to challenging problems
- Not a high-end techie in an engineering sense, but I figure most things out eventually
- Not afraid to work hard, whatever it takes to get the job done
- I can tolerate some routine, as long as I have the opportunity to make improvements if needed
- Tend to lead quietly by example, rather than by visibly and vocally taking charge
- Knowing that I do good work is more important than getting approval from others
- I tend not to follow fads and crowds; sometimes I'm ahead of the curve, sometimes I'm behind the curve

Where I Want to Be

- Get an advanced degree; not sure what subject area yet, though
- Haven't really settled on one industry or profession yet; working with systems of any kind is more appealing than any particular profession that I've learned about so far
- Develop my leadership and communication skills to become a more "obvious" leader
- Collaborate with others while still having the freedom to work independently (may be become an independent contractor or consultant at some point?)
- Have the opportunity to work internationally, at least for a few years
- I like the big bucks that corporate executives earn, but I don't want to live in the public eye like that or have to "play the game" to get ahead
- Believe I would be good manager, but not sure I want to spend all my time just managing people
- What to be known as an independent thinker and creative problem solver, as somebody who can analyze tough situations and figure out solutions that others might not consider
- Are there jobs where I could focus on troubleshooting, improving processes, or designing new systems?

What experiences from your past give you insight into where you would like to go in the future?

Where do you stand now in terms of your education and career, and what do you know about yourself?

What would you like your future to be? What do you like and dislike? What would you like to explore? If you haven't figured everything out yet, that's fine—as long as you've started to think about the future.

Figure 1 Writing the Story of You

Writing the "story of you" is a helpful way to think through where you've been in your life and career so far, where you are now, and where you would like to go from here. Remember that this is a private document designed to help you clarify your thoughts and plans, although you probably will find ways to adapt some of what you've written to various job-search documents, including your résumé.

You might find it helpful to think about the "story of you," the things you are passionate about, your skills, your ability to help an organization reach its goals, the path you've been on so far, and the path you want to follow in the future (see Figure 1). Think in terms of an image or a theme you'd like to project. Are you academically gifted? An effective leader? A well-rounded professional with wide-ranging talents? A creative problem solver? A technical wizard? Writing your story is a valuable planning exercise that helps you think about where you want to go and how to present yourself to target employers.

LEARNING TO THINK LIKE AN EMPLOYER

Employers judge their recruiting success by quality of hire, *and you can take steps to be—and look like—a high-quality hire.*

When you know your side of the hiring equation a little better, switch sides and look at it from an employer's perspective. To begin with, recognize that companies take risks with every hiring decision—the risk that the person hired won't meet expectations and the risk that a better candidate has slipped through their fingers. Many companies judge the success of their recruiting efforts by *quality of hire*, a measure of how closely new employees meet the company's needs.[2] Given this perspective, what steps can you take to present yourself as the low-risk, high-reward choice?

Of course, your perceived ability to perform the job is an essential part of your potential quality as a new hire. However, hiring managers consider more than just your ability to handle the job. They want to know if you'll be reliable and motivated—if you're somebody who "gets it" when it comes to being a professional in today's workplace. A great way to get inside the heads of corporate recruiters is to "listen in" on their professional conversations by reading periodicals such as *Workforce Management* and blogs such as Fistful of Talent and The HR Capitalist.

Follow the online conversations of professional recruiters to learn what their hot-button issues are.

RESEARCHING INDUSTRIES AND COMPANIES OF INTEREST

Learning more about professions, industries, and individual companies is a vital step in your job search. It also impresses employers, particularly when you go beyond the easily available sources such as a company's own website. "Detailed research, including talking to our customers, is so rare it will almost guarantee you get hired," explains the recruiting manager at Alcon Laboratories.[3]

Table 1 lists some of the many websites where you can learn more about companies and find job openings. Start with The Riley Guide, which offers advice for online job searches as well as links to hundreds of specialized websites that post openings in specific industries and professions. Your college's career center placement office probably maintains an up-to-date list as well.

To learn more about contemporary business topics, peruse leading business periodicals and newspapers with significant business sections (in some cases, you may need to go through your library's online databases in order to access back issues).

Employers expect you to be familiar with important developments in their industries, so stay on top of business news.

TABLE 1   Selected Job-Search Websites

Website*	URL	Highlights
Riley Guide	www.rileyguide.com	Vast collection of links to both general and specialized job sites for every career imaginable; don't miss this one—it could save you hours of searching
TweetMyJobs.com	http://tweetmyjobs.com	The largest Twitter job board, with thousands of channels segmented by geography, job type, and industry
CollegeRecruiter.com	www.collegerecruiter.com	Focused on opportunities for graduates with fewer than three years of work experience
Monster	www.monster.com	One of the most popular job sites, with hundreds of thousands of openings, many from hard-to-find small companies; extensive collection of advice on the job search process
MonsterCollege	http://college.monster.com	Focused on job searches for new college grads; your school's career center site probably links here
CareerBuilder	www.careerbuilder.com	One of the largest job boards; affiliated with more than 150 newspapers around the country
Jobster	www.jobster.com	Uses social networking to link employers with job seekers
USAJOBS	www.usajobs.gov	The official job-search site for the U.S. government, featuring everything from jobs for economists to astronauts to border patrol agents
IMDiversity	www.imdiversity.com	Good resource on diversity in the workplace, with job postings from companies that have made a special commitment to promoting diversity in their workforces
Dice.com	www.dice.com	One of the best sites for high-technology jobs
Net-Temps	www.net-temps.com	Popular site for contractors and freelancers looking for short-term assignments
InternshipPrograms.com	http://internshipprograms.com	Posts listings from companies looking for interns in a wide variety of professions
Simply Hired Indeed	www.simplyhired.com www.indeed.com	Specialized search engines that look for job postings on hundreds of websites worldwide; they find many postings that aren't listed on job board sites such as Monster

Note: This list represents only a small fraction of the hundreds of job-posting sites and other resources available online; be sure to check with your college's career center for the latest information.
Sources: Individual websites, all accessed 13 March 2015.

In addition, thousands of bloggers, microbloggers, and podcasters offer news and commentary on the business world. AllTop is another good resource for finding people who write about topics that interest you. In addition to learning more about professions and opportunities, this research will help you get comfortable with the jargon and buzzwords currently in use in a particular field, including essential *keywords* to use in your résumé.

Take advantage of job-search apps as well, including those offered by job posting websites and major employers You can use them to learn more about the company as well as specific jobs. See "Job Search Strategies: Maximize Your Mobile" for more tips on using a smartphone in your job search.

MOBILE APP

Indeed.com's mobile app lets you search for jobs and apply from your phone.

TRANSLATING YOUR GENERAL POTENTIAL INTO A SPECIFIC SOLUTION FOR EACH EMPLOYER

An essential task in your job search is presenting your skills and accomplishments in a way that is relevant to the employer's business challenges.

An important aspect of the employer's quality-of-hire challenge is trying to determine how well a candidate's attributes and experience will translate into the demands of a specific position. As a job candidate, customizing your résumé to each job opening is an important step in showing employers that you will be a good fit. As you can see from the sample résumés in Figures 4 through 6, customizing your résumé is not difficult if you have done your research. From your initial contact all the

---

DIGITAL + SOCIAL + MOBILE: TODAY'S COMMUNICATION ENVIRONMENT

Job Search Strategies: Maximize Your Mobile

The mobile business communication revolution is changing the way employers recruit new talent and the way job candidates look for opportunities. Many companies have optimized their careers websites for mobile access, and some have even developed mobile apps that offer everything from background information on what it's like to work there to application forms that you can fill out right on your phone.

However, don't be too quick to abandon a job application or an investigation into an employer just because the firm doesn't have a careers app or a mobile-friendly job site. Creating apps and mobile-friendly websites takes time and money, and many employers are still in the process of optimizing their online career materials for mobile devices. In a recent survey, 40 percent of mobile users said they would abandon a nonmobile job application—a distressingly high number in a slow job market. Don't miss a great opportunity just because an employer hasn't caught up to your mobile habits.

In addition to researching companies and applying for openings, integrating a mobile device into your job search strategy can help with networking and staying on top of your active job applications. For instance, some companies don't wait long after extending an offer; if they don't hear from the top candidate in a short amount of time, they'll move on their next choice. By staying plugged in via your mobile device, you won't let any opportunities pass you by.

Think of ways to use your mobile device to enhance your personal brand and your online portfolio. If you want to work in retail, for example, you could take photos of particularly good or particularly bad merchandising displays and post them with commentary on your social media accounts. Employers doing background research you on will see these

posts and recognize you as a candidate who is invested in his or her career and the industry as a whole. Many of the tools you can use to build your personal brand are available as mobile apps, including blogging platforms, Twitter, Facebook, and LinkedIn.

In addition, dozens of apps are available to help with various aspects of your job search. Résumé-creation apps let you quickly modify your résumé if you come across a good opportunity. Business-card scanning apps make it easy to keep digital copies of business cards, so you'll never lose important contact information. Note-taking apps are a great way to plan for interviews and record your post-interview notes. Use your phone's scheduling capability to make sure you never miss an interviewing or a filing deadline. Polish your interviewing skills with your phone's audio and video recording features or a practice-interview app. If an employer wants to interview you via Cisco Webex or another online meeting system, those apps are available for your phone or tablet as well.

You've been paying a lot for your mobile service—now make that mobile work for you by helping you land a great job.

CAREER APPLICATIONS

1. Would it be a good idea to present your online portfolio on your smartphone during a job interview? Why or why not?
2. Is it wise for applicants to shun a company that doesn't have a mobile-friendly careers website or a career app? Why or why not?

Sources: David Cohen, "Social Recruiting Goes Mobile," AllFacebook blog, 23 December 2013, http://allfacebook.com; Ryan Rancatore, "The 33 Best iPhone Apps For Personal Branding," Personal Branding 101 blog, 27 December 2009, http://personalbranding101.com; Jule Gamache, "The Rise of Mobile Job Search," Come Recommended blog, 12 June 2013, http://comerecommended.com.

way through the interviewing process, in fact, you will have opportunities to impress recruiters by explaining how your general potential translates to the specific needs of the position.

TAKING THE INITIATIVE TO FIND OPPORTUNITIES

When it comes to finding the right opportunities for you, the easiest ways are not always the most productive ways. The major job boards such as Monster and classified services such as Craigslist might have thousands of openings, but thousands of job seekers are looking at and applying for these same openings. Moreover, posting job openings on these sites is often a company's last resort, after it has exhausted other possibilities.

To maximize your chances, take the initiative and go seek opportunities. Identify the companies you want to work for and focus your efforts on them. Get in touch with their human resources departments (or individual managers, if possible), describe what you can offer the company, and ask to be considered if any opportunities come up.[4] Reach out to company representatives on social networks. Your message might appear right when a company is busy looking for someone but hasn't yet advertised the opening to the outside world. And be sure to take advantage of the growing number of career-related mobile apps (see Figure 2).

Don't hesitate to contact interesting companies even if they haven't advertised job openings to the public yet; they might be looking for somebody just like you.

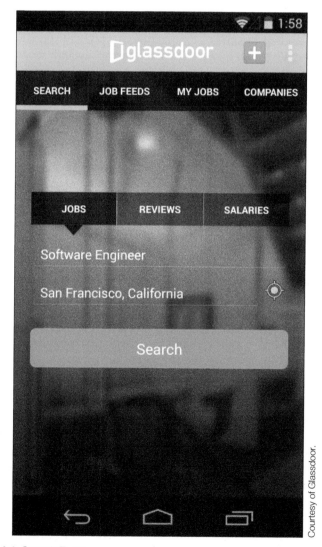

Courtesy of Glassdoor.

Figure 2   Mobile Job Search Tools
Put your mobile phone or tablet to work in your job search, using some of the many employment apps now available.

BUILDING YOUR NETWORK

Networking is the process of making informal connections with mutually beneficial business contacts. Networking takes place wherever and whenever people talk: at industry functions, at social gatherings, at alumni reunions—and all over the Internet, from LinkedIn and Twitter to Facebook and Google+. In addition to making connections through social media tools, you might get yourself noticed by company recruiters.

Networking is more essential than ever because the vast majority of job openings are never advertised to the general public. To avoid the time and expense of sifting through thousands of applications and the risk of hiring complete strangers, most companies prefer to ask their employees for recommendations first.[5] The more people who know you, the better chance you have of being recommended for one of these hidden job openings.

Start thinking like a networker now; your classmates could turn out to be some of your most important business contacts.

Start building your network now, before you need it. Your classmates could end up being some of your most valuable contacts, if not right away then possibly later in your career. Then branch out by identifying people with similar interests in your target professions, industries, and companies. Read news sites, blogs, and other online sources. Follow industry leaders on Twitter. You can also follow individual executives at your target companies to learn about their interests and concerns.[6] Be on the lookout for career-oriented *Tweetups*, in which people who've connected on Twitter get together for in-person networking events. Connect with people on LinkedIn and Facebook, particularly in groups dedicated to particular career interests. Depending on the system and the settings on individual users' accounts, you may be able to introduce yourself via public or private messages. Just make sure you are respectful of people, and don't take up much of their time.[7]

MOBILE APP
Stay in touch with your professional network with LinkedIn's mobile app.

Participate in student business organizations, especially those with ties to professional organizations. Visit *trade shows* to learn about various industries and rub shoulders with people who work in those industries.[8] Don't overlook volunteering; you not only meet people but also demonstrate your ability to solve problems, manage projects, and lead others. You can do some good while creating a network for yourself.

Networking is a mutual beneficial activity, so look for opportunities to help others in some way.

Remember that networking is about people helping each other, not just about other people helping you. Pay close attention to networking etiquette: Try to learn something about the people you want to connect with, don't overwhelm others with too many messages or requests, be succinct in all your communication efforts, don't give out other people's names and contact information without their permission to do so, never email your résumé to complete strangers, and remember to say thank you every time someone helps you.[9]

To become a valued network member, you need to be able to help others in some way. You may not have any influential contacts yet, but because you're researching industries and trends as part of your own job search, you probably have valuable information you can share via your online and offline networks. Or you might simply be able to connect one person with another who can help. The more you network, the more valuable you become in your network—and the more valuable your network becomes to you.

Finally, be aware that your online network reflects on who you are in the eyes of potential employers, so exercise some judgment in making connections. Also, many employers now contact people in a candidate's public network for background information, even if the candidate doesn't list those people as references.[10]

SEEKING CAREER COUNSELING

Don't overlook the many resources available through your college's career center.

Your college's career center probably offers a wide variety of services, including individual counseling, job fairs, on-campus interviews, and job listings. Counselors can advise on career planning and provide workshops on job search techniques, résumé preparation, job readiness training, interview techniques, self-marketing, and more.[11] You can also find career planning advice online. Many of the websites listed in Table 1 offer articles and online tests to help you choose a career path, identify essential skills, and prepare to enter the job market.

AVOIDING MISTAKES

Don't let a silly mistake knock you out of contention for a great job.

While you're making all these positive moves to show employers you will be a quality hire, take care to avoid the simple blunders that can torpedo a job search, such as not catching

Striving to Excel

Pros are good at what they do, and they never stop improving. No matter what your job might be at any given time—even if it is far from where you aspire to be—strive to perform at the highest possible level. Not only do you have an ethical obligation to give your employer and your customers your best effort, but excelling at each level in your career is also the best way to keep climbing up to new positions of responsibility. Plus, being good at what you do delivers a sense of satisfaction that is hard to beat.

In many jobs and in many industries, performing at a high level requires a commitment to continuous learning and improvement. The nature of the work often changes as markets and technologies evolve, and expectations of quality tend to increase over time as well. View this constant change as a positive thing, as a way to avoid stagnation and boredom.

Striving to excel can be a challenge when there is a mismatch between the job's requirements and your skills and knowledge. If you are underqualified for a job, you need to identify your weaknesses quickly and come up with a plan to address them. A supportive manager will help you identify these areas and encourage improvement through training or mentoring. Don't wait for a boss to tell you your work is sub-par, however. If you know you're floundering, don't wait until you've failed to get help.

If you are overqualified for a job, it's easy to slip into a rut and eventually underperform simply because you aren't being challenged. However, current and future bosses aren't going to judge you on how well you performed relative to your needs and expectations; they're going to judge you on how well you performed relative to job's requirements. Work with your boss to find ways to make your job more challenging if possible, or start looking for a better job if necessary, but be sure to maintain your level of performance until you can bring your responsibilities and talents into closer alignment.

CAREER APPLICATIONS

1. Should you ever try to sell yourself into a job for which you are not yet 100 percent qualified? Explain your answer.
2. Do you agree that you have an ethical obligation to excel at your job? Why or why not?

mistakes in your résumé, misspelling the name of a manager you're writing to, showing up late for an interview, tweeting something unprofessional, failing to complete application forms correctly, asking for information that you can easily find yourself on a company's website, or making any other error that could flag you as someone who is careless or disrespectful. Assume that every employer will conduct an online search on you. Busy recruiters will seize on these errors as a way to narrow the list of candidates they need to spend time on, so don't give them a reason to toss out your résumé.

Planning Your Résumé

2 LEARNING OBJECTIVE
Explain the process of planning your résumé, including how to choose the best résumé organization.

Although you will create many messages during your career search, your **résumé**, a structured, written summary of your education, employment background, and job qualifications, will be the most important document in this process. You will be able to use it directly in many instances, adapt it to a variety of uses such an e-portfolio or a social media résumé, and reuse pieces of it in social networking profiles and online application forms. Even if you apply to a company that doesn't want to see résumés from applicants, the process of developing your résumé will prepare you for interviewing and preemployment testing.

Developing a résumé is one of those projects that really benefits from multiple planning, writing, and completing sessions spread out over several days or weeks. You are trying to summarize a complex subject (yourself!) and present a compelling story to strangers in a brief document. Follow the three-step writing process (see Figure 3 on the next page) and give yourself plenty of time.

Before you dive into your résumé, be aware that you will find a wide range of opinions about résumés, regarding everything from appropriate length, content, design, distribution methods, and acceptable degrees of creativity to whether it even makes sense to write a traditional résumé in this age of online applications. For example, you may encounter a prospective employer that wants you to tweet your résumé or submit all the links that make up your online presence, rather than submit a conventional résumé.[12] You may run across examples of effective résumés that were produced as infographics, interactive

1 Plan →	2 Write →	3 Complete
Analyze the Situation Recognize that the purpose of your résumé is to get an interview, not to get a job. **Gather Information** Research target industries and companies so that you know what they're looking for in new hires; learn about various jobs and what to expect; learn about the hiring manager, if possible. **Choose Media and Channels** Start with a traditional paper résumé and develop scannable, plain text, PDF, and social/online versions, as needed. Consider other formats as supplements. **Organize the Information** Choose an organizational model that highlights your strengths and downplays your shortcomings; use the chronological approach unless you have a strong reason not to.	**Adapt to Your Audience** Plan your wording carefully so that you can catch a recruiter's eye within seconds; translate your education and experience into attributes that target employers find valuable. **Compose the Message** Write clearly and succinctly, using active, powerful language that is appropriate to the industries and companies you're targeting; use a professional tone in all communications.	**Revise the Message** Evaluate content and review readability and then edit and rewrite for conciseness and clarity. **Produce the Message** Use effective design elements and suitable layout for a clean, professional appearance; seamlessly combine text and graphical elements. When printing, use quality paper and a good printer. **Proofread the Message** Review for errors in layout, spelling, and mechanics; mistakes can cost you interview opportunities. **Distribute the Message** Deliver your résumé, carefully following the specific instructions of each employer or job board website.

Figure 3   Three-Step Writing Process for Résumés
Following the three-step writing process will help you create a successful résumé in a short time. Remember to pay particular attention to the "you" attitude and presentation quality; your résumé will probably get tossed aside if it doesn't speak to audience needs or if it contains mistakes.

videos, simulated search engine results, puzzles, games, graphic novels—you name it, somebody has probably tried it.

When you hear conflicting advice or see trendy concepts that you might be tempted to try, remember the most important question in business communication: What is the most effective way to adapt your message to the individual needs of each member of your audience? An approach that is wildly successful with one company or in one industry could be a complete disaster in another industry. To forge your own successful path through this maze of information, get inside the heads of the people you are trying to reach—try to think the way they think—and then apply the principles of effective communication you are learning in this course.

ANALYZING YOUR PURPOSE AND AUDIENCE

Planning an effective résumé starts with understanding its true function—as a brief, persuasive business message intended to stimulate an employer's interest in meeting you and learning more about you (see Table 2). In other words, the purpose of a résumé is not to get you a job but rather to get you an interview.[13]

As you conduct your research on various professions, industries, companies, and individual managers, you will have a better perspective on your target readers and their information needs. Learn as much as you can about the individuals who may be reading your résumé. Many professionals and managers are bloggers, Twitter users, and LinkedIn members, for example, so you can learn more about them online even if you've never met them. Any bit of information can help you craft a more effective message.

You will see lots of ideas and even some conflicting advice about résumés; use what you know about effective business communication to decide what is right for your résumés.

Once you view your résumé as a persuasive business message, it's easier to decide what should and shouldn't be in it.

Thanks to Twitter, LinkedIn, and other social media, you can often learn valuable details about individual managers in your target employers.

TABLE 2 Fallacies and Facts About Résumés	
Fallacy	**Fact**
The purpose of a résumé is to list all your skills and abilities.	The purpose of a résumé is to kindle employer interest and generate an interview.
A good résumé will get you the job you want.	All a résumé can do is get you in the door.
Your résumé will always be read carefully and thoroughly.	In most cases, your résumé needs to make a positive impression within a few seconds; only then will someone read it in detail. Moreover, it will likely be screened by a computer looking for keywords first—and if it doesn't contain the right keywords, a human being may never see it.
The more good information you present about yourself in your résumé, the better, so stuff your résumé with every positive detail.	Recruiters don't need that much information about you at the initial screening stage, and they probably won't read it.

By the way, if employers ask to see your "CV," they're referring to your *curriculum vitae*, the term used instead of *résumé* in academic professions and in many countries outside the United States. Résumés and CVs are essentially the same, although CVs can be much more detailed and include personal information that is not included in a résumé.

REAL-TIME UPDATES

LEARN MORE BY VISITING THIS WEBSITE

Converting your résumé to a CV

If you need to convert your U.S-style résumé to the *curriculum vitae* format used in many other countries (and in many academic positions in the United States), this website will tell you everything you need to know. Go to http://real-timeupdates.com/ebc12 and click on Learn More in the Students section.

GATHERING PERTINENT INFORMATION

If you haven't been building an employment portfolio thus far, you may need to do some research on yourself at this point. Gather all the pertinent personal history you can think of, including all the specific dates, duties, and accomplishments from any previous jobs you've held. Compile all your educational accomplishments, including formal degrees, training certificates, professional and technical certifications, academic awards, and scholarships. Also, gather information about school or volunteer activities that might be relevant to your job search, including offices you have held in any club or professional organization, presentations given, and online or print publications. You probably won't use every piece of information you come up with, but you'll want to have it at your fingertips.

SELECTING THE BEST MEDIA AND CHANNELS

You should expect to produce your résumé in several media and formats. "Producing Your Résumé" discusses your options.

ORGANIZING YOUR RÉSUMÉ AROUND YOUR STRENGTHS

Although there are a number of ways to organize a résumé, most are some variation of chronological, functional, or a combination of the two. The right choice depends on your background and your goals.

The Chronological Résumé

In a **chronological résumé**, the work experience section dominates and is placed immediately after your contact information and introductory statement (see Figure 6 for an example). The chronological approach is the most common way to organize a résumé, and many employers prefer this format because it presents your professional history in a clear, easy-to-follow arrangement.[14] If you're just graduating from college and have limited professional experience, you can vary this chronological approach by putting your educational qualifications before your experience.

Develop your work experience section by listing your jobs in reverse chronological order, beginning with the most recent one and giving more space to the most recent positions you've held. For each job, start by listing the employer's name and location, your

The chronological résumé is the most common approach, but it might not be right for you at this stage in your career.

official job title, and the dates you held the position (write "to present" if you are still in your most recent job). Next, in a short block of text, highlight your accomplishments in a way that is relevant and understandable to your readers. If the general responsibilities of the position are not obvious from the job title, provide a little background to help readers understand what you did.

The Functional Résumé

The functional résumé is often considered by people with limited or spotty employment history, but many employers are suspicious of this format.

A **functional résumé**, sometimes called a *skills résumé*, emphasizes your skills and capabilities, identifying employers and academic experience in subordinate sections. This arrangement stresses individual areas of competence rather than job history. The functional approach has three benefits: (1) Without having to read through job descriptions, employers can get an idea of what you can do for them; (2) you can emphasize previous job experience through the skills you gained in those positions; and (3) you can deemphasize any lengthy unemployment or lack of career progress. However, you should be aware that because the functional résumé can obscure your work history, many employment professionals are suspicious of it.[15] Moreover, it lacks the evidence of job experience that supports your skills claims. If you don't believe the chronological format will work for you, consider the combination résumé instead.

The Combination Résumé

If you don't have a lot of work history to show, consider a combination résumé to highlight your skills while still providing a chronological history of your employment.

A **combination résumé** meshes the skills focus of the functional format with the job history focus of the chronological format. Figures 4 and 5 show examples of combination résumés. The chief advantage of this format is that it allows you to highlight your capabilities and education when you don't have a long or steady employment history, without raising concerns that you might be hiding something about your past.

As you look at a number of sample résumés, you'll probably notice many variations on the three basic formats presented here. Study these other options in light of the effective communication principles you've learned in this course and the unique circumstances of your job search. If you find one that seems like the best fit for your unique situation, by all means use it.

ADDRESSING AREAS OF CONCERN

Many people have gaps in their careers or other issues that could be a concern for employers. Here are some common issues and suggestions for handling them in a résumé:[16]

- **Frequent job changes.** If you've had a number of short-term jobs of a similar type, such as independent contracting and temporary assignments, you can group them under a single heading. Also, if past job positions were eliminated as a result of layoffs or mergers, find a subtle way to convey that information (if not in your résumé, then in your cover letter). Reasonable employers understand that many professionals have been forced to job hop by circumstances beyond their control.
- **Gaps in work history.** Mention relevant experience and education you gained during employment gaps, such as volunteer or community work.
- **Inexperience.** Mention related volunteer work and membership in professional groups. List relevant course work and internships.
- **Overqualification.** Tone down your résumé, focusing exclusively on the experience and skills that relate to the position.
- **Long-term employment with one company.** Itemize each position held at the firm to show growth within the organization and increasing responsibilities along the way.
- **Job termination for cause.** Be honest with interviewers and address their concerns with proof, such as recommendations and examples of completed projects.

REAL-TIME UPDATES

LEARN MORE BY READING THIS ARTICLE

Smart strategies to explain gaps in your work history

Get three key pieces of advice if you have been or were out of work for a period of time. Go to http://real-timeupdates.com/ebc12 and click on Learn More in the Students section.

- **Criminal record.** You don't necessarily need to disclose a criminal record or time spent incarcerated on your résumé, but you may be asked about it on job application forms. Laws regarding what employers may ask (and whether they can conduct a criminal background check) vary by state and profession, but if you are asked and the question applies to you, you are legally bound to answer truthfully. Use the interview process to explain any mitigating circumstances and to emphasize your rehabilitation and commitment to being a law-abiding, trustworthy employee.[17]

Writing Your Résumé

3 LEARNING OBJECTIVE
Describe the tasks involved in writing your résumé, and list the major sections of a traditional résumé.

With the necessary information and a good plan in hand, you're ready to begin writing. If you feel uncomfortable writing about yourself, you're not alone. Many people, even accomplished writers, can find it difficult to write their own résumés. If you get stuck, imagine you are somebody else, writing a résumé for this person called you. By "being your own client" in this sense, you might find the words and idea flow more easily. You can also find a classmate or friend who is writing a résumé and swap projects for a while. Working on each other's résumés might speed up the process for both of you.

If you're uncomfortable writing your own résumé, you might try to trade with a classmate and write each other's résumé.

KEEPING YOUR RÉSUMÉ HONEST

Estimates vary, but one comprehensive study uncovered lies about work history in more than 40 percent of the résumés tested.[18] And dishonest applicants are getting bolder all the time—going so far as to buy fake diplomas online, pay a computer hacker to insert their names into prestigious universities' graduation records, and sign up for services that offer phony employment verification.[19] "It's becoming common to cheat," observes Professor George Gollin of the University of Illinois, Urbana, mentioning the 200,000 fake college degrees sold every year as one example.[20]

REAL-TIME UPDATES
LEARN MORE BY WATCHING THIS VIDEO
Learn to use LinkedIn's résumé builder
See how to build and customize a résumé on LinkedIn and then use it on other social networking sites. Go to http://real-timeupdates .com/ebc12 and click on Learn More in the Students section.

Applicants with integrity know they don't need to stoop to lying. If you are tempted to stretch the truth, bear in mind that professional recruiters have seen all sorts of fraud by job applicants, and frustrated employers are working aggressively to uncover the truth. Nearly all employers do some form of background checking, from contacting references and verifying employment to checking criminal records and sending résumés through verification services.[21] Employers are also beginning to craft certain interview questions specifically to uncover dishonest résumé entries.[22]

Résumé fraud has reached epidemic proportions, but employers are fighting back with more rigorous screening techniques.

More than 90 percent of companies that find lies on résumés refuse to hire the offending applicants, even if that means withdrawing formal job offers.[23] And if you do sneak past these filters and get hired, you'll probably be exposed on the job when you can't live up to your own résumé. Given the networked nature of today's job market, lying on a résumé could haunt you for years—and you could be forced to keep lying throughout your career to hide the misrepresentations on your original résumé.[24]

MOBILE APP
Need a simple résumé in a hurry? Resume App Pro and Resume Builder Pro let you build one right on your phone.

ADAPTING YOUR RÉSUMÉ TO YOUR AUDIENCE

The importance of adapting your résumé to your target readers' needs and interests cannot be overstated. In a competitive job market, the more you look like a good fit—a quality hire—the better your chances of securing interviews. Address your readers' business concerns by showing how your capabilities meet the demands and expectations of the position and the organization as a whole.

Translate your past accomplishments into a compelling picture of what you can do for employers in the future.

For example, an in-house public relations (PR) department and an independent PR agency perform many of the same tasks, but the outside agency must also sell its services to multiple clients. Consequently, it needs employees who are skilled at attracting and keeping paying customers, in addition to being skilled at PR. If you are applying for both in-house and agency PR jobs, you need to adapt your résumé for each of these audiences.

Building Careers and Writing Résumés

REAL-TIME UPDATES

LEARN MORE BY READING THIS INFOGRAPHIC

See how an applicant tracking system handles your résumé

Once you see how the system works, you'll understand why it's so crucial to customize the wording on your résumé for every job opening. Go to http://real-timeupdates.com/ebc12 and click on Learn More in the Students section.

Military service and other specialized experiences may need to be "translated" into terms more readily understandable by your target readers.

An essential step in adapting your résumé is using the same terminology as the employer uses to describe job responsibilities and professional accomplishments. In Figures 4 through 6, you can see how the sample résumés do this, echoing key terms and phrases from the job postings. With the rise of automated **applicant tracking systems**, which attempt to analyze the content of résumés in order to find good matches with company job descriptions, aligning your language to the employer's will help you get past the keyword filters these systems use to rank incoming résumés.

If you are applying for business positions after military service or moving from one industry to another, you may need to "translate" your experience into the language of your target employers. For instance, military experience can help you develop many skills that are valuable in business, but military terminology can sound like a foreign language to people who aren't familiar with it. Isolate the important general concepts and present them in the business language your target employers use.

COMPOSING YOUR RÉSUMÉ

Draft your résumé using short, crisp phrases built around strong verbs and nouns.

Write your résumé using a simple and direct style. Use short, crisp phrases instead of whole sentences and focus on what your reader needs to know. Avoid using the word *I*, which can sound both self-involved and repetitive by the time you outline all your skills and accomplishments. Instead, start your phrases with strong action verbs such as these:[25]

accomplished	coordinated	initiated	participated	set up
achieved	created	installed	performed	simplified
administered	demonstrated	introduced	planned	sparked
approved	developed	investigated	presented	streamlined
arranged	directed	launched	proposed	strengthened
assisted	established	maintained	raised	succeeded
assumed	explored	managed	recommended	supervised
budgeted	forecasted	motivated	reduced	systematized
chaired	generated	negotiated	reorganized	targeted
changed	identified	operated	resolved	trained
compiled	implemented	organized	saved	transformed
completed	improved	oversaw	served	upgraded

For example, you might say, "Created a campus organization for students interested in entrepreneurship" or "Managed a fast-food restaurant and four employees." Whenever you can, quantify the results so that your claims don't come across as empty puffery. Don't just say that you're a team player or detail oriented—show that you are by offering concrete proof.[26] Here are some examples of phrasing accomplishments using active statements that show results:

Instead of This	Write Active Statements That Show Results
Responsible for developing a new filing system	Developed a new filing system that reduced paperwork by 50 percent
I was in charge of customer complaints and all ordering problems	Handled all customer complaints and resolved all product order discrepancies
I won a trip to Europe for opening the most new customer accounts in my department	Generated the highest number of new customer accounts in my department
Member of special campus task force to resolve student problems with existing cafeteria assignments	Assisted in implementing new campus dining program that balances student wishes with cafeteria capacity

Providing specific supporting evidence is vital, but make sure you don't go overboard with details.[27] Carefully select the most compelling evidence so that your message is clear and immediate.

In addition to clear writing with specific examples, the particular words and phrases used throughout your résumé are critically important. The majority of résumés are now subjected to *keyword searches* in an applicant tracking system or other database, in which a recruiter searches for résumés most likely to match the requirements of a particular job. Résumés that don't closely match the requirements may never be seen by a human reader, so it is essential to use the words and phrases that a recruiter is most likely to search on. (Although most experts used to advise including a separate *keyword summary* as a standalone list, the trend nowadays is to incorporate your keywords into your introductory statement and other sections of your résumé.)[28]

> Include relevant *keywords* in your introductory statement, work history, and education sections.

Identifying these keywords requires some research, but you can uncover many of them while you are looking into various industries and companies. In particular, study job descriptions carefully. In contrast to the action verbs that catch a human reader's attention, keywords that catch a computer's attention are usually nouns that describe the specific skills, attributes, and experiences an employer is looking for in a candidate. Keywords can include the business and technical terms associated with a specific profession, industry-specific jargon, names or types of products or systems used in a profession, job titles, and college degrees.[29]

REAL-TIME UPDATES

LEARN MORE BY VISITING THIS WEBSITE

Find the keywords that will light up your résumé

This list of tips and tools will help you find the right keywords to customize your résumé for every opportunity. Go to http://real-timeupdates.com/ebc12 and click on Learn More in the Students section.

Name and Contact Information

Your name and contact information constitute the heading of your résumé; include the following:

- Name
- Address (both permanent and temporary, if you're likely to move during the job-search process)
- Email address
- Phone number(s)
- The URL of your personal webpage, e-portfolio, or social media résumé (if you have one)

> Be sure to provide complete and accurate contact information; mistakes in this section of the résumé are surprisingly common.

If the only email address you have is through your current employer, get a free personal email address from one of the many services that offer them. It's not fair to your current employer to use company resources for a job search, and doing so sends a bad signal to potential employers. Also, if your personal email address is anything like precious.princess@something.com or PsychoDawg@something.com, get a new email address for your business correspondence.

> Use a professional-sounding email address for business correspondence, such as *firstname.lastname@something.com*).

Introductory Statement

Of all the parts of a résumé, the brief introductory statement that follows your name and contact information probably generates the most disagreement. You can put one of three things here:[30]

> You can choose to open with a career objective, a qualifications summary, or a career summary.

- **Career objective.** A career objective identifies either a specific job you want to land or a general career track you would like to pursue. Some experts advise against including a career objective because it can categorize you so narrowly that you miss out on interesting opportunities, and it is essentially about fulfilling your desires, not about meeting the employer's needs. In the past, most résumés included a career objective, but in recent years more job seekers are using a qualifications summary or a career summary. However, if you have little or no work experience in your target profession, a career objective might be your best option. If you do opt for an objective, word it in a way that relates your qualifications to employer needs.
- **Qualifications summary.** A qualifications summary offers a brief view of your key qualifications. The goal is to let a reader know within a few seconds what you

can deliver. You can title this section generically as "Qualifications Summary" or "Summary of Qualifications," or, if you have one dominant qualification, you can use that as the title. Consider using a qualifications summary if you have one or more important qualifications but don't yet have a long career history. Also, if you haven't been working long but your college education has given you a dominant professional "theme," such as multimedia design or statistical analysis, you can craft a qualifications summary that highlights your educational preparedness.

- **Career summary.** A career summary offers a brief recap of your career with the goal of presenting increasing levels of responsibility and performance (see Figure 6 for an example). A career summary can be particularly useful for managers who have demonstrated the ability to manage increasingly larger and more complicated business operations—a key consideration when companies look to hire upper-level executives.

Whichever option you choose, make sure it includes many of the essential keywords you identified in your research—and adapt these words and phrases to each job opportunity as needed.

Education

If you're still in college or have recently graduated, education is probably your strongest selling point. Present your educational background in depth, choosing facts that support your professional theme. Give this section a heading such as "Education," "Technical Training," or "Academic Preparation," as appropriate. Then, starting with the most recent, list the name and location of each school you have attended, the month and year of your graduation (say "anticipated graduation: ____" if you haven't graduated yet), your major and minor fields of study, significant skills and abilities you've developed in your course work, and the degrees or certificates you've earned. Fine-tune your message by listing courses that are most relevant to each job opening, and indicate any scholarships, awards, or academic honors you've received.

The education section should also include relevant training sponsored by business or government organizations. Mention high school or military training only if the associated achievements are pertinent to your career goals.

Whether you list your grade point average depends on the job you want and the quality of your grades. If you don't show your GPA on your résumé—and there's no rule saying you have to—be prepared to answer questions about it during the interview process because many employers will assume that your GPA is not spectacular if you didn't list it on your résumé. If you choose to show a grade point average, be sure to mention the scale, especially if it isn't a four-point scale. If your grades are better within your major than in other courses, you can also list your GPA as "Major GPA" and include only those courses within your major.

Work Experience, Skills, and Accomplishments

This section can be called "Work Experience," "Professional Experience," or "Work and Volunteer Experience," if you have limited work experience and want to bolster that with volunteer experience. Like the education section, the work experience section should focus on your overall theme in a way that shows how your past can contribute to an employer's future. Use keywords to call attention to the skills you've developed on the job and to your ability to handle responsibility. Emphasize what you accomplished in each position, not just the generic responsibilities of the job.

List your jobs in reverse chronological order, starting with the most recent. Include military service and any internships and part-time or temporary jobs related to your career objective. Include the name and location of the employer, and if readers are unlikely to recognize the organization, briefly describe what it does. When you want to keep the name of your current employer confidential, you can identify the firm by industry only ("a large video game developer"). If an organization's name or location has changed since you worked there, state the current name and location and include the old information preceded by "formerly..." Before or after each job listing, state your job title and give the

If you have a reasonably focused skill set but don't yet have a long career history, a qualifications summary is probably the best type of introductory statement for you.

If you are early in your career, your education is probably your strongest selling point.

When you describe past job responsibilities, identify the skills and knowledge that you can apply to a future job.

years you worked in the job; use the phrase "to present" to denote current employment. Indicate whether a job was part time.

Devote the most space to the jobs that are most recent or most closely related to your target position. If you were personally responsible for something significant, be sure to mention it. Facts about your skills and accomplishments are the most important information you can give a prospective employer, so quantify them whenever possible.

One helpful exercise is to write a 30-second "commercial" for each major skill you want to highlight. The commercial should offer proof that you really do possess the skill. For your résumé, distill the commercials down to brief phrases; you can use the more detailed proof statements in cover letters and as answers to interview questions.[31]

If you have a number of part-time, temporary, or entry-level jobs that don't relate to your career objective, you have to use your best judgment when it comes to including or excluding them. Too many minor and irrelevant work details can clutter your résumé, particularly if you've been in the professional workforce for a few years. However, if you don't have a long employment history, including these jobs shows your ability and willingness to keep working.

> Devote the most space to jobs that are related to your target position.

Activities and Achievements

This optional section can be used to highlight activities and achievements outside of a work or educational context—but only if they make you a more attractive job candidate. For example, traveling, studying, or working abroad and fluency in multiple languages could weigh heavily in your favor with employers who do business internationally.

Because many employers are involved in their local communities, they tend to look positively on applicants who are active and concerned members of their communities as well. Consider including community service activities that suggest leadership, teamwork, communication skills, technical aptitude, or other valuable attributes.

You should generally avoid indicating membership or significant activity in religious or political organizations (unless, of course, you're applying to such an organization) because doing so might raise concerns for people with differing beliefs or affiliations. However, if you want to highlight skills you developed while involved with such a group, you can refer to it generically as a "not-for-profit organization."

Finally, if you have little or no job experience and not much to discuss outside of your education, indicating involvement in athletics or other organized student activities lets employers know that you don't spend all your free time hanging around your apartment playing video games. Also consider mentioning publications, projects, and other accomplishments that required relevant business skills.

> Include personal accomplishments only if they suggest special skills or qualities that are relevant to the jobs you're seeking.

Personal Data and References

In nearly all instances, your résumé should not include any personal data beyond the information described in the previous sections. When applying to U.S. companies, never include any of the following: physical characteristics, age, gender, marital status, sexual orientation, religious or political affiliations, race, national origin, salary history, reasons for leaving jobs, names of previous supervisors, names of references, Social Security number, or student ID number.

However, be aware that standards can vary in other countries. For example, some international employers might require you to include your citizenship, nationality, or marital status.[32]

The availability of references is assumed, so you don't need to put "References available upon request" at the end of your résumé. However, be sure to have a list of several references ready when you begin applying for jobs. Prepare your reference sheet with your name and contact information at the top. For a finished look, use the same design and layout you use for your résumé. Then list three or four people who have agreed to serve as references. Include each person's name, job title, organization, address, telephone number, email address (if the reference prefers to be contacted by email), and the nature of your relationship.

Figures 4 through 6 show how a job applicant can put these guidelines to work in three job-search scenarios.

> When applying to U.S. companies, your résumé should not include any personal data such as age, marital status, physical description, or Social Security number.

> Prepare a list of references but don't include them on your résumé.

The Scenario

You are about to graduate and have found a job opening that is in your chosen field. You don't have any experience in this field, but the courses you've taken in pursuit of your degree have given you a solid academic foundation for this position.

The Opportunity

The job opening is for an associate market analyst with Living Social, the rapidly growing advertising and social commerce service that describes itself as "the online source for discovering valuable local experiences." (A market analyst researches markets to find potentially profitable business opportunities.)

The Communication Challenge

You don't have directly relevant experience as a market analyst, and you might be competing against people who do. Your education is your strongest selling point, so you need to show how your coursework relates to the position.

Don't let your lack of experience hold you back; the job posting makes it clear that this is an entry-level position. For example, the first bullet point in the job description says "Become an expert in market data . . .," and the required skills and experience section says that "Up to 2 years of experience with similar research and analysis is preferred." The important clues here are *become* (the company doesn't expect you to be an expert already) and *preferred* (experience would be great if you have it, but it's not required).

Keywords and Key Phrases

You study the job posting and highlight the following elements:

1. Working in a team environment
2. Research, including identifying trendy new businesses
3. Analyzing data using Microsoft Excel
4. Managing projects
5. Collaborating with technical experts and sales staff
6. Creating new tools to help maximize revenue and minimize risks
7. Bachelor's degree is required
8. Natural curiosity and desire to learn
9. Detail oriented
10. Hands-on experience with social media

Emma Gomes

(847) 555–2153
emma.gomes@mailsystem.net
emmawrites.blogspot.com

Address:
860 North 8th Street, Terre Haute, IN 47809

Permanent Address:
993 Church Street, Barrington, IL 60010

Summary of Qualifications

- In-depth academic preparation in marketing analysis techniques
- Intermediate skills with a variety of analytical tools, including Microsoft Excel and Google Analytics
- Front-line experience with consumers and business owners
- Multiple research and communication projects involving the business applications of social media

Education

B.S. in Marketing (Marketing Management Track), Indiana State University, Terre Haute, IN, anticipated graduation: May 2014

Program coursework

- 45 credits of core business courses, including Business Information Tools, Business Statistics, Principles of Accounting, and Business Finance
- 27 credits of marketing and marketing management courses, including Buyer Behavior, Marketing Research, Product and Pricing Strategy, and seminars in e-commerce and social media

Special projects

- "Handcrafting a Global Marketplace: The Etsy Phenomenon," in-depth analysis of how Etsy transformed the market for handmade craft items by bringing e-commerce capabilities to individual craftspeople
- "Hybrid Communication Platforms for Small Businesses," team service project for five small businesses in Terre Haute, recommending best practices for combining traditional and social-media methods of customer engagement and providing a customized measurement spreadsheet for each company

Work and Volunteer Experience

Independent math tutor, 2009-present. Assist students with a variety of math courses at the elementary, junior high, and high school level; all clients have achieved combined test and homework score improvements of at least one full letter grade, with an average improvement of 38 percent

Volunteer, LeafSpring Food Bank, Terre Haute, IN (weekends during college terms, 2012–present). Stock food and supply pantries; prepare emergency baskets for new clients; assist director with public relations activities, including website updates and social media news releases.

Customer care agent, Owings Ford, Barrington, IL (summers, 2011–2013). Assisted the service and sales managers of this locally owned car dealership with a variety of customer-service tasks; scheduled service appointments; designed and implemented improvements to service-center waiting room to increase guest comfort; convinced dealership owners to begin using Twitter and Facebook to interact with current and potential customers.

Professional Engagement

- Collegiate member, American Marketing Association; helped establish the AMA Collegiate Chapter at Indiana State
- Participated in AMA International Collegiate Case Competition, 2011-2012

Awards

- Dean's List: 2012, 2013
- Forward Youth award, Barrington Chamber of Commerce, 2010

Notice how Gomes adapts her résumé to "mirror" the keywords and phrases from the job posting:

1. Offers concrete evidence of teamwork (rather than just calling herself a "team player," for example)
2. Emphasizes research skills and experience in multiple instances
3. Calls out Microsoft Excel, as well as Google Analytics, a key online tool for measuring activity on websites
4. Indicates the ability to plan and carry out projects, even if she doesn't have formal project management experience
5. Indicates some experience working in a supportive or collaborative role with technical experts and sales specialists (the content of the work doesn't translate to the new job, but the concept does)
6. Suggests the ability to work with new analytical tools
7. Displays her B.S. degree prominently
8. Demonstrates a desire to learn and to expand her skills
9. Tracking the progress of her tutoring clients is strong evidence of a detail-oriented worker—not to mention someone who cares about results and the quality of her work
10. Lists business-oriented experience with Facebook, Twitter, and other social media

Figure 4   Crafting Your Résumé, Scenario 1: Positioning Yourself for an Ideal Opportunity
Even for an ideal job-search scenario, where your academic and professional experiences and interests closely match the parameters of the job opening, you still need to adapt your résumé content carefully to "echo" the specific language of the job description.[42]

Building Careers and Writing Résumés

The Scenario

You are about to graduate but can't find job openings in the field you'd like to enter. However, you have found an opening that is in a related field, and it would give you the chance to get some valuable work experience.

The Opportunity

The job opening is for a seller support associate with Amazon, the online retail giant. Employees in this position work with merchants that sell products through the Amazon e-commerce system to make sure merchants are successful. In essence, it is a customer service job, but directed at these merchants, not the consumers who buy on Amazon.

The Communication Challenge

This isn't the job you ultimately want, but it is a great opportunity with a well-known company.

You note that the position does not require a college degree, so in that sense you might be a bit over-qualified. However, you also see a strong overlap between your education and the responsibilities and required skills of the job, so be sure to highlight those.

Keywords and Key Phrases

You study the job posting and highlight the following elements:

1. Be able to predict and respond to merchant needs; good business sense with the ability to appreciate the needs of a wide variety of companies
2. Strong written and oral communication skills
3. High degree of professionalism
4. Self-starter with good time management skills
5. Logically analyze problems and devise solutions
6. Comfortable with computer-based tools, including Microsoft Excel
7. Desire to expand business and technical skills
8. Customer service experience
9. Collaborate with fellow team members to resolve difficult situations
10. Record of high performance regarding quality of work and personal productivity

---

Emma Gomes
(847) 555–2153
emma.gomes@mailsystem.net
emmawrites.blogspot.com

Address:
860 North 8th Street, Terre Haute, IN 47809

Permanent Address:
993 Church Street, Barrington, IL 60010

Summary of Qualifications

- Front-line customer service experience with consumers and business owners
- Strong business sense based on work experience and academic preparation
- Intermediate skills with a variety of software tools, including Microsoft Excel and Google Analytics
- Record of quality work in both business and academic settings

Education

B.S. in Marketing (Marketing Management Track), Indiana State University, Terre Haute, IN, expected graduation May 2014

Program coursework

- 45 credits of core business courses, including Business Information Tools, Business Statistics, Principles of Accounting, and Business Finance
- 27 credits of marketing and marketing management courses, including Marketing Fundamentals, Buyer Behavior, Marketing Research, Retail Strategies and seminars in e–commerce and social media

Special projects

- "Handcrafting a Global Marketplace: The Etsy Phenomenon," in-depth analysis of how the Etsy e-commerce platform helps craftspeople and artisans become more successful merchants
- "Hybrid Communication Platforms for Small Businesses," team service project for five small businesses in Terre Haute, recommending best practices for combining traditional and social–media methods of customer engagement and providing a customized measurement spreadsheet for each company

Work and Volunteer Experience

Independent math tutor, 2009-present. Assist students with a variety of math courses at the elementary, junior high, and high school level; all clients have achieved combined test and homework score improvements of at least one full letter grade, with an average improvement of 38 percent

Volunteer, LeafSpring Food Bank, Terre Haute, IN (weekends during college terms, 2012–present). Stock food and supply pantries; prepare emergency baskets for new clients; assist director with public relations activities, including website updates and social media news releases.

Customer care agent, Owings Ford, Barrington, IL (summers, 2011–2013). Assisted the service and sales managers of this locally owned car dealership with a variety of customer-service tasks; scheduled service appointments; designed and implemented improvements to service-center waiting room to increase guest comfort; convinced dealership owners to begin using Twitter and Facebook to interact with current and potential customers.

Professional Engagement

- Collegiate member, American Marketing Association; helped establish the AMA Collegiate Chapter at Indiana State
- Participated in AMA International Collegiate Case Competition, 2011-2012

Awards

- Dean's List: 2012, 2013
- Forward Youth award, Barrington Chamber of Commerce, 2010

Gomes modified her summary of qualifications to increase emphasis on customer service.

She adjusts the selection of highlighted courses to reflect the retail and e-commerce aspects of this particular job opening.

She adjusts the wording of this Etsy project description to closely mirror what Amazon is—an e-commerce platform serving a multitude of independent merchants.

She provides more detail regarding her customer support experience.

The final sections are still relevant to this job opening, so she leaves them unchanged.

Notice how Gomes adapts her résumé to "mirror" the keywords and phrases from the job posting:

1. Suggests strong awareness of the needs of various businesses
2. Examples of experience with written business communication; she can demonstrate oral communication skills during phone, video, or in-person interviews
3. Results-oriented approach to tutoring business suggests high degree of professionalism, as do the two awards
4. The ability to work successfully as an independent tutor while attending high school and college is strong evidence of self-motivation and good time management
5. Indicates ability to understand problems and design solutions
6. Suggests the ability to work with a variety of software tools
7. Demonstrates a desire to learn and to expand her skills
8. Highlights customer service experience
9. Offers concrete evidence of teamwork (rather than just calling herself a "team player," for example)
10. Tracking the progress of her tutoring clients is strong evidence of someone who cares about results and the quality of her work; Dean's List awards also suggest quality of work; record of working while attending high school and college suggests strong productivity

Figure 5 Crafting Your Résumé, Scenario 2: Repositioning Yourself for Available Opportunities
If you can't find an ideal job opening, you'll need to adjust your plans and adapt your résumé to the openings that are available. Look for opportunities that meet your near-term financial needs while giving you the chance to expand your skill set so that you'll be even more prepared when an ideal opportunity does come along.[43]

Emma Gomes
(847) 555–2153
emma.gomes@mailsystem.net
Twitter: www.twitter.com/emmagomes
1605 Queen Anne Avenue North, Seattle, WA 98109

Market and Strategy Analyst

- Five years of experience in local and online retailing, with three years of focus on market opportunity analysis
- Strong business sense developed through more than 60 marketing programs across a range of retail sectors, including hospitality, entertainment, and fashion
- Recognized by senior management for ability to make sound judgment calls in situations with incomplete or conflicting data
- Adept at coordinating research projects and marketing initiatives across organizational boundaries and balancing the interests of multiple stakeholders
- Advanced skills with leading analysis and communication tools, including Excel, PowerPoint, and Google Analytics

Professional Experience

Associate Market Analyst, LivingSocial, Seattle, WA (July 2011-present). Analyzed assigned markets for such factors as consumer demand, merchandising opportunities, and seller performance; designed, launched, and managed marketing initiatives in 27 retailing categories, including fashions and accessories; met or exceeded profit targets on 90 percent of all marketing initiatives; appointed team lead/trainer in recognition of strong quantitative and qualitative analysis skills; utilized both established and emerging social media tools and helped business partners use these communication platforms to increase consumer engagement in local markets.

Seller support associate, Amazon, Seattle, WA (July 2009–June 2011). Worked with more than 300 product vendors, including many in the fashion and accessories sectors, to assure profitable retailing activities on the Amazon e-commerce platform; resolved vendor issues related to e-commerce operations, pricing, and consumer communication; anticipated potential vendor challenges and assisted in the development of more than a dozen new selling tools that improved vendor profitability while reducing Amazon's vendor support costs by nearly 15 percent.

Education

Evening MBA program, University of Washington, Seattle, WA; anticipated graduation: May 2015. Broad-based program combining financial reporting, marketing strategy, competitive strategy, and supply chain management with individual emphasis on quantitative methods, financial analysis, and marketing decision models.

B.S. in Marketing (Marketing Management Track), Indiana State University, Terre Haute, IN, May 2009. Comprehensive coursework in business fundamentals, accounting and finance, marketing fundamentals, retailing, and consumer communications.

Professional Engagement

- Member, American Marketing Association
- Member, International Social Media Association
- Active in National Retail Federation and Retail Advertising & Marketing Association

Awards

- Living Social Top Ten Deals (monthly employee achievement award for designing the most profitable couponing deals); awarded seven times, 2011—2013
- Social Commerce Network's Social Commerce Innovators: 30 Under 30; 2012

Notice how Gomes adapts her résumé to "mirror" the keywords and phrases from the job posting:

- Highlights her experience in market and business analysis and her continuing education in this area
- Mentions skill at coordinating cross-functional projects
- Lists experiences that relate to the collection and analysis of retail data
- Emphasizes the work she has done with fashion-related retailing and retailing in general
- Identifies experience and education that relates to quantitative and qualitative analysis (this point overlaps #1 and #3 to a
- degree)
- Mentions project management experience
- Lists areas that suggest effective communication skills
- Lists education, with emphasis on coursework that relates most directly to the job posting
- Mentions work experience and educational background related to these topics
- Includes these programs in the list of software tools she uses

Figure 6 Crafting Your Résumé, Scenario 3: Positioning Yourself for More Responsibility
When you have a few years of experience under your belt, your résumé strategy should shift to emphasize work history and accomplishments. Here is how Emma Gomes might reshape her résumé if she had held the two jobs described in Figures 4 and 5 and is now ready for a bigger challenge.[44]

Completing Your Résumé

Completing your résumé involves revising it for optimum quality, producing it in the various forms and media you'll need, and proofreading it for any errors before distributing it or publishing it online.

REVISING YOUR RÉSUMÉ

Revising your résumé for clarity and conciseness is essential. Recruiters and hiring managers want to find key pieces of information about you, including your top skills, your current job, and your education, in a matter of seconds. Many are overwhelmed with résumés, and if they have to work to find or decode this information, chances are they'll toss yours aside and move on to the next one in the pile. Remember the fundamental purpose of the résumé—to get you an interview, not to get you a job. Weed out details and irrelevant information until your résumé is tight, clear, and focused.

Revise your résumé until it is as short and clear as possible.

The ideal length of your résumé depends on the depth of your experience and the level of the positions for which you are applying. As a general guideline, if you have fewer than five years of professional experience, keep your conventional résumé to one page. For online résumé formats, you can always provide links to additional information. If you have more experience and are applying for a higher-level position, you may need to prepare a somewhat longer résumé.[33] For highly technical positions, longer résumés are often the norm as well because the qualifications for such jobs can require more description.

If your employment history is brief, keep your résumé to one page.

PRODUCING YOUR RÉSUMÉ

No matter how many media and formats you eventually choose for producing your résumé, a clean, professional-looking design is a must. Recruiters and hiring managers typically skim your essential information in a matter of seconds, and anything that distracts or delays them will work against you.

Effective résumé designs are clear, clean, and professional.

Choosing a Design Strategy for Your Résumé

You'll find a wide range of résumé designs in use today, from text-only examples that follow a conventional layout to full-color infographics with unique designs. As with every type of business message, keep your audience, your goals, and your resources in mind. Don't choose a style just because it seems trendy or flashy or different. For example, you can find a lot of eye-catching infographic résumés online, but many of those are created by graphic designers applying for visual jobs in advertising, fashion, web design, and other areas in which graphic design skills are a must. In other words, the intended audience expects an applicant to have design skills, and the résumé is a good opportunity to demonstrate those. In contrast, a colorful, graphically intense résumé might just look odd to recruiters in finance, engineering, or other professions.

Don't pick a résumé style just because it's trendy or different; make sure it works for your specific needs.

The sample résumés in Figures 4 through 6 use a classic, conservative design that will serve you well for most business opportunities. Notice how they feature simplicity, an easy-to-read layout, effective use of white space, and clear typefaces. Recruiters can pick out the key pieces of information in a matter of seconds.

With any résumé design, make sure that readers can find essential information in a matter of seconds.

You can certainly enhance your résumé beyond this style, but do so carefully and always with an eye on what will help the reader. Make subheadings easy to find and easy to read. Avoid big blocks of text, and use lists to itemize your most important qualifications. Color is not necessary by any means, but if you add color, make it subtle and sophisticated. Above all, don't make the reader work to find the key points of story. Your résumé should be a high-efficiency information-delivery system, not a treasure hunt.

Depending on the companies you apply to, you might want to produce your résumé in as many as six formats (all are explained in the following sections):

- Printed traditional résumé
- Printed scannable résumé

Be prepared to produce versions of your résumé in multiple formats.

- Electronic plain-text file
- Microsoft Word file
- Online résumé
- PDF file

Unfortunately, no single format or medium will work for all situations, and employer expectations continue to change as technology evolves. Find out what each employer or job posting website expects, and provide your résumé in that specific format.

Considering Photos, Videos, Presentations, and Infographics

Do not include or enclose a photo in résumés that you send to employers or post on job websites.

As you produce your résumé in various formats, you will encounter the question of whether to include a photograph of yourself on or with your résumé. For print or electronic documents that you will be submitting to employers or job websites, the safest advice is to avoid photos. The reason is that seeing visual cues of the age, ethnicity, and gender of candidates early in the selection process exposes employers to complaints of discriminatory hiring practices. In fact, some employers won't even look at résumés that include photos, and some applicant tracking systems automatically discard résumés with any extra files.[34] However, photographs are acceptable and expected for social media résumés and other online formats where you are not actively submitting a résumé to an employer.

In addition to the six main résumé formats, some applicants create PowerPoint or Prezi presentations, videos, or infographics to supplement a conventional résumé. Two key advantages of a presentation supplement are flexibility and multimedia capabilities. For instance, you can present a menu of choices on the opening screen and allow viewers to click through to sections of interest. (Note that most of the things you can accomplish with a presentation can be done with an online résumé, which is probably more convenient for most readers.)

A video résumé can be a compelling supplement as well, but be aware that some employment law experts advise employers not to view videos, at least not until after candidates have been evaluated solely on their credentials. The reason for this caution is the same as with photographs. In addition, videos are more cumbersome to evaluate than paper or electronic résumés, and some recruiters refuse to watch them.[35] However, not all companies share this concern over videos, so you'll have to research their individual preferences. In fact, the online retailer Zappos encourages applicant videos and provides a way to upload videos on its job application webpage.[36]

An infographic résumé attempts to convey a person's career development and skill set graphically through a visual metaphor such as a timeline or subway map or as a poster with array of individual elements. A well-designed infographic could be an intriguing element of the job-search package for candidates in certain situations and professions because it can definitely stand out from traditional résumés and can show a high level of skill in visual communication. However, infographics are likely to be incompatible with most applicant tracking systems and with the screening habits of most recruiters, so while you might stand out with an infographic, you might also get tossed out if you try to use an infographic in place of a conventional résumé. In virtually every situation, an infographic should complement a conventional résumé, not replace it. In addition, successful infographics require skills in graphical design, and if you lack those skills, you'll need to hire a designer.

Producing a Traditional Printed Résumé

Use high-quality paper when printing your résumé.

Even though most of your application activity will take place online, having a copy of a conventional printed résumé is important for taking to job fairs, interviews, and other events. Many interviewers expect you to bring a printed résumé to the interview, even if you applied online. The résumé can serve as a note-taking form or discussion guide, and it is tangible evidence of your attention to professionalism and detail.[37] When printing a résumé, choose a heavier, higher-quality paper designed specifically for résumés and other important documents. White or slightly off-white is the best color choice. Avoid papers with borders or backgrounds.

Printing a Scannable Résumé

You might encounter a company that prefers *scannable résumés*, a type of printed resume that is specially formatted to be compatible with optical scanning systems that convert printed documents to electronic text. These systems were quite common just a few years ago, but their use appears to be declining rapidly as more employers prefer email delivery or website application forms.[38] A scannable résumé differs from the traditional format in two major ways: It should always include a keyword summary, and it should be formatted in a simpler fashion that avoids underlining, special characters, and other elements that can confuse the scanning system. If you need to produce a scannable résumé, search online for "formatting a scannable résumé" to get detailed instructions.

Some employers still prefer résumés in scannable format, but most now want electronic submissions.

Creating a Plain-Text File of Your Résumé

A *plain-text file* (sometimes known as an ASCII text file) is an electronic version of your résumé that has no font formatting, no bullet symbols, no colors, no lines or boxes, and no other special formatting. The plain-text version can be used in two ways. First, you can include it in the body of an email message, for employers who want email delivery but don't want file attachments. Second, you can copy and paste the sections into the application forms on an employer's website.

A plain-text version is easy to create with your word processor. Start with the file you used to create your résumé, use the "Save As" choice to save it as "plain text" or whichever similarly labeled option your software has, and verify the result by using a basic text editor (such as Microsoft Notepad). If necessary, reformat the page manually, moving text and inserting space as needed. For simplicity's sake, left-justify all your headings rather than trying to center them manually.

A plain-text version of your résumé is simply a computer file without any of the formatting that you typically apply using word-processing software.

Make sure you verify the plain-text file that you create with your word processor; it might need a few manual adjustments using a text editor such as NotePad.

Creating a Word File of Your Résumé

In some cases, an employer or job-posting website will want you to upload a Microsoft Word file or attach it to an email message. (Although there are certainly other word-processing software programs available, Microsoft Word is the de facto standard in business these days.) This method of transferring information preserves the design and layout of your résumé and saves you the trouble of creating a plain-text version. However, before you submit a Word file to anyone, make sure your computer is free of viruses. Infecting a potential employer's computer will not make a good first impression.

Some employers and websites want your résumé in Microsoft Word format; make sure your computer is thoroughly scanned for viruses first, however.

Creating a PDF Version of Your Résumé

Creating a PDF file is a simple procedure, but you need the right software. Adobe Acrobat (not the free Adobe Reader) is the best-known program, but many others are available, including some free versions. You can also use Adobe's online service to create PDFs without buying software. The advantages of creating PDFs are that you preserve the formatting of your résumé (unlike pasting plain text into an email message), and you create a file type that is less vulnerable to viruses than word-processer files.

Creating an Online or Social Media Résumé

A variety of online résumé formats, variously referred to as *e-portfolios*, *interactive résumés*, or *social media résumés*, provide the opportunity to create a dynamic, multimedia presentation of your qualifications. You can expand on the information contained in your basic résumé with links to projects, publications, screencasts, online videos, course lists, blogs, social networking profiles, and other elements that give employers a more complete picture of who you are and what you can offer.

You have a number of options for hosting an online résumé. Start with your college's career center; many such centers offer hosting for e-portfolios, for example, where you can showcase your academic achievements. You can also chose one of the commercial résumé hosting services, such as LinkedIn, VisualCV, and Gozaik. In addition to being free (for basic services, at least), these sites provide easy-to-use tools for creating your online

You have many options for creating an online résumé, from college-hosted e-portfolios to multimedia résumés on commercials websites.

profile. You can also use them to peruse examples of various résumés, from students just about to enter the workforce full-time all the way up to corporate CEOs.

Regardless of the approach you take to creating an online résumé, keep these helpful tips in mind:

- **Remember that your online presence is a career-management tool.** The way you are portrayed online can work for you or against you, and it's up to you to create a positive impression.
- **Take advantage of social networking.** Use whatever tools are available to direct people to your online résumé, such as including your URL in your Twitter profile.
- **During the application process, don't expect or ask employers to retrieve a résumé from a website.** Submit your résumé using whatever method and medium each employer prefers. If employers then want to know more about you, they will likely do a web search on you and find your site, or you can refer them to your site in your résumé or application materials.

PROOFREADING YOUR RÉSUMÉ

Your résumé can't be "pretty good" or "almost perfect"—it needs to be *perfect*, so proofread it thoroughly and ask several other people to verify it, too.

Employers view your résumé as a concrete example of your attention to quality and detail. Your résumé doesn't need to be good or pretty good—it needs to be *perfect*. Although it may not seem fair, just one or two errors in a job application package are enough to doom a candidate's chances.[39]

REAL-TIME UPDATES

LEARN MORE BY READING THIS ARTICLE

Don't let these mistakes cost you an interview

Make sure you don't commit these nine costly blunders. Go to http://real-timeupdates.com/ebc12 and click on Learn More in the Students section.

Your résumé is one of the most important documents you'll ever write, so don't rush or cut corners when it comes to proofreading. Check all headings and lists for clarity and parallelism, and be sure your grammar, spelling, and punctuation are correct. Double-check all dates, phone numbers, email addresses, and other essential data. Ask at least three other people to read it, too. As the creator of the material, you could stare at a mistake for weeks and not see it.

DISTRIBUTING YOUR RÉSUMÉ

When distributing your résumé, pay close attention to the specific instructions provided by every employer, job website, or other recipient.

How you distribute your résumé depends on the number of employers you target and their preferences for receiving résumés. Employers usually list their requirements on their websites, so verify this information and follow it carefully. Beyond that, here are some general distribution tips:

- **Mailing printed résumés.** Take some care with the packaging. Spend a few extra cents to mail these documents in a flat 9 × 12 envelope, or better yet, use a Priority Mail flat-rate envelope, which gives you a sturdy cardboard mailer and faster delivery for just a few more dollars.
- **Emailing your résumé.** Some employers want applicants to include the text of their résumés in the body of an email message; others prefer an attached Microsoft Word or PDF file. If you have a reference number or a job ad number, include it in the subject line of your email message.
- **Submitting your résumé to an employer's website.** Many employers, including most large companies, now prefer or require applicants to submit their résumés online. In some instances, you will be asked to upload a complete file. In others, you will need to copy and paste sections of your résumé into individual boxes in an online application form.
- **Posting your résumé on job websites.** You can post your résumé on general-purpose job websites such as Monster and CareerBuilder, on more specialized websites such as Jobster or Jobfox, or with staffing services such as Volt. Roughly 100,000 job boards are now online, so you'll need to spend some time looking for sites that specialize in your target industries, regions, or professions.[40] Before you upload your résumé to any site, however, learn about its privacy protection. Some sites allow you

---

CHECKLIST ✔ Writing an Effective Résumé

A. Plan your résumé.
- Analyze your purpose and audience carefully to make sure your message meets employers' needs.
- Gather pertinent information about your target companies.
- Select the required media types by researching the preferences of each employer.
- Organize your résumé around your strengths, choosing the chronological, functional, or combination structure. (Be careful about using the functional structure.)

B. Write your résumé.
- Keep your résumé honest.
- Adapt your résumé to your audience to highlight the qualifications each employer is looking for.
- Choose a career objective, qualifications summary, or career summary as your introductory statement—and make it concise, concrete, and reader-focused.

- Use powerful language to convey your name and contact information, introductory statement, education, work experience, skills, work or school accomplishments, and activities and achievements.

C. Complete your résumé.
- Revise your résumé until it is clear, concise, compelling—and perfect.
- Produce your résumé in all the formats you might need: traditional printed résumé, scannable, plain-text file, Microsoft Word file, PDF, or online.
- Proofread your résumé to make sure it is absolutely perfect.
- Distribute your résumé using the means that each employer prefers.

---

to specify levels of confidentiality, such as letting employers search your qualifications without seeing your personal contact information or preventing your current employer from seeing your résumé. Don't post your résumé to any website that doesn't give you the option of restricting the display of your contact information. Only employers that are registered clients of the service should be able to see your contact information.[41]

Don't post a résumé on any public website unless you understand its privacy and security policies.

For a quick summary of the steps to take when planning, writing, and completing your résumé, refer to "Checklist: Writing an Effective Résumé."

ON THE JOB: SOLVING COMMUNICATION DILEMMAS AT VMWARE

You work as a recruiter in the human resources department at VMWare, where part of your responsibility involves using the applicant tracking system to identify promising job candidates. Solve these challenges by using what you've learned about presenting oneself effectively on a résumé.

1. You've learned to pay close attention to the introductory statement on résumés in order to match applicants' interests with appropriate job openings. You've selected four résumés for an accountant position. Which of the following is the most compelling statement for this position?
   a. Career objective: An entry-level financial position in a large company
   b. Qualifications summary: Proven track record of using accounting and financial talent and business savvy in shepherding companies toward explosive growth

   c. Qualifications summary: Solid academic grounding in business administration with experience in cash management and basic accounting procedures
   d. Career objective: To learn all I can about accounting in an exciting environment with a company whose reputation is as outstanding as VMWare's.

2. Of the education sections included in the résumés, which of the following is the most effective?
   a. **Morehouse College, Atlanta, GA, 2009–2013.** Received BA degree with a major in Business Administration and a minor in Finance. Graduated with a 3.65 grade point average. Played varsity football and basketball. Worked 15 hours per week in the library. Coordinated the local student chapter of the American Management Association. Member of Alpha Phi Alpha social fraternity.

b. **I attended Wayne State University in Detroit, Michigan, for two years and then transferred to the University of Michigan at Ann Arbor, where I completed my studies.** My major was economics, but I also took many business management courses, including employee motivation, small business administration, history of business start-ups, and organizational behavior. I selected courses based on the professors' reputation for excellence, and I received mostly A's and B's. Unlike many college students, I viewed the acquisition of knowledge—rather than career preparation—as my primary goal. I believe I have received a well-rounded education that has prepared me to approach management situations as problem-solving exercises.

c. **University of Connecticut, Storrs, Connecticut. Graduated with a BA degree in 2013.** Majored in Physical Education. Minored in Business Administration. Graduated with a 2.85 average.

d. **North Texas State University and University of Texas at Tyler.** Received BA and MBA degrees. I majored in business as an undergraduate and concentrated in financial management during my MBA program. Received a special $2,500 scholarship offered by Rotary international recognizing academic achievement in business courses. I also won the MEGA award in 2012. Dean's List.

3. Which of the résumés does the best job of portraying each candidate's work experience?

a. **McDonald's, Peoria, IL, 2009–2010. Part-time cook.** Worked 15 hours per week while attending high school. Prepared all menu items. Received employee-of-the-month award for outstanding work habits. **University Grill, Ames, IA, 2011–2015. Part-time cook.** Worked 20 hours per week while attending college. Prepared hot and cold sandwiches. Helped manager purchase ingredients. Trained new kitchen workers. Prepared work schedules for kitchen staff.

b. Although I have never held a full-time job, I have worked part-time and during summer vacations throughout my high school and college years. During my freshman and sophomore years in high school, I bagged groceries at the A&P store three afternoons a week, where I was generally acknowledged as one of the hardest-working employees. During my junior and senior years, I worked at the YMCA as an after-school counselor for elementary school children. I know I made a positive difference in their lives because I still get letters from some of them. During summer vacations while I was in college, I did construction work for a local homebuilder. The job paid well, and I also learned a lot about carpentry. I also worked part-time in college in the student cafeteria.

c. **Macy's Department Store, Sherman Oaks, CA, Summers, 2011–2014. Sales Consultant, Furniture Department.** Interacted with a diverse group of customers while endeavoring to satisfy their individual needs and make their shopping experience efficient and enjoyable. Under the direction of the sales manager, prepared employee schedules and completed departmental reports. Demonstrated computer skills and attention to detail while assisting with inventory management, working the cash register, and handling a variety of special orders and customer requests. Received the CEO Award (for best monthly sales performance) three times.

d. **Athens, GA, Civilian Member of Public Safety Committee, January–December 2015.**
   - Organized and promoted a lecture series on vacation safety and home security for the residents of Athens, GA; recruited and trained seven committee members to help plan and produce the lectures; persuaded local businesses to finance the program; designed, printed, and distributed flyers; wrote and distributed press releases; attracted an average of 120 people to each of three lectures
   - Developed a questionnaire to determine local residents' home security needs; directed the efforts of 10 volunteers working on the survey; prepared written report for city council and delivered oral summary of findings at town meeting; helped persuade city to fund new home security program
   - Initiated the Business Security Forum as an annual meeting at which local business leaders could meet to discuss safety and security issues; created promotional flyers for the first forum; convinced 19 business owners to fund a business security survey; arranged press coverage of the first forum

4. While you are analyzing four résumés suggested by your applicant tracking system, a fellow employee hands you the following résumé and says this person would be great for the opening in accounting. What action will you take?

a. Definitely recommend that VMWare take a look at this outstanding candidate.

b. Reject the application. He doesn't give enough information about when he attended college, what he majored in, or where he has worked.

c. Review the candidate's web-based e-portfolio, in which he has posted many of his school projects. If the assessment contains the missing information and the candidate sounds promising, recommend him for a closer look. If vital information is still missing, send the candidate an email requesting additional information. Make the decision once you receive all necessary information.

d. Consider the candidate's qualifications relative to those of other applicants. Recommend him if you cannot find three or four other applicants with more directly relevant qualifications.

Darius Jaidee
809 N. Perkins Rd, Stillwater, OK 74075
Phone: (405) 369-0098
Email: dariusj@okstate.edu

Career Objective: To build a successful career in financial management

Summary of Qualifications: As a student at the University of Oklahoma, Stillwater, completed a wide variety of assignments that demonstrate skills related to accounting and management. For example:

Planning skills: As president of the university's foreign affairs forum, organized six lectures and workshops featuring 36 speakers from 16 foreign countries within a nine-month period. Identified and recruited the speakers, handled their travel arrangements, and scheduled the facilities.

Communication skills: Wrote more than 25 essays and term papers on various academic topics, including at least 10 dealing with business and finance. As a senior, wrote a 20-page analysis of financial trends in the petroleum industry, interviewing five high-ranking executives in accounting and finance positions at ConocoPhillip's refinery in Ponca City, Oklahoma, and company headquarters in Houston, Texas.

Accounting and computer skills: Competent in all areas of Microsoft Office, including Excel spreadsheets and Access databases. Assisted with bookkeeping activities in parents' small business, including the conversion from paper-based to computer-based accounting (Peachtree software). Have taken courses in accounting, financial planning, database design, web design, and computer networking.

For more information, including employment history, please access my e-portfolio at http://dariusjaidee.com.

Learning Objectives Checkup

Assess your understanding of the principles in this chapter by reading each learning objective and studying the accompanying exercises. You can check your responses against the answer key.

Objective 1: List eight key steps to finding the ideal opportunity in today's job market.

1. How does writing the "story of you" help you plan your job search and craft your résumé?
   a. It helps you focus your résumé on your needs, rather than on the employer's.
   b. It helps you think about where you want to go and how to present yourself to target employers.
   c. It allows you to avoid writing a traditional structured résumé.
   d. It helps you plan the speech you should make at the beginning of every job interview.

2. ____ ____ ____ is a measure of how closely new employees meet a company's needs.

3. What is the first step that employers usually take when they need to find candidates to interview for a job opening?
   a. They search online for personal websites and e-portfolios that might contain information about potential candidates.
   b. They look inside the company for likely candidates.
   c. They post job openings on job boards such as Monster.com and CareerBuilder.com.
   d. They run ads in the local newspaper.

4. Which of these most accurately characterizes the respective approaches that employers use to find new employees and employees use to find new opportunities?
   a. Employers and employees look in the same places, in the same general sequence.
   b. The respective approaches of employers and employees are essentially opposite, with employers starting inside the firm and gradually moving toward help wanted ads as a last resort and employees starting with help wanted ads and moving in the other direction.
   c. Because websites are the only places that employers now communicate news of job openings, the web is the only place employees should look.
   d. The approaches of employees and employers have nothing in common.

5. Which of the following best describes the process of networking as it applies to your career?
   a. Making sure you are plugged into the online scene so that you don't miss out on any new Internet developments
   b. Making informal connections with a broad sphere of mutually beneficial business contacts
   c. Asking as many people as possible to alert you to interesting job opportunities
   d. Making sure you get to know everyone in your company shortly after accepting a new position

6. If you don't yet have significant work experience but still want to become a valued network member, which of the following tactics should you consider?
   a. Limit your networking to people whose work experience is similar to yours so that you can share similar information.
   b. Create a convenient, foldable, business-card-size version of your résumé that you can give to everyone you meet so they don't have to carry a full-size copy of your résumé.
   c. Avoid networking until you have enough work experience to be able to offer insider tips on the job market in your industry.
   d. Research recent trends in the business world in order to have interesting and useful information at your fingertips whenever you encounter people in your network.

Objective 2: Explain the process of planning your résumé, including how to choose the best résumé organization.

7. A/an _____ résumé highlights employment experience, listing jobs in reverse order from most recent to earliest.

8. A/an ____ résumé focuses on a person's particular skills and competencies, without itemizing his or her job history.

9. A/an _____ résumé uses elements of both the chronological and functional formats.

10. Which of the following is an advantage of the chronological résumé?
    a. It helps employers easily locate necessary information.
    b. It highlights your professional growth and career progress.
    c. It emphasizes continuity and stability in your employment background.
    d. It performs all of these communication functions.

11. Why are many employers suspicious of the functional résumé?
    a. It allows applicants to hide or downplay lengthy periods of unemployment or a lack of career progress.
    b. It doesn't scan into computer databases as effectively as other résumé formats.
    c. It doesn't provide any information about education.
    d. It encourages applicants to include accomplishments that were the result of teamwork rather than individual efforts.

12. Which of the following is a disadvantage of the combination résumé?
    a. It is impossible to convert to scannable format.
    b. It tends to be longer than other formats and can be repetitious.
    c. It doesn't work for people who have extensive job experience.
    d. The combination résumé has no disadvantages.

Objective 3: Describe the tasks involved in writing your résumé and list the major sections of a traditional résumé.

13. Which of the following sections should be included in any résumé, regardless of the format you've chosen?
    a. Contact information, education, and work experience
    b. Contact information, education, and personal references
    c. Personal data, contact information, and education
    d. Education, personal references, and career objectives

14. Why do some experts recommend against using a career objective as the introductory statement on your résumé?
    a. It can limit your possibilities as a candidate, particularly if you want to be considered for a variety of positions.

b. It shows that you're selfish and thinking only about your own success.

c. It shows that you're unrealistic because no one can plan a career that might last for 40 or 50 years.

d. It helps focus you as a candidate in the minds of potential employers.

15. How does a qualifications summary differ from a career summary?

a. They are identical.

b. A qualifications summary offers a brief view of your most important skills and attributes, whereas a career summary is a recap of your career progress.

c. No one uses a qualifications summary anymore, whereas a career summary is still popular.

d. The career summary is best for recent graduates, whereas the qualifications summary is best for people with a decade or two of experience.

16. Which should come first on your résumé, your education or your work experience?

a. Education should come first.

b. Work experience should come first.

c. It depends on which is more meaningful to an employer, given where you are in your career at this moment.

d. The best résumés today use a two-column format in which education and work experience are listed side by side.

17. How much personal data should you put on a résumé aimed at U.S. employers?

a. You should list your age, marital status, and physical handicaps that might require special accommodation.

b. You should list your age, marital status, a general assessment of your health (without mentioning any specific problems), and religious affiliation.

c. You should not list any personal data on your résumé.

d. You should not list anything related to health or nationality, but you should list age, gender, and salary history (assuming you've had at least one full-time job).

Objective 4: Characterize the completing step for résumés, including the six most common formats in which you can produce a résumé.

18. Which of the following best describes the level of quality you should achieve when producing your résumé?

a. With the advent of email and social networking, most companies are much more relaxed about grammar, spelling, and other old-school concerns, so don't sweat the details.

b. The typical recruiter in a major corporation sees so many résumés on any given day that most errors pass by unnoticed.

c. Your résumé needs to be perfect.

d. Your résumé should reflect your work habits, so if you're more of a strategic thinker and don't worry about insignificant details, make sure your résumé reflects that.

19. Most résumés are now subjected to _____ _____ in an applicant tracking system or other database, in which a recruiter looks for résumés most likely to match the requirements of a particular job.

20. A/an _____ _____ version of your résumé has the same content as a traditional résumé but has had all the formatting removed so that it can be easily emailed or copied into online forms.

21. Which of these is a significant advantage of an online résumé?

a. You can expand on the information contained in your basic résumé with links to projects, publications, screencasts, online videos, course lists, social networking profiles, and other elements.

b. You can build up your résumé over time and don't have to worry about having every little detail in place when you launch your job search.

c. You can use lots of color.

d. You can use the flexibility of the web to provide extensive details on your life history

Quick Learning Guide

LEARNING OBJECTIVES

1 List eight key steps to finding the ideal opportunity in today's job market.

2 Explain the process of planning your résumé, including how to choose the best résumé organization.

3 Describe the tasks involved in writing your résumé, and list the major sections of a traditional résumé.

4 Characterize the completing step for résumés, including the six most common formats in which you can produce a résumé.

KEY TERMS

applicant tracking systems Computer systems that capture and store incoming résumés and help recruiters find good prtospects for current openings

chronological résumé The most common résumé format; it emphasizes work experience, with past jobs shown in reverse chronological order

combination résumé Format that includes the best features of the chronological and functional approaches

functional résumé Format that emphasizes your skills and capabilities while identifying employers and academic experience in subordinate sections; many recruiters view this format with suspicion

networking The process of making connections with mutually beneficial business contacts

résumé A structured, written summary of a person's education, employment background, and job qualifications

CHECKLIST

Writing an Effective Résumé

A. Plan your résumé.
- Analyze your purpose and audience carefully to make sure your message meets employers' needs.
- Gather pertinent information about your target companies.
- Select the required media types by researching the preferences of each employer.
- Organize your résumé around your strengths, choosing the chronological, functional, or combination structure. (Be careful about using the functional structure.)

B. Write your résumé.
- Keep your résumé honest.
- Adapt your résumé to your audience to highlight the qualifications each employer is looking for.
- Choose a career objective, qualifications summary, or career summary as your introductory statement—and make it concise, concrete, and reader-focused.

- Use powerful language to convey your name and contact information, introductory statement, education, work experience, skills, work or school accomplishments, and activities and achievements.

C. Complete your résumé.
- Revise your résumé until it is clear, concise, compelling—and perfect.
- Produce your résumé in all the formats you might need: traditional printed résumé, scannable, plain-text file, Microsoft Word file, PDF, or online.
- Proofread your résumé to make sure it is absolutely perfect.
- Distribute your résumé using the means that each employer prefers.

Apply Your Knowledge

To review chapter content related to each question, refer to the indicated Learning Objective.

⭐ 1. How can you "think like an employer" if you have no professional business experience? [LO-1]

2. If you were a team leader at a summer camp for children with special needs, should you include this in your employment history if you are applying for work that is unrelated? Explain your answer. [LO-3]

3. Can you use a qualifications summary if you don't yet have extensive professional experience in your desired career? Why or why not? [LO-3]

⭐ 4. Some people don't have a clear career path when they enter the job market. If you're in this situation, how would your uncertainty affect the way you write your résumé? [LO-3]

⭐ 5. Between your sophomore and junior years, you quit school for a year to earn the money to finish college. You worked as a loan-processing assistant in a finance company, checking references on loan applications, typing, and filing. Your manager made a lot of the fact that he had never attended college. He seemed to resent you for pursuing your education, but he never criticized your work, so you thought you were doing okay. After you'd been working there for six months, he fired you, saying that you'd failed to be thorough enough in your credit checks. You were actually glad to leave, and you found another job right away at a bank, doing similar duties. Now that you've graduated from college, you're writing your résumé. Will you include the finance company job in your work history? Explain. [LO-3]

Practice Your Skills

Message for Analysis

Read the following résumé information and then (1) analyze the strengths or weaknesses of the information and (2) revise the résumé so that it follows the guidelines presented in this chapter.

6. Message A: Writing a Résumé [LO-3]

Sylvia Manchester
765 Belle Fleur Blvd.
New Orleans, LA 70113
(504) 312-9504
smanchester@rcnmail.com

Personal: Single, excellent health, 5'7", 136 lbs.; hobbies include cooking, dancing, and reading.

Job Objective: To obtain a responsible position in marketing or sales with a good company.

Education: BA degree in biology, University of Louisiana, 1998. Graduated with a 3.0 average. Member of the varsity cheerleading squad. President of Panhellenic League. Homecoming queen.

Work Experience

Fisher Scientific Instruments, 2014 to now, field sales representative. Responsible for calling on customers and explaining the features of Fisher's line of laboratory instruments. Also responsible for writing sales letters, attending trade shows, and preparing weekly sales reports.

Fisher Scientific Instruments, 2011–2013, customer service representative. Was responsible for handling incoming phone calls from customers who had questions about delivery, quality, or operation of Fisher's line of laboratory instruments. Also handled miscellaneous correspondence with customers.

Medical Electronics, Inc., 2008–2011, administrative assistant to the vice president of marketing. In addition to handling typical secretarial chores for the vice president of marketing, I was in charge of compiling the monthly sales reports, using figures provided by members of the field sales force. I also was given responsibility for doing various market research activities.

New Orleans Convention and Visitors Bureau, 2005–2008, summers, tour guide. During the summers of my college years, I led tours of New Orleans for tourists visiting the city. My duties included greeting conventioneers and their spouses at hotels, explaining the history and features of the city during an all-day sightseeing tour, and answering questions about New Orleans and its attractions. During my fourth summer with the bureau, I was asked to help train the new tour guides. I prepared a handbook that provided interesting facts about the various tourist attractions, as well as answers to the most commonly asked tourist questions. The Bureau was so impressed with the handbook they had it printed up so that it could be given as a gift to visitors.

University of Louisiana, 2005–2008, part-time clerk in admissions office. While I was a student in college, I worked 15 hours a week in the admissions office. My duties included filing, processing applications, and handling correspondence with high school students and administrators.

Exercises

Each activity is labeled according to the primary skill or skills you will need to use. To review relevant chapter content, you can refer to the indicated Learning Objective.

7. **Career Management: Researching Career Opportunities [LO-1]** Based on the preferences you identified in your career self-assessment and the academic, professional, and personal qualities you have to offer, perform an online search for a career that matches your interests (starting with the websites listed in Table 1). Draft a brief report for your instructor, indicating how the career you select and the job openings you find match your strengths and preferences.

Message Strategies: Writing a Résumé; Collaboration: Team Projects [LO-3] Working with another student, change the following statements to make them more effective for a résumé by using action verbs.

8. Have some experience with database design.

9. Assigned to a project to analyze the cost accounting methods for a large manufacturer.
10. I was part of a team that developed a new inventory control system.
11. Am responsible for preparing the quarterly department budget.
12. Was a manager of a department with seven employees working for me.
13. Was responsible for developing a spreadsheet to analyze monthly sales by department.
14. Put in place a new program for ordering supplies.
15. **Message Strategies: Writing a Résumé; Communication Ethics: Resolving Ethical Dilemmas [LO-3]** Assume that you achieved all the tasks shown in Exercises 8 through 14 not as an individual employee but as part of a work team. In your résumé, must you mention other team members? Explain your answer.
16. **Completing a Résumé [LO-4]** Using your revised version of the résumé in Message for Analysis A, create a plain-text file that Sylvia Manchester could use to include in email messages.
17. **Completing a Résumé [LO-4]** Imagine you are applying for work in a field that involves speaking in front of an audience, such as sales, consulting, management, or training. Record a two- to three-minute video demonstration of your speaking and presentation skills. Record yourself speaking to an audience, if one can be arranged.

Expand Your Skills

Critique the Professionals

Locate an example of an online résumé (a sample or an actual résumé). Analyze the résumé following the guidelines presented in this chapter. Using whatever medium your instructor requests, write a brief analysis (no more than one page) of the résumé's strengths and weaknesses, citing specific elements from the résumé and support from the chapter. If you are analyzing a real résumé, do not include any personally identifiable data, such as the person's name, email address, or phone number, in your report.

Sharpen Your Career Skills Online

Bovée and Thill's Business Communication Web Search, at http://websearch.businesscommunicationnetwork.com, is a unique research tool designed specifically for business communication research. Use the Web Search function to find a website, video, PDF document, podcast, or presentation that offers advice on creating effective online résumés. Write a brief email message to your instructor or a post for your class blog, describing the item that you found and summarizing the career skills information you learned from it.

Improve Your Grammar, Mechanics, and Usage

The following exercises help you improve your knowledge of and power over English grammar, mechanics, and usage. Turn to the "Handbook of Grammar, Mechanics, and Usage" at the end of this text and review Frequently Confused Words, Frequently Misused Words, and Frequently Misspelled Words. Then review the following items and indicate the preferred choice within each set of parentheses.

18. Everyone (*accept, except*) Barbara King has registered for the company competition.
19. We need to find a new security (*device, devise*).
20. The Jennings are (*loath, loathe*) to admit that they are wrong.
21. That decision lies with the director, (*who's whose*) in charge of this department.
22. In this department, we see (*a lot, alot*) of mistakes like that.
23. In my (*judgement, judgment*), you'll need to redo the cover.
24. He decided to reveal the information, (*irregardless, regardless*) of the consequences.
25. Why not go along when it is so easy to (*accomodate, accommodate*) his demands?
26. When you say that, do you mean to (*infer, imply*) that I'm being unfair?
27. All we have to do is try (*and, to*) get along with him for a few more days.

Cases

Website links for selected companies mentioned in cases can be found in the Student Assignments section at http://real-time updates.com/ebc12.

CAREER SKILLS/EMAIL SKILLS

28. Career Planning: Researching Career Opportunities [LO-1] Knowing the jargon and "hot button" issues in a particular profession or industry can give you a big advantage when it comes to writing your résumé and participating in job interviews. You can fine-tune your résumé for both human readers and applicant tracking systems, sound more confident and informed in interviews, and present yourself as a professional-class individual with an inquiring mind.

Your task: Imagine a specific job category in a company that has an informative, comprehensive website (to facilitate the research you'll need to do). This doesn't have to be a current job opening, but a position you know exists or is likely to exist in this company, such as a business systems analyst at Apple or a brand manager at Unilever.

Explore the company's website and other online sources to find the following: (1) a brief description of what this job entails, with enough detail that you could describe it to a fellow student; (2) some of the terminology used in the profession or industry, both formal terms that might serve as keywords on your résumé and informal terms and phrases that insiders are likely to use in publications and conversations; (3) an ongoing online conversation among people in this profession, such as a LinkedIn Group, a popular industry or professional blog that seems to get quite a few comments, or an industry or professional publication that attracts a lot of comments; and (4) at least one significant issue that will affect people in this profession or companies in this industry over the next few years. For example, if your chosen profession involves accounting in a publicly traded corporation, upcoming changes in international financial reporting standards would be a significant issue. Similarly, for a company in the consumer electronics industry, the recycling and disposal of e-waste is an issue. Write a brief email message summarizing your findings and explaining how you could use this information on your résumé and during job interviews.

29. Career Management: Researching Career Opportunities [LO-1] Perhaps you won't be able to land your ultimate dream job right out of college, but that doesn't mean you shouldn't start planning right now to make that dream come true.

Your task: Using online job search tools, find a job that sounds just about perfect for you, even if you're not yet qualified for it. It might even be something that would take 10 or 20 years to reach. Don't settle for something that's not quite right—find a job that is so "you" and so exciting that you would jump out of bed every morning, eager to go to work (such jobs really do exist!). Start with the job description you found online and then supplement it with additional research so that you get a good picture of what this job and career path are all about. Compile a list of all the qualifications you would need in order to have a reasonable chance of landing such a job. Now compare this list with your current résumé. Write a brief email message to your instructor that identifies all the areas in which you would need to improve your skills, work experience, education, and other qualifications in order to land your dream job.

30. Planning a Résumé [LO-2] If you haven't begun your professional career yet or you are pursuing a career change, the employment history section on your résumé can sometimes be a challenge to write. A brainstorming session with your wise and creative classmates could help.

Your task: In a team assigned by your instructor, help each other evaluate your employment histories and figure out the best way to present your work backgrounds on a résumé. First, each member of the team should compile his or her work history, including freelance projects and volunteer work if relevant, and share this information with the team. After allowing some time for everyone to review each other's information, meet as a team (in person if you can, or online otherwise). Discuss each person's history, pointing out strong spots and weak spots, and then brainstorm the best way to present each person's employment history.

Note: If there are aspects of your employment history you would rather not share with your teammates, substitute a reasonably similar experience of the same duration.

31. Writing a Résumé [LO-3] The introductory statement of a résumé requires some careful thought, both in deciding which of the three types of introductory statement to use and what information to include in it. Getting another person's perspective on this communication challenge can be helpful. In this activity, in fact, someone else is going to write your introductory statement for you, and you will return the favor.

Your task: Pair off with a classmate. Provide each other with the basic facts about your qualifications, work history, education, and career objectives. Then meet in person or online for an informal interview, in which you ask each other questions to flesh out the information you have on each other. Assume that each of you has chosen to use a qualifications summary for your résumé. Now write each other's qualifications summary and then trade them for review. As you read what your partner wrote about you, ask yourself if this feels true to what you believe about yourself and your career aspirations. Do you think it introduces you effectively to potential employers? What might you change about it?

32. Message Strategies: Completing a Résumé [LO-4] Creating presentations and other multimedia supplements can be a great way to expand on the brief overview that a résumé provides.

Your task: Starting with any version of a résumé you've created for yourself, create a PowerPoint presentation that expands on your résumé information to give potential employers a more complete picture of what you can contribute. Include samples of your work, testimonials from current or past employers and colleagues, videos of speeches you've made, and anything else that tells the story of the professional "you." If you have a specific job or type of job in mind, focus your presentation on that. Otherwise, present a more general picture that shows why you would be a great employee for any company to consider. Be sure to review information about creating professional-quality presentations.

33. Message Strategies: Completing a Résumé [LO-4] In the right circumstances, brief videos can be an effective complement to a traditional job-search communication package.

Your task: Find a job opening that interests you (something you are at least partially qualified for at this stage of your career) and produce a two-minute video profile of yourself, highlighting the skills mentioned in the job description. For tips on producing effective video, visit www.indie-film-making.com.

MyBCommLab

Go to the Assignments section of your MyLab to complete these writing exercises.

34. How does a chronological résumé differ from a functional résumé, and when is each appropriate? [LO-2]

35. Explain the difference between a qualifications summary and a career summary. [LO-3]

Endnotes

1. Ladan Nikravan, "Socially Exceptional Recruiting," *Talent Management*, 6 March 2015, www.talentmgt.com; VMWare website, accessed 13 March 2015, www.vmware.com; VMWare Careers profile on LinkedIn, accessed 12 March 2015, www.linkedin.com/company/vmware/careers; VMWare University Twitter account, accessed 13 March 2015, https://twitter.com/vmwareu; VMWare Community portal, accessed 13 March 2015, https://communities.vmware.com; James Molloy profile on LinkedIn, accessed 13 March 2015, www.linkedin.com/in/jmolloy.

2. Courtland L. Bovée and John V. Thill, *Business in Action*, 5th ed. (Boston: Pearson Prentice Hall, 2011), 241–242.

3. Anne Fisher, "How to Get Hired by a 'Best' Company," *Fortune*, 4 February 2008, 96.

4. Eve Tahmincioglu, "Revamping Your Job-Search Strategy," *MSNBC.com*, 28 February 2010, www.msnbc.com.

5. Jessica Dickler, "The Hidden Job Market," *CNNMoney.com*, 10 June 2009, http://money.cnn.com.

6. Tara Weiss, "Twitter to Find a Job," *Forbes*, 7 April 2009, www.forbes.com.

7. Miriam Saltpeter, "Using Facebook Groups for Job Hunting," Keppie Careers blog, 13 November 2008, www.keppiecareers.com.

8. Anne Fisher, "Greener Pastures in a New Field," *Fortune*, 26 January 2004, 48.

9. Liz Ryan, "Etiquette for Online Outreach," Yahoo! Hotjobs website, accessed 26 March 2008, http://hotjobs.yahoo.com.

10. Eve Tahmincioglu, "Employers Digging Deep on Prospective Workers," *MSNBC.com*, 26 October 2009, www.msnbc.com.

11. Career and Employment Services, Danville Area Community College website, accessed 23 March 2008, www.dacc.edu/career; Career Counseling, Sarah Lawrence College website, accessed 23 March 2008, www.slc.edu/occ/index.php; Cheryl L. Noll, "Collaborating with the Career Planning and Placement Center in the Job-Search Project," *Business Communication Quarterly* 58, no. 3 (1995): 53–55.

12. Rachel Emma Silverman, "No More Résumés, Say Some Firms," *Wall Street Journal*, 24 January 2012, http://online.wsj.com.

13. Randall S. Hansen and Katharine Hansen, "What Résumé Format Is Best for You?" QuintCareers.com, accessed 7 August 2010, www.quintcareers.com.

14. Hansen and Hansen, "What Résumé Format Is Best for You?"

15. Katharine Hansen, "Should You Consider a Functional Format for Your Resume?" QuintCareers.com, accessed 7 August 2010, www.quintcareers.com.

16. Kim Isaacs, "Resume Dilemma: Criminal Record," Monster.com, accessed 23 May 2006, www.monster.com; Kim Isaacs, "Resume Dilemma: Employment Gaps and Job-Hopping," Monster.com, accessed 23 May 2006, www.monster.com; Susan Vaughn, "Answer

the Hard Questions Before Asked," *Los Angeles Times*, 29 July 2001, W1–W2.

17. John Steven Niznik, "Landing a Job with a Criminal Record," *About.com*, accessed 12 December 2006, http://jobsearchtech.about.com.

18. "How to Ferret Out Instances of Résumé Padding and Fraud," *Compensation & Benefits for Law Offices*, June 2006, 1.

19. "Resume Fraud Gets Slicker and Easier," *CNN.com*, accessed 11 March 2004, www.cnn.com.

20. "Resume Fraud Still Major Problem HR Needs to Address," *HR Focus*, July 2012, 13–15.

21. Cari Tuna and Keith J. Winstein, "Economy Promises to Fuel Résumé Fraud," *Wall Street Journal*, 17 November 2008, http://online.wsj.com; Lisa Takeuchi Cullen, "Getting Wise to Lies," *Time*, 1 May 2006, 59; "Resume Fraud Gets Slicker and Easier"; Employment Research Services website, accessed 18 March 2004, www.erscheck.com.

22. "How to Ferret Out Instances of Résumé Padding and Fraud."

23. Jacqueline Durett, "Redoing Your Résumé? Leave Off the Lies," *Training*, December 2006, 9; "Employers Turn Their Fire on Untruthful CVs," *Supply Management*, 23 June 2005, 13.

24. Cynthia E. Conn, "Integrating Writing Skills and Ethics Training in Business Communication Pedagogy: A Résumé Case Study Exemplar," *Business Communication Quarterly*, June 2008, 138–151; Marilyn Moats Kennedy, "Don't Get Burned by Résumé Inflation," *Marketing News*, 15 April 2007, 37–38.

25. Rockport Institute, "How to Write a Masterpiece of a Résumé," accessed 9 August 2010, www.rockportinstitute.com.

26. Lora Morsch, "25 Words That Hurt Your Resume," *CNN.com*, 20 January 2006, www.cnn.com.

27. Liz Ryan, "The Reengineered Résumé," *BusinessWeek*, 3 December 2007, SC12.

28. Katharine Hansen, "Tapping the Power of Keywords to Enhance Your Resume's Effectiveness," QuintCareers.com, accessed 7 August 2010, www.quintcareers.com.

29. Hansen, "Tapping the Power of Keywords to Enhance Your Resume's Effectiveness."

30. Anthony Balderrama, "Resume Blunders That Will Keep You from Getting Hired," *CNN.com*, 19 March 2008, www.cnn.com; Michelle Dumas, "5 Resume Writing Myths," Distinctive Documents blog, 17 July 2007, http://blog.distinctiveweb.com; Kim Isaacs, "Resume Dilemma: Recent Graduate," Monster.com, accessed 26 March 2008, http://career-advice.monster.com.

31. Karl L. Smart, "Articulating Skills in the Job Search," *Business Communication Quarterly* 67, no. 2 (June 2004): 198–205.

32. "When to Include Personal Data," ResumeEdge.com, accessed 25 March 2008, www.resumeedge.com.

33. "Résumé Length: What It Should Be and Why It Matters to Recruiters," *HR Focus*, June 2007, 9.

34. John Hazard, "Resume Tips: No Pictures, Please and No PDFs," Career-Line.com, 26 May 2009, www.career-line.com; "25 Things You Should Never Include on a Resume," HR World website 18 December 2007, www.hrworld.com.

35. John Sullivan, "Résumés: Paper, Please," *Workforce Management*, 22 October 2007, 50; "Video Résumés Offer Both Pros and Cons During Recruiting," *HR Focus*, July 2007, 8.

36. Jobs page, Zappos website, accessed 24 March 2011, http://about .zappos.com/jobs.

37. Rachel Louise Ensign, "Is the Paper Résumé Dead?" *Wall Street Journal*, 24 January 2012, http://online.wsj.com.

38. Nancy M. Schullery, Linda Ickes, and Stephen E. Schullery, "Employer Preferences for Résumés and Cover Letters," *Business Communication Quarterly*, June 2009, 163–176.

39. "10 Reasons Why You Are Not Getting Any Interviews," *Miami Times*, 7–13 November 2007, 6D.

40. Deborah Silver, "Niche Sites Gain Monster-Sized Following," *Workforce Management*, March 2011, 10–11.

41. "Protect Yourself from Identity Theft When Hunting for a Job Online," *Office Pro*, May 2007, 6.

42. Job description keywords and key phrases quoted or adapted in part from "Associate Market Analyst" job opening posted on LivingSocial website, accessed 9 July 2012, http://corporate.livingsocial.com.

43. Job description keywords and key phrases quoted or adapted in part from "Seller Support Associate" job opening posted on Amazon website, accessed 12 July 2012, https://us-amazon.icims.com/jobs.

44. Job description keywords and key phrases quoted or adapted in part from "Senior Strategy Analyst" job opening posted on Nordstrom website, accessed 17 July 2012, http://careers .nordstrom.com.

Answer Key for "Learning Objectives Checkup"

1. b
2. quality of hire
3. b
4. b
5. b
6. d
7. chronological
8. functional
9. combination
10. d
11. a
12. b
13. a
14. a
15. b
16. c
17. c
18. c
19. keyword searches
20. plain text
21. a

Answer Key for "Improve Your Grammar, Mechanics, and Usage" Exercises

18. except (4.1)
19. device (4.1)
20. loath (4.1)
21. who's (4.1)
22. a lot (4.2)
23. judgment (4.3)
24. regardless (4.2)
25. accommodate (4.3)
26. imply (4.2)
27. to (4.2)

Applying and Interviewing for Employment

From Chapter 16 of *Excellence in Business Communication*, Twelfth Edition. John V. Thill, Courtland L. Bovée. Copyright © 2017 by Pearson Education, Inc. All rights reserved.

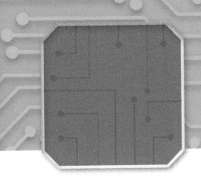

Applying and Interviewing for Employment

LEARNING OBJECTIVES

After studying this chapter, you will be able to

1 Explain the purposes of application letters and describe how to apply the AIDA organizational approach to them.

2 Describe the typical sequence of job interviews, the major types of interviews, and the attributes employers look for during an interview.

3 List six tasks you need to complete to prepare for a successful job interview.

4 Explain how to succeed in all three stages of an interview.

5 Identify the most common employment messages that follow an interview and explain when you would use each one.

ON THE JOB: COMMUNICATING AT
ZAPPOS

Unconventional Approaches to Finding Unconventional Employees

When a company communicates its core values with the help of a cartoon amphibian named Core Values Frog, you can guess the company doesn't quite fit the stuffy corporate stereotype. While it is passionately serious about customer satisfaction and employee engagement, the Las Vegas–based online shoe and clothing retailer Zappos doesn't take itself too seriously. In fact, one of the 10 values the frog promotes is "Create fun and a little weirdness."

Fun and a little weirdness can make a workplace more enjoyable, but CEO Tony Hsieh's commitment to employees runs

Zappos CEO Tony Hsieh makes sure the company's interviewing process finds the candidates who are compatible with an offbeat customer- and colleague-focused culture.

much deeper than that. The company makes frequent reference to "the Zappos Family," and it embraces the ideals of taking care of one another and enjoying time spent together. These activities can range from parades in the workplace and other goofy events to the Wishez program, in which employees can ask one another to fulfill personal wishes, from lighthearted desires such as getting backstage access at concerts to serious matters such as getting help during tough financial times.

To find employees who will thrive in and protect the unconventional Zappos culture, the company takes an unorthodox path when it comes to recruiting and interviewing. For example, in stark contrast to the companies that refuse to look at videos as part of job application packages, Zappos encourages applicants to send videos of themselves. And in perhaps its boldest recruiting move yet, the company no longer posts job openings. Instead, it now requires would-be employees to join a customized social network called Inside Zappos. The network lets candidates learn more about what it's like to work at Zappos, and it lets the company learn more about the candidates—including how they interact with other people.

The Zappos interviewing process is designed to find passionate, free-thinking candidates who fit the culture, from the offbeat antics to the serious commitment to customers and fellow employees. Some of the questions interviewees can expect to encounter include "What was the best mistake you made on the job?" and "On a scale of 1 to 10, how weird are you?"

Speaking of offbeat interviews, the company recently screened software engineering candidates using 30-minute coding challenges, in which the first programmer to solve the problem was "fast-tracked to Vegas" for the next round of interviews. Coding contests are not all that unusual for recruiting programmers, but it's unlikely that many feature an open bar, as the Zappos competition did.

A strong customer- and employee-focused culture, a strong commitment to maintaining that culture, and a recruiting strategy that finds the right people for that culture—this relentless focus on doing business the Zappos way keeps paying off. The company continues to grow and to be ranked as one of the best places to work in the United States.[1]

WWW.ZAPPOS.COM

Submitting Your Résumé

Your résumé is the centerpiece of your job search package, but it needs support from several other employment messages, including application letters, job-inquiry letters, application forms, and follow-up notes.

1 LEARNING OBJECTIVE
Explain the purposes of application letters and describe how to apply the AIDA organizational approach to them.

WRITING APPLICATION LETTERS

Whenever you mail, email, hand-deliver, or upload your résumé, you should include an **application letter**, also known as a *cover letter*, to let readers know what you're sending, why you're sending it, and how they can benefit from reading it. (Even though this message is often not a printed letter anymore, many professionals still refer to it as a letter.) Take the same care with your application letter that you took with your résumé. A poorly written application letter can prompt employers to skip over your résumé, even if you are a good fit for a job.[2] Staffing specialist Abby Kohut calls the application letter "a writing-skills evaluation in disguise" and emphasizes that even a single error can get you bounced from contention.[3]

Always accompany your résumé with an application letter (printed or email) that motivates the recipient to read the résumé.

The best approach for an application letter depends on whether you are applying for an identified job opening or are *prospecting*—taking the initiative to write to companies even though they haven't announced a job opening that is right for you.[4] In many ways, the difference between the two is like the difference between solicited and unsolicited proposals. Figure 1 on the next page shows an application message written in response to a posted job opening. The writer knows exactly what qualifications the organization is seeking and can "echo" those attributes back in his letter.

As with proposals, the best approach for an application letter depends on whether your application is solicited or unsolicited.

Writing a prospecting letter is more challenging because you don't have the clear target you have with a solicited letter, and the message is unexpected. You will need to do more research to identify the qualities that a company would probably seek for the position you hope to occupy (see Figure 2). Also, search for news items that involve the company, its customers, the profession, or the individual manager to whom you are writing. Using this information in your application letter helps you establish common ground with your reader—and it shows that you are tuned in to what is going on in the industry.

MOBILE APP
The CareerBuilder app lets you search and apply for jobs from your phone or tablet.

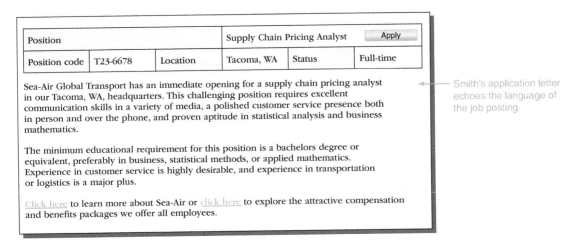

Position			Supply Chain Pricing Analyst		Apply
Position code	T23-6678	Location	Tacoma, WA	Status	Full-time

Sea-Air Global Transport has an immediate opening for a supply chain pricing analyst in our Tacoma, WA, headquarters. This challenging position requires excellent communication skills in a variety of media, a polished customer service presence both in person and over the phone, and proven aptitude in statistical analysis and business mathematics.

The minimum educational requirement for this position is a bachelors degree or equivalent, preferably in business, statistical methods, or applied mathematics. Experience in customer service is highly desirable, and experience in transportation or logistics is a major plus.

Click here to learn more about Sea-Air or click here to explore the attractive compensation and benefits packages we offer all employees.

Smith's application letter echoes the language of the job posting.

27225 Eucalyptus Avenue
Long Beach, CA 90806
March 13, 2017

Sea-Air Global Transport
5467 Port of Tacoma Rd., Suite 230
Tacoma, WA 98421

Dear Hiring Manager:

Sea-Air Global Transport consistently appeared as a top transportation firm in the research I did for my senior project in global supply chain management, so imagine my delight when I discovered the opening for an export pricing analyst in your Tacoma headquarters (Position Code: T23-6678). With a major in business and a minor in statistical methods, my education has been ideal preparation for the challenges of this position.

In fact, my senior project demonstrates most of the skills listed in your job description, including written communication skills, analytical abilities, and math aptitude. I enjoyed the opportunity to put my math skills to the test as part of the statistical comparison of various freight modes.

As you can see from my résumé, I also have more than three years of part-time experience working with customers in both retail and commercial settings. This experience taught me the importance of customer service, and I want to start my professional career with a company that truly values the customer. In reviewing your website and reading several articles on Lloyd's List and other trade websites, I am impressed by Sea-Air's constant attention to customer service in this highly competitive industry.

My verbal communication skills would be best demonstrated in an interview, of course. I would be happy to meet with a representative of your company at their earliest convenience. I can be reached at dalton.k.smith@gmail.com or by phone at (562) 555-3737.

Sincerely,

Dalton Smith

The first sentence grabs attention by indicating knowledge of the company and its industry.

The reference to his résumé emphasizes his customer service orientation and also shows he has done his homework by researching the company.

The letter doesn't include a handwritten signature because it was uploaded to a website along with his résumé.

The opening paragraph identifies the specific job for which he is applying.

In this discussion of his skills, he echoes the qualifications stated in the job posting.

In the close, he politely asks for an interview in a way that emphasizes yet another job-related skill.

Figure 1   Solicited Application Message
In this response to an online job posting, Dalton Smith highlights his qualifications while mirroring the requirements specified in the posting. Following the AIDA model, he grabs attention immediately by letting the reader know he is familiar with the company and the global transportation business.

For either type of letter, follow these tips to be more effective:[5]

- Resist the temptation to stand out with gimmicky application letters; impress with knowledge and professionalism instead.
- If the name of an individual manager is findable, address your letter to that person. (And if it is findable, make sure you find it, because other applicants will.) Search LinkedIn, the company's website, industry directories, Twitter, and anything else

Ineffective

457 Mountain View Rd.
Clear Lake, IA 50428
June 16, 2017

Ms. Patricia Downing, Store Manager
Walmart
840 South Oak
Iowa Falls, IA 50126

Dear Ms. Downing:

Do you have any openings for people who want to move into store management? I am really looking for an opportunity to get a job like yours, even if it takes starting at a low level and working my way up.

Allow me to list some highlights from my enclosed résumé. First, I have a BA degree in retailing, which included such key courses as retailing, marketing, management, and business information systems. Second, I have worked as a clerk and as an assistant manager in a large department store. Third, I have experience in the customer-facing aspect of retailing, as well as operations, marketing, and personnel supervision.

Successful retailing is about more than systems and procedures. It is also about anticipating customer needs, fostering positive relationships with the community, and delivering the type of service that keeps customers coming back. Retailers that fail in any of these areas are doomed to decline in today's hypercompetitive sales environment. I am the sort of forward-thinking, customer-focused leader who can help you avoid this fate.

I will call you next Wednesday at 2:00 to explain why I would make a great addition to your team.

Sincerely,

Glenda Johns

Glenda Johns
Enclosure

The writer commits three major mistakes in the first paragraph: asking a question that she could answer herself by visiting the company's website, failing to demonstrate any knowledge of the company, and making the message all about her.

This paragraph merely repeats information from the enclosed résumé, which wastes the reader's time and wastes the opportunity for the writer to present a more complete picture of herself.

Johns attempts to show that she understands retailing, but this paragraph comes across as an arrogant lecture. The tone is particularly inappropriate, given that she is writing to the store's top manager.

The call to action is overly aggressive, and it presumes that the reader will be available and willing to take a phone call from a complete stranger about a job opening that might not even exist.

Effective

457 Mountain View Rd.
Clear Lake, IA 50428
June 16, 2017

Ms. Patricia Downing, Store Manager
Walmart
840 South Oak
Iowa Falls, IA 50126

Dear Ms. Downing:

Even with its world-class supply chain, admired brand name, and competitive prices, Walmart obviously would not be the success it is without enthusiastic, service-driven associates and managers. If you have or foresee an opening for such a professional, someone eager to learn the Walmart way and eventually move into a management position, please consider me for the opportunity.

As an associate or management trainee, I can bring a passion for retailing and the perspective I've gained through academic preparation and four years of experience. (Please refer to my enclosed résumé for more information.)

Working as a clerk and then as an assistant manager in a large department store taught me how to anticipate customer needs, create effective merchandising, and deliver service that keeps customers coming back. Moreover, my recent BA degree in retailing, which encompassed such courses as retailing concepts, marketing fundamentals, management, and business information systems, prepared me with in-depth awareness of contemporary retailing issues and strategies.

I understand Walmart prefers to promote its managers from within, and I would be pleased to start out with an entry-level position until I gain the necessary experience. Could we have a brief conversation about the possibilities of joining your team? I am available by phone at 641-747-2222 or email at glendajohns@mailnet.com.

Sincerely,

Glenda Johns

Glenda Johns
Enclosure

Johns gets the reader's attention by demonstrating good awareness of the company and the type of people it hires, presents herself as just such a professional, and then asks to be considered for any relevant job openings.

Johns uses the body of her letter to expand on the information presented in her résumé, rather than simply repeating that information.

The close builds the reader's interest by demonstrating knowledge of the company's policy regarding promotion.

The call to action is respectful, and it makes a response easy for the reader by providing both phone and email contact information.

Figure 2 Unsolicited Application Letter: Poor and Improved
Demonstrating knowledge of the employer's needs and presenting your qualifications accordingly are essential steps in an unsolicited application letter.

you can think of to locate an appropriate name. Ask the people in your network if they know a name. If you can't find a name, addressing your letter to "Dear Hiring Manager" is perfectly acceptable.

- Clearly identify the opportunity you are applying for or expressing interest in.
- Show that you understand the company and its marketplace.
- Never volunteer salary history or requirements unless an employer has asked for this information.
- Keep it short—no more than three or four brief paragraphs. Remember that all you are trying to do at this point is move the conversation forward one step.
- Show some personality, while maintaining a business-appropriate tone. The letter gives you the opportunity to balance the facts-only tone of your résumé.
- Project confidence without being arrogant.
- Don't just repeat information from your résumé; use the conversational tone of the letter to convey additional professional and personal qualities and your reasons for wanting this particular job.

Because application letters are persuasive messages, the AIDA approach is ideal, as the following sections explain.

Getting Attention

The opening paragraph of your application letter needs to clearly convey the reason you're writing and give the recipient a compelling reason to keep reading.

The opening paragraph of your application letter must accomplish two essential tasks: (1) explaining why you are writing and (2) giving the recipient a reason to keep reading by demonstrating that you have some immediate potential for meeting the company's needs. Consider this opening:

> With the recent slowdown in corporate purchasing, I can certainly appreciate the challenge of new fleet sales in this business environment. With my high energy level and 16 months of new-car sales experience, I believe I can produce the results you listed as vital in the job posting on your website.

This applicant does a smooth job of echoing the company's stated needs while highlighting his personal qualifications and providing evidence that he understands the broader market. He balances his relative lack of experience with enthusiasm and knowledge of the industry. Table 1 suggests some other ways you can spark interest and grab attention in your opening paragraph.

Building Interest and Increasing Desire

Use the middle section of your application letter to expand on your opening and present a more complete picture of your strengths.

The middle section of your letter presents your strongest selling points in terms of their potential benefit to the organization, thereby building interest in you and creating a desire to interview you. Be specific and back up your assertions with convincing evidence:

> **Poor:** I completed three college courses in business communication, earning an A in each course, and have worked for the past year at Imperial Construction.

> **Improved:** Using the skills gained from three semesters of college training in business communication, I developed a collection system for Imperial Construction that reduced annual bad-debt losses by 25 percent.

In a solicited letter, be sure to discuss each major requirement listed in the job posting. If you are deficient in any of these requirements, stress other solid selling points to help strengthen your overall presentation. Don't restrict your message to just core job duties, either. Also highlight personal characteristics that apply to the targeted position, such as your ability to work hard or handle responsibility:

TABLE 1	Tips for Getting Attention in Application Letters
Tip	**Example**
Unsolicited Application Letters	
Show how your strongest skills will benefit the organization.	If you need a regional sales specialist who consistently meets sales targets while fostering strong customer relationships, please consider my qualifications.
Describe your understanding of the job's requirements and show how well your qualifications fit them.	Your annual report stated that improving manufacturing efficiency is one of the company's top priorities for next year. Through my postgraduate research in systems engineering and consulting work for several companies in the industry, I've developed reliable methods for quickly identifying ways to cut production time while reducing resource use.
Mention the name of a person known to and highly regarded by the reader.	When Janice McHugh of your franchise sales division spoke to our business communication class last week, she said you often need promising new marketing graduates at this time of year.
Refer to publicized company activities, achievements, changes, or new procedures.	Today's issue of the *Detroit News* reports that you may need the expertise of computer programmers versed in robotics when your Lansing tire plant automates this spring.
Use a question to demonstrate your understanding of the organization's needs.	Can your fast-growing market research division use an interviewer with two years of field survey experience, a B.A. in public relations, and a real desire to succeed? If so, please consider me for the position.
Use a catchphrase opening if the job requires ingenuity and imagination.	*Haut monde*—whether referring to French, Italian, or Arab clients, it still means "high society." As an interior designer for your Beverly Hills showroom, not only could I serve and sell to your distinguished clientele, but I could also do it in all these languages. I speak, read, and write them fluently.
Solicited Application Letters	
Identify where you discovered the job opening; describe what you have to offer.	Your job posting on Monster.com for a cruise-line social director caught my eye. My eight years of experience as a social director in the travel industry would equip me to serve your new Caribbean cruise division well.

While attending college full-time, I worked part-time during the school year and up to 60 hours a week each summer in order to be totally self-supporting while in college. I can offer your organization the same level of effort and perseverance.

Mention your salary requirements only if the organization has asked you to state them. If you don't know the salary appropriate for the position and someone with your qualifications, you can find typical salary ranges at the Bureau of Labor Statistics website, www.bls.gov, or a number of commercial websites. If you do state a target salary, tie it to the value you would offer:

> Don't bring up salary in your application letter unless the recipient has asked you to include your salary requirements.

For the past two years, I have been helping a company similar to yours organize its database marketing efforts. I would therefore like to receive a salary in the same range (the mid-60s) for helping your company set up a more efficient customer database.

Toward the end of this section, refer the reader to your résumé by citing a specific fact or general point covered there:

As you can see in the attached résumé, I've been working part-time with a local publisher since my sophomore year. During that time, I've used client interactions as an opportunity to build strong customer service skills.

Motivating Action

In the final paragraph of your application letter, respectfully ask for specific action and make it easy for the reader to respond.

The final paragraph of your application letter has two important functions: to ask the reader for a specific action (usually an interview) and to facilitate a reply. Offer to come to the employer's office at a convenient time or, if the firm is some distance away, to meet with its nearest representative or arrange a telephone or Skype interview. Include your email address and phone number, as well as the best times to reach you:

> After you have reviewed my qualifications, could we discuss the possibility of putting my marketing skills to work for your company? I am available at (360) 555-7845 from 2 p.m. to 10 p.m. Monday to Friday or by email at john.wagner462@gmail.com.

After editing and proofreading your application letter, give it a final quality check by referring to "Checklist: Writing Application Letters." Then send it along with your résumé promptly, especially if you are responding to an advertisement or online job posting.

FOLLOWING UP AFTER SUBMITTING A RÉSUMÉ

Think creatively about a follow-up letter; show that you've continued to add to your skills or that you've learned more about the company or the industry.

Deciding if, when, and how to follow up after submitting your résumé and application letter is one of the trickiest parts of a job search. First and foremost, keep in mind that employers continue to evaluate your communication efforts and professionalism during this phase, so don't say or do anything to leave a negative impression. Second, adhere to whatever instructions the employer has provided. If a job posting says "no calls," for example, don't call. Third, if the job posting lists a *close date*, don't call or write before then, because the company is still collecting applications and will not have made a decision about inviting people for interviews. Wait a week or so after the close date. If no close date is given and you have no other information to suggest a timeline, you can generally contact the company starting a week or two after submitting your résumé.[6]

When you follow up by email or telephone, you can share an additional piece of information that links your qualifications to the position (keep an eye out for late-breaking news about the company, too) and ask a question about the hiring process as a way to gather some information about your status. Good questions to ask include:[7]

- Has a hiring decision been made yet?
- Can you tell me what to expect next in terms of the hiring process?
- What is the company's timeframe for filling this position?
- Could I follow up in another week if you haven't had the chance to contact me yet?
- Can I provide any additional information regarding my qualifications for the position?

Whatever the circumstances, a follow-up message can demonstrate that you're sincerely interested in working for the organization, persistent in pursuing your goals, and committed to upgrading your skills.

CHECKLIST ✔ Writing Application Letters

- Take the same care with your application letter that you took with your résumé.
- If you are *prospecting* using an unsolicited message, do deep research to identify the qualities the company likely wants.
- For solicited messages in response to a posted job opening, word your message in a way that echoes the qualifications listed in the posting.
- Open the letter by capturing the reader's attention in a businesslike way.
- Use specific language to clearly state your interests and objectives.
- Build interest and desire in your potential contribution by presenting your key qualifications for the job.
- Link your education, experience, and personal qualities to the job requirements.
- Outline salary requirements only if the organization has requested that you provide them.
- Request an interview at a time and place that is convenient for the reader.
- Make it easy to comply with your request by providing your complete contact information and good times to reach you.
- Adapt your style for cultural variations, if required.

If you don't land a job at your dream company on the first attempt, don't give up. You can apply again if a new opening appears, or you can send an updated résumé with a new unsolicited application letter that describes how you have gained additional experience, taken a relevant course, or otherwise improved your skill set. Many leading employers take note of applicants who came close but didn't quite make it and may extend offers when positions open up in the future.[8]

REAL-TIME UPDATES

LEARN MORE BY VISITING THIS INTERACTIVE WEBSITE

Prepare for your next interview with these Pinterest pins

The Pinterest pinboard maintained by St. Edward's University offers dozens of helpful resources. Go to http://real-timeupdates.com/ebc12 and click on Learn More in the Students section.

Understanding the Interviewing Process

An **employment interview** is a meeting during which both you and the prospective employer ask questions and exchange information. The employer's objective is to find the best talent to fill available job openings, and your objective is to find the right match for your goals and capabilities.

As you get ready to begin interviewing, keep two vital points in mind. First, recognize that the process takes time. Start your preparation and research early; the best job offers usually go to the best-prepared candidates. Second, don't limit your options by looking at only a few companies. By exploring a wide range of firms and positions, you might uncover great opportunities that you would not have found otherwise. You'll increase the odds of getting more job offers, too.

2 LEARNING OBJECTIVE
Describe the typical sequence of job interviews, the major types of interviews, and the attributes employers look for during an interview.

Start preparing early for your interviews—and be sure to consider a wide range of options.

THE TYPICAL SEQUENCE OF INTERVIEWS

Most employers interview an applicant multiple times before deciding to make a job offer. At the most selective companies, you might have a dozen or more individual interviews across several stages.[9] Depending on the company and the position, the process may stretch out over many weeks, or it may be completed in a matter of days.[10]

Employers start with the *screening stage*, in which they filter out applicants who are unqualified or otherwise not a good fit for the position. Screening can take place on your school's campus, at company offices, via telephone (including Skype or another Internet-based phone service), or through a computer-based screening system. Time is limited in screening interviews, so keep your answers short while providing a few key points that confirm your fit for the position. If your screening interview will take place by phone, try to schedule it for a time when you can be focused and free from interruptions.[11]

The next stage of interviews, the *selection stage*, helps the organization identify the top candidates from all those who qualify. During these interviews, show keen interest in the job, relate your skills and experience to the organization's needs, listen attentively, and ask questions that show you've done your research.

If the interviewers agree that you're a good candidate, you may receive a job offer, either on the spot or a few days later by phone, mail, or email. In other instances, you may be invited back for a final evaluation, often by a higher-ranking executive. The objective of the *final stage* is often to sell you on the advantages of joining the organization.

MOBILE APP
Add the Skype mobile app to your phone to be ready for video interviews.

During the screening stage of interviews, use the limited time available to confirm your fit for the position.

During the selection stage, continue to show how your skills and attributes can help the company.

During the final stage, the interviewer may try to sell you on working for the firm.

COMMON TYPES OF INTERVIEWS

Be prepared to encounter a variety of interviewing approaches. These can be distinguished by the way they are structured, the number of people involved, and the purpose of the interview.

Structured Versus Unstructured Interviews

In a **structured interview**, the interviewer (or a computer program) asks a series of questions in a predetermined order. Structured interviews help employers identify candidates who don't meet basic job criteria, and they allow the interview team to compare answers from multiple candidates.[12]

A structured interview follows a set sequence of questions, allowing the interview team to compare answers from all candidates.

In an open-ended interview, the interviewer adapts the line of questioning based on your responses and questions.

In contrast, in an **open-ended interview**, the interviewer adapts his or her line of questioning based on the answers you give and any questions you ask. Even though it may feel like a conversation, remember that it's still an interview, so keep your answers focused and professional.

Panel and Group Interviews

In a panel interview, you meet with several interviewers at once; in a group interview, you and several other candidates meet with one or more interviewers at once.

Although one-on-one interviews are the most common format, some employers use panel or group interviews as well. In a **panel interview**, you meet with several interviewers at once.[13] Try to make a connection with each person on the panel, and keep in mind that each person has a different perspective, so tailor your responses accordingly.[14] For example, an upper-level manager is likely to be interested in your overall business sense and strategic perspective, whereas a potential colleague might be more interested in your technical skills and ability to work in a team. In a **group interview**, one or more interviewers meet with several candidates simultaneously. A key purpose of a group interview is to observe how the candidates interact.[15] Group interviews can be tricky because you want to stand out while coming across as a supportive team player. Be sure to treat your fellow candidates with respect, while looking for opportunities to demonstrate the depth of knowledge you have about the company and its needs.

Behavioral, Situational, Working, and Stress Interviews

In a behavioral interview, you are asked to describe how you handled situations from your past.

Interviewing techniques also vary based on the types of questions you are asked. Perhaps the most common type of interview these days is the **behavioral interview**, in which you are asked to relate specific incidents and experiences from your past.[16] In contrast to generic questions that can often be answered with "canned" responses, behavioral questions require candidates to use their own experiences and attributes to craft answers. Studies show that behavioral interviewing is a much better predictor of success on the job than traditional interview questions.[17] To prepare for a behavioral interview, review your work or college experiences to recall several instances in which you demonstrated an important job-related attribute or dealt with a challenge such as uncooperative team members or heavy workloads. Get ready with responses that quickly summarize the situation, the actions you took, and the outcome of those actions.[18]

In situational interviews, you're asked to explain how you would handle various hypothetical situations.

A **situational interview** is similar to a behavioral interview except that the questions focus on how you would handle various hypothetical situations on the job. The situations will likely relate closely to the job you're applying for, so the more you know about the position, the better prepared you'll be.

In a working interview, you perform actual work-related tasks.

A **working interview** is the most realistic type of interview: You actually perform a job-related activity during the interview. You may be asked to lead a brainstorming session, solve a business problem, engage in role playing, or even make a presentation.[19]

Stress interviews help recruiters see how you handle yourself under pressure.

The most unnerving type of interview is the **stress interview**, during which you might be asked questions designed to unsettle you or might be subjected to long periods of silence, criticism, interruptions, and or even hostile reactions by the interviewer. The theory behind this approach is that you'll reveal how well you handle stressful situations, although some experts find the technique of dubious value.[20] If you find yourself in a stress interview, recognize what is happening and collect your thoughts for a few seconds before you respond.

You might encounter two or more types of interview questions within a single interview, so stay alert and try to understand the type of question you're facing before you answer each one.

INTERVIEW MEDIA

Expect to use a variety of media when you interview, from in-person conversations to virtual meetings.

Expect to be interviewed through a variety of media. Employers trying to cut travel costs and the demands on staff time now interview candidates via telephone, email, instant messaging, virtual online systems, and videoconferencing, in addition to traditional face-to-face meetings.

Treat a telephone interview as seriously as you would an in-person interview.

To succeed at a telephone interview, make sure you treat it as seriously as an in-person interview. Be prepared with a copy of all the materials you have sent to the employer, including your résumé and any correspondence. In addition, prepare some note cards with key message points you'd like to make and questions you'd like to ask. And remember that you won't be able to use a pleasant smile, a firm handshake, and other nonverbal signals to create a good impression. A positive, alert tone of voice is therefore vital.[21]

Email and IM are also sometimes used in the screening stage. Although you have almost no opportunity to send and receive nonverbal signals with these formats, you do have the major advantage of being able to review and edit each response before you send it. Maintain a professional style in your responses, and be sure to ask questions that demonstrate your knowledge of the company and the position.[22]

> When interviewing via email or IM, be sure to take a moment to review your responses before sending them.

Many employers use video technology for both live and recorded interviews. For instance, Zappos uses video interviews on Skype to select the top two or three finalists for each position and then invites those candidates for in-person interviews.[23] Recruiters can also use mobile apps for interviews. With recorded video interviews, an online system asks a set of questions and records the respondent's answers. Recruiters then watch the videos as part of the screening process.[24] Prepare for a video interview as you

REAL-TIME UPDATES

LEARN MORE BY WATCHING THIS VIDEO

Video interviewing on Skype

Watch this video for essential tips on preparing for and participating in an online video interview. Go to http://real-timeupdates.com/ebc12 and click on Learn More in the Students section.

would for an in-person interview—including dressing and grooming—and take the extra steps needed to become familiar with the equipment and the process. If you're interviewing from home, arrange your space so that the webcam doesn't pick up anything distracting or embarrassing in the background. During any video interview, remember to sit up straight and focus on the camera.

> In a video interview, speak to the camera as though you are addressing the interviewer in person.

Online interviews can range from simple structured questionnaires and tests to sophisticated job simulations that are similar to working interviews (see Figure 3). These simulations help identify good candidates, give applicants an idea of what the job is like, and reduce the risk of employment discrimination lawsuits because they closely mimic actual job skills.[25]

> Computer-based virtual interviews range from simple structured interviews to realistic job simulations to meetings in virtual worlds.

WHAT EMPLOYERS LOOK FOR IN AN INTERVIEW

Interviews give employers the chance to go beyond the basic data of your résumé to get to know you and to answer two essential questions. The first is whether you can handle the responsibilities of the position. Naturally, the more you know about the demands of the position, and the more you've thought about how your skills match those demands, the better you'll be able to respond.

> Suitability for a specific job is judged on the basis of such factors as
> - Academic preparation
> - Work experience
> - Job-related personality traits

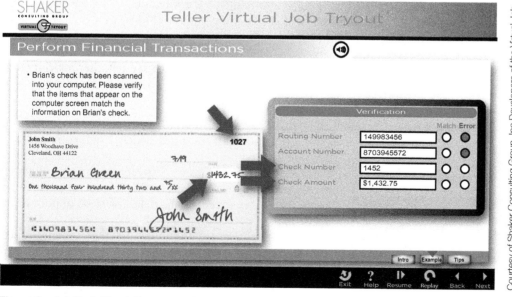

Figure 3   Job Task Simulations
Computer-based job simulations are an increasingly popular approach to testing job-related skills.

Compatibility with an organizational culture and a position is judged on such factors as personal background, attitudes, and communication style.

The second essential question is whether you will be a good fit with the organization and the target position. All good employers want people who are confident, dedicated, positive, curious, courteous, ethical, and willing to commit to something larger than their own individual goals. Companies also look for fit with their individual cultures. Just like people, companies have different "personalities." Some are intense; others are more laid back. Some emphasize teamwork; others expect employees to forge their own way and even to compete with one another. Expectations also vary from job to job within a company and from industry to industry. An outgoing personality is essential for sales but less so for research, for instance.

PREEMPLOYMENT TESTING AND BACKGROUND CHECKS

Preemployment tests attempt to provide objective, quantitative information about a candidate's skills, attitudes, and habits.

In an effort to improve the predictability of the selection process, many employers now conduct a variety of preemployment evaluations and investigations. Here are types of assessments you are likely to encounter during your job search:[26]

- **Integrity tests.** Integrity tests attempt to measure how truthful and trustworthy a candidate is likely to be.
- **Personality tests.** Personality tests are designed to gauge such aspects as attitudes toward work, interests, managerial potential, dependability, commitment, and motivation.
- **Cognitive tests.** Cognitive tests measure a variety of attributes involved in acquiring, processing, analyzing, using, and remembering information. Typical tests involve reading comprehension, mathematics, problem solving, and decision making.
- **Language proficiency.** You may be asked to take a reading or writing test.
- **Job knowledge and job skills tests.** These assessments measure the knowledge and skills required to succeed in a particular position. An accounting candidate, for example, might be tested on accounting principles and legal matters (knowledge) and asked to create a simple balance sheet or income statement (skills).
- **Substance tests.** A majority of companies perform some level of drug and alcohol testing. Many employers believe such testing is necessary to maintain workplace safety, ensure productivity, and protect companies from lawsuits, but others view it as an invasion of employee privacy.
- **Background checks.** In addition to testing, most companies conduct some sort of background check, including reviewing your credit record, checking to see whether you have a criminal history, and verifying your education. Moreover, you should assume that every employer will conduct a general online search on you. To help prevent a background check from tripping you up, verify that your college transcripts are current, look for any mistakes or outdated information in your credit record, plug your name into multiple search engines to see whether anything embarrassing shows up, and scour your social network profiles and connections for potential problems.

Preemployment assessments are a complex and controversial aspect of workforce recruiting. For instance, even though personality testing is widely used, some research suggests that commonly used tests are not a reliable predictor of job success.[27] However, expect to see more innovation in this area and greater use of testing in general in the future as companies try to reduce the risks and costs of poor hiring decisions.

If you're concerned about any preemployment test, ask the employer for more information or ask your college career center for advice. You can also get more information from the Equal Employment Opportunity Commission, at www.eeoc.gov.

REAL-TIME UPDATES

LEARN MORE BY LISTENING TO THIS PODCAST

Expert tips for successful phone interviews

Recruiting experts offer invaluable advice on nailing a phone interview. Go to http://real-timeupdates.com/ebc12 and click on Learn More in the Students section.

Preparing for a Job Interview

Now that you're armed with insights into the interviewing and assessment process, you're ready to begin preparing for your interviews. Preparation will help you feel more confident and perform better under pressure, and preparation starts with learning about the organization.

3 LEARNING OBJECTIVE
List six tasks you need to complete to prepare for a successful job interview.

LEARNING ABOUT THE ORGANIZATION AND YOUR INTERVIEWERS

Employers expect serious candidates to demonstrate an understanding of the company's operations, its markets, and its strategic and tactical challenges.[28] You've already done some initial research to identify companies of interest, but when you're invited to an interview, it's time to dig a little deeper (see Table 2). Making this effort demonstrates your interest in the company, and it identifies you as a business professional who knows the importance of investigation and analysis.

In addition to learning about the company and the job opening, try to find out as much as you can about the managers who will be interviewing you, if you can get their names. Search LinkedIn in particular. It's also perfectly acceptable to ask your contact at the company for the names and titles of the people who will be interviewing you.[29] Think about ways to use whatever information you find during your interview. For example, if an interviewer lists membership in a particular professional organization, you might ask whether the organization is a good forum for people to learn about vital issues in the profession or industry. This question gives the interviewer an opportunity to talk about his

Interviewers expect you to know some basic information about the company and its industry.

TABLE 2 Investigating an Organization and a Job Opportunity

Where to Look and What You Can Learn

- **Company website, blogs, and social media accounts:** Overall information about the company, including key executives, products and services, locations and divisions, employee benefits, job descriptions
- **Competitors' websites, blogs, and social media accounts:** Similar information from competitors, including the strengths these companies claim to have
- **Industry-related websites and blogs:** Objective analysis and criticism of the company, its products, its reputation, and its management
- **Marketing materials (print and online):** The company's marketing strategy and customer communication style
- **Company publications (print and online):** Key events, stories about employees, new products
- **Your social network contacts:** Names and job titles of potential contacts within a company
- **Periodicals (newspapers and trade journals, both print and online):** In-depth stories about the company and its strategies, products, successes, and failures; you may find profiles of top executives
- **Career center at your college:** Often provides a wide array of information about companies that hire graduates
- **Current and former employees:** Insights into the work environment

Points to Learn About the Organization

- Full name
- Location (headquarters and divisions, branches, subsidiaries, or other units)
- Ownership (public or private; whether it is owned by another company)
- Brief history
- Products and services
- Industry position (whether the company is a leader or a minor player; whether it is an innovator or more of a follower)
- Key financial points (such as stock price and trends, if a public company)
- Growth prospects (whether the company is investing in its future through research and development; whether it is in a thriving industry)

Points to Learn About the Position

- Title
- Functions and responsibilities
- Qualifications and expectations
- Possible career paths
- Salary range
- Travel expectations and opportunities
- Relocation expectations and opportunities

or her own interests and experiences for a moment, which builds rapport and might reveal vital insights into the career path you are considering. Just make sure your questions are sincere and not uncomfortably personal.

THINKING AHEAD ABOUT QUESTIONS

Planning ahead for the interviewer's questions will help you handle them more confidently and successfully. In addition, you will want to prepare insightful questions of your own.

Planning for the Employer's Questions

You can expect to face a number of common questions in your interviews, so be sure to prepare for them.

Many general interview questions are "stock" queries you can expect to hear again and again during your interviews. Get ready to face these six at the very least:

- **What is the hardest decision you've ever had to make?** Be prepared with a good example (that isn't too personal), explaining why the decision was difficult, how you made the choice you made, and what you learned from the experience.
- **What is your greatest weakness?** This question seems to be a favorite of some interviewers, although it probably rarely yields useful information. One good strategy is to mention a skill or attribute you haven't had the opportunity to develop yet but would like to in your next position.[30] Another option is to discuss a past shortcoming you took steps to correct.
- **Where do you want to be five years from now?** This question tests (1) whether you're merely using this job as a stopover until something better comes along and (2) whether you've given thought to your long-term goals. Your answer should reflect your desire to contribute to the employer's long-term goals, not just your own goals. Whether this question often yields useful information is also a matter of debate, but be prepared to answer it.[31]
- **What didn't you like about previous jobs you've held?** Answer this one carefully: The interviewer is trying to predict whether you'll be an unhappy or difficult employee.[32] Describe something that you didn't like in a way that puts you in a positive light, such as having limited opportunities to apply your skills or education. Avoid making negative comments about former employers or colleagues.
- **Tell me something about yourself.** One good strategy is to briefly share the "story of you"—quickly summarizing where you have been and where you would like to go—in a way that aligns your interests with the company's. Alternatively, you can focus on a specific skill you know is valuable to the company, share something business-relevant that you are passionate about, or offer a short summary of what colleagues or customers think about you.[33] Whatever tactic you choose, this is not the time to be shy or indecisive, so be ready with a confident, memorable answer.
- **How do you spend your free time?** This question can pop up late in an interview, after the interviewer has covered the major work-related questions and wants to get a better idea of what sort of person you are.[34] Prepare an answer that is honest and that puts you in a positive light, without revealing more than you are comfortable revealing or suggesting that you might not fit in the corporate culture. Sports, hobbies, reading, spending time with family, and volunteer work are all "safe" answers.

Continue your preparation by planning a brief answer to each question in Table 3.

As you prepare answers, look for ways to frame your responses as brief stories (30 to 90 seconds) rather than simple declarative answers.[35] Cohesive stories tend to stick in the listener's mind more effectively than disconnected facts and statements.

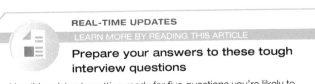
Look for ways to frame your responses as brief stories rather than as dry facts or statements.

TABLE 3 Twenty-Five Common Interview Questions

Questions About College
1. What courses in college did you like most? Least? Why?
2. Do you think your extracurricular activities in college were worth the time you spent on them? Why or why not?
3. When did you choose your college major? Did you ever change your major? If so, why?
4. Do you feel you did the best scholastic work you are capable of?
5. How has your college education prepared you for this position?

Questions About Employers and Jobs
6. Why did you leave your last job?
7. Why did you apply for this job opening?
8. Why did you choose your particular field of work?
9. What are the disadvantages of your chosen field?
10. What do you know about our company?
11. What do you think about how this industry operates today?
12. Why do you think you would like this particular type of job?

Questions About Work Experiences and Expectations
13. What was your biggest failure?
14. Describe an experience in which you learned from one of your mistakes.
15. What motivates you? Why?
16. What do you think determines a person's progress in a good organization?
17. Are you a leader or a follower?
18. What have you done that shows initiative and willingness to work?
19. Why should I hire you?

Questions About Work Habits
20. Do you prefer working with others or by yourself?
21. What type of boss do you prefer?
22. Have you ever had any difficulty getting along with colleagues or supervisors? With instructors? With other students?
23. What would you do if you were given an unrealistic deadline for a task or project?
24. How do you feel about overtime work?
25. How do you handle stress or pressure on the job?

Sources: Alison Green, "The 10 Most Common Job Interview Questions," *U.S. News & World Report*, 24 January 2011, http://money.usnews.com; "Most Common Interview Questions," Glassdoor blog, 29 December 2011, www.glassdoor.com; *The Northwestern Endicott Report* (Evanston, Ill.: Northwestern University Placement Center).

Planning Questions of Your Own

Remember that an interview is a two-way conversation: The questions you ask are just as important as the answers you provide. By asking insightful questions, you can demonstrate your understanding of the organization, steer the discussion into areas that allow you to present your qualifications to best advantage, and verify for yourself whether this is a good opportunity. Plus, interviewers expect you to ask questions and look negatively on candidates who don't have any questions to ask. For good questions that you might use as a starting point, see Table 4 on the next page.

> Preparing questions of your own helps you understand the company and the position, and it sends an important signal that you are truly interested.

BOOSTING YOUR CONFIDENCE

Interviewing is stressful for everyone, so some nervousness is natural. However, you can take steps to feel more confident. Start by reminding yourself that you have value to offer the employer, and the employer already thinks highly enough of you to invite you to an interview.

If some aspect of your appearance or background makes you uneasy, correct it if possible or offset it by emphasizing positive traits such as warmth, wit, intelligence, or charm. Instead of dwelling on your weaknesses, focus on your strengths. Instead of worrying about how you will perform in the interview, focus on how you can help the organization succeed. As with public speaking, the more prepared you are, the more confident you'll be.

> The best way to build your confidence is to prepare thoroughly and address shortcomings as best you can. In other words, take action.

TABLE 4   Ten Questions to Consider Asking an Interviewer

Question	Reason for Asking
1. What are the job's major responsibilities?	A vague answer could mean that the responsibilities have not been clearly defined, which is almost guaranteed to cause frustration if you take the job.
2. What qualities do you want in the person who fills this position?	This will help you go beyond the job description to understand what the company really wants.
3. How do you measure success for someone in this position?	A vague or incomplete answer could mean that the expectations you will face are unrealistic or ill defined.
4. What is the first problem that needs the attention of the person you hire?	Not only will this help you prepare, but it can also signal whether you're about to jump into a problematic situation.
5. Would relocation be required now or in the future?	If you're not willing to move often or at all, you need to know those expectations now.
6. Why is this job now vacant?	If the previous employee got promoted, that's a good sign. If the person quit, that might not be such a good sign.
7. What makes your organization different from others in the industry?	The answer will help you assess whether the company has a clear strategy to succeed in its industry and whether top managers communicate this to lower-level employees.
8. How would you define your organization's managerial philosophy?	You want to know whether the managerial philosophy is consistent with your own working values.
9. What is a typical workday like for you?	The interviewer's response can give you clues about daily life at the company.
10. What are the next steps in the selection process? What's the best way to follow up with you?	Knowing where the company is in the hiring process will give you clues about following up after the interview and possibly give you hints about where you stand.

Sources: Heather Huhman, "5 Must-Ask Questions at Job Interviews," Glassdoor blog, 7 February 2012, www.glassdoor.com; Joe Conklin, "Turning the Tables: Six Questions to Ask Your Interviewer," *Quality Progress*, November 2007, 55; Andrea N. Browne, "Keeping the Momentum at the Interview; Ask Questions, Do Your Research, and Be a Team Player," *Washington Post*, 29 July 2007, K1.

POLISHING YOUR INTERVIEW STYLE

Staging mock interviews with a friend is one good way to hone your style.

Competence and confidence are the foundation of your interviewing style, and you can enhance them by giving the interviewer an impression of poise, good manners, and good judgment. You can develop a smooth style by staging mock interviews with a friend or using an interview simulator on your phone or tablet (see Figure 4). Record these mock interviews so you can evaluate yourself. Your college's career center may have computer-based systems for practicing interviews as well.

After each practice session, look for opportunities to improve. Have your mock interview partner critique your performance, or critique yourself if you're able to record your practice interviews, using the list of warning signs shown in Table 5. Pay close attention to the length of your planned answers as well. Interviewers want you to give complete answers, but they don't want you to take up valuable time or test their patience by chatting about minor or irrelevant details.[36]

Evaluate the length and clarity of your answers, your nonverbal behavior, and the quality of your voice.

In addition to reviewing your answers, evaluate your nonverbal behavior, including your posture, eye contact, facial expressions, and hand gestures and movements. Do you come across as alert and upbeat or passive and withdrawn? Pay close attention to your speaking voice as well. If you tend to speak in a monotone, for instance, practice speaking in a livelier style, with more inflection and emphasis. And watch out for "filler words" such as *uh* and *um*. Many people start sentences with a filler without being conscious of doing so. Train yourself to pause silently for a moment instead as you gather your thoughts and plan what to say.

REAL-TIME UPDATES
LEARN MORE BY READING THIS INFOGRAPHIC

Get a quick reminder of the key steps in preparing for an interview

Use these tips to refresh your memory before an interview. Go to http://real-timeupdates.com/ebc12 and click on Learn More in the Students section.

PRESENTING A PROFESSIONAL IMAGE

Dress conservatively and be well groomed for every interview.

Clothing and grooming are important elements of preparation because they reveal something about a candidate's personality, professionalism, and ability to sense the unspoken

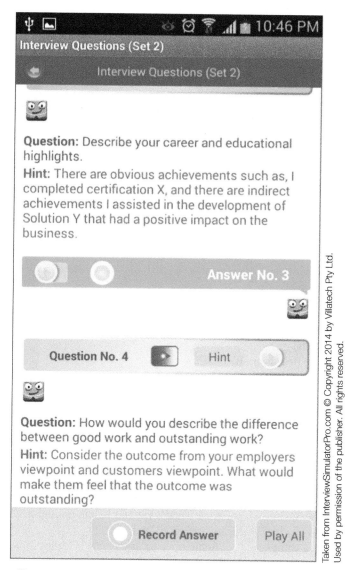

Figure 4   Interview Simulators

A number of mobile apps are available to help you practice and polish your interviewing skills.

"rules" of a situation. Your research into various industries and professions should give you insight into expectations for business attire. If you're not sure what to wear, ask someone who works in the same industry or even visit the company at the end of the day and see what employees are wearing as they leave the office. You don't need to spend a fortune on interview clothes, but your clothes must be clean, pressed, and appropriate. The following look will serve you well in most interview situations:[37]

- Neat, "adult" hairstyle
- For more formal environments, a conservative business suit (for women, that means no exposed midriffs, short skirts, or plunging necklines) in a dark solid color or a subtle pattern such as pinstripes; white shirt and understated tie for men; coordinated blouse for women
- For less formal environments, smart-looking "business casual," including a pressed shirt or blouse and nice slacks or a skirt
- Limited jewelry (men, especially, should wear very little jewelry)
- No visible piercings other than one or two earrings (for women only)
- No visible tattoos
- Stylish but professional-looking shoes (no extreme high heels or casual shoes)
- Clean hands and nicely trimmed fingernails

TABLE 5 Warning Signs: 25 Attributes Interviewers Don't Like to See

1. Poor personal appearance	13. Poor scholastic record
2. Overbearing, overaggressive, or conceited demeanor; a "superiority complex"; a know-it-all attitude	14. Unwillingness to start at the bottom; expecting too much too soon
3. Inability to express ideas clearly; poor voice, diction, or grammar	15. Tendency to make excuses
4. Lack of knowledge or experience	16. Evasive answers; hedging on unfavorable factors in record
5. Poor preparation for the interview	17. Lack of tact
6. Lack of interest in the job	18. Lack of maturity
7. Lack of planning for career; lack of purpose or goals	19. Lack of courtesy and common sense, including answering mobile phones, texting, or chewing gum during the interview
8. Lack of enthusiasm; passive and indifferent demeanor	20. Being critical of past or present employers
9. Lack of confidence and poise; appearance of being nervous and ill at ease	21. Lack of social skills
10. Insufficient evidence of achievement	22. Marked dislike for schoolwork
11. Failure to participate in extracurricular activities	23. Lack of vitality
12. Overemphasis on money; interest only in the best offer	24. Failure to look interviewer in the eye
	25. Limp, weak handshake

Sources: Donna Fuscaldo, "Seven Deadly Interview Sins," Glassdoor blog, 4 April 2012, www.glassdoor.com; "Employers Reveal Outrageous and Common Mistakes Candidates Made in Job Interviews, According to New CareerBuilder Survey," CareerBuilder.com, 12 January 2011, www.careerbuilder.com; *The Northwestern Endicott Report* (Evanston, Ill.: Northwestern University Placement Center).

- Little or no perfume or cologne (some people are allergic and many people are put off by strong smells)
- Subtle makeup (for women)
- Exemplary personal hygiene

COMMUNICATING ACROSS CULTURES

Successfully Interviewing Across Borders

Interviewing for a job in another country can be one of the most exciting steps in your career. To succeed, you need to pay close attention to the important elements of the interviewing process, including personal appearance, an awareness of what interviewers are really trying to learn about you, and things you should learn about the organization you're hoping to join.

Some countries and cultures place a much higher importance on dress and personal grooming than many employees in the United States are accustomed to; moreover, expectations of personal appearance can vary dramatically from country to country. Ask people who've been to the country before and observe local businesspeople when you arrive. Many people interpret inappropriate dress as more than a simple fashion mistake; they view it as an inability or unwillingness to understand another culture. Even if you are interviewing via Skype, as is often the case in the early rounds, make sure your on-screen appearance is appropriate.

For instance, business image consultant Ashley Rothschild points out that you could get away with wearing a boldly colored suit in Italy but probably not in Japan. Business professionals tend to dress formally in Italy, but as a worldwide fashion leader, the country has a broad definition of what is appropriate business attire.

Smart recruiters always analyze both nonverbal signals and verbal messages to judge whether an applicant truly has the qualities necessary for a job. In international employment situations, you'll probably be under even closer scrutiny. Recruiters abroad will want to know if you really have what it takes to succeed in unfamiliar social settings, how your family will handle the transition, and whether you can adapt your personal work style and habits enough to blend in with the hiring organization.

Remember to ask plenty of questions and do your research, both before and after the interview. Some employees view overseas postings as grand adventures, only to collide headfirst with the reality of what it's like to live and work in a completely different culture. For instance, if you've grown accustomed to the independent work style you enjoy in your current job or in school, could you handle a more structured work environment with a hierarchical chain of command? Make sure to get a sense of the culture both within the company and within its social community before you commit to a job in another country.

CAREER APPLICATIONS

1. Explain how you could find out what is appropriate dress for a job interview in South Africa.
2. Would it be appropriate to ask an interviewer to describe the culture in his or her country? Explain your answer.

Sources: Sharon Ann Holgate, "Gaining an Edge in Overseas Interviews," *Science Careers,* 4 August 2014; http://sciencecareers.sciencemag.org; Jean-Marc Hachey, "Interviewing for an International Job," excerpt from *The Canadian Guide to Working and Living Overseas,* 3rd ed., accessed 23 February 2004, www.workingoverseas.com; Rebecca Falkoff, "Dress to Impress the World: International Business Fashion," Monster.com, accessed 23 February 2004, www.monster.com; Mary Ellen Slater, "Navigating the Details of Landing an Overseas Job," *Washington Post,* 11 November 2002, E4.

An interview is not the place to express your individuality or to let your inner rebel run wild. Send a clear signal that you understand the business world and know how to adapt to it. You won't be taken seriously otherwise.

If you want to be taken seriously, dress and act seriously.

BEING READY WHEN YOU ARRIVE

When you go to your interview, take a small notebook, a pen, a list of the questions you want to ask, several copies of your résumé (protected in a folder), an outline of what you have learned about the organization, and any past correspondence about the position. You may also want to take a small calendar, a transcript of your college grades, a list of references, and a portfolio containing samples of your work, performance reviews, and certificates of achievement.[38] Think carefully if you plan to use a tablet computer or any other device for note taking or reference during an interview. You don't want to waste any of the interviewer's time fumbling with it. Also, turn off your mobile phone; in a recent survey of hiring professionals, answering calls or texting while in an interview was identified as the most common mistake job candidates make during their interviews.[39]

> **REAL-TIME UPDATES**
> **LEARN MORE BY WATCHING THIS PRESENTATION**
> **Simple tips for a professional interview look**
> Not sure how to get the right look? Follow this advice. Go to http://real-timeupdates.com/ebc12 and click on Learn More in the Students section.

Be sure you know when and where the interview will be held. The worst way to start any interview is to be late. Verify the route and time required to get there, even if that means traveling there ahead of time. Plan to arrive early, but don't approach the reception desk until 5 minutes or so before your appointed time.[40] Chances are the interviewer won't be ready to receive you until the scheduled time.

Be ready to go the minute you arrive at the interviewing site; don't fumble around for your résumé or your list of questions.

If you have to wait for the interviewer, use this time to review the key messages about yourself you want to get across in the interview. Conduct yourself professionally while waiting. Show respect for everyone you encounter, and avoid chewing gum, eating, or drinking. Anything you do or say at this stage may get back to the interviewer, so make sure your best qualities show from the moment you enter the premises. To review the steps for planning a successful interview, see "Checklist: Planning for a Successful Job Interview."

Interviewing for Success

At this point, you have a good sense of the overall process and know how to prepare for your interviews. The next step is to get familiar with the three stages of every interview: the warm-up, the question-and-answer session, and the close.

> **4 LEARNING OBJECTIVE**
> Explain how to succeed in all three stages of an interview.

> **CHECKLIST ✔ Planning for a Successful Job Interview**
>
> - Learn about the organization, including its operations, markets, and challenges.
> - Learn as much as you can about the people who will be interviewing you, if you can find their names.
> - Plan for the employer's questions, including questions about tough decisions you've made, your perceived shortcomings, what you didn't like about previous jobs, and your career plans.
> - Plan questions of your own to find out whether this is really the job and the organization for you and to show that you've done your research.
> - Bolster your confidence by removing as many sources of apprehension as you can.
>
> - Polish your interview style by staging mock interviews.
> - Present a professional appearance with appropriate dress and grooming.
> - Be ready when you arrive and bring along a pen, paper, a list of questions, copies of your résumé, an outline of your research on the company, and any correspondence you've had regarding the position.
> - Double-check the location and time of the interview and map out the route beforehand.
> - Relax and be flexible; the schedule and interview arrangements may change when you arrive.

THE WARM-UP

Of the three stages, the warm-up is the most important, even though it may account for only a small fraction of the time you spend in the interview. Studies suggest that many interviewers make up their minds within the first 20 seconds of contact with a candidate.[41] Don't let your guard down if the interviewer engages in what feels like small talk; these exchanges are every bit as important as structured questions.

Body language is crucial at this point. Stand or sit up straight, maintain regular but natural eye contact, and don't fidget. When the interviewer extends a hand, respond with a firm but not overpowering handshake. Repeat the interviewer's name when you're introduced ("It's a pleasure to meet you, Ms. Litton"). Wait until you're asked to be seated or the interviewer has taken a seat. Let the interviewer start the discussion, and be ready to answer one or two substantial questions right away. The following are some common openers:[42]

- Why do you want to work here?
- What do you know about us?
- Tell me a little about yourself.

THE QUESTION-AND-ANSWER STAGE

Questions and answers usually consume the greatest part of the interview. Depending on the type of interview, the interviewer will likely ask about your qualifications, discuss some of the points mentioned in your résumé, and ask about how you have handled particular situations in the past or would handle them in the future. You'll also be asking questions of your own.

Answering and Asking Questions

Let the interviewer lead the conversation and never answer a question before he or she has finished asking it. Not only is this type of interruption rude, but the last few words of the question might alter how you respond. As much as possible, avoid one-word yes-or-no answers. Use the opportunity to expand on a positive response or explain a negative response. If you're asked a difficult question or the offbeat questions that companies such as Zappos and Google are known to use, pause before responding. Think through the implications of the question. For instance, the recruiter may know that you can't answer a question and only wants to know how you'll respond under pressure or whether you can construct a logical approach to solving a problem.

Whenever you're asked if you have any questions, or whenever doing so naturally fits the flow of the conversation, ask a question from the list you've prepared. Probe for what the company is looking for in its new employees so that you can show how you meet the firm's needs. Also try to zero in on any reservations the interviewer might have about you so that you can dispel them.

Listening to the Interviewer

Paying attention when the interviewer speaks can be as important as giving good answers or asking good questions. The interviewer's facial expressions, eye movements, gestures, and posture may tell you the real meaning of what is being said. Be especially aware of how your answers are received. Does the interviewer nod in agreement or smile to show approval? If so, you're making progress. If not, you might want to introduce another topic or modify your approach.

Handling Potentially Discriminatory Questions

A variety of federal, state, and local laws prohibit employment discrimination on the basis of race, ethnicity, gender, age (at least if you're between 40 and 70), marital status, religion, national origin, or disability. Interview questions designed to elicit information on these topics are potentially illegal.[43] Table 6 compares some specific questions that employers are and are not allowed to ask during an employment interview.

The first minute of the interview is crucial, so stay alert and be on your best business behavior.

Recognize that you could face substantial questions as soon as your interview starts, so make sure you are prepared and ready to go.

MOBILE APP
Monster's mobile app offers helpful tips to help you prepare for your next job interviews.

Listen carefully to questions before you answer.

Paying attention to both verbal and nonverbal messages can help you turn the question-and-answer stage to your advantage.

TABLE 6 Acceptable Versus Potentially Discriminatory Interview Questions

Interviewers May Ask This.. .	But Not This
What is your name?	What was your maiden name?
Are you over 18?	When were you born?
Did you graduate from high school?	When did you graduate from high school?
[No questions about race are allowed.]	What is your race?
Can you perform [specific tasks]?	Do you have physical or mental disabilities?
	Do you have a drug or alcohol problem?
	Are you taking any prescription drugs?
Would you be able to meet the job's requirement to frequently work weekends?	Would working on weekends conflict with your religion?
Do you have the legal right to work in the United States?	What country are you a citizen of?
Have you ever been convicted of a felony?	Have you ever been arrested?
This job requires that you speak Spanish. Do you?	What language did you speak in your home when you were growing up?

Sources: Dave Johnson, "Illegal Job Interview Questions," *CBS Money Watch*, 27 February 2012, www.cbsnews.com; "5 Illegal Interview Questions and How to Dodge Them," *Forbes,* 20 April 2012, www.forbes.com; Deanna G. Kucler, "Interview Questions: Legal or Illegal?" *Workforce Management*, accessed 28 September 2005, www.workforce.com.

If an interviewer asks a potentially unlawful question, consider your options carefully before you respond. You can answer the question as it was asked, you can ask tactfully whether the question might be prohibited, you can simply refuse to answer it, or you can try to answer "the question behind the question."[44] For example, if an interviewer inappropriately asks whether you are married or have strong family ties in the area, he or she might be trying to figure out if you're willing to travel or relocate—both of which are acceptable questions. Only you can decide which is the right choice based on the situation.

Even if you do answer the question as it was asked, think hard before accepting a job offer from this company if you have alternatives. Was the off-limits question possibly accidental (it happens) and therefore not really a major concern? If you think it was intentional, would you want to work for an organization that condones illegal or discriminatory questions or that doesn't train its employees to avoid them?

If you believe an interviewer's questions to be unreasonable, unrelated to the job, or an attempt to discriminate, you have the option of filing a complaint with the U.S. Equal Employment Opportunity Commission or with the agency in your state that regulates fair employment practices.

Federal, state, and local laws prohibit employment discrimination based on a variety of factors, and well-trained interviewers know to avoid questions that could be used to discriminate in the hiring process.

Think about how you might respond if you were asked a potentially unlawful question.

THE CLOSE

Like the warm-up, the end of the interview is more important than its brief duration would indicate. These last few minutes are your final opportunity to emphasize your value to the organization and to correct any misconceptions the interviewer might have. Be aware that many interviewers will ask whether you have any more questions at this point, so save one or two from your list.

REAL-TIME UPDATES

LEARN MORE BY WATCHING THIS VIDEO

Stay calm by pressing your "panic reset button"

Learn how to reset your emotions if you feel like you're starting to panic in a job interview. Go to http://real-timeupdates.com/ebc12 and click on Learn More in the Students section.

Concluding Gracefully

You can usually tell when the interviewer is trying to conclude the session. He or she may ask whether you have any more questions, check the time, summarize the discussion, or simply tell you that the allotted time for the interview is up. When you get the signal, be sure to thank the interviewer for the opportunity and express your interest in the

Conclude an interview with courtesy and enthusiasm.

organization. If you can do so comfortably, try to pin down what will happen next, but don't press for an immediate decision.

If this is your second or third visit to the organization, the interview may end with an offer of employment. If you have other offers or need time to think about this offer, it's perfectly acceptable to thank the interviewer for the offer and ask for some time to consider it. If no job offer is made, the interview team may not have reached a decision yet, but you may tactfully ask when you can expect to know the decision.

Discussing Salary

Research salary ranges in your job, industry, and geographic region before you try to negotiate salary.

If you receive an offer during the interview, you'll naturally want to discuss salary. However, let the interviewer raise the subject. If asked your salary requirements during the interview or on a job application, you can say that your requirements are open or negotiable or that you would expect a competitive compensation package.[45]

How far you can negotiate depends on several factors, including market demand for your skills, the strength of the job market, the company's compensation policies, the company's financial health, and any other job offers you may be considering. Remember that you're negotiating a business deal, not asking for personal favors, so focus on the unique value you can bring to the job. The more information you have, the stronger your position will be.

Negotiating benefits may be one way to get more value from an employment package.

If salary isn't negotiable, look at the overall compensation and benefits package. You may find flexibility in a signing bonus, profit sharing, retirement benefits, health coverage, vacation time, and other valuable elements.[46]

To review the important tips for successful interviews, see "Checklist: Making a Positive Impression in Job Interviews."

INTERVIEW NOTES

Keeping a careful record of your job interviews is essential.

Maintain a notebook or simple database with information about each company, interviewers' answers to your questions, contact information for each interviewer, the status of follow-up communication, and upcoming interview appointments. Carefully organized

---

CHECKLIST ✔ Making a Positive Impression in Job Interviews

A. Be ready to make a positive impression in the warm-up stage.
- Be alert from the moment you arrive; even initial small talk is part of the interviewing process.
- Greet the interviewer by name, with a smile and direct eye contact.
- Offer a firm (not crushing) handshake if the interviewer extends a hand.
- Take a seat only after the interviewer invites you to sit or has taken his or her own seat.
- Listen for clues about what the interviewer is trying to get you to reveal about yourself and your qualifications.
- Exhibit positive body language, including standing up straight, walking with purpose, and sitting up straight.

B. Convey your value to the organization during the question-and-answer stage.
- Let the interviewer lead the conversation.
- Never answer a question before the interviewer finishes asking it.
- Listen carefully to the interviewer and watch for nonverbal signals.
- Don't limit yourself to simple yes-or-no answers; expand on the answer to show your knowledge of the company (but don't ramble on).
- If you encounter a potentially discriminatory question, decide how you want to respond before you say anything.
- When you have the opportunity, ask questions from the list you've prepared; remember that interviewers expect you to ask questions.

C. Close on a strong note.
- Watch and listen for signs that the interview is about to end.
- Quickly evaluate how well you've done and correct any misperceptions the interviewer might have.
- If you receive an offer and aren't ready to decide, it's entirely appropriate to ask for time to think about it.
- Don't bring up salary but be prepared to discuss it if the interviewer raises the subject.
- End with a warm smile and a handshake and thank the interviewer for meeting with you.

notes will help you decide which company is the right fit for you when it comes time to choose from among the job offers you receive.

Following Up After the Interview

Staying in contact with a prospective employer after an interview shows that you really want the job and are determined to get it. Doing so also gives you another chance to demonstrate your communication skills and sense of business etiquette. Following up brings your name to the interviewer's attention once again and reminds him or her that you're actively looking and waiting for the decision.

Any time you hear from a company during the application or interview process, be sure to respond quickly. Companies flooded with résumés may move on to another candidate if they don't hear back from you within 24 hours.[47]

5 **LEARNING OBJECTIVE** Identify the most common employment messages that follow an interview and explain when you would use each one.

FOLLOW-UP MESSAGE

Send a follow-up message within two days of the interview, even if you feel you have little chance of getting the job. These messages are often referred to as "thank-you notes," but they give you an important opportunity to go beyond merely expressing your appreciation. You can use the message to reinforce the reasons you are a good choice for the position, modify any answers you gave during the interview if you realize you made a mistake or have changed your mind, and respond to any negatives that might have arisen in the interview (see Figure 5 on the next page).[48] Email is usually acceptable for follow-up messages, unless the interviewer has asked you to use other media.

A follow-up message after an interview is more than a professional courtesy; it's another chance to promote yourself to an employer.

MESSAGE OF INQUIRY

If you're not advised of the interviewer's decision by the promised date or within two weeks, you might make an inquiry. A message of inquiry (which can be handled by email if the interviewer has given you his or her email address) is particularly appropriate if you've received a job offer from a second firm and don't want to accept it before you have an answer from the first. The following message illustrates the general model for a direct request:

Use the model for a direct request when you write an inquiry about a hiring decision.

When we talked on April 7 about the fashion coordinator position in your Park Avenue showroom, you indicated that a decision would be made by May 1. I am still enthusiastic about the position and eager to know what conclusion you've reached. — *Identifies the position and introduces the main idea*

To complicate matters, another firm has now offered me a position and has asked that I reply within the next two weeks. — *Places the reason for the request second*

Because your company seems to offer a greater challenge, I would appreciate knowing about your decision by Thursday, May 12. If you need more information before then, please let me know. — *Makes a courteous request for specific action last, while clearly stating a preference for this organization*

REQUEST FOR A TIME EXTENSION

If you receive a job offer while other interviews are still pending, you can ask the employer for a time extension. Open with a strong statement of your continued interest in the job, ask for more time to consider the offer, provide specific reasons for the request, and assure the reader that you will respond by a specific date (see Figure 6).

LETTER OF ACCEPTANCE

When you receive a job offer you want to accept, reply within five days. Begin by accepting the position and expressing thanks. Identify the job you're accepting. In the next paragraph, cover any necessary details. Conclude by saying that you look forward to reporting

Use the model for positive messages when you write a letter of acceptance.

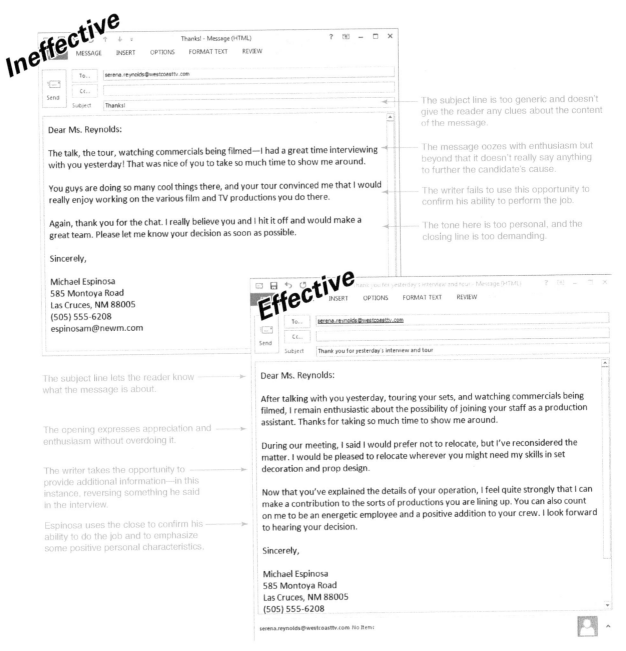

Figure 5 Follow-Up Message: Ineffective and Effective
Use the follow-up message after an interview to express continued interest in the opportunity, to correct or expand on any information you provided in the interview, and to thank the interviewer for his or her time.
Source: MS Outlook 2013, © Microsoft.

for work. As always, a positive letter should convey your enthusiasm and eagerness to cooperate:

Confirms the specific terms of the offer with a good-news statement at the beginning

> I'm delighted to accept the graphic design position in your advertising department at the salary of $3,875 per month.

Covers miscellaneous details in the body

> Enclosed are the health insurance forms you asked me to complete and sign. I've already given notice to my current employer and will be able to start work on Monday, January 18.

Closes with another reference to the good news and a look toward the future

> The prospect of joining your firm is exciting. Thank you for giving me this opportunity, and I look forward to making a positive contribution.

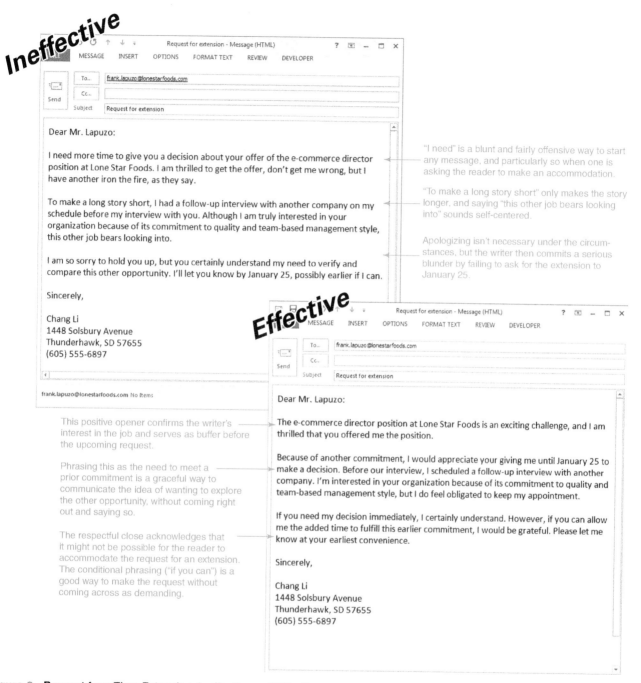

Figure 6   Request for a Time Extension: Ineffective and Effective
Needing more time to decide on a job offer is not uncommon, particularly for candidates with desirable credentials. However, make the request in a respectful and subtle way. The reader understands you are comparing opportunities and looking for the best offer, so you don't need to belabor this point.
Source: MS Outlook 2013, © Microsoft.

Be aware that a job offer and a written acceptance of that offer can constitute a legally binding contract, for both you and the employer. Before you send an acceptance letter, be sure you want the job.

Written acceptance of a job offer can be considered a legally binding contract.

LETTER DECLINING A JOB OFFER

After all your interviews, you may find that you need to write a letter declining a job offer. Use the techniques for negative messages: Open warmly, state the reasons for refusing the offer, decline the offer explicitly, and close on a pleasant note that

If you decide to decline a job offer, do so tactfully, using the model for negative messages.

expresses gratitude. By taking the time to write a sincere, tactful letter, you leave the door open for future contact:

Uses a buffer in the opening paragraph → Thank you for your hospitality during my interview at your Durham facility last month. I'm flattered that you would offer me the computer analyst position that we talked about.

Precedes the bad news with tactfully phrased reasons for the applicant's unfavorable decision → I was fortunate to receive two job offers during my search. Because my desire to work abroad can more readily be satisfied by another company, I have accepted that job offer.

Lets the reader down gently with a sincere and cordial ending → I deeply appreciate the time you spent talking with me. Thank you again for your consideration and kindness.

LETTER OF RESIGNATION

Letters of resignation should always be written in a gracious and professional style that avoids criticism of your employer or your colleagues.

If you get a job offer while employed, you can maintain good relations with your current employer by writing a thoughtful letter of resignation to your immediate supervisor. Follow the advice for negative messages and make the letter sound positive, regardless of how you feel. Say something favorable about the organization, the people you work with, or what you've learned on the job. Then state your intention to leave and give the date of your last day on the job. Be sure you give your current employer at least two weeks' notice.

Uses an appreciative opening to serve as a buffer → My sincere thanks to you and to all the other Emblem Corporation employees for helping me learn so much about serving the public these past two years. You have given me untold help and encouragement.

States reasons before the bad news itself, using tactful phrasing to help keep the relationship friendly, should the writer later want letters of recommendation → You may recall that when you first interviewed me, my goal was to become a customer relations supervisor. Because that opportunity has been offered to me by another organization, I am submitting my resignation. I will miss my friends and colleagues at Emblem, but I want to take advantage of this opportunity.

Discusses necessary details in an extra paragraph → I would like to terminate my work here two weeks from today (June 13) but can arrange to work an additional week if you want me to train a replacement.

Tempers any disappointment with a cordial close → My sincere thanks and best wishes to all of you.

To verify the content and style of your follow-up messages, consult the tips in "Checklist: Writing Follow-Up Messages."

CHECKLIST ✔ Writing Follow-Up Messages

A. Thank-you messages
- Write a brief thank-you letter within two days of the interview.
- Acknowledge the interviewer's time and courtesy.
- Restate the specific job you're applying for.
- Express your enthusiasm about the organization and the job.
- Add any new facts that may help your chances.
- Politely ask for a decision.

B. Messages of inquiry
- If you haven't heard from the interviewer by the promised date, write a brief message of inquiry.
- Use the direct approach: main idea, necessary details, specific request.

C. Requests for a time extension
- Request an extension if you have pending interviews and need time to decide about an offer.
- Open on a friendly note.

- Explain why you need more time and express continued interest in the company.
- In the close, promise a quick decision if your request is denied and ask for a confirmation if your request is granted.

D. Letters of acceptance
- Send this message within five days of receiving the offer.
- State clearly that you accept the offer, identify the job you're accepting, and confirm vital details such as salary and start date.
- Make sure you want the job; an acceptance letter can be treated as a legally binding contract.

E. Letters declining a job offer
- Use the indirect approach for negative messages.
- Open on a warm and appreciative note and then explain why you are refusing the offer.
- End on a sincere, positive note.

F. Letters of resignation
- Send a letter of resignation to your current employer as soon as possible.
- Begin with an appreciative buffer.
- In the middle section, state your reasons for leaving and actually state that you are resigning.
- Close cordially.

ON THE JOB: SOLVING COMMUNICATION DILEMMAS AT ZAPPOS

You recently joined the recruiting team at Zappos' headquarters in Las Vegas. You're looking to hire experienced customer support specialists who remain calm when things get chaotic and who are comfortable communicating in the Zappos style with a diverse range of customers. Using what you know about job applications and interviewing, address these challenges. (To learn more about working at Zappos, you can visit https://jobs.zappos.com/)

1. The first step for someone hoping to get a job at Zappos is to become an "Insider" by joining the Inside Zappos social network. Because written communication skills are such an important part of the job, you pay close attention to how people present themselves in their networking profiles. Based on the following opening paragraphs, which of these four candidates has done the best job of capturing your attention and interest?
   a. With 4.5 years of customer service experience, solid performance reviews, and a firm commitment to excellence in customer service, I trust I don't sound overconfident when I say that I posses the qualities a fine organization such as Zappos needs to help achieve its goals and objectives.
   b. You do wacky. I do wacky. Let's make this happen.
   c. Given your reputation for hiring coolest cats in town, the big question is why the heck don't I work there yet? I'm driven, way smarter than average, and would feel right at home in Vegas, baby!
   d. In addition to being an enthusiastic Zappos customer, I am also a customer service professional myself. A brilliant idea came to me last week while I was having yet another satisfying interaction with your customer support crew: I want to be part of the team that can create such positive experiences for customers.

2. You like to put applicants at ease right away, so you usually start interviews by asking an offbeat question to break the tension while also prompting the candidate to reveal something about his or her personality and knowledge. Which of these questions would you choose to start an interview?
   a. Who is the most ridiculously demanding customer you ever encountered?
   b. If we gave you a jetpack to fly all over town surprising customers with product deliveries, would you take the job?
   c. Ever have one of those days when life seems like one endless job interview?
   d. So... buying that weekly lottery ticket still hasn't worked out, eh?

3. Zappos likes employees who can think on their feet, even when faced with outlandish questions and circumstances. Which of these questions would you use to judge a candidate's ability to grasp a problem and begin developing a solution?
   a. You're a scientist with the Environmental Protection Agency, specializing in toxic waste from electronic products. You're testifying before a congressional committee, and a senator wants to know how many mobile phone batteries will be thrown away in the next 10 years. Without access to any additional information, how would you start to construct an estimate of this number?
   b. Guess how old I am.
   c. Why do telephone numbers in movies and TV shows always start with 555?
   d. How would you explain the concept of a human family to a creature from another planet?

4. At the end of each interview, you make a point to ask candidates if they have any questions for you. Which of the following responses impresses you the most?
   a. No, thanks. I think I'm all set. You've done a wonderful job of answering whatever questions I might've come in with.
   b. Oh, I don't need to take any more of your time. I'm a pretty good independent thinker. If I have any questions, I'll just look you up online when I get back to home.
   c. Absolutely. Can you give me the inside scoop? Is this fun Zappos family environment stuff for real or just a show to impress people on the outside?
   d. Yes, thanks, I do. Now that Amazon has acquired Zappos, do you think there will be opportunities to spread the Zappos spirit through the entire Amazon operation? Or is there a risk that the Zappos spirit might be lost now that it's part of a much larger company?

Learning Objectives Checkup

Assess your understanding of the principles in this chapter by reading each learning objective and studying the accompanying exercises. You can check your responses against the answer key.

Objective 1: Explain the purposes of application letters and describe how to apply the AIDA organizational approach to them.

1. What is the primary reason for sending an application letter?
   a. To encourage the reader to look at your résumé
   b. To ask for a job
   c. To itemize your qualifications
   d. To ask for an application form
2. Why are unsolicited application letters more challenging to write than solicited application letters?
   a. Nobody wants to receive unsolicited application letters.
   b. With an unsolicited letter, you have to do the research to identify the qualities the company would likely be looking for and convince someone to consider you for a job that might not even be open yet.
   c. Solicited application letters are shorter, making it more likely than recruiters will bother to read them.
   d. Unsolicited letters do not lend themselves to the AIDA model.
3. Which of the following is a good technique to gain attention in the opening paragraph of any application letter?
   a. Make sure you "jump off the page" with an eye-catching design.
   b. Explain how you have some immediate potential to meet the company's needs.
   c. Invoke a sense of dramatic mystery by withholding either the job you are applying for or some key facts about yourself.
   d. Go deep; structure your letter more along the lines of a comprehensive informational report.
4. What are the two vital functions of the final paragraph of an application letter?
   a. To ask the reader for an interview (or other appropriate action) and to express how happy would you be to work for the company
   b. To ask the reader for an interview (or other appropriate action) and to make it easy for the reader to reply
   c. To ask the reader for an interview (or other appropriate action) and to state your salary expectations
   d. To encourage the reader to read your résumé and to highlight at least three key points from your résumé

Objective 2: Describe the typical sequence of job interviews, the major types of interviews, and the attributes employers look for during an interview.

5. Which of these interview stages happens first?
   a. The selection stage
   b. The screening stage
   c. The filtering stage
   d. The sorting stage
6. A/an _____ interview, often used in the screening stage, features a series of prepared questions in a set order.
7. How does a behavioral interview differ from a situational interview?
   a. A behavioral interview asks you to relate incidents and experiences from your past, whereas a situational interview puts you in actual work situations and asks you to perform some task, such as leading a brainstorming session.
   b. They are essentially the same thing, although behavioral interviews are generally conducted by computer rather than a live interviewer.
   c. A situational interview asks you to relate incidents and experiences from your past, whereas a behavioral interview asks how you would respond to various hypothetical situations in the future.
   d. A behavioral interview asks you to relate incidents and experiences from your past, whereas a situational interview asks how you would respond to various hypothetical situations in the future.
8. What are the two most important factors employers look for during interviews?
   a. Fit with the organization and motivation
   b. Motivation and ability to perform the job
   c. Motivation and years of experience
   d. Ability to perform the job and compatibility with the organization
9. Which of the following preemployment tests might you encounter while applying for jobs?
   a. Integrity tests
   b. Substance tests
   c. Personality tests
   d. All of the above

Objective 3: List six tasks you need to complete to prepare for a successful job interview.

10. If an interviewer asks you to describe your biggest weakness, which of the following is a good strategy for your response?
    a. The interviewer is just trying to rattle you, so what you say is less important than staying cool and calm while you say it.
    b. Frame your response in terms of skills you plan to develop in the future, specifically a skill that will benefit the company.
    c. Respectfully explain to the interviewer that the question is illegal.
    d. Explain that you don't have any major weaknesses.

11. What is the best strategy for asking questions of your own during an interview?
    a. Try to ask all of them at the beginning of the interview so that you don't run out of time.
    b. Wait until after the interview and then email your questions to the interviewer.
    c. Try to work your questions in naturally throughout the course of the interview.
    d. Wait until the interviewer asks if you have any questions.

12. If you believe that you have a particular disadvantage related to some aspect of your appearance, interviewing skills, job skills, or work experience, how should you handle the situation when preparing for an interview?
    a. Plan to make a joke about your weakness early in the interview; this will break the tension and allow you to focus on the interviewer's questions.
    b. Compensate by focusing on your strengths, both while you're preparing and during the interview.
    c. Correct the perceived shortcoming if possible; if not, focus on your positive attributes.
    d. Ignore the situation; there's nothing you can do about a weakness at this point.

13. If you're not sure what style of clothing to wear to a particular interview and you're not able to ask someone at the company for advice, what should you do?
    a. Dress in a fairly conservative style; it's better to be a little too dressy than too casual.
    b. Dress as you would like to dress on the job.
    c. Dress in an eye-catching style that will make a lasting impression on the interviewer.
    d. Arrive early with several different changes of clothes; try to see what people there are wearing, then find a place to change into whichever outfit you have that most closely matches.

Objective 4: Explain how to succeed in all three stages of an interview.

14. Studies show that many interviewers, particularly those with poor training, make up their minds about candidates
    a. In the first 20 seconds of the interview
    b. In the final 20 seconds of the interview
    c. On the basis of the résumé
    d. On the basis of the cover letter

15. Which of the following is an advisable response to an interviewer who asks you about your marital status, how many children you have, and what their ages are?
    a. Answer the questions; it is perfectly within the interviewer's right to ask you such personal questions, even if they are not directly related to the job you are applying for.
    b. Tell the interviewer that such questions are illegal and threaten to sue for invasion of privacy.
    c. Sidestep the questions by asking if the interviewer has some specific concerns about your commitment to the job, your willingness to travel, or some other factor.
    d. If you want the job, refuse to answer the questions but promise that you won't report the illegal questioning to the EEOC.

16. What should you do if the interviewer tells you the salary for the job being offered?
    a. Always take whatever the company offers.
    b. Respond with a figure higher than what is offered.
    c. Respond with a figure lower than what is offered.
    d. Ask if there is any room to negotiate on salary.

Objective 5: Identify the most common employment messages that follow an interview and explain when you would use each one.

17. After a job interview, you should send a follow-up message
    a. Within two days after the interview
    b. Only if you think you got the job
    c. That follows the AIDA organizational model
    d. That does all of the above

18. A letter declining a job offer should follow
    a. The direct approach
    b. The AIDA model
    c. A negative news approach
    d. The polite plan

Quick Learning Guide

LEARNING OBJECTIVES

1 Explain the purposes of application letters and describe how to apply the AIDA organizational approach to them.

2 Describe the typical sequence of job interviews, the major types of interviews, and the attributes employers look for during an interview.

3 List six tasks you need to complete to prepare for a successful job interview.

4 Explain how to succeed in all three stages of an interview.

5 Identify the most common employment messages that follow an interview and explain when you would use each one.

KEY TERMS

application letter Message that accompanies a résumé to let readers know what you're sending, why you're sending it, and how they can benefit from reading it

behavioral interview Interview in which you are asked to relate specific incidents and experiences from your past

employment interview Formal meeting during which you and an employer ask questions and exchange information

group interview Interview in which one or more interviewers meet with several candidates simultaneously

open-ended interview Interview in which the interviewer adapts his or her line of questioning based on the answers you give and any questions you ask

panel interview Interview in which you meet with several interviewers at once

situational interview Similar to a behavioral interview, except the questions focus on how you would handle various hypothetical situations on the job

stress interview Interview in which you might be asked questions designed to unsettle you or subject you to long periods of silence, criticism, interruptions, and or hostile reactions by the interviewer

structured interview Interview in which the interviewer (or a computer) asks a series of prepared questions in a set order

working interview Interview in which you perform a job-related activity

CHECKLIST ✔

Making a Positive Impression in Job Interviews

A. Be ready to make a positive impression in the warm-up stage.
- Be alert from the moment you arrive; even initial small talk is part of the interviewing process.
- Greet the interviewer by name, with a smile and direct eye contact.
- Offer a firm (not crushing) handshake if the interviewer extends a hand.
- Take a seat only after the interviewer invites you to sit or has taken his or her own seat.
- Listen for clues about what the interviewer is trying to get you to reveal about yourself and your qualifications.
- Exhibit positive body language, including standing up straight, walking with purpose, and sitting up straight.

B. Convey your value to the organization during the question-and-answer stage.
- Let the interviewer lead the conversation.
- Never answer a question before the interviewer finishes asking it.
- Listen carefully to the interviewer and watch for nonverbal signals.
- Don't limit yourself to simple yes-or-no answers; expand on the answer to show your knowledge of the company (but don't ramble on).
- If you encounter a potentially discriminatory question, decide how you want to respond before you say anything.
- When you have the opportunity, ask questions from the list you've prepared; remember that interviewers expect you to ask questions.

C. Close on a strong note.
- Watch and listen for signs that the interview is about to end.
- Quickly evaluate how well you've done and correct any misperceptions the interviewer might have.
- If you receive an offer and aren't ready to decide, it's entirely appropriate to ask for time to think about it.
- Don't bring up salary but be prepared to discuss it if the interviewer raises the subject.
- End with a warm smile and a handshake and thank the interviewer for meeting with you.

Apply Your Knowledge

To review chapter content related to each question, refer to the indicated Learning Objective.

⭐ 1. If you lack one important qualification for a job but have made it past the initial screening stage, how should you prepare to handle this issue during the next round of interviews? Explain your answer. [LO-3]

2. What is an interviewer likely to conclude about you if you don't have any questions to ask during the interview? [LO-3]

⭐ 3. Why is it important to distinguish unethical or illegal interview questions from acceptable questions? Explain. [LO-4]

4. What should you do if your mind goes blank after an interviewer asks you a question? [LO-4]

Practice Your Skills

Messages for Analysis

Read the following messages and then (1) analyze the strengths or weaknesses of each document and (2) revise each document so that it follows this chapter's guidelines.

5. **Message A: Writing an Application Letter [LO-1]**

I'm writing to let you know about my availability for the brand manager job you advertised. As you can see from my enclosed résumé, my background is perfect for the position. Even though I don't have any real job experience, my grades have been outstanding, considering that I went to a top-ranked business school.

I did many things during my undergraduate years to prepare me for this job:

- Earned a 3.4 out of a 4.0, with a 3.8 in my business courses
- Elected representative to the student governing association
- Selected to receive the Lamar Franklin Award
- Worked to earn a portion of my tuition

I am sending my résumé to all the top firms, but I like yours better than any of the rest. Your reputation is tops in the industry, and I want to be associated with a business that can pridefully say it's the best.

If you wish for me to come in for an interview, I can come on a Friday afternoon or anytime on weekends when I don't have classes. Again, thanks for considering me for your brand manager position.

6. **Message B: Writing Application Follow-Up Messages [LO-1]**

Did you receive my résumé? I sent it to you at least two months ago and haven't heard anything. I know you keep résumés on file, but I just want to be sure that you keep me in mind. I heard you are hiring health-care managers and certainly would like to be considered for one of those positions.

Since I last wrote you, I've worked in a variety of positions that have helped prepare me for management. To wit, I've become lunch manager at the restaurant where I work, which involved a raise in pay. I now manage a waitstaff of 12 girls and take the lunch receipts to the bank every day.

Of course, I'd much rather be working at a real job, and that's why I'm writing again. Is there anything else you would like to know about me or my background? I would really like to know more about your company. Is there any literature you could send me? If so, I would really appreciate it.

I think one reason I haven't been hired yet is that I don't want to leave Atlanta. So I hope when you think of me, it's for a position that wouldn't require moving. Thanks again for considering my application.

7. **Message C: Thank-You Message [LO-5]**

Thank you for the really marvelous opportunity to meet you and your colleagues at Starret Engine Company. I really enjoyed touring your facilities and talking with all the people there. You have quite a crew! Some of the other companies I have visited have been so rigid and uptight that I can't imagine how I would fit in. It's a relief to run into a group of people who seem to enjoy their work as much as all of you do.

I know that you must be looking at many other candidates for this job, and I know that some of them will probably be more experienced than I am. But I do want to emphasize that my two-year hitch in the Navy involved a good deal of engineering work. I don't think I mentioned all my shipboard responsibilities during the interview.

Please give me a call within the next week to let me know your decision. You can usually find me at my dormitory in the evening after dinner (phone: 877-9080).

8. **Message D: Letter of Inquiry [LO-5]**

I have recently received a very attractive job offer from the Warrington Company. But before I let them know one way or another, I would like to consider any offer that your firm may extend. I was quite impressed with your company during my recent interview, and I am still very interested in a career there.

I don't mean to pressure you, but Warrington has asked for my decision within 10 days. Could you let me know by Tuesday whether you plan to offer me a position? That would give me enough time to compare the two offers.

9. **Message E: Letter Declining a Job Offer [LO-5]**

I'm writing to say that I must decline your job offer. Another company has made me a more generous offer, and I have decided to accept. However, if things don't work out for me there, I will let you know. I sincerely appreciate your interest in me.

Exercises

Each activity is labeled according to the primary skill or skills you will need to use. To review relevant chapter content, you can refer to the indicated Learning Objective.

10. **Career Management: Preparing for Interviews [LO-3]** Google yourself, Bing yourself, scour your social networking profiles, review your Twitter messages, and explore every other possible online source you can think of that might have something about you. If you find anything potentially embarrassing, remove it if possible. Write a summary of your search-and-destroy mission (you can skip any embarrassing details in your report to your instructor!).

    Career Management: Researching Target Employers [LO-3] Select a medium or large company (one that you can easily find information on) where you might like to work. Use Internet sources to gather some preliminary research on the company; don't limit your search to the company's own website.

11. What did you learn about this organization that would help you during an interview there?

12. What Internet sources did you use to obtain this information?

13. Armed with this information, what aspects of your background do you think might appeal to this company's recruiters?

14. Based on what you've learned about this company's culture, what aspects of your personality should you try to highlight during an interview?

15. **Career Management: Interviewing; Collaboration: Team Projects [LO-4]** Divide the class into two groups. Half the class will be recruiters for a large chain of national department stores, looking to fill manager trainee positions (there are 16 openings). The other half of the class will be candidates for the jobs. The company is specifically looking for candidates who demonstrate these three qualities: initiative, dependability, and willingness to assume responsibility.

    - Have each recruiter select and interview an applicant for 10 minutes.
    - Have all the recruiters discuss how they assessed the applicant in each of the three desired qualities. What questions did they ask or what did they use as an indicator to determine whether the candidate possessed the quality?
    - Have all the applicants discuss what they said to convince the recruiters that they possessed each of these qualities.

16. **Career Management: Interviewing [LO-3]** Write a short email to your instructor, discussing what you believe are your greatest strengths and weaknesses from an employment perspective. Next, explain how these strengths and weaknesses would be viewed by interviewers evaluating your qualifications.

17. **Career Management: Interviewing [LO-3]** Prepare written answers to 10 of the questions listed in Table 3.

Message Strategies: Employment Messages, Communication Ethics: Resolving Ethical Dilemmas [LO-5] You have decided to accept a new position with a competitor of your company. Write a letter of resignation to your supervisor, announcing your decision.

18. Will you notify your employer that you are joining a competing firm? Explain.

19. Will you use the direct or the indirect approach? Explain.

20. Will you send your letter by email, send it by regular mail, or place it on your supervisor's desk?

Expand Your Skills

Critique the Professionals

Find an online video of a business professional being interviewed by a journalist. Using whatever medium your instructor requests, write a brief assessment (no more than one page) of the professional's performance and any tips that you picked up that could you use in job interviews.

Sharpen Your Career Skills Online

Bovée and Thill's Business Communication Web Search, at http://websearch.businesscommunicationnetwork.com, is a unique research tool designed specifically for business communication research. Use the Web Search function to find a website, video, PDF document, podcast, or presentation that offers advice on successful interviewing techniques. Write a brief email message to your instructor or a post for your class blog, describing the item that you found and summarizing the career skills information you learned from it.

Improve Your Grammar, Mechanics, and Usage

The following exercises help you improve your knowledge of and power over English grammar, mechanics, and usage. Turn to the Handbook of Grammar, Mechanics, and Usage at the end of this text and review Numbers. Then look at the following items and indicate the preferred choice in each group of sentences.

21. a. We need to hire one office manager, four bookkeepers, and 12 clerk-typists.
    b. We need to hire one office manager, four bookkeepers, and twelve clerk-typists.
    c. We need to hire 1 office manager, 4 bookkeepers, and 12 clerk-typists.

22. a. The market for this product is nearly 6 million people in our region alone.
    b. The market for this product is nearly six million people in our region alone.
    c. The market for this product is nearly 6,000,000 million people in our region alone.

23. a. Make sure that all 1,835 pages are on my desk no later than 9:00 a.m.

b. Make sure that all 1835 pages are on my desk no later than nine o'clock in the morning.

c. Make sure that all 1,835 pages are on my desk no later than nine o'clock a.m.

24. a. Our deadline is 4/7, but we won't be ready before 4/11.

b. Our deadline is April 7, but we won't be ready before April 11.

c. Our deadline is 4/7, but we won't be ready before April 11.

25. a. 95 percent of our customers are men.

b. Ninety-five percent of our customers are men.

c. Of our customers, ninety-five percent are men.

26. a. More than half the U.S. population is female.

b. More than ½ the U.S. population is female.

c. More than one-half the U.S. population is female.

27. a. Last year, I wrote 20 15-page reports, and Michelle wrote 24 three-page reports.

b. Last year, I wrote 20 fifteen-page reports, and Michelle wrote 24 three-page reports.

c. Last year, I wrote twenty 15-page reports, and Michelle wrote 24 three-page reports.

28. a. Our blinds should measure 38 inches wide by 64 and one-half inches long by 7/16 inches deep.

b. Our blinds should measure 38 inches wide by 64-1/2 inches long by 7/16 inches deep.

c. Our blinds should measure 38 inches wide by 64-1/2″ long by 7/16 inches deep.

29. a. Deliver the couch to 783 Fountain Rd., Suite 3, Procter Valley, CA 92074.

b. Deliver the couch to 783 Fountain Rd., Suite three, Procter Valley, CA 92074.

c. Deliver the couch to seven eighty-three Fountain Rd., Suite three, Procter Valley, CA 92074.

30. a. Here are the corrected figures: 42.7% agree, 23.25% disagree, 34% are undecided, and the error is 0.05%.

b. Here are the corrected figures: 42.7% agree, 23.25% disagree, 34.0% are undecided, and the error is .05%.

c. Here are the corrected figures: 42.70% agree, 23.25% disagree, 34.00% are undecided, and the error is 0.05%.

Cases

Website links for selected companies mentioned in cases can be found in the Student Assignments section at http://realtimeupdates.com/ebc12.

Application Messages

VIDEO SKILLS

31. Media Skills: Video; Message Strategies: Employment Messages [LO-1] With its encouragement of video applications and abandonment of traditional job postings, Zappos might be starting a mini-trend toward a new style of employment application.

Your task: Identify a company where you would like to work and assume that it encourages candidates to submit video introductions. Plan, record, and produce a short video (no longer than three minutes) that you might submit to this employer. Don't worry too much about fancy production quality, but make sure your content and presentation match the company's style and brand image. For example, a fun and goofy video would be great for Zappos but not for many other companies.

EMAIL SKILLS

32. Message Strategies: Employment Messages [LO-1] Use one of the websites listed in Table 1 to find a job opening in your target profession. If you haven't narrowed down to one career field yet, choose a business job for which you will have at least some qualifications at the time of your graduation.

Your task: Write an email message that would serve as your application letter if you were to apply for this job. Base your message on your actual qualifications for the position, and be sure to "echo" the requirements listed in the job description. Include the job description in your email message when you submit it to your instructor.

MICROBLOGGING SKILLS

33. Message Strategies: Employment Messages [LO-1] If you want to know whether job candidates can express themselves clearly on Twitter, why not test them as part of the application process? That's exactly what the Minneapolis advertising agency Campbell Mithun does. Rather than having them using conventional application methods, the company asks intern candidates to tweet their applications in 13 messages.[49]

Your task: Find a job opening on Twitter by searching on any of the following hashtags: #hiring, #joblisting, or #nowhiring.[50] Next, write an "application letter" composed of 13 individual tweets (140 characters maximum). If your class is set up with private Twitter accounts, go ahead and send the tweets. Otherwise, email them to your instructor or post them on your class blog, as your instructor indicates.

EMAIL SKILLS

34. Message Strategies: Employment Messages [LO-1] Finding job openings that align perfectly with your professional interests is wonderful, but it doesn't always happen. Sometimes you have to widen your search and go after whatever opportunities happen to be available. Even when the opportunity is not ideal, however, you still need to approach the employer with enthusiasm and a focused, audience-centric message.

Your task: Find a job opening for which you will be qualified when you graduate (or close to being qualified, for the purposes of this activity), but make it one that is outside your primary field of interest. Write an email application letter for this opening, making a compelling case that you are the right candidate for this job.

Interviewing

BLOGGING SKILLS/TEAM SKILLS

35. Career Management: Researching Target Employers [LO-3] Research is a critical element of the job search process. With information in hand, you increase the chance of finding the right opportunity (and avoiding bad choices), and you impress interviewers in multiple ways by demonstrating initiative, curiosity, research and analysis skills, an appreciation for the complex challenges of running a business, and willingness to work to achieve results.

Your task: With a small team of classmates, use online job listings to identify an intriguing job opening that at least one member of the team would seriously consider pursuing as graduation approaches. (You'll find it helpful if the career is related to at least one team member's college major or on-the-job experience so that the team can benefit from some knowledge of the profession in question.) Next, research the company, its competitors, its markets, and this specific position to identify five questions that would (1) help the team member decide if this is a good opportunity and (2) show an interviewer that you've really done your homework. Go beyond the basic and obvious questions to identify current, specific, and complex issues that only deep research can uncover. For example, is the company facing significant technical, financial, legal, or regulatory challenges that threaten its ability to grow or perhaps even survive in the long term? Or is the market evolving in a way that positions this particular company for dramatic growth? In a post for your class blog, list your five questions, identify how you uncovered the issue, and explain why each is significant.

TEAM SKILLS

36. Career Management: Interviewing [LO-4] Interviewing is a skill that can be improved through observation and practice.

Your task: You and all other members of your class are to write letters of application for an entry-level or management-trainee position that requires an engaging personality and intelligence but a minimum of specialized education or experience. Sign your letter with a fictitious name that conceals your identity. Next, polish (or create) a résumé that accurately identifies you and your educational and professional accomplishments.

Now, three members of the class who volunteer as interviewers divide up all the anonymously written application letters. Then each interviewer selects a candidate who seems the most convincing in his or her letter. At this time, the selected candidates identify themselves and give the interviewers their résumés.

Each interviewer then interviews his or her chosen candidate in front of the class, seeking to understand how the items on the résumé qualify the candidate for the job. At the end of the interviews, the class decides who gets the job and discusses why this candidate was successful. Afterward, retrieve your letter, sign it with the right name, and submit it to the instructor for credit.

TEAM SKILLS

37. Career Management: Interviewing [LO-4] Select a company in an industry in which you might like to work and then identify an interesting position within the company. Study the company and prepare for an interview with that company.

Your task: Working with a classmate, take turns interviewing each other for your chosen positions. Interviewers should take notes during the interview. When the interview is complete, critique each other's performance. (Interviewers should critique how well candidates prepared for the interview and answered the questions; interviewees should critique the quality of the questions asked.) Write a follow-up letter thanking your interviewer and submit the letter to your instructor.

Following Up After an Interview

LETTER WRITING SKILLS

38. Message Strategies: Employment Messages [LO-5] Because of a mix-up in your job application scheduling, you accidentally applied for your third-choice job before going after the one you really wanted. What you want to do is work in retail marketing with the upscale department store Neiman Marcus in Dallas; what you have been offered is a job with Longhorn Leather and Lumber, 65 miles away in the small town of Commerce, Texas.

You review your notes. Your Longhorn interview was three weeks ago with the human resources manager, R. P. Bronson, who has just written to offer you the position. The store's address is 27 Sam Rayburn Drive, Commerce, TX 75428. Mr. Bronson notes that he can hold the position open for 10 days. You have an interview scheduled with Neiman Marcus next week, but it is unlikely that you will know the store's decision within this 10-day period.

Your task: Write to Mr. Bronson, requesting a reasonable delay in your consideration of his job offer.

LETTER WRITING SKILLS/EMAIL SKILLS

39. Message Strategies: Employment Messages [LO-5] Fortunately for you, your interview with Neiman Marcus (see the previous case) went well, and you've just received a job offer from the company.

Your task: Write a letter to R. P. Bronson at Longhorn Leather and Lumber, declining his job offer, and write an email message to Clarissa Bartle at Neiman Marcus, accepting her job offer. Make up any information you need when accepting the Neiman Marcus offer.

LETTER WRITING SKILLS

40. Message Strategies: Employment Messages (Letters of Resignation) [LO-5] Leaving a job is rarely stress free, but it's particularly difficult when you are parting ways with a mentor who played an important role in advancing your career. A half-dozen years into your career, you have benefited greatly from the advice, encouragement, and professional connections offered by your mentor, who also happens to be your current boss. She seemed to believe in your potential from the beginning and went out of her way on numerous occasions to help you. You returned the favor by becoming a stellar employee who has made important contributions to the success of the department your boss leads.

Unfortunately, you find yourself at a caree impasse. You believe you are ready to move into a management position, but your company is not growing enough to create many opportunities.

Worse yet, you joined the firm during a period of rapid expansion, so there are many eager and qualified internal candidates at your career level interested in the few managerial jobs that do become available. You fear it may be years before you get the chance to move up in the company. Through your online networking activities, you found an opportunity with a firm in another industry and have decided to pursue it.

Your task: You have a close relationship with your boss, so you will announce your intention to leave the company in a private, one-on-one conversation. However, you also recognize the need to write a formal letter of resignation, which you will hand to your boss during this meeting. This letter is addressed to your boss, but as formal business correspondence that will become part of your personnel file, it should not be a "personal" letter. Making up whatever details you need, write a brief letter of resignation.

MyBCommLab

Go to the Assignments section of your MyLab to complete these writing exercises.

41. How can you prepare for a situational or behavioral interview if you have no experience with the job for which you are interviewing? [LO-2]

42. Why are the questions you ask during an interview as important as the answers you give to the interviewer's questions? [LO-3]

Endnotes

1. Zappos Inside Zappos page, accessed 8 August 2014, https://jobs.zappos.com; Blair Hanley Frank, "Zappos Ditches Job Posts, Replaces Them with a Social Network," *GeekWire*, 27 May 2014, www.geekwire.com. "Wishez Is Live," Zappos Family blog, 17 November 2010, http://blogs.zappos.com; Tony Hsieh, "Amazon & Zappos, 1 Year Later," Zappos CEO & COO blog, 22 July 2010, http://blogs.zappos.com; Todd Raphael, "7 Interview Questions from Zappos," Todd Raphael's World of Talent blog, 22 July 2010, http://community.ere.net; Jeffrey M. O'Brien, "Zappos Knows How to Kick It," *Fortune*, 22 January 2009, http://about.zappos.com/ press-center; "Zappos Family Seattle Coding Challenge and Tech Tweet Up," Zappos Family blog, 22 March 2011, http://blogs.zappos.com.
2. Matthew Rothenberg, "Manuscript vs. Machine," The Ladders, 15 December 2009, www.theladders.com; Joann Lublin, "Cover Letters Get You in the Door, So Be Sure Not to Dash Them Off," *Wall Street Journal*, 6 April 2004, B1.
3. Lisa Vaas, "How to Write a Great Cover Letter," The Ladders, 20 November 2009, www.theladders.com.
4. Allison Doyle, "Introduction to Cover Letters," *About.com*, accessed 13 August 2010, http://jobsearch.about.com.
5. Alison Green, "Are You Making These 8 Mistakes on Your Cover Letter?" *U.S. News & World Report*, 18 July 2012, http://money.usnews.com; Doyle, "Introduction to Cover Letters"; Vaas, "How to Write a Great Cover Letter"; Toni Logan, "The Perfect Cover Story," *Kinko's Impress* 2 (2000): 32, 34.

6. Lisa Vaas, "How to Follow Up a Résumé Submission," The Ladders, 9 August 2010, www.theladders.com.
7. Alison Doyle, "How to Follow Up After Submitting a Resume," *About.com*, accessed 13 August 2010, http://jobsearch.about.com; Vaas, "How to Follow Up a Résumé Submission."
8. Anne Fisher, "How to Get Hired by a 'Best' Company," *Fortune*, 4 February 2008, 96.
9. Fisher, "How to Get Hired by a 'Best' Company."
10. Sarah E. Needleman, "Speed Interviewing Grows as Skills Shortage Looms; Strategy May Help Lock in Top Picks; Some Drawbacks," *Wall Street Journal*, 6 November 2007, B15.
11. Scott Beagrie, "How to Handle a Telephone Job Interview," *Personnel Today*, 26 June 2007, 29.
12. John Olmstead, "Predict Future Success with Structured Interviews," *Nursing Management*, March 2007, 52–53.
13. Anne Fisher, "How to Get Hired by a 'Best' Company," *Fortune*, 4 February 2008, 96.
14. Erinn R. Johnson, "Pressure Sessions," *Black Enterprise*, October 2007, 72.
15. "What's a Group Interview?" About.com Tech Careers, accessed 5 April 2008, http://jobsearchtech.about.com.
16. Fisher, "How to Get Hired by a 'Best' Company."
17. Katherine Hansen, "Behavioral Job Interviewing Strategies for Job-Seekers," QuintCareers.com, accessed 13 August 2010, www.quintcareers.com.

18. Hansen, "Behavioral Job Interviewing Strategies for Job-Seekers."

19. Chris Pentilla, "Testing the Waters," *Entrepreneur*, January 2004, www.entrepreneur.com; Terry McKenna, "Behavior-Based Interviewing," *National Petroleum News*, January 2004, 16; Nancy K. Austin, "Goodbye Gimmicks," *Incentive*, May 1996, 241.

20. William Poundstone, "Beware the Interview Inquisition," *Harvard Business Review*, May 2003, 18.

21. Peter Vogt, "Mastering the Phone Interview," Monster.com, accessed 13 December 2006, www.monster.com; Nina Segal, "The Global Interview: Tips for Successful, Unconventional Interview Techniques," Monster.com, accessed 13 December 2006, www.monster.com.

22. Segal, "The Global Interview."

23. Barbara Kiviat, "How Skype Is Changing the Job Interview," *Time*, 20 October 2009, accessed 13 August 2010, www.time.com.

24. HireVue website, accessed 4 April 2008, www.hirevue.com; in2View website, accessed 4 April 2008, www.in2view.biz; Victoria Reitz, "Interview Without Leaving Home," *Machine Design*, 1 April 2004, 66.

25. Gina Ruiz, "Job Candidate Assessment Tests Go Virtual," *Workforce Management*, January 2008, www.workforce.com; Connie Winkler, "Job Tryouts Go Virtual," *HR Magazine*, September 2006, 131–134.

26. U.S. Equal Employment Opportunity Commission, "Employment Test and Selection Procedures," EEOC website, accessed 24 July 2012, www.eeoc.gov; Jonathan Katz, "Rethinking Drug Testing," *Industry Week*, March 2010, 16–18; Ashley Shadday, "Assessments 101: An Introduction to Candidate Testing," *Workforce Management*, January 2010, www.workforce.com; Dino di Mattia, "Testing Methods and Effectiveness of Tests," *Supervision*, August 2005, 4–5; David W. Arnold and John W. Jones, "Who the Devil's Applying Now?" *Security Management*, March 2002, 85–88; Matthew J. Heller, "Digging Deeper," *Workforce Management*, 3 March 2008, 35–39.

27. Frederick P. Morgeson, Michael A. Campion, Robert L. Dipboye, John R. Hollenbeck, Kevin Murphy, and Neil Schmitt, "Are We Getting Fooled Again? Coming to Terms with Limitations in the Use of Personality Tests in Personnel Selection," *Personnel Psychology* 60, no. 4 (Winter 2007): 1029–1049.

28. Austin, "Goodbye Gimmicks."

29. Hannah Morgan, "The Ultimate Interview Prep Checklist," *U.S. News & World Report*, 23 April 2014, http://money.usnews.com.

30. Rachel Zupek, "How to Answer 10 Tough Interview Questions," CNN.com, 4 March 2009, www.cnn.com; Barbara Safani, "How to Answer Tough Interview Questions Authentically," The Ladders, 5 December 2009, www.theladders.com.

31. Nick Corcodilos, "How to Answer a Misguided Interview Question," *Seattle Times*, 30 March 2008, www.seattletimes.com.

32. Katherine Spencer Lee, "Tackling Tough Interview Questions," *Certification Magazine*, May 2005, 35.

33. Scott Ginsberg, "10 Good Ways to 'Tell Me About Yourself,'" The Ladders, 26 June 2010, www.theladders.com.

34. Richard A. Moran, "The Number One Interview Trap Question," *Business Insider*, 23 April 2014, www.businessinsider.com.

35. Joe Turner, "An Interview Strategy: Telling Stories," Yahoo! HotJobs, accessed 5 April 2008, http://hotjobs.yahoo.com.

36. "A Word of Caution for Chatty Job Candidates," *Public Relations Tactics*, January 2008, 4.

37. Randall S. Hansen, "When Job-Hunting: Dress for Success," QuintCareers.com, accessed 5 April 2008, www.quintcareers.com; Alison Doyle, "Dressing for Success," *About.com*, accessed 5 April 2008, http://jobsearch.about.com.

38. William S. Frank, "Job Interview: Pre-Flight Checklist," *The Career Advisor*, accessed 28 September 2005, http://careerplanning.about.com.

39. "Employers Reveal Outrageous and Common Mistakes Candidates Made in Job Interviews, According to New CareerBuilder Survey," CareerBuilder.com, accessed 24 March 2011, www.careerbuilder.com.

40. Alison Green, "10 Surefire Ways to Annoy a Hiring Manager," *U.S. News & World Report*, accessed 24 July 2012, http://money.usnews.com.

41. T. Shawn Taylor, "Most Managers Have No Idea How to Hire the Right Person for the Job," *Chicago Tribune*, 23 July 2002, www.ebsco.com.

42. "10 Minutes to Impress," *Journal of Accountancy*, July 2007, 13.

43. Steven Mitchell Sack, "The Working Woman's Legal Survival Guide: Testing," *FindLaw.com*, accessed 22 February 2004, www.findlaw.com.

44. Todd Anten, "How to Handle Illegal Interview Questions," Yahoo! HotJobs, accessed 7 August 2009, http://hotjobs.yahoo.com.

45. "Negotiating Salary: An Introduction," *InformationWeek*, accessed 22 February 2004, www.informationweek.com.

46. "Negotiating Salary."

47. Lisa Vaas, "Resume, Meet Technology: Making Your Resume Format Machine-Friendly," The Ladders, accessed 13 August 2010, www.theladders.com.

48. Alison Green, "How a Thank-You Note Can Boost Your Job Chances," *U.S. News & World Report*, 27 June 2012, http://money.usnews.com; Joan S. Lublin, "Notes to Interviewers Should Go Beyond a Simple Thank You," *Wall Street Journal*, 5 February 2008, B1.

49. Tiffany Hsu, "Extreme Interviewing: Odd Quizzes, Weird Mixers, Improve Pitches. Can You Get Past the Hiring Gatekeepers?" *Los Angeles Times*, 19 February 2012, B1.

50. From Ritika Trikha, "The Best Tips for Tweeting Your Way to a Job," *U.S. News & World Report*, 24 July 2012, http://money.usnews.com.

Answer Key for "Learning Objectives Checkup"

1. a
2. b
3. b
4. b
5. b
6. structured
7. d
8. d
9. d
10. b
11. c
12. c
13. a
14. a
15. c
16. d
17. a
18. c

Answer Key for "Improve Your Grammar, Mechanics, and Usage" Exercises

21. c (3.4)
22. a (3.4)
23. a (3.4)
24. b (3.4)
25. b (3.4)
26. a (3.4)
27. b (3.4)
28. b (3.4)
29. a (3.4)
30. c (3.4)

Index